SOCIETY AND THE VICTORIANS
FOUR PERIODS OF PUBLIC EDUCATION

FOUR PERIODS OF PUBLIC EDUCATION AS REVIEWED IN 1832, 1839, 1846, 1862

James Kay-Shuttleworth

With an introduction by
NORMAN MORRIS
Senior Lecturer in Education,
University of Manchester

THE HARVESTER PRESS 1973

THE HARVESTER PRESS LIMITED
Publishers

50 Grand Parade
Brighton Sussex
BN2 2QA England

SOCIETY & THE VICTORIANS
General Editor: John Spiers

This series makes available again important books by and about the Victorians. Selections mainly focus on the politics and social history of the period, and great importance is attached to presenting each volume in the context of current research. Each title chosen has either been out of print and difficult to find, or exceedingly rare for many years. Scholars of established reputations provide substantial new introductions, and almost all titles included have textual notes and a full bibliography. Texts are reprinted from the best editions.

'Four Periods of Public Education as reviewed in 1832, 1839, 1846 and 1862' first published in 1862 by Longman, Green, Longman, and Roberts, London

This edition first published in 1973 by The Harvester Press

Introduction © Norman Morris 1973

'Society & The Victorians' No.14
ISBN: 0 901759 63 5
LC Card No. 72–86831

Typesetting by Campbell Graphics Limited, Newcastle upon Tyne
Printed in England by The Scolar Press Limited, Menston

All rights reserved.

Contents

Introduction by Norman Morris   page vii

FOUR PERIODS OF PUBLIC EDUCATION

Introduction

James Phillips Kay, the son of a cotton manufacturer, was born at Rochdale in 1804. He added his wife's family name to his own on his marriage in 1842 and died as Sir James Kay-Shuttleworth Bt. in 1877.

Oddly enough, his own life falls neatly into four periods. As a young doctor in Manchester, he was one of the founders of the Manchester Statistical Society and earned a wide reputation as a social scientist. This took him south in 1834 as an Assistant Commissioner to the new Poor Law Board and to several years of distinguished pioneer work in the education of pauper children. When an embryo 'Ministry of Education' was set up in 1839 he was a natural choice for appointment as its first Secretary, as both an experienced civil servant and a notable authority on the education of lower class children. This was his third period, on which his reputation mainly rests. Overwork and a consequential break-down in health led to his resignation in 1849 and he spent the rest of his life in retirement as the elder statesman of British education. His name has become synonymous with the first years of State intervention in education in this country and with the foundation of our national system.

Mass education came to England and Wales in the nineteenth century, later than in some countries, but the reasons for its arrival and the form which it took were peculiarly native. Prior to 1800 schooling, particularly for children of the labouring poor, was sporadic and voluntary; by the last decades of the century it was universal and compulsory, with central and local governmental agencies to enforce both provision and attendance. Such a revolution in attitudes and practice, involving large-scale organisation and expenditure, was clearly neither accidental nor purely doctrinaire. It had its roots in the vast changes brought about by the industrial revolution and was shaped by the pressures of its time. Of all the social innovations of the nineteenth century elementary education was one of the most necessary for national survival—not, as is sometimes suggested, to ensure that the male proletariat enfranchised in 1867 could exercise power with a minimum of understanding, or even to feed the factories with a disciplined work force able to read instructions, but as an essential instrument of social control. At the time of the 1867 Representation of the People Act the country was already covered by a system of elementary schools, for girls as well as boys, which many people considered to be nearly complete. The fact that we had a system at the end of the century which could protect society from the dangers of extended suffrage or meet the demands of advancing technology was a spin-off from the work already carried out by an older generation before 1870.

Kay-Shuttleworth became, even in his life-time, the folk-hero of this initial phase. It would be interesting to examine the reasons for his elevation and to consider why so much attention has centred around him. His published writings on education, of which *Four Periods* is perhaps the best known, were no more voluminous than those of many of his contemporaries and he was by no means a creative thinker; he made no claim to originality for any of the ideas which he promoted. His period of public office as paid secretary to the newly-formed Committee of Council on Education lasted for only ten years and it is difficult to understand why popular opinion decided to attribute the policies pursued during that period to Kay-Shuttleworth, the civil servant, rather than to his political masters. This is quite different from the treatment given to his successor, Lingen, who was probably a far more able administrator; in Lingen's case it is Robert Lowe, the politician, who commands the limelight whilst Lingen, on very shaky evidence, is relegated to the shadows. Nevertheless, Kay-Shuttleworth is an essential object of study for the educational historian. If he voiced no original ideas and helped to build up an administrative structure which was called into serious question by a Royal Commission within ten years of his departure from office, he embodied in his writings, in his public utterances and in his official acts the spirit of progressive education in the first half of the century. He gave shape and point to what many of the best minds were thinking and assisted in translating the mood of a whole generation of educationists into bricks and mortar.

For Kay-Shuttleworth education was a social question. The industrial revolution had not only changed the face of Britain, scarring it with mills and mines; it had transformed social relationships and altered people. From being mainly rural and agrarian Britain was becoming urban and industrial. Population rose rapidly. To the ruling classes, accustomed to country life or the leisurely pace of a small market town, it seemed that the kingdom had been invaded by endless waves of new barbarians. They sprang from nowhere, occupied the towns in enormous swarms and stayed there in indescribable squalor. Whatever their previous life, these people were now rootless. Whatever ties they might have had in a previous existence with established communities and a settled way of living were broken. Their own backgrounds were diverse. They were not only foreign to their adopted home, they were often alien to each other. As wage-earners in a laissez-faire economy they owed little loyalty to their new employers and even when they discovered the strength which came from workers' unity this only widened the gulf between them and polite society. There were immediate problems of health and sanitation; Kay-Shuttleworth, who began his career as a physician in the worst slums of the first great industrial agglomeration at the worst period of its history, was to draw world-wide attention to these aspects in his description of Manchester in 1832. There were problems of police and discipline. But to radical thinkers these were only the effects of the urban disease. Beyond the physical aspects, and pervading them, was the problem of alienation; how could the new class of industrial workers be re-integrated into society in such a way that old class divisions would remain intact?

The immediate dangers of crime, pauperism and riot could be dealt with by coercion. 'At this hour', Kay-Shuttleworth wrote in 1839, 'military force alone retains in subjection great masses of the operative population, beneath whose outrages, if not thus restrained, the wealth and institutions of society would fall.' But in the long-term there had to be a return to government by consent. The future safety of the nation lay in winning acquiescence. The options were plain and Kay-Shuttleworth put them clearly: 'But the critical events of this very hour are full of warning, that the ignorance—nay the barbarism—of large portions of our fellow-countrymen, can no longer be neglected, if we are not prepared to substitute a military tyranny or anarchy for the moral subjection which has hitherto been the only safeguard of England.' (See below, page 228).

Here, then, were the alternatives: social collapse, continuous repression or political brain-washing; history is full of examples of each solution. In choosing the third Kay-Shuttleworth was consciously evolutionary. Control over the minds of its members was essential to the stability of any society and it had always been a function of organised religion to exercise a normative influence. The foundation of society was the inculcation of a morality adapted to the framework of the existing social structure under the control of responsible religious bodies. Times might change but old ways were best and the churches were still eager to play their orthodox role. The evangelical revival in the previous century was, in effect, only a re-statement of the teaching mission of the church which had been previously conducted, with fair success, through services and sermons, through catechism or personal contact and, perhaps sporadically, in parochial or charity schools. The development of elementary schools under religious sanction in the nineteenth century represented, therefore, no break with the past. The new factors were simply the size of the problem and the need to adapt historic machinery to new conditions.

It is a common error to think of the nineteenth century as the age of child labour. Children of the poor had always worked but under conditions which society was able to tolerate. Whether employed on the land or in cottage industries, or whether they were too young for any form of work, they were in reach of responsible supervision. The factory system changed all this. The familiar picture of young slaves squatting under looms, crawling through low tunnels underground or climbing inside chimneys can be misleading. These were occupations in which a small child could be a profitable economic unit. Even these were gradually proscribed by law. But beyond those who found opportunity to be exploited were the untamed hordes for whom warehousing, railways and heavier or more dangerous industries had little use. It was the nineteenth century which first created a serious problem of child unemployment. Since both parents might be away from home for long hours, the urban problem was not one of child exploitation but of unsupervised child leisure. A private-adventure child-minding industry developed which seemed to many to be worse than the disease it claimed to cure. Infancy and early childhood were normally spent in the streets and alleys without adult contact and it was for this reason that the churches were forced to conclude, early in the century, that old methods of church attendance or even the newer Sunday schools were insufficient. If children were to be civilised, nothing short of *day* schools, with longer periods of exposure to control, would be effective.

This was the rationale behind Kay-Shuttleworth's 'First Period'. He wrote as a sociologist who came to his conclusions after careful observation of the urban situation, backed by measurement and statistics. He saw the problems in terms of morals and behaviour and the answer in terms of education. By the time that he became active, in the 1830s, the churches had already built up a net-work of day elementary schools. These had now to be moulded into an effective weapon.

An orthodox radical, he believed in the use of governmental machinery to eradicate dead wood and make institutions work efficiently. This is the key to the remaining Periods in which he is less concerned with ideas than with practice. In order to provide schools quickly with extremely limited resources the denominations had been forced to accept low standards, including a monitorial system under which the main instruction was carried out by unpaid pupils between the ages of nine and thirteen. The taught, when they attended, were off the streets but what little learning took place was mechanical and what Victorians quaintly called *intellectual*; the main *moral* purpose of education, to subject and form young minds through contact with reliable adults, was frustrated. The fault lay not in the intentions of school managers but in their lack of finance to do better and the radical answer was the simple one—to give them added resources from public funds. Grants, which poured from the Treasury in the years following 1833, were designed not so much to spread the availability of education as to improve its quality. Voluntary bodies provided the schools, the State's role was to stimulate efficiency by breaking down monitorialism, improving school furniture and building layout, increasing stock and equipment and, in general, modernising the curriculum. These principles were adopted at government level and formed the basis on which a new State department, the Education Office, was established in 1839. As Secretary to this department Kay-Shuttleworth was therefore engaged to carry through a brief whose general lines were already politically determined and would have been pursued even if he had not been himself available for office.

The essence of the plan—sometimes referred to as the Kay-Shuttleworth system—was to foster desirable developments by means of specific subsidies. After 1846 there were grants not only for school buildings and school master's houses but for books, furniture and apparatus of all kinds. Particularly important were payments to encourage the employment of qualified teachers and the use of a new race of apprentice teachers, between thirteen and nineteen years old, to replace the younger monitors and feed the profession. Together with grants to Training Colleges and a system of Queen's Scholarships, no effort was spared to increase the supply of good-quality adult teachers and to make it financially possible for the schools to employ them. These are the developments which Kay-Shuttleworth defends and expounds in his 'Second' and his 'Third Period'. There is no doubt that under the guidance of one of the best informed educationists of the day, elementary schools took a great leap forward.

There were, however, difficulties which became apparent in the 'Fourth Period', after he had left office. The system which Kay-Shuttleworth helped to father was highly centralised and bureaucratised. The Office in Whitehall maintained contact with each individual set of managers; each school might receive a number of different subsidies, each of which had to be calculated, paid out and accounted for separately. It was unlikely that this system, devised to meet the needs of education when schools were few, could be allowed to continue indefinitely as schools grew in number. Some rationalisation of government assistance had to be found. Basically, the Revised Code of 1862 was an attempt to find a formula on which each school could be given a block grant which it could spend as it pleased; the public interest was safeguarded by making part of the grant dependent on the efficiency of the instruction given.

The educational arguments, for and against this experiment, were nicely balanced but Kay-Shuttleworth saw only disadvantages. His 'Fourth Period', like all the others, is written personally but now there is a note of bitterness. He is still a campaigner but now he is fighting in defence of his own reputation. He had always advocated secular learning as an aid to moral understanding but now, it appeared, the emphasis was to be reversed; the formation of moral attitudes was to be, at best, peripheral to a new purpose—the achievement of examination passes in secular subjects. In his eagerness to refute the validity of the Revised Code he was unwilling to concede any criticism even of the over-centralised and over-weighted administrative structure which he had developed. To those who pointed out that the Kay-Shuttleworth system could only be extended on the backs of an ever-increasing army of clerks and an endless stream of paper flowing back and forth between the centre and the localities, he replied that this was how civil service departments normally functioned. Historians, perhaps influenced by Kay-Shuttleworth's own strictures, have tended to condemn Payment by Results as anti-educational. It is less certain, however, that history would have welcomed a national education service run on the same lines as the Post Office or the Admiralty.

Four Periods, like most of Kay-Shuttleworth's publications, is very much a personal document rather than an analytical record of events. He was on the inside of so much that happened in education that he cannot be overlooked. Historians have, indeed, tended to accept and echo his views. Nevertheless, it is important to understand that his perspectives were his own. The long, blow-by-blow account of his own connection with teacher training is probably out of proportion. More serious is the twist which he gives to the role of the churches. Despite lengthy negotiations with the sects he failed to obtain agreement on the establishment of an inter-denominational training college under state auspices; two years later he negotiated the basis for an agreement on parochial schools, incorporated in Graham's Factory Bill of 1843, only to see the relevant clauses withdrawn, at a very late stage, because of non-conformist opposition. Both of these experiences convinced him that sectarian rivalry was blocking educational progress—a view which others held and which historians have tamely endorsed. This judgment is, however, superficial in both instances. In the former case, the government's main objective was to take a hand in the training and certification of teachers and its first idea was to set up its own institution which would, of necessity, have to be undenominational. The Anglican church found this objectionable but accepted the principle of state certification in denominational colleges. This was by no means an unreasonable or unprogressive stance to take. But by emphasising what was opposed rather than what was supported Kay-Shuttleworth diverted attention from a very real revolution—the quiet transference of the traditional right to license teachers from church to state.

The case of the school clauses in the Factory Bill of 1843 was more complex. Their withdrawal followed what was probably the most vigorous demonstration of dissenting fury in the whole of the century. But to say, as Kay-Shuttleworth did, that Tory ministers were simply defeated by sectarian differences, is to ignore deep political under-currents. The year 1843 was one of potential revolution. In the war which the middle classes waged against church and land both sides sought working class support. The Anti-Corn Law League, with its emphasis on the cost of food, had already found a platform useful to the middle class cause. Now the government presented it with another slogan. It is a moot point whether freedom of conscience would have proved a stronger rallying-cry for mass agitation than cheap bread but Peel's government declined to wait and see; the education clauses were abandoned.

On all this, Kay-Shuttleworth is silent. It is a matter for gratitude that Britain's first chief educational civil servant was an educationist before he was an administrator. He certainly did not claim to be an objective historian and *Four Periods* should be read as he intended it, as the thoughts of a man engaged in making history rather than writing it.

FOUR PERIODS

OF

PUBLIC EDUCATION

LONDON
PRINTED BY SPOTTISWOODE AND CO.
NEW-STREET SQUARE

FOUR PERIODS

OF

PUBLIC EDUCATION

AS REVIEWED IN

1832—1839—1846—1862

IN PAPERS BY

SIR JAMES KAY-SHUTTLEWORTH, BART.

LONDON
LONGMAN, GREEN, LONGMAN, AND ROBERTS
1862

TO

THE MARQUIS OF LANSDOWNE, K.G.

&c. &c.

AND

THE EARL RUSSELL

&c. &c.

THE MINISTERS OF THE CROWN

TO WHOSE SAGACITY, MODERATION, AND FIRMNESS THE COUNTRY

OWES THE ESTABLISHMENT OF

THE COMMITTEE OF THE PRIVY COUNCIL ON EDUCATION

AND THE ADOPTION OF

THE MINUTES OF 1846

THIS VOLUME

IS GRATEFULLY DEDICATED BY THEIR FAITHFUL SERVANT

THE AUTHOR

March 1862

CONTENTS.

FIRST PERIOD.

	PAGES
The Moral and Physical Condition of the Working Classes of Manchester in 1832	3 to 84
Sketch of the Progress of Manchester in thirty years, from 1832 to 1862	87 to 170

SECOND PERIOD.

Preface	175 to 178
The Order in Council creating the Committee of the Privy Council on Education (April 10, 1839)	179
The Minute as to the Proposed National Normal School (April 13, 1839)	179
The Minute as to the Inspection of Schools (June 3, 1839)	182
A Pamphlet issued by direction of the Government, entitled 'Recent Measures for the Promotion of Education in England,' explaining the intentions of the Ministry in 1839	187 to 286
First steps in Workhouses and Schools of Industry for Pauper Children, respecting the Apprenticeship of Pupil Teachers. A few brief extracts from Reports (1837 to 1840)	287 to 292
First Report on the Origin and Organisation of the Training College at Battersea, and the introduction of some of the Pupil Teachers as Students (1841)	294 to 386
Second Report on the Schools for the Training of Parochial Schoolmasters at Battersea	387 to 431

THIRD PERIOD.

EXPLANATION OF THE MINUTES OF 1846.

CHAPTER I.

Preliminaries to the establishment of the Committee of Council on Education . . . . 437 to 456

CHAPTER II.

The Nature and Objects of the Appointment of Inspectors of Schools, and the Mode of Appointing Inspectors . . . 457 to 470

CHAPTER III.

The Minutes of August and December, 1846, considered in relation to their influence on the Schoolmaster, the School, and the Poor . . . . 471 to 493

CHAPTER IV.

Minutes of August and December, 1846, considered in their Religious and Political Aspect . . . . . . 494 to 522

CHAPTER V.

The Outlay from Public Grants and Private Contributions required by the Minutes of August and December, 1846 . . 523 to 530

Appendices A. B. C. . . . . 531 to 551

FOURTH PERIOD.

Two Letters to Earl Granville, K.G. &c.

                                                                     PAGES

1. On the Recommendations of the Royal Commissioners' Report dated March 18, 1861 . . . . 555 to 573

2. On the Minute of the Committee of Council on Education, dated July 29th, 1861, establishing a Revised Code of Regulations for the Distribution of the Parliamentary Grant . . 574 to 638

Appendices . . . . 639 to 644

FIRST PERIOD

THE CONDITION OF THE WORKING CLASSES OF MANCHESTER IN 1832

FOLLOWED BY

A SKETCH OF THE PROGRESS OF MANCHESTER

IN THIRTY YEARS

FROM 1832 TO 1862

THE MORAL AND PHYSICAL CONDITION

OF THE

WORKING CLASSES OF MANCHESTER

IN 1832.

SELF-KNOWLEDGE, inculcated by the maxim of the ancient philosopher, is a precept not less appropriate to societies than to individuals. The physical and moral evils by which we are personally surrounded, may be more easily avoided when we are distinctly conscious of their existence; and the virtue and health of society may be preserved, with less difficulty, when we are acquainted with the sources of its errors and diseases.

The sensorium of the animal structure, to which converge the sensibilities of each organ, is endowed with a consciousness of every change in the sensations to which each member is liable; and few diseases are so subtle as to escape its delicate perceptive power. Pain thus reveals to us the existence of evils, which, unless arrested in their progress, might insidiously invade the sources of vital action.

Society were well preserved, did a similar faculty preside, with an equal sensibility, over its constitution; making every order immediately conscious of the evils affecting any portion of the general mass, and thus rendering their removal equally necessary for the immediate ease, as it is for the ultimate welfare of the whole social system. The mutual dependence of the individual members of society and of its various orders, for the supply of their necessities and the gratification of their desires, is acknowledged, and it imperfectly compensates for the want of a faculty, resembling that pervading consciousness which presides over the animal economy. But a knowledge of the moral and physical evils oppressing one order of the community, is by these means slowly communicated to those which are remote; and general efforts are seldom made for the relief of partial ills, until they threaten to convulse the whole social constitution.

Some governments have attempted to obtain, by specific measures, that knowledge for the acquisition of which there is no natural faculty. The statistical investigations of Prussia, of the Netherlands, of Sweden, and of France, concerning population, labour, and its commercial and agricultural results; the existing resources of the country, its taxation, finance, &c. are minute and accurate. The economist may, however, still regret, that many most interesting subjects of inquiry are neglected, and that the reports of these governments fail to give a perfect portraiture of the features of each individual part of the social body. Their system, imperfect though it be, is greatly superior to any yet introduced into this country. Here, statistics are neglected; and when any emergency demands a special inquiry, information is obtained by means of committees of the Commons, whose labours are so multifarious, as to afford them time for little else than the investigation of general conclusions, derived from the experience of those supposed to be most conversant with the subject. An approximation to truth may thus be made, but the results are never so minutely accurate as those obtained from statistical investigations; and, as they are generally deduced from a comparison of opposing testimonies, and sometimes from partial evidence, they frequently utterly fail in one most important respect, namely—in convincing the public of the facts which they proclaim.

The introduction into this country of a singularly malignant contagious malady, which, though it selects its victims from every order of society, is chiefly propagated amongst those whose health is depressed by disease, mental anxiety, or want of the comforts and conveniences of life, has directed public attention to an investigation of the state of the poor. In Manchester, Boards of Health were established, in each of the fourteen districts of Police, for the purpose of minutely inspecting the state of the houses and streets. These districts were divided into minute sections, to each of which two or more inspectors were appointed from among the most respectable inhabitants of the vicinity, and they were provided with tabular queries, applying to each particular house and street. Individual exceptions only exist, in which minute returns were not furnished to the Special Board: and as the investigation was prompted equally by the demands of benevolence, of personal security, and of the general welfare, the results may be esteemed as accurate as the nature of the investigation would permit. The other facts contained in this pamphlet have been obtained from the public offices of the town, or are the results of the author's personal observation.

The township of Manchester chiefly consists of dense masses of houses, inhabited by the population engaged in the great manufactories of the cotton trade. Some of the central divisions are occupied by warehouses and shops, and a few streets by the dwellings of some of the more wealthy inhabitants; but the opulent merchants chiefly reside in the country, and even the superior servants of their establishments inhabit the suburban townships. Manchester, properly so called, is chiefly inhabited by shopkeepers and the labouring classes.[1] Those districts

---

[1] To the stranger, it is also necessary to observe, that the investigations on whose results the conclusions of this pamphlet are founded, were of necessity

where the poor dwell are of very recent origin. The rapid growth of the cotton manufacture has attracted hither operatives from every part of the kingdom, and Ireland has poured forth the most destitute of her hordes to supply the constantly increasing demand for labour. This immigration has been, in one important respect, a serious evil. The Irish have taught the labouring classes of this country a pernicious lesson. The system of cottier farming, the demoralisation and barbarism of the people, and the general use of the potato as the chief article of food, have encouraged the growth of population in Ireland more rapidly than the *available* means of subsistence have been increased. Debased alike by ignorance and pauperism, they have discovered, with the savage, what is the minimum of the means of life, upon which existence may be prolonged. The paucity of the amount of means and comforts *necessary for the mere support of life*, is not known by a more civilised population, and this secret has been taught the labourers of this country by the Irish. As competition and the restrictions and burdens of trade diminished the profits of capital, and consequently reduced the price of labour, the contagious example of ignorance and a barbarous disregard of forethought and economy, exhibited by the Irish, spread. The colonisation of savage tribes has ever been attended with effects on civilisation as fatal as those which have marked the progress of the sand flood over the fertile plains of Egypt. Instructed in the fatal secret of subsisting on what is barely necessary to life,— yielding partly to necessity, and partly to example,— the labouring classes have ceased to entertain a laudable pride in furnishing their houses, and in multiplying the decent comforts which minister to happiness. What is superfluous to the mere exigencies of nature is

conducted *in the township of Manchester only;* and that the inhabitants of a great part of the adjacent townships are in a condition superior to that described in these pages. The most respectable portion of the operative population has, we think, a tendency to avoid the central districts of Manchester, and to congregate in the suburban townships.

too often expended at the tavern; and for the provision of old age and infirmity, they too frequently trust either to charity, to the support of their children, or to the protection of the poor laws.

When this example is considered in connection with the unremitted labour of the whole population engaged in the various branches of the cotton manufacture, our wonder will be less excited by their fatal demoralisation. Prolonged and exhausting labour, continued from day to day, and from year to year, is not calculated to develop the intellectual or moral faculties of man. The dull routine of a ceaseless drudgery, in which the same mechanical process is incessantly repeated, resembles the torment of Sisyphus — the toil, like the rock, recoils perpetually on the wearied operative. The mind gathers neither stores nor strength from the constant extension and retraction of the same muscles. The intellect slumbers in supine inertness; but the grosser parts of our nature attain a rank development. To condemn man to such monotonous toil is, in some measure, to cultivate in him the habits of an animal. He becomes reckless. He disregards the distinguishing appetites and habits of his species. He neglects the comforts and delicacies of life. He lives in squalid wretchedness, on meagre food, and expends his superfluous gains in debauchery.

The population employed in the cotton factories rises at five o'clock in the morning, works in the mills from six till eight o'clock, and returns home for half an hour or forty minutes to breakfast. This meal generally consists of tea or coffee, with a little bread. Oatmeal porridge is sometimes, but of late rarely used, and chiefly by the men; but the stimulus of tea is preferred, and especially by the women. The tea is almost always of a bad, and sometimes of a deleterious quality; the infusion is weak, and little or no milk is added. The operatives return to the mills and workshops until twelve o'clock, when an hour is allowed for dinner. Amongst those who obtain the lower rates of wages this meal generally consists of boiled potatoes.[1] The mess of potatoes is put into one large dish; melted lard and butter are poured upon them, and a few pieces of fried fat bacon are sometimes mingled with them, and but seldom a little meat. Those who obtain better wages, or families whose aggregate income is larger, add a greater proportion of animal food to this meal, at least three times in the week; but the quantity consumed by the labouring population is not great. The family sits round the table, and each rapidly appropriates his portion on a plate, or they all plunge their spoons into the dish, and with an animal eagerness satisfy the cravings of their appetite. At the expiration of the hour, they are all again employed in the workshops or mills, where they continue until seven o'clock or a later hour, when they generally again indulge in the use of tea, often mingled with spirits accompanied by a little bread. Oatmeal or potatoes are however taken by some a second time in the evening.

The comparatively innutritious qualities of these articles of diet are most evident. We are, however, by no means prepared to say that an individual living in a healthy atmosphere, and engaged in active employment in the open air, would not be able to continue protracted and severe labour, without any suffering, whilst nourished by this food. We should rather be disposed, on the contrary, to affirm, that any ill effects must necessarily be so much diminished, that, from the influence of habit, and the benefits derived from the constant inhalation of an uncontaminated atmosphere, during healthy exercise in agricultural pursuits, few if any evil results would ensue. But the population nourished on this aliment is crowded into one dense mass, in cottages separated by narrow, unpaved, and almost pestilential streets, in an atmosphere loaded with the smoke and exhalations of a large manufacturing city. The operatives are congregated in rooms and work-

---

[1] The diet and household management of the factory operatives have undergone a great change since this was written. Tea, coffee, wheaten bread, and animal food, are now much more consumed.— J. P. K. S. 1862.

shops during twelve[1] hours in the day, in an enervating, heated atmosphere, which is frequently loaded with dust or filaments of cotton, or impure from constant respiration, or from other causes. They are engaged in an employment which absorbs their attention, and unremittingly employs their physical energies.[2] They are drudges who watch the movements, and assist the operations, of a mighty material force, which toils with an energy ever unconscious of fatigue. The persevering labour of the operative must rival the mathematical precision, the incessant motion, and the exhaustless power of the machine.

Hence, besides the negative results—the abstraction of moral and intellectual stimuli — the absence of variety — banishment from the grateful air and the cheering influences of light, the physical energies are impaired by toil, and imperfect nutrition. The artisan too seldom possesses sufficient moral dignity or intellectual or organic strength to resist the seductions of appetite. His wife and children, subjected to the same process, have little power to cheer his remaining moments of leisure. Domestic economy is neglected, domestic comforts are too frequently unknown. A meal of coarse food is hastily prepared, and devoured with precipitation. Home has little other relation to him than that of shelter — few pleasures are there — it chiefly presents to him a scene of physical exhaustion, from which he is glad to escape. His house is ill furnished, uncleanly, often ill ventilated — perhaps damp; his food, from want of forethought and domestic economy, is meagre and innutritious; he generally becomes debilitated and hypochondriacal, and, unless supported by principle, falls the victim of dissipation. In all these respects, it is grateful to add, that those among the operatives of the mills, who

---

[1] The Factories Regulation Acts, restricting the hours of labour for women and children, had not then passed. Practically the restriction shortens the men's time to about an average of ten hours.

[2] A gentleman, whose opinions on these subjects command universal respect, suggests to me, that the intensity of this application is exceedingly increased by the system of paying, not for time, but according to the result of labour.

are employed *in the process of spinning*, and especially of fine spinning (who receive a high rate of wages and who are elevated on account of their skill), are more attentive to their domestic arrangements, have better furnished houses, are consequently more regular in their habits, and more observant of their duties than those engaged in other branches of the manufacture.

The other classes of artisans of whom we have spoken, are frequently subject to a disease, in which the sensibility of the stomach and bowels is morbidly excited; the alvine secretions are deranged, and the appetite impaired. Whilst this state continues, the patient loses flesh, his features are sharpened, the skin becomes sallow, or of the yellow hue which is observed in those who have suffered from the influence of tropical climates. The strength fails, the capacities of physical enjoyment are destroyed, and the paroxysms of corporeal suffering are aggravated by deep mental depression. We cannot wonder that the wretched victim of this disease, invited by those haunts of misery and crime the gin shop and the tavern, as he passes to his daily labour, should endeavour to cheat his suffering of a few moments, by the false excitement procured by ardent spirits; or that the exhausted artisan, driven by ennui and discomfort from his squalid home, should strive, in the delirious dreams of a continued debauch, to forget the remembrance of his reckless improvidence, of the destitution, hunger, and uninterrupted toil, which threaten to destroy the remaining energies of his enfeebled constitution.

The example which the Irish have exhibited of barbarous habits and savage want of economy, united with the necessarily debasing consequences of uninterrupted toil, have lowered the state of the people.

The inspection conducted by the District Boards of Health, chiefly referred to the state of the streets and houses, inhabited by the labouring population — to local nuisances, and more general evils. The greatest portion of these districts, especially of those situated beyond Great

Ancoats-street, are of very recent origin; and from the want of proper police regulations are untraversed by common sewers. The houses are ill soughed, often ill ventilated, unprovided with privies, and, in consequence, the streets, which are narrow, unpaved, and worn into deep ruts, become the common receptacles of mud, refuse, and disgusting ordure.

The Inspectors' reports do not comprise all the houses and streets of the respective districts, and are in some other respects imperfect. The returns concerning the various defects which they enumerate must be received, as the reports of evils too positive to be overlooked. Frequently, when they existed in a slighter degree, the questions received no reply.

Predisposition to contagious disease is encouraged by everything which depresses the physical energies, amongst the principal of which agencies may be enumerated imperfect nutrition; exposure to cold and moisture, whether from inadequate shelter, or from want of clothing and fuel, or from dampness of the habitation; uncleanliness of the person, the street, and the abode; an atmosphere contaminated, whether from the want of ventilation, or from impure effluvia; extreme labour, and consequent physical exhaustion; intemperance; fear; anxiety; diarrhœa, and other diseases. The whole of these subjects could not be included in the investigation, though it originated in a desire to remove, as far as possible, those ills which depressed the health of the population. The list of inquiries to which the inspectors were requested to make tabular replies is placed in the appendix, for the purpose of enabling the reader to form his own opinion of the investigation from which the classified results are deduced.

The state of the streets powerfully affects the health of their inhabitants. Sporadic cases of typhus chiefly appear in those which are narrow, ill ventilated, unpaved, or which contain heaps of refuse, or stagnant pools. The confined air and noxious exhalations, which abound in such places, depress the health of the people, and on this account contagious diseases are also most rapidly propagated there. The operation of these causes is exceedingly promoted by their reflex influence on the manners. The houses, in such situations, are uncleanly, ill provided with furniture; an air of discomfort if not of squalid and loathsome wretchedness pervades them, they are often dilapidated, badly drained, damp: and the habits of their tenants are gross—they are ill fed, ill clothed, and uneconomical—at once spendthrifts and destitute—denying themselves the comforts of life, in order that they may wallow in the unrestrained licence of animal appetite. An intimate connection subsists, among the poor, between the cleanliness of the street and that of the house and person. Uneconomical habits and dissipation are almost inseparably allied; and they are so frequently connected with uncleanliness, that we cannot consider their concomitance as altogether accidental. The first step to recklessness may often be traced in a neglect of that self-respect, and of the love of domestic enjoyments, which are indicated by personal slovenliness, and discomfort of the habitation. Hence, the importance of providing by police regulations or general enactment, against those fertile sources alike of disease and demoralisation, presented by the gross neglect of the streets and habitations of the poor. When the health is depressed by the concurrence of these causes, contagious diseases spread with a fatal malignancy among the population subjected to their influence. The records[1] of the Fever Hospital of Manchester prove that typhus *prevails almost exclusively* in such situations.

The following table, arranged by the Committee of Classification appointed by the Special Board of Health, from the reports of Inspectors of the various District Boards of Manchester, shows the extent to which the imperfect state of the streets of Manchester may tend to promote demoralisation and disease among the poor.

---

[1] Abundant evidence of this fact was collected by Mr. Wallis, lately House Surgeon to the House of Recovery.

Manchester in 1832

No. of District.	No. of streets inspected.	No. of streets unpaved.	No. of streets partially paved.	No. of streets ill ventilated.	No. of streets containing heaps of refuse, stagnant pools, ordure, &c.
1	114	63	13	7	64
2	180	93	7	23	92
3	49	2	2	12	28
4	66	37	10	12	52
5	30	2	5	5	12
6	2	1	0	1	2
7	53	13	5	12	17
8	16	2	1	2	7
9	48	0	0	9	20
10	29	19	0	10	23
11	0	0	0	0	0
12	12	0	1	1	4
13	55	3	9	10	23
14	33	13	0	8	8
Total	687	248	53	112	352

A minute inspection of this table will render the extent of the evil affecting the poor more apparent. Those districts which are almost exclusively inhabited by the labouring population are Nos. 1, 2, 3, 4, and 10. Nos. 13 and 14, and 7, also contain, besides the dwellings of the operatives, those of shopkeepers and tradesmen, and are traversed by many of the principal thoroughfares. No. 11 was not inspected, and Nos. 5, 6, 8, and 9, are the central districts containing the chief streets, the most respectable shops, the dwellings of the more wealthy inhabitants, and the warehouses of merchants and manufacturers. Subtracting, therefore, from the various totals, those items in the reports which concern these divisions only, we discover in those districts which contain a large portion of poor, namely, in Nos. 1, 2, 3, 4, 7, 10, 13, and 14, that among 579 streets inspected, 243 were altogether unpaved, 46 partially paved, 93 ill ventilated, and 307 contained heaps of refuse, deep ruts, stagnant pools, ordure, &c.; and in the districts which are almost exclusively inhabited by the poor, namely, Nos. 1, 2, 3, 4, and 10, among 438 streets inspected, 214 were altogether unpaved, 32 partially paved, 63 ill ventilated, and 259 contained heaps of refuse, deep ruts, stagnant pools, ordure, &c.

The replies to the questions proposed in the second table relating to houses, contain equally remarkable results, which have been carefully arranged by the Classification Committee of the Special Board of Health, as follows :—

District.	No. of houses inspected.	No. of houses reported as requiring whitewashing.	No. of houses reported as requiring repair.	No. of houses in which the soughs wanted repair.	No. of houses damp.	No. of houses reported as ill ventilated.	No. of houses wanting privies.
1	850	399	128	112	177	70	326
2	2489	898	282	145	497	109	755
3	213	145	104	41	61	52	96
4	650	279	106	105	134	69	250
5	413	176	82	70	101	11	66
6	12	3	5	5			5
7	343	76	59	57	86	21	79
8	132	35	30	39	48	22	20
9	128	34	32	24	39	19	25
10	370	195	53	123	54	2	232
11							
12	113	33	23	27	24	16	52
13	757	218	44	108	146	54	177
14	481	74	13	83	68	7	138
Total	6951	2565	960	939	1435	452	2221

It is, however, to be lamented, that even these numerical results fail to exhibit a perfect picture of the ills which are suffered by the poor. The replies to the questions contained in the Inspectors' table refer only to cases of the most positive kind, and the numerical results would, therefore, have been exceedingly increased, had they embraced those in which the evils existed in a scarcely inferior degree. Some idea of the want of cleanliness prevalent in their habitations, may be obtained from the report of the number of houses requiring whitewashing; but this column fails to indicate their gross neglect of order, and absolute filth. Much less can we obtain satisfactory statistical results concerning the want of furniture, especially of bedding, and of food, clothing, and fuel. In these respects the habitations of the Irish are most destitute. They can scarcely be said to be furnished. They contain one or two chairs, a mean table, the most scanty culinary apparatus, and one or two beds, loathsome with filth. A whole family is often accommodated on a single bed, and sometimes a heap of filthy straw and a covering of old sacking hide them in one undistinguished heap, debased alike by penury, want of economy, and dissolute habits. Frequently, the Inspectors found two or more families crowded into one small house, containing only two apartments, one in which they slept, and another in which they ate; and often more than one family lived in a damp cellar, containing only one room, in whose pestilential atmosphere from twelve to sixteen persons were crowded. To these fertile sources of disease were sometimes added the keeping of pigs and other animals in the house, with other nuisances of the most revolting character.

As the visits of the Inspectors were made in the day, when the population is engaged in the mills, and the vagrants and paupers are wandering through the town, they could not form any just idea of the state of the pauper lodging-houses. The establishments thus designated are fertile sources of disease and demoralisation. They are frequently able to accommodate from twenty to thirty or more lodgers, among whom are the most abandoned characters, who, reckless of the morrow, resort thither for the shelter of the night—men who find safety in a constant change of abode, or are too uncertain in their pursuits to remain beneath the same roof for a longer period. Here, without distinction of age or sex, careless of all decency, they are crowded in small and wretched apartments; the same bed receiving a succession of tenants until too offensive even for their unfastidious senses. The Special Board being desirous that these lodging-houses should be inspected by the Overseers, the Churchwardens obtained a report of the number in each district, which cannot fail to be a source of surprise and apprehension.

PAUPER LODGING-HOUSES.

	No. of houses.		No. of houses.
District No. 1	0	District No. 9	0
2	108	10	12
3	51	11	26
4	0	12	—
5	6	13	60
6	0	14	1
7	3		
8	0		267

The temporary tenants of these disgusting abodes, too frequently debased by vice, haunted by want, and every other consequence of crime, are peculiarly disposed to the reception of contagion. Their asylums are frequently recesses where it lurks, and they are active agents in its diffusion. They ought to be as much the objects of a careful vigilance from those who are the guardians of the health, as from those who protect the property of the public.

In some districts of the town exist evils so remarkable as to require more minute description. A portion of low, swampy ground, liable to be frequently inundated, and to constant exhalation, is included between a high bank over which the Oxford Road passes, and a bend of the river Medlock, where its course is impeded by a weir. This unhealthy spot lies so low that the chimneys of its houses, some of them three stories high, are little above the level of the road. About two hundred of these habitations are crowded together in an extremely narrow space, and they are chiefly inhabited by the lowest Irish. Many of these houses have also cellars, whose floor is scarcely elevated above the level of the water flowing in the Medlock. The soughs are destroyed, or out of repair: and these narrow abodes are in consequence always damp, and are frequently flooded to the depth of several inches, because the surface water can find no exit. This district has sometimes been the haunt of hordes of thieves and desperadoes who defied the law, and is always inhabited by a class resembling savages in their appetites and habits. It is surrounded on every side by some of the largest factories of the town, whose chimneys vomit forth dense clouds of smoke, which hang heavily over this insalubrious region.

The subjoined document resulted from an inspection made by a Special Sub-committee of Members of the Board of Health, and the signatures of the gentlemen forming that Sub-Committee were appended to it.[1]

Near the centre of the town, a mass of buildings, inhabited by prostitutes and thieves, is intersected by nar-

---

[1] TO THE MAGISTRATES OF THE DISTRICT.

GENTLEMEN,

The undersigned having been deputed by the Special Board of Health to inquire into the state of Little Ireland, beg to report that in the main street and courts abutting, the sewers are all in a most wretched state, and quite inadequate to carry off the surface water, not to mention the slops thrown down by the inhabitants in about two hundred houses.

The privies are in a most disgraceful state, inaccessible from filth, and too few for the accommodation of the number of people,—the average number being two to two hundred and fifty people. The upper rooms are, with few exceptions, very dirty, and the cellars much worse; all damp, and some occasionally overflowed. The cellars consist of two rooms on a floor, each nine to ten feet square, some inhabited by ten persons, others by more: in many, the people have no beds, and keep each other warm by close stowage on shavings, straw, &c.; a change of linen or clothes is an exception to the common practice. Many of the back rooms where they sleep have no other means of ventilation than from the front rooms.

Some of the cellars on the lower ground were once filled up as uninhabitable; but one is now occupied by a weaver, and he has stopped up the drain with clay, to prevent the water flowing from it into his cellar, and mops up the water every morning.

We conceive it will be impossible effectually to remove the evils enumerated; and offer the following suggestions with a view to their partial amelioration.

First, to open up the main sewer from the bottom, and to relay it.

Secondly, to open and unchoke the lateral drains, and secure a regular discharge of the water, &c., into the main sewer.

Thirdly, to enforce the weekly cleansing and purification of the privies.

Fourthly, if practicable, to fill up the cellars.

Fifthly, to provide the inhabitants with quicklime, and induce them to whitewash their rooms, where it can be done with safety.

Sixthly, if possible, to induce the inhabitants to observe greater cleanliness in their houses and persons.

In conclusion, we are decidedly of opinion that should cholera visit this neighbourhood, a more suitable soil and situation for its malignant development cannot be found than that described and commonly known by the name of Little Ireland.

row and loathsome streets, and close courts defiled with refuse. These nuisances exist in No. 13 District, on the western side of Deansgate, and chiefly abound in Wood-street, Spinning Field, Cumberland-street, Parliament-passage, Parliament-street, and Thomson-street. In Parliament-street there is only one privy for three hundred and eighty inhabitants, which is placed in a narrow passage, whence its effluvia infest the adjacent houses, and must prove a most fertile source of disease. In this street also, cesspools with open grids have been made close to the doors of the houses, in which disgusting refuse accumulates, and whence its noxious effluvia constantly exhale. In Parliament-passage about thirty houses have been erected, merely separated by an extremely narrow passage (a yard and a half wide) from the wall and back door of other houses. These thirty houses have one privy.

The state of the streets and houses in that part of No. 4, included between Store-street and Travis-street, and London Road, is exceedingly wretched — especially those built on some irregular and broken mounds of clay, on a steep declivity descending into Store-street. These narrow avenues are rough, irregular gullies, down which filthy streams percolate; and the inhabitants are crowded in dilapidated abodes, or obscure and damp cellars, in which it is impossible for the health to be preserved.

Unwilling to weary the patience of the reader by extending such disgusting details, it may suffice to refer generally to the wretched state of the habitations of the poor in Clay-street, and the lower portion of Pot-street; in Providence-street, and its adjoining courts; in Back Portugal-street; in Back Hart-street, and many of the courts in the neighbourhood of Portland-street, some of which are not more than a yard and a quarter wide, and contain houses, frequently three stories high, the lowest of which stories is occasionally used as a receptacle of *excrementitious matter :* — to many streets in the neighbourhood of Garden-street, Shudehill:— to Back Irk-street, and to the state of almost the whole of that mass of cottages filling the insalubrious valley through which the Irk flows, and which is denominated Irish town.

The Irk, black with the refuse of dye-works erected on its banks, receives excrementitious matters from some sewers in this portion of the town — the drainage from the gas-works, and filth of the most pernicious character from bone-works, tanneries, size manufactories, &c. Immediately beneath Ducie-bridge, in a deep hollow between two high banks, it sweeps round a large cluster of some of the most wretched and dilapidated buildings of the town. The course of the river is here impeded by a weir, and a large tannery, eight stories high (three of which stories are filled with skins exposed to the atmosphere, in some stage of the processes to which they are subjected), towers close to this crazy labyrinth of pauper dwellings. This group of habitations is called 'Gibraltar,' and no sight can well be more insalubrious than that on which it is built. Pursuing the course of the river on the other side of Ducie-bridge, other tanneries, size manufactories, and tripe-houses occur. The parish burial ground occupies one side of the stream, and a series of courts of the most singular and unhealthy character the other. Access is obtained to these courts through narrow covered entries from Long Millgate, whence the explorer descends by stone stairs, and in one instance by three successive flights of steps to a level with the bed of the river. In this last-mentioned (Allen's) court he discovers himself to be surrounded, on one side by a wall of rock, on two others by houses three stories high, and on the fourth by the abrupt and high bank down which he descended, and by walls and houses erected on the summit. These houses were, a short time ago, chiefly inhabited by fringe, silk, and cotton weavers, and winders, and each house contained in general three or four families. An adjoining court (Barrett's) on the summit of the bank, separated from Allen's court only by a low wall, contained, besides a pig-stye — a tripe manufactory in a low cottage, which was in a state of loathsome filth. Portions of animal matter were decaying in it, and one of the inner rooms was converted into a kennel, and contained a litter of puppies. In the court, on the opposite side, is a tan yard where skins are prepared without bark in open pits, and here is also a catgut manufactory. Many of the windows of the houses in Allen's court open over the river Irk, whose stream (again impeded, at the distance of one hundred yards by a weir) separates it from another tannery, four stories high and filled with skins, exposed to the currents of air which pass through the building. On the other side of this tannery is the parish burial ground, chiefly used as a place of interment for paupers. A more unhealthy spot than this (Allen's) court it would be difficult to discover, and the physical depression consequent on living in such a situation may be inferred from what ensued on the introduction of cholera here. A matchseller, living in the first story of one of these houses, was seized with cholera, on Sunday, July 22nd: he died on Wednesday, July 25th; and owing to the wilful negligence of his friends, and because the Board of Health had no intimation of the occurrence, he was not buried until Friday afternoon, July 27th. On that day, five other cases of cholera occurred amongst the inhabitants of the court. On the 28th, seven, and on the 29th two. The cases were nearly all fatal. Those affected with cholera were on the 28th and 29th removed to the Hospital, the dead were buried, and on the 29th the majority of the inhabitants were taken to a house of reception, and the rest, with one exception, dispersed into the town, until their houses had been thoroughly fumigated, ventilated, whitewashed, and cleansed; notwithstanding which dispersion, other cases occurred amongst those who had left the court.

These facts are thus minutely related, because we are anxious to direct public attention to the advantage which would accrue from widening this portion of Long Millgate, by taking down the whole of the houses on the Irk side of the street, from a factory which projects into it, on that side, as far as Ducie-bridge, and thus improving this important entrance to the town, from Bury, and from the north-east of Lancashire.

The houses of the poor, especially throughout the whole of the Districts Nos. 1, 2, 3, 4, are too generally built back to back, having therefore only one outlet, no yard, no privy, and no receptacle of refuse. Consequently the narrow, unpaved streets, in which mud and water stagnate, become the common receptacles of offal and ordure. Often low, damp, ill-ventilated cellars[1] exist beneath the houses; an improvement on which system consists in the erection of a stage over the first story, by which access is obtained to the second, and the house is inhabited by two separate families. More than one disgraceful example of this might be enumerated. The streets, in the districts where the poor reside, are generally unsewered, and the drainage is consequently superficial. The houses are often built with a total neglect of order, on the summit of natural irregularities of the surface, or on mounds left at the side of artificial excavations on the brick grounds, with which these parts of the town abound.

One nuisance frequently occurs in these districts of so noxious a character, that it ought, at the earliest period, to be suppressed by legal interference. The houses of the poor sometimes surround a common area, into which the doors and windows open at the back of the dwelling. Porkers, who feed pigs in the town, often contract with the inhabitants to pay some small sum for the rent of their area, which is immediately covered with pigstyes, and converted into a dung-heap and receptacle of the putrescent garbage, upon which the animals are fed, as also of the refuse which is now heedlessly flung into it from all

---

[1] I have placed in the Appendix No. II. a Note, written in 1862, containing the results of the inquiries of the Statistical Society of Manchester, as to the number of cellar dwellings in Manchester and Liverpool, in 1834-5-6.

the surrounding dwellings. The offensive odour which sometimes arises from these areas cannot be conceived.

There is no *Common* Slaughter-house in Manchester, and those which exist are chiefly situated in the narrowest and most filthy streets in the town. The drainage from these houses, deeply tinged with blood, and impregnated with other animal matters, frequently flows down the common surface drain of the street, and stagnates in the ruts and pools. Moreover, sometimes in the yards of these houses — from the want of a vigilant circumspection — offal is allowed to accumulate with the grossest neglect of decency and disregard to the health of the surrounding inhabitants. The attention of the commissioners of police cannot be too soon directed to the propriety of obtaining powers to erect a Common Slaughter-house on some vacant space, and to compel the butchers of the town to slaughter all animals killed in the township in the building thus provided.

The Districts Nos. 1, 2, 3, and 4, are inhabited by a turbulent population, which, rendered reckless by dissipation and want,— misled by the secret intrigues, and excited by the inflammatory harangues of demagogues, has frequently committed daring assaults on the liberty of the more peaceful portions of the working classes, and the most frightful devastations on the property of their masters. Machines have been broken, and factories gutted and burned at mid-day, and the riotous crowd has dispersed ere the insufficient body of police arrived at the scene of disturbance. The civic force of the town is totally inadequate to maintain the peace, and to defend property from the attacks of lawless depredators; and *a more efficient, and more numerous corps ought to be immediately organised*, to give power to the law, so often mocked by the daring front of sedition, and outraged by the frantic violence of an ignorant and deluded rabble. The police form, in fact, so weak a screen against the power of the mob, that popular violence is now, in almost every instance, controlled by the presence of a military force.

The wages[1] obtained by operatives in the various branches of the cotton manufacture are, in general, such, as with the exercise of that economy without which wealth itself is wasted, would be sufficient to provide them with all the decent comforts of life—the average wages of all persons employed in the mills (young and old) being from nine to twelve shillings per week. Their means are too often consumed by vice and *improvidence.* But the wages of certain classes are exceedingly meagre. The introduction of the power-loom, though ultimately destined to be productive of the greatest general benefits, has, in the present restricted state of commerce, occasioned some temporary embarrassment, by diminishing the demand for certain kinds of labour, and, consequently, their price. The hand-loom weavers, *existing in this state of transition*, still continue a very extensive class, and though they labour fourteen hours and upwards daily, earn only from five to seven or eight shillings per week.[2] They consist chiefly of Irish, and are affected by all the causes of moral and physical depression which we have enumerated. Ill fed—ill clothed—half sheltered and ignorant;—weaving in close damp cellars, or crowded workshops, it only remains that they should become, as is too frequently the case, demoralised and reckless, to render perfect the portraiture of savage life. Amongst men so situated, the moral check has no influence in preventing the rapid increase of the population. The existence of cheap and redundant labour in the market has, also, a *constant* tendency to lessen its general price, and hence the wages of the English operatives have been exceedingly reduced by this immigration of Irish—their comforts consequently diminished—their manners debased—and the natural

---

[1] 'The wages are paid weekly, not once a fortnight, or once a month, as is the case in collieries and many other places. The youngest child in the mill earns three shillings per week, and the best female spinner twenty-one shillings. The total paid is £356—averaging nine shillings and three pence per week to each person employed.'—*Letter to Lord Althorp in Defence of the Cotton Factories of Lancashire.* By Holland Hoole, Esq.

[2] Evidence of Joseph Foster before the Emigration Committee, 1827.

influence of manufactures on the people thwarted. We are well convinced that without the numerical and moral influence of this class, on the means and on the character of the people who have had to enter into competition with them in the market of labour, we should have had less occasion to regret the physical and moral degradation of the operative population.

The poor-laws, as at present administered[1], retain all the evils of the gross and indiscriminate bounty of ancient monasteries. They also fail in exciting the gratitude of the people, and they extinguish the charity of the rich. The custom is not now demanded as the prop of any superstition; nor is it fit that institutions, well calculated to assuage the miseries which feudalism inflicted on its unemployed and unhappy serfs, should be allowed to perpetuate indigence, improvidence, idleness and vice, in a commercial community. The artificial structure of society, in providing security against existing evils, has too frequently neglected the remote moral influence of its arrangements on the community. Humanity rejoices in the consciousness that the poorest may obtain the advantages of skilful care in disease, and that there are asylums for infirmity, age, and decrepitude; but the unlimited extension of benefits, devised by a wise intelligence for the relief of evils which no human prescience could elude, has a direct tendency to encourage amongst the poor apathy concerning present exigencies, and the neglect of a provision for the contingencies of the future.

A rate levied on property for the support of indigence is, in a great degree, a tax on the capital, from whose employment are derived the incentives of industry and the rewards of the frugal, ingenious, and virtuous poor. If the only test of the application of this fund be *indigence*, without reference to *desert*—be *want*, irrespective of *character*—motives to frugality, self-control and industry are at once

---

[1] This was published before the passing of the Poor Law Amendment Act.

removed, and the strong barrier which nature had itself erected to prevent the moral lapse of the entire population is wantonly destroyed. The tax acts as a new burden on the *industrious* poor, already suffering from an enormous pressure, and not only drags within the limits of pauperism unwilling victims, but paralyses with despair the efforts of those whose exertions might otherwise have prolonged their struggle with adversity. The wages of the worthy are often given to encourage the sluggard, the drunkard, and the man whose imprudence entails on the community the precocious burden of his meagre and neglected offspring.

The feeble obstacle raised in the *country* to the propagation of a pauper population, by making the indigent chargeable on the estates of the land-owners, is even there rendered almost entirely inefficacious by the too frequent non-residence of the gentry, or the indifference with which this apparently inevitable evil is regarded. In the South of England the fatal error has been committed of paying a certain portion of the wages of able-bodied labourers out of the fund obtained by the poor-rates; and a population is thus created, bound like slaves to toil, and having also like them a right to be maintained. But, in the large towns, the feeble check to the increase of pauperism, which thus exists in some rural districts, is entirely removed. The land is let to speculators who build cottages, the rents of which are collected weekly, a commutation for the rates being often paid by the landlord when they are demanded, which seldom occurs in the lowest description of houses. A married man having thus by law an unquestioned right to a maintenance proportioned to the number of his family, direct encouragement is afforded to improvident marriages. The most destitute and immoral marry to increase their claim on the stipend appointed for them by law, which thus acts as a bounty on the increase of a squalid and debilitated race, who inherit from their parents disease, sometimes deformity, often vice, and always beggary.

The number of labourers thus created diminishes the

already scanty wages of that portion of the population still content to endeavour by precarious toil to maintain their honest independence. Desperate is the struggle by which, under such a system, the upright labourer procures for his family the comforts of existence. Many are dragged by the accidents of life to an unwilling acceptance of this legalised pension of the profligate, and some, over informed by misfortune in the treachery of their own hearts, are seduced to palter with temptation, and at length to capitulate with their apparent fate.

Fearful demoralisation attends an impost whose distribution diminishes the incentives to prudence and virtue. When reckless of the future, the intelligence of man is confined to the narrow limits of the present. He thus debases himself beneath the animals, whose instincts teach them to lay up stores for the season of need. The gains [1] of the pauper are, in prosperity, frequently squandered in taverns, whilst his family exists in hungered and ragged misery, and few sympathies with the sufferings of his aged relatives or neighbours enter his cold heart, since he knows they have an equal claim with himself, on that pittance which the law awards. The superfluities which nature would prompt him in a season of abundance to hoard for the accidents of the future, are wasted with reckless profusion; because *the law takes care of the future.* Selfish profligacy usurps the seat of the household virtues of the English labourer.

Charity once extended an invisible chain of sympathy between the higher and lower ranks of society, which has been destroyed by the luckless pseudophilanthropy of the law.[2] Few aged or decrepid pensioners now gratefully receive the visits of the higher classes — few of the poor seek the counsel, the admonitions, and assistance of the

---

[1] See evidence of Mr. Allen concerning pauperism in Spitalfields.

[2] If the relief of indigence from the poor-rate were a matter of Christian charity, in any other sense than being a humane provision of an enlightened system of police, developed in a Christian nation, this might be just; but otherwise it involves a confusion of charity with police.—J. P. K. S. 1862.

rich in the period of the inevitable accidents of life. The bar of the overseer is however crowded with the sturdy applicants for a legalised relief, who regard the distributor of this bounty as their stern and merciless oppressor, instructed by the compassionless rich to reduce to the lowest possible amount the alms which the law wrings from their reluctant hands. This disruption of the natural ties has created a wide gulf between the higher and lower orders of the community, across which the scowl of hatred banishes the smile of charity and love.

That government have appointed a Commission of inquiry into the evils arising from the administration of the Poor-laws, must be a source of satisfaction to every well-wisher to the poor. Since it would be unjust to annul the existing provision for a rapidly increasing indigence which the law has itself fostered, the improvement of its present administration is all that the most sanguine can expect as an immediate result of this inquiry. Every change which assimilates the *method of distributing* this legal charity to that by which a well-regulated private bounty is administered, must be hailed.[1] The present official organisation in the large towns is incapable of producing these results. The parish officers and sidesmen are not sufficiently numerous to enable them (if they were permitted by law) to make a discrimination — concerning the characters of individuals, their actual condition, and the accidents or faults that may have occasioned it — equal to that which is observed in the most judicious distribution of private bounty. Since desert does not enhance the claim which indigence can enforce, the only relation which the parish officer now has with the applicant for relief is that of the investigation and proof of his indigence; and, to this end, those now em-

---

[1] This rule is not applicable to the simple relief of indigence. That is a pure regulation of police, giving security to life in order to give security to property and peace to society, by the suppression of vagabondage and crime. But it is applicable to all the moral relations of pauper children and indigent age in workhouses.—1862.

ployed may be sufficiently proper agents. But if we would substitute any portion of that sympathy with the distresses of the poor, and that gratitude for relief afforded — that acknowledged right to administer good counsel, and that willingness to receive advice — that privilege of inquiring into the arrangements of domestic economy, instructing the ignorant, and checking the perverse—all which attend the beneficent path of private charity, much superior men must be employed in the office of visiting the houses of the poor, and being the almoners of the public. Such an office can only be properly filled by men of some education, but especially of high moral character, and possessing great natural gentleness. An attempt should be constantly made to relieve the mind of the independent poor from the necessity of receiving an eleemosynary dole, by recommending the worthy to employment. It is not sufficient that the Sidesman or Churchwarden should give a few hours daily to an examination of all applicants in our enormous townships, but the towns should be minutely subdivided, each district having its local board, which (besides an executive parish overseer resident in the district, and thus possessing every means of becoming minutely acquainted with the character of the inhabitants), should also be furnished with its board of superior officers. By such means: by adopting the test of desert[1], at least to determine the *amount* of relief bestowed: by discouraging or even rejecting those whose indigence is the consequence of dissipation, of idleness, and of wilful imprudence; and by making the overseers themselves the means of instructing the poor, that every labourer is the surest architect of his own fortune—by constituting them the patrons of virtue and the censors of vice, and besides being the almoners of the public charity, the sources of a powerful moral agency —

---

[1] There is no moral test applicable to destitution of the means of living. Society decides that it is for the public interest that even the most worthless indigent should be kept alive. The pauper's claim is for life, not on account of desert, but of indigence.—J. P. K. S. 1862.

much good might be effected.¹ The enormous expenditure, incurred by the present system, might be exceedingly reduced, and the alms might at length (by a process whose success would depend on the gradual moral improvement of society), be confined to such of the aged, the decrepid, and the unfortunate, as being without the hope of assistance from the charity of relations or friends, were thus reluctantly driven, by a hard necessity, to have recourse to the *fund of the poor*. *Societies for mutual relief should be everywhere encouraged*, and a constant effort should be vigorously maintained to disburden the public of this enormous tax, by every other *means which would contribute to the virtuous independence of the working classes.*

At present this alarming impost increases so rapidly, that it threatens ultimately to absorb the fund which ought to be employed solely in rewarding the labour of the industrious poor, and hence, to reduce the whole population to the condition of helots.

The fund derived from the poor's-rate for the relief of the indigent, is, in Manchester, as judiciously administered as the state of the law will permit. Too much praise can scarcely be given to the zealous exertions of those gentlemen who fill the offices of Churchwardens and Sidesmen. Yet the effect of the present state of the law is but too apparent here.

Pauperism is everywhere accompanied with moral and physical degradation. Impressed with this opinion, we endeavoured to discover, from such facts as might be ascertained at the town's offices, how this calamitous law affected Manchester.

Unfortunately, the distribution of the poor-rates is not registered separately for each of the police divisions. We are therefore only able to compare the four sections of the town visited by the overseers. The first and second

---

¹ The scheme here suggested is clearly impracticable as a method of administration for the relief of indigence: but it is also impossible, in the strictest relief of indigence as a matter of police, to overlook all the moral relations of men.—1862.

of these four sections, which we shall denominate the Newtown and the Ancoats districts, comprise Nos. 1, 2, and 4, and therefore contain almost exclusively poor inhabitants. On the other hand, the third, or central division, besides Nos. 5, 6, 9, and a small part of No. 8, which are inhabited by a great number of shopkeepers and tradesmen, contains also Nos. 10, 11, and 14, which have a very large proportion of poor. The fourth, or Portland-street District, besides Nos. 3, 7, and 13, containing many poor, likewise comprises No. 12, and the greater part of No. 8, in which the poor inhabitants are relatively much less numerous.

We have subjoined a table exhibiting the population of each of the police divisions, according to the last census, and arranged in the four sections visited by the overseers of the poor, so as to exhibit their relative population.

Newtown.	Ancoats.	Central.	Portland Street.
No. 2...25,581 $\frac{3}{5}$ of 4... 9337$\frac{4}{5}$	No. 1...31,573 $\frac{2}{5}$ of 4... 6225$\frac{1}{5}$	No. 5... 7275 6... 1274 9... 3318 10... 3886 11...13,635 14... 6834 $\frac{1}{4}$ of 8... 686	No. 3... 11,431 7... 9784 $\frac{3}{4}$ of 8... 2058 12... 1859 13... 7269
34,918$\frac{4}{5}$	37,798$\frac{1}{5}$	36,908	32,401

The cases relieved at the Churchwardens' offices are classed as Irish and English cases: the first consist exclusively of Irish cases *without settlements*, but under the denomination of English cases, are included *all who have obtained settlements, whether English or Irish;* and this class comprises a very great proportion of Irish. We have been enabled, by the liberality of the Churchwardens, and Mr. Gardiner's politeness, to obtain returns of the relative proportion of these cases during the four winter months of the four years from 1827 to 1831 inclusive, The general table is inserted in the Appendix[1], but

[1] See Appendix No. III.

from this we have deduced some more minutely classified results, which we conceive strongly to corroborate the opinions which we have hazarded, concerning the origin and growth of pauperism.

The table contained in the Appendix exhibits, in the first place, an alarming increase of pauperism in the whole township. The total number of *cases* (each representing, on the average, two and a half individuals) relieved in the township, in the months of November, December, January, and February of 1827 and 1828, was 30,717, or included 76,792 individual acts of relief, each continued for an indefinite period. This number had, in the same months of 1830-31, increased to 45,842, or, at a period when the population amounted to 142,026, it included 114,605 individual acts of relief, each of which comprised indefinite portions of the four months, or had *almost doubled in four years*. Supposing these acts to have been administered at all times to different persons, then, more than four-fifths of the whole population were relieved for an indefinite portion of the four winter months.

The relative proportion of Irish cases without settlements, and of English and Irish cases with settlements, and their relative increase during these four years, are perhaps still more remarkable.

Districts.	Nov. 1827 to Feb. 1828.		Nov. 1828 to Feb. 1829.		Nov. 1829 to Feb. 1830.		Nov. 1830 to Feb. 1831.	
	Irish.	English.	Irish.	English.	Irish.	English.	Irish.	English.
NEWTOWN. No. 2 & ⅗ No. 4	1559	6059	1490	5434	3911	8023	4051	9129
ANCOATS. No. 1 & ⅖ No. 4	1482	6701	2155	7158	2690	8022	3818	9027
CENTRAL. Nos. 5, 6, 9, 10, 11, 14, & ¼ No. 8	366	7422	532	7161	742	9668	909	10,214
PORTLAND ST. Nos. 3, 7, 12, 13, and ¾ of No. 8	264	6864	577	6974	1186	8591	1114	7580

The proportion of Irish cases *without settlements*, in the

Ancoats and Newtown Divisions, containing Nos. 1, 2, and 4, and its relative increase, are exceedingly greater than in the Central and Portland-street Districts; notwithstanding that the number of Irish in these latter sections is much augmented by the inclusion of Nos. 3, 7, 10, and 13.

By the following table, this increase may be more easily compared :—

Districts.	Nov. 1827 to Feb. 1828.		Nov. 1828 to Feb. 1829.		Nov. 1829 to Feb. 1830.		Nov. 1830 to Feb. 1831.	
	Irish.	English.	Irish.	English.	Irish.	English.	Irish.	English.
NEWTOWN AND ANCOATS.	3041	12,760	3645	12,592	6601	16,045	7869	18,156
CENTRAL AND PORTLAND ST.	630	14,286	1109	14,136	1928	18,259	2023	17,794

The Newtown and Ancoats Districts have always contained a greater proportion of Irish than any other portion of the town; but the increase of pauperism in the Central and Portland Districts, must evidently be ascribed to the recent rapid colonisation of Irish in Divisions 3, 7, and 10; since, whilst the Irish cases, having no *settlements*, have increased from 600 to 2000, or are more than trebled, — the cases having settlements, which have been relieved, have only increased from 14,000 to 17,000, or about two-ninths. In the same period, the rapid relative increase of the Irish cases having *no settlements*, in the Newtown and Ancoats Districts, renders it extremely probable, that the increase of those cases which *have obtained settlements*, is in a great measure to be imputed to the Irish; and that pauperism, therefore, spreads most rapidly in an ignorant and demoralised population. These tables also abundantly testify, that *pauperism chiefly prevails in those portions of the town, where the sources and evidences of moral and physical depression, to which we have alluded, are the most numerous.*[1]

[1] I have no doubt whatever that this remark was founded on accurate observation; and varied experience of thirty years confirms it.—1862.

The relative proportion of the population to the cases and individuals relieved, in the four Sections visited by the Overseers, is displayed in the following table:—

Districts.	Cases relieved for indefinite periods of the four winter months, 1830-31.	Population.			Individual acts of relief for indefinite periods of time.
NEWTOWN	13,180	$34,918\frac{4}{5}$ of which	$\frac{2}{5}=$	$13,967\frac{1}{5}$	32,950
ANCOATS	12,890	$37,798\frac{1}{5}$	$\frac{1}{3}=$	$12,599\frac{2}{3}$	32,225
Total	26,070	72,717	$\frac{3}{8}=$	$27,143\frac{7}{8}$	65,175
CENTRAL	11,123	36,908	$\frac{3}{10}=$	$11,072\frac{4}{10}$	$27,807\frac{1}{2}$
PORTLAND	8694	32,401	$\frac{1}{4}=$	8100	21,735
Total	19,817	69,309			49,542

The following table [1] shows the relative proportion of cases relieved in the four Overseers' Sections during three portions of the year 1830-31, each containing four months.

Districts.	Nov. Dec. Jan. Feb.		Mar. Apr. May, June.		July, Aug. Sept. Oct.	
	Irish.	English.	Irish.	English.	Irish.	English.
NEWTOWN	4051	9129	3896	7958	3409	7996
ANCOATS	3818	9027	3333	7801	3280	8107
CENTRAL	909	10,214	815	9474	695	9287
PORTLAND	1114	7580	897	7050	863	7766
	9892	35,950	8941	32,283	8247	33,156

The population of the township is 142,026; *and the cost of parochial relief in one year*, each continued through indefinite periods of time, *were* 321,172, of which cast 67,700 *concerned Irish who had obtained no settlements.*

The sources of vice and physical degradation are allied with the causes of pauperism. Amongst the poor, the most destitute are too frequently the most demoralised— virtue is the surest economy—vice is haunted by profligacy

---

[1] See Appendix No. II.

and want. Where there are most paupers, the gin shops, taverns, and beer houses are most numerous. The following table enumerates the taverns of the town. Gin shops are held under the same licence, and are attached to three-fourths of these establishments.

NO. OF LICENSED TAVERN AND INNKEEPERS IN THE TOWNSHIP OF MANCHESTER.

No. 1 . . . 62	No. 6 . . . 39	No. 11 . . . 37
2 . . . 44	7 . . . 19	12 . . . 16
3 . . . 48	8 . . . 10	13 . . . 25
4 . . . 31	9 . . . 36	14 . . . 13
5 . . . 46	10 . . . 4	
		Total . . . 430

To this number may perhaps be added 322 gin shops. These last establishments especially abound in the poorest and most destitute districts, where their proportion to the taverns is at least four-fifths. We were unable to procure, from the officers of excise in Manchester, information concerning the relative proportion of the beer houses in the several divisions of the town; but we are informed by Mr. Shawcross, of the police department, that their number is at least three hundred. If we subtract fifty respectable inns, which, however, have generally taprooms attached to them, one thousand haunts of intemperance exist in Manchester.

The Districts 1, 2, 3, and 4, may be conceived to represent most correctly the exclusively labouring population; but in estimating the relative number of all these sources of vice frequented by the population of these districts, it is necessary to include those of the adjoining divisions 5 and 6, where a much smaller proportion of poor resides. The result is, that in Nos. 1, 2, 3, 4, 5, and 6, there are 270 taverns, 216 gin shops (estimated as four-fifths of taverns), 188 beer houses (estimated as being distributed through the divisions of the town in the same ratio as the taverns), total 674: or more than two-thirds of the whole number of taverns, gin shops, and beer houses of the town, may therefore be considered as chiefly ministering to the vicious propensities of the inhabitants of Nos. 1, 2, 3, and 4. Some idea may be formed of the influence of these establishments on the health and morals of the people from the following statement; for which we are indebted to Mr. Braidley, the Boroughreeve. He observed the number of persons entering a gin shop in five minutes, during eight successive Saturday evenings, and at various periods from seven o'clock until ten. The average result was, 112 men and 163 women, or 275 in forty minutes, which is equal to 412 per hour.

The report of the Committee on gaols reveals the gross mismanagement of the licence system in London, and shows that taverns are the rendezvous of criminals and profligates of the lowest order. The scenes of depravity which occur in them, without the shadow of concealment —the constant temptations to moral errors which they unblushingly offer to those orders of society which have the least power of repelling them — the seductions to grosser sins by which they enthral the idle and unwary — the maxims of iniquity, and the arts of dishonesty, which are undisguisedly taught in them, by the miscreants who find a daily shelter there — all these glaring abuses demand the prompt and energetic interference of authority with the regulations of establishments, which, without the pretence of necessity, or the veil of one virtuous amusement, are public schools of vice.

The decency of our towns is violated, even in this respect, that every street blazons forth the invitations of these haunts of crime. Gin shops and beer houses encouraged by the law (which seems to value rather the amount of the public revenue, than the prevalence of private virtue) and taverns, over which the police can at present exercise but an imperfect control, have multiplied with such rapidity that they will excite the strong remonstrances which every lover of good order is prepared to make with government, against the permission, much less the sanction, of such public enormities. Two physicians of great experience who practise in two of our largest manufacturing towns, inform us, that delirium tremens (a disease occasioned by continued intemperance) has increased, within the sphere of their observation, in an alarming ratio since the passing of the Beer Act; and another, who superintends one of the largest public Lunatic Asylums in the provinces, discovers that one great cause of the prevalence of insanity of late years is an addiction to the use of ardent spirits.

The amount of crime is one chief means of ascertaining the moral condition of a community. To the perfection of this estimate it is, however, essential that crimes committed against the person should be distinguished from those against property.[1] 'The moral guilt of the latter depending considerably upon the equality of the distribution of wealth throughout the country, the degree of ease in which the people live ought also to be brought into view; and when we compare the criminal calendars of different nations, we ought not to omit to refer to their respective modes of administering justice, and to the attention paid in each country to that branch of it which we call preventive. That *prevention* is by far the more important care, in point both of duty and expediency, is a truth which governments are beginning to perceive; though in most countries repression, and in not a few vindictiveness[2], still form the spirit of the penal code.' 'So long as the will of man is free, and it is in his power either to conform to the law, or to violate it, the care of the legislature should be to turn that will into the right channel.'

The state of the registers, required for an accurate investigation of the amount of crime committed in Manchester, was such as to demand more time in their classification, than, under the circumstances in which this pamphlet was prepared, we were able to give the subject. We have obtained, however, an account of the number of persons committed at the New Bailey Court House, Salford, for the different offences under which their commit-

---

[1] 'Foreign Quarterly Review,' vol. v. p. 404.
[2] Works of Charles Lucas—also 'De la Justice de la Prévoyance'—and 'De la Mission de la Justice Humaine.'—*Par M. Depéctiaux.*

Manchester in 1832

ment is recorded. The amount of crime exhibited in this table results therefore from a much greater population than that contained in the township; the out-townships being also included, or a population of at least 240,000.

	1829.	1830.	1831.	Total.
Number of Felons	580	559	638	1777
Persons committed for want of sureties to keep the peace—non-payment of fines—neglect of family, &c.	819	960	996	2775
For want of sureties to appear at the Sessions . .	192	153	182	527
For disobeying orders in Bastardy	174	151	181	506
Rogues and Vagabonds	620	743	835	2198
				7713

We subjoin, in a note, a table extracted from a very valuable pamphlet published by Mr. Ridgway, entitled 'An Inquiry into the State of the Manufacturing Population, and the Causes and Cures of the Evils therein existing,'[1] by which the reader may be enabled to form a more accurate opinion concerning the relative extent to which crime prevails in Manchester.

There is, however, a licentiousness capable of corrupting the whole body of society, like an insidious disease, which eludes observation, yet is equally fatal in its effects.

[1] 1827.   1827.

Manufacturing Counties.	Population.	Crime.	Crime to Population, 1, to	Agricultural Counties.	Population.	Crime.	Crime to Population. 1, to
Cheshire . .	304,130	497	612	Berkshire. .	143,400	208	690
Lancashire .	1,226,600	2459	495	Essex . . .	319,400	451	708
Middlesex .	1,295,100	3381	353	Hertford . .	144,300	205	704
Northumberl.	220,500	96	2300	Kent . . .	468,900	632	742
Nottingham .	206,300	298	695	Hampshire .	314,000	341	920
Stafford . .	378,600	569	665	Westmoreld.	55,800	20	2790
Warwick . .	310,500	602	515	Wiltshire . .	245,000	365	671
York . . .	1,321,600	1223	1080	Devonshire .	484,200	432	1121
Average . . . 840				 1043			

Criminal acts may be statistically classed—the victims of the law may be enumerated—but the number of those affected with the moral leprosy of vice cannot be exhibited with mathematical precision. Sensuality has no record[1], and the relaxation of social obligations may co-exist with a half dormant, half restless impulse to rebel against all the preservative principles of society; yet these chaotic elements may long smoulder, accompanied only by partial eruptions of turbulence or crime.

In the absence of direct evidence, we are unwilling that any statements should rest on our personal testimony; but we again refer with confidence to that of an intelligent and impartial observer.[2]

One other characteristic of the social body, in its present constitution, appears to us too remarkable and important to be entirely overlooked.

Religion is the most distinguished and ennobling feature of civil communities. Natural attributes of the human mind appear to ensure the culture of some form of worship; and as society rises through its successive stages, these forms are progressively developed, from the grossest observances of superstition, until the truths and dictates of revelation assert their rightful supremacy.

The absence of religious feeling, the neglect of all religious ordinances, afford substantive evidence of so great a moral degradation of the community, as to ensure a concomitant civic debasement. The social body cannot be constructed like a machine, on abstract principles which merely include physical motions, and their numerical results in the production of wealth. The mutual relation of men is not merely dynamical, nor can the composition of their forces be subjected to a purely mathematical calculation. Political economy, though its object be to

---

[1] No record exists by which the number of illegitimate births can be ascertained. Even this evidence would form a very imperfect rule by which to judge of the comparative prevalence of sensuality.

[2] 'Inquiry into the State of the Manufacturing Population.' p. 24.—Ridgway.

ascertain the means of increasing the wealth of nations, cannot accomplish its design, without at the same time regarding their happiness, and as its largest ingredient the cultivation of religion and morality.

With unfeigned regret, we are therefore constrained to add, that the standard of morality is exceedingly debased, and that religious observances are neglected amongst the operative population of Manchester. The bonds of domestic sympathy are too generally relaxed; and as a consequence, the filial and paternal duties are uncultivated. The artisan has not time to cherish these feelings, by the familiar and grateful arts which are their constant food, and without which nourishment they perish. An apathy benumbs his spirit. Too frequently the father, enjoying perfect health and with ample opportunities of employment, is supported in idleness on the earnings of his oppressed children; and on the other hand, when age and decrepitude cripple the energies of the parents, their adult children abandon them to the scanty maintenance derived from parochial relief.

That religious observances are exceedingly neglected, we have had constant opportunities of ascertaining, in the performance of our duty as Physician to the Ardwick and Ancoats Dispensary, which frequently conducted us to the houses of the poor on Sunday. With rare exceptions, the adults of the vast population of 84,147 contained in Districts Nos. 1, 2, 3, 4, spend Sunday either in supine sloth, in sensuality, or in listless inactivity. A certain portion only of the labouring classes enjoys even healthful recreation on that day, and a very small number frequent the places of worship.

The fruits of external prosperity may speedily be blighted by the absence of internal virtue. With pure religion and undefiled, flourish frugality, forethought, and industry—the social charities which are the links of kindred, neighbours, and societies—and the amenities of life, which banish the jealous suspicion with which one order regards another. In vain may the intellect of man be tortured to devise expedients by which the supply of the necessaries of life may undergo an increase, equivalent to that of population, if the moral check be overthrown. Crime, diseases, pestilence, intestine discord, famine, or foreign war — those agencies which repress the rank overgrowth of a meagre and reckless race — will, by a natural law, desolate a people devoid of prudence and principle, whose numbers constantly press on the limits of the means of subsistence. We therefore regard with alarm the state of those vast masses of our operative population which are acted upon by all other incentives, rather than those of virtue; and are visited by the emissaries of every faction, rather than by the ministers of an ennobling faith.

The present means or methods of religious instruction are, in the circumstances in which our large towns are placed, most evidently inadequate to their end. The labours of some few devoted men — of whom the world is not worthy — in the houses of the poor, are utterly insufficient to produce a deep and permanent moral impression on the people. Some of our laws, as now administered, encourage indigence and vice, and hence arises an increased necessity for the daily exertions of the teachers of religion, to stem that flood of prevailing immorality which threatens to overthrow the best means that political sagacity can devise for the elevation of the people.

The exertions of Dr. Tuckerman, of Boston, in establishing 'a ministry for the poor' have been, until very recently, rather the theme of general and deserved praise, than productive of laudable imitation. This ministration is effected, chiefly by a visitation of the houses of the poor, and he proposes as its objects, religious instruction, uninfluenced by sectarian spirit or opinions:— the relief of the most pressing necessities of the poor — first by a well-regulated charity, and secondarily, by instruction in domestic economy — exhortations to industry — admonition concerning the consequences of vice, and by obtaining work for the deserving and unemployed. The minister should also encourage the education of the children, should prove the friend of the poor in periods of perplexity, and, when the labourer is subdued by sickness, should breathe into his ear the maxims of virtue, and the truths of religion. He might also act as a medium of communication and a link of sympathy, between the higher and lower classes of society. He might become the almoner of the rich, and thus daily sow the seeds of a kindlier relationship than that which now subsists between the wealthy and the destitute. He might also serve as a faithful reporter of the secret miseries which are suffered in the abodes of poverty, unobserved by those to whom he may come to advocate the cause of the abandoned. The prevalence of the principles and the practice of the precepts of Christianity, we may hope, will thus ultimately be made to bind together the now incoherent elements of society.

The success of Dr. Tuckerman's labours in Boston had, before the commencement of a similar plan in Manchester, given rise to several societies for the Christian instruction of the people in the Metropolis, and in other parts of the kingdom. Six such societies are now in operation in Manchester and its out-townships — five amongst the Independent, and one amongst the Unitarian Dissenters. The objects proposed by these associations, and the means by which these objects are prosecuted, may be estimated by the perusal of an extract from the report of that connected with the Mosley-street Independent Chapel, placed in the Appendix. But we regret to add that their number is utterly insufficient to affect the habits of more than a small portion of the population. The vast portions of the town included in the Ancoats, Newtown, and Portland districts, are utterly unoccupied by this beneficent system; and, when it is further observed, that in those districts reside the most indigent and immoral of our poor, it will be at once apparent what need there is of the immediate extension of the same powerful agency to them.

Having enumerated so many causes of physical depression, perhaps the most direct proof of the extent to which the effect co-exists in natural alliance with poverty, may be derived from the records of the medical charities of the town. During the year preceding July 1831 — 21,196 patients were treated at the Royal Infirmary — 472 at the House of Recovery — 3,163 at the Ardwick and Ancoats Dispensary, of which (subtracting one-sixth as belonging to the township of Ardwick) 2,636 were inhabitants of Manchester — perhaps 2,000 at the Workhouse Dispensary, and 1,500 at the Children's — making a total of 27,804, without including the Lock Hospital and the Eye Institution. 'If to this sum,'[1] says Mr. Roberton, engaged in making a similar calculation, 'we were further to add the incomparably greater amount of all ranks visited or advised as private patients by the whole body (not a small one) of professional men; those prescribed for by chemists and druggists, scarcely of inferior pretension; and by herb doctors and quacks; those who swallow patent medicines; and lastly the subjects of that ever flourishing branch — domestic medicine; we should be compelled to admit that not fewer, perhaps, than three-fourths of the inhabitants of Manchester annually are, or fancy they are, under the necessity of submitting to medical treatment.'

Ingenious deductions, by Mr. Roberton, from facts contained in the records of the Lying-in Hospital of Manchester, prove, in a different manner, the extreme dependence of the poor on the charitable institutions of the town. The average annual number of births (deduced from a comparison of the last four years), attended by the officers of the Lying-in Charity, is 4,300; and the number of births to the population may be assumed as 1 in 28 inhabitants. This annual average of births, therefore, represents a population of 124,400, and assuming that of Manchester and the environs to be 230,000, more than

---

[1] 'Remarks on the Health of English Manufacturers, and on the need which exists for the Establishment of Convalescents' Retreats,' by J. Roberton.

one-half of its inhabitants are therefore either so destitute or so degraded, as to require the assistance of public charity in bringing their offspring into the world.

The children thus adopted by the public are often neglected by their parents. The early age at which girls are admitted into the factories prevents their acquiring much knowledge of domestic economy; and even supposing them to have had accidental opportunities of making this acquisition, the extent to which women are employed in the mills does not, even after marriage, permit the general application of its principles. The infant is the victim of the system; it has not lived long, ere it is abandoned to the care of a hireling or a neighbour, while its mother pursues her accustomed toil. Sometimes a little girl has the charge of the child, or even of two or three collected from neighbouring houses. Thus abandoned to one whose sympathies are not interested in its welfare, or whose time is too often also occupied in household drudgery, the child is ill fed, dirty, ill clothed, exposed to cold and neglect; and in consequence, more than one-half of the offspring of the poor (as may be proved by the bills of mortality of the town) die before they have completed their fifth year. The strongest survive; but the same causes which destroy the weakest impair the vigour of the more robust; and hence the children of our manufacturing population are proverbially pale and sallow, though not generally emaciated, nor the subjects of disease. We cannot subscribe to those exaggerated and unscientific accounts of the physical ailments to which they are liable, which have been lately revived with an eagerness and haste equally unfriendly to taste and truth; but we are convinced that the operation of these causes, continuing unchecked through successive generations, would tend to depress the health of the people; and that consequent physical ills would accumulate in an unhappy progression.

Before the age when, according to law, children can be admitted into the factories, they are permitted to run wild in the streets and courts of the town, their parents often being engaged in labour and unable to instruct them. Five infant schools have been established in Manchester and the suburban townships, in which 600 children (a miserable portion of those who are of age to learn) receive instruction. 'In Britain and Ireland all sects and all parties approve of infant schools; in France those who are best qualified to form a judgment fully appreciate their value, and public tranquillity is alone wanted to secure the universal adoption of them in that country: in Geneva they are received so zealously as to have become improved by the systematic addition of gardens, in which the children pass more hours than in the schoolroom; in North America they are gaining ground with the rapidity and steadiness with which everything prospers in the United States: and the republicans of the West, abandoning a deeply rooted and barbarous prejudice, are in some places even providing infant schools for their young slaves. At the Cape of Good Hope the just union of the white and coloured races is begun, not more by the newly imparted equality of rights, than by these establishments being opened in common to the offspring of both; they are in like manner begun to be offered to all classes without invidious distinction in India; and in the *Ultima Thule* of civilisation, New South Wales, the innocent children of both the convict and the free are, in some measure, rescued by infant schools from abominations which affect the young, in a manner to which our distance from the scene renders us careless.'[1] The importance of this system, to our large manufacturing towns, is such that we hope funds will be speedily granted by government, so that it may be extended, until all the children of the poor are rescued from ignorance, and from the effects of that bad example, to which they are now subjected in the crowded lanes of our cities.

With a general system of education, we hope will also

---

[1] 'Westminster Review,' No. xxxiv.

be introduced institutions, in which the young females of the poor may be instructed in domestic economy, and where those pernicious traditional prejudices, which, combined with neglect, occasion the great mortality of their children, may be removed, and they may receive wholesome advice concerning their duties as wives and mothers.

We have avoided alluding to evidence which is founded on general opinion, or depends merely on matters of perception; and have chiefly availed ourselves of such as admitted of a statistical classification. We may, however, be permitted to add, that our own experience, confirmed by that of those members of our profession on whose judgment we can rely with the greatest confidence, induces us to conclude, that diseases assume a lower and more chronic type in Manchester than in smaller towns and in agricultural districts; and a residence in the Hospitals of Edinburgh, and practice in its Dispensaries amongst the most debased part of its inhabitants, enables us to affirm, with confidence, that the diseases occurring here admit of less active antiphlogistic or depletory treatment than those incident to the degraded population of the old town of that city.

Frequent allusion has been made to the supposed rate of mortality in Manchester, as a standard by which the health of the manufacturing population may be ascertained. From the mortality of towns, however, their comparative health cannot be invariably deduced. There is a state of physical depression which does not terminate in fatal organic changes, which, however, converts existence into a prolonged disease, and is not only compatible with life, but is proverbially protracted to an advanced age.

The difficulty of obtaining returns of burials, from all the places of interment, in the town and suburbs of Manchester, prevented the estimation of the rate of mortality, when the former edition of this pamphlet was published. Since that period a Parliamentary paper has been published (No. 729) containing a return of the number of burials occurring annually in Manchester, from 1821 to 1830; and the Board of Health have obtained returns for the last four years, which are confirmatory of this Parliamentary document. We have, from these returns and the census, constructed a table, showing the mortality of every year from 1821 to 1831, inclusive.

The population, by the census of the townships of Ardwick, Broughton, Cheetham Hill, Chorlton-upon-Medlock, Hulme, Manchester, and Salford, in 1811 was 108,993 :— in 1821, it was 152,683 :— and in 1831, 224,143; or the increase in the first of these periods was to that of the latter, nearly as 44 parts of 115 are to 71 parts of the same number. Hence, supposing the sources of increase from births and immigration to remain nearly the same in the intermediate periods, we obtain a rule to distribute the increase of population between 1821 and 1831. Dividing this period into two equal parts, the rate of increase during the first five years would be 44 of 115 equal parts of the whole increase, or in 1826 the population would be $152,683 + 27,369$ ($\frac{44}{115}$ of the whole increase)$= 180,052$ which $+ 44,091$ ($\frac{71}{115}$, which ratio is assumed to occur during the second five years)$= 224,143$, the population of the town in 1831. These sums being again distributed by the same rule to half of the first and second cycles of five years, and the products thus obtained divided by five, a tolerably accurate approximation to the half-yearly increase of the population is obtained. By this rule, the following Table of the annual rate of mortality was constructed.

Some error appears to have occurred in the returns of interments for the first two years; therefore omitting them, the mean annual rate of interments acting as a divisor on the mean numbers of the population from 1823 to 1831 inclusive, will give an approximation to the mean rate of mortality, or $188,666 \div 5356 = 35\cdot22$, the mean rate of the annual mortality of Manchester.

Diseases, we have said, assume in this town a compara-

Year.	Interments of Churchmen.	Interments of Dissenters.	Total of Interments.	Population.	Rate of Mortality.
1821	1561	1726	3287	152,683	46·45
1822	1285	1044	2329	156,663	67·223
1823	1585	3230	4815	160,664	33·36
1824	1428	3219	4647	166,117	35·74
1825	1398	3530	4928	173,083	35·12
1826	1548	3804	5352	180,052	33·64
1827	1604	3235	4839	186,462	38·53
1828	1615	4106	5721	192,874	33·73
1829	1479	3719	5198	201,691	38·80
1830	1590	4383	5973	212,913	35·64
1831			6736	224,143	33·27

tively chronic type; and *a general prevalence of such maladies* is compatible even with a *low* rate of mortality. Acute diseases (which are eminently fatal) prevail, on the contrary, in a population where the standard of health is high, and attack the most robust and plethoric. Thus, a high rate of mortality may often be observed in a community, where the number of persons affected with disease is small; and on the other hand, general physical depression may concur with the prevalence of chronic maladies, and yet be unattended with a great proportion of deaths. We have elsewhere discussed the origin, and shown the great prevalence of dyspepsia, gastralgia[1], enteralgia, and chronic bronchitis and phthisis[2], in Manchester; and this reference to the subject may therefore be sufficient here.

The preceding statements must, we fear, be received as valid evidence that many sources of physical depression exist in Manchester. The Special Board of Health, in the course of their inquiries, discovered that they possessed very limited means of removing the evils whose existence was ascertained by the reports of the District Inspectors. Some thousands of houses were whitewashed. Several additional gangs of scavengers were employed; and the result of their operations was evident in the im-

---

[1] Second Number of the 'North of England Medical and Surgical Journal:' On Gastralgia and Enteralgia.
[2] Third Number of the 'North of England Medical and Surgical Journal.'

proved condition of the public thoroughfares of the town: but to repair and sewer the unpaved streets, courts, &c., and to remove the gross accumulations of filth which they contain, would have entailed upon the town an expenditure for which the fiscal authorities were unwilling to become responsible. Letters were also addressed to the landlords of all houses reported to be out of repair, and of those in which the soughs required repair — which were damp — ill ventilated — or which had no privies, informing them of the defects reported, and requesting them to assist the Special Board in their efforts to ameliorate the physical condition of the poor, by remedying these evils. The disease of the body politic is not superficial, and cannot be cured, or even temporarily relieved, by any specific: its sources are unfortunately remote, and the measures necessary to the removal of its disorders include serious questions on which great difference of opinion prevails.

Visiting Manchester, the Metropolis of the commercial system, a stranger regards with wonder the ingenuity and comprehensive capacity, which, in the short space of half a century, have here established the staple manufacture of this kingdom. He beholds with astonishment the establishments of its merchants — monuments of fertile genius and successful design:— the masses of capital which have been accumulated by those who crowd upon its mart, and the restless but sagacious spirit which has made every part of the known world the scene of their enterprise. The sudden creation of the mighty system of commercial organisation which covers this county, and stretches its arms to the most distant seas, attests the power and the dignity of man. Commerce, it appears to such a spectator, here gathers in her storehouses the productions of every clime, that she may minister to the happiness of a favoured race.

When he turns from the great capitalists, he contemplates the fearful strength only of that multitude of the labouring population, which lies like a slumbering giant at their feet. He has heard of the turbulent riots of the people—of machine breaking—of the secret and sullen organisation which has suddenly lit the torch of incendiarism, or well nigh uplifted the arm of rebellion in the land. He remembers that political desperadoes have ever loved to tempt this population to the hazards of the swindling game of revolution, and have scarcely failed. In the midst of so much opulence, however, he has disbelieved the cry of need.

Believing that the natural tendency of unrestricted commerce (unchecked by the prevailing want of education, and the incentives afforded by imperfect laws to improvidence and vice), is to develop the energies of society, to increase the comforts and luxuries of life, and to *elevate the physical condition* of every member of the social body, we have exposed, with a faithful, though a friendly hand, the condition of the lower orders connected with the manufactures of this town, because we conceive that the evils affecting them result *from foreign and accidental causes*. A system, which promotes the advance of civilisation, and diffuses it over the world—which promises to maintain the peace of nations, by establishing a permanent international law, founded on the benefits of commercial association, cannot be inconsistent with the happiness of the *great mass of the people*. There are men who believe that the labouring classes are condemned for ever, by an inexorable fate, to the unmitigated curse of toil, scarcely rewarded by the bare necessaries of existence, and often visited by the horrors of hunger and disease—that the heritage of ignorance, labour, and misery, is entailed upon them as an eternal doom. Such an opinion might appear to receive a gloomy confirmation, were we content with the evidence of fact, derived only from the history of uncivilised races, and of feudal institutions. No modern Rousseau now rhapsodises on the happiness of the state of nature. Moral and physical degradation are inseparable from barbarism. The unsheltered, naked savage,

E

starving on food common to the denizens of the wilderness, never knew the comforts contained in the most wretched cabin of our poor.

Civilisation, to which feudality is inimical, but which is most powerfully promoted by commerce, surrounds man with innumerable inventions. It has thus a constant tendency to multiply, without limit, the comforts of existence, and that by an amount of labour, at all times undergoing an indefinite diminution. It continually expands the sphere of his relations, from a dependence on his own limited resources, until it has combined into one mighty league, alike the members of communities, and the powers of the most distant regions. The cultivation of the faculties, the extension of knowledge, the improvement of the arts, enable man to extend his dominion over matter, and to minister, not merely to all the exigencies, but to the capricious tastes and the imaginary appetites of his nature. When, therefore, every zone has contributed its most precious stores—science has revealed her secret laws—genius has applied the mightiest powers of nature to familiar use, making matter the patient and silent slave of the will of man—if want prey upon the heart of the people, we may strongly presume that, besides the effects of existing manners, some accidental barrier exists, arresting their natural and rightful supply.

The evils affecting the working classes, *so far from being the necessary results of the commercial system, furnish evidence of a disease which impairs its energies, if it does not threaten its vitality.*

The increase of the manufacturing establishments, and the consequent colonisation of the district, have been exceedingly more rapid than the growth of its civic institutions. The eager antagonisation of commercial enterprise has absorbed the attention, and concentrated the energies, of every member of the community. In this strife the remote influence of arrangements has sometimes been neglected, not from the want of humanity, but from the pressure of occupation, and the deficiency of time.

Thus, some years ago, the internal arrangements of mills (now so much improved) as regarded temperature, ventilation, cleanliness, and the proper separation of the sexes, &c., were such as to be extremely objectionable. The same cause has, we think, chiefly occasioned the want of police regulations, to prevent the gross neglect of the streets and houses of the poor.

The great and sudden fluctuations to which trade is liable, are often the sources of severe embarrassment. Sometimes the demand for labour diminishes, and its price consequently falls in a corresponding ratio. On the other hand, the existing population has often been totally inadequate to the required production; and capitalists have eagerly invited a supply of labour from distant counties and the sister kingdom. The colonisation of the Irish was thus first encouraged; and has proved one chief source of the demoralisation, and consequent physical depression of the people.

The effects of this immigration, even when regarded as a simple economical question, do not merely include an equation of the comparative cheapness of labour; its influence on civilisation and morals, as *they tend to affect the production of wealth*, cannot be neglected.

In proof of this, it may suffice to present a picture of the natural progress of barbarous habits. Want of cleanliness, of forethought and economy, are found in almost invariable alliance with dissipation, reckless habits, and disease. The population gradually becomes physically less efficient as the producers of wealth—morally so from idleness—politically *worthless* as having few desires to satisfy, and *noxious* as dissipators of capital accumulated. Were such manners to prevail, the horrors of pauperism would accumulate. A debilitated race would be rapidly multiplied. Morality would afford no check to the increase of the population: crime and disease would be its only obstacles—the licentiousness which indulges its capricious appetite, till it exhausts its power—and the disease which, at the same moment, punishes crime, and sweeps away a hecatomb of its victims. A dense mass, impotent alike of great moral or physical efforts, would accumulate; children would be born to parents incapable of obtaining the necessaries of life, who would thus acquire, through the mistaken humanity of the law, a new claim for support from the property of the public. They would drag on an unhappy existence, vibrating between the pangs of hunger and the delirium of dissipation — alternately exhausted by severe and oppressive toil, or enervated by supine sloth. Destitution would now prey on their strength, and then the short madness of debauchery would consummate its ruin. Crime, which banishes or destroys its victims, and disease and death, are severe but brief natural remedies, which prevent the unlimited accumulation of the horrors of pauperism. Even war and pestilence, when regarded as affecting a population thus demoralised, and politically and physically debased, seem like storms which sweep from the atmosphere the noxious vapours whose stagnation threatens man with death.

Morality is therefore worthy of the attention of the economist, even when considered as simply ministering to the production of wealth. Civilisation creates artificial wants, introduces economy, and cultivates the moral and physical capabilities of society. Hence the introduction of an uncivilised race does not tend even primarily to increase the power of producing wealth, in a ratio by any means commensurate with the cheapness of its labour, and may ultimately retard the increase of the fund for the maintenance of that labour. Such a race is useful only as a mass of animal organisation, which consumes the smallest amount of wages. The low price of the labour of such people depends, however, on the paucity of their wants, and their savage habits. When they assist the production of wealth, therefore, their barbarous habits and consequent moral depression must form a part of the equation. They are only necessary to a state of commerce *inconsistent* with such a reward for labour as is calculated to maintain the standard of civilisation. A few years pass, and they become burdens to a community whose morals and physical power they have depressed; and dissipate wealth which they did not accumulate.

Conscious of the evils resulting from the immigration of Irish, we nevertheless tremble at the thought of applying unmodified poor-laws to Ireland. In England the system of parochial relief has a most prejudicial influence, in chaining redundant labour to a narrow locality, and thus aggravating the pressure of partial ills, and in relaxing those bonds of the social constitution, industry, forethought, and charity.[1] Much less could the habits of the Irish be corrected by a parliamentary enactment: and to attempt the removal of their misery, by a constant supply of their wants, would be to offer direct encouragement to idleness, improvidence, and dissipation. It would ultimately render every individual dependent on the State, and change Ireland into a vast infirmary, divided into as many wards as there are parishes, whose endowment would swallow up the entire rental of the country. Such a measure, says Mr. Senior, would[2] 'divide Ireland into as many distinct counties as there are parishes, each peopled by a population *ascripta glebæ;* multiplying without forethought; impelled to labour principally by the fear of punishment; drawing allowance for their children, and throwing their parents on the parish; considering wages not a matter of contract but of right; attributing every evil to the injustice of their superiors; and, when their own idleness or improvidence has occasioned a fall of wages, avenging it by firing the dwellings, maiming the cattle, or murdering the persons of the landlords and overseers; combining, in short, the insubordination of the freeman with the sloth and recklessness of the slave.'

We believe, however, that an impost on the rental of Ireland might be applied with advantage in employing its

---

[1] Chalmers's 'Christian and Civic Economy of Large Towns:' 'Speech before the General Assembly:' 'Political Economy,' p. 398, &c., &c.

[2] 'Letter to Lord Howick on a Legal Provision for the Irish Poor,' &c., &c. p. 33.

redundant labour in great public works—such as draining bogs, making public roads, canals, harbours, &c., by which the entire available capital of the country would be increased, and the people would be trained in industrious habits, and more civilised manners. England would then cease to be, to the same extent as at present, the receptacle of the most demoralised and worthless hordes of the sister country.

The Irish, who were invited to colonise the country at a period when the demand for labour was greater than the native population could supply, have suffered more than any other class from the introduction of the power-loom. The state of transition in employment consequent on a new invention (by which the powers of production are increased, its cost diminished, and the demand for a peculiar kind of labour almost extinguished), will always be followed by an embarrassment, whose pressure and duration will be determined, *cæteris paribus*, by the extent of the market for manufactures. If by the want of commercial treaties—by the imposition of injudicious duties on foreign produce, which provoke jealous retaliation—the existence of arbitrary restrictions and monopolies, the extent of the market for manufactures be diminished, the demand for labour will be confined within the same limits. A new invention will thus be robbed of half its rewards, since we deprive other nations of the power of buying our manufactures, by refusing to accept what they offer in exchange. We depress the spirit of their enterprise; and we discourage our own. The relations of commerce are those of unlimited reciprocity—not of narrow and bigoted exclusion. We encourage genius and industry in proportion as we permit them to receive their reward in the riches of every clime. We dam up not only the well-spring of our own wealth and happiness, but of that of other nations, when we refuse to barter the results of the ingenuity and perseverance of our artisans, for the products of the bounty of other climates, or the arts and genius of other people. Unrestricted commerce, on the other hand, would rapidly promote the advance of civilisation, by cultivating the physical and mental power of individuals and nations to multiply the amount of natural products, and to create those artificial staple commodities, by the barter of which they acquire the riches of other regions. Every new invention in agriculture or manufactures — every improvement in the powers of transmission, would enable its possessors, by the same amount of labour, to obtain a greater quantity of foreign products in exchange. The labour of man would be constantly, to an indefinite extent, diminished[1], whilst its reward would be, at the same time, perpetually increased. Human power would be employed 'in its noblest occupation, that of giving a direction to the mere physical power which it had conquered.'[2]

But, under a restrictive system, the demand for the results of labour is limited, not by the wants of the whole world, but of the market from which commodities are received in exchange. Even then, as civilisation multiplies the desires, and stimulates the industry and ingenuity of man, the quantity of products permitted to be bartered for our manufactures has a constant tendency to increase. Unfortunately, however, the restrictions which fetter commerce are so numerous, and the monopolies which exclude free trade from the fairest portions of the earth are so extensive, as to render the progressive increase in the demand for the results of our labour and capital slow. Population, nevertheless, increases the supply of labour in at least as great a ratio as the demand existing under a restrictive system. Every invention, therefore, which diminishes the quantity of labour necessary to produce the objects of barter, lessens its price, and excludes, for an indefinite period, a great part of the population from

---

[1] 'Observations on the Influence of Machinery upon the Working Classes of the Community,' by John Kennedy, Esq. : 'Memoirs of the Literary and Philosophical Society of Manchester,' vol. v. second series. Also, 'The Economy of Machinery and Manufactures,' by Charles Babbage, Esq.

[2] 'Results of Machinery,' p. 193.

employment. By this system the profits of capital are increased, though not in the same ratio as the wages of labour are for a time diminished. But, were the restrictions abolished, each new invention would not only enable man to purchase, by a smaller amount of labour, a larger portion of foreign products, but would, by these means, powerfully stimulate the genius and industry of other nations, whose demand for our manufactures would increase in a ratio at least equal to their accumulation. In other words, improvements in machinery *diminish the cost of production;* but if the demand for manufactures be limited by arbitrary enactments, *the increased employment* which would also be their natural and inevitable result, *is prevented*, until commerce is able, in some other way, to compensate for the evils of injudicious legislation. We have *capital and labour*—but to obtain the greatest amount of commercial advantages, we must also have an *unlimited power of exchange.*

We believe, therefore, that chiefly to *this cause* must be attributed the combined misery of severe labour and want entailed on that wretched but extensive class, the handloom weavers of the cotton trade.

Were an unlimited exchange permitted to commerce, the hours of labour might be reduced, and time afforded for the education and religious and moral instruction of the people. With a virtuous population, engaged in free trade, the existence of redundant labour would be an evil of brief duration, rarely experienced. The unpopular, but alas, too necessary proposals of emigration would no longer be agitated. Ingenuity and industry would draw from the whole world a tribute more than adequate to supply the ever-increasing demands of a civilised nation.

The duties imposed on the introduction of foreign corn were originally intended, by raising the price of grain, to act as a compensation to the landowner for the supposed unequal pressure of taxation upon him. This inequality of the public burdens has, however, been exceedingly exaggerated, and those taxes, which are said to be derived from land on which corn is grown, are also procured from many other descriptions of property which are not protected. The faults of our present financial system[1] are so numerous, that if the principle of relieving the inequality of the pressure of taxation be admitted, we must pay back in bounties one third of what is obtained by taxes. The scarcity and dearness of food certainly bring to the agricultural population no benefit, after the brief demand for labour necessary to bring fresh soils into cultivation is past. The landowner alone receives any advantage from the high price of food, and that much less than has generally been supposed. The fluctuating scale by which the duties on corn are at present regulated, has produced the most disastrous effects among the agricultural tenantry: rents have been paid out of capital, and estates have been injured, in consequence of the embarrassments of the cultivators. A tax *on the staple commodity of life* enhances the price of all other food, by increasing the wages of labour, and the rent of land; and, as it enters as an element into the cost of every article produced (and that in a ratio constantly accumulating with the amount of labour employed), it presses heavily, though indirectly, on the superior classes, and upon all other consumers. Not the least injurious effects of the present Corn-law are the burden of supporting an unemployed population, which it entails on society at large, and the insecurity of property which results from the near approach to destitution of a large portion of its members. But since this system simultaneously contracts the market of the capitalist (by excluding one most important object of barter), and increases the cost of production, its direct effects are felt in the manufacturing districts, which have long been maintaining an unequal struggle with foreign competitors. In the cotton trade, to the expense of importing the raw material, and that chiefly from one of those countries where bounties on manufactures exist, is added the press-

---

[1] Sir H. Parnell, on Financial Reform.

ure of one tax, on the raw material, and of another, which, by raising the price of labour, increases that of the manufactured result. Industry, invention, the most subtle sagacity, and the most daring enterprise appear at length almost baffled by the difficulties they encounter. The profits of capital are reduced to the most meagre attenuation—the rapidity of production, of transmission and return, appear to have reached their utmost limit. Injudicious duties on foreign produce have provoked retaliation, and the manufactures of other countries are supported by artificial expedients in rivalry with our own. The difficulty of changing the system is every day increased, until, ere long, it may become a serious question with other countries, whether the advantages to be derived from free trade can compensate for the sacrifice of the capital embarked in their commercial establishments. The cotton manufacture is rapidly spreading all over the continent, and particularly in Switzerland and France; and America threatens us with a more formidable competition.

Under these circumstances, every part of the system appears necessary to the preservation of the whole. The profits of trade will not allow a greater remuneration for labour, and competition even threatens to reduce its price. *Whatever time is subtracted from the hours of labour [1] must be accompanied with an equivalent deduction from its rewards;* the restrictions of trade prevent other improvements, and we fear that the condition of the working

---

[1] The effect of such a measure is thus correctly described in an able and perspicuous pamphlet lately published, entitled, 'A Letter to Lord Althorp, in Defence of the Cotton Factories of Lancashire,' by Holland Hoole.

'If Mr. Sadler's bill becomes a law, the masters will have the choice of two evils. Either they must reduce the hours of labour to the limit proposed to be fixed for children (fifty-eight hours per week) or they must place their establishments without the pale of this enactment, by discharging all persons under eighteen years from their factories.'

'In the former case a reduction of the wages of all persons employed, whether children or adults, corresponding with the reduction of the time of labour must inevitably take place.' 'Not a few of the master cotton spinners have determined to adopt the other course above mentioned, namely, to discharge from their employment all the hands under eighteen years of age, as soon as the proposed law comes into operation.'

classes cannot be much improved, until the burdens and restrictions of the commercial system are abolished.

We will yield to none in an earnest and unqualified opposition to the present restrictions and burdens of commerce, and chiefly because they lessen the wages of the lower classes, increase the price of food, and prevent the reduction of the hours of labour:—because they will retard the application of a general and efficient system of education, and thus not merely depress the health, but debase the morals of the poor. Those politicians who propose a serious reduction of the hours of labour, unpreceded by the relief of commercial burdens, seem not to believe that this measure would inevitably depress the wages of the poor, whilst the price of the necessaries of life would continue the same. They appear, also, not to have sufficiently reflected that, if this measure *were unaccompanied by a general system of education*, the time thus bestowed would be wasted or misused. If this depression of wages, coincident with an increase of the time generally spent by an uneducated people in sloth or dissipation, be carefully reflected upon, the advocates of this measure will, perhaps, be less disposed to regard it as one calculated to confer unqualified benefits on the labouring classes. To retrace the upward path from evil and misery is difficult. Health is only acquired after disease, by passing through slow and painful stages. Neither can the evils which affect the operative population be instantly relieved by the exhibition of any single notable remedy.

Men are, it must be confessed, too apt to regard with suspicion those who differ from them in opinion, and rancorous animosity is thus engendered between those whose motives are pure, and between whose opinions only shades of difference exist. We believe that no objection to a reduction of the hours of labour would exist amongst the enlightened capitalists of the cotton trade, if the difficulty of maintaining, under the present restrictions, the commercial position of the country did not forbid it.

Were these restrictions abolished, they would cease to fear the competition of their foreign rivals, and the working classes of the community would find them to be the warmest advocates of every measure which could conduce to the physical comfort, or moral elevation of the poor.

A general and efficient system of education would be devised — a more intimate and cordial association would be cultivated between the capitalist and those in his employ — the poor would be instructed in habits of forethought and economy; and, in combination with these great and general efforts to ameliorate their condition, when the restrictions of commerce had been abolished, a reduction in the hours of labour would tend to elevate the moral and physical condition of the people.

We are desirous of adding a few observations on each of these measures. Ere the moral and physical condition of the operative population can be much elevated, a system of national education so extensive and liberal as to supply the wants of the whole labouring population must be introduced. Ignorance is twice a curse — first from its necessarily debasing effects, and then because rendering its victim insensible to his own fate, he endures it with supine apathy. The ignorant are, therefore, properly, the care of the state. Our present means of instruction are confined to Sunday Schools, and a few Lancasterian and National Schools, quite inadequate to the wants of the population. The absence of education is like that of cultivation, the mind untutored becomes a waste, in which prejudices and traditional errors grow as rankly as weeds. In this sphere of labour, as in every other, prudent and diligent culture is necessary to obtain genial products from the soil; noxious agencies are abroad, and, while we refuse to sow the germs of truth and virtue, the winds of heaven bring the winged seeds of error and vice. Moreover, as education is delayed, a stubborn barrenness affects the faculties — want of exercise renders them inapt — he that has never been judiciously instructed, has not only to master the first elements of truth, and to unlearn error, but in proportion as the period has been delayed, will be the difficulty of these processes. What wonder then that the teachers of truth should make little impression on an unlettered population, and that the working classes should become the prey of those *who flatter their passions, adopt their prejudices, or even descend to imitate their manners.*

If a period ever existed when public peace was secured by refusing knowledge to the population, that epoch has lapsed. The policy of governments may have been little able to bear the scrutiny of the people. This may be the reason why the fountains of English literature have been sealed — and the works of our reformers, our patriots, and our confessors — the exhaustless sources of all that is pure and holy, and of good report amongst us — *have not been made accessible and familiar to the poor.* Yet literature of this order is destined to determine the structure of our social constitution, and to become the mould of our national character; and they who would dam up the flood of truth from the lower ground, cannot prevent its silent transudation. A little knowledge is thus inevitable, and it is proverbially a dangerous thing. Alarming disturbances of social order generally commence with *a people only partially instructed.* The preservation of *internal peace*, not less than the improvement of our national institutions, depends on the education of the working classes.

Government, unsupported by popular opinion, is deprived of its true strength, and can only retain its power by the hateful expedients of despotism. Laws which obtain not general consent are dead letters, or obedience to them must be purchased by blood. But ignorance perpetuates the prejudices and errors which contend with the just exercise of a legitimate authority, and makes the people the victims of those ill-founded panics which convulse society, or seduces them to those tumults which disgrace the movements of a deluded populace. Unacquainted with the real sources of their own distress, misled by the artful misrepresentations of men whose element is disorder, and whose food faction can alone supply, the people have too frequently neglected the constitutional expedients by which redress ought only to have been sought, and have brought obloquy on their just cause, by the blind ferocity of those insurrectionary movements, in which they have assaulted the institutions of society. That good government may be stable, the people must be so instructed that they may love that *which they know to be right.*

The present age is peculiarly calculated to illustrate the truth of these observations. When we have equally to struggle against the besotted idolatry of ancient modes, which would retain error, and the headlong spirit of innovation, which, under the pretence of reforming, would destroy — now, hurried wildly onwards to the rocks on which we may be crushed; and then sucked back into the deep,— between this Scylla and that Charybdis, shall we hesitate to guide the vessel of the state, by the power of an enlightened popular opinion ! The increase of intelligence and virtue amongst the mass of the people will prove our surest safeguard, in the absence of which, the possessions of the higher orders might be, to an ignorant and brutal populace, like the fair plains of Italy to the destroying Vandal. The wealth and splendour, the refinement and luxury of the superior classes, might provoke the wild inroads of a marauding force, before whose desolating invasion every institution which science has erected, or humanity devised, might fall, and beneath whose feet all the arts and ornaments of civilised life might be trampled.

Even our national power rests on this basis, which power is sustained[1] 'not so much by the number of the people, as by the ability and character of that people;' and we should tremble to behold the excellent brightness and terrible form of a great nation resting, like the 'image' of the prophet, on a population, in which the

---

[1] 'Cobbett's Cottage Economy.' Introduction.

elements of strength and weakness are so commingled, as to ensure the dissolution of every cohesive principle, in that portion of society, which is thus not inaptly portrayed by the feet which were part of iron and part of clay.

The education afforded to the poor must be substantial. The mere elementary rudiments of knowledge are chiefly useful, as a means to an end. The poor man will not be made a much better member of society, by being only taught to read and write. His education should comprise such branches of general knowledge as would prove sources of rational amusement, and would thus elevate his tastes above a companionship in licentious pleasures. Those portions of the exact sciences which are connected with his occupation, should be familiarly explained to him, by popular lectures, and *cheap treatises*. To this end, Mechanics' Institutions (partly conducted by the artisans themselves, in order that the interest they feel in them may be constantly excited and maintained) should be multiplied by the patrons of education, among the poor. The ascertained truths of political science should be early taught to the labouring classes, and *correct* political information should be constantly and industriously disseminated amongst them. Were the taxes on periodical publications removed, men of great intelligence and virtue might be induced to conduct journals, established for the express purpose of directing to legitimate objects that restless activity by which the people are of late agitated. Such works, sanctioned by the names of men distinguished for their sagacity, spirit, and integrity, would command the attention and respect of the working classes. The poor might thus be also made to understand their political position in society, and the duties that belong to it — 'that[1] they are in a great measure the architects of their own fortune; that what others can do for them is trifling indeed, compared with what they can do for

---

[1] McCulloch, on the Rise, Progress, and Present State of the British Cotton Manufacture. 'Edinburgh Review,' No. 91.

themselves; that they are infinitely more interested in the preservation of public tranquillity than any other class of society; that mechanical inventions and discoveries are always supremely advantageous to them; and that their real interests can only be effectually promoted, by displaying greater prudence and forethought.' They should be instructed in the nature of their domestic and social relations. The evils which imprudent marriages entail on those who contract them, on their unhappy offspring, and on society at large, should be exhibited in the strongest light. The consequence of idleness, improvidence, and moral deviations, should be made the subjects of daily admonition; so that a young man might enter the world, not, as at present, without chart or compass, blown hither and thither by every gust of passion, but, with a knowledge of the dangers to which he is exposed, and of the way to escape them.

The relation between the capitalist and those in his employ, might prove a fruitful source of the most beneficial comments. The misery which the working classes have brought upon themselves, by their mistaken notions on this subject, is incalculable, not to mention the injury which has accrued to capitalists, and to the trade of this country.

Much good [1] would result from a more general and cordial association of the higher and lower orders. In Liverpool a charitable society exists denominated the 'Provident,' whose members include a great number of the most influential inhabitants. The town is subdivided into numerous districts, the inspection and care of each of which is committed to one or two members of the association. They visit the people in their houses — sympathise with their distresses, and minister to the wants of the necessitous; but above all, they acquire by their charity, the right of inquiring into their arrangements —

---

[1] 'An Address to the Higher Classes on the present State of Feeling among the Working Classes.'

of instructing them in domestic economy — of recommending sobriety, cleanliness, forethought, and method.

Every capitalist might contribute much to the happiness of those in his employ, by a similar exercise of enlightened charity. He might establish provident associations and libraries amongst his people. Cleanliness, and a proper attention to clothing and diet[1] might be enforced. He has frequent opportunities of discouraging the vicious, and of admonishing the improvident. By visiting the houses of the operatives, he might advise the multiplication of household comforts and the culture of the domestic sympathies. Principle and interest admonish him to receive none into his employ, unless they can produce the most satisfactory attestations to their character.

Above all, he should provide instruction for the children of his workpeople: he should stimulate the appetite for useful knowledge, and supply it with appropriate food.

Happily, the effect of such a system is not left to conjecture. In large towns serious obstacles oppose its introduction; but in Manchester more than one enlightened capitalist confesses its importance, and has made preparations for its adoption. In the country, the facilities are greater; and many establishments might be indicated, which exhibit the results of combined benevolence and intelligence. One example may suffice.

Twelve hundred persons are employed in the factories of Mr. Thomas Ashton, of Hyde. This gentleman has erected commodious dwellings for his workpeople, with each of which he has connected every convenience that can minister to comfort. He resides in their immediate vicinity, and has frequent opportunities of maintaining a cordial association with his operatives. Their houses are well furnished, clean, and their tenants exhibit every indication of health and happiness. Mr. Ashton has also built a school, where 640 children, chiefly belonging to his establishment, are instructed on Sunday, in reading,

---

[1] 'True Theory of Rent,' by T. Perronnet Thomson, Esq.

F

writing, arithmetic, &c. A library, connected with this school, is eagerly resorted to, and the people frequently read after the hours of labour have expired. An infant school is, during the week, attended by 280 children, and in the evenings others are instructed by masters selected for the purpose. The factories themselves are certainly excellent examples of the cleanliness and order which may be attained, by a systematic and persevering attention to the habits of the artisans.

The effects of such enlightened benevolence may be, to a certain extent, exhibited by statistical statements. The population, before the introduction of machinery, chiefly consisted of colliers, hatters, and weavers. Machinery was introduced in 1801, and the following table exhibits its consequences in the augmentation of the value of property, the diminution of poor rates, and the rapid increase of the amount assessed for the repairs of the highway, during a period, in which the population of the township increased from 830 to 7,138.

Township of Hyde, in the Parish of Stockport, in the County of Chester.

Year.	Estimated value of property assessable to the Poor's Rate.	Sums assessed for the Relief of the Poor.	Sums assessed for the Repairs of the Highway.	Population.	REMARKS.
	£ s.	£ s. d.	£ s. d.		
1801	693 10	533 12 0	2 11 6	830	Machinery introduced.
2	697 0	394 19 4	51 19 5		
3	697 0	336 8 0	52 3 $0\frac{3}{4}$		
4	697 10	325 10 0	52 5 $9\frac{1}{4}$		
5	724 0	385 17 4	100 6 $11\frac{1}{2}$		
6	786 0	339 6 0	110 12 $11\frac{1}{2}$		
7	829 0	276 6 8	172 7 $9\frac{1}{2}$		
8	898 10	223 1 4	177 6 10		
9	915 0	286 16 8	152 17 9		
1810	935 0	345 10 0	146 18 $3\frac{1}{2}$		
1	945 10	417 6 4	199 19 $3\frac{1}{2}$	1806	Riots, Machinery broken in various places.
2	975 15	471 8 4	168 11 1		
3	986 0	687 7 8	148 18 $11\frac{1}{4}$		
4	997 0	630 6 8	144 18 $8\frac{1}{4}$		Power looms introduced.
5	1029 15	508 18 0	99 9 $3\frac{1}{2}$		
6	1079 5	390 2 0	156 9 $5\frac{1}{4}$		
7	1109 15	502 3 6	150 2 $8\frac{1}{2}$		
8	1142 0	421 2 0	171 15 9		
9	1242 0	431 6 0	201 8 $7\frac{1}{2}$		
1820	1272 0	355 4 8	229 11 7		
1	1371 15	274 7 0	265 1 1	3355	New County Rate made: from this time the County Rate, together with the salary of the serving officer, average £200 per annum.
2	1429 5	435 10 6	440 12 $0\frac{3}{4}$		
3	1570 0	479 8 0	454 8 $8\frac{3}{4}$		
4	1792 0	348 17 0	506 2 $2\frac{1}{2}$		
5	1957 0	398 11 0	524 19 $3\frac{1}{2}$		
6	2093 10	438 7 6	573 10 $7\frac{3}{4}$		
7	2354 15	479 6 3	598 10 5		
8	2533 0	502 7 4	732 4 $3\frac{1}{2}$		
9	2623 0	790 11 9	681 19 $6\frac{1}{2}$		
1830	2727 0	549 16 0	578 10 1		
1	2783 0	[1] 834 18 9	359 5 $5\frac{1}{2}$	7138	
Total in 31 yrs. .		13,994 13 7	8405 19 7		
Average		451 10 0	271 7 2		

[1] A considerable balance in the Overseer's hands.

This table exhibits a cheering proof of the advantages which may be derived from the commercial system, under judicious management. We feel much confidence in inferring that where so little pauperism exists, the taint of vice has not deeply infected the population; and concerning their health we can speak from personal observation. The rate of mortality, from statements[1] with which Mr. Ashton has politely furnished us, appears to be exceedingly low. In thirteen years (during the first six of which, the number of rovers, spinners, piecers and dressers was 100, and during the last seven, above 200) only eight deaths occurred, though the same persons were, with rare exceptions, employed during the whole period. Supposing, for the sake of convenience, that the deaths were nine; then by ascribing three to the first six years, and six to the last seven, the mortality during the former period was 1 in 200, and during the latter, 1 in 233. The number of weavers during the first six years was 200,

---

[1] Minute of Deaths among the Spinners, Piecers and Dressers, employed at the works of Mr. Thomas Ashton, in Hyde, from 1819 to 1832, thirteen years, viz.: Spinners — Rd. Robinson, James Seville, David Cordingly, Eli Taylor. Piecers — Jas. Rowbotham, Wm. Green. Dressers — John Cocker, Samuel Broadhurst.

There are employed at these works 61 rovers and spinners, 120 piecers, and 38 dressers: total 219; among whom there are at this time 10 spinners, whose ages are respectively from forty up to fifty-six years; and among the dressers there are 12 whose ages are equal to that of the above spinners. We have no orphans at this place, neither have we any family receiving parochial relief; nor can we recollect the time when there was any such. The different clubs or sick lists among the spinners, dressers, overlookers and mechanics employed here, allow ten or twelve shillings per week to the members during sickness, and from six to eight pounds to a funeral; which applies also to the member's wife, and, in some cases, one half or one fourth to the funeral of a child. The greatest amount of contributions to these funds has in no one year exceeded five shillings and sixpence from each member.

The weavers (chiefly young women) have also a funeral club, the contributions to which are fourpence per member to each funeral. In the above period of thirteen years there have happened among them only forty funerals.

Total number of persons employed, twelve hundred, who maintained about two thousand.   JOSEPH TINKER, Book-keeper.

Hyde, 27th March, 1832.

and during the last seven 400; and in this body of workmen 40 deaths occurred in thirteen years. By ascribing 13 of these deaths to the first six years, and 27 to the last seven, the mortality, during the former period, was 1 in 92, and during the latter, 1 in 103.

These facts indicate that the present hours of labour do not injure the health of a population, *otherwise favourably situated*, but that, when evil results ensue, they must chiefly be ascribed to the combination of this *with other causes of moral and physical depression.*

Capitalists, whose establishments are situated in the country, enjoy many opportunities of controlling the habits and ministering to the comforts of those in their employ, which cannot exist in a large manufacturing town. In the former, the land in the vicinity is generally the property of the manufacturer, and upon this he may build commodious houses, and surround the operative with all the conveniences and attractions of a home. In the town, the land is often in the possession of non-resident proprietors, anxious only to obtain the largest amount of chief rent. It is therefore let in separate lots to avaricious speculators, who (unrestrained by any general enactment, or special police regulation) build without plan, wretched abodes in confused groups, intersected by narrow, unpaved or undrained streets and courts. By this disgraceful system the moral and physical condition of the poor undergoes an inevitable depression.

In Manchester [1] 'it is much to be regretted that the surveyors of highways, or some other body of gentlemen specially appointed, were not, forty years ago, invested with authority to regulate the laying out of building-land within the precincts of the town, and to enforce the observance of certain conditions, on the part of the owners and lessees of such property.' Private rights ought not to be exercised so as to produce a public injury. The

---

[1] Dr. Lyon on the Medical Topography and Statistics of Manchester.—'North of England Medical and Surgical Journal,' vol. i. p. 17.

law, which describes and punishes offences against the person and property of the subject, should extend its authority by establishing a social code, in which the rights of communities should be protected from the assaults of partial interests. By exercising its functions in the former case, it does not wantonly interfere with the liberty of the subject, nor in the latter, would it violate the reverence due to the sacred security of property.

The powers obtained by the recent changes in the Police Act of Manchester are retrospective, and exclusively refer to the removal of existing evils: their application must also necessarily be slow. We conceive that special police regulations should be framed for the purpose of preventing the recurrence of that gross neglect of decency and violation of order, whose effects we have described.

Streets should be built according to plans determined (after a conference with the owners) by a body of Commissioners, specially elected for the purpose—their width should bear a certain relation to the size and elevation of the houses erected. Landlords should be compelled, on the erection of any house, to provide sufficient means of drainage, and each to pave his respective area of the street. Each habitation should be provided with a due receptacle for every kind of refuse, and the owner should be obliged to whitewash the house, at least once every year. Inspectors of the state of houses should be appointed: and the repair of all those, reported to be in a state inconsistent with the health of the inhabitants, should be enforced at the expense of the landlords. If the rents of houses are not sufficient to remunerate the owners for this repair, their situation must in general be such, or their dilapidation so extreme, as to render them so undesirable to the comfort, or so prejudicial to the health of the tenants, that they ought no longer to be inhabited.

Sources of physical depression, arising from the neglect of these arrangements, abound to such an extent in Manchester, that it has been sagaciously suggested that some powerful counteracting causes must also be in operation, or we should otherwise frequently be subjected to the visitation of fatal epidemic diseases. What all those causes may be it would perhaps be vain to speculate, but it might be demonstrated that the establishment of the House of Recovery has had a most salutary influence in checking the spread of typhus fever.

The associations of workmen, for protecting the price of labour, have too frequently been so directed, as to occasion increased distress to the operatives, embarrassment to the capitalist, and injury to the trade of the country, whereas, were they properly conducted, they might exercise a generally beneficial influence. No combination can permanently raise the wages of labour above the limit defined by the relation existing between population and capital; but partial monopolies, and individual examples of oppression might, by this means, be removed, and occasions exist, when, on the occurrence of a fresh demand, the natural advance of the price of labour might be hastened. So long, however, as these associations needlessly provoke animosity by the slander of private character, by vexatious and useless interference, and by exciting turbulence and alarm, many of their most legitimate purposes cannot be pursued. Distrust will then prevent masters and workmen from framing regulations for their mutual benefit, such as modes of determining the quantity or quality of work produced, and the collection of correct statistical information—or from combining in applications to government for improvements of the laws which affect commerce. Capitalists, fearing combination amongst their workmen, will conceal the true state of the demand, and thus at one period, the operative will be deprived of that reward of his labour, which he would otherwise obtain, and, at another, will receive no warning of the necessary reduction of manufacturing establishments; which change may thus occur at a period, when, having made no provision for it, he may be least able to encounter the privation of his ordinary means of support. The risks attending the outlay of capital, the extension of the sphere of enterprise, and even the execution of contracts are, by the uncertainty thus introduced into circumstances affecting the supply of labour, exceedingly augmented. Larger stocks must be maintained, less confidence will attend commercial transactions, and an increase of price is necessary to cover these expenses and risks. '[1]If an establishment consist of several branches which can be only carried on jointly, as, for instance, of iron mines, blast furnaces, and a colliery, in which there are distinct classes of workmen, it becomes necessary to keep on hand a larger stock of materials than would otherwise be required, if it were certain that no combinations would arise. The proprietors of one establishment in the trade which has been mentioned, think it expedient always to keep above ground a supply of coal, for six months, which is in that instance equal in value to about £10,000.'

The efforts of these associations have not unfrequently occasioned the introduction of machinery into branches of labour, whence skill has been driven to undertake the severer and ill-rewarded occupation of ordinary toil. When machinery thus *suddenly* excludes skilled labour, much greater temporary distress is occasioned to the operative, than by the natural and gradual progress of mechanical improvements. By employing the power of these associations, at periods when an advance of wages has been impossible, or to resist a fall which the influence of natural causes rendered inevitable, the workmen have not only prevented the accumulation of the fund for the maintenance of labour, at a period when the advance of population was unchecked, but they have dissipated their own savings, as well as the monies of the union, in useless efforts, and, when pride and passion have combined to prolong the struggle, their furniture and clothes have been sold, and their family reduced to the extremes of misery.

---

[1] 'The Economy of Machinery and Manufactures,' by Chas. Babbage, Esq., p. 250.

The effects of these 'strikes' are frequently shared by unwilling sufferers, first, among those whose labour cannot be conducted independently of the body which has refused to work, and secondly, by those whose personal will is controlled by the threats or the actual violence of the rest. During the 'strike,' habits of idleness or dissipation are not unfrequently contracted—suspicion degenerates into hatred—and a wide gulf is created between the masters and the workmen. The kindlier feelings are extinguished, secret leagues are formed, property is destroyed, such of the operatives as do not join the combination, are daily assaulted, and at length licence mocks the law with the excesses of popular tumult.

It is impossible that the distrust, thus created, should not sometimes occasion the exclusion from the trade, of the entire body of workmen concerned, and the introduction of a new colony of operatives into the district. The labourers thus immigrating are not seldom an uncivilised and foreign race, so that, if ever the slightest tendency to cordial co-operation existed between the capitalist and the operative, that is now dissolved. The obstinacy with which this struggle with the manufacturer has sometimes been conducted has occasioned the removal of establishments to another district, or even to a foreign country, and these contests are always unfavourable to the introduction of fresh capital into the neighbourhood where they occur.

The more deserving and intelligent portions of the labouring class are often controlled by the greater boldness and activity of that portion which has least knowledge and virtue. Thus, we fear, that the power of the Co-operative Unions has been directed to mischievous objects, and the funds, the time, and energies of the operatives, have been wasted on unfeasible projects. Moreover, they who, as they are the weakest, ought to be, and generally are, the firmest advocates of liberty, have been misled into gross violations of the liberty of their fellow workmen. The power of these unions, to create disorder, or to attain improper objects, would be destroyed, if every assault were prosecuted, or the violation of the liberty of the subject prevented by the assiduous interference of an efficient police. The radical remedy for these evils is such an education as shall teach the people in what consists their true happiness, and how their interests may be best promoted.

The tendency to these excesses would be much diminished, did a cordial sympathy unite the higher with the lower classes of society. The intelligence of the former should be the fountain whence this should flow. If the *results* of labour be solely regarded, in the connection of the capitalist with those in his employ, the first step is taken towards treating them as a mere animal power necessary to the mechanical processes of manufacture. This is a heartless, if not a degrading association. The contract for the rewards of labour conducted on these principles issues in suspicion, if not in rancorous animosity.

The operative population constitutes one of the most important elements of society, and when numerically considered, the magnitude of its interests and the extent of its power assume such vast proportions, that the folly which neglects them is allied to madness. If the higher classes are unwilling to diffuse intelligence among the lower, those exist who are ever ready to take advantage of their ignorance; if they will not seek their confidence, others will excite their distrust; if they will not endeavour to promote domestic comfort, virtue, and knowledge among them, their misery, vice, and prejudice will prove volcanic elements, by whose explosive violence the structure of society may be destroyed. The principles developed in this Pamphlet, as they are connected with facts occurring within a limited sphere of observation, may be unwittingly supposed to have relation to that locality alone. The object of the author will, however, be grossly misunderstood, if it be conceived, that he is desirous of placing in invidious prominence defects which he may have observed in the social constitution of his own town.

He believes the evils here depicted to be incident, in a much larger degree, to many other great cities, and the means of cure here indicated to be equally capable of application there. His object is simply to offer to the public *an example* of what he conceives to be too generally the state of the working classes, throughout the kingdom, and to illustrate by *specific instances*, evils everywhere requiring the immediate interference of legislative authority.

APPENDIX No. I.

TABLE No. 1, p. 28.

INQUIRIES CONCERNING THE STATE OF HOUSES.

District.   No.

Name of Street, Court, &c.	No.	No.	Name of Street, Court, &c.	No.	No.
1. Is the House in good Repair?			12. Is a private privy attached to the house?.		
2. Is it clean?			13. Will the tenants assist in cleansing the streets and houses?		
3. Does it require Whitewashing?					
4. Are the rooms well ventilated, or can they be without change in windows, &c.?			14. Will they allow the Town's Authorities to whitewash them, if they cannot conveniently do it themselves?		
5. Is the house damp, or dry?			15. Are the tenants generally healthy or not?.		
6. Are the cellars inhabited?					
7. Are these inhabited cellars damp or ever flooded?			16. What is their occupation?		
8. Are the soughs in a bad state?			17. Remarks concerning food, clothing, and fuel		
9. Who is the proprietor?					
10. What number of families or lodgers does the house contain?.			18. Habits of life		
11. What is the state of the beds, closets, and furniture?			19. General Observations		

TABLE No. 2, p. 28.

INQUIRIES CONCERNING THE STATE OF STREETS, COURTS, ALLEYS, &c.

District.   No.   Inspectors.

Names of Streets, Courts, Alleys, &c.	Name.	Name.	Name.
Is the street, court, or alley narrow, and is it ill ventilated?			
Is it paved or not?			
If not, is it under the Police Act?			
Does it contain heaps of refuse, pools of stagnant fluid, or deep ruts?			
Are the public and private privies well situated, and properly attended to?			
Is the street, court, or alley, near a canal, river, brook, or marshy land?			
General Observations			

APPENDIX No. II.

EXTRACTS FROM REPORTS OF CHRISTIAN INSTRUCTION SOCIETIES. (*Note, page* 67.)

Mosley Street Christian Instruction Society.

'Its members agreed to consider a certain section of the Town, adjacent to the Chapel, as the field of their labour, and to visit periodically all the abodes of the poor within the limits so marked out, for the purpose of conversing with the inmates on the great truths of the Gospel, lending them tracts and books on those momentous subjects, and inducing them to attend public worship, and to live themselves, and train up their children, as immortal beings. From that time to the present about forty individuals have followed out this undertaking within a district of which Market Street, Mosley Street, and Deansgate, on the South side, as far as Bootle Street, have constituted the boundaries. At the commencement of the present year, returns were made, from which the following facts were ascertained. The dwellings visited by the Society were about 350, containing nearly 600 families, which consisted of about 1800 *resident* members. In those families there were, children under ten years of age, 453; children sent to Day Schools, 149; children sent to Sunday Schools only, 240; children old enough for school but not sent, 93. There were, of families possessing Bibles, 327; of families in which the adults did not regularly neglect public worship, only 150; of Catholic families, 60; of families the heads of which were *avowed* infidels, 5. To make the description of the Society's district answerable to the impressions of it on the minds of the visitors, there would have to be added, to these facts, details of drunkenness and sabbath-breaking, of vice and misery, of the complete negation of moral and religious sentiment, of flagrant vice, and shameless profligacy, of squalid poverty, of wasting sickness, and of hopeless death. When the visitors attained some extensive knowledge of the domestic circumstances and spiritual wants of the people whom they had taken under their charge, they became desirous to join, to their own agency, that of one who might give his whole time to such cases as were perpetually demanding more attention than they could possibly pay; cases of protracted illness, of approaching death, and of awakened inquiry, &c. For this office they selected a member of the church, Mr. Robinson, who has since devoted himself with the utmost diligence to the labours of his honourable, but arduous and extremely self-denying, vocation. Two preaching stations have been established; one in Queen Street, Deansgate, and one in Gee's Buildings, near Lloyd Street. Both are occupied on Sunday evening; Mr. Robinson being engaged at one place, while private members of the church most kindly and acceptably supply the other.'

London Christian Instruction Society.

'Its design is, irrespective of the particular denominations of Christians, to advance evangelical Religion amongst the inhabitants of the Metropolis and its Vicinity, by promoting the observance of the Sunday—the preaching of the Gospel—the establishment of Prayer Meetings and Sunday Schools—the circulation of Religious Tracts, accompanied with systematic visitation—and by the establishment of gratuitous Circulating Libraries—with every other legitimate method which the Committee may from time to time approve, for the accomplishment of the great object contemplated by the Society. To facilitate the operations of the Society, the Metropolis is divided, by the establishment of Associations, into districts, to each of which is appointed a Superintendent, with the approbation of the Committee, who presides over the proceedings of the Society in the District to which he belongs, and reports to the Committee, at their conference with the whole body of the Superintendents, the state of the District committed to his care. At the present time there are sixty-five Associations, which engage the benevolent attention of 1173 gratuitous visitors, who have, during the past year, visited 31,591 families, being an increase of 4677 families since the last report. So that, by this agency alone, religious tracts and books are now placed within the reach of at least 150,000 individuals. Through the benevolent efforts of the Visitors during 1830, 1260 cases of extreme distress were relieved, 617 copies of the Sacred Scriptures were brought into circulation, and 2303 children were sent to the various Sabbath Schools, and more than 1200 individuals were induced to attend public worship. Many zealous Visitors have included within their spheres of benevolence, the hospitals, workhouses, police stations, and manufactories, that are found in their respective neighbourhoods. Connected with the numerous Associations are *ninety-three stations* for reading the Scriptures, exhortation, and prayer. These meetings are usually held in the apartments of the poor, who appear gratified with the opportunity of showing their respect for the Visitors by lending their abodes for such a purpose. At various stations not less than 200 sermons were preached to congregations, varying from 100 to 1000 persons.'

Appendix No. II

Greenock City Mission.

'This Society is engaged, 1st, In visiting the lower classes in their own houses; 2nd, In collecting into one house individuals living in the same neighbourhood, for the purpose of reading and expounding the Scriptures; and 3rd, In an investigation into the state of the community generally. From this investigation, it appears that Greenock contains 6200 families, and 26,500 inhabitants, of whom 8360 are below 12 years of age: 4370 are betwixt 12 and 20: 13,970 are above 20 years. About 3000 children attend day schools, therefore there must be nearly 2000 betwixt 6 and 14 years of age, who do not attend school. It is not the business of the Directors to propose a remedy for this apparent neglect of education, but it certainly suggests the propriety of exertions being made, to have parish schools established in Greenock, being the *legal* means of affording cheap education to all classes. The number attending Sabbath evening schools is nearly 2000, and there being about 5000 youths in Greenock, betwixt 7 and 16 years of age, it follows that 3000 receive no Sabbath school instruction. And allowing liberally for those whose parents instruct them at home, a number will still remain sufficiently great to show the necessity of more vigorous efforts to afford the means of religious instruction to the young. As far as could be ascertained, there are 500 individuals, chiefly grown up, who cannot read. The Directors particularly call attention to the subject of church accommodation and church attendance, information in regard to which is next in order. The number of sittings said to be taken in churches is, 8850, being only at the rate of two-thirds of a sitting to each person above 20 years of age — of course, one-third or 4621 persons above 20 years, have no sittings in any church, and there is *no* provision at all for those *below* 20. It must be allowed that in a Christian community, every individual above 12 or 14 years of age ought to have a sitting in church, so that 9000 in Greenock, above 14 years of age, are without sittings in any church. But, in fact, there is little more than church accommodation in town, for the number of sittings said to be taken, and several of the churches are not full; it follows therefore, that not nearly one-half of the population above 12 years, attend church on any one Sabbath!! About 3100 families state they belong to the Established Church, 1500 families are Dissenters, and 360 families are Catholics; nearly 1200 families could not distinctly tell to what Church they belonged!! Seven thousand two hundred persons are communicants, being only one-half of the population above 20 years of age! Surely such a statement as this needs no comment, and the Directors merely draw from it a pressing argument for increased exertions to support this Society, whose object is to attend to those at home, who either cannot or will not come to the house of God. It is remarkable that there are no fewer than 1450 widows who keep house, being betwixt a fourth and fifth of the whole number of householders. The number of paupers, or those who enjoy *regular* assistance from the parish funds, is about one thousand. It is unnecessary to state the number of families in want of Bibles, the Grenock Bible Society and Association having kindly offered to supply any deficiency of this kind.'

Glasgow City Mission.

'The object of the Mission is "To promote the Religious Interests of the Poor of Glasgow and its vicinity." It enacts that the Agents of the Society be chosen from all denominations of professing Christians: that they be men of approved piety, prudence, and zeal; and who, by their acquirements, especially in Divinity, may appear fitted for the duties of the agency: that the Agents occupy themselves, at least four hours daily, in the service of the Society, excepting Saturday, which is allowed them for study; that they select such hours of call as will best suit the convenience of the people; and that no calls be made *at the hour of dinner;* that preaching stations be appointed in the districts visited by the Agents, to which the poor shall be invited : and that the co-operation of ordained ministers and preachers of the Gospel be solicited to maintain worship at the said stations, &c. Lastly, that no Agent be required to act contrary to the laws prescribed to him, by that body of Christians with which he is connected. Of the 20 Agents employed in 1828, 6 were members of the Church of Scotland ; 10 seceders, of the various sects ; 2 Independents; 1 a Reformed Presbyterian ; and 1 a Baptist.

'The printed "Instructions to the Agents" are liberal and judicious; but they are too long to admit of being inserted. Every Agent has his own allotted district. He is required to keep a schedule, in which he enters the number of hours employed in the service of the Society, and the number of families visited each day. He is also required to keep a regular journal or diary for the inspection of the Directors. An idea of the work done by the Agents may be formed from the statement, that in the month of October, 1828, when only 16 Agents were in employment, *four thousand and seventy families* were visited in the ordinary course of visitation. *Two hundred and eighty-eight* sick and dying had special visits paid to them; 239 meetings were held, attended by as many as 2514 poor ; chiefly of such a class as otherwise might not have heard the Gospel. The number of families, the subjects of regular visitation, in 1828, was about *twelve thousand.* These devoted Agents read and expound the Holy Scriptures to the poor, and converse with them on every topic connected with their own religious instruction, and that of their children. They supply them with books and tracts. They enlist their children as scholars in the various Sunday schools, which happily are to be found in every neighbourhood. In cases of extreme want and destitution, they are also often the means of obtaining pecuniary help, through the benevolence of opulent individuals, to whom they consider it a part of their duty to make such cases known.

Manchester in 1832

*No. I.—Irish), which received Parochial Relief in the Township of Manchester, in the four winter months of the years 1827-8, 1828-9, 1829-30, 1830-31, and of the sums thus expended.

	NEWTOWN.		ANCOATS.		CENTRAL.		PORTLAND STREET.	
	No. of Cases.	Amount paid.	No. of Cases.	Amount paid.	No. of Cases.	Amount paid.	No. of Cases.	Amount paid.
		£ s. d.		£ s. d.		£ s. d.		£ s. d.
1827 and 1828.								
November.	English 1456	208 18 3	English 1694	207 17 0	English 1818	245 13 0	English 1670	226 3 6
	Irish 369	54 10 6	Irish 348	38 0 6	Irish 1874	246 10 6	Irish 1732	229 9 0
December.	English 1534	204 12 0	English 1708	209 11 6	English 1911	262 2 6	English 1738	237 9 0
	Irish 396	52 17 6	Irish 379	41 10 6	Irish 195	19 19 0	Irish 133	12 17 0
January.	English 1551	213 1 2	English 1674	205 8 8	English 1819	232 8 19	English 1724	223 19 6
	Irish 400	54 14 6	Irish 386	42 3 0	Irish 171	16 19 —	Irish 131	13 1 6
February.	English 1508	210 2 6	English 1625	193 10 0				
	Irish 394	51 14 0	Irish 369	39 10 0				
	7618	1050 10 5	8183	977 10 0	7788	1023 13 0	7128	932 19 0
1828 and 1829.								
November.	English 1291	153 9 6	English 1620	191 1 6	English 1684	208 7 5	English 1689	205 18 0
	Irish 309	34 0 0	Irish 488	56 12 6	Irish 122	12 5 0	Irish 144	14 10 0
December.	English 1339	159 7 0	English 1701	207 18 6	English 1784	216 17 0	English 1737	211 8 6
	Irish 342	37 8 0	Irish 507	57 4 0	Irish 134	15 7 0	Irish 130	15 5 6
January.	English 1347	161 8 0	English 1836	221 9 0	English 1847	231 6 6	English 1748	219 19 6
	Irish 335	39 7 0	Irish 547	62 9 0	Irish 133	15 0 0	Irish 147	15 8 0
February.	English 1457	179 1 6	English 2001	244 4 6	English 1847	236 4 0	English 1800	227 6 0
	Irish 474	55 7 6	Irish 613	72 4 6	Irish 143	15 4 9	Irish 156	16 4 6
	6924	819 3 0	9313	1113 2 0	7694	950 16 9¾	7551	925 19 6
1829 and 1830.								
November.	English 2053	292 2 1	English 2069	245 9 6	English 2278	319 5 6	English 2030	269 0 0
	Irish 530	114 19 6	Irish 639	68 5 0	Irish 166	19 13 6	Irish 228	22 6 6
December.	English 1597	285 14 6	English 1960	228 5 0	English 2346	320 14 0	English 2121	282 5 5
	Irish 585	122 3 4	Irish 640	65 14 14½	Irish 168	19 14 6	Irish 259	24 2 2
January.	English 1931	267 15 2	English 1934	231 14 7⅓	English 2481	363 6 6	English 2150	278 19 6
	Irish 961	127 18 10	Irish 694	74 5 11	Irish 198	23 8 8	Irish 320	28 16 6
February.	English 2042	290 11 11	English 2059	245 9 6	English 2563	365 9 3	English 2290	307 2 9
	Irish 1035	137 8 9	Irish 717	80 6 0	Irish 210	25 18 0	Irish 379	34 18 6
	11,934	1638 14 1	10,712	1239 0 8	10,410	1467 14 5	9777	1247 1 3
1830 and 1831.								
November.	English 2365	322 1 6	English 2210	278 1 6½	English 2395	321 15 1	English 1765	202 5 6
	Irish 925	125 8 6	Irish 925	125 8 6	Irish 204	24 9 6	Irish 230	23 1 6
December.	English 2374	360 9 5	English 2333	314 5 0	English 2597	351 3 9¾	English 1864	225 12 8
	Irish 1128	157 17 6	Irish 978	107 17 0	Irish 233	30 10 0	Irish 989	29 5 2
January.	English 2477	428 14 4	English 2328	336 8 10⅝	English 2673	377 8 10	English 1984	242 12 10½
	Irish 1022	146 4 4	Irish 994	107 9 0	Irish 243	32 10 0	Irish 304	30 17 0
February.	English 2213	335 6 3	English 2201	278 7 0	English 2549	348 1 0	English 1967	231 8 6
	Irish 976	133 6 3	Irish 921	96 8 0	Irish 229	29 0 6	Irish 291	30 19 0
	13,180	2009 1 6	12,890	1643 9 3	11,123	1514 19 4⅝	8694	1015 18 6⅝

*No. 2.

PAROCHIAL RELIEF administered in eight months of the year 1831, in the TOWNSHIP of MANCHESTER.

1831.	NEWTOWN.			ANCOATS.			CENTRAL.			PORTLAND STREET.		
	No. of Cases.		Amount paid.	No. of Cases.		Amount paid.	No. of Cases.		Amount paid.	No. of Cases.		Amount paid.
			£ s. d.			£ s. d.			£ s. d.			£ s. d.
March.	English	2037	285 12 8	English	1943	250 19 6	English	2430	334 19 4	English	1764	199 3 10
	Irish	1099	138 2 4	Irish	804	86 6 6	Irish	226	28 8 6	Irish	236	25 0 0
April.	English	2022	317 3 4½	English	1917	264 8 6	English	2879	332 4 0½	English	1769	213 5 0
	Irish	984	127 16 9	Irish	806	85 15 0	Irish	202	23 18 2	Irish	230	25 3 0
May.	English	1931	293 16 6	English	1961	254 7 6	English	2285	314 6 9½	English	1735	204 14 2½
	Irish	902	116 11 6	Irish	841	88 14 6	Irish	180	21 12 2	Irish	214	21 9 0
June.	English	1968	286 6 8	English	1980	249 4 6	English	2380	327 15 10	English	1782	207 2 6
	Irish	911	117 7 6	Irish	882	94 1 0	Irish	207	24 3 0	Irish	217	21 13 0
		11,854	1682 17 3½		11,134	1373 16 6		10,289	1403 7 10		7947	917 11 6½
July.	English	1986	306 14 10½	English	1969	275 18 6	English	2378	323 15 0	English	1730	218 5 8
	Irish	888	117 7 2	Irish	856	92 12 6	Irish	199	25 1 0	Irish	220	24 10 7½
August.	English	1987	291 15 11½	English	2024	271 1 9	English	2324	305 15 8	English	1687	205 8 6
	Irish	856	115 19 10	Irish	813	83 10 6	Irish	175	21 6 6	Irish	227	24 12 0
Sept.	English	2086	294 3 11	English	2023	274 18 4½	English	2284	307 18 6	English	1754	201 12 6
	Irish	856	110 0 6	Irish	823	85 1 0	Irish	152	16 19 0	Irish	205	20 3 6
Oct.	English	1937	289 10 10	English	2091	258 19 2	English	2301	312 10 2	English	1732	179 7 6
	Irish	809	106 1 9	Irish	788	80 12 0	Irish	169	19 4 2	Irish	211	20 17 0
		11,405	1631 7 10		11,387	1422 19 9½		9982	1332 10 0		7766	894 7 3½

APPENDIX No. IV.

Inserted in 1862.

I shall hereafter show that the inquiries of the Statistical Society of Manchester disclosed the fact, that in 1834 upwards of 15,000 persons in a population of 200,000 were living in cellar dwellings. The condition of a very large proportion of these dwellings beneath the level of unsewered streets was, to the last degree, insalubrious—it was often pestilential. I have sometimes, as a Dispensary physician, had to make my way to the bed of a patient suffering from typhus, by stepping from one brick to another placed for my convenience on the flagged floor, covered with some inches of water. This occurred to me twice in Little Ireland, where, on one of these occasions, nearly a whole family perished of typhus. The cellars were inundated during a flood in the Medlock. It occurred also in 'Irish town,' in the valley of the Irk; and during the prevalence of cholera I remember carrying away some bad cases in canvas slings, on the shoulders of hospital-bearers, from flooded cellars not far from Knotmill. The following letter was read to the Statistical Section of the British Association for the Advancement of Science, at its Annual Meeting in Liverpool, in 1837. A statement had been made in the Report of the Manchester Statistical Society, on the state of the working classes in Liverpool, that 31,000 persons in Liverpool, out of a population of 230,000 persons, or taking the working population as two-thirds of the whole, 20 per cent. of that class were living in cellars. This was disbelieved, and the police were directed to make an exhaustive inquiry. The following is the Report of the Head Constable of Liverpool to Mr. Adam Hodgson:—

' Watch Office, Sept. 14, 1837.

'Sir,

'I have great pleasure in fulfilling the promise casually made to you yesterday, during the conversation in the Statistical section on inhabited cellars of Liverpool. I had an accurate return made in the morning by the inspectors, and the following is the result:—North district, 4004 inhabited cellars; South district, 3858. Total, 7862. Allowing five inmates to each cellar, and that number is rather under the average (this is only an estimate), the number of persons living in cellars in this town will therefore be 39,310!

'Permit me to observe, that although persons who live in cellars are always poor, poverty is not exactly the cause of their selecting such domiciles. The rent of rooms is not comparatively higher than that of cellars, frequently the reverse; but cellars offer advantages to two descriptions of persons which give them a preference.

'1st. They serve as places for carrying on little retail trades. These trades, in nine cases out of ten, are the reverse of profitable, but still they hold out a slight inducement to those whose hopes are better than their habits: poor women, who keep mangles, also generally live in cellars.

'2nd. A very numerous class prefer the cellar, for this reason—that it renders them independent of their landlords. It is a complete dwelling in itself; the inhabitants enter and leave through their own, and not through their landlord's, door, and consequently ejectment is not only a difficulty, but in many cases an impossibility, without pecuniary compromise. Those, therefore, who are unwilling to pay rent, or occasionally unable to pay it, and whose domestic habits are not very refined, prefer the cellar.

' I must confess that I did not believe, until this morning, that so great a number of persons resided in such objectionable places.

' I am, Sir, your obedient servant,

' M. J. WHITTY, Head Constable.

' Adam Hodgson, Esq.'

SKETCH OF THE PROGRESS OF MANCHESTER

IN THIRTY YEARS

FROM 1832 TO 1862

SKETCH OF THE PROGRESS OF MANCHESTER IN THIRTY YEARS

FROM 1832 TO 1862

The description of the moral and physical condition of the working classes in Manchester, which precedes relates to a period immediately before the first Treasury grants for the promotion of Public Education in 1833. I had then been about nine years occupied in the study and practice of medicine. I had been thus led to a close observation of the condition of the population of great cities. As a young student, I acted as assistant to Dr. Alison—the late Professor of Medicine in the University of Edinburgh—first, during an epidemic typhus in the wynds, closes, and many storied barrack-houses of the old town of Edinburgh. Next, as his and Professor Graham's clinical assistant in the wards of the Royal Infirmary, and of the Queensbury Fever Hospital; and then as resident, having charge of the medical wards of the Royal Infirmary. In these capacities I had for some years opportunities of observing the habits and condition of the Scotch and Irish Celtic population during epidemics of the fatal typhus of the old town of Edinburgh.

One autumn I spent with the poor of Dublin, among whom typhus always lurked, and often broke forth with epidemic violence.

I had visited the chief cities of Europe, and been careful to observe the comparative condition of the people.

Then for several years I had been a Dispensary Physician in Ancoats, the poorest district of Manchester, and had spent many hours daily among the labourers and factory operatives, often visited by typhus fever.

When Asiatic cholera appeared, I was Secretary to the Board of Health of Manchester, and Physician to the Knotmill Cholera Hospital. The account of the moral and physical condition of the working classes of Manchester was written after I had been some months in daily attendance on this cholera hospital; and also occupied in tracing every successive case of the disease in the house in which it occurred, in order to ascertain the means by which cholera was propagated, and, if that were impossible, then the conditions promoting its diffusion. My previous experience in Edinburgh, Dublin, and Manchester, had enabled me to suggest to the Board of Health inquiries as to such circumstances in the state of the streets, sewers, drains, cesspools, nuisances, state of dwellings, and courts, as I knew affected the health of the inhabitants. In framing these questions, and moving the Board of Health to confide the investigation to the most intelligent and wealthy inhabitants, I had a double object in view. I wished to bring under the notice of the chief merchants and manufacturers the condition of the streets, courts, and houses of that part of the town in which the poor dwelt. The report would, I knew, be faithful; and, as it would proceed from an indisputable authority, it would be a sure basis of future municipal improvement. Then I also wished to show the most influential inhabitants the close connection between the public health, involving the sanitary security of all classes, and the physical well-being of the people. They would come to know by the history of this epidemic how far the causes of disease were preventible. They would ascertain that cholera and typhus found their victims among classes whose health was depressed by moral and physical evils, which were the proper objects of public solicitude. In a preface to the second edition of my pamphlet in 1832, I anticipated the formation of a permanent department of public health in the following words :—

'Cholera can only be eradicated by raising the physical and moral condition of the community in such a degree as to remove the predisposition to its reception and propogation, which is created by poverty and immorality. Were this notion, as it ought to be, widely diffused,—did it become, as it will, the conviction of every intelligent man,—what additional force would be added to the arguments suggested by sympathy and selfishness!

'The presence of this new danger will so affect the public mind that Boards of Health, established in conformity with the Orders in Council, will become permanent organised centres of medical police, where municipal powers will be directed by scientific men, to the removal of those agencies which most powerfully depress the physical condition of the inhabitants. But I chiefly depend on the strong impression made upon *the public mind*, when I confidently expect that its energy will be directed to promote, not only by general enactment, but by individual exertion, every scheme devised for the moral elevation of the working classes.'

Subsequently to the publication of this pamphlet, a Statistical Society was formed in Manchester, which prosecuted inquiries into the state of education in this and other towns. In 1834, Sir Ben. Heywood 'read before the Statistical Section of the British Association for the Advancement of Science, the results of an inquiry into the condition of 4102 families belonging to the working classes, which he had conducted at his own expense in 1 and 2 Police Districts of the town of Manchester.' The Statistical Society then 'selected paid agents, on whose care and diligence they could rely, to visit from house to house among the working classes of the towns of Manchester, Salford, Bury, Ashton, Stalybridge, and Dukenfield, and to fill up a list of queries with which they were furnished.' 'The inquiry occupied seventeen months in the years 1834-5-6.' 'The information obtained was afterwards analysed by the Committee, and compressed into a condensed form.' These investigations were conducted by gentlemen since distinguished—one, by his success as a political author—and the rest, for their eminence as bankers or merchants in Manchester or Liverpool. The results confirmed, to a remarkable extent, the account which I had published of the moral and physical condition of the working classes of Manchester; and I shall avail myself of them in the more grateful task of describing, in contrast with them, the ameliorative change which has in the interval taken place.

It may be desirable to remind my younger readers that the condition of the working classes, described in the following pages, preceded a course of legislation and of administrative improvement which, in the accumulated results of thirty years of beneficial progress, has amounted to a social and political revolution. In 1832 neither Manchester nor Salford was directly represented in Parliament. Their municipal administration were conducted by commissioners of police, whose imperfect powers constantly frustrated the zealous exertions of some of the most public spirited townsmen. The Municipal Corporations' Act had not become law. Factories were 'running' at least twelve hours daily, and often much longer, without any protection for women and children. Warehouses were often open till ten o'clock at night or later, and generally far into the evening. Print and bleach works not unfrequently toiled all night. The system of bounties and restrictions crippled trade and enhanced the cost of the necessaries of life.

It is no part of my present purpose to dilate upon the violation of the principles of political economy in our fiscal and commercial legislation which depressed the wages of labour, enhanced the cost of the necessaries of life, occasioned extreme uncertainty in commercial arrangements, and by the sudden changes in the rates and facilities of exchange, in monetary circulation and credit, created sudden embarrassments, not simply destructive of private fortunes, and exceedingly discouraging to all legitimate trade, but causing the most severe suffering to the hardy but rude spinners and weavers of the cotton districts. I prefer to place in a note an admirable summary prepared by Mr. David Chadwick of the consequences of a more statesmanlike system of legislation and government, both on the wages of labour and the prices of food.[1]

[1] *VII.—General Remarks.*

'The results of the present inquiry prove that a large proportion of the operative classes in the various branches of trade are receiving more wages at the present time than they have done during the last twenty years.

'It may be safely affirmed that the *low prices* of provisions and clothing, together with the *high rate* of wages, and the facilities for education and mental culture now existing, have placed within the reach of the working classes more physical comforts, and the means of obtaining more social and intellectual enjoyment, than at any previous period.

'(1.) In the *cotton trade* the *advance* of wages has averaged from 10 to 25 per cent. during the twenty years 1839-59.

'(2.) In the *silk trade* an advance of wages has taken place in all the branches equal to more than 10 per cent.

'(3.) In *calico printing, dyeing, and bleaching,* and in *silk and fustian dyeing,* a decline in wages has occurred in those branches which no longer require any special or peculiar skill; and also in the higher class of skilled workmen, such as "*machine printers;*" but the wages of this class now range from 25s. to 50s. per week, the average rate being 38s.

'(4.) In the *building trades* the *increase* in the rate of wages during the twenty years, has averaged from 11 to 32 per cent.

'(5.) In the *mechanical trades* there has been a general advance in nearly all branches. In some instances this advance is equal to 45 per cent.

'A reduction has occurred in the high wages formerly paid to brass moulders (now 30s.) and to engravers to calico printers, though the wages of the latter now range from 25s. to 48s. per week.

'(6.) In the *miscellaneous trades,* including upwards of eighty classes of workmen, the rate of wages has generally been maintained, and in some cases has been considerably advanced.

'The advance of wages, in the great majority of the cases, has been directly occasioned by *improvements of machinery,* whereby the increased production has lessened the cost, and thereby caused a largely increased *demand.*

'This is shown in a remarkable manner in the cotton trade, the extraordinary extension of which (as illustrated in the Tables in the Appendix) is entirely owing to the cheapening of the means of production. But the remarkable case of the large advance of wages in the building trades presents a peculiar exception to that of other trades.

'The operatives in these trades, by restricting the number of apprentices

Though these crises in trade were generally attended by popular tumults, the authorities depended rather on the troops of the line than on a well organised police for the restraint of a rude, ignorant, and turbulent population. The principles governing the rate of wages—the fluctuations of commerce — the state of credit—were not generally understood among even the middle classes, and among the unlettered poor were questions on which delusions existed, inflaming their passions to wild excesses. Yet there was neither a well-disciplined town nor county police. The 'runners' of a sagacious and rough chief constable, spies and informers, and the soldiers, were the

and other arbitrary regulations, have *prevented* the *supply* of labour from being equal to the *demand,* and thereby enhanced its value.

'The Table DD. is a carefully prepared statement of the amount expended in food, clothing, &c., by a working man with a wife and three children, whose earnings average 30s. per week,— as compared with the cost of the same in 1849 and 1839.

'This return shows that out of an average income of 30s. per week, 20s. 6½d., or rather more than *two-thirds,* are expended in *provisions,* leaving 9s. 5½d., or rather less than *one-third,* for clothing, rent, and sundries. It also shows that the same articles of provisions which, in 1859, cost 20s. 6½d., would in 1849 have cost £1 1s. 5½d., and in 1839, £1 4s. 7d., being a reduction in the cost of provisions of the same quality and quantity during the twenty years, of 4s. ½d. or 20 per cent., or nearly 14 per cent. on the amount of his average income.

'This reduction arises principally from the repeal of the Corn Laws and the reduction of the duties upon tea, coffee, sugar, and soap.

'The Return CC. shows that the number of depositors in the Manchester and Salford Savings Bank, was 11,700, in 1839; 24,700, in 1849; and 45,447, in 1859. That the amount of deposits remaining in the bank was, in 1839, £331,000; in 1849, £614,000; and in 1859, £1,160,085. The increase in the number of depositors and the amount deposited may, to a great extent, be ascribed to the improved resources and the extension of provident habits amongst the working classes in the district generally.

'I believe it is admitted by the great mass of the intelligent working men, that their physical and social position has much improved during the last twenty years; and it is hoped that the continued progress of sanitary improvements in rendering their " homes " more healthy, will further greatly contribute to this result.

'As a body, they are now much better educated, and are much less addicted to the sin of drunkenness; they have much greater self-respect and intelligence.'

Extracted from ' *The Rate of Wages in* 200 *Trades and Branches of Labour in Manchester and Salford, and the Manufacturing District of Lancashire, during twenty years, from* 1839 *to* 1859, *&c.*' By David Chadwick, F.S.S., Treasurer of Salford.

instruments by which the peace was preserved, or disorder was suppressed. The overworked population had scarcely any means of education except Sunday schools, dame schools, and adventure schools. They were ignorant, harassed with toil, inflamed with drink, and often goaded with want, owing to sudden depressions in trade, caused by the defective fiscal, monetary, and commercial system upheld by the law. They broke out into fierce tumults, in which I have seen mobs gut the mills, destroy the machinery, or burn the factories at mid-day. They were at the mercy of leaders who either encouraged senseless 'strikes,' accompanied with the 'picketing' of mills — the mobbing or assassination of 'knobsticks'— or the occasional murder of masters; or they became the victims of those arts of demagogues so graphically exposed in Samuel Bamford's patriotic 'Autobiography of a Radical.' Thus they were led to the manufacture of pikes, moonlight drilling, secret associations encouraged by spies, 'blanket' expeditions, and to the catastrophe of the 'Peterloo Massacre.' Those who desire it, may learn what was the political condition of the district as affecting the security of property and the public peace, by reading the Journal of General Sir Charles Napier, when commander of the northern district. The account which I published in 1832 of the moral and physical condition of the working classes of Manchester, must be regarded as the work of a physician who was unwilling to enter into the whole of the political and social questions involved in the state of the population with which he was in contact, but who could not avoid some reserved allusion to them. It was published with the hope of strengthening the hands of those who in their several spheres of action were represented by Mr. George William Wood, Sir Thomas Potter, Sir Benjamin Heywood, and Mr. (afterwards Alderman) John Shuttleworth. Each of these gentlemen was the centre of energetic efforts for improvement — all consciously tending, with more or less of harmony, to raise Manchester and Salford from the condition of rude, unorganised, overgrown villages into one great city, worthy of being the emporium of the cotton manufacture and the metropolis of trade.

In 1831 the town was under the government of the Boroughreve and the Commissioners of Police, who had, with limited powers, vigorously commenced the work of improvement. The Charter of Incorporation gave a fresh impulse to this zeal, enlarged its capacities of action, and the growing public spirit opened for itself new spheres of improvement. One gentleman has been remarkably identified with the wise and able acts of the Corporation. No town clerk has possessed greater influence among members of both houses of Parliament than Mr. Joseph Heron, who has laboured for twenty-five years to secure to the city greater municipal power—to vindicate its rights against adverse interests—and especially to render its government a source of wise beneficence to the people by the improvement of their sanitary condition and household comfort.

The Town Council has confided the several departments of municipal action to committees. A very rapid summary of the results of the labours of some of these committees, though necessarily deformed with an accumulation of statistics, is indispensable to a correct estimate of the progress made in Manchester towards a much higher condition of civilisation than that which I described in 1831–32. None are more convinced than the most intelligent and benevolent of its citizens, that what has been done, though great, leaves quite as much undone. But the task is well begun; and if the rate of mortality still proves an imperfect social condition, that active and earnest spirit which has faithfully striven with the evils exposed in 1831–2, will not fail to grapple with those which remain to be overcome.

As the condition of the streets and courts forms one of the most prominent topics of my pamphlet in 1831, I give a brief sketch of the work done by the Paving, Sewering, and Highways Committee. They have made twenty miles of sewering, at the expense of the public rates. Under the provisions of the Manchester Improvement Act of 1851, they have also paved and sewered, at the cost of the owners of adjoining property, streets containing an area of 970,033 yards, at an expense of £314,550. In 1861, 1578 streets and courts had been paved, flagged, drained, &c., in thirty years. The length of the streets thus improved was sixty miles; and the area flagged and paved about 205 acres. Ninety miles of main sewers, and forty-nine miles of cross-sewers and eyes had been constructed, and 12,948 siphon-traps had been laid in connection[1] with them.

In 1832, out of 687 streets inspected in Manchester by the gentlemen who undertook this duty, on the invitation of the Board of Health, 352 streets were reported to be foul, with heaps of refuse, stagnant pools, ordure, &c. Some of these streets were almost impassable to a cart—most of them were in a condition disgusting to the senses and prejudicial to the public health. The paving, sewering, and scavenging of the streets has almost banished this loathsome evil; and the Nuisance Committee's Inspectors report on all neglect of drains, ashpits, cesspools, or of heaps of offensive matter; or on the prevention of noisome smells, all attempts to remove manure at improper hours, and generally on all forms of negligence as to other matters likely to be injurious to public health and safety.

The mode in which pigs were kept in houses and close streets—the position of size and tripe manufactories, and slaughter-houses, and their odious foulness—were fertile sources of disease in 1831. Though the Corporation has not erected public *abattoirs*, which is the only effectual remedy for one part of these evils, very stringent regulations have been adopted to secure the proper construction of slaughter-houses and their cleanliness.

---

[1] Similar works have been executed, at a very great cost, in the other townships comprised within the municipal borough,—viz., Chorlton-upon-Medlock, Hulme, Ardwick, Cheetham, and Beswick, and in the borough of Salford. In Salford, from 1844 to 1860, the paving and sewering of 282 streets had cost £61,546.

The smoke from manufactories has also been greatly diminished by the regulations and inspection of the Smoke Committee.

In procuring a supply of water for the city of Manchester, the Corporation have constructed very extensive works in the valley of Longdendale on the river Etherow, at a cost of £827,000. The whole outlay (including £538,000 paid for the property of the former Water Works Company) has been £1,356,459.[1] The valleys of the Pennine chain on its southern slope above Glossop now contain large lakes, which are the reservoirs of the rain-fall on a wide watershed, whence a full supply of water gravitates to every household in Manchester. In 1840 the quantity of water supplied by the Manchester and Salford Water Works Company was one million and a half gallons daily; whereas the daily supply had increased in 1860, under the administration of the Corporation, to eleven millions and a half. The revenue received for water supplied in 1840 was £22,400, and it had increased in 1860 to £72,000.[2]

The Commissioners of Police, by a wise foresight, chiefly prompted by the late Mr. George William Wood, founded gas works at the expense of the ratepayers, and devoted the annual profits of this enterprise to the improvement of the town, by creating new thoroughfares, like Market and John Dalton Streets, and by widening old streets. The Commissioners, partly from this source, and partly from the highway rates of the township of Manchester, expended £383,000 on these streets before the Charter of Incorporation was granted to the Borough. Since 1839 these public improvements have been judiciously prosecuted by the Town Council with such vigour that upwards of £720,000, derived solely from the profits of the gas works, have been expended upon them. The tradition of Mr. George William Wood's wise design, to improve the facilities for public traffic by the substitu-

---

[1] Account supplied by the Town Clerk.
[2] 'Progress of Manchester.' By David Chadwick, Esq.

tion of wide and straight thoroughfares for tortuous and narrow lanes, or intricate zigzag streets without plan, has been faithfully preserved by Mr. Alderman Nield and others; and the gas works have been successfully managed under the skilful and diligent chairmanship of Alderman Shuttleworth. These improvements have been so embellished by the rapidly growing wealth and taste of the city, that a large part of the street architecture in the centres of trade is transformed. Many of the warehouses are chaste structures of brick and stone. Some are even palaces of Italian art. One bank recently built may rival any club in Pall Mall. There are, of course, one or two examples of a grotesque taste. But if the city had secured the site between Lever Street and Oldham Street for a combination of the Town Hall, Post Office, Law Courts, and Exchange, Manchester might also have possessed the noblest public building in Great Britain.

The Committee of the Manchester Statistical Society, which conducted the inquiries into the condition of the working classes in that town in 1834, reports (though the inquiry does not profess to be exhaustive) that 3571 cellar dwellings were examined in the borough of Manchester. The average number of persons living in each cellar was 4·17; therefore, nearly 15,000 persons in a then estimated population of 200,000 were living in cellars.[1] Of 28,186 dwellings examined, 8322 were reported as 'not comfortable.' At that time a large class of these houses had no back yards and conveniences; many were built round close courts; others in back premises, approached from the main street only by entries; and very many were in immediate contact with foul nuisances, with trades so conducted as to be foci of contagion, or with effluvia so noxious to the health of the neighbourhood, as to make it liable to epidemic disease. The attention of

---

[1] The motives leading to a preference of this kind of dwelling over single rooms, and to its selection in other cases, are given by the Head Constable of Liverpool in the Appendix No. IV., previously inserted at a time when 30,310 persons were living in cellars in that town.

H

the Corporation has been directed to the improvement of dwellings, and particularly to that of cellar dwellings, since 1854, when the powers vested in the Corporation were referred to a committee. From the 1st of November, 1854, to the 21st August, 1861, the total number of cellars inspected was 1577, of which number 1123 were ordered to be altered, and 454 to be discontinued as separate dwellings. Of these 997 have either been altered, or alterations were in progress when the Building Sanitary Regulations Committee reported, and 370 had been discontinued as separate dwellings. Many cellars ordered to be discontinued as separate dwellings are said to have been so satisfactorily altered as to induce the Committee to refrain from taking further steps to secure an exact compliance with their original notice. As examples of the other forms of sanitary interference superintended by this Committee, I place in a note [1] an extract from their report of the 18th October, 1861.[2]

---

[1] *To the Chairman and Members of the Building and Sanitary Regulations Committee.*

GENTLEMEN,—I very respectfully present to you the annual tabular statement of the business transacted by you from the 1st May, 1860, to the 30th April, 1861.

Table No. 1 shews that the Sub-Committees have inspected 123 properties, comprising 594 tenements, occupied by 2970 persons, for whose accommodation there existed 258 privies and 136 ashpits. After inspection, the Committee, on the recommendation of the Sub-Committees, required 277 privies and 173 ashpits to be constructed. Of the former 256, and of the latter 159, have been completed; 21 privies and 14 ashpits have not been completed; 42 ashpits were ordered to be ventilated, which has been done.

Table No. 2 shews that during the year 17 urinals were ordered to be constructed at public-houses and beer-houses; of which number 7 have been completed and 10 not completed.

Table No. 3 shews that 3 places of worship, 15 warehouses, 8 workshops, and 352 houses have been erected during the year.

Table No. 4 states that 27 buildings reported as having been dangerous, were, under the direction of the Committee and City Surveyor, made secure; that 77 owners or builders of properties were served with the Committees' regulations, notwithstanding which, 8 houses were built contrary to the regulations, and that 22 courts and 78 passages were referred to Committees for paving and sewering.

[2] See Extracts from Dr. Headlam Greenhow's Report (in Appendix D.), 1859.

The improvement of the public elementary schools of the city has been chiefly due to the exertions and sacrifices of the Church and other religious communions, aided to the extent of about one-third the whole outlay by the grants made by the government since 1833. But the wisdom and zeal which founded the Public Free Library will long hallow the memory of Sir John Potter, a worthy son of Sir Thomas Potter, thrice elected Mayor of Manchester, as well as its representative in Parliament. This Library, with its three branches, was established at a cost exceeding £18,000, the chief part of the original outlay having been procured from a public subscription, collected by the persevering energy of Sir John Potter, and largely enriched by his munificence. On the 5th of September, 1861, these libraries contained 56,554 volumes. The average daily issues of books were 1369, or 409,021 in 1860–61. The annual expenses are now paid from the borough rates under the Public Libraries' Act.

Public parks for the recreation of the working classes have, in like manner, been created at a cost of £35,000 for the two boroughs of Manchester and Salford.

The Manchester and Salford Baths and Laundries Company have raised £36,135 by shares since 1856, and have four separate establishments. The total number of bathers in 1860 was 177,183, who paid £2503 16s. 5d. In the same year, the number of persons who washed clothes in the laundries was 31,094, and they paid £481 19s. 9½d. The total receipts in this year were £2985 16s. 2½d., and the expenditure £2439 15s. 2d., leaving a profit of £546 1s. 0½d. The directors, therefore, were enabled to pay a dividend of 1½ per cent. on the 30th December, 1860, to the shareholders.

Great as are the proofs given in the preceding details of the progress made in municipal and social improvement, the more abundant means of elementary education, and since 1846, the great development of their efficiency, will bear a comparison with any or all of these departments of ameliorative change. The population of Manchester has accumulated more rapidly than its natural increase by immigration from the valleys of the Lancashire, Yorkshire, and Derbyshire highlands, and from Ireland. In 1834 the Statistical Society reported that out of 28,186 heads of families examined in Manchester, 4953 were Irish, and that there were also 9841 Irish lodgers in these families. Thus, at least 30,000 inhabitants in 200,000 were then Irish; and, as the inquiry was not exhaustive, the number was certainly greater. The number of Irish in 1862 is probably double that in 1834; and that their habits and influences on the rest of the population are similar to those observed in 1831, may be deemed probable from an examination of the Table in the note[1], showing the number of Irish poor, without settlements, who were relieved in one year, 1860-1, as compared with the whole of the remaining indigent population, including the Irish who had obtained settlements. This table should be compared with the tables at pages 30-1-2-3 in 1831-2. The proportion of Irish to the population is smaller in Salford.

A population, assembled from districts so rude, was necessarily, in a large part of its elements, semi-barbarous. Mingled with it was the original quaint, honest, and enduring population of the Lancashire homesteads and hand-looms, — a race full of rare qualities,

[1] *Township of Manchester.*

The number of Persons (exclusive of Lunatics in Asylums, and Vagrants) in receipt of Relief during the half-years ended September, 1860, and March, 1861; and Cost of such Relief.

	Out-Door.		In-Door.	
	Number of Persons.	Amount of Relief.	Number of Persons.	Cost of Maintenance.
Irish Poor.				
Half-year, ended Sept. 1860.	2412	£2086 0 1	1471	£1941
Do do. March 1861.	3965	2338 18 8	1752	2226
English, &c., Poor.				
Half-year, ended Sept. 1860.	3522	3714 11 7	3471	5950
Do do. March, 1861.	4513	3777 12 6	3681	6942

—hardy, broken to toil, full of loyalty to the traditions of family and place,— genial, humorous, but coarse,— easily tempted by drink to hurtful excesses, and in periods of prolonged and pinching want apt to be goaded to tumult, and in blind fury to wreak its wrath on machines and mills. This race, mixed with the Irish, Scotch, Welsh, and border elements, presented a singular problem to the educator; for the children were taken at eight years of age, or earlier, to work in factories and mines. Both women and men were required by the exigencies of the ever increasing trade. The mother gave, and still gives, up her infant of a few weeks' or even days' age to a hireling, that she may work in the mills. Young girls were, and still are, kept at home to tend the house and to nurse, and thus grievously interrupt their schooling in order that the family may have the larger earnings of the mother. High wages stimulated and still provoke sensuality in an untaught and coarse population. Gin shops, beer shops, and taverns multiplied before schools and churches effectually began their work. The tares were rank before the husbandman asked himself the question, whether the wheat could contend with them for the soil.

Two exhaustive inquiries, one of which was conducted by the Statistical Society in the years 1834-5, and the other by the Committee on the Manchester and Salford Local Education Bill, in 1852[1], afford the means of comparison so as to show the progress made in schools in seventeen years, and a recent investigation by the chief constables completes this comparison to 1861. But the last fifteen years have been marked by a still greater improvement, if measured by the greater efficiency of the schools. The statistics 'available however to demon-

[1] I shall avail myself freely of the results of this inquiry as recorded in the important evidence of Canon Richson, before the Committee of the House of Commons, in 1852. The inquiry owes much of its completeness and success to Canon Richson's statistical experience and skill, and to the zeal with which he superintended the inquiry. Mr. Joseph Adshead's evidence before the same Committee contains also many valuable facts. See Report ordered to be printed, June 21, 1852.

strate this' want the completeness of those of 1834-5, and 1852. Even prior to 1852 a large part of the change had consisted in the substitution of public elementary day schools, under the management of the religious bodies, for Dame Schools, and Private Adventure Schools.

The Dame Schools are described in the Report of the Committee of the Statistical Society in 1834-5 as 'in the most deplorable condition. The greater part of them are kept by females, but some by old men, whose only qualification for this employment seems to be their unfitness for every other. Many of these teachers are engaged at the same time in some other employment, such as shopkeeping, sewing, washing, &c., which renders any regular instruction among their scholars absolutely impossible. Indeed, neither parents nor teachers seem to consider this as the principal object in sending their children to these schools, but generally say that they go there in order to be taken care of, and to be out of the way at home' (p. 5).

'These schools are generally found in very dirty unwholesome rooms—frequently in close damp cellars, or old dilapidated garrets. In one of these schools eleven children were found in a small room in which one of the children of the mistress was lying in bed ill of the measles. Another child had died in the same room of the same complaint a few days before, and no less than thirty of the usual scholars were then confined at home with the same disease' (p. 6).

'In another school all the children, to the number of twenty, were squatted on the bare floor, there being no benches, chairs, or furniture of any kind in the room. The master said his terms would not allow him to provide forms; but he hoped that as his school increased, and his circumstances thereby improved, he should be able some time or other to provide this luxury' (p. 6).

'In by far the greater number of these schools, there were only two or three books among the whole number of scholars. In others there was not one; and the children depended for their instruction on the chance of some one of them bringing a book, or a part of one, from home. Books, however, were occasionally provided by the mistress, and in this case the supply is somewhat greater; but in almost all cases it is exceedingly deficient' (p. 6).

'One of these schools is kept by a blind man, who hears his scholars read their lessons, and explains them with great simplicity; he is, however, liable to interruption in his academic labours, as his wife keeps a mangle, and he is obliged to turn it for her' (p. 6).

'Occasionally, in some of the more respectable districts there are still to be found one or two of the old primitive Dame Schools, kept by a tidy, elderly female, whose school has an appearance of neatness and order, which strongly distinguishes it from this class of schools. The terms, however, are here somewhat higher, and the children evidently belong to a more respectable class of parents. The terms of the Dame Schools vary from $2d.$ to $7d.$ a week, and average $4d.$ The average yearly receipts of each mistress are about £17 10$s.$ The number of children attending these Dame Schools is 4722; but it appears to the Committee that no instruction really deserving the name is received in them; and in reckoning the number of those to be considered as partaking of the advantages of useful education, these children must be left almost entirely out of the amount' (p. 7).

'The "Common Day Schools," kept by private adventure teachers, in 1834–5, are described by the Statistical Society's Committee as in rather better condition than those last mentioned, but are still very little fitted to give a really useful education to the children of the lower classes. The masters are generally in no way qualified for their occupation, take little interest in it, and show very little disposition to adopt any of the improvements that have elsewhere been made in the system of instruction. The terms are generally low; and it is no uncommon thing to find the master professing to regulate his exertions by the rate of payment received from his pupils — saying that he gives enough for 4*d*., 6*d*., or 8*d*. a week; but that if the scholars would pay higher, he would teach them more. The payments vary from 3*d*. to 1*s*. 6*d*. per week, the greater number being from 6*d*. to 9*d*.; and the average receipts of the master are 16*s*. or 17*s*. a week' (pp. 8 and 9).

'There are very few schools in which the sexes are entirely divided,—almost every boys' school containing some girls, and every girls' school a few boys. They are chiefly the children of mechanics, warehousemen, or small shopkeepers, and learn reading, writing, and arithmetic, and, in a few of the better description of schools, a little grammar and geography. In a great majority of these schools there seems to be a great want of orderly system. The confusion arising from this defect, added to the very low qualifications of the master, the number of scholars under the superintendence of one teacher, the irregularity of the attendance, the great deficiency of books, and the injudicious plan of instruction, or, rather, the want of any plan, render them inefficient for any purposes of real education' (p. 9).

'Religious instruction is seldom attended to, beyond the rehearsal of a catechism; and moral education, real cultivation of mind, and improvement of character totally neglected. "Morals!" said one master, in answer to the inquiry whether he taught them " morals." "How am I to teach morals to the like of these?" The girls' schools are generally in much better condition than the boys' schools, and bear a greater appearance of cleanliness, order, and regularity. This seems to arise in part from the former being more constantly employed, and the scholars being fewer in number to each teacher' (p. 10).

In 1834–5 there were 11,512 scholars in attendance in Manchester on these two classes of schools, of whom 4722 were in the Dames' Schools; whereas, in schools connected with the religious bodies there were only 3818 scholars. In 1852 the proportions were reversed. The children in Dame and Adventure Day Schools were reduced to 4334; and those in the schools under the direction of the Religious Communions had quadrupled, having become 15,270. At the same time, the numbers in superior private schools had increased from 2934 in 1834-5, to 3772 in 1852. In Salford the scholars of the Dame and Private Adventure Schools had been reduced from 3357 in 1834-5, to 1217 in 1852; whereas the children attending National, British, and Denominational Schools had increased from 1566 in 1834-5, to 4246 in 1852; the superior Private Schools, from 882 to 1125.

The population of Manchester had increased from 200,000 to 303,358, and that of Salford, with the townships of Broughton and Pendleton, from 55,000 in 1834-5, to 84,764 in 1851.

The number of Sunday Scholars had, in this period of seventeen years, increased from 24,104, in Manchester, to 38,699; and in Salford, &c., from 6566 to 12,233, or in a much more rapid ratio than the population.[1] For, while the population had increased at the rate of 50 per cent., the Sunday Scholars were 66 per cent. more numerous, and the scholars of superior Private Schools, and National, British, and Denominational Schools had become more than two and a half times as great, or had increased at the rate of about 260 per cent.

The change, even up to the year 1852, was not, however, to be measured by the gradual extinction of the worthless Dame and Adventure Schools, and the erection of capacious and well ventilated elementary school-rooms,

[1] The statistics submitted by Mr. Joseph Adshead to the Committee of the House of Commons, on the Manchester and Salford Local Education Bill, differed in some degree from those presented by Canon Richson on behalf of the Manchester Committee. Mr. Adshead's 'Comparative Summary of Sunday Schools, with Population, &c., in 1834 and 1851,' was as follows:

Population of townships of Manchester, Chorlton-upon-Medlock, Hulme, Ardwick, Beswick, Cheetham, in 1834, is reduced by him to 182,016; and the number of Sunday scholars increased to 31,953. In 1851 the population is stated from the census, at 303,358; and the number of Sunday scholars, in the above township, as 53,869. Whilst, therefore, the population had, according to this account, increased about 56 per cent., the number of Sunday scholars had increased at the rate of 66 per cent. Both estimates have been made in good faith: it is unnecessary here to explain the causes of the discrepancy.

under the management of the religious bodies, nor by the great increase of scholars attracted to them. From about 1844, a class of trained teachers had been in course of introduction. In 1847 the Pupil-Teacher-system commenced; and from that time forward the Trained Certificated Teachers, aided by grants under the Minutes of 1846, gradually gave, with the aid of their apprentices, an entirely new organisation to the schools. The internal arrangement, fittings, apparatus, books, and methods of instruction, were transformed. The Manchester Statistical Society had, in 1834-5, reported respecting the two schools on Dr. Bell's monitorial system; and one school, with 1040 scholars, conducted on the Lancasterian system, that, 'they seem to be well conducted according to the systems they pursue; but it appears to the Committee that some of these systems are capable of much improvement. In the Lancasterian school, for example, and in others where a very large number of scholars are placed under the direction of one master, the plan of instruction is too mechanical; and, while the children make considerable progress in such branches of knowledge as can be taught in this manner, particularly in writing and arithmetic, many other branches of useful knowledge, and still more the general cultivation of their mental powers, are often totally neglected.'

The Lancasterian school thus commented upon was, excepting the admirable monitorial schools of the Borough Road, and those of the Kildare Place, in Dublin, the best English monitorial school which I ever visited. It contained many paid monitors, and comprised among its scholars children of small shopkeepers, overlookers, superior mechanics, and handicraftsmen. The intelligence of a large proportion of the scholars, aided by trained and paid monitors, enabled this school to approach, in some of its features, the successful examples to which I have alluded. These schools had, by paying their monitors and retaining their services to a riper age, taken the first step towards the Pupil-Teacher-system. Their paid monitors were under stricter discipline, more docile, better instructed, more skilful; and the whole organisation of the school was consequently better ordered, and the instruction more exact and efficient. But it was necessarily limited to what boys from twelve to fourteen, or at most fifteen, years of age could teach. They, too, received their instruction in a monitorial class in the school hours, and the efficiency of the school, therefore, depended on the time which the master could devote to this class. His attention, skill, and energy were, therefore, concentrated on it. The school of 1040 children in Manchester was taught by them.

The results in the Borough Road and the Kildare Place schools were remarkable; but even these schools were, as in Manchester, liable to the criticism of the Committee of the Statistical Society. The fatal defect of the system was that it was inapplicable in districts in which the monitors could not be selected from intelligent and well-ordered families, who could afford, with the aid of a slight remuneration, to allow them to remain three years at least beyond the usual school age, in order that they might have the special care and attention of the master. The causes of the failure of the monitorial system in ordinary practice will be found to be fully described in subsequent pages of this volume.

On the contrary, the pupil teacher begins his work at a more mature age than the monitor usually abandoned his, except in such schools as those of the Borough Road and Kildare Place. He is apprenticed to the teacher, and, therefore, strictly subordinate to him. He is paid an annual stipend contingent on his good conduct, attention to his duties, and success in an annual examination by the Queen's inspector. He receives daily one hour and a half of instruction out of the usual school hours from the teacher. His character and his religious and moral training are under the special charge of the parochial or other minister, and their certificate and that of Managers' are annually required. The result of these arrangements has been an almost unprecedented success. The Queen's scholars are preferred to all other students in the Training Colleges, not merely on account of their more exact attainments, habits of application, and aptitude to learn and to teach, but on account of their more docile dispositions, stricter sense of duty, and, as far as observation extends, greater consciousness of religious obligation. Not only so, a director of the Guarantee Society, which undertakes the suretyship of persons holding mercantile and government offices with pecuniary responsibility, assures me that, though the Society has given security for a great number of young men who had passed through their apprenticeships as pupil teachers, it has suffered no loss on their account. The certificated masters are the Queen's scholars ripened by two years' training in college, and sent forth with a renewal of obligation to the government, in addition to their direct responsibilities to the managers of schools. Their certificates are not awarded until after two years' good service in the same school, and are liable to be withdrawn for misconduct. Their augmentation grants are annually dependent on the satisfaction which they give to the managers and the Queen's inspector; and this augmentation, as well as their salary derived from local sources, grows with faithful and successful service. This system has, between 1847 and 1862, transformed the monitorial schools into well organised establishments, supplied with a staff of certificated teachers and of assistant or pupil teachers, grappling with the difficulties attending the instruction of the children of an unlettered sensual population, of very migratory habits, unconscious from experience of the advantages of instruction, and apt to sacrifice the mental and moral training of the scholars to some caprice or transient want, or to the gratification of low animal instincts.

While this great improvement in the efficiency of day schools has been in progress, the proportionate increase in scholars has been very great. An inquiry conducted at the suggestion of Mr. David Chadwick by the Head Constables, Captain Palin and Mr. Taylor, gave the following results as to the numbers of Sunday and day scholars in Manchester and Salford in 1861 :—

The pupils in day schools under the religious communions had increased in Manchester successively from 3818 in 1834-5, to 15,270 in 1852, and then to 22,837 in 1861: while in Salford they had augmented from 1566 in 1834-5, to 4246 in 1852, and to 7850 in 1861. In the two boroughs, therefore, the day scholars in charge of the religious bodies had increased in 27 years from 5,384 to 30,687 ; or they were nearly six times more numerous.

For other particulars respecting the public and private day schools, and also concerning Sunday schools, I must refer to the subjoined Note[1], containing two Tables, extracted from Mr. David Chadwick's papers on the Progress of Manchester (1861).

The growth of the cotton manufacture had been so rapid, that before 1830, even in the great centre of the trade, the means of religious instruction and public worship were strangely defective. But Mr. Joseph Adshead stated in his evidence before the Committee of the House of Commons on the Manchester and Salford Education Bill (June 21, 1852), that the amount of accommodation for public worship, in connection with the whole of the religious bodies in the borough of Manchester, had remarkably increased between 1831 and 1851. In that borough in 1851, there were 121 churches and chapels, containing sittings for 95,729, or for nearly one-third of the whole population. Of these 40 per cent. belonged to the Church of England, 7 per cent. to the Roman Catholics (whose chapels are, however, thronged during several successive services in the same day), and 53 per cent. to the several denominations of Dissenters. Whereas in

[1] The present average attendance at day schools in Manchester was stated as 31,923; in Salford, 9,925; total, 41,848. And in Sunday-schools, in Manchester, 42,687 ; in Salford, 13,272 ; total, 55,959 ; as particularised in the following Tables, prepared for this paper by Captain Palin and Mr. Taylor:—

First Period

1831 there had been only 50 churches and chapels, with sittings for 51,742 persons. There was, therefore, in 20 years an increase of 43,987 sittings, or 86½ per cent., during a period in which the population had increased 66⅔ per cent.

I am indebted to the labours of Mr. David Chadwick, as a statistician, for the following information, which he has collected with much difficulty and expense. The

Return showing the Number of Schools of all Denominations within the City of Manchester, and the number of Scholars attending them.

Day & Sunday Schools.	Sunday Schools.	Total.	If under Government Inspection, and if Church of England, Roman Catholic, or Dissenting.	Day Scholars.				Sunday Scholars.
				Under 7 years.	Under 14 years.	Above 14 yrs.	Total.	
8	2	10	Church of England . .	463	700	12	1175	} 14,904
34	..	34	Ditto under Inspection.	6040	6845	45	12,930	
5	..	5	Roman Catholic . . .	570	384	15	969	} 5150
7	..	7	Ditto under Inspection .	1226	1516	12	2754	
18	44	62	Dissenting	1157	1544	21	2722	} 20,803
6	..	6	Ditto under Inspection .	772	1470	45	2287	
191	..	191	Private Schools, Academies, and all Establishments not directly connected with a Place of Worship	2678	5943	465	9086	1830
269	46	315		12,906	18,402	615	31,923	42,687

Return showing the Number of Schools of all Denominations in Salford, including Broughton and Pendleton, and the Number of Scholars attending them.

No. of Schools.	If under Government Inspection, and if Church of England, Roman Catholic, or Dissenting.	Day Scholars.				Sunday Scholars.
		Under 7 years.	Under 14 yrs.	Above 14 yrs.	Total.	
1	Church of England	10	43	1	54	6757
18	Ditto, under Inspection . .	2499	2634	13	5146	
2	Roman Catholic	318	456	2	776	1040
4	Dissenting	160	232	10	402	8557
5	Ditto, under Inspection . .	642	764	66	1472	
48	Private Schools, Academies, and all Establishments not directly connected with a Place of Worship . .	489	1402	184	2075	
78		4118	5531	276	9925	16,354

account given by Mr. Joseph Adshead was confined to the city of Manchester; that collected by Mr. David Chadwick comprises the borough of Salford and adjoining districts. The aggregate population in 1840 was 315,000, with sittings in churches and chapels for 86,442. In 1850, the population had increased to 405,000, with sittings for 126,331. In 1860, the population was 470,000, and the sittings were 184,016.

This account is not so encouraging as that given by Mr. Adshead for the twenty years from 1831 to 1851, and for the city of Manchester alone. In Manchester, Salford, and the adjoining districts, the proportion of sittings to the population, from Mr. David Chadwick's statistics, appear to have been in 1840, one sitting to nearly three and two-thirds persons of all ages; in 1850, one sitting to about three and one-fifth; and in 1860, one sitting to nearly two persons and three-fifths. (See Table on p. 112.)

I gave in 1831 some account of the operation of the City Missionaries and District Visiting Societies. Mr. Adshead in his evidence before the Committee of the House of Commons (on the 7th June, 1852), thus describes the principles and progress of the Manchester and Salford City Mission, affording a gratifying answer to the 'regret' which I had expressed in 1831, that the 'number' of these missionaries was 'utterly insufficient to affect the habits of more than a small portion of the population.' Ancoats, Newtown, and Portland districts,' in which 'reside the most indigent and immoral of our poor,' were then 'unoccupied.' 'In 1832,' says Mr. Adshead, 'a few persons joined together to devise the best means of providing an agency by which' these 'classes of persons might be morally and religiously benefited.' 'The Committee of this Association is composed of members of the Church of England, Independents, Baptists, Wesleyans, and Presbyterians; and although comprising these several religious opinions, the greatest unanimity has prevailed in advancing the object of the Mission.' 'The guiding principle' 'was not to proselytise, but to evangelise. The first

TABLE—showing the Increase of Churches and Chapels, with the Amount of Seat-room for decennial periods, in the City of Manchester and Borough of Salford, and adjoining Districts.

Denomination.	1840.			1850.			1860.		
	Churches and Chapels.	Seat-room.	Population.	Churches and Chapels.	Seat-room.	Population.	Churches and Chapels.	Seat-room.	Population.
Church of England .	28	34,246		48	46,896		85	82,411	
Dissenters	77	46,246	315,000	120	70,605	405,000	130	91,605	470,000
Roman Catholics . .	4	6000		7	8850		10	10,000	
	109	86,492		175	126,331		225	184,016	

year of the operations of this Mission, they had 29 missionaries; they have now (1852) 70 missionary agents, who are daily employed in visiting the operative classes in Manchester and Salford.' They 'are regarded as friends of the operative classes, which will appear from the following particulars of their operations from 1837 to 1852:—Visits made to the abodes of the operative classes 2,247,420; meetings held, 65,815; persons who have attended such meetings, 1,289,462; tracts distributed, 3,212,859; turned from the error of their ways, or as it is said in the Reports, "hopefully converted to God," 4658; visitations to the sick, 248,159; of the last it is said in the Reports ("died hopefully in the faith of the Gospel"), 3583; infidels reclaimed, 211; prostitutes returned to society, 141; drunkards reclaimed, 987; children induced to attend Sunday schools, 6285; adult persons induced to attend public worship, 5036. The amount contributed from the commencement of the Society in 1837 to 1852 was " £44,971 15s." '

In 1861 the number of missionaries had increased to 100; of house visits to 379,902 in that year, and to a total of 5,266,289; the visits to the sick to 50,059 in the year, and to a total of 600,544. The other acts of ministration were in similar proportion, as will be seen in the tabular [1] summary, where the outlay in 1861 is

[1] ' Organised infidel opposition is scarcely known, and the Bible reader and his teaching receives a welcome among all classes of working men, such as was seldom witnessed in the earlier years of the Society's history.

' The cases reported as " Reclaimed Infidels," by the Missionaries for the last few years have become less and less; and that, too, whilst those under other heads of usefulness have all increased. The present year furnishes only seven. This is another corroborative evidence at least that scepticism in Manchester, so far as any avowed form of it is concerned, is greatly reduced. It is therefore deemed needless any longer, to specify such instances under a distinct column among the results of Missionary labour.'—*From Manchester City Mission Report*, 1860.

The following summary was also presented to me by Mr. Geldard, the Secretary to the *City Mission*:—' The various meetings of men collected together weekly, at their respective places of employment, for the purpose of religious services, strongly confirm this encouraging statement. Full 2000 men are, by these means, instructed by the Missionary, in addition to 5000 or

Summary of Labour, Results, and Income, as Reported from the Commencement in 1837 to 1861.

Date.	No. of Missionaries. From 20 to 60	Visits.	Visits to the Sick.	Meetings held.	Average Attendance.	Tracts Circulated.	Induced to attend Public Worship.	Hopeful Conversions.	Become Communicants.	Hopeful Deaths.	Infidels Reclaimed.	Fallen Women Restored.	Drunkards Reformed.	Children sent to Sunday Schools.	Children sent to Day Schools. Not previously reported.	Income. £ s. d.
From 1837 to 1852		2,247,420	248,159	65,815	19	3,212,859	5036	4658	1046	3583	211	141	987	6285		42,127 11 5
1853	69	285,890	26,266	6443	16	98,062	601	594	98	724	20	21	132	919		4686 6 1
1854	80	327,909	37,280	7357	15	86,000	955	568	145	873	17	23	190	1692		4770 7 11
1855	75	353,214	40,754	8096	25	96,963	663	517	133	720	17	18	186	1166		4829 13 5
1856	70	319,704	34,442	8441	22	72,145	786	497	183	821	27	27	182	1232	2346	5443 7 5
1857	80	313,169	36,993	8203	20	89,637	616	608	114	831	24	22	201	1153	1884	5378 1 9
1858	80	337,720	39,390	9469	33	272,116	728	665	148	998	24	27	229	1144	1743	5707 4 5
1859	86	337,227	39,920	10,455	36	326,213	804	776	188	1059	14	56	220	1033	939	5366 6 4
1860	88	364,134	47,281	12,253	29	367,396	721	756	181	1349	7	78	196	831	1400	6375 3 11
1861	100	379,902	50,059	12,244	25	325,118	656	805	188	1281	—	176	227	1009	1685	6261 9 3
Totals...		5,266,289	600,544	148,776		4,946,509	11,566	10,444	2424	12,239	361	589	2750	16,464	9997	90,945 11 11

recorded as amounting to £6261 9s. 8d., and the whole outlay from the commencement of the City Mission to £90,945 11s. 11d.

One part of the operations of the City Mission is supported by a separate fund. Mr. Le Mare had been a Member of the Local Committee on the Manchester and Salford Education Bill. He was aware, from the investigations of that Committee, to how great an extent the apathy of parents co-operated with their waste of the means of comfortable living, and sometimes with their poverty, to induce a neglect of the schooling of their children.

6000 met with in their daily house-to-house visitations. Any sceptical objections or indisposition to attend these meetings are exceptions to the general rule, and the opportunities seem likely to multiply every month. They are held among the lurrymen or carters, in the employ of the large carriers — the passenger and goods porters of the London and North Western — the Lancashire and Yorkshire, the East Lancashire and the Manchester, Sheffield and Lincolnshire Railway Companies; almost all the men under the town councils of Manchester and Salford,—viz. the police, the lamplighters, the gas works and main men, the paviours, the night scavengers, the men in breweries, dye works, print works, machine shops, tan yards, file works, alum works, &c.; also, cabmen and ostlers. The large tea meetings held occasionally with these men and their wives, are abundant proof of the popular feeling entertained towards the religious teacher. The men in the employ of the Council Lamp and Scavenging Committee, with their wives, took tea together a few days since — nearly 600 in the whole — when the chairman, Ivie Mackie, Esq., stated that the improvement among the men was so marked, that, instead of the Committee being occupied at their fortnightly meeting for an hour and a half, as it used to be, in hearing complaints against delinquents for neglect of work, they now had scarcely any brought before them. At a similar large meeting of the Railway Porters of the Goods Department of the London and North Western Railway, Mr. Kay, their superintendent, who was in the chair, said that about 500 copies of the Scriptures had lately been sold to those under his charge, and during the past year, only four men had been brought before him because of drunkenness or other fault — a smaller number by far than he had ever before known. Two tea meetings will soon take place for the men and their wives, and friends connected with the gas works and main men under the Gas Works Committee. These together will number about 1000.

When the lurrymen or carters, in April last, obtained the boon of shorter hours, by a wise arrangement made between the merchants and the carriers, they desired, entirely of their own accord, to celebrate the event, and to testify their gratitude by attending, in a company 800 strong, at Christ Church on the Sunday afternoon, to hear a sermon from the Rev. Canon Stowell.

Mr. Forbes, one of the City Missionaries, as early as January, 1849, had devised a scheme for the remedy of this evil, and had to a limited extent carried it into execution. Mr. Le Mare subsequently resolved on a similar effort on a more extended scale. The principles on which these two Supplemental School funds are administered, and the agency employed—the City Missionaries—are the same. The intention is to arouse parents to a sense of their duty of sending their children to school, and to aid and encourage them in the discharge of it by paying part of the school-pence. The fund collected by Mr. Le Mare has, during six years, averaged £372 15s. 7d. per annum. That raised by Mr. Forbes, is from £110 to £120 per annum. 'The proportion of school-fees paid by the parents at first was 38 per cent.; but from the last year (1860–61) it has been 51 per cent.' Mr. Le Mare reports in 1858, that 'the number of children receiving instruction' through these means was 'altogether about 2800, of whom 1800 were aided by the fund' under his charge, 'and the residue by other means,' such as Mr. Forbes's separate fund. In 1861, the Committee of Mr. Forbes's fund report that 562 children had been thus kept at school at a cost of £241 4s. 5d., of which £129 5s. 7½d. was paid by the family, and £111 18s. 9½d. by the subscribers to the Supplementary School fund. Benevolent and useful as are these forms of action, they ought to be regarded as only transient expedients, adapted less to the real need than the apathy and sensual condition of a population in receipt, for the most part, of high wages, but unlettered, unconscious of the value of education to their children, and wasting their resources in coarse living and in drink. The application of such palliatives is, by no means, a subject of unmixed gratification. The period during which they can be continued, and the classes to which they can be extended, are legitimate subjects of a vigilant jealousy. The charity which ceases to quicken the sense of duty is often a pernicious dole.

The gentlemen who have charge of these funds are doubtless, however, well aware of the necessity for this caution.

While churches, schools, and missionaries are striving, by their moral agencies, to wean the population from sensual and criminal habits, the police watch and restrain the criminal classes. The proportion of the constabulary to the population does not bear a strict relation to the need for their interference; but it may be regarded as one among many indications of the comparative security of the person, of property, and the public peace. In the counties of England and Wales, apart from the boroughs, the amount of this force[1] for 1860 was 1 in 1417 of the population; in the boroughs maintaining a separate Police Force (excepting the City of London and the Metropolitan Police District) it was 1 in 720, and in the City of Manchester 1 in 502 inhabitants. In the City of Manchester in 1841 the police numbered 817, and in 1859–60 their force amounted to 617.

The proportion of the criminal classes to the population was more favourable in the seats of the cotton and linen manufactures than in any other districts in England and Wales, except the metropolis. The following are the proportions:—

	Criminal Classes.	Prostitutes.
1. The Metropolis	1 in 183·8	1 in 366·8
2. Seats of Cotton and Linen Manufactures	1 in 131·4	1 in 506·4
3. Seats of small Mixed Textile Fabrics	1 in 126·7	1 in 357·2
4. Seats of Woollen and Worsted Manufactures	1 in 121·0	1 in 596·8
5. Pleasure Towns	1 in 103·8	1 in 248·2
6. Commercial Ports	1 in 99·9	1 in 182·0
7. Agricultural Towns	1 in 91·5	1 in 241·0
8. Seats of Hardware Manufacture	1 in 67·8	1 in 423·3

Mr. David Chadwick has furnished me with another

---

[1] Judicial Statistics, 1860, England and Wales. Presented to Parliament, p. 5.

result of his laborious statistical investigations (see Appendix C), showing the number of persons 'taken into custody, summarily convicted, convicted on indictment, and discharged or acquitted, in each year, from 1841 to 1860. From these returns it appears that 3249 persons were on the average summarily convicted in each of the first six years of this term to 1846 inclusive, and 3703 in each of the last six years, or from 1854 to 1860. The number of criminals convicted on trial, was in each of six years, from 1841 to 1846 inclusive, on the average, 571; whereas in the last six years to 1860, the annual average was 586. In the city of Manchester, therefore, crime has remained stationary during twenty years, in which the population has more than doubled. The number of prisoners in the Manchester City Gaol has, however, increased from 303 in 1851, to 508 in 1861, which is an indication, either of a change in the character of the punishments inflicted, or of an increase in the class of crimes punished by imprisonment (see Appendix C). I place some facts also in a note [1] extracted from the Official Summary and Tables of Judicial Statistics, relating

---

[1] 'Burglary and house-breaking' are stated to be most frequent in the country districts. ([a]) 'In the city of Manchester, however, 269 cases of this crime occurred in 1860, or one offence in 1127·8 of the population, while in Liverpool only 51 cases were reported, or an offence against every 7341·2 of the population. In Manchester the number of indictable offences reported was 5975; in Liverpool, 4194,—the population of the latter town exceeding that of the former by 17,000. In 1859 the cases of house-breaking and burglary were in Manchester, 227; in Liverpool, 79. The total of the indictable offences was in Manchester, 6126; in Liverpool, 3901: showing a still greater disproportion in the total number of crimes than in 1860.' On the other hand, offences entitled 'Shooting at, wounding, stabbing, &c.,' to do bodily harm,' amounted to 106 in Liverpool, and only to 13 in Manchester.([b]) In Liverpool there were 18,306 summary convictions, out of 37,214 proceeded against; and in the City of Manchester only 4742 out of 8508 proceeded against; and in Salford 1101 ([c]), out of 1877 proceeded against. In explanation of this enormous disparity in the offences punishable by Justices, the following numbers may be compared ([d]), which account for its chief sources:—

---

[a] Judicial Statistics, p. 6.   [b] Ibid, p. 15.   [c] Ibid, p. 22.   [d] Ibid, p. 27.

chiefly to a comparison of the criminal returns of Manchester and Liverpool. It concerns the police to watch and detect the skilful burglars, who are attracted by the defenceless state of warehouses and houses to Manchester.

It ought also to be remarked that, while the population of England and Wales has increased from 17,927,609 in 1851, to 20,066,145 in 1861, the number of persons committed or bailed for trial in 1851, amounted to 27,960, and in 1860 it was reduced to 15,999. The comparative returns in the county of Lancaster [1] in 1851, reported 3459 persons committed or bailed for trial in a population of 2,031,236, and in 1860 they were 2701 in a population of 2,465,366. If, therefore, crime has remained stationary in Manchester during a period in which its population has doubled, and in England and Wales crime has diminished six-fourteenths, while the population increased about one-eighth, the condition of Manchester will bear a comparison with that of England and Wales as to the relative proportions of crime to the population.

Both crime and pauperism are affected by the rapid accumulation of a rude immigrant population. Mr. David Chadwick's Table of the increase of the population in England and Wales, and in the County of Lancaster, as

Offences.	Liverpool Borough.	Manchester City.	Salford Borough.
Assaults on Peace Officers, resisting, obstructing, &c.	1126	276	66
Drunkenness, and drunk and disorderly	10,963	2329	—
Local Acts and Borough Bye-laws, offences against	14,459	120	113
Offences punishable as misdemeanours	1337	—	—
Revenue Laws, offences against	444	—	—
Mercantile Acts, offences against	330	—	—
Larceny by offenders under 16	482	90	48
Larceny under value of 5s. and on pleading guilty	1419	157	172

[1] Judicial Statistics, p. 54.

compared with that of Manchester (see note [1]), proves how vast that immigration has been. The accumulation of wealth in the City has kept pace with that of inhabitants; for the assessments for the poor-rate (see Table Appendix D) have increased from £307,510 in 1820 to £789,203 in 1860, in which period the population had about doubled. The average annual amount of the poor-rate from 1820 to 1829, both inclusive, was £59,965, and in the ten years from 1851 to 1860, both inclusive, the annual average was £141,667, being in 1860 £131,533. So that, while the poor-rate is much more than double—being two-fifths less than three times its amount in 1820, population has more than doubled in the same period. The rate of increase in pauperism has, therefore, quite kept pace with that of wealth and population since 1821. Taking into account the fact that the value of the property assessed has more than doubled, that wages have improved, employment has been more

[1] *Population of England and Wales, of the County of Lancaster, and of the Manchester Districts, from* 1801 *to* 1851.

	1801.	1811.	Increase 1801-11.	1821.	Increase 1811-21
England and Wales	8,892,536	10,164,256	Per cent. 14	12,000,236	Per cent. 18
County of Lancaster	673,486	828,499	22	1,052,948	27
Manchester Salford Chorlton and Barton-upon-Irwell Poor-Law Districts	124,339	149,801	20·5	201,506	34·5

	1831.	Increase 1821-31.	1841.	Increase 1831-41.	1851.	Increase 1841-51.
England and Wales	13,896,797	Per cent. 16	15,914,148	Per cent. 14	17,927,609	Per cent. 13
County of Lancaster	1,336,854	27	1,667,054	24	2,031,236	22
Manchester Salford Chorlton and Barton-upon-Irwell Poor-Law Districts	284,238	41	366,050	42·86	471,382	28·77

This Table is extracted from Mr. David Chadwick's 'Rate of Wages,' p. 34.

steady, and the prices of food and clothing have fallen, the present charge for indigence can only be explained by the class of causes which we shall find that we are obliged to resort to, in order to account for the maintenance of a high rate of mortality.

The character and extent of the sanitary improvements, made with so much public spirit in Manchester and Salford during the last thirty years, lead to the expectation of a decrease in the annual mortality. This is strengthened by the better condition of the people in many particulars affecting health and life. Their dwellings are improved —the hours of labour are more reasonable—wages are higher—the price of food and clothing is reduced—they have more abundant means of innocent recreation, of education for their children, and of religious instruction. Owing in a great degree to neglect and mismanagement, one half the children born in 1831 died in five years. The chief part of this mortality occurred in the first two years. There is, therefore, reason to fear that it has been little, if at all, reduced by the increase of Infant Schools; for they do not receive children until they are three or four years old. The rate of mortality continues so high, that to ascertain its level and causes is a painful but unavoidable duty. In 1831 I estimated the mean rate of mortality for nine years to 1831 inclusive, in Manchester and Salford, and the then suburban townships of Ardwick, Broughton, Cheetham, Chorlton-upon-Medlock, and Hulme, as 1 in 35·22, or as 28·03 deaths per thousand; in 1831 the rate was 30·05 deaths per thousand. But it must be borne in mind that this rate was reduced by the inclusion of the suburban townships, which continue to be more healthy than the central townships. This apparent rate had improved between 1841–50, when the annual mortality of Manchester, as estimated by Dr. Wm. Farr, was 33 per 1000 living, and in Salford, 28 per 1000. The Registrar-General, in his Seventh Annual Report (1845, p. 338), states the mean duration of life or males in Manchester in 1841 to be 24·2 years, or 16·0 years less than 40·2 years, the duration of life in all England.

The Table in which the Registrar General compared the per centage of annual mortality at each quinquennial period at all ages in 1841, in Manchester, Liverpool, and Surrey, is so instructive that I have placed it in an Appendix (A).

The summary is as follows for all ages:—

Per centage of Mortality at all ages.

	Males.	Females.
Manchester Town Sub-registration Districts	3·655	3·212
Manchester Country Sub-Districts	2·193	1·971
Liverpool	3·583	3·151
Richmond and Kingston	2·042	1·749
Chertsey and Epsom	1·935	1·680
Croydon	2·236	1·985
Godstone, Reigate, and Dorking	1·536	1·616
Guildford, Farnham, and Hambledon	1·781	1·787
Surrey	1·856	1·756

Confining this retrospect to the general rate of mortality in the first instance, I am enabled, by Mr. David Chadwick, to give (from data furnished to him by the Registrar-General) the following estimate of the deaths per thousand in Manchester and Salford, at successive periods from 1851 to 1858.

	1851.	1853.	1856.	1858.
Manchester	29·49	34·37	30·35	34·09
Salford	25·1	28·11	26·16	34·11

Mr. Royston, the Secretary to the Manchester and Salford Sanitary Association, estimates the annual deaths per thousand, through two decennial periods, from 1840, to be on the average as follows:—

	1841 to 1850.	1851 to 1860.
Registration District of Manchester	33	31½
Township of Manchester	36	34
Town of Liverpool	36	33¼

'This shows a reduction in the annual rate of mortality in the district of Manchester of 1½ to every 1000 of the population, which represents a saving of 3500 lives during the last ten years; the per centage of reduction is greater in the Township, being at the rate of 2 to every 1000, which arises from the circumstance, that during the last few years, some of the out-Townships have much increased, and become more urban in their character.'

'Being desirous of finding at what period the additional improvement began to take place in Liverpool[1], I examined every year separately, and found the mortality to be as follows:—

	1858.	1859.	1860.
Manchester	36	$30\frac{3}{4}$	$30\frac{1}{2}$
Liverpool	36	$30\frac{1}{2}$	$28\frac{1}{2}$ '

Mr. David Chadwick finds that in 1854 the death-rate per 1000 on the population of 1851, in thirty-one principal towns, containing a population of nearly seventeen millions, was 24·44. In all England the Registrar-General reports that the deaths are annually at the rate of 23·54 per thousand on the actual population; in country districts 20·26 per thousand; and in town districts 28·16 per thousand. Sixty-one thousand of the deaths in England are referable to the imperfect operations of the sanitary arrangements of our towns. I place on the following page, a Table extracted from Mr. David Chadwick's 'Vital Statistics of Towns,' affording the means of comparison between towns in which the rate of mortality is highest.

That the high rate of mortality in Manchester is still in some degree dependent on the over-crowding of the population in their dwellings, on bad ventilation: want of cleanliness, and on imperfect sanitary arrangement is rendered probable by the great difference between the death-rates in the more salubrious suburban districts, inhabited by a better housed and more moral and comfortable class, and the death-rates in Manchester and Salford separately. This is confirmed by Dr. Greenhow's Report.[2]

---

[1] This I consider both disheartening and encouraging — disheartening, to find that we have been passed in the race by our neighbours,—and encouraging, because it shows that the improvements made by the authorities in Liverpool during the last few years are beginning now to bear good fruit. May it stimulate us to 'go and do likewise.'

[2] See Appendix E.

Population enumerated, 1841 and 1851; and Deaths Registered during the Years 1851-1858.

REGISTRATION DISTRICT.	POPULATION.		Per Centage of Increase.	DEATHS.								Average for Three years.
	1841.	1851.		1851.	1852.	1853.	1854.	1855.	1856.	1857.	1858.	
London (Metropolis Dis.)	1,948,417	2,362,236	21·23	55,488	54,638	60,069	73,697	61,942	57,274	59,103	64,122	
Mortality per 1000				23·48		25·42			24·24		27·14	
Birmingham*	138,215	173,951	25·85	4989	4567	4947	6020	4662	4729	5578	5795	
Mortality per 1000				28·68		28·45			27·18		33·31	
Ashton*	50,977	66,852	31·14	1554	1470	1634	2055	1598	1521	1903	2095	
Mortality per 1000				23·24		24·44			22·75		31·33	
Liverpool*	223,003	258,236	15·79	8754	8648	8293	10,370	9096	8225	9117	9579	
Mortality per 1000				33·89		31·11			31·85		37·09	
West Derby*	88,680	153,279	72·84	3782	4019	3649	4427	4175	4146	4621	5202	
Mortality per 1000				24·67		23·8			27·04		33·93	
Leeds*	88,741	101,343	14·2	3181	3370	2822	3238	2641	2713	2901	3221	
Mortality per 1000				31·38		27·84			26·77		31·78	
Ecclesall Bierlow*	31,625	37,914	19·88	919	988	1052	1106	1111	1046	1236	1393	
Mortality per 1000				24·23		27·77			27·58		36·73	
Sheffield*	85,293	103,626	21·49	3108	3261	3434	3569	2931	2828	3422	3697	
Mortality per 1000				29·99		33·13			27·29		35·67	
Bradford*	132,161	181,964	37·68	5132	5018	5182	4855	4395	4768	4555	5152	
Mortality per 1000				28·02		28·47			26·2		28·31	
Bristol*	64,266	65,716	2·25	1831	1916	1948	1772	1793	1582	1610	2004	
Mortality per 1000				27·86		29·64			24·07		30·49	
Wolverhampton*	80,721	104,158	29·03	2956	2752	3228	3902	3080	2980	3611	3139	
Mortality per 1000				28·37		30·99			28·61		30·13	
Salford*	70,224	87,523	24·63	2198	2487	2461	2650	2527	2290	2517	2986	
Mortality per 1000				25·1		28·11			26·16		34·11	
Manchester*	192,403	228,433	18·72	6737	7597	7851	7792	7939	6933	7545	7789	
Mortality per 1000				29·49		34·37			30·35		34·09	
The County of Lancaster	1,698,609	2,067,301	21·7	54,928	60,634	59,677	59,288	59,888	56,049	60,811	64,007	
Mortality per 1000				26·56		28·86			27·11		30·96	

* These are Superintendent Registrars' Districts, usually co-extensive with Poor Law Unions.

'The number of deaths[1] average in

Manchester	34	per thousand annually.
Salford	29	,, ,,
Ardwick,	25	,, ,,
Cheetham and Crumpsall	17	,, ,,
Pendleton	24	,, ,,
Broughton	15	,, ,,

Whilst this great difference exists in the several townships of the same parish and district, I believe it will be found that as great a disparity in the rate of mortality exists between various parts of each of the said townships.'

Mr. Royston, the Deputy-Treasurer, calls the attention of the Manchester and Salford Sanitary Association to the fact published by the Registrar-General in his Sixteenth Annual Report, that the rate of mortality in England varies in the different registration districts from 15 to 36 annual deaths per thousand of population.

'England and Wales are divided into 624 districts, which are classified as follows:—

In	3	Districts the Annual Mortality was 15 to every 1000.		
	14	,,	,,	16 ,,
	47	,,	,,	17 ,,
	87	,,	,,	18 ,,
	96	,,	,,	19 ,,
	111	,,	,,	20 ,,
	90	,,	,,	21 ,,
	48	,,	(and all England)	22 ,,
	26	,,	,,	23 ,,
	29	,,	,,	24 ,,
	24	,,	,,	25 ,,
	18	,,	,,	26 ,,
	13	,,	,,	27 ,,
	18	,,	,,	28 ,,
				and up to 36
	624			

These Tables are based on the Mortality in the 10 years, 1841 to 1850, and the population for the same years.

'It will be seen that there are 64 districts, containing a population of about 1,000,000, in which the mortality

---

[1] Variation of the Death-rate in England, by William Royston.

does not exceed 17 per 1000; and, in reference to these 64 districts, the Registrar-General observes that "the health and the circumstances of the population by no means approach any ideal standard of perfection; and although nature has done much for the inhabitants, the health of the people in those districts admits of improvement; and it may be assumed with certainty that the mortality of the English people, in very variable but generally favourable conditions, does not exceed 17 per 1000; the deaths of 17 in 1000 may therefore be considered, in our present imperfect state, natural deaths, and all the deaths above that number may be referred to artificial causes." According to this rule, it would appear that during the ten years on which these Tables are based, viz. 1841 to 1850, 846,000 more deaths took place than should have done.'

The average mortality of the Township of Manchester, from 1851 to 1860, is, we have seen, estimated by Mr. Royston at 34 per thousand. Before proceeding to separate the elements of which this high rate of deaths is composed, it is necessary to examine the comparative rate of infant mortality during the last thirty years, and its present proportion to the whole rate of deaths.

In 1831 the infant mortality of Manchester was such that I stated that 'more than one-half of the offspring of the poor die before they have completed their fifth year.' In 1841 the Registrar-General reports that out of 100,000 born in Manchester, 49,910 only were alive at six years of age; 50,090 infants having perished in five years. Of these, 38,368 died under two years of age.

The relative duration of life among Males in Manchester, and in all England, was, in 1841, estimated by the Registrar-General as follows (p. 338, Seventh Annual Report):—

Precise Age.	Manchester.	England.	Manchester below the average.
	Expectation of Life.		
	Years.	Years.	Years.
0	24·2	40·2	16·0
1	33·1	46·7	13·6
10	40·6	47·1	6·5
20	33·3	39·9	6·6
30	26·6	33·1	6·5
40	20·6	26·6	6·0
50	15·2	20·0	4·8
60	10·3	13·6	3·3
70	6·8	8·5	1·7 [1]
80	4·6	4·9	
90	3·2	2·7	
100	1·2	1·5	

The degree in which this Infant mortality is attributed to crowded dwellings, and a lower physical state of the population, can only be imperfectly estimated by a comparison of the rate in the town and suburban districts. Moral and social causes operate in more than a proportionate degree, with the better physical condition of the inhabitants of these districts, to diminish this mortality of infants. But that preventible sanitary evils, which were legitimate subjects of legislative provision and of municipal administration, were not eradicated in 1841, was only too apparent from the following facts, extracted from the Registrar-General's Seventh Annual Report:—

	1841. Annual Mortality per cent.		Age.
	Males.	Females.	
Manchester — Town Sub-Districts of Registrars, viz.:			
Ancoats	34·637	27·413	0
Deansgate	17·827	16·872	1
St. George	7·829	7·954	2
London Road	5·644	6·046	3
Market Street	4·205	4·415	4
Manchester—Country Sub-Districts of Registrars, viz.:			
Blackley	22·094	15·397	0
Cheetham	7·451	6·327	1
Failsworth	3·004	3·635	2
Newton	2·042	2·353	3
Prestwich	1·723	2·311	4

[1] The facts for Manchester are too few to admit of a comparison above the age of 80.

The number of children living under two years of age was not distinguished in the Census Tables of 1851, and the ages of those living in 1861 have not yet been ascertained. It is not possible, therefore, accurately to compare the three decennial periods from 1841 to 1861 as respects the per centage of deaths under two years of age. This can, however, be done approximatively for those under five up to 1860, by estimating those living under five in 1861 as bearing the same proportion to the whole population as in 1851. The mean of the deaths under five registered from 1851 to 1860, both inclusive, compared with the estimated population of 1860, is the basis of the following statement, as far as it respects 1860.

Infant Mortality of Children under Five Years of Age, from 1841 to 1860, both inclusive.[1]

	Living under five years of age.		Deaths under five years of age.		Per centage of Annual Mortality under five years of age.	
	Manchester.	Salford.	Manchester.	Salford.	Manchester.	Salford.
1841	24,917	9648	2788	1031	11·189	10·68
Seven yrs., of which 1841 was the centre.			3218	1115	12·908[a]	11·324[a]
1851	28,652	11,514	3098	1058	10·58	9·18
1860	30,050[b]	13,798[b]	3408[c]	1259[c]	11·34	9·05

[a] This per centage is calculated on the population of 1841.
[b] Estimated from population of 1861.
[c] The mean of five years, from 1856 to 1860 inclusive.

The rate of infant mortality has continued so high in Manchester during the last thirty years, that it is necessary

[1] In the Ancoats district, inhabited almost exclusively by an operative population, and the smaller shop-keepers supplying them, the deaths under 5 years of age were above the average rate of Manchester in 1859. The population of Ancoats, in 1851, was 73,737; the total deaths in 1859, were 1493; and the deaths under 5 years of age were 785; or they accounted for more than half the mortality of the year. I am not enabled to state the number living under 5.

to a correct estimate of the causes of the mortality at all ages to separate that of infants. When the deaths under five years are deducted from the whole deaths, the rate of mortality is greatly reduced. In the Appendix (B) are some remarks, and a diagram prepared by Mr. William Royston[1], making this result very apparent. In like manner, comparing Brampton in Cumberland with Manchester, the whole death-rate of Brampton is 17 per thousand, as compared with 34 in Manchester; but as in Manchester the deaths under five are 17 per thousand, and in Brampton only 5 per thousand, it follows that 'at all ages the variation is only 5' (*i.e.* M. 34—17=17 death-rate, and B. 17—5=12: now M. 17—B. 12=5), 'being a reduction of the balance against Manchester from 17 to 5 per thousand.' Mr. Royston further gives an interesting Table showing the effect of immigration on the proportion of the population from 15 up to 45 years of age (see Appendix B). He also shows 'that above 5 years and up to 35, the mortality is 50 per cent. greater in Manchester than in Brampton; but that from 35 to 65 years of age, the mortality is 100 per cent. greater; thus proving that the statement of Dr. Farr was no exaggeration, that, in London, Birmingham, and Manchester, the mortality among working men was probably double what it was in the healthy districts.'

What, then, are the causes operating to cause this high rate of mortality in Manchester, after twenty-five years of sanitary improvement in the drainage, water supply, paving, scavenging, and ventilation of the central parts of the town, and in a partial improvement of the condition of houses, the closing of the worst cellar dwellings, and the better state of others?

The mortality is greater in the central than the suburban districts. The least intelligent, civilised, and moral

---

[1] Variation of the death-rate in England, pp. 5, 6.

part of the population inhabits those central districts. The immigration of labourers is not a simple phenomenon of the introduction of a large class at the most healthy periods of life, if they bring with them semi-barbarous habits, and are unable to resist temptations to brutal excesses, when in receipt of higher wages, and exposed to the temptations of town life. No doubt sanitary police, especially as respects the suppression of cellar dwellings, the inspection and regulation of lodging-houses, the removal of slaughter-houses to the outskirts, the extirpation of nuisances, the periodic cleansing of ashpits and cesspools after brief intervals, the opening of close courts, the sewering, paving, and scavenging of the city and borough, can be still considerably improved. What has been done should create a just civic pride in completing this great work of municipal improvement.

But a larger part of the inhabitants of the central townships consists of factory operatives; and among them the employment of the married women and girls in mills has a fatal influence on the health and life of infants, by neglect and mismanagement in nursing. This employment of married women in factories also deranges the comfort of the workman's household. He escapes from a slatternly home and an ill-cooked meal to the tavern. The price paid for the cheap labour of married women is a high rate of infant mortality, and of waste in drink, fatal to health and life.

Mr. David Chadwick, in his 'Rate of Wages' (p. 5), gives the proportionate number of men, women, boys, and girls in a cotton mill employing 500 persons, and the average wages to each class. There were 95 men, or 19 per cent., at 18s. 6d. average weekly wages; 251 women, or 50·2 per cent., at 10s. 2d. weekly wages; 33 boys, or 6·6 per cent., at 7s. weekly wages; and 121 girls, or 24·2 per cent., at 5s. average weekly wages. The wages of all classes of factory operatives appear to have increased from 10 to 25 per cent. during the last twenty years. It is, therefore, clear that the employment of women and girls is excessive[1]; and that for the reasons previously stated, it tends to promote intemperance, and thus, by a waste of hardly-earned resources, to perpetuate the misdirection of women's work, and with it infant mortality. This is an evil to be cured by the growth of intelligence, and of a higher sense of responsibility and duty among the working classes and mill owners. Legislative interference with the labour of married women could also be applied as a form of protection in well-defined cases. The charge of an

[1] *Proportion and Wages of Adults and Children in a Cotton Mill of 500 Workers.*

Class of Work.	Men.	Women.	Boys.	Girls.	Total.
	No.	No.	No.	No.	No.
1. Stokers, engineers, lodge-keepers and warehousemen, mechanics, and porters	20	2	5	...	27
2. Cotton mixing and blowing	7	...	1	...	8
3. Carding	17	36	4	15	72
4. Self-acting mule spinning	24	...	10	1	35
5. Throstle spinning, winding, and warping	7	39	12	11	69
7. Power-loom weavers	10	173	...	92	275
8. Beaming, twisting, and sizing	10	1	1	2	14
	95	251	33	121	500
	£ s. d.	£ s. d.	£ s. d.	£ s. d.	£ s. d.
Average of Total Wages of Workers in ALL departments taken together	87 17 6	127 11 10	11 11 0	30 5 0	257 5 4
Average Wages to each Person	0 18 6	0 10 2	0 7 0	0 5 0	0 10 3½

infant child is a distinct duty not to be neglected, except under the pressure of one even more urgent.

In all evils, having principally a moral source, like pauperism, or neglect of the nurture or education of children, the degree in which palliatives can be applied without injuriously masking the mischief and postponing the application of efficient remedies is questionable. But the moral and intellectual elevation of the people, by schools and religious training, is a work requiring generations of effort. Parents more lettered and less sensual will be less prone to neglect infants and children of riper age. A population imbued with a religious sense of responsibility would not bear such a burden on the conscience. But is nothing meanwhile to be done, in the name of humanity, to prevent the premature extinction of infant life? Shall we say, that it is better that the more feeble germs of the life of such a sensual race should perish by undue exposure and mismanagement, than that the race itself should degenerate? Or shall we more hopefully say, inspired by the charity which Christ has taught, that these infants are objects of compassionate interference? If they were born one degree lower in the scale of society the parents would be paupers, and they would be in the excellent Industrial School for pauper children at Swinton.

Infant schools, to a great extent, take charge of them at three years of age. In the infant school they are in a well-ventilated room — they are in healthful exercise in various forms of amusement and drill — their manners, temper, tone of thought, and habits of application are under intelligent training. That is a form of interference justified by the results of experience. The infant school, for children from three to five, ought to be self-supporting. There might also be connected with the infant school, in all districts in which married women are much employed from home, a nursery, managed — as a school of domestic training — under the superintendence of the schoolmistress by girls, who should be paid and instructed in infant management. This nursery ought to be entirely self-supporting.

It should provide for the food and nursing of the infants during twelve hours of the day. Establishments of the kind, but capable of much improvement, exist in France. I do not here enter on the simple details of their economy.

On mature reflection I consider them to be legitimate palliatives. They bear the same relation to the management of infants by ignorant, careless, or harsh hirelings, that the infant school does to the old dame school, or the much worse modern dame school.

There remains the important question, in what cases the law should interfere. What are the conditions under which mothers should be allowed to delegate to other persons the personal care of infant children during the first years of nurture, in order to increase the earnings of the family? This subject is one too intricate and extensive for more than a passing allusion here. But in presence of the proportions which the labour of women bears to that of men in factories, and of the rate of infant mortality in Manchester, this question is one deserving consideration.

The employment of girls in manufactories interferes with their domestic training. Factory girls are, to a lamentable extent, ignorant of household management. The Infant Nursery might be a most important school. Married women, besides their inaptitude in cooking and household economy, are away from home during ten or twelve hours in the day; though it may be very questionable how far their work compensates for the want of thrift, for the absence of domestic management, and for the waste of wages in drink and in coarse feeding. The discomfort of the home reacts on the habits of all, and especially of the husband. This discomfort costs far more than the decent proprieties of a well-ordered house. In this vicious circle of cause and effect, there is a destructive force accumulating with the accelerated revolution of this weight of evil, which sweeps before it comfort, peace, morality, health, and life itself.

In 1851, the Chairman of the Licensed Victuallers' Association of Manchester and Salford said at their annual dinner, that 'there were 600 licensed victuallers in Manchester and Salford, whose annual rental, taken on a moderate scale, amounted to £48,000; paying for assessed taxes, £6000; for income tax, £4800; for licenses, £10,800; for police and highway rates, £2400; for poor-rate, £9000; for gas rent, £9000; for water, £1800; total, £91,800. *He thought those figures were sufficient to show that they should not be treated as an insignificant body.*' 'They employed 3000 servants, whose wages, calculated at the low average of 12s. per week each, amounted to £93,600 per annum.'

There are, says Dr. Lees[1], 1500 (1852) beer-houses in the two boroughs, which he estimates to cost £168,700 per annum. Dr. Lees proceeds, as will be seen, to estimate the whole annual outlay on intoxicating liquors in Manchester and Salford in 1852 at £1,400,000 at least.

A Committee of the Manchester and Salford Temperance

---

[1] From the best information obtainable, we learn that the 1500 beer-sellers pay annually for rent, at an average of £18 each, £27,000; for poor-rates, police rates, highway rates, and water rates, at the very least, £6500; for gas rent, £3000; for family expenses, viz., eating, drinking, clothing, schooling, and incidental family matters (including the bad debts they complain of), say 25s. per week each establishment, or £97,500; for 1500 servants, being one for each house, and allowing for wages, maintenance, wear and tear, &c., 8s. per week each, or in the aggregate, £31,200, per annum; and for painting, repairing, beautifying, &c., including lamps, signs, breakages, &c., say £2 per annum each, or in the aggregate, £3000; making the total cost of the beer houses per annum, £168,700.

Hence we learn that the costs out of pocket for keeping 600 public houses, is, at a low estimate . . .	£286,680
Ditto for 1500 beer houses	£168,700
Making the total yearly cost of the public-houses and beer-shops of Manchester and Salford	£455,380

This sum, being, as we have intimated, for *costs out of pocket*, must necessarily come out of the *profits* of business; and if we allow the drink trade to realise an average profit of 32 per cent., or say, 6s. 5d. in the pound; it follows, that to supply a profit equal to the necessary expenses of maintaining these establishments, the inhabitants of Manchester and Salford must spend *in* the public-houses and beer-shops, considerably more than £1,400,000 a year!—*Inquiry into the Cost and Consequences of Intoxicating Drinks in Manchester and Salford.* By J. J. Lees, 1852.

Society in 1854 watched during ten successive Sundays 'the houses in which intoxicating drinks are usually sold,' and kept an 'exact report of the number of visits paid to each.' For this purpose the city of Manchester 'was divided into 63 wards, each district superintended by a captain, with one general superintendent over the whole.'

They thus found, as will be seen below[1], that 215,318 Sunday visits were paid to 1437 houses for the purchase of intoxicating liquors, and that among the visitors were 71,699 women and 23,585 children.

If the money expended in the abuse of intoxicating drinks could be diverted to the rent of better houses, probably four-fifths of the families of Manchester and Salford

[1] From the 'Alliance' newspaper of August 10th, 1854. The following is a general summary. It will be seen that while the proceedings of the Committee extended over ten Sundays, yet, as no house was taken twice, a fair average of the attendance at each has been arrived at. The Committee are aware of no particular cause which could operate to render the results of one Sunday's census different from another; and it would have rendered observation much more difficult had not due caution and secrecy been observed. The Committee have every reason to believe in the perfect accuracy of the figures:—

General Summary of Visits during Legal Hours.

Date.	Houses.				Men.	Women.	Children.	Total.	
April 2	2				936	278	429	1643	
„ 9	8				2163	902	51	3116	
„ 16	36				9789	5277	851	15,917	
„ 23	57				7056	3981	692	11,729	
„ 30	95				7078	6378	935	14,391	
May 7	100				6699	4088	1109	11,896	
„ 14	234				18,239	9566	2559	30,364	
„ 21	329				27,684	16,322	6201	50,207	
„ 28	354				25,602	16.299	6528	48,429	
June 4	222				14,878	8518	4230	27,626	
Total	1437				120,124	71,609	23,585	215,318	
	Vaults.	Public-house.	Beer-house.	Total					avge.
	114			114	29,568	17,926	4147	51,641	453
		127		127	14,880	7947	2835	25,662	202
			746	746	51,474	27,512	11,544	90,530	121
Mixed	37	122	281	440	24,202	17,726	5059	47,485	106¼
Total	151	259	1027	1437	120,124	71,609	23,585	215,318	149½

might afford dwellings containing at least three ample bedrooms. Another less considerable portion would, with the occupation of ten-pound houses, obtain the franchise.

A large number of rate-payers and inhabitants of Manchester agreed to a memorial to the magistrates at their Brewster Sessions, on the 6th of August, 1859. In this memorial they represented that there were in that city 485 licensed victuallers' houses, and 1538 beer-houses. The police had reported that 'no improvement had taken place in the conduct of the licensed victuallers and beer retailers. Of the public-houses, 61 are reported as the resort of thieves and prostitutes, being upwards of 12 per cent.;' 'and of the beer-shops 68 are similarly reported, or nearly 5 per cent.' 'Of robberies from the person by prostitutes and others, 75 occurred in the premises of licensed victuallers, being nearly $16\frac{1}{2}$ per cent. on the number of the houses; and of robberies from the person in beer-houses there were 37 cases, being a percentage of $2\frac{1}{2}$ on the number of the houses.'

The memorialists presented statistics to show that there existed in the city of Manchester in 1858 one place for the sale of intoxicating liquors for every 29 houses; one for every $171\frac{1}{2}$ inhabitants (men, women, and children); 7 such places for every school (including both public and private schools); and 15 to every church or chapel in the city.

Another fact, most material in the consideration of the proper province and object of legislation on the sale of intoxicating liquors transpires in a Table furnished by the Chief Constable, Captain Palin, to Mr. David Chadwick (See Appendix C). While the number of licensed victuallers' houses with or without spirit vaults, was 498 in 1841, it was only 485 in 1859–60, though the vaults attached to these houses had increased one-fourth since 1847. Whereas the beer-houses, which numbered 769 in 1841, had increased to 1646 in 1859–60, or were more than twice as numerous.

The United Kingdom Alliance struggles by various

means against these evils. The mischief, which is one chief source of a revenue[1] of nearly twenty millions, probably causes an outlay of between sixty and seventy millions in the United Kingdom, by far the larger part of which is paid from the earnings of the poor, in a great degree by a waste of those resources, if not by a use of them fatal to health or life, domestic morality and peace; and directly causing crime and disorder.

There is, therefore, little occasion for wonder that in Manchester the Local Alliance Committee obtained 6826 signatures for the enactment of the Maine Law as a permissive measure. The magnitude of the evil is reflected in the extreme form of interference sought. The Grand Jury of the County Palatine, at the Assize held in Liverpool in August, 1859, made the following presentment to the late Baron Watson:—

'My Lord Judge,—The grand jury of this assize for the county palatine of Lancaster desire to make the following presentment to your lordship: In the charge with which your Lordship opened this assize, you directed the attention of the grand jury to those acts of violence which occupy a prominent place in the calendar. You informed them that it contained "thirty-five cases of cutting, stabbing, and wounding, by which eight persons

---

[1] Public revenue from Excise for the year ending March 31st, 1861.

	£	s.	d.
Hops	582,727	9	5
Malt	6,208,813	8	10
Spirits	9,225,538	19	10
Sugar used in brewing	180	1	0
	£16,017,259	19	1
Part also of Licenses	1,492,687	7	3
Income from Customs:—			
Rum	1,733,445	12	6
Brandy	747,150	12	9
Geneva	107,263	6	7
Other sorts of spirits	35,755	5	0
	£20,133,562	3	2

had come to their deaths." Your Lordship concluded your charge by directing the attention of the jury to those means of prevention which might be wisely adopted to check the growth of crime. The grand jury have carefully borne in mind both parts of your Lordship's charge. They find that the acts of violence to which your Lordship directed their attention have been of an aggravated description. A large proportion resulted from quarrels commenced within the walls of licensed public-houses, after drinking prolonged for hours, and indeed until it had produced a brutal frenzy. After savage blows struck in the house—sometimes producing severe injury—the combat has been renewed in the yard, or the adjoining road, or the street, and in some cases an unmanly use has been made of knives—stabs, with dangerous bleeding or immediate loss of life, or blows and kicks have been given with such barbarity as to cause death. In cases where the grand jury had not before them evidence of the commencement of the quarrel in a particular public-house, it has been clear that the parties had been infuriated with drink. The grand jury desire emphatically to express their opinion that, apart from the moral mischief which the excessive use of intoxicating drinks occasions in families and in society, all the poisons sold to malefactors, or wantonly or carelessly used, cause far fewer deaths than the unregulated sale of beer or spirits. The chaplains of our gaols have for many years called the attention of the magistrates of this county to drunkenness as the chief source of crime. But the magistrates have only a very limited power over beer-houses, inasmuch as they cannot limit the number of licenses; and their discretion as to the suspension or removal of the license of public-houses is subjected to embarrassing restrictions. It is especially to be regretted that the law does not enable the magistrates to secure the personal residence of the licensed victualler in his public-house. The grand jury, nevertheless, suggest that in all cases of intoxication causing any breach of the peace, the police should be directed to ascertain, and report to the justices in petty sessions, what were the houses in which the several parties had been permitted to obtain drink in excess. They would urge that the justices should pursue these inquiries, so as to impress on all who are intrusted with the sale of intoxicating liquors that they become parties to disorder —to much moral mischief—to breaches of the peace and acts of brutal violence, ending in homicide—by permitting drink to be taken in excess. They therefore frustrate the intentions of the legislature—that the license should be held on condition of co-operation with the justices of the peace to prevent the abuse of intoxicating drinks, and should be withdrawn if this condition were not fulfilled. The grand jury conceive that the justices in petty sessions may be strengthened in the discharge of such duties if, from this assize, their attention be called to all those cases of violence caused by intoxication, and commencing in public-houses, which have been sent for trial by your Lordship, and that they be requested to consider whether they should take such measures with respect to the licenses of such publicans as may issue in their suspension or removal. Some such immediate exercise of the authority of the justices, followed by a vigorous and persevering administration of the law, has become indispensable. The grand jury, however, feel that if these efforts were successful they would leave untouched the mischievous influences of beer-houses, kept by a ruder class of persons than the licensed victuallers. Either, on the one hand, the sale of beer and spirituous liquors may be safely made an open trade, both without reference to the character of the dealers or to any guarantee for their good conduct; or, if such a trade cannot be suffered without control, then the security which the legislature has required from the licensed victuallers should be rendered thoroughly effectual, and extended to beer-houses. Such security should be sought, not only in the provisions of the statute, but also by an administration of the law, prompt, earnest, and free from personal or party favour or interest. The present law neither effectually promotes wholesome restraint, nor is it consistent with an unfettered trade. It is administered by two classes of functionaries, on two conflicting ill-defined principles, so as to cause a confusion most injurious to those who are supported by manual labour, and to become a fruitful source of crime. The grand jury are of opinion that the laws as to the sale of intoxicating drinks in beer-houses and public-houses should be assimilated, and that the authority administering the law should be made uniform, and should be such as to secure a prompt, pure, and faithful enforcement of the intention of the legislature. The grand jury venture to say that no graver question of domestic legislation awaits the action of the executive government. The grand jury cannot conclude this presentment without expressing their earnest concurrence with your Lordship as to the supreme importance which you attached to all the moral means for the prevention of crime afforded by the religious bringing up of our youth, by private example, and by efficient schools. They likewise desire to rejoice with your Lordship in the marked success which has hitherto attended the institutions of late created, for the reformation especially of females and of juvenile offenders. They would further urge that the associations of "patronage," which aid the reformed adult prisoner, on his discharge, to obtain an honest livelihood by work, deserve confidence, and that an immediate extension of such societies is rendered desirable by the practical abolition of the punishment of transportation.

'J. P. KAY SHUTTLEWORTH, *Foreman.*'

I cannot hesitate, therefore, to attribute the present high rate of mortality in Manchester and Salford in a great degree to intemperance. But one fertile source of this intemperance, as well as a consequence of it in the vicious circle of causation, is, I repeat, the excessive employment of women in the manufactories of the cotton trade. This explains the continuance of the high rate of infant mortality, notwithstanding that sanitary improvements have been so general and efficient as to have reduced the frequency and violence of epidemic diseases in Manchester since 1847. The chief means of improving the health and prolonging the life of the poorer classes now consist in the elevation of moral and religious feeling, and of general intelligence. The withdrawal of a large part of the married women from work out of their own homes, except in cases of absolute necessity, is indispensable to improve the domestic training of girls. The radical cure for an excessive infant mortality lies in the same power of the wife over her household which will enable her to wean her husband from the tavern. Crime and disease will be proportionately diminished, and the annual death-rate will be reduced. This excessive employment of married women is neither an unavoidable necessity in factory work, nor needed for the sufficiency of the income of families in the cotton district; but, on the contrary, it is a wasteful source of expense, and a cause of intemperance, disease, and death.

The power to issue licenses should be vested in a Surveyor-General, not liable to political influence, aided by the police and an efficient staff of inspectors, co-operating with the county and borough Magistrates, but independent of them. The license should no longer confer a value on property held by a brewer or landed proprietor, but should be granted to the licensed victualler personally, as a man of approved good character, and should be revocable by the Surveyor-General. On complaint of Justices of the Peace, or of the Grand or Petty Jury, or Chairman of Quarter Sessions, or on the recommendation of any Jury as to any serious disorder, crime, or abuse of privilege, the Surveyor-General should have no option as to the revocation of the license, unless, after inquiry, he convinced the authority complaining of some serious defect in the evidence. Holders of licenses should be subject to a preliminary warning from the Surveyor-General, which should be communicated to the Local Justices, and by them to the Police; and to a second warning, which should be advertised in the local papers at the expense of the holder. If after this second warning complaint were made, slighter offences should cause the withdrawal of the license. No beer-houses should be held without such a license. All holders of licenses should be regarded as persons selected for their good character and capacity to co-operate with the Police for the prevention of drunkenness.

The power of the licensed victuallers to prevent the adoption of such a system arises from two causes. It is probable that the return of the House of Commons in a general election costs from £600,000 to one million of money. A large part of this sum is spent in besotting the lower class of voters with drink. The power of the licensed victuallers in a contested election is, therefore, not small. The brewers in town and country make the public-houses the spouts through which they empty their vats. A large brewing firm is prosperous in proportion to the number of licensed public-houses which it possesses or rents. The spirit dealers, in like manner, by advances of money — possession of houses — and otherwise, provide for the attractions of the gin-shops. The capital invested, and the vast imperial revenue derived from the abuse of intoxicating liquors, render any effort to save the working classes from this source of ruin to their comfort, health, or life, a question which arrays against it formidable interests. No Chancellor of the Exchequer would, however, deliberately seek to raise a revenue at so frightful a sacrifice of national well-being. The horrors of excessive mortality and crime, clearly attributable mainly to the expenditure of upwards of sixty millions annually on beer, spirits, and tobacco, are now brimful and run over. The progress of sanitary improvement unmasks them. Drunkenness must be regarded by the law as a misdemeanour endangering the public peace, health, and life, and filling the criminal calendar with offenders. It must be restrained by a reformed license system, faithfully administered by a firm, equal, and vigilant central authority. The misdemeanour must also be punished summarily. The stocks were a good method of expressing a public loathing of the self-degrading character of this offence. The working men ought to know, that the right application of the money now ruinously expended would raise a larger number of them within the £10 franchise, than would, according to the calculations of its advocates, be admitted by the reduction of the franchise to a £6 rating qualification. No man who has not this power of self-restraint ought to possess the franchise.

In every class of workmen there are frugal men who save,— who establish the building clubs —become possessors of their own cottages — or, with a provident forethought, even build several dwellings. The first step towards these results is often a deposit in the savings' bank ; though, especially in rural districts, a secret hoard, hid in crevices of walls— in mattresses—under a flag in the floor, or in some other ' nook'— is a favourite device.[1] The building club is attractive, by the high rate of interest which is given, and the generally sound security and good management of these clubs. They let out the fund at a high rate of interest, to aid workmen and others building cottages, on which they take security by holding the building lease, with a promissory note. The regularity of factory-work affords a check to extreme intemperance during the week, but this is often more than compensated by gross feeding and drinking on Saturday night and Sunday. The handicraft trades, out-door labourers' occupations, and work in mines, are much more embarrassed by the absence of the men ' on a spree.' Intemperance is not, however, the habit of a class. The wives and families of all classes of workmen are much employed in mills. It is not, therefore, possible to trace in the classification of

---

[1] One of the colliers of a Lancashire estate built several cottages. His wife kept his own and his sons' hoards. When it was necessary to pay the builders, she produced the money from hoards hidden in this way in many different parts of the cottage.

depositors in the savings' bank any marked distinction in favour of any class, either as to the average amount belonging to each depositor, or as to the number of depositors. The most numerous class in the Manchester and Salford Bank for Savings on the 20th November, 1861, was that of domestic servants (24,697, with an average deposit of £24); then clerks, shopmen, warehousemen, porters, and their wives (22,189, with an average of £24); the whole body of operatives employed in silk and cotton spinning and weaving, and in calico-printing, bleaching, dyeing, in packing and making-up, with their wives, had opened 22,493 accounts, of which 5083 remained open in Nov. 20th, 1861, containing £143,515 16s. 3d., with an average deposit of rather more than £28. In like manner, 14,624 mechanics and handicraftsmen had opened accounts, of which 4024 remained open on the 20th Nov., 1861, containing £113,703 0s. 10d., or an average deposit of £28.

The provident members of each class are, therefore, probably more numerous in proportion as their occupation places them either in the families, or under the immediate influence, by personal intercourse in the warehouse, or in their work, of members of the middle classes. Apart from this influence, no other source of a great difference in the proportionate numbers of frugal members appears to exist in any class.

But it is gratifying to observe that the amount of deposits relatively to the whole population has steadily increased. Adopting the estimate of the Manchester Statistical Society, and of Mr. David Chadwick, as to the population of Manchester, Salford, and the adjoining districts, in the decennial periods from 1831 to 1861, and reducing this population to the decennial periods from the opening of the bank in 1827, the following is an approximate result :—

Year.	Population.	Accounts open.	On Inhabitants.	Balance.	Average amount of balance.			Rate per head of total balance to whole population.		
				£	£	s.	d.	£	s.	d.
1827	170,000	4998	34	144,911	28	19	11	0	17	0
1837	270,000	10,245	26	298,342	29	2	5	1	1	0
1847	370,000	21,735	17	580,915	26	14	7	1	11	1
1857	446,000	39,333	11¼	986,319	25	1	6	2	4	0
1860	464,000	47,337	9¾	1,228,500	25	19	0	2	12	11

The number of frugal persons who confide their savings to this bank, and the amount of their whole deposits, have, therefore, steadily increased relatively to the whole population, though the average amount of the balance on each account has diminished. Those who deposited in from 1827 to 1837 were evidently of a class less mixed with the mass of the operative population, and probably more under the personal influence of the middle class than after 1837. Setting the increase of benefit and building clubs against the previous custom of hiding hoards, it seems probable that the sum saved in 1860 per head is three times as great as in 1827.

In the year following the second edition of the account of the 'Moral and Physical Condition of the Working Classes of Manchester,'— a District Provident Society was formed, on the type of one founded in Liverpool at the suggestion of Mrs. Fry, and the operations of which I had, with my friend, Mr. William Langton, carefully examined. After preliminary meetings summoned by the Borough-reeve in the Town Hall, in February, 1833, a general meeting was held in the Exchange dining-room, under the presidency of the Chief Constable, at which resolutions were adopted embodying the principles and defining the practical operations of the Society. The design was to collect the transient savings of the working classes for the purchase of clothing, furniture, and fuel; or for rent; or as a preliminary to more permanent deposits in the savings' banks. This was accomplished by a weekly visitation and collection from house to house. The savings might at any time be withdrawn, in whole or in part. The checks were well devised, and worked without fraud or friction. It was, however, found necessary to employ a paid agency to a great extent, owing to the increasing tendency of the more wealthy inhabitants to live in the remoter suburbs and in the country,—a tendency now greatly increased by the greater facilities for locomotion, especially by railways. There was also a Mendicity department, conducted by a machinery closely resembling that of London.

I extremely regret to observe that the operations of this most useful Society have gradually become more languid; for, unless the City Missionaries were also agents of the Society, their labours do not, in promoting frugality, supersede it. I will not here attempt to determine whether the work of the City Missionaries ought not to include that which has been hitherto the peculiar work of the agents of the Provident Society. I incline to think that the City Missionaries would greatly increase their own opportunities for intercourse with the poor, and augment their usefulness, by taking up this now comparatively neglected sphere of beneficent labour. In the Reports for 1853-4-5, it is stated that 'the Society originally contemplated the encouragement of habits of provident economy among the poor by means of periodical house-to-house collections of small deposits through the agency of volunteer district visitors.' This machinery has 'steadily decreased in efficiency. It is not without regret that the Committee have felt themselves unable to check this decline. They are willing to believe that a plan which the Society was formerly amongst the most prominent to encourage, has more recently been extensively adopted by individuals in connection with the various congregational associations, and similar institutions in the town; and that, though they have fewer names on their roll of visitors, there may be no real diminution in the kindly intercourse between the rich and poor of this great town, which it was the Society's aim to foster. Nevertheless they conceive that it would not be difficult for any one who is already engaged in regular visitation to superadd to his or her engagement the charge of one or more sections in the Provident Society's district map.'

Certain modifications in the action of the Society, and its annual results, are recorded in the Note below.[1]

The preceding facts and deductions concentrate in one main conclusion.

The removal of purely physical evils, such as inordinate toil, a bad sanitary condition of the town or neighbourhood, even the better condition of the dwelling, higher wages, cheaper food and clothing, however important as

---

[1] In order in some degree to provide a means of supplying, as near as possible to the homes of the poor, the desired opportunity of saving, the Society in 1848 initiated a system of district dépôts for the receipt of small sums. With one exception these dépôts have been highly successful, and, subject to a temporary check in cases of unavoidable removal, have succeeded in attaching increasing bodies of depositors, whose individual payments are, generally speaking, regular though often of very small amount.

The Society now maintains dépôts in St. Michael's district, in Ancoats, in Grosvenor Street, Lower Mosley Street, and Pendleton. Each is kept open under the superintendence of two at least on each occasion of the members or officers of the Society, from seven to half-past eight, every Monday night.

The following Table shows the Amount deposited with and withdrawn from the Society in each year, from its formation to the end of 1860.

Year.	Deposits.			Repayments.			Year.	Deposits.			Repayments.		
	£	s.	d.	£	s.	d.		£	s.	d.	£	s.	d.
1833	351	10	8	110	13	8	Forward	69,134	3	10½	68,640	10	4½
1834	4169	7	11½	3297	4	3½	1848	2088	11	10	2045	0	3½
1835	7856	17	8	7059	6	10	1849	2256	7	11	2295	9	2
1836	8489	1	9½	8964	17	4½	**1850**(a)	1759	11	8	1876	19	5½
1837	4735	19	5½	5084	14	7½	1851	1353	15	10	1420	14	5½
1838	5582	19	2½	5482	9	6½	1852	1333	16	6	1352	2	0
1839	4468	14	10½	4843	19	9	1853	1229	13	8½	1282	2	11½
1840	4696	11	9	4561	17	1½	1854	954	6	5	970	14	5
1841	4249	12	11	4470	3	7	1855	1001	14	9	1003	1	10½
1842	3200	13	5	3142	15	0	1856	1455	13	7	1365	16	10
1843	4935	7	3	4702	14	7½	1857	1843	2	6	1781	18	8
1844	5053	13	4	4815	8	10½	1858	2093	2	7	1906	5	1½
1845	5157	5	8	5171	15	7	1859	3286	17	7	3077	3	3
1846	3847	1	1	4192	19	6	1860	3464	0	8½	3482	18	6½
1847	2339	6	10	2739	10	0							
	69,134	3	10½	68,640	10	4½	Total	93,254	19	5½	92,500	17	5

(a) No Premium given from this date.

elements of the comfort of the working classes, do not insure their well-being. If the population of the lowest faubourgs of Paris had in 1830 or in 1848 permanently taken possession of the Quartier St. Germain, or converted the Palace of the Tuileries and the Louvre into a Phalanstère, that revolution would not only not have insured their welfare, but would certainly have precipitated them into the direst misery amidst the ruins of society. But even temporarily, before the catastrophe was complete, and while they enjoyed a possible revenue from the sale of the crown jewels, and of the articles of luxury and *vertu* which they had not wantonly destroyed, they would merely have converted the palaces into styes like their own lodgings ' *au cinquième.*'

The removal of physical evils is indispensable to the elevation of the working classes. But in itself, though followed in the mixed constitution of man by a certain amount of moral advantage, this change consists more in the removal of obstacles to moral progress, and in the provision of a secure foundation for the higher and nobler structure.

It is, on the contrary, in the nature of that which improves the mind and raises the moral character of a class, to secure a triumph over physical evils. Neither form of beneficent labour should be neglected. Each co-operates with the other. But that which derives its power from mental, moral, and religious agencies is incalculably stronger. It is, therefore, to education and to religion that society must mainly owe its progress.

Manchester and Salford have, therefore, in thirty years made vast progress, not only in population and wealth, but in social organisation. The municipal authority has been administered with wisdom and vigour. The sanitary condition of both towns is greatly improved. The wages and prices of clothing and food of the working population place them in a position commanding a much larger share of the comforts of life. The hours of labour are reduced to a reasonable limit. The means of innocent recreation are greatly increased. The provision for public worship, the City Mission, the Provident Society, the Savings' Banks, and the growth of the number and efficiency of Day Schools, conspire as moral forces to penetrate the sensual habits of a population which has continued to accumulate from the rudest districts by immigration. Yet the waste of earnings on coarse feeding, and the abuse of intoxicating liquor, is maintained, though it degrades its victims to worse and more crowded dwellings, and to the loss of home comfort and wholesome diet, and subjects married women to work in mills. The ill-ventilated, uncleanly, crowded cottage, surrounded by influences which depress the health, in a close court or narrow back street, is the price paid for a misuse of earnings sufficient to pay the rent of a house, with three ample bed-rooms, in a salubrious neighbourhood,—to enable the wife to remain in charge of her household duties,— especially to nurture her infant children—and to provide wholesome food, innocent recreation for the family, and regular schooling for the children.

The well-paved and sewered streets, the improving or closing of cellars, the increase of proper conveniences to cottages, an ample supply of pure water, and the suppression of the grossest nuisances, unmask the evils which still so depress the health of the population that the rate of mortality is 34 in 1000 in 1860, and the rate of infant mortality 11·34 per cent. under five years of age, having been 11·189 in 1841. Those evils now are mainly the habits of an unlettered sensual population, which has not yet learned self-restraint, and fails to second the efforts of a spirited and intelligent municipal power, by that right use of the more abundant means of well-being, which can only be fully enjoyed by a thoroughly civilised and Christian people.

It was because I had always foreseen this result, that I attached more importance to the moral expedients for the extirpation of pauperism and crime when I wrote in 1831, than to the influence of restraints in the administration of the law. Such restraints are not without their moral consequences; and I co-operated with zeal in the extirpation of able-bodied pauperism in the Eastern Counties and in the Metropolis, by the workhouse system. But in the manufacturing districts of the North, the forms of able-bodied pauperism were not, as in the agricultural districts, and in the cities fed from them, remains of the helotry of the middle ages, aggravated by recent maladministration. In the North, they were attributable, except in crises of trade, to exactly the same causes as those which still keep up a high rate of mortality in the towns. A semi-barbarous population, rapidly accumulated from the rudest regions, has been disciplined by the organisation of labour and the Police of the municipalities, but has not learned self-restraint, providence, or the real sources of domestic and social well-being. That is the lesson which this population has to learn by every form of instruction and training before the rate of mortality can fall nearer to the average of all England.

The efficacy of the moral forces at work is wasted by the constant accumulation of obstacles. The population of Manchester and Salford and the adjacent townships [1] has increased from 1801 to 1811 at the rate of 20·5 per cent.; from 1821 to 1831, at 34·5; from 1831 to 1841, at 41; from 1841 to 1851, at the rate of 28·77 per cent.; while in all England the rate of increase in these fifty years has never exceeded 18 per cent. in any decennial period, and has ranged from 13 per cent. to 18. It is clear, therefore, that the growth of the population in Manchester and Salford has been to a great extent due to immigration. This population has been derived from Ireland, from the hills and moors of the Pennine chain, of the border, of Derbyshire, and of Wales. The immigrants have been singularly rude. The Irish have commonly filtrated through Liverpool; the hill migrants through some other of the manufacturing towns and villages of Lancashire.

---

[1] 'Rate of Wages.' By Mr. David Chadwick, p. 33.

This preliminary training has only broken them to work at out-door labour or in factories. They have not been in any other sense civilised by it. They had lived in a semi-savage state in Irish cabins, or moorland huts, or the rudest cottages built of boulders, one storey high. They had exchanged the solitude of a cottier's, or shepherd's, or herdsman's, or lead miner's, or quarryman's life for the throngs of the manufacturing districts. The meagre diet of potatoes, or oatmeal and bacon, or 'brassy,'[1] was succeeded by that purchased by the work of the wife and children in the mill, and of the father in the building trades or out-door labour. A semi-barbarous race seldom resists the satanic attraction of the 'firewater,' and is indifferent to the domestic comfort of a well-furnished and well-ordered home. High wages, bad example, and constant temptation, together with the waste of force caused by the exchange of the air of the mountain or plain for that of the close city, and the expenditure of animal energy in toil, render the use of beer, if it could be taken in moderation, and in combination with wholesome food, perhaps the best support for the strength of a workman. But the abuse follows close on the heels of the use, especially in such a race. The brain is inflamed by excess; a vicious habit is formed. The vendors of intoxicating liquors to a constant succession of uncivilised immigrants are now the hostile force with which all the higher moral agencies of society have to contend. They must be defeated, or no further progress can be made.

The immigration of this uncivilised population everywhere throughout Lancashire keeps down the level of the condition of the working classes, but it has been indispensable to the progress of trade. Mr. Robert Hyde Greg, in the evidence embodied by Sir George Cornewall Lewis, in his 'Report on the State of the Irish Poor in Great Britain' in 1834, said, 'Supposing that all external competition' for labour 'could have been shut out, wages

[1] The mutton of sheep found dead on the moors.

might have temporarily advanced so much as to have transferred our manufactures to other places,— perhaps to the coal districts of Wales, or to Ireland itself, where cheap labour is found united to the noblest falls of water. What would then have been the rate of labour, and the amount of the poor's rates? If the competition of Irish labour has done anything towards averting such a catastrophe, its tendency has been to raise, not to depress, the rate' of the wages 'of labour.'[1] Mr. Houldsworth doubts whether, without this immigration, the trade 'could' have met 'foreign competition',[2] especially that of the Americans. It is clear that the entire '*plant*' of the trade in mills, docks, reservoirs, mines, roads, canals, railways, and other great works, as well as warehouses and cottages, must have cost a vastly greater outlay of capital. Lancashire has built up its present power with the help of a rude uncivilised immigrant class. In the evidence which I gave to Sir George Cornewall Lewis in 1834, I said,[3] 'The introduction of masses of inhabitants into the large towns of England, greatly below the civilisation common to its working classes, is an evil which much economical benefit would be required to compensate. This colonisation[4] is not without its influence on the manners of the inhabitants.' 'A knowledge of the minimum of comfort, and of the means of subsistence upon which life can be supported, is thus obtained.' I attributed ' a great deal of the discomfort in the habitations of the working classes of Manchester, and the adoption of an inferior diet, to the example of the Irish,' and of other rude immigrant classes. 'In some of the neighbouring towns, in all other respects similarly situated to Manchester, but not colonised by Irish, the dwellings of the poor contain more furniture, and are cleaner, and their diet is superior to that of a great portion of the population of Manchester.' In the interval since 1834, I have had abundant opportunity to

---

[1] Sir George Cornewall Lewis's Report, p. 36.
[2] P. 35.
[3] Sir George C. Lewis's Report, p. 40.
[4] Ibid. p. 39.

examine the bases of this opinion, as applicable, not simply to the Irish, but to all other semi-civilised immigrants; and with this qualification, I have no doubt whatever that the moral influence of *the immigration of semi-barbarous masses is prejudicial, by example, and personal intercourse, to the habits of the population with which they mingle.*

These classes are also strange impediments to the salutary influence of the higher moral agencies. The ignorant, unkempt, and stultish children of a half-brutish class of immigrants from the moors or border, render progress in a school difficult, or if they are numerous, almost impossible. A school encumbered with this burden exhibits classes of half-savage scholars, big rude dullards in the lower classes, some disorder, much inattention, none of the higher moral condition which is detected at a glance by an experienced eye. In the street they are wild and boisterous, if not turbulent. In like manner, the City Missionary finds a street of such families exchanging toil for the tavern, and mingled labour and excess for supine sloth. They keep their children with great irregularity at school, if they send them there at all. Except the Roman Catholics, they are seldom seen in a place of religious instruction and worship. The physician finds their houses, courts, alleys, and barracks, dens of fever.

These are evils to surmount which generations of effort are required. The Day and Sunday Schools must do their work with children. The Evening School and Mechanics' Institution must combine their functions for youth between school age and manhood with the precedent and co-operating influences of civilisation. A second generation of educated parents will not be indifferent to the schooling of their children. A third may be willing to make more abundant provision for it; and with a higher capacity for the discharge of such a duty, may claim some control of elementary schools, proportionate to its more abundant contribution to their support. With the growth of intelligence, there will, doubtless, be an increase of the power of self-restraint, and a partial triumph of mind over sense.

This cannot occur in a Christian country, without the awakening of the conscience from its sleep, to the acknowledgment of the higher responsibilities of our being. Then religion will be at hand, with the revelation which brought life and immortality to light.

First Period.—Mortality in Manchester, Liverpool, and Surrey.

ANNUAL MORTALITY per Cent.

1.—Extra-Metropolitan part of SURREY.
2.—SOUTH EASTERN DIVISION.

Age.	Manchester Town Sub-districts.*		Manchester County Sub-Districts.†		Liverpool.‡		Richmond and Kingston.		Chertsey and Epsom.		Croydon.		Godstone, Reigate, and Dorking.		Guildford, Farnham, and Hambledon.		Surrey.		Age.
	Males.	Females.	Males.	Females.	Males.	Females.	Males.	Females.	Males.	Females.	Males.	Females.	Males.	Females.	Males.	Females.	Males.	Females.	
0	34·637	27·413	22·094	15·397	30·419	25·609	16·588	13·048	15·082	10·126	17·788	13·448	13·702	9·296	13·130	9·863	14·729	10·791	0
1	17·227	16·872	7·451	6·327	17·035	16·810	4·713	4·544	4·598	3·658	6·558	6·292	3·177	2·517	3·966	2·762	4·386	3·657	1
2	7·829	7·954	3·004	3·635	8·004	8·237	2·590	2·334	1·917	2·17	4·026	4·383	1·597	1·665	1·953	1·852	2·284	2·328	2
3	5·644	6·046	2·042	2·353	6·211	5·432	2·059	1·530	1·504	1·680	2·392	3·591	1·507	1·531	1·502	1·735	1·716	1·889	3
4	4·205	4·415	1·722	2·311	4·422	4·183	1·574	1·882	1·272	1·237	3·270	2·811	·912	1·178	·974	1·038	1·437	1·515	4
0	14·767	13·208	7·431	6·254	14·377	12·771	5·508	4·556	4·592	3·856	6·436	6·007	4·123	3·323	4·203	3·515	4·772	4·066	0
5	1·527	1·569	1·020	·766	1·735	1·590	·877	·830	·735	·664	1·871	1·440	·669	·655	·601	·737	·875	·830	5
10	·575	·694	·523	·605	·631	·597	·309	·499	·348	·608	1·000	·658	·318	·363	·318	·508	·443	·520	10
15	·960	·948	·725	·690	·987	·789	·625	·628	·765	·717	·676	·799	·621	·756	·775	·904	·690	·754	15
20	1·358	1·283	·877	1·026	1·268	1·220	·989	·702	1·021	·746	·774	·847	·633	·949	·781	1·106	·816	·842	20
25	2·101	1·842	1·245	1·384	2·162	1·808	1·407	1·080	1·095	1·012	1·245	·873	1·006	1·215	1·039	1·216	1·135	1·051	25
35	1·964	1·964	1·933	1·933	3·367	2·637	1·641	1·372	1·609	1·303	1·770	1·554	1·174	1·330	1·330	1·374	1·459	1·357	35
45	3·220	2·943	3·015	3·373	5·305	4·668	3·636	2·813	2·969	2·468	3·099	2·468	1·215	3·087	2·602	2·617	2·829	2·683	45
55	5·702	4·660	7·685	6·616	10·634	9·370	6·924	5·345	6·110	4·744	7·160	5·164	2·283	5·655	6·176	6·067	6·389	5·460	55
65	10·638	9·014	17·038	13·149	20·740	18·232	13·371	12·601	14·28?	13·456	15·883	15·046	6·359	13·103	14·399	12·625	14·398	13·119	65
75	20·382	16·615	24·949	36·719	32·230	30·851	35·734	27·716	28·307	21·919	32·233	29·707	15·312	25·338	30·335	34·632	32·238	27·862	75
85	30·641	26·598											42·843		52·278	38·075	56·169	39·029	85
95 and upwards.	§																		95 and upwards.
All ages.	3·655	3·312	2·193	1·971	3·583	3·151	2·042	1·749	1·935	1·680	2·236	1·985	1·536	1·616	1·781	1·747	1·856	1·756	All ages.

* Manchester Town Sub-districts are :— Ancoats, Deansgate, St. George, London Road, Market Street.
† Manchester Country Sub-districts are :— Blackley, Cheetham, Failsworth, Newton, Prestwich.
‡ Liverpool comprises the whole of the Liverpool district.
§ The facts after the age of 95 are too few and uncertain to deserve attention in any of the districts. The results are not given here for Manchester.
Note.—The mortality against the age of 5 is the mortality amongst persons of the age of 5 and under 10, and so of other ages.
The Table is read thus :—The mortality in Manchester amongst boys of the age of 0 and under 5, is 14·767 per cent. annually ; of men of the age of 45 and under 55, it is 3·220 per cent. ; at the same ages in the extra-metropolitan part of Surrey, the mortality is only 4·772 per cent. and 1·459 per cent.

(Extracted from pp. 332-3 of Seventh Annual Report of Registrar-General, 1845.)

APPENDIX B.

'It is well known that the chief cause of the excessive mortality in large towns is the deaths of children under 5 years of age; this first induced me to think that it might be interesting to show the death line under 5 years, and I have accordingly done so. The upper line of the following diagram indicates the death-rate at all ages, beginning with Glendale, in Northumberland, with 15 deaths per 1000, and ending with Liverpool, with 35 deaths per 1000,—so that we have here a difference of 20 per 1000 between the two extremes. The lower line indicates the deaths exclusive of those under the age of 5 years, and shows a rate of 11 per 1000 for Glendale, and 18 for Liverpool,—thus proving that in Glendale the deaths under 5 are only 4 per 1000, while in Liverpool they are 17, which is represented by the space between the two lines. These being the facts, we have thus reduced the difference in the mortality from 20 to 7 per 1000,—proving very clearly that it is the deaths under the age of 5 years which are the chief cause of the great variation in the death-rate,—of these above one-half die under one year of age, and nearly a quarter from one to two. These calculations are based on the deaths for five years, viz. 1851 to 1855, and the population of the census of 1851.'

DIAGRAM.

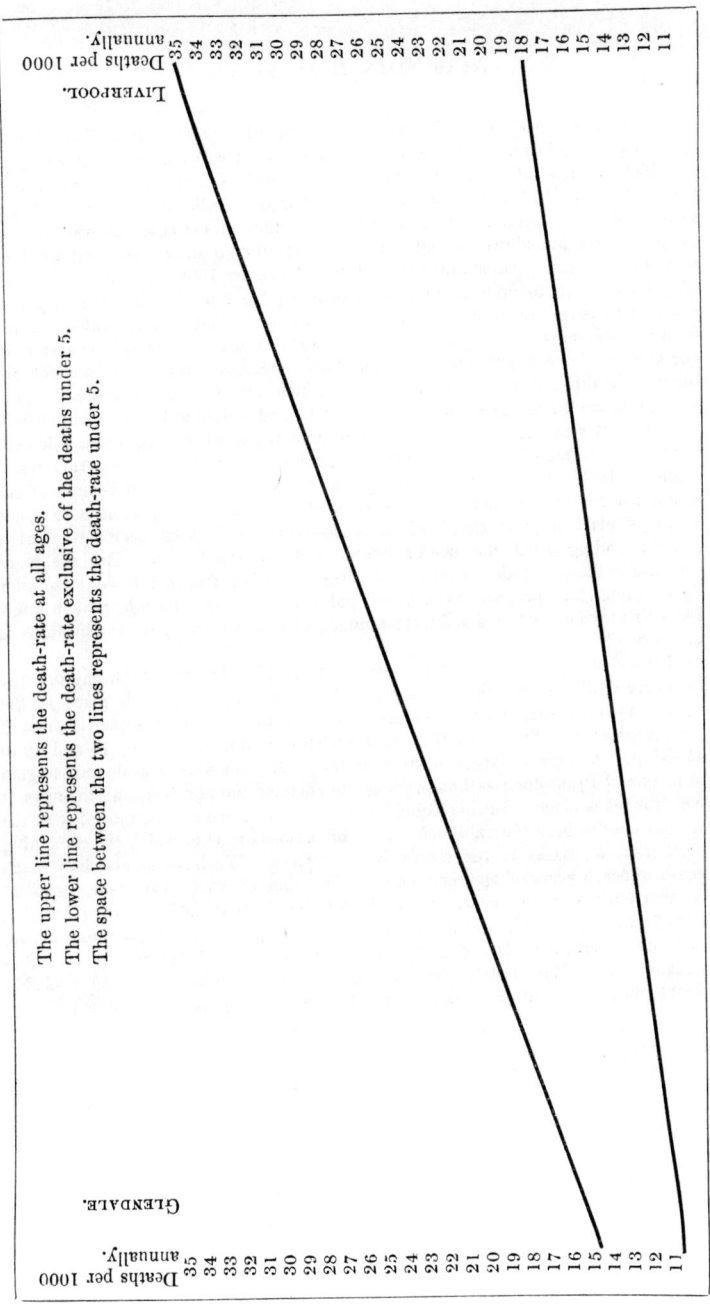

The upper line represents the death-rate at all ages.
The lower line represents the death-rate exclusive of the deaths under 5.
The space between the two lines represents the death-rate under 5.

APPENDIX B (*continued*).

'We will now endeavour to ascertain at what other periods of life the death-rate is excessive in large towns; and, in doing so, we will compare our own city, in which the rate at all ages is 34 per 1000, with Brampton, in Cumberland, where the rate is 17 per 1000: in Manchester the deaths under 5 are 17 per 1000, and in Brampton only 5 per 1000,—so that at all ages the variation is 17 per 1000; but above the age of 5, the variation is only 5,—being a reduction of the balance against Manchester from 17 to 5 per 1000. Before proceeding, it may be as well to premise that in contrasting the mortality in different places many disturbing causes may arise. The most important is that which springs from the difference in the proportion of persons at the same ages; because if in one place we have a greater proportion of the population at those ages which are the most healthy, as a matter of course the mortality in those places will be the lowest; hence those towns that are sustained and enlarged by immigration will have a greater per centage of the population at the healthy ages, which will tend to reduce the rate of mortality from what it would have been but for this immigration. In Liverpool it is calculated that this cause makes a difference of six deaths per 1000 per annum. To show the effect of this immigration, it may not be out of place to state that without it Liverpool would soon decrease,—in the 5 years ending 1858 the deaths exceeded the births by 55. But the mere decrease in the population would be the least important feature; it would so alter the character and proportions of the population as regards its age, that in a few years there would not be a sufficient number of adults to carry on the business of the town.

'Let us now proceed with our comparison of Manchester with Brampton: the following Table shows the proportion of the population in each place at the various ages in 1851, and that the per centage of the population under the age of 15 was greater in Brampton than in Manchester; from the age of 15 and up to 45 the per centage is larger in Manchester; and after 45, the scale turns again in favour of Brampton;—thus proving the effect of immigration, and the ages at which it takes place. In this Table I have also given the rate of mortality at the various ages in both towns, which shows the periods of life at which the remaining portion of the excess in the mortality takes place. We have named how much arises under 5 years of age, and now we find that above 5 years and up to 35 the mortality is 50 per cent. greater in Manchester than in Brampton; but that from 35 to 65 years of age the mortality is 100 per cent. greater;—thus proving that the statement of Dr. Farr was no exaggeration,—"that in London, Birmingham, and Manchester, the mortality among working men was probably double what it was in the healthy districts by which they were surrounded."'

APPENDIX B (continued).

Table showing the Per Centage of the Population, and the Deaths at the following Ages, in Manchester and in Brampton. The Population used is that of 1851, and the Deaths the Average of the Years 1850, 1851, and 1852.

	Under 5 Years.	5 to 10 Years.	10 to 15 Years.	15 to 25 Years.	25 to 35 Years.	35 to 45 Years.	45 to 55 Years.	55 to 65 Years.	Above 65 Years.	
MANCHESTER, Population 228,433.	28,652	23,889	23,239	48,483	39,447	29,250	19,337	10,066	6,070	Population at each age.
	12·54	10·45	10·17	21·22	17·26	12·8	8·46	4·46	2·64	Per centage at each age on total population.
BRAMPTON, Population 11,323 .	1,496	1,339	1,287	2,100	1,559	1,208	989	665	680	Population at each age.
	13·21	11·82	11·36	18·54	13·76	10·66	8·73	5·87	6·05	Per centage at each age on total population.
MANCHESTER, Deaths 7,125	3,532	289	133	347	502	513	563	501	745	Deaths at each age.
	12·33	1·2	·57	·71	1·27	1·75	2·91	4·97	12·27	Per centage at each age on population at same age.
BRAMPTON Deaths 197	62	11	5	14	11	14	10	15	55	Deaths at each age.
	4·14	·82	·38	·66	·7	1·15	1·01	2·25	8·08	Per centage at each age on population at same age.

The Appendix B is taken from 'Variation of the Death Rate in England.' By William Royston. Pp. 7, 8, 9.

APPENDIX C.

Return of the Number of Persons Apprehended within the City of Manchester, and how disposed of, &c., for 19 years and 9 months.

Years.	Taken into Custody.	Summarily Convicted.	Convicted on Indictment.	Discharged by Magistrates, and Acquitted on Trial.	Number of Public Houses. With Vaults.	Without Vaults.	Total.	Number of Beerhouses.	Number of Licensed Marine Store Dealers.	Number of Brothels.	Strength of Police Force.
1841 ..	13,345	2,138	824	10,383	NoRet.	NoRet.	498	769	NoRet.	309	317
1842 ..	8,341	1,503	414	6,424	"	"	NoRet.	NoRet.	"	NoRet.	383
1843 ..	12,147	2,981	590	76	"	"	502	781	"	330	398
1844 ..	10,702	3,961	540	6,201	"	"	490	941	"	332	413
1845 ..	9,635	5,117	535	3,983	"	"	482	1,006	"	300	435
1846 ..	7,629	3,795	527	3,307	"	"	487	1,089	"	303	469
1847 ..	6,587	3,091	654	2,842	259	223	482	1,100	"	308	469
1848 ..	6,477	2,885	646	2,746	264	211	475	1,143	"	314	469
1849 ..	4,687	2,311	527	1,849	266	214	480	1,230	"	366	469
1850 ..	4,578	2,058	594	1,926	265	216	481	1,298	1,054	297	467
1851 ..	4,890	2,176	722	1,992	271	210	481	1,312	996	312	467
1852 ..	5,166	2,494	730	1,942	273	208	481	1,465	1,174	289	476
1853 ..	5,362	2,627	623	2,112	274	210	484	1,572	1,148	254	482
1854 ..	5,955	2,584	805	2,566	272	213	485	1,576	1,624	259	529
1855 ..	6,054	3,077	748	2,229	272	215	487	1,581	1,561	263	532
1856 to Sep. 30	4,470	2,372	505	1,593	273	216	489	1,552	1,414	302	546
1856-7 .	7,797	4,144	602	3,051	273	212	485	1,573	1,827	325	576
1857-8 .	7,643	4,325	605	2,713	283	202	485	1,538	1,301	382	605
1858-9 .	6,788	3,946	520	2,322	307	177	484	1,628	1,314	401	604
1859-60	7,387	4,359	541	2,487	318	167	485	1,646	1,231	404	617

This Table was prepared by Captain Palin, Chief Constable, for Mr. David Chadwick.

SALFORD POLICE FORCE.

	1840.	1861.
Number of Police	31	105
Cost of Force	£1,861 10 3	£4,931 7 6 after deducting Government Grant, £1,493 11 8
Number of Apprehensions	2275	1525
,, Public-houses	97	97
,, Vaults	10	75
,, Beer-houses	250	387
,, Pawnbrokers	7	34

This Table was prepared by Mr. JAMES TAYLOR, Chief Constable.

Return showing the average number of Prisoners in the Manchester City Gaol, with cost per head per day, after deducting earnings.

Date of opening.	Year.	Average Number of Prisoners.	Cost per head per day.	Nett Earnings per Annum.	Cost per head per day, deducting Earnings, &c.
March 11th 1850.	1851	303	$19\frac{3}{4}d.$	£ s. d. 162 8 8	$19\frac{1}{4}d.$
	1852	469	$12\frac{1}{4}d.$	683 7 0	$11\frac{1}{4}d.$
	1853	420	$12d.$	845 15 8	$10\frac{3}{4}d.$
	1854	438	$12\frac{1}{2}d.$	1,086 0 3	$10\frac{3}{4}d.$
	1855	514	$12\frac{3}{4}d.$	1,282 5 2	$11d.$
	1856	569	$12\frac{1}{2}d.$	1,170 10 4	$11d.$
	1857	557	$11\frac{3}{4}d.$	1,310 15 1	$10\frac{1}{4}d.$
	1858	512	$13d.$	1,510 12 4	$11d.$
	1859	540	$11\frac{3}{4}d.$	1,694 4 7	$9\frac{3}{4}d.$
	1860	514	$11\frac{3}{4}d.$	2,425 4 3	$8\frac{3}{4}d.$
	1861	508	$12\frac{3}{4}d.$	2,776 5 5	$9\frac{1}{4}d.$

This Table was prepared by C. B. J. LANE, Governor, Manchester City Gaol.

APPENDIX

POOR-RATES:—*Value of Property Assessed, Number and Amount of the*

Year.	Rate per £.	No. of Assessments.	Amount of Assessments.	Amount of Poor's-Rate.	Amount of Rate collected.	Per Cent.	No of Collectors.	Paid to Constables.	Paid to County Rates.
	s. d.		£ s. d.	£ s. d.	£ s. d.			£ s. d.	£ s. d
1820	4 6	19,811	307,510 10 0	69,189 17 3	42,313 16 6¾	61·1	6	3,074 6 4	10,124 7 8
1821	4 6	20,824	313,147 10 0	70,458 3 9	44,077 7 0	62·5	.	2,127 4 9	12,075 8 9
1822	3 0	22,213	296,112 15 0	44,416 18 3	36,144 6 6	81·3	.	1,967 16 11	7,804 4 5
1823	2 0	24,115	305,200 15 0	30,520 1 6	24,800 10 9½	81·2	.	2,037 7 4	7,461 9 0
1824	2 0	25,215	317,063 0 0	31,706 6 0	24,911 16 11¾	78·5	.	1,706 10 4	9,017 0 8
1825	2 6	26,402	334,737 10 0	41,842 3 9	31,086 5 1¼	74·3	.	2,464 5 2	10,440 15 7
1826	5 0	27,013	346,176 5 0	86,544 1 3	59,371 10 7½	68·6	.	3,218 8 6½	12,365 9 5
1827	5 0	27,306	352,588 5 0	88,147 1 3	66,204 11 3½	75·1	10	3,356 2 3	12,774 19 3
1828	4 0	27,464	337,861 0 0	67,572 4 0	55,080 10 0½	81·5	.	3,501 16 8	6,485 18 8
1829	4 0	28,100	346,288 0 0	69,257 12 0	56,590 8 7½	81·7	.	4,014 19 11	4,924 19 3
1830	No	Rate	. . .	. . .	. . .	.	.	3,227 18 4	8,611 4 4
1831	3 0	28,667	360,121 0 0	54.018 3 0	45,722 10 4½	84·6	.	3,708 3 9	6,000 0 2
1832	4 0	29,317	362,839 5 0	72,567 17 0	61,044 15 9½	84·1	.	3,652 7 7	5,841 4 2
1833	3 0	29,690	367,141 10 0	55,071 4 6	47,585 19 5	8·64	.	3,106 9 11	6,728 15 6
1834	2 6	30,722	409,191 0 0	51,148 17 6	45,108 0 8	88·1	.	3,810 13 5	5,583 2 5
1835	2 0	31,540	429,814 0 0	42,981 8 0	38,871 3 0	90·4	.	3,831 10 10	5,831 9 10
1836	1 4	33,099	467,476 5 0	31,165 1 8	28.127 3 4	90·2	.	4,320 7 1	3,437 0 8
1837	1 8	34,535	568,883 5 0	47,406 18 9	40,532 19 8	85·6	6	5,185 12 5	4,546 8 6
1838	1 6	34,793	574,341 10 0	43,075 12 3	37,018 5 8½	85·9	.	5,018 4 4	7,162 0 6
1839 {	2 0	35,827	. . .	58,953 17 0	49,646 5 8½	84·2	.	. .	. .
	1 0	35,827	589,538 10 0	29,476 18 6	24,001 19 1½	81·4	.	2,210 1 8	7,947 13 6
1840	2 4	35,632	597,921 15 0	69,757 10 9	57,683 8 9½	82·6	.	. .	. .
1841	2 4	35,661	601,351 15 0	70,152 16 8	56,666 12 8½	80·7	.	. .	. .
1842	3 4	36,009	602,620 15 0	100,436 15 10	79,361 8 6	79·0	7	. .	. .
1843	4 0	36,603	590,938 0 0	118,179 13 0	96,278 9 6	81·4	.	. .	. .
1844	3 0	37,033	596,531 15 0	89,480 1 3	75,806 4 10	84·7	.	. .	. .
1845	3 0	37,407	617,156 5 0	92,573 8 9	79,695 17 4	86·0	.	. .	. .
1846	5 0	37,761	633,017 16 0	158,254 9 0	135,491 18 8½	85·6	.	. .	. .
1847	4 6	38,024	643,821 0 0	144,026 15 6	122,662 19 0	85·1	.	. .	. .
1848	6 8	38,151	647,568 15 0	215,856 5 0	174,245 15 8	81·0	.	. .	. .
1849	4 0	38,728	657,863 5 0	131,573 17 0	107,531 19 5	81·6	.	. .	. .
1850	3 6	38,974	665,669 0 0	116,492 1 6	96,699 9 10	83·0	.	. .	. .
1851	4 0	40,113	677,446 10 0	135,489 6 0	114,020 2 1	84·1	.	. .	. .
1852	4 0	41,540	691,354 0 0	138.270 16 0	117,156 17 0	84·7	.	. .	. .
1853	3 6	42,549	721,082 0 0	126,189 7 0	105,860 5 10	84·4	.	. .	. .
1854	3 6	43,681	732,408 10 0	128,171 9 9	107,589 17 4	83·9	8	. .	. .
1855	4 0	43,718	737,325 10 0	147,465 2 0	123,545 19 0	83·7	.	. .	. .
1856	4 0	43,689	741,991 10 0	148 398 6 0	124,055 11 10	83·6	.	. .	. .
1857	4 0	43,521	757,106 10 0	151,421 6 0	126,953 7 2	83·8	.	. .	. .
1858	4 0	44,045	769,690 10 0	153,938 2 0	130,920 12 1	85·0	.	. .	. .
1859	4 0	42,265	778,985 10 0	155,797 2 0	136,005 3 0	87·2	.	. .	. .
1860	3 4	41,916	789,203 10 0	131,533 18 4	115,944 17 1	88·1	7	. .	. .
		1,409,500	21,637,085 16 0						

Average rate in the £ for 20 years, 1820—1840 = 2*s.* 11*d.*
" " " 21 years, 1840—1860 = 3*s.* 9¾*d.*
{ Average rate in the £ for the whole 40 years, 1820—1860, being 3*s.* 5½*d.*

	Assessments	Per Cent.
Increase in the number of assessments in 20 years, 1820—1840 =	15,821,	or 79·86.
" " " 20 years, 1840—1860 =	6,284,	or 17·64.

D.

Assessments, and Rates Collected in Manchester 1820 *to* 1860.

Year.	Paid Parish Highway Rates. £ s. d.	Sir Chas. Shaw paid Chief Commissioners of Police. £ s. d.	Paid to Borough Rate. £ s. d.	Paid to Guardians. £ s. d.	Overseers' Expenses. £ s. d.	Total paid out of Poor-Rates. £ s. d.	Balance in hand at the end of each Year. £ s. d.
1820	.	.	.	.	28,380 4 0½	41,578 18 0½	12,029 2 2
1821	316 7 9	.	.	.	24,525 4 9	39,044 6 0	15,767 15 6
1822	316 7 9	.	.	.	20,550 9 0½	30,638 18 1½	25,038 19 5½
1823	.	.	.	.	21,248 0 3	30,746 16 7	20,827 1 0½
1824	316 7 9	.	.	.	22,058 13 7	33,098 12 4	10,029 7 5½
1825	316 7 9	.	.	.	26,243 19 7½	39,465 8 1½	3,241 3 2
1826	316 7 9	.	.	.	42,383 0 5½	58,283 6 2	1,582 17 10
1827	1,565 11 0	.	.	.	36,882 7 8½	54,579 0 2½	15,803 1 9¼
1828	1,598 6 6	.	.	.	29,831 19 3¼	41,418 1 1¼	29,521 4 7½
1829	774 9 6	.	.	.	48,203 1 5	57,917 10 1	31,724 6 8
1830	.	.	.	.	41,787 5 11	53,626 8 7	5,767 5 8½
1831	.	.	.	.	47,191 7 9	56,899 11 8	2,505 1 7
1832	388 0 3	.	.	.	53,411 13 4	63,293 5 4	9,377 7 8
1833	.	.	.	.	33,634 4 6	43,463 9 11	11,532 15 6
1834	.	.	.	.	27,645 9 6½	37,039 5 4½	18,044 10 7
1835	.	.	.	.	33,523 8 8½	43,186 9 4½	23,186 4 6
1836	193 12 5	.	.	.	30,815 3 7½	38,766 3 9½	21,708 11 6
1837	387 4 9	.	.	.	37,603 8 5	47,722 14 1	18,432 13 10
1838	.	.	.	.	36,190 1 9	48,370 6 3	13,987 10 11
1839 {	.	.	.	.	.	.	.
	387 4 9	9,000 0 0	.	.	40,650 12 7	60,195 12 6	17,027 13 0
1840	387 4 9	16,391 12 8	22,104 15 6	.	46,192 15 3	85,076 8 2	6,393 7 1
1841	751 16 3	16,896 1 8	9,701 15 6	31,001 0 0	4,206 10 6	62,557 3 11	*1,654 8 5
1842	.	14,478 19 2	7,000 0 0	58,350 18 11	3,752 9 4	83,582 7 5	6,276 1 4
1843	.	.	31,191 14 6	49,073 8 2	3,475 13 0	83,740 15 8	25,941 8 7
1844	751 16 3	.	34,840 19 6	44,000 0 0	3,313 16 3	82,906 12 0	25,044 11 1
1845	.	.	42,766 16 4	54,000 0 0	3,505 13 10	100,272 10 2	7,588 11 11
1846	.	.	42,273 10 3	60,000 0 0	3,707 4 9	105,980 15 0	†30,167 11 3
1847	563 17 3	.	37,189 14 1	122,000 0 0	4,037 12 7	163,791 3 11	3,285 4 11
1848	.	.	33,707 15 2	90,000 0 0	4,389 12 6	128,097 7 8	39,510 15 10
1849	563 17 3	.	43,760 5 4	70,000 0 0	5,784 1 1	120,108 3 8	‡40,991 18 10
1850	1,503 12 7	.	43,148 2 0	50,000 0 0	21,063 18 9	115,715 13 4	§25,549 11 2
1851	.	.	42,322 19 0	60,000 0 0	5,660 2 2	107,983 1 2	33,703 2 7
1852	.	.	47,052 4 0	54,585 16 8	5,051 4 9	106,689 5 5	49,583 15 0
1853	.	.	45,165 19 11	60,000 0 0	5,196 0 10	110,362 0 9	48,820 13 4
1854	.	.	52.509 16 0	65,000 0 0	5,264 19 9	122,774 15 9	35,807 6 8
1855	.	.	49,687 9 7	80,000 0 0	5,677 18 10	135,365 8 5	25,033 12 0
1856	.	.	42,155 11 8	80,000 0 0	5,701 15 7	127,857 7 3	24,811 17 11
1857	.	.	47,296 3 9	77,000 0 0	6,108 0 9	130,404 4 6	22,740 13 2
1858	.	.	45,133 18 2	80,000 0 0	7,056 12 5	132 190 10 7	28,201 9 10
1859	.	.	45,453 8 3	84,945 0 10	5,542 19 10	135,941 8 11	32,497 13 3
1860	.	.	44,872 12 8	60,000 0 0	5,345 9 11	110,218 2 7	39,788 14 8

* Went into Union. † New Poor Law order of accounts. ‡ Removal Department returned to Overseers. § One Quarter's relief of Poor.

Per Cent.

Increase in the value of property assessed in 20 years, 1820—1840 = £290,411, or 94·44.
" " " " 20 years, 1840—1860 = £191,282, or 31·99.

APPENDIX E.

I HAVE excluded from the sketch of the progress of Manchester all medical details not indispensable to an estimate of the three chief causes of the high rate of mortality still maintained there. To enter into the various questions of vital statistics subordinate to the three prominent sources of this mortality would be inconsistent with the main objects of this volume. But I place in this Appendix corroborative evidence that I have not without sufficient ground attributed this high rate of mortality chiefly :—1. To the sanitary defects in the construction of dwellings and their conveniences; to their being too closely crowded; and to the degree in which the removal of nuisances still baffles the efforts of the Corporations of Manchester and Salford. 2. To the mismanagement or neglect of children under five years of age. And 3. To intemperance.

In support of the first two of these causes I append the following extracts from the *Report of Dr. Headlam Greenhow*, to the Public Health Department of the Privy Council, *on Diarrhœa in Manchester*, presented to both Houses of Parliament in 1859.

It is especially satisfactory to me to find that the particular nuisances to which in 1831 I had directed the attention of the Board of Health, and of the committees of inspection appointed by it,—the absence or bad position of privies; the overcrowding of dwellings; the want of ventilation of courts, alleys, and small streets; the imperfect removal of excrementitious matter; the defects in scavenging—though less in degree, are exactly those which, in Dr. Greenhow's opinion, combine with the neglect or mismanagement of infants as two main sources of the high rate of mortality.

I also append an analysis of the causes of deaths among children under five years of age in the Ancoats district in 1859.

'MANCHESTER.— Cholera occasioned 891 deaths in Manchester in 1849, but visited it very lightly in 1854; indeed, the deaths from cholera, dysentery, and diarrhœa were more numerous in Manchester in 1852, when cholera was not supposed to be epidemic in this country, than in 1854, when it prevailed severely in an epidemic form in several parts of England. Excluding the 891 deaths from cholera in 1849, but including those in other years, 7032 persons died of diarrhœal disease; that is to say, of diarrhœa, cholera, and dysentery, in the registration district of Manchester during the eleven years 1848-58. Of these deaths, 4924 occurred during the seven years 1848-54, and 2836 during the five years 1854-8; being an annual average of 703 during the earlier, and of 567 during the later period. The deaths from diarrhœa have thus materially decreased of late years; and, as the population has increased, the diminution in proportion to the number of inhabitants is even larger than is represented by these figures.' 'The average annual death-rate from diarrhœal disease, which was 3·20 per 1000 persons during the septennial period 1848-54, had fallen to 2·28 during the five years 1854-8, or nearly one-third.' 'Satisfactory as is this great reduction in the mortality from diarrhœa in Manchester, there yet remains a wide margin for improvement, seeing that the present death-rate from this disease is more than seven times higher than the normal rate. There can be little hesitation in attributing this improvement in the public health of Manchester, more especially as regards diarrhœa, mainly, if not exclusively, to the efforts made by the civic authorities to amend the sanitary state of the city.

'Manchester is a densely-built town; the interspaces between the streets being small, and almost entirely covered with buildings.'

'The streets and courts of Manchester are, generally speaking, well kept and cleanly, the little heaps of refuse so commonly to be observed in most towns being here found only exceptionally. During a very minute inspection of the town, but few places were observed requiring notice, on account of their filthy condition.' 'These, together with a few small courts and back passages, were in this respect the only strikingly exceptionable places observed. Courts abound in the interspaces between the streets, and are often narrow, ill ventilated, and, being sometimes entered under an archway, are so entirely surrounded by buildings as to form mere wells of stagnant air, which is often rendered offensive by the effluvia from privies. Indeed, these latter form the prevailing nuisance of Manchester. Although apparently well looked after, they cannot fail, more especially in close, warm, still weather, to be a source of great annoyance to the inhabitants ; and, if their influence on the public health may be judged of by experience in other places, they are one of the primary causes of the prevalence of diarrhœa. Privies are the only kind of convenience attached to the dwellings of the labouring classes, water-closets being apparently discountenanced by the local authorities.

'It is stated in the official regulations published by the Sanitary Committee of the Council, "that water-closets will only be allowed under special arrangements with the Committee, and the owner or occupier agreeing with the Water Works Committee for Water, for the purpose of cleansing the pipes ; also defraying one half of the cost of removing the ashes." Privies are, therefore, in general use; in the older portion of the town, where they did not formerly exist, their construction has been enforced in the proportion of one privy for every four houses; and, when necessary, houses have, it is said, been removed, to afford room for their construction. Every recently built dwelling-house is provided with a privy and ash-pit. Very stringent regulations have been adopted on this subject by the civic authorities. (*The regulations are then quoted.*)

'It results from these regulations that, in laying out ground for building purposes, the space between the backs of parallel rows of houses is usually just sufficient to admit of the construction of privies, ash-pits, and passages in accordance with the requirements of the Sanitary Committee. In some instances, the space is not even quite enough to comply with the spirit of the law, although the letter be scrupulously adhered to.' (*Instances are related.*) 'Sometimes there are rooms over privies, as in ' streets named. ' There is usually in such cases a ventilating shaft or flue for carrying away the exhalations from the privy to the open air, the flue constructed for this purpose sometimes passing through the rooms above the privy. In other places, perhaps of more recent construction, a space for the dispersion of effluvia is left between the top of the privy and the floor of the room above ; examples of this arrangement are met with in the neighbourhood of Brown and Caledon Streets. Small sculleries, with bedrooms over them, are occasionally erected as projections from the backs of houses ; these interfere materially with the passage of the air through the interspaces behind the houses, the ventilation being often so impeded that offensive exhalations are but slowly dispersed into the general atmosphere.

'When it is considered that this system of constructing privies in very confined spaces is common throughout Manchester, it may well be termed the monster sanitary defect of this important city. This evil, curiously enough, is less conspicuous in the older than in the newer portions of the town; for, although the older houses are often loftier, and occasionally let out in tenements of a single room each, the yards are usually larger, and the privies often less objectionably placed than in the more modern streets. Pigs were observed in a few places, but by no means commonly. Strictly speaking, the keeping of pigs in the town is not prohibited; but whenever complaints are made concerning them, their removal is ordered; and, practically, this has almost sufficed to banish them from the denser portions of the city. Many cellar dwellings are found in Manchester, and often the houses stand back to back with each other. The water supply is almost, if not entirely, obtained from the public waterworks.'

'Nearly two-thirds of the deaths' from diarrhœa 'were those of infants under one year of age, and considerably more than four-fifths those of children who had not attained the age of five years. If the deaths during the five years comprised in this investigation had amounted to 1000, they would have been distributed among the several stages of life in the following manner:—

Under 1 year	603·1
From 1 to 5 years	273·6
„ 5 to 60 years	68·7
Over 60 years	57·6
	1000·0

'The proportion of infant deaths' from diarrhœa 'varied considerably in different years; the per centage of infant deaths was 57·6 in 1854, 62·0 in 1855, 50·5 in 1856, 54·4 in 1857, and 59·6 in 1858.'

'The proportion of infant deaths also varied in the several registration districts, having been much larger in the town districts than in Newton, Cheetham, Failsworth, Blackley, and Prestwich, which are termed the five suburban districts.'

'The annexed Table shows the mortality at all ages' from diarrhœa 'per 1000 persons in each of the urban sub-districts, and in the five suburban districts here treated, as though they formed but a single district:—

Ancoats	2·63
Deansgate	2·37
London Road	2·27
Market Street	1·84
St. George's	2·15
Five Suburban Districts	0·96

'The peculiar arrangement of the privies prevails more or less in every part of Manchester, but is not equally objectionable in all. The differences of diarrhœal death-rate appear to coincide with these local differences of construction. Ancoats district, which is very densely built, has the highest rate of mortality in proportion to its population. This is the more striking, as the proportion of infant deaths is somewhat less in Ancoats than in the other districts. The connection between the mortality from diarrhœa and the existence of privies in the immediate neighbourhood of dwellings was repeatedly ascertained, and the comparative immunity of places freer from this local nuisance was also apparent, both from the evidence of the inhabitants and the small number of deaths recorded in the death register.'

'CHORLTON comprises Ardwick, Chorlton, and Hulme, which form integral portions of the city of Manchester, besides several less populous townships.'

'The same evils were found to exist in it as in Manchester, but in a minor degree, the ground being less densely covered with buildings, so that, with few exceptions, there is a wider space between the rows of houses. It is true the same regulations relative to new houses apply to Hulme, Ardwick, and Chorlton, as to Manchester; and, in some cases, they have been as closely adhered to; but this is exceptional, and more commonly the air at the back of the houses is less stagnant in Chorlton than in Manchester.'

'SALFORD Registration District comprehends the borough of Salford, together with Pendleton, Pendlebury, and Broughton. In common with Manchester and Chorlton, it was visited by cholera in 1849, and almost entirely escaped the visitation of 1854. In the former of these years, 234 deaths were occasioned by the epidemic. It also participated, but less severely in proportion to its population, in the diarrhœal epidemic of 1852. Exclusive of the deaths from cholera in 1849, but including the deaths from cholera, dysentery, and diarrhœa in the other years of the series, 2748 deaths were caused by diarrhœal disease in Salford during the eleven years 1848–58. Of these, 1863 occurred during the seven years 1848–54, and 1239 during the five years 1854-8, being an annual average of 266 during the earlier, and of 248 during the later period. There has thus been a decrease in the diarrhœal mortality of Salford, as well as in that of the adjoining districts. The population of Salford in 1851 consisted of 87,523 persons; and if it has increased in the same ratio since 1851 as during the preceding ten years, it would consist in 1856 of nearly 98,000 persons. If this estimate be correct, the average annual diarrhœal death rate, which was 3·03 per 1000 persons during the septennial period 1848-54, has only been 2·55 during the five years 1854-8. Thus the diminution of mortality, although unquestionable, has been smaller in Salford than in either Manchester or Chorlton. The rate of mortality from all causes has likewise been less during the last five than during the seven preceding years. It was 27·83 per 1000 persons during the seven years 1848-54, and has only been 26·58 during the five years 1854-58.

'Some parts of Salford are very densely covered with buildings, but others are much less densely built than Manchester, which in many respects it closely resembles, but with this difference, that the privy nuisance is, in some respects, even worse in Salford than in Manchester. Houses placed back to back, and cellar dwellings, are common in Salford. Houses are not often let in single-room tenements, and are rarely overcrowded, usually containing only the members of a single family. The sanitary arrangements in some of the more recently built houses are quite satisfactory; those in some of the older streets very much the reverse. There are no waterclosets to the dwellings of the poorer classes; the soil from the privies being removed by the municipal authorities, forms a source of revenue which would be lost if waterclosets were in general use. The water supply is the same as that of Manchester, being exclusively derived from the Manchester Waterworks; wells, formerly in common use, have been altogether disused and covered over. The rule respecting privies is, that they shall be constructed for cottage property to the satisfaction of the Sanitary Committee, and, although sometimes one of these conveniences is allowed to serve for six houses, the Committee generally require that there shall be one for every four houses. In some parts of the town privies are well apart from dwellings; in others they are, as in Manchester, situated in very small yards, and in close proximity to the houses. In very many instances they are either actually within the houses, having dwelling rooms immediately over them, or in the centre of rows, having houses on either side; being, in fact, constructed in what were formerly houses, the upper floor being left unoccupied or employed for ventilation. Sometimes, but more rarely, houses have been entirely removed, and privies erected on their site. It would be easy to give examples of these several arrangements.' Instances are related. 'In several of these places the inhabitants residing in the adjoining houses complained of the privies, and sometimes diarrhœa had prevailed among them. Four courts are there described with privies in houses, below occupied rooms, in which the annual diarrhœal rate of mortality rose to 7·2 per 1000.

'More than half the deaths were those of infants under the age of one year, and more than four-fifths those of children who had not reached the fifth anniversary of their birth. If the entire mortality during the five years had been 1000, it would be distributed among the several stages of life in the following manner:—

Under 1 year	578·2
From 1 to 5 years	277·4
„ 5 to 60 years	72·2
Over 60 years	72·2
	1000

'The proportion of infant deaths varied from year to year, being 55·8 per cent. of the entire diarrhœal mortality in 1854, 58·1 in 1855, 49·4 in 1856, 54·9 in 1857, and 59·6 per cent. in 1858.'

'As in Coventry and Nottingham, so in Manchester, the large diarrhœal mortality of children is partly attributed by the medical men to the neglect arising from the employment of women in factories. Infants, it is said, are frequently left by their mothers, at the age of three or four weeks, for the greater portion of the day, during which they are fed upon bread and water, and more rarely upon arrow-root and milk. Coffee, meat, and "little drops" of gin are also sometimes given to infants; and the system of drugging with Godfrey's Cordial is so common, that one druggist is reputed to sell thirty gallons per week of this narcotic. Mr. Leigh, one of the sub-registrars, and likewise a medical practitioner, who has devoted much attention to the sanitary state of Manchester, attributes the frequency of atrophy in young children to this system of drugging them with opiates, and the large mortality among children from diarrhœa, to neglect; parents, he says, send for medicines to druggists at the commencement of an illness, and only call in medical advice when the case has assumed a serious character. But it was also stated by some of the medical gentlemen that diarrhœa prevails likewise among persons not of the poorest class, and among adults, to neither of whom the above-mentioned causes are applicable.'

'The local distribution of diarrhœal disease has varied less in Manchester than in some of the towns previously visited; but where such variations have been observed, they appear to have been in a direct ratio to the tainting of the air with the exhalations from foul privies or ash-pits. The inhabitants themselves sometimes complained of the effluvia, and also, in a few instances, attributed the prevalence of diarrhœa among their households to this cause. In all probability, the general diffusion of deaths from diarrhœa in Manchester should be referred to the uniform manner in which stinking ash-pits and privies are distributed throughout the town; and the slightly higher mortality of Salford to the larger proportion of privies in common use by the inmates of several houses, causing the accumulation of ordure in larger quantities in the midst of the population, and to the closer proximity of this nuisance, in but too many instances, to the dwellings.'

Extracts from the concluding Summary.

'A very large number of the deaths were those of young children, but the proportion has varied in different places. With the exception of Merthyr Tydfil and Dudley, more than half the deaths were those of infants in the first year after birth. The deaths of infants have borne the largest proportion to those of all ages in the three manufacturing towns, Coventry, Nottingham, and Manchester, in each of which evidence has been adduced of the mismanagement of infants, arising from the employment of mothers in factory labour. The different proportions in each place would seem to countenance the opinion that the assigned cause is not without influence, seeing that a much larger proportion of the women of Coventry were employed in the special manufactures of that city in 1851 than of those of either Manchester or Nottingham. The four years between the completion of the first and the termination of the fifth year after birth is the next most fatal period of life, and the deaths in these four years being added to those of the first year, very nearly equalise the mortality in most of the places during the first five years of life. But here again variations exist, which would appear to denote the operation of different influences in the several districts. Manchester and Salford have been the districts most fatal to children; next to them Coventry; whilst in Leeds, Merthyr Tydfil, and Nottingham, the proportion of deaths of children under five years of age from diarrhœa, in proportion to the whole mortality from this disease, has been smaller than in the other places. The following Table, based upon the assumption that 1000 deaths have occurred in each district, shows at a glance the proportion which the deaths from diarrhœal disease at each period of life bears to the total mortality from this disease in the several places.

The figures have already been given separately for each place, but they are here placed side by side for all the places, and an additional column has been added to show the mortality under five years of age:—

Name of District.	Under 1 Year.	From 1 to 5 Years.	Under 5 Years.	From 5 to 60 Years.	Over 60 Years.	All Ages.
Coventry . . .	675·9	176·8	852·7	69·3	78·0	1·000
Birmingham . .	549·0	267·0	816·0	87·0	97·0	1·000
Wolverhampton .	522·2	310·1	832·3	94·0	73·7	1·000
Dudley . . .	477·3	359·8	837·1	89·4	73·5	1·000
Merthyr Tydfil .	385·4	370·3	755·7	128·5	115·8	1·000
Nottingham . .	608·0	136·0	744·0	105·0	151·0	1·000
Leeds . . .	535·5	250·5	786·0	92·0	122·0	1·000
Manchester . .	603·1	273·6	876·7	65·7	57·6	1·000
Chorlton . . .	599·3	239·4	838·7	90·1	71·2	1·000
Salford . . .	578·8	277·4	856·2	72·2	72·2	1·000

'The proportion of infant deaths in each place varied in the several years, but there has been no uniformity in this respect in the different districts; even such as are contiguous, like Manchester, Chorlton, or Salford, or near to each other, like Birmingham, Wolverhampton, and Dudley, having differed from one another.

'However great the influence of season, of age, or of the mismanagement of young children in causing a large mortality from diarrhœa, the concurrence at least of some other cause might be expected from the very different rate of mortality which prevails in different districts. The present inquiry has very clearly established the existence of two principal local causes of this disease. These are the breathing an atmosphere tainted with the products of animal decomposition, more especially, although perhaps not exclusively, that of human excrement, and the drinking of impure water.'

'Confirmation of the opinion here expressed, that the diarrhœal mortality of towns is mainly due to the accumulation of night-soil within their precincts, is afforded by the beneficial results accruing from such local exertions as have had for their object the suppression or diminution of this evil, and which have been attended by success, almost in exact proportion to the greater or less completeness with which this object has been attained.'

Causes of Death in the Ancoats District of Manchester in 1859 *among Children under five years of age.*

Population of Ancoats Sub-Registration District in 1861 . 55,983
Deaths under five years 785
Deaths of illegitimate children 64
Total deaths 1493

Furnished by ARTHUR RANSOME, Esq., Honorary Secretary to the Manchester and Salford Sanitary Association.

Diseases.	Deaths under 1 year,	Deaths from 1—2.	Deaths from 2—5.	Total.
Scarlatina	5	20	55	80
Bronchitis	17	11	16	44
Pneumonia	29	27	17	73
Marasmus	30	6	8	44
Tabes, Mesen.	17	4	5	26
Hooping-cough & debility	30	. .	1	31
Premature births	13	. .	. .	13
Convulsions	109	8	5	122
Dentition	19	11	1	31
Fever	3	4	9	16
Hooping-cough	13	11	9	33
Syphilis	9	2	. .	11
Diarrhœa	88	32	7	127
Dysentery	4	2	1	7
Measles	2	1	5	8
Dropsy	. .	2	. .	2
Croup	2	1	6	9
Small-pox	. .	. .	1	1
Hydrocephalus	2	2	3	7
Diphtheria	1	4	2	7
Other causes	42	27	24	93
	435	175	175	785

SECOND PERIOD

1839

THE FORMATION OF THE COMMITTEE OF COUNCIL ON EDUCATION

1837 TO 1840

THE COMMENCEMENT OF THE PUPIL-TEACHER SYSTEM

1841 TO 1843

THE ESTABLISHMENT OF THE FIRST TRAINING COLLEGE

SECOND PERIOD.

1. *The Order in Council creating the Committee of the Privy Council on Education.* April 10, 1839.
2. *The Minutes as to the National Normal School* (April 13, 1839), *and as to the Inspection of Schools* (June 3, 1839).
3. *A Pamphlet issued by direction of the Government, entitled 'Recent Measures for the Promotion of Education in England,' explaining the Intentions of the Ministry in* 1839.
4. *First Steps in Workhouses and Schools of Industry for Pauper Children respecting the Apprenticeship of Pupil Teachers. A few brief Extracts from Reports.* 1837 to 1840.
5. *Two Reports describing the Origin and Organisation of the Training College at Battersea, and the Introduction of some of the Pupil Teachers as Students.* 1841 and 1843.

PREFACE

In entering on the chief features of a new period, it may be well to recapitulate. The account given in the First Period of the condition of the Working Classes in Manchester in 1832, and of the progress of that city in thirty years, exhibits the relative power of moral and physical forces on the well-being of the people. The growth of Manchester in wealth has been accompanied by a corresponding improvement in all the means of physical well-being in the operative population. They have better wages—more regular employment—cheaper food and clothing—the houses and streets which they inhabit are generally in a better sanitary condition—they have a more abundant supply of pure water—their labour is restrained within reasonable limits—institutions have sprung up since 1832 to encourage providence, cleanliness, and a knowledge of sanitary laws, and to provide the means of innocent recreation. The limitation of the hours of attendance in warehouses, and the Saturday half-holiday, are signs of the sincerity of the desire which exists in Manchester that no obstacle should prevent social improvement.

These changes belong rather to the ameliorations of the physical than of the moral condition of the population; but they do not consist simply in the removal of impediments to moral progress. Necessarily, in our complex nature, moral and physical improvement are in some degree correlative.

When, therefore, the extension and the greater efficiency of moral agencies is combined with the amelioration of the physical relations of the population, we are naturally led to seek the proofs of the effects of these combined improvements in the diminution of the rate of mortality. Efficient Schools have increased in number; Churches and Chapels have been built with zeal; a City Mission labours with activity in the houses of the poor; Free Public Libraries, Mechanics' Institutions, Evening Schools, and Savings' Banks, combine their attractions with the warning voice of religious teachers to wean the workman from sensuality. But the population is swollen by the immigration of a large mass of semi-barbarous colonists, who are drawn thither by the unexampled demand for labour caused by the growth of the cotton manufacture during these thirty years. The pauperism of Manchester is thus largely fed by the Irish and other immigrants. It has been customary in Manchester to relieve the indigent Irish from the poor-rate, though they have obtained no settlement. The number of unsettled Irish thus relieved amounts to two-thirds of the number of English and settled Irish who obtain relief. Doubtless the amount of intemperance, and of those crimes which are its direct consequence, are at least in similar proportions. If to the deteriorating influence of this Irish population be added the similarly barbarising influence of uncivilised English immigrants, we have before us two powerfully counteracting forces which resist the influence of physical and moral agencies now at work.

This immigrant barbarism is one main source of that increase of beer-houses which has been recorded. The intemperance of this population, and its apathy as to those parental and familiar duties which would keep the mother of an infant child at home, and would secure the early and regular attendance of any young children at the Infant School, are among the causes of the excessive infant mortality, and of the permanence for thirty years of a high rate of general mortality. The civilisation of such a population must be gradual. It is the work of successive generations. These obstacles to the combined influence of all forms of social improvement are analysed in Manchester. It is clear, then, that sanitary defects, though much improvement may still be made, are not now the chief source of the high rate of mortality that is attributable to the low mental and moral state of a population so rude, that prosperity itself inflames its sensual appetites, and thus defeats the wisdom and public spirit of the corporation, as well as the zeal of the School managers and of the religious communions.

The demonstration of the nature of the obstacles to social progress afforded by the sketch of the progress of Manchester in thirty years throws much light on the value of those moral forces which have been called into operation by the improvements in Public Education in Great Britain since 1833, and especially since 1846. It also accounts for the difficulty which has been experienced by the promoters of Schools in securing all those results among their scholars which they were so sanguine as to expect might, at an early period, flow from their labours. They had first to train and discipline before they could instruct their scholars, —an uncivilised, ignorant population, supporting their own sensual excesses in some degree by the too early labour of their children, is necessarily indifferent to their education. Such scholars attend School irregularly — change their Schools capriciously — are ignorant, undisciplined, dull, inattentive, wayward, if not obstinate and turbulent. They are the elements of disorder in Schools. They are the dead-weights which the teacher has to carry. He has no help in their training at home: there they are neglected, or harshly treated. They come to school unkempt, ragged, dirty, insubordinate, if they come at all. But they are often truant: they are often kept away to go an errand — to nurse a child — to do some household work — which a dexterous housewife would otherwise provide for. In short, Barbarism and the School are at war. In this warfare the School will be the victor; but time is an indispensable element of success. The account, therefore, of the First Period in Public Education has been devoted to an analysis of the character of the population of one of our most prosperous cities, and to a description of the difficulties encountered by generous and enlightened citizens in their efforts to promote the Christian civilisation of their fellow-townsmen.

The Second Period opens a more agreeable task to the Author. Successive publications here record the means adopted by the Government to elevate the standard of education in elementary Schools, by the first steps in the introduction of Pupil Teachers, and by the proposal of a National Normal Training School, the defeat of which was one reason why the Battersea Training College was established. These several documents naturally tell the story of the progress made in this Second Period.

The account given of foreign education in the defence of the Government measures in 1839 was limited to the briefest space, on account of the indisposition of the public at that time to believe that anything was to be learned from foreign institutions.

The Author, therefore, availed himself only of those authorities whose testimony would tend to recommend their statements to popular attention. He is glad to be enabled now to refer to the Fourth Volume of the 'Report of the Royal Commission on Education of 1858,' published in 1861, containing the Reports of the Assistant Commissioners appointed to inquire into the State of Popular Education in Continental Europe. The Reports of Mr. Matthew Arnold, the Professor of Poetry at Oxford, and one of the Inspectors of Schools, 'On Systems of Popular Education in use in France, Holland, and the French Cantons of Switzerland,' and that of the Rev. Mark Pallison, B.D., now Master of Lincoln College, Oxford, 'On the State of Elementary Education in Germany,' are valuable contributions to our knowledge of these subjects, and worthy of the most attentive perusal.

I.

ORDER IN COUNCIL, CREATING THE COMMITTEE OF THE PRIVY COUNCIL ON EDUCATION.

At the Court at Buckingham Palace, the 10th of April, 1839.

Present:

THE QUEEN'S MOST EXCELLENT MAJESTY IN COUNCIL.

'IT is this day ordered by Her Majesty in Council, that the Most Honourable Henry, Marquis of Lansdowne, Lord-President of the Council; the Right-Honourable John William, Viscount Duncannon, Lord Privy Seal; the Right-Honourable Lord John Russell, One of H.M.'s Principal Secretaries of State; and the Right-Honourable Thomas Spring Rice, Chancellor of H.M.'s Exchequer, be, and they are hereby appointed, a Committee to superintend the Application of any Sums voted by Parliament for the purpose of promoting Public Education.

' (Signed)   C. C. GREVILLE.'

II.

THE NATIONAL NORMAL SCHOOL OF 1839.

Extract from the Minutes of the Committee of Council appointed to superintend the Application of any Sums voted by Parliament for the purpose of promoting Public Education.

April 13th, 1839.

Read, The following scheme for the future guidance of the Committee, viz. :—

'*Normal School.* — To found a school, in which candidates for the office of teacher in schools for the poorer classes may acquire the knowledge necessary to the exercise of their future profession, and may be practised in the most approved methods of religious and moral training and instruction.

'*Model School.* — This school to include a Model School, in which children of all ages from three to fourteen, may be taught and trained, in sufficient numbers to form an Infant School, as well as schools for children above seven.

'*Religious Instruction in Model School.* — Religious instruction to be considered as general and special.

'*General.* — Religion to be combined with the whole matter of instruction, and to regulate the entire system of discipline.

'*Special.* — Periods to be set apart for such peculiar doctrinal instruction as may be required for the religious training of the children.

'*Chaplain.* — To appoint a chaplain to conduct the religious instruction of children whose parents or guardians belong to the Established Church.

'*Dissenters.* — The parent or natural guardian of any other child to be permitted to secure the attendance of the licensed minister of his own persuasion, at the period appointed for special religious instruction, in order to give such instruction apart.

'*Licensed Minister.* — To appoint a licensed minister to give such special religious instruction wherever the number of children in attendance on the Model School belonging to any religious body dissenting from the Established Church is such as to appear to this Committee to require such special provision.

'*Scriptures read daily in School.* — A portion of every day to be devoted to the reading of the Scriptures in the School, under the general direction of the Committee, and superintendence of the Rector. *Roman Catholics.* — Roman Catholics, if their parents or guardians require it, to read their own version of the Scriptures, either at the time fixed for reading the Scriptures, or at the hours of special instruction.

'*Simultaneous Method Classes.* — To arrange the classes in separate rooms or sections of the same apartment, divided by partitions, so as to enable the simultaneous method to be applied to 40 or 50 children of similar proficiency.

'*Gallery.* — To adopt means to assemble a greater number of children for simultaneous instruction on subjects not so technical as to require a division into classes of 50.

'*Instruction in Industry.* — To include instruction in industry as a special department of the moral training of the children.

'*Special Character of Secular Instruction.* — To give such a character to the matter of instruction in the school as to keep it in close relation with the condition of workmen and servants.

'*Physical Training.* — Besides the physical training of the children in various employments, to introduce such exercises during the hours of recreation as will develop their strength and activity.

'*Moral Training.* — To render the moral training of the children at all times an object of special solicitude.

'NORMAL SCHOOL.

'*Candidate Teachers to reside.* — To provide apartments for the residence of the candidate teachers.

'*Class-Rooms.* — To construct the class-rooms so as to afford the candidate teachers an opportunity of attending each class in the Model School without distracting the attention of the children or of the teacher.

'*Means of Instruction and Training.* — To provide means for the instruction of the candidate teachers in the theory of their art, and for furnishing them with whatever knowledge is necessary for success in it.

'*Rector: his duties.*— To appoint a Rector to give lectures upon the method and matter of instruction, and on the whole art of training children of the poor. To regulate the reading and exercises of the candidate teachers, and to examine them. To determine the order in which they may be admitted to the practice of their art in the school, and at length intrusted with the conjoint management of classes, and to superintend their ultimate examination, subject to the rules of this Committee.

'*Religious Instruction of Candidate Teachers.*—The religious instruction of the candidate teachers to form an essential and prominent element of their studies, and no certificate to be granted unless the authorised religious teacher has previously attested his confidence in the character, religious knowledge, and zeal of the candidate whose religious instruction he has superintended.

'*Chaplain to instruct Teachers belonging to Established Church.* — The religious instruction of all candidate teachers connected with the Established Church to be committed to the Chaplain, and the special religious instruction to be committed (in any case in which a wish to that effect is expressed) to the licensed Minister of the religious persuasion of the candidate teacher, who is to attend the school at stated periods, to assist and examine the candidate teachers in their reading on religious subjects, and to afford them spiritual advice.

'*Internal Discipline of Normal School.* — The candidate teachers in all other respects to conform to such regulations as respects the entire internal economy of the household as may be issued by the Rector, with the approval of this Committee.

'*Number of Children in Model School. Boarders.* — To provide accommodation in the Model School for at least 450 children, who should lodge in the household, viz. 120 infants, 200 boys and girls receiving ordinary instruction, and 50 boys and 50 girls receiving superior instruction, and 30 children probably absent from sickness or other causes.

'*Day School.* — To establish a day school of 150 or 200 children of all ages and both sexes, in which the candidate teachers may realise the application of the best methods of instruction, under the limitations and obstructions which must arise in a small village or town day school.'

III.

A MINUTE OF THE COMMITTEE OF COUNCIL ON EDUCATION,

Of the 3rd day of June, 1839.

At the Court at Buckingham Palace, the 3rd of June, 1839.

Present:

THE QUEEN'S MOST EXCELLENT MAJESTY IN COUNCIL.

WHEREAS there was this day read at the Board a Report from the Committee of Council appointed to superintend the application of any sums voted by Parliament for the purpose of promoting Public Education; which Report, dated the 1st of June, was in the words following; viz.:—

'Your Majesty having been pleased, by your Order in Council of the 10th of April, 1839, to appoint us a Committee of Council to superintend the application of any Sums voted by Parliament for the purpose of promoting Public Education, we, the Lords of the said Committee, have this day met, and agreed humbly to present to Your Majesty the following Report:

'The Lords of the Committee recommend that the sum of Ten Thousand Pounds, granted by Parliament in 1835 towards the erection of Normal or Model Schools, be given in equal proportions to the National Society and the British and Foreign School Society. That the remainder of the subsequent Grants of the years 1837 and 1838, yet unappropriated, and any Grant that may be voted in the present year, be chiefly applied in aid of Subscriptions for building, and, in particular cases, for the support of Schools connected with those Societies; but that the rule hitherto adopted of making a Grant to those places where the largest proportion is subscribed be not invariably adhered to, should application be made from very poor and populous districts, where Subscriptions to a sufficient amount cannot be obtained.

'The Committee do not feel themselves precluded from making Grants in particular cases, which shall appear to them to call for the aid of Government, although the applications may not come from either of the two mentioned Societies.

'The Committee are of opinion, that the most useful application of any sums voted by Parliament would consist in the employment of those monies in the establishment of a Normal School, under the direction of the State, and not placed under the management of a voluntary society. The Committee, however, experience so much difficulty in reconciling conflicting views respecting the provisions which they are desirous to make in furtherance of Your Majesty's wish, that the children and teachers instructed in this School should be duly trained in the principles of the Christian religion, while the rights of conscience should be respected, that it is not in the power of the Committee to mature a plan for the accomplishment of this design without further consideration, and they therefore postpone taking any steps for this purpose until greater concurrence of opinion is found to prevail.

'The Committee recommend that no further Grant be made, now or hereafter, for the establishment or support of Normal Schools, or of any other Schools, unless the right of inspection be retained, in order to secure a conformity to the regulations and discipline established in the several Schools, with such improvements as may from time to time be suggested by the Committee.

'A part of any Grant voted in the present year may be usefully applied to the purposes of inspection, and to the means of acquiring a complete knowledge of the present state of Education in England and Wales.'

Her Majesty, having taken the said Report into consideration, was pleased, by and with the advice of Her Privy Council, to approve thereof.

(Signed)   C. C. GREVILLE.

AN EXPLANATION OF

THE INTENTIONS OF HER MAJESTY'S GOVERNMENT

ENTITLED

RECENT MEASURES FOR THE PROMOTION OF EDUCATION IN ENGLAND

PUBLISHED IN 1839

RECENT MEASURES

&c

CHAPTER I.

INTRODUCTION—STATE OF EDUCATION IN ENGLAND—EFFECTS ON CRIME—REPORTS OF CHAPLAINS OF GAOLS—NECESSITY FOR INTERFERENCE OF GOVERNMENT.

ALL plans which have been proposed for promoting National Education in England by calling into operation the powers of the Executive Government, have necessarily been subjected to the most searching scrutiny. The advocates of education must not, however, accept the earnestness with which public attention is directed to this subject as a measure of the degree in which the necessity of an extension and improvement of the elementary education of the poorer classes is recognised. It is indeed generally known that even the art of reading has been acquired by a portion only of the rising population, and by a smaller part of the adult working class; and that, as respects the rudimentary knowledge which might develop the understanding, and afford the labourer a clear view of his social position,—its duties, its difficulties, and rewards,—and thus enable him better to employ the powers with which Providence has gifted him, to promote his own comfort and the well-being of society, he is generally destitute, and, what is worse, abandoned to the ill-regulated and often pernicious agencies by which he is surrounded. It is commonly confessed that no sufficient means exist to train the habits of the children of our poorer classes,—to inspire them with healthful, social, and household sympathies,—with a love of domestic peace and social order,—with an enlightened reverence for revealed truth,—and with the sentiment of piety and devotion.

But while these proofs of the fatal void in our national institutions are admitted, we fear we may not attribute the eagerness with which every proposal for the improvement and extension of popular education is discussed solely to an earnest and enlightened sympathy with the condition of the working classes. We must admit as a necessary element of our estimate of the popular feeling, the fact that the connection which exists in every well-devised plan for National Education between the secular and the religious instruction and moral training of the people, rouses the advocates of the antagonist principles involved in questions of civil and religious liberty, which have caused political struggles deeply affecting the middle and higher classes of society, but in the consequences of which the lower classes have hitherto had comparatively little practical interest.

The ferment occasioned by the recent settlement of some of these grave questions has not yet subsided; and to the state of public opinion, which has had its source in their prolonged discussion, we must attribute, in a great degree, the suspicion with which every proposal for the promotion of National Education is regarded, and the singular excitement produced by its announcement.

We are the last to deprecate public discussion — we invite it: we rejoice in the activity of the public mind — we have nothing to fear excepting from its apathy; our hopes are all concentrated in the right of private opinion — in the freedom with which, in this country, every question of public policy is debated, and in the consequent spread of a knowledge of the principles on which the changes demanded by the advance of civilisation are based.

In the first movements of popular excitement, misrepresentation and clamour may mislead individuals or entire political or religious bodies into an opposition to plans, which on more attentive consideration they would have cordially approved. Nay, in any society in which the right of public discussion is admitted, it is the lot of every improvement to be misunderstood and misrepresented at its first announcement; the frame of society receives a shock at every change, even for the better, and in the first moments of surprise the entire community bestirs itself to ascertain whence comes the disturbance, and what is its object.

To enable every person interested in this national question to ascertain what is the plan of her Majesty's Government, and thus to prevent or to remove the consequences of industriously circulated misrepresentations; —to invite public discussion, and at the same time to provide it with a plain exposition of the principles and arrangements which we conceive to be involved in that plan, we have published the Report of the Committee of Council approved by her Majesty, with a few observations.

Evidence has been collected from time to time by Committees of the House of Commons, by voluntary societies, and by individuals, incontestably proving that the provision for the education of the poorer classes in England is most limited in extent and defective in quality. In the year 1816, the 'Report from the Select Committee of the House of Commons on the Education of the Lower Orders in the Metropolis,' of which Mr. Brougham was Chairman, states the Committee 'have found reason to conclude that a very large number of poor children are wholly without the means of instruction, although their parents appear to be generally very desirous of obtaining that advantage for them.' 'They feel persuaded that the greatest advantages would result to this country from Parliament taking proper measures, in concurrence with the prevailing disposition of the community, for supplying the deficiency of the means of instruction which exists at present, and for extending the blessing to the poor of all descriptions.'

In their Report in the year 1818, this Committee states 'that a very great deficiency exists in the means of educating the poor wherever the population is thin and scattered over country districts. The efforts of individuals combined in societies are almost wholly confined to populous places.'

On the 4th of May, 1835, Lord Brougham brought the subject of National Education before the House of Lords, by moving a series of resolutions, among which were the following :—

'1. That although the number of schools, where some of the elementary branches of education are taught, are greatly increased within the last twenty years; yet, that there exists a great deficiency of such schools, especially in the metropolis and other great towns, and that the means of elementary education are peculiarly deficient in the counties of Middlesex and Lancaster.

'2. That the kind of education given at the greater number of schools now established for the poorer classes of the people is of a kind by no means sufficient for their instruction, being for the most part confined to reading, writing, and a little arithmetic; whereas, at no greater expense, and in the same time, the children might easily be instructed in the elements of the more useful branches of knowledge, and thereby trained to sober, industrious, prudent, and virtuous habits.

'3. That the number of Infant Schools is exceedingly deficient, and especially in those great towns where they are most wanted, for improving the morals of the people, and preventing the commission of crimes.

'4. That, while it is expedient to do nothing which may relax the efforts of private beneficence, in forming and supporting schools, or which may discourage the poorer classes of the people from contributing to the cost of educating their children, it is incumbent upon Parliament to aid in providing the effectual means of instruction, where these cannot be obtained, for the people.

'5. That it is incumbent upon Parliament to encourage, in like manner, the establishment of Infant Schools, especially in the larger towns.

'6. That, for the purpose of improving the kind of education given at schools for the people at large, it is expedient to establish, in several parts of the country, seminaries where good schoolmasters may be trained, and taught the duties of their profession.'

The Committee on the education of the poorer classes, over which Mr. Slaney presided in 1838, in their Report say, 'they apprehend that they have ample grounds for stating, throughout this vast metropolis, the means of useful daily instruction are lamentably deficient. It must be borne in mind, that in the various valuable Reports made by the Statistical Societies of Manchester and London, and in much of the evidence adduced before your Committee, the worthless nature of the education supposed to be given in the common Day and Dame Schools, has been dwelt upon; so that in many places it may be left almost out of account.'

Your Committee now turn to the state of education in the large manufacturing and seaport towns, where the population has rapidly increased within the present century; they refer for particulars to the evidence taken before them, which appears to bear out the following results:—

'1. That the kind of education given to the children of the working classes is lamentably deficient.

'2. That it extends (bad as it is) to but a small proportion of those who ought to receive it.

'3. That, without *some strenuous and persevering efforts be made on the part of the Government*, the greatest evils to all classes may follow from this neglect.'

Place.	Population.	Children of Working Classes at Daily Schools, &c.		Total.
		Day and Dame Schools very indifferent.	Other better Schools.	
1836. Liverpool	230,000	11,336	14,024	25,360*
1834. Manchester	200,000	11,520	5680	17,200*
1835. Salford †	50,810	3340	2015	5355*
—— Bury	20,000	1648	803	2451
1835. { Ashton, Dukenfield, Staleybridge }	47,800	. . .	. . .	2496
1837. Birmingham	100,000	8180	4697	12,877‡
1837. Bristol	112,438	4135	1119	5254
1838. Brighton§ { B. and F. / National. }	40,634 in 1831	Not including Private Schools. { 1367 / 863 }	{ 3033 / 3247 }	{ 4400 / 4110 }
1838. Leeds . B. & F.	123,393 in 1831	No return of Dame or Day, but only of Public Schools.	2971	—
1838. Sheffield ‖	96,692 in 1831	3359	5905	9264
Northampton . { B. and F. / National. }	20,000	{ 1011 / 996 }	{ 1215 / 1202 }	{ 2226 / 2198 }
Reading . B. & F.	15,595 in 1831	297	962	1259
Exeter	28,242 in 1831	2045	1830 Including Evening.	3875
1836. York ¶	25,259 in 1831	1494	2697	4191

The returns made to the Education Inquiry, undertaken in 1833 on the motion of Lord Kerry, were, from the great imperfection of our administrative machinery, exceedingly incorrect, as has been proved by the subsequent investigations of societies and individuals. At the period of this inquiry, the population of England and Wales was

* Vide Reports of Statistical Society.
† Report of Manchester Statistical Society on a Manufacturing District, read at British Association. Ridgway, 1837.
‡ Vide Evidence, Riddall Wood.
§ Where 'B. & F.' or 'National' are mentioned, it only means that the returns came through the Secretaries of those Societies.
‖ Report (B. & F.) excluding superior and middling Schools.
¶ Report of Statistical Society of Manchester, 1837.

Note. The general result of all these Towns is, that about one in twelve receive some sort of daily instruction, but only about one in twenty-four an education likely to be useful. In Leeds, only one in forty-one; in Birmingham, one in thirty-eight; in Manchester, one in thirty-five.

14,314,102 ; and the number of children between the ages of three and fifteen, estimated as bearing the same ratio to the population as in 1821, was 4,294,230 ; and the returns to the Education Inquiry give 1,276,947 children as in receipt of daily instruction. We must recur to the Report of the Parliamentary Committee of 1838 for the quality of that instruction, which, being for the most part conveyed in Dame and common Day Schools, is to be regarded as almost worthless, if not, in many instances, pernicious. The number returned as attending Sunday Schools, in 1833, was 1,548,890, which is to be regarded as a cheering indication of the extent of the means at present in existence for procuring an observance of the Sunday among the children of the labouring classes, and of conveying to them a limited amount of religious instruction upon that day, but cannot be accepted as an indication of the amount of the efficient means for the intellectual development and moral and religious training of the children of our working classes. The children between the ages of three and seven, estimated as bearing the same ratio to the population as in 1821, was 1,574,551 ; and all under this age must be regarded as fit only for Dame and Infant Schools.

But we have already remarked, that the returns to the Parliamentary Inquiry of 1833 are utterly insufficient to test the quality and extent of education in England and Wales ; we must therefore have recourse to some of the laborious investigations, conducted impartially by Statistical Societies, into the extent of education provided for the poorer classes in certain districts.

In the Report of the Manchester Statistical Society, respecting the state of education in Manchester, Salford, Liverpool, Bury, and York, we find the population estimated as 533,000 ; and it has been calculated that the number of children of the working classes, from three to thirteen, for whom daily education should be provided, is 80,050 (one-third having been deducted from the whole number of children between three and thirteen, for those privately educated, or employed, or sick, or prevented by casualties from attending School, and deducting the number attending superior private Schools); of these children 21,957 attend Endowed and Charity Schools, National and Lancasterian, and Schools attached to public institutions, and Infant Schools.

Further, of the total number of 80,050 children who ought to be educated, 29,259 receive an almost worthless instruction in Dame and common Day Schools, leaving 28,834 uneducated in any Week-day Schools. Therefore 58,093 *children out of* 80,050, *either receive no weeekly instruction, or instruction only in Dame or common Day Schools.*

The Reports of the Manchester Statistical Society show the inefficiency of the instruction given in the Dame and common Day Schools, which is confirmed by the Report of the Parliamentary Committee of 1838, which we have already quoted. In our Appendix, No. 1, we have given, in a tabular form, summaries of the results of these investigations.

Whenever inquiries of a similar character have been conducted in rural districts, they have exhibited an equally lamentable deficiency of the means of primary instruction; and as the physical agencies of civilisation are in less active operation in rural districts than in towns, we fear that a large portion of our labouring population have already realised the description given by Adam Smith of the working classes of a nation whose instruction has been neglected by the Government.

What might be accomplished for the advancement of civilisation, and for the eradication of crime, by the introduction of a more efficient primary education of the working classes, may in some slight degree be estimated from the following facts, showing the proportion of offenders to their respective intellectual conditions in the years 1836, 1837, and 1838 :—

	1836.	1837.	1838.
Wholly uninstructed, or having received only the first rudiments of learning	85·85	87·93	87·81
Able to read and write well	10·56	9·46	8·77
Instructed beyond reading and writing	0·91	0·43	0·34
Intellectual condition not known	2·68	2·18	2·08
	100	100	100

From this rule of moral inefficiency we fear we cannot exclude any class of Schools as at present conducted, for the methods of teaching which at present prevail commit the instruction of the children even of our National and Lancasterian Schools chiefly, if not solely, to the most proficient boys and girls; and from these it is apparent that little or no *moral influence* capable of elevating the character of the scholars can proceed. The training of the habits and affections, and the adoption of systematic means to develop either the faculties or the feelings of the children, are therefore necessarily neglected. Such acquirements as are made in these Schools result almost solely from an effort of the memory, which receives a meagre supply of the most rudimentary knowledge, while in a great number, if not the majority, of instances, as this knowledge is received with distaste, it is not retained long after the children leave the School, and besides, exerting no influence on the character in after life, is of little use in enabling its possessor even to improve his physical condition. But what is most lamentable, we may say most fearful, is the fact which Professor Pillans and Mr. Wood have fully exposed, that the religious instruction consists, chiefly, if not solely, in committing to memory catechisms and formularies which are neither explained nor understood, and that thus not only are the great truths of Christianity not recommended to the rational capacity of the child, but the sympathies which they are calculated to rouse and to develop, and which form so essential a part of a lively faith and an operative sentiment of devotion, are left uncultivated. While, however, we depict, with deep regret, the defects of the existing system of primary education, we render our hearty thanks to those individuals and societies, particularly the National and British and Foreign, which have taken even the first step in the intellectual advancement of the people; but we request them to contemplate with us with apprehension the facts disclosed in the following Table, resulting from an examination respecting the education of 1052 prisoners in the Penitentiary at Millbank:—

EDUCATION OF PRISONERS IN THE PENITENTIARY.

		Total Number.	Of whom could not read.	Proportion of those who could not read to Total.
Schools connected with the Church.	National School	66	1	1 in 66
	Charity Schools, not on the National System	96	7	1 in 14
	Sunday School—Church of England	96	18	1 in 5
Schools connected with Dissenters.	Sunday Schools—Dissenters	28	1	1 in 28
	Lancasterian, or Dissenting Schools	19	1	1 in 19
Common Day Schools		598	43	1 in 4
Attended no School of any kind		149		

SUMMARY.

Total Number educated in Schools connected with the Church . 258 of whom could not read 26, or 1 in 10

Total Number educated in Schools connected with Dissenters . 47 of whom could not read 2, or 1 in 23

Total Number educated in common Day Schools . . . . 598 of whom could not read 43, or 1 in 14

Total of the above . 903 of whom could not read 71, or 1 in 13
Number who attended no School of any kind 149

1052

The results contained in the foregoing Table are abundantly confirmed in all their details by the records of the prisons for juvenile offenders in this country.

Lord John Russell, in his Letter to the Lord President

of the Council, says, 'The reports of the chaplains of gaols show that to a large number of unfortunate prisoners a knowledge of the fundamental truths of natural and revealed religion has never been imparted.'

The Report of the Chaplain respecting the prisoners of the county gaol at Bedford in 1838, states 'that their great leading characteristic was ignorance, heathenish ignorance of the simplest truths.' At Midsummer Quarter Session he reported, that ' as to the condition, mentally and morally, of his unhappy charge, he regretted to say it could scarcely be more ignorant or degraded. It was his conviction that no pen could depict in colours sufficiently dark the moral and spiritual ignorance and debasement of the vastly greater number of those unhappy beings who pass through the prisons.'[1]

Respecting the county gaol of Hertford, the Visiting Magistrates report, 'The schoolmaster has been regular and diligent in discharging the duties of his office. During the year there have been 72 discharged, exclusive of those who did not fall under his notice and instruction, of whom 30 had been taught to read the Psalms and New Testament imperfectly, or so far to improve themselves as to read well. Of the rest, some have progressed to a knowledge of most words of two syllables, and the remainder were totally ignorant, the short periods of their imprisonment not admitting of improvement.'

The Report of the Chaplain of the House of Correction at Preston says, 'The following Table shows the amount of ignorance in the 1129 individuals committed for various offences during the year, and the connection subsisting between that and the causes which have led to their offences :—

---

[1] Gaol Returns under 4 Geo. IV. c. 64, and 5 Geo. IV. c. 12, dated 20th Feb. 1839.

DEGREES OF EDUCATION.	CAUSES OF CRIME.								
	Drinking.	Uncertain.	Idleness and Bad Company.	Temptation.	Want.	Confirmed Bad Habits.	Weak Intellects.	Combination of Workmen.	Total.
1. Unable to read . . .	139	215	49	5	59	72	7	8	554
2. Barely capable of reading .	57	92	12	4	24	32	1		222
3. Can read the Testament . .	46	61	5	2	19	21		1	155
4. Can read fluently . . .	14	14	1	1	3	4		1	38
5. Can read well, and write a little	71	50	6	3	17	5			152
6. Can read and write well . .	4	3		1					8
	331	435	73	16	122	134	8	10	1129

'If we consider the educated criminals as represented by the amount of those who are able to "read and write well," the proportion is remarkably small; and the inference surely must be, that education prevents or restrains crime, either by the operation of those good and religious principles which it should be its great object to communicate, or, at the least, by giving a taste and capacity for pursuits incompatible with the low and debasing propensities which open the door to crime for the ignorant and sensual. On the other hand, it is evident that the greatest absolute amount of crime is the result of ignorance and drinking combined. It is also, I think, specially worthy of observation, that, as the scale of instruction rises, intoxication begins to exhibit itself as a gradually increasing cause of crime, until, with the educated, it appears paramount over every other which can be distinctly ascertained.'

The following is an extract from the Report of the Chaplain of the County Gaol at Warwick, on the condition of the criminals confined in that prison, presented at the Michaelmas Sessions in 1836:—

'Their condition, as regards education, is this: of every twenty-four who are committed, on an average seven have been taught to read and write; eight can read only; and nine can do neither; most of those who can write can read tolerably well, though their writing is generally a very poor performance; but at least the half of those who can read only, do it very badly. With regard to those important parts of education, religion and morality, generally speaking, no instruction whatever appears to have been given to them; for, in a vast majority of instances, the persons who come to prison are utterly ignorant both of the simplest truths of religion, and of the plainest precepts of morality. Further, it seldom happens that any effort has been made to bring the reasoning faculties into healthy exercise; and the mind being thus left blank, as far as regards everything that is good, it ceases to be a wonder that evil principles should so readily be adopted. Indeed, where such a miserable system of education is found, as appears to prevail in many places, it were much better that nothing were attempted; for people often appear to learn only just sufficient to render ignorance conceited, and to supply them with fresh incentives to vice. As far as regards religious worship, it is very true that at some period of their lives most of the prisoners have attended a place of worship of some denomination, but very few have been taught to consider this as an imperative duty, but rather as a matter of indifference, which perhaps it may be better to do than leave undone.'

Many similar extracts might be given from the Reports of other chaplains of gaols, all confirmatory of the brutal state of ignorance exhibited by almost all the offenders who come under their observation; but these may suffice. We have, however, placed in the Appendix a Table containing a summary of the proficiency of the prisoners in Norwich Castle in reading and writing at the time of their commitment, taken at different periods, from 1826 to 1835.[1]

But the consequences flowing from this neglect are not fully exhibited in such returns. The expense of the penal administration for the prevention, detection, and punishment of crime in England and Wales, amounts to

---

[1] See Appendix, Table No. II.

£1,213,082,[1] and the number of juvenile offenders in the prisons last year was 12,000.

On the 12th of February, 1839, by her Majesty's command, Lord John Russell laid upon the table of the House of Commons the letter which he addressed by her Majesty's command to the President of the Council, with Lord Lansdowne's reply. His Lordship's letter commences with words which cannot be too attentively considered,—'My Lord, I have received her Majesty's command to make a communication to your Lordship on a subject of the greatest importance. Her Majesty has observed, with deep concern, the want of instruction which is still observable among the poorer classes of her subjects. All the inquiries which have been made show a deficiency in the general education of the people, which is not in accordance with the character of a civilised and Christian nation.'

In the Treatise on the Wealth of Nations, Adam Smith thus describes the condition of a people whose education is neglected by the Government:—

'In the progress of the division of labour, the employment of the far greater part of those who live by labour, that is, of the great body of the people, comes to be confined to a few very simple operations—frequently to one or two. But the understandings of the greater part of men are necessarily formed by their ordinary employments. The man whose whole life is spent in performing a few simple operations, of which the effects too are perhaps always the same, or very nearly the same, has no occasion to exert his understanding, or to exercise his invention, in finding out expedients for removing difficulties which never occur. He naturally loses, therefore, the habit of exertion, and generally becomes as stupid and ignorant as is possible for a human creature to become. The torpor of his mind renders him not only incapable of relishing or bearing a part in any rational conversation, but of conceiving any generous, noble, or tender sentiment, and consequently of

---

[1] See Returns for 1834 and 1838.

forming any just judgment concerning many even of the ordinary duties of private life. Of the great and extensive interests of his country he is altogether incapable of judging; and unless very particular pains have been taken to render him otherwise, he is equally incapable of defending his country in war. The uniformity of his stationary life naturally corrupts the courage of his mind, and makes him regard with abhorrence the irregular, uncertain, and adventurous life of a soldier. It corrupts even the activity of his body, and renders him incapable of exerting his strength with vigour and perseverance in any other employment than that to which he has been bred. His dexterity at his own particular trade seems in this manner to be acquired at the expense of his intellectual, social, and martial virtues. But in every improved or civilised society, this is the state into which the labouring poor, that is, the great body of the people, must necessarily fall, unless Government takes some pains to prevent it.'—B. v. c. i.

The calamity thus foreseen by our great economist is realised in the condition of our rural population. The abuses of the poor laws, together with the almost universal neglect of instruction, have reduced this class to a state of mental and physical torpor. The gradual absorption of our domestic manufactures in the great vortices of trade, left in the south-eastern counties of England a larger population on the soil than could be supported in comfort by agricultural labour only; yet the labourer, reduced to the condition of a serf, was incapable of any independent exertions to procure employment by removing to the great seats of commerce, or embarking in some new sphere of enterprise, like the more adventurous, because more intelligent, Scottish population. Though the labouring class in these counties must often have suffered from continued want, few or none could be induced to emigrate—few or no recruits for the army could be procured—their struggles were confined to stupid contests with the overseer, in which they suffered their wages to be swindled away. Then, when they found industry had no reward—that all were bound to toil, but had a right to be maintained like helots—acts of secret and sullen revenge ensued. They sought to extort by fear what they could no longer procure by virtuous exertion. Property seemed their enemy; therefore they wrapped in one indiscriminating flame the stacks and homesteads of the southern counties, seeking the improvement of their condition by the destruction of capital.

On the other hand, the rapid progress of our physical civilisation has occasioned the growth of masses of manufacturing population, the instruction, and moral, and religious elevation of which have hitherto been neglected by the State. These communities exhibit alarming features; labouring classes, unmatched in the energy and hardihood with which they pursue their daily toil, yet thriftless, incapable of husbanding their means, or resisting sensual gratification; high wages and want under the same roof; while other portions of the same classes are struggling on the barest pittance with continual labour, abstinent by necessity. From opposite quarters misery and discontent are goading both. The Rev. Mr. Close, perpetual Curate of Cheltenham, says, in a sermon just published, 'It is a well-known fact that, in the manufacturing districts, where the highest wages are obtained, the greatest poverty often prevails; where money is easily acquired, it is as quickly spent, and often in feasting as well as drunkenness; persons in this rank of life will not unfrequently discover a degree of extravagance in the gratification of their appetites, which would astonish those who are much their superiors in station; expending a week's wages in one feast, heedless of the wants of their families to-morrow.' At the next door to the highly-paid artisan, who has squandered his week's earnings on the Sunday's feast, pines the hand-loom weaver, exhausted with continual penury and toil.

Physical prosperity stimulates all the animal appetites, and, if unaided by moral restraint, wastes her resources, and, instead of connecting content and peace with plenty, continually rouses the population to feverish exertion. Notwithstanding the high wages of the artisan, the wife commits her infant to an hireling, and leaves her domestic duties to work in the manufactory. The parents, to enable ill-regulated means to satisfy increasing wants, lead their children of a tender age to the same scene of continual exertion. Domestic virtue and household piety have little opportunity to thrive in a population alternating between protracted labour and repose, or too frequent sensual gratification. When all the animal powers are thus continually called into action, adversity is met with sullen discontent, or with fierce outbreaks of passionate disquiet. Whoever will promise less toil and more money, is a prophet in the manufacturing districts; and — in the absence of those who would teach, that comfort can only be secured by a cultivation of those domestic sympathies and household virtues, which spring from a well-regulated mind, and prove that happiness depends upon those internal moral resources, without which the greatest prosperity is often a curse — prophets will always be found ready to teach the population to seek a remedy for the evils they endure by violent attempts at social change. To the ignorant man, who has only the sense of the continual necessity to labour, in order to gratify his unappeased desires for sensual gratification, and to meet the wants created by wasted means, who can be more welcome than he who comes with the golden promise of high wages and ease, instead of leading him to an enlightened estimate of his domestic and social duties, and teaching him how much a resolute will, under the influence of morality and religion, may do, even in adverse circumstances, to render the lot of the poor man peaceful and happy? Less work and more means have always, therefore, been the promises of every impostor who has practised on the ignorance, discontent, and suffering of the manufacturing population.

We shall have to speak, in subsequent pages, of the political and social combinations which have of late prevailed in the manufacturing districts; the Trades' Unions, in which incendiarism, personal violence, and even assassination, are practised for the unattainable object of sustaining the rate of wages above the level resulting from the natural laws of trade; and the more recent armed associations for political purposes, in which the working classes have been exhorted to obtain by force privileges withheld by the constitutional representatives of the people; results, which are all ascribable to the fact that the physical development of the population has been more rapid than the growth of our intellectual, moral, and religious institutions.

On the other hand, it is cheering to know, that the accumulation of the people in masses renders them more accessible to the beneficial influence of well-regulated social institutions. Having once encountered the necessity of supplying the intellectual and moral wants of the labouring classes, knowledge and virtue will, with adequate agencies, make more rapid progress among a concentrated than a scattered population. So long as our artisans lived in cottages scattered over the moors of our northern, and the wolds of our southern counties, little danger might arise to the State from their universal ignorance, apathy, and want; but if the necessity for raising their moral and intellectual condition could, under such circumstances, have been as pressing as it now is, the difficulty of civilising them would have been almost insuperable. In the concentrated population of our towns, the dangers arising from the neglect of the intellectual and moral culture of the working class are already imminent; and the consequences of permitting another generation to rise, without bending the powers of the executive government and of society to the great work of civilisation and religion, for which the political and social events of every hour make a continual demand, must be social disquiet little short of revolution. But the same masses of population are equally open to all the beneficial influences derivable from a careful cultivation of their domestic and social habits;

from the communication of knowledge enabling them to perceive their true relation to the other classes of society, and how dependent their interests are upon the stability of our institutions and the preservation of social order.

The law recognises the duty devolving on property, as respects the education of the factory children; and we rejoice to believe that, under the guidance of men of high intelligence and benevolence, such as many of the most wealthy manufacturers are, we shall soon realise what are the fruits of a well-devised system of intellectual, moral, and religious training, in rendering the communities, in whose well-being they have so deep a stake, examples of what may be effected by applying to the moral elevation of the population the same sagacity and perseverance which have occasioned its physical prosperity. A short time only will elapse before, in some of our great towns, the most influential inhabitants will combine for the erection and support of Model Schools. Such institutions will create and diffuse a more correct estimate of the value of Education, and will promote its spread.

For another neglected class also the State has interfered. Under the parochial system, the orphan, deserted, and illegitimate children—waifs of society—were scattered through the parochial workhouses of England, where they were promiscuously mingled with the idiots, the sick, the sturdy vagabond, and profligate women. From the parochial workhouses, the gaols and hulks recruited the ranks of crime. These children are now under the care of Boards of Guardians, separated from the adult paupers, and measures are in progress to educate them so as to render them efficient and virtuous members of society.

For the juvenile offenders the Government is carefully preparing a system of reformatory discipline and training, in which all the resources of the educator will be exhausted to redeem these outcasts from the depravity consequent on neglect and evil example.

Besides these signs of coming improvement, we hail, as a presage of no little importance, the fact that the subject of National Education has occupied the attention of the Houses of Parliament during five nights of anxious discussion. We never were so sanguine as to expect that the great embarrassments with which it is surrounded could be at once dispelled; but we have a confident belief that every hour increases the anxiety of all friends of our constitutional liberties and national institutions, to preserve both by the education of the people.

CHAPTER II.

RESULTS OF REFORMATION IN EUROPEAN PROTESTANT STATES — SCOTLAND — PRUSSIA — CONFEDERATION OF THE RHINE — SWITZERLAND — SWEDEN — NORWAY — DENMARK — HOLLAND, ETC.— CONDITION IN CATHOLIC STATES — BELGIUM — FRANCE — COMPARATIVE RESOURCES IN ENGLAND.

ONE of the early consequences of the Reformation in Europe, with the exception of England, was the establishment of a system of elementary instruction. It was a natural consequence of the assertion of the right of private judgment, that every Government should charge itself with the duty of raising the standard of knowledge among the mass of the people. Thus a century and a half have elapsed since the system of parochial education was established by an Act of the Scottish Parliament, and we may now trace, in the industry, enterprise, and foresight of our Scottish fellow-subjects, and above all, in their household virtues and earnest patriotism—in their domestic piety and reverence for the public institutions and ceremonial of religion, the consequences of a system of National Education, which, whatever be its imperfections—and they are numerous,— is in many respects adapted to the genius of their nation. Prussia, as early as 1736, declared the elementary education of the people to be an essential part of the policy of the State. In that year she provided for the erection and repair of school-houses by the communes; regulated the duties and privileges of the teachers; appropriated portions of the Church revenues to the provision of their salaries; and provided from the public funds means to meet the contingent expenses of the Schools. This law underwent successive improvements in the years 1763 and

1765. These edicts also provided for the inspection and due regulation of the Schools; for the transmission of Reports to the Government; for the examination of teachers by the School inspectors; and for the elevation of some of the principal Schools of the newly acquired territory of Silesia to the character of Normal Schools. The preamble to the first of these statutes describes the condition of the elementary instruction of Prussia, in terms singularly appropriate to that of the primary education of England at this moment. The training of the rising population was extremely inefficient, on account of the incompetency of the teachers: in wide districts of the country the training of the children of the working class was almost utterly neglected. The spread of true religion—the maintenance of social order—the diffusion of useful knowledge and virtuous habits, and the cultivation of the industrial arts—could not be secured excepting by a system of education capable of raising the people from ignorance, and, in some districts, from semi-barbarism.[1]

---

[1] The late President of the United States, in his Letters on Silesia, thus describes the Schools which Frederick the Great established in every village of Silesia. 'At the time of the conquest of Silesia,' says Mr. Adams, 'education had seldom been made an object of the concern of Governments, and Silesia, like the rest of Europe, was but wretchedly provided either with Schools or teachers. In the small towns and villages, the schoolmasters were so poorly paid, that they could not subsist without practising some other trade besides their occupation as instructors; and they usually united the character of the Village Fiddler with that of the Village Schoolmaster. Even of these there were so few, that the children of the peasants in general, throughout the province, were left untaught. This was especially the case in Upper Silesia. Frederick issued an ordinance, that a School should be kept in every village, and that a competent subsistence should be provided for the schoolmaster, by the joint contributions of the lord of the village, and of the tenants: the superintendence of the Schools was prescribed as the duty of the Clergy.'

Mr. Adams then relates how Frederick carried into execution his great design; he describes the mission of Felbiger, to acquire a knowledge of the latest improvements in the art of teaching, and the consequent establishment of Model Schools at Breslau and Glatz, for the training of educators for the primary Schools.

'After all these preparatory measures had been carried into effect,' he says, 'an ordinance was published in the year 1765, prescribing the mode of teaching as adopted in the seminaries, and the manner in which the

We have not space to describe the consequences which followed the exertions of the Prussian Government, until the disastrous war of 1806 involved Prussia in embarrassments, which, for a time, impeded the progress of her social institutions. Nevertheless, even when she was subjected to the incursion of foreign armies, or to a foreign yoke, her Normal Schools had, between 1806 and 1816,

Clergy should superintend the efficacious establishment of the system. The regulations of this ordinance prove the earnestness with which the King of Prussia laboured to spread the benefits of useful knowledge among his subjects. The teachers are directed to give plain instruction, and upon subjects applicable to the ordinary concerns of life; not merely to load the memory of their scholars with words, but to make things intelligible to their understanding; to habituate them to the use of their own reason, by explaining every object of the lesson, so that the children themselves may be able to explain it upon examination. The candidates for school-keeping must give specimens of their ability, by teaching at one of the schools connected with the seminary, in presence of the professors, that they may remark and correct any thing defective in the candidate's method. The school tax must be paid by the lord and tenants, without distinction of religions. The boys must all be sent to school from their sixth to their thirteenth year, whether the parents are able to pay the school-tax or not, for the poor, the school money must be raised by collections. Every parent or guardian who neglects to send his child or pupil to school, without sufficient cause, is obliged to pay a double tax, for which the guardian shall have no allowance. Every curate must examine weekly the children of the school in his parish. A general examination must be held annually by the deans of the districts of the schools within their respective precincts; and a report of the condition of the schools, the talents and attention of the schoolmasters, the state of the buildings, and the attendance of the children, made to the office of the Vicar-General, who is bound to transmit all these reports to the royal domain offices, from which orders are issued to supply the deficiencies in the schools.. This system was at first prepared only for the Catholic schools; but it was afterwards adopted by most of the Lutheran consistories.

'The system had at first many difficulties to contend with. The indolence of the Catholic clergy was averse to the new and troublesome duty imposed upon them. Their zeal was alarmed at the danger arising from this diffusion of light to the stability of their Church; they considered alike the spirit of innovation, and the spirit of inquiry, as their natural enemies. But the firmness of the Government overcame every obstacle. There are now more than 3500 schools established in the province. Before the Seven Years' war, there had not been more than one periodical journal or gazette published in the province at one time; while there are now no fewer than seventeen newspapers and magazines, which appear by the day, the week, the month, and the quarter, and many of them upon subjects generally useful, and which contain very valuable information on all the most interesting topics of discussion.'

increased from six to sixteen. A special department for the superintendence of public worship, public instruction, and medicine, was created by an ordinance issued on the Peace of Tilsit in 1810, and successive ordinances have regulated the whole details of public instruction, into the system of which we cannot now enter.

At the present moment, the extent of the existing provision for the education of the poorer classes, is remarkable. There are forty-five schools for the training of teachers in the several provinces, which are constantly educating 2583 teachers; but so vigilant is the Prussian Government, that the official reports state that a considerable number of the teachers still entrusted with the management of schools, have hitherto not obtained certificates of competency, and the annual supply of teachers is not adequate to the demand created by casualties, and the retirement of teachers from age and other causes. To the supply of these wants the attention of the Government is constantly directed.

In 1838, Prussia contained a population of 14,000,000; the number of public schools was 22,910, in which 27,575 teachers were employed, who educated 2,171,745 children (or one teacher to seventy-eight scholars); besides which, 117,982 children were educated at Middle and Burgher schools. The number of children between five and fifteen, or of an age to go to school, was 2,830,328; the number of children receiving instruction in the schools was 2,289,727, so that only 540,601 children were not at school, in the whole body of children, between the ages of five and fifteen. The proportion of children at school to the population, being as one to six, it may be considered that the extent of the provision for education in Prussia is complete as to quantity, though as regards quality, it is still susceptible of considerable improvement. In the great towns of Prussia, the proportion of children at school to the population was, in Berlin, one in ten; in Breslau, one in nine; in Cologne with Deuz, one in eight; in Konigsberg, one in nine; in Danzig, one in eleven; in Magdeburg, one in eight; in Elberfeld with Barmen, one in seven; in Aix-la-Chapelle, one in thirteen; in Posen, one in thirteen; in Stettin, one in ten. The interference with primary instruction in towns occasioned by the early employment of children in the manufactories, by the less settled habits of the population, and by other causes, is greater than in the country; and the proportion of one in eight has been generally deemed a complete provision for the education of the poorer classes in towns. Though the number of children attending school in the principal cities of Prussia falls short of this proportion, it is greatly superior to the whole number attending school in the great towns of this country, even including the ill-regulated common day and dame schools. The Prussian regulations respecting education are adapted to the character of the people, and in harmony with the general policy of the Government. The state of education in Prussia may be employed as a means of comparison between the extent and quality of the means of instruction existing in that country and our own, while we carefully bear in mind that any measures which may be adopted by the Government of this country may be required to differ as widely from the ordinances of Prussia as the character of the English people and the nature of the laws and institutions of this country differ from those of the Prussian nation.

The condition of education in some of the states of Germany is, perhaps, superior to that of any other portion of Europe. The development of primary instruction in Saxe Weimar and Wurtemburg has, during the present century, been promoted by one of the greatest minds of modern times, which embodied the national characteristics of the genius of his countrymen so as to command their universal homage. We avail ourselves of a luminous account of the state of education in Germany, and its legitimate consequences, given in the Journal of Education[1], by the

[1] 'The change for the better, consequent on the system of instruction introduced into Prussia, seems to be inferior to that which has followed the

learned and experienced traveller, Mr. Loudon, whose powers of observation and impartiality will command

introduction of National Schools into Wirtemburg, Baden, Bavaria, and generally in all those states included in what was formerly denominated the Confederation of the Rhine. In Wirtemburg, indeed, the inhabitants have been pretty well supplied with the means of education for near a century past; but during the last thirty years, the system has been very greatly extended and improved. At present, not only in Wirtemburg, but also in Baden, Hesse, &c., a public school is established in every parish, and in some instances, in every hamlet. The Master receives, as in Scotland, a fixed salary from the parish, exclusive of a small fee from the pupils, varying according to their age, and the subjects in which they are instructed. The fees are fixed by Government, and are everywhere the same. Exclusive of the salaries and fees, the Masters are furnished with a house, a garden, and in most instances, a few acres of ground, corresponding to the glebes of the Scotch Clergy. The law requires that the children should be instructed in reading, writing, and arithmetic, and it is specially enacted that they shall be instructed in the principles of German grammar and in composition. The books used in the schools of Wirtemburg and Baden, and generally throughout Germany, are very superior to those used in similar establishments in this country. They consist of geographical, biographical, and historical works, and of elementary treatises on moral science, natural history, and the principles and practice of some of the most important and useful arts. In all the larger schools, the boys and girls are kept separate, and the latter, in addition to reading, writing, and arithmetic, are taught all sorts of needle-work, the knitting of stockings, the making of clothes, &c. receiving at the same time lessons in the art of cookery, the management of children, &c. The supervision of the schools is intrusted, in every parish or commune, to a committee, consisting of a few of the principal inhabitants; the clergy of the parish, whether Protestants or Catholics, being always ex-officio members of the Committee. This body is intrusted with the duty of inspecting the school, and is bound to see that the Master does his duty, and that the children regularly attend. No particular system of religion is allowed to be taught in any of the schools of Wirtemburg, and most of the other Germanic States. The tuition of this important branch is left entirely to the Clergy, and the parents of the children, so that the sons and daughters of Catholics, Lutherans, Calvinists, Quakers, &c. frequent the same schools, and live in the most perfect harmony.

' In Bavaria, the beneficial consequences resulting from the establishment of a system of National Education have been more signal than in any other European country. Half a century ago, the Bavarians were the most ignorant, debauched, and slovenly people between the Gulf of Genoa and the Baltic. (For proofs of what is now stated, see Riesbeck's "Travels in Germany," vol. i. cap. xi.) That they are at present patterns of morality, intelligence, and cleanliness, it would be going too far to affirm; but we are bold to say, that no people has ever made a more rapid advancement in the career of civilisation, than they have made during the last thirty years. The late and present Kings of Bavaria, have been truly the fathers of their country; for they have not only swept away myriads of abuses, and established a representative system of government, but they have laid the only universal respect, and whose statements are so important as to deserve quotation, without abridgment. We have, therefore, placed them in a note.

The schools in the Protestant Cantons of Switzerland have long been under the direction of a Council of Education, appointed by the Government, and are frequented by one-sixth to one-tenth of the population. Considerable

> sure foundations of permanent and real improvement, in the organisation of a truly admirable system of National Education. A school has been established in every parish of Bavaria, to which, as already observed, every one is obliged to send his children, from the age of six to fourteen. Lyceums, Colleges, and Universities, have also been instituted for the use of those who are desirous of prosecuting their studies, and every facility is afforded for the acquisition of the best instruction at the lowest price. In Bavaria the schools are inspected, and reports regularly made upon their condition by properly qualified officers, appointed for that purpose by Government. There is a particular department in the Ministry of the Interior appropriated to the supervision of the different kinds of schools. We subjoin a list of the places of primary education, and the number of teachers, pupils, &c. in Bavaria in 1828.
>
> | | |
> |---|---|
> | Public or National Schools | 5394 |
> | Normal Schools | 7 |
>
> TEACHERS AND PUPILS.
>
> | | |
> |---|---|
> | Inspectors of Schools | 286 |
> | Teachers | 7114 |
> | Pupils of all classes, about | 498,000 |
>
> 'Now, as the population of Bavaria is almost exactly four millions, it follows that not less than one-eighth of the entire population is at school. This is a very high proportion, and shows conclusively how universally education is diffused. In Scotland, it is supposed that the individuals at school amount to about one-tenth of the entire population.
>
> 'Throughout Germany the greatest attention is paid, not merely to the acquirements of the Teachers, but also to their capacity for teaching. To ensure proficiency in this respect, normal or pattern schools have been established in all the principal towns, which are attended by those who are candidates for the situation of Master; who, besides being instructed in the branches they are to be employed in teaching, are at the same time instructed in the best methods of teaching, and in the conduct proper to be followed in the management of scholars. Some of these schools very justly enjoy a very high reputation; and their establishment has had the most powerful and salutary influence on the system of instruction. No one is admitted to the pattern schools under thirteen years of age, and candidates are obliged to have made considerable proficiency in various branches. At the famous Normal School of Rastadt, the pupils, among other indispensable requisites, are expected to be masters of the elements of music.'—See *Quarterly Journal of Education*, vol. i. p. 29.

improvements have been introduced into the system of Swiss education during the last sixteen years. Berne, Geneva, Basle, and Argovia have been long distinguished by their zeal, and the Canton de Vaud has recently made great exertions for the improvement of the methods pursued in its schools. Fribourg has been distinguished by the labours of Père Girard, whose schools in that town were the most successful development of the system of mutual instruction, which the Continent has yet witnessed. His method resembled, in some important respects, that pursued by Mr. Wood in the Edinburgh Sessional Schools. In the Protestant Cantons, the average number of pupils to each school is about 90, and the proportion to each teacher 70. No detailed accounts of the Normal Schools of Switzerland have reached this country, but we are informed by intelligent travellers that two Normal Schools exist in the Canton of Berne; a very good one at Lausanne, in the Canton de Vaud; two in Argovia; a very large school at Küsnacht, near Zurich; one in Thurgovia, presided over by Vehrli, whose name is familiar to all who take an interest in the progress of education; two in St. Gall; a school in Appenzell, pronounced to be well conducted, and one at Schaffhausen, another in the Catholic Canton of Grisons, and a third in that of Lucerne. Besides these, there are doubtless others of which at present we have no account, and generally it may be stated, that the Protestant Cantons of Switzerland are nearly foremost in Europe, as respects primary education. Throughout these Cantons the superintendence of the schools by a Council of Education, appointed by the Government, and acting by means of Training Schools, and a system of active inspection, has been found not only efficient in promoting the progress of education, but in perfect harmony with the free constitutions of the Swiss Cantons.

In Sweden, Gustavus Vasa, in 1527, diffused the Lutheran doctrine over the whole country. This change in the religious institutions of the country harmonised with the wants and character of the people of that age. Though, however, the Swedish clergy are still in numbers equal to their task, and though their ecclesiastical discipline is admirable, the Church has ceased to be influenced by the genius of Protestantism. A spiritual tyranny represses the right of private judgment, and the people continue superstitious. In 1684, Charles XI. enacted that every one of his subjects should be able to read, that the curate should examine him in religion before he was admitted to the Holy Sacrament, and that nobody should be married who had not been confirmed. These enactments appear to account for the fact that the Swedish peasantry were, until towards the close of the last century, regarded as the most religious and best instructed working class in Europe. Before the present century, education in Sweden was almost solely parental ; few children attended public schools, but in order to entitle them to the privileges of citizenship, they were instructed and trained by their parents at home. Since the latter part of the last century a rapid deterioration has taken place in Swedish manners and in the moral condition of the population. Mr. Laing traces this degeneration to the influence of a defective social system, in which some of the worst institutions of feudalism corrupt a people aroused from the incurious apathy of the middle ages. The system of parental instruction has been found insufficient to struggle against the demoralising influence of misrule and imperfect laws, discouraging industry and merit, and impoverishing the mass—and the evil example of corrupt manners among the privileged classes. Of late years only has any attempt been made to provide a remedy for these formidable evils.

An elementary school for the training of teachers in the best methods has been established at Stockholm, and a Committee for the revision of Public Education, formed by an order of the King in 1825, have reported their opinions on schools for the common people, on elementary schools, and on the universities. They recommend that a school be established in every parish for the children of the poorer class, where they may be instructed in reading, writing, arithmetic, religion, biblical history, church singing, linear drawing, history, geography, and gymnastic exercises. They also recommend that libraries of useful books be attached to each school. These measures have since the Report of the Committee, been in a state of progressive execution, and Sweden will soon enjoy institutions suited to the character of her people and the wants of the age.

A parochial system of primary instruction is established in Norway resembling that of Scotland, but partaking of the primitive character of the institutions of that country. The funds for the support of schools are generally derived from endowments, from local taxes, subscriptions, &c. Manufacturers employing more than thirty workmen are obliged to provide schools for their children, and to pay the teachers. Several training schools for teachers exist, and it is the intention of the Government to extend and improve them. The population of Norway being thinly scattered over wide mountainous districts, the Government, besides the paid parochial teachers, has provided a class of itinerant teachers, who successively visit the hamlets of their districts, assembling and instructing the children in the usual elementary knowledge. In 1833, the population being about 1,000,000, Mr. Ewerloff stated the *fixed schools*, in Norway, to be 183, instructing 13,693 children of both sexes, and the number of ambulatory schools as 1610, instructing 132,632 children. Besides which there were in the vicinity of towns 55 regular schools, supported by the citizens, in which 600 or 700 children were instructed. (*Journal of Education.*)

In Denmark a general code of regulations for schools has existed since 1817, the condition of the primary instruction having previously to that period made satisfactory progress. The elementary schools of Denmark now amount to 4600, educating 278,500 children. The population is 2,000,000, and it is estimated that there are 300,000 children of an age to go to school. The entire population of Denmark may, therefore, be said to be receiving instruction.

Holland has long enjoyed the advantages of an advancing civilisation. The institutions of the central states of Europe for the promotion of primary education procured, at an early period in the Batavian Republic, spontaneous efforts from a sagacious people for the training and instruction of the poorer classes. The direct interference of the Government was reserved for the present century; and this is in no slight degree to be attributed to the labours of Pestalozzi in Switzerland, which called forth similar exertions from Van den Ende, from Prinsèn, and from Falk. Early in the present century the Normal School at Haarlem was established under the direction of Prinsèn. The superintendence of education was thrown upon the Minister of the Interior, assisted by the Inspector-General of Instruction. From this department a series of well-devised regulations have in successive years emanated, which have been gradually carried into execution by a system of inspection so devised as to be in perfect harmony with the municipal institutions of the country, and the character and feelings of the inhabitants. The inspectors form the medium of communication between the Government, the municipal councils, the provincial authorities, and the committees and directors of schools. It is their duty to foster the exertions of the local communities, and to direct them to useful objects. The inspection of schools; the examination of teachers, and their special authorisation; together with the diffusion of information concerning the best methods of teaching, the proper apparatus, and most useful books, are among the inspectors' duties. Every inspector visits the schools of his district at least twice every year; he has power to appoint local school commissions; but is himself under the authority of a commission of inspectors of each department, which assembles three times a year in the chief town of the province, to examine the reports of the local inspectors, and to discuss and settle all matters relating to the internal regulation of schools. Deputies from each departmental commission are sent to the council of inspectors at the Hague, which assembles annually to confer with the Inspector-General and the Minister of the Interior. Two normal schools now exist in Holland, in which a large body of teachers is trained; but it is a part of the discipline of the Dutch schools to select the most promising pupils, first, as assistants in the more mechanical arrangements of the school, and then to be trained successively in every department, and at the same time to receive such instruction as may fit them, when they arrive at maturity, successfully to perform the duties of teachers in primary schools. Many of the pupils thus reared in the primary schools finish their education in the normal schools. Holland is now one of the best instructed countries in Europe; and the singular prudence, industry, moral habits, and religious feeling of the Dutch people are chiefly attributable to a system of education interwoven with the institutions and with the habits and feelings of the nation. Mr. Nicholls thus describes the connection between the religious and educational institutions of Holland. 'As respects religion, the population of Holland is divided, in about equal proportions, into Catholic, Lutheran, and Protestants of the Reformed Calvinistic Church, and the ministers of each are supported by the state. The schools contain, without distinction, the children of every sect of Christians. The religious and moral instruction afforded to the children is taken from the pages of Holy Writ, and the whole course of education is mingled with a frequent reference to the great general evidences of revelation. Biblical history is taught, not as a dry narrative of facts, but as a storehouse of truths, calculated to influence the affections, to correct and elevate the manners, and to inspire sentiments of devotion and virtue. The great principles and truths of Christianity, in which all are agreed, are likewise carefully inculcated; but those points which are the subjects of difference and religious controversy, form no part of the instructions of the schools. This department of religious teaching is confided to the ministers of each persuasion who discharge this portion of their duties out of the school : but within the schools the common ground of instruction is faithfully preserved, and they are consequently altogether free from the spirit of jealousy and proselytism. We witnessed the exercise of a class of the children of notables in Haarlem (according to the simultaneous method) respecting the death and resurrection of our Saviour, by a minister of the Lutheran Church. The class contained children of Catholics, Calvinists, and other denominations of Christians, as well as Lutherans ; and all disputable doctrinal points were carefully avoided. The Lutherans are the smallest in number, the Calvinists the largest, and the Catholics about midway between the two; but all appear to live together in perfect amity, without the slightest distinction in the common intercourse of life; and this circumstance so extremely interesting in itself, no doubt facilitated the establishment of the general system of education here described, the effects of which are so apparent in the highly moral and intellectual condition of the Dutch people.'

The proceedings of the States of Germany probably suggested to Frederick the great designs which he conceived for the moral, intellectual, and religious improvement of Silesia. From these States the influence of advancing civilisation spread into Switzerland, Sweden, Denmark, and Holland. The wars which succeeded the French Revolution kept back for a time the educational institutions of these states; yet even under a foreign yoke, and in the confusion consequent on rapid political changes, a gradual progress was made; every interval of quiet was, in Germany and Prussia, applied to the reparation of the consequences of foreign invasion, and the general peace was no sooner proclaimed than the Government of every Protestant state on the Continent sought to rescue the people from the demoralisation consequent on a disorganising war, and to prepare the means of future defence in the development of the moral force of her people, England alone appears in this respect to have misunderstood the genius of Protestantism. With the wealthiest and most enlightened aristocracy, the richest and most influential church, and the most enterprising middle class, her lower orders are, as a mass, more ignorant and less civilised than those of any other large Protestant country in Europe.

By reference to the following table, extracted from various authorities, it will be perceived how far we are correct in tracing to the Reformation the great impulse which education has given to the civilisation of Europe.

Proportion of Scholars in Elementary Schools to whole Population.

	Pupil.	Inhabitants.
Thurgovia, Switzerland (1832)	1 in	4·8
Zurich, Switzerland (1832)	1 in	5
Argovia, Switzerland (1832)	1 in	5·3
Bohemia (1833)	1 in	5·7
Wurtemburg	1 in	6
Prussia (1838)	1 in	6
Baden (1830)	1 in	6
Drenthe, Province of, Holland (1835)	1 in	6
Saxony	1 in	6
Province of Overyssel (1835)	1 in	6·2
Canton of Neufchatel (1832)	1 in	6·4
Frise (1833)	1 in	6·8
Norway (1834)	1 in	7
Denmark (1834)	1 in	7
Scotland (1834)	1 in	10·4
Bavaria (1831)	1 in	8
Austria (1832)	1 in	10
Belgium	1 in	11·5
England	1 in	11·5
Lombardy (1832)	1 in	12·6
France	1 in	17·6
Ireland	1 in	18
Roman States	1 in	50
Lucca	1 in	53
Tuscany	1 in	66
Portugal	1 in	88
Russia	1 in	367

In England we have no normal schools deserving of the name; Scotland owes to spontaneous individual exertions the only model schools which exist in that country;

and in Ireland, the Board of Education, obstructed by peculiar difficulties, is proceeding to complete the fabric of an institution for the training of teachers, as a part of the great mission of civilisation with which it is entrusted in that distracted country. Meanwhile the Catholic States of Europe have caught the impulse communicated from Germany to the Protestant Governments. When Belgium was incorporated in the kingdom of the Netherlands, the present King of Holland planned, and carried on for fourteen years, a series of measures for securing to the poorer classes an efficient education, which up to the Belgian Revolution were eminently successful. The entire proceedings of the Dutch Government, as related in the Reports of the Inspector-General of Education, are descriptive of the benefits derivable from a judicious and persevering application of the powers of the Executive to the improvement and extension of primary instruction; while the consequences of the law proclaiming the liberty of teaching, or in other words, abandoning primary education to the spontaneous agencies of society, are to be found in the almost complete ruin of all institutions for the primary education of the people in Belgium.

Since the year 1833, the Minister of the Department of Public Instruction in France has been assiduously employed in the execution of the law of June, 1833, relating to primary instruction in that country. The translation of the reports of M. Cousin on the state of primary instruction in Prussia and in Holland, has made the English public universally acquainted with the inquiry which M. Cousin executed by direction of the French Government in those countries, on the results of which the French law of instruction was founded, and which has served as a guide to the Department of Public Instruction in the execution of that law in France.

In the Report of M. Gillon, on the part of the Commission charged with the examination of the French budget of 1839, it is stated that there are seventy-six normal schools in France, training 2500 teachers. No department now wants an establishment for the training of teachers; but ten are associated with others for the support of a common establishment, and many instructors throughout France are engaged in rearing educators from their most successful pupils.

The state of primary instruction at the end of the year 1837, was as follows:—

Communes without schools	. .	5663	
Communes provided with schools	. .	29,750	
Boys' schools { Communal	. .	30,065 }	39,504
Private	. .	9439 }	
Girls' schools { Communal	. .	5283 }	14,426
Private	. .	9143 }	
			53,930

The want of schools in some departments is still very great. The number of children attending school amounts to 2,654,492, whereas it is calculated from recent official returns of the population that the number of children between the age of five and twelve years, is upwards of 4,800,000; but one-fourth of the children in the schools are above twelve years of age; the number of children therefore between five and twelve in actual attendance on the schools is 1,989,000; and on these premisses it is calculated that there are

Boys	{ At school	. .	1,164,000 }	2,550,000
	{ Not attending school	.	1,386,000 }	
Girls	{ At school	. .	822,000 }	2,250,000
	{ Not attending school	.	1,428,000 }	

From these facts it appears that only five-twelfths of the whole number of children attend school.

The Report proceeds to deplore the fact that 2,811,000 children in France receive no other instruction than that which is given by their parents, the greater part of whom are the hardest worked and the most ignorant of the population. In 1830, however, the number of children of both sexes attending the primary schools was only 1,642,206, since which period an increase of 1,009,000 has occurred. In 1830 there were only 10,000 schools

for girls; now there are 14,000. The Report continues:
—Young people seldom instruct themselves when their
infancy has been neglected. Of this, sufficient proof is
given by the return made respecting those who are called
by their age to partake in the operations of the military
service. A table has been prepared, in which they are
classed according to the degree of instruction. From
1833 to 1836, the proportion of this class who could
neither read nor write was nearly one-half. It should
be remarked that this return relates to young men who
should have been at school between the years 1825 and
1828, a period when primary instruction was encouraged
in France more by the zeal of voluntary associations than
by the intervention of the State. Now the whole influence of the Administration is applied to induce children
to accept the instruction which is offered them, and it is
evident that the number of the illiterate has diminished.

If, continues the Report, the influence of ignorance on
crime were doubted, all uncertainty would be dispelled
by the official table of the persons accused and convicted,
just published by the Minister of Justice, for the Administration of 1836, and which differs but little from previous
returns.

Accused.	Men.	Women.	Total.
Neither able to read nor to write	3172	1067	4239
Imperfectly instructed in reading and writing.	1853	220	2073
Well instructed in reading and writing ...	620	45	665
Having an instruction one degree superior .	248	7	255
	5893	1339	7232

France cannot be cited as a country exhibiting the
effects of a well-devised system of Education on the
moral and religious condition of the people, because
sufficient time has not yet been afforded for the success
of the exertions of the French Government in the improvement and extension of the means of primary

education in that country; neither can France be cited as an example that a high degree of secular instruction is found connected with a diminution of violence, but an increase of the crimes of fraud.

Mr. Porter has shown that M. Guerry's conclusion respecting the diminution of the crimes of violence and the increase of the crimes of fraud in the direct ratio of the extent of primary instruction in France was drawn from one year only (1831), but was not found to be supported, as far as the extent of this increase of the crimes of fraud is concerned, by an examination of the same facts in a series of five years, including that selected by M. Guerry, The yearly average of 1829–30–31–32–33, was as follows in the four *most* instructed departments, and in the *four* least instructed, the population being nearly the same in the departments compared.

	Crimes against person.	Crimes against property.	Total No, of Criminals.	No. upon whom sentence of death, and of forced labour for life, and for terms of years, was passed.
Four most instructed Departments	45	136	181	35
For least instructed Departments	66	132	198	41·6

See Trans. of Statistical Society of London, vol. i. p. 97, folio edition.

This result reduces the annual average excess of offenders against property in the four most instructed departments to 4 in 132, or about three per cent. We have before shown that France cannot be regarded as a country enjoying the benefits of a well-devised system of primary instruction, either as respects the extent or quality of the existing means of education, and we are inclined to agree with the following remarks of Mr. Porter on these facts as applicable to a country in that stage of civilisation:—
' Crimes against property may be considered as among the consequences of civilisation, since it is evident that the temptation to commit them must be greatest when the

artificial wants of man are the most numerous and urgent, and where the accumulation of the means for their gratification is most considerable.'

We have already shown that nearly all the crime in France is committed by persons who are ignorant; and, within a fraction, all the crime is confined to those whose instruction has been limited to reading and writing merely. Mr. Porter proves that this was equally true in the year selected by M. Guerry, and that therefore the excess of crimes against property in the four most instructed departments in that year is *attributable solely to the physical influences of civilisation on the uninstructed part of the population.* If we separate the criminals of the eight departments under examination according to this classification, we shall find that, in the year 1831, they were divided as follow:—

	Four *most* Instructed Departments.	Four *least* Instructed Departments.
Class 1. Those wholly uninstructed...	101	158
2. Those who read and write imperfectly............	103	12
3. Those who read and write well	24	13
4. Those still further educated ..	4	4
	232	187

The deductions of M. Guerry are thus entirely disproved from his own data,—a result which it is to be regretted should have been overlooked in some recent discussions.[1]

The influence of instruction superior to that of mere

---

[1] The following extract from Mr. Porter's paper contains facts too important to be omitted, though, perhaps, too elaborate for the text.

'We have seen that in the more enlightened departments the proportion of persons who can read and write is 73 in 100, while in the least instructed it is no more than 13 in 100. The population of the first being 1,142,454, it follows that only 308,463 persons are wholly uninstructed; and the number of offenders in this class being 101, it further follows that one person in 3054 among them has been brought before the tribunals; whereas, among the three instructed classes the offenders are 131 among 833,991 instructed persons, or only 1 in 6366.

'In the least instructed departments a similar examination gives us the reading and writing may be estimated also from the subjoined Table, from which 'it will be seen that out of 50 persons sentenced to death, not one belonged to the well-educated class; that 47 in that class were subjected to only slight correctional punishments, and 4 to simple surveillance; leaving only 49 well-educated persons out of the whole population of more than 32 millions, or 1 in 664,678 persons, who, in the course of the year 1833 were considered deserving of punishments in any degree severe.'

Punishments.	Cannot read or write.	Read and write imperfectly.	Read and write well.	Superior degree of instruction.	Total.
Death	34	10	6	...	50
Perpetual Labour	90	44	4	3	141
Labour for different periods	483	235	67	17	802
Solitary Confinement	437	213	64	23	737
Transportation	1	...	...	3	4
Imprisonment	13	4	1	3	21
Correctional Punishments	1544	628	198	47	2417
Children detained	16	7	2	...	25
Surveillance	10	8	3	4	25
	2628	1149	345	100	4222
	3777 89·4 per cent.		8·2 per cent	2·4 per cent.	100 per cent.

Results exactly similar are contained in the returns for 1834, 1835, and 1836, which it would, however, be superfluous to insert.

following result:—the population being 1,134,280, of whom only 13 in 100 are instructed, there will be 986,824 wholly ignorant, and 147,456 who can read or write. The number of wholly ignorant offenders being 158, gives in that class only 1 offender in 6245 persons; whereas the instructed classes, amounting in number to 147,456, include 29 offenders, or 1 in every 5084 individuals.

'It is not difficult to account for these results. In situations where education is pretty generally imparted, the wholly ignorant will find themselves at a disadvantage, through the greater portion of employments being occupied by those who are instructed. The ignorant man is therefore more impelled to lawless courses than in other situations, where the great bulk of the people, being equally uninstructed, all have a nearly equal chance of obtaining honest employment.'

But if this be the state of primary education in the Continental States, what, we are entitled to ask, ought to be its condition in England? Our political atmosphere has been comparatively serene; our social institutions have not suffered the shock of any disastrous revolution; our country has not been ravaged, as has been the fate of every Continental state, by any armies. The great territorial possessions of our aristocracy, are but so many stores of wealth and power, by which the civilisation of the people might be promoted. In every English proprietor's domain there ought to be, as in many there are, school-houses with well trained masters, competent and zealous to rear the population in obedience to the laws, in submission to their superiors, and to fit them to strengthen the institutions of their country by their domestic virtues, their sobriety, their industry, and forethought,—by the steadiness of purpose with which they pursue their daily labour,—by the enterprise with which they recover from calamity,—and by the strength of heart with which they are prepared to grapple with the enemies of their country. How striking is the contrast which the estates of the landed proprietors of almost all other European countries bear in all that relates to material wealth—to the domains of our English aristocracy! On the Continent you are met on every side by the proofs of meagre or exhausted resources. In England we have no excuse; we have proofs of how much can be affected, and at how little cost, by the well directed energy of individuals; and we have in our eye examples among our peerage which cannot but be imitated as soon as they are generally known and appreciated.

Our great commercial cities and manufacturing towns contain middle classes whose wealth, enterprise, and intelligence have no successful rivals in Europe; they have made this country the mart of the whole earth; they have covered the seas with their ships, exploring every inlet, estuary, or river which affords them a chance of successful trade. They have colonised almost every accessible region;

and from all these sources, as well as from the nightly and daily toil of our working classes in mines, in manufactories, and workshops, in every form of hardy and continued exertion on the sea and on the shore, wealth has been derived, which has supported England in unexampled struggles; yet between the merchants and manufacturers of this country and the poorer class there is little or no alliance, excepting that of mutual interest. But the critical events of this very hour are full of warning, that the ignorance—nay the barbarism—of large portions of our fellow-countrymen, can no longer be neglected, if we are not prepared to substitute a military tyranny or anarchy for the moral subjection which has hitherto been the only safeguard of England. At this hour military force alone retains in subjection great masses of the operative population, beneath whose outrages, if not thus restrained, the wealth and institutions of society would fall. The manufacturers and merchants of England must know what interest they have in the civilisation of the working population; and ere this we trust they are conscious, not merely how deep is their stake in the moral, intellectual, and religious advancement of the labouring class, but how deep is their responsibility to employ for this end the vast resources at their command.

In one other respect England stands in the strongest contrast with the Continental States as to the extent of her means for educational improvement. It is scarcely credible that, with primary education in utter ruin, we should possess educational endowments to the extent of half a million annually, which are either, to a large extent, misapplied, or are used for the support of such feeble and inefficient methods of instruction as to render little service to the community. Whenever the Government shall bend its efforts to combine, for the national advantage, all these great resources, we have no fears for our country. We perceive in it energies possessed by no other nation—partly attributable to the genius of our race; to a large extent derived from the spirit of our policy, which has admitted constant progression in our social institutions; in no small degree to our insular situation, which makes the sea at once the guardian of our liberties and the source of our wealth. But any further delay in the adoption of energetic measures for the elementary education of her working classes is fraught both with intestine and foreign danger — no one can stay the physical influences of wealth — some knowledge the people will acquire by the mere intercourse of society — many appetites are stimulated by a mere physical advancement. With increasing wants comes an increase of discontent, among a people who have only knowledge enough to make them eager for additional enjoyments, and have never yet been sufficiently educated to frame rational wishes and to pursue them by rational means. The mere physical influences of civilisation will not, we fear, make them more moral or religious, better subjects of the State, or better Christians, unless to these be superadded the benefits of an education calculated to develope the entire moral and intellectual capacity of the whole population.

A great change has taken place in the moral and intellectual state of the working classes during the last half century. Formerly, they considered their poverty and sufferings as inevitable, as far as they thought about their origin at all; now, rightly or wrongly, they attribute their sufferings to political causes; they think that by a change in political institutions their condition can be enormously ameliorated. The great Chartist petition, recently presented by Mr. Attwood, affords ample evidence of the prevalence of the restless desire for organic changes, and for violent political measures, which pervades the manufacturing districts, and which is every day increasing. This agitation is no recent matter; it has assumed various other forms in the last thirty years, in all of which the manufacturing population have shown how readily masses of ignorance, discontent, and suffering may be misled. At no period within our memory have the manufacturing districts been free from some form of agitation for unattainable objects referable to these causes. At one period, Luddism prevailed; at another, machine-breaking; at successive periods the Trades' Unions have endeavoured in strikes, by hired bands of ruffians, and by assassination, to sustain the rate of wages above that determined by the natural laws of trade; panics have been excited among the working classes, and severe runs upon the Savings' Banks effected from time to time. At one time they have been taught to believe that they could obtain the same wages if an eight hours' bill were passed as if the law permitted them to labour twelve hours in the day; and mills were actually worked on this principle for some weeks, to rivet the conviction in the minds of the working class. The agitation becomes constantly more systematic and better organised, because there is a greater demand for it among the masses, and it is more profitable to the leaders. It is vain to hope that this spirit will subside spontaneously, or that it can be suppressed by coercion. Chartism, an armed political monster, has at length sprung from the soil on which the struggle for the forcible repression of these evils has occurred. It is as certain as any thing future is certain, that the anarchical spirit of the Chartist association will, if left to the operation of the causes now in activity, become every year more formidable. The Chartists think that it is in the power of Government to raise the rate of wages by interfering between the employer and the workman; they imagine that this can be accomplished by a maximum of prices and minimum of wages, or some similar contrivance; and a considerable portion of them believe that the burden of taxation and of all 'fixed charges' (to use Mr. Attwood's expression) ought to be reduced by issuing inconvertible paper, and thus depreciating the currency. They are confident that a Parliament chosen by universal suffrage would be so completely under the dominion of the working classes as to carry these measures into effect; and therefore they petition for universal suffrage, treating all truly remedial measures as unworthy of their notice, or as obstacles to the attainment of the only objects really important. Now the sole effectual means of preventing the tremendous evils with which the anarchical spirit of the manufacturing population threatens the country is, by giving the working people a good secular education, to enable them to understand the true causes which determine their physical condition and regulate the distribution of wealth among the several classes of society. Sufficient intelligence and information to appreciate these causes might be diffused by an education which could easily be brought within the reach of the entire population, though it would necessarily comprehend more than the mere mechanical rudiments of knowledge.

We are far from being alarmists; we write neither under the influence of undue fear, nor with a wish to inspire undue fear into others. The opinions which we have expressed are founded on a careful observation of the proceedings and speeches of the Chartists, and of their predecessors in agitation in the manufacturing districts for many years, as reported in their newspapers; and have been as deliberately formed as they are deliberately expressed. We confess that we cannot contemplate with unconcern the vast physical force which is now moved by men so ignorant and so unprincipled as the Chartist leaders; and without expecting such internal convulsions as may deserve the name of *civil war*, we think it highly probable that persons and property will, in certain parts of the country, be so exposed to violence as materially to affect the prosperity of our manufactures and commerce, to shake the mutual confidence of mercantile men, and to diminish the stability of our political and social institutions. That the country will ultimately recover from these internal convulsions we think, judging from its past history, highly probable; but the recovery will be effected by the painful process of teaching the working classes, by actual experience, that the violent measures which they desire do not tend to improve their condition.

It is astonishing to us, that the party calling themselves Conservative should not lead the van in promoting the diffusion of that knowledge among the working classes which tends beyond any thing else to promote the security of property and the maintenance of public order. To restore the working classes to their former state of incurious and contented apathy is impossible, if it were desirable. If they are to have knowledge, surely it is the part of a wise and virtuous Government to do all in its power to secure to them useful knowledge, and to guard them against pernicious opinions.

We have already said that all instruction should be hallowed by the influence of religion; but we hold it to be equally absurd and short-sighted to withhold secular instruction, on the ground that religion is alone sufficient.

We do not, however, advocate that form of religious instruction which merely loads the memory, without developing the understanding, or which fails to stir the sympathies of our nature to their inmost springs. There is a form of instruction in religion which leaves the recipient at the mercy of any religious or political fanatic who may dare to use the sacred pages as texts in support of imposture. We have seen that even a maniac may lead the people to worship him as the Messiah, whose second coming, spoken of in the pages of Holy Writ, was fulfilled. Many of the Chartists proclaim themselves Missionaries of Christianity. They know how to rouse the superstition of an ignorant population in favour of their doctrines, by employing passages of Scripture the true meaning of which the uninstructed mass do not reach. They continually set before them those verses which speak of the rich man as an oppressor—which show with how much difficulty the rich shall enter the kingdom of heaven. Poverty is the Lazarus whom they place in Abraham's bosom—wealth the Dives whom they doom to hell. They find passages in the writings of the Apostles speaking of a community of goods among the early Christians: on this they found the doctrines of the Socialists. Our Saviour, in the synagogue of Nazareth, opened the Scripture at the prophecy in which Isaiah describes His divine mission: 'The Spirit of the Lord is upon me, because he hath anointed me to preach the gospel to the poor, &c.' From these and similar passages, they gather the sanctions of their own Mission. Christianity in their hands becomes the most frantic democracy, and democracy is clothed with the sanctions of religion. Even the arming of the Chartist association is derived from our Saviour's injunction, 'he that hath no sword, let him sell his garment and buy one.' To such purposes may the Scriptures be wrested by unscrupulous men who have practised on the ignorance, discontent, and suffering of the mass.

Their power will continue as long as the people are without sufficient intelligence to discern in what the fearful error of such impiety consists. There are times in which it is necessary that every man should be prepared to give a reason for the faith that is in him. We loathe a merely speculative religion, which does not purify the motives, and which robs piety alike of humility and charity; but when the teachers of the great mass of the people unite the imposture of religious and political fanatics, preaching anti-social doctrines as though they were a gospel of truth, the knowledge of the people must be increased, and their intellectual powers strengthened, so as to enable them to grapple with the error and to overcome it.

Next to the prevalence of true religion, we most earnestly desire that the people should know how their interests are inseparable from those of the other orders of society; and we will not stop to demonstrate so obvious a truth as that secular knowledge, easily accessible, but most powerful in its influence, is necessary to this end.

If, on the other hand, an opponent of popular education should admit the existence of the evil and the sufficiency of the remedy, but should refuse to apply it because it would violate his notions of the duty of the Government to diffuse the orthodox faith, we can only say that such a person is unfit for the government of men in the nineteenth century, and that he is sacrificing to his own opinions upon abstruse questions of theology, the certain and demonstrable temporal happiness of millions of his fellow-creatures.

CHAPTER III.

RECENT PROCEEDINGS OF HER MAJESTY'S GOVERNMENT — LORD JOHN RUSSELL'S LETTER TO THE LORD PRESIDENT OF THE COUNCIL — MINUTE OF THE COMMITTEE OF COUNCIL OF THE THIRD OF JUNE.

Since the reform of the Representation, the state of education in England has, during three sessions, occupied the attention of Committees of the House of Commons. It has also incidentally been brought under the notice of various Commissions of Inquiry and departments of administration; but the Government has not yet proposed to Parliament any general plan for the improvement and extension of primary education. The difficulty of devising a system consistent with the principles of civil and religious liberty, and at the same time capable of combining all parties and all religious denominations, has hitherto appeared to be insurmountable. The Government has therefore confined its interference to preliminary and experimental measures, which only indicate the embarrassment with which this question is surrounded, and its desire to surmount them.

Lord Althorp procured the consent of the House of Commons to a vote of £20,000, for the building of Schoolhouses in England and Wales, which has since been annually voted, as well as the sum of £10,000 for similar purposes in Scotland. The appropriation of these grants was confided to the Treasury, by which, in England and Wales, they were distributed, through the medium of the National Society, and of the British and Foreign School Society.[1] On the 30th of August, 1833, the Chancellor

---

[1] *Copy of Treasury Minute, dated 30th August,* 1833.

My Lords read the Act of the last Session, by which a sum of £20,000 is

of the Exchequer proposed the rules contained in the subjoined note, to regulate the distribution of the sums annually voted by the House of Commons. Respecting the proceedings of the Treasury on these rules, the Archbishop of Canterbury, in the recent debate in the House of Lords said, 'he would appeal to the consciences of the Clergy in general, whether with respect to the grant of £20,000, which of late years had been given by the Government, very laudably and liberally, to the Schools connected with the National School Society, and the Lancasterian School

---

granted to His Majesty to be issued in aid of private subscriptions for the erection of Schools for the Education of the Children of the Poorer Classes in Great Britain.

The Chancellor of the Exchequer feeling it absolutely necessary that certain fixed Rules should be laid down by the Treasury for their guidance in this matter, so as to render this sum most generally useful for the purposes contemplated by the grant, submits the following arrangements for the consideration of the Board.

1st. That no portion of this sum be applied to any purpose whatever, except for the erection of new School-houses; and that in the definition of a School-house, the residence for Masters or Attendants be not included.
2nd. That no application be entertained unless a sum be raised by private contribution, equal at the least to one-half of the total estimated expenditure.
3rd. That the amount of private subscription be received, expended, and accounted for, before any issue of public money for such School be directed.
4th. That no application be complied with, unless upon the consideration of such a Report, either from the National School Society, or the British and Foreign School Society, as shall satisfy this Board that the case is one deserving of attention, and there is a reasonable expectation that the School may be permanently supported.
5th. That the applicants whose cases are favourably entertained, be required to bind themselves to submit to any audit of their accounts which this Board may direct, as well as to such periodical Reports respecting the state of their Schools, and the number of scholars educated, as may be called for.
6th. That in considering the applications made to the Board, a preference be given to such applications as come from large cities and towns, in which the necessity of assisting in the erection of Schools is most pressing, and that due inquiries also be made before any such application be acceded to, whether there may not be charitable funds, or public and private endowments, that might render any further grants inexpedient or unnecessary.

In these suggestions My Lords concur.

Society, they had ever complained of the share which the Dissenters in the Lancasterian Schools had had in that grant. They took the share belonging to them, not only without complaint, but with thankfulness, and never inquired into the proportion in which it was distributed. They were satisfied with the grant, considering it as a temporary expedient. Lord Althorp said, when he brought forward the resolution, that he proposed it only as an experiment. It was an experiment, however, which had succeeded extremely well, and the money, as far as it went, had been most usefully expended. They considered it then as an experiment—as a temporary expedient—and no better could have been imagined as such; but, at the same time, they looked forward to the period when a permanent system would be established by Parliament,—when a plan of education would be definitively settled. They conceived that the whole matter would be referred to the consideration of the legislature, and that the liberality of Parliament would be, as it had been, distributed equally to all who might be entitled to it.'

The exertions of the National and British and Foreign School Societies, in connexion with the assistance thus granted, are thus acknowledged in Lord John Russell's letter to the Lord President. 'It is some consolation to her Majesty to perceive that, of late years, the zeal for popular education has increased; that the Established Church has made great efforts to promote the building of Schools, and that the National, and British and Foreign School Societies, have actively endeavoured to stimulate the liberality of the benevolent and enlightened friends of general education.

'Still,' his Lordship continues, 'much remains to be done; and among the chief defects yet subsisting, may be reckoned the insufficient number of qualified Schoolmasters—the imperfect method of teaching which prevails in, perhaps, the greater number of the Schools—the absence of any sufficient inspection of the Schools, and examination of the nature of the instruction given—the want of a Model School, which might serve for the example of those Societies and Committees which anxiously seek to improve their own methods of teaching; and finally, the neglect of this great subject among the enactments of our voluminous legislation.

'Some of these defects appear to admit of an immediate remedy; and I am directed by Her Majesty to desire, in the first place, that your Lordship, with four other of the Queen's servants, should form a Board or Committee for the consideration of all matters affecting the Education of the People.

'For the present it is thought advisable that this Board should consist of

The Lord President of the Council.
The Lord Privy Seal.
The Chancellor of the Exchequer.
The Secretary of State for the Home Department, and
The Master of the Mint.

'It is proposed that the Board should be intrusted with the application of any sums which may be voted by Parliament for the purposes of Education in England and Wales.'

A Committee of Council on Education was accordingly appointed on the 10th of April, 1839—and it should be observed that the functions of the Committee are limited to 'superintend the application of any sums voted by Parliament for the purpose of promoting public Education.' These functions are therefore precisely similar to those which were exercised by the Treasury in the years 1835, 6, 7, and 8.

The Committee of Council is equally amenable to Parliament, annually, for all its proceedings: the sum confided to it is not greater than that intrusted to the Treasury As it consists of five responsible Members of the Cabinet, instead of only one, the security for correct administration is augmented, and its proceedings are, in all respects, rendered more open to observation, by their separation from the mass of details with which the Treasury is encumbered, and their transference to a department where they can obtain more constant and deliberate attention from the Executive. In all these respects the change is a great improvement, though it appears to have been the source of much groundless alarm.

But we perceive the Archbishop of Canterbury, in the recent debate in the House of Lords, remarked, 'He knew not if there was any objection in principle to the Committee appointed, but he should have thought the Lords of the Treasury were just as competent to judge of these matters as the Noble Lords named.'

In his letter to the Lord President of the Council, Lord John Russell proceeds to state, that 'among the first objects to which any grant may be applied, will be the establishment of a Normal School. In such a School a body of schoolmasters may be formed, competent to assume the management of similar institutions in all parts of the country. In such a School, likewise, the best modes of teaching may be introduced, and those who wish to improve the Schools of their neighbourhood may have an opportunity of observing their results.

'In any Normal or Model School to be established by the Board, four principal objects should be kept in view: namely, religious instruction, general instruction, moral training, and habits of industry. Of these four, I need only allude to the first. With respect to religious instruction, there is, as your Lordship is aware, a wide, or apparently wide, difference of opinion among those who have been most forward in promoting education.

'The National Society, supported by the Established Church, contend that the schoolmaster should be invariably a Churchman; that the Church Catechism should be taught in the School to all the scholars; that all should be required to attend church on Sundays, and that the Schools should be, in every case, under the superintendence of the clergyman of the parish.

'The British and Foreign School Society, on the other hand, admit Churchmen and Dissenters equally as schoolmasters, require that the Bible should be taught in their Schools, but insist that no catechism should be admitted.

'Others, again, contend that secular instruction should be the business of the School, and that the ministers of different persuasions should each instruct separately the children of their own followers.

'In the midst of these conflicting opinions, there is not practically that exclusiveness among the Church societies, nor that indifference to religion among those who exclude dogmatic instruction from the School, which their mutual accusations would lead bystanders to suppose.

'Much, therefore, may be effected by a temperate attention to the fair claims of the Established Church, and the religious freedom sanctioned by law.

'On this subject I need only say, that it is her Majesty's wish that the youth of this kingdom should be religiously brought up, and that the rights of conscience should be respected.'

The necessity for the immediate establishment of Normal Schools is demonstrated by the account given in the subjoined Table of the number of teachers (engaged in daily instruction, in various classes of Schools) who had received any previous preparation for their vocation, in the five large northern towns to which we have before referred, and in Westminster.

Accordingly the Minute of the proceedings of the Committee of Privy Council on Education, of the 11th of April, 1839, related chiefly to the plan of a Normal School. This plan was subsequently postponed, in consequence of the difficulty of obtaining a concurrence of public opinion respecting the means to be adopted for the religious instruction of the children and teachers of different religious denominations in that School. We shall only remark here, that 'religion' was, in this School, 'to be combined with the whole matter of instruction, and to regulate the entire system of discipline,' as respected the children trained therein; and that 'the religious instruction of the candidate teachers' was 'to form an essential and prominent

Explanation of Measures of 1839

Number of Teachers of various Classes of Day and Evening Schools, and the number who have received any Education for their Employment, in the undermentioned places:—

	Dame Schools.			Common Boys' & Girls' Schools.			Superior Private Schools.			Evening Schools.			Infant Schools.			Endowed and Charity Schools.		
	Number of Teachers.	Number educated for their employment.	Not ascertained.	Number of Teachers.	Number educated for their employment.	Not ascertained.	Number of Teachers.	Number educated for their employment.	Not ascertained.	Number of Teachers.	Number educated for their employment.	Not ascertained.	Number of Teachers.	Number educated for their employment.	Not ascertained.	Number of Teachers.	Number educated for their employment.	Not ascertained.
nchester .	230	..	8	179	29	11	114	24	9	83	7	4	5	..	..	24	5	5
ford . .	65	10	..	42	8	..	29	14	..	28	7	..	3	..	..	13	2	..
erpool .	244	2	..	194	18	2	143	71	11	43	6	..	17	1	..	50	18	7
y . . .	30	2	..	17	2	..	8	6	..	6	..	..	2	..	..	4	2	..
k . . .	37	..	..	23	2	..	30	10	3	2	..	..	3	1	..	31	19	3
Totals .	606	14	8	455	59	13	324	125	23	162	20	4	30	2	..	122	46	15
stminster 3 districts) Martin-in e-Fields, . Clemen anes, St. ary-le- rand, St. aul, Co- nt Gar- n, and the voy .	21	1	5	33	9	4	32	18	2	..	..	..	5	3	1	14	7	3
John and Margaret	63	12	..	41	20	..	24	20	..	..	..	..	6	4	..	23	12	2
eorge, St. mes, and . Anne, ho . .	46	7	..	55	25	..	73	54	1	..	..	..	6	5	..	18	10	..
Totals .	130	20	5	129	54	4	129	92	3	..	..	..	17	12	1	55	29	5

element of their studies, and no certificate' was 'to be granted, unless the authorised religious teacher' had 'previously attested his confidence in the character, religious knowledge, and zeal of the candidate whose religious instruction he' had 'superintended.' The postponement of the establishment of a Normal School, has been represented as the temporary postponement only of this particular plan, which, notwithstanding repeated assurances to the contrary in Parliament, it is contended may still be carried into execution during the recess. A perusal of the clause of the Report of the Committee of Council of the 3rd of June, which announces the postponement of any attempt to create a Normal School, will convince any candid reader that, as the whole proceedings of the Committee are annually dependent on the opinion and votes of the House, the Committee could only have referred to the 'greater concurrence of opinion,' as far as it influenced the decisions of Parliament, or, in other words, to the opinion of Parliament. The postponement of any proceedings respecting the Normal School was announced in the following terms, in the Report of the Committee of Council on the 3rd of June:—

'The Committee are of opinion that the most useful application of any sums voted by Parliament, would consist in the employment of those moneys in the establishment of a Normal School, under the direction of the State, and not placed under the management of a voluntary Society. The Committee, however, experience so much difficulty in reconciling conflicting views respecting the provisions which they are desirous to make in furtherance of your Majesty's wish, that the children and teachers instructed in this School should be duly trained in the principles of the Christian religion, while the rights of conscience should be respected; that it is not in the power of the Committee to mature a plan for the accomplishment of this design without further consideration; and they therefore postpone taking any steps for this purpose until greater concurrence of opinion is found to prevail.'

As the Committee of Council have postponed to another year the establishment of a Normal School, we shall reserve to the close of these remarks our comments on the plan which they submitted to Parliament, and we proceed to point out in what respects the plan now proposed by the Committee of Council for the appropriation of any sums voted by Parliament for the purpose of promoting public education, differs from that formerly adopted by the Treasury.

1. 'The Lords of the Committee recommend that the sum of £10,000, granted by Parliament in 1835, towards the erection of Normal or Model Schools, be given in equal proportions to the National Society, and the British and Foreign School Society.

2. 'That the remainder of the subsequent grants of the years 1837 and 1838 yet unappropriated, and any grant which may be voted in the present year, be chiefly applied in aid of subscriptions for building, and, in particular cases, for the support of Schools connected with those societies; but that the rule hitherto adopted of making a grant to those places where the largest proportion is subscribed be not invariably adhered to, should application be made from very poor and populous districts, where subscriptions to a sufficient amount cannot be obtained.'

Thus far no objection appears to have been raised to the plan.

3. 'The Committee do not feel themselves precluded from making grants in particular cases which shall appear to them to call for the aid of Government, although the applications may not come from either of the two mentioned societies.'

The special exception thus made to the general rule may have been the source of some apprehension, and it certainly has been the subject of much misrepresentation. We find it difficult, however, to believe that if in any particular locality great destitution, combined with extreme ignorance and demoralisation, should be found to prevail, to which the plan of either of the two societies should be found to be absolutely inapplicable without some variation in deference to the right of conscience, any reasonable man, to whom authority to decide such a question was committed, having before him the Minutes of the Committee of Council, would not determine it somewhat in the following manner. The Minutes of the Committee plainly limit the application of the sums voted by Parlia-

ment to Schools connected with the two societies, with the exception of these particular cases. It is therefore evident that any deviation from the plans by which the two societies are distinguished from each other, and from other societies (*i. e.* the method of giving religious instruction), ought in such cases to be admitted on the plea of absolute necessity—the choice being between, on the one hand, ignorance and barbarism, and on the other, the erection of a School in which a variation from the plans of the two societies is admitted; and that, as the distinguishing characteristics of the two societies relate to religious instruction, this variation should be only such as would be required for the success of the School. One principle [1] . . . .
. . . is especially applicable to these cases,—viz., that while the Government is most anxious that religious instruction should be united to secular, and will therefore grant all proper facilities for that purpose, the State is peculiarly charged with the duty of rendering secular instruction accessible to all, and with the improvement of the quality of such secular instruction, by assistance from the public funds and by constant superintendence.[2] . . . . . .
. . . . The particular regulation embraced in this clause of the Minute of the Committee of Council, provides for a cautious experimental application of the principle as a temporary expedient. Arrangements similar to those proposed by the Committee of the British and Foreign School, in their memorial dated 14th April 1838, would probably suffice in such exceptional cases, viz., 'That the Holy Scriptures should be read and taught in' such 'Schools, such instruction to form a part of the usual occupation of the School, and to be communi-

---

[1] Certain words omitted.

[2] Interlocutory remarks from Report of Debate in the House of Lords, and another sentence omitted, in consequence of a correspondence which was printed in the Preface to the tenth and succeeding editions of this Pamphlet. It is not necessary now to revive the memory of this discussion.

cated by the schoolmaster, but that the children of Catholics and Jews might, if their parents required it, be absent at such time, and that the children of Dissenters should not be compelled to learn any religious formulary or catechism to which their parents objected.'

4. 'The Committee recommend that no further grant be made, now or hereafter, for the establishment and support of Normal Schools, or of any other Schools, unless the right of inspection be retained, in order to secure a conformity to the regulations and discipline established in the several Schools, with such improvements as may from time to time be suggested by the Committee. A part of any grant voted in the present year may be usefully applied to the purposes of inspection, and to the means of acquiring a complete knowledge of the present state of education in England and Wales.'

We have seen that the inspection of Schools by a skilled agency is regarded by the Continental Governments as second only to the foundation of Normal Schools in its influence on the advancement of primary education. We have observed how well organised are the arrangements for the inspection of Schools in Holland. M. Cousin says, 'The Dutch legislators made no attempt at a master-piece of codification, in which the whole subject of primary instruction was to be divided and classed according to the rules of philosophical analysis; they went straight to their point by the shortest and the safest road; and as inspection must be the fundamental basis of primary Schools, it was inspection they established by law.' And in another place he says—'There are, by the law both of Prussia and Holland, salaried officers called Inspectors, selected because they are found to possess the requisite qualifications, who are responsible to Government for the whole of the primary Schools within a given district.' (Their powers are, therefore, vastly more extensive than any thing contemplated in the Minute of the Committee of Council). 'This is the true kind of government,' he adds, 'for primary Schools; and to determine how the organisation of that government shall be most skilfully contrived is, in my mind, the vital question in a system of popular education.' M. Guizot, in his Report to the King of the French, on the execution of the Law of the 28th of June 1833, attaches at least equal importance to this measure, and describes in detail the means by which this inspection is accomplished throughout the whole of France. Lord Lansdowne, in the debate in the House of Lords, 'appealed to the experience of those Noble Lords who had sat upon the Committee of Inquiry into the state of Education in Ireland. He appealed to the experience of those Noble Lords whether they were not met at every step of their inquiry by evidence showing that some inspection of those Schools on behalf of the public was absolutely indispensable to their success as a means of education.'

The subjoined evidence of the Rev. J. C. Wigram, the Secretary of the National School Society, and of Mr. Dunn, the Secretary of the British and Foreign School Society, leads to the same conclusion.[1]

---

[1] 'Rev. J. C. Wigram,—

'Chairman.] Do you not think that if the Government makes grants of money for the purpose of aiding Schools on either system, that they may fairly make it a condition that a due inspection of the Schools should take place, and that adequate returns should be made to Parliament to show that the Schools are well and efficiently conducted?—I think it would be very desirable that they should do so; and I think that they might promote that object very much, and with great benefit, by giving grants in aid of some places to the schoolmasters of certain districts, upon examinations reported, with all particulars, with respect to a certain number of Schools; for instance, that a return should be made of the particulars which they might determine, respecting not less than fifty Schools, and that some pecuniary reward should be given, to a different amount, to the five or six masters whose scholars were best conducted. Those examinations might be triennial, or at distant intervals; and in order to prevent the same man from always getting the reward, the prizes might be given with due reference to the circumstances of the School, and for different qualifications in the state of the School. It might be one year given for the intellectual state of the School; another year for retaining the scholars for a longer period; and other qualifications might be introduced. It has been done by the National Society to a small extent in many parts of the country, and with great benefit.'

'Henry Dunn, Esq.—

'Do you not think that one of the first steps towards any general plan of education for the humbler classes would be, the formation of such a board

After recommending the appointment of a Board of Education, the Committee of the British and Foreign School, in a Memorial addressed to Lord John Russell on the 14th of April 1838, say —

'It has been suggested that great advantages would result if these Commissioners were brought, in the disposal of the public funds, into immediate correspondence with the Individual or Local Committee sustaining each separate School, instead of acting through the agency of any society or societies; this point seems well worthy of consideration; but, however this may be decided, the Committee would suggest—1st. That the Board should not interfere in any way with the religious instruction imparted in any School. 2nd. That it should not impose any terms or restrictions, except such as might be necessary in order to secure efficient teaching, and an adequate share of secular information.'

On this subject the Archbishop of Canterbury, in the recent debate on Education, said, ' He conceived that the public when they made a grant for relief, should be assured

as the two great parties who have interested themselves in education in this country would have confidence in?—I think it would; and that then their efforts should be directed to improve the existing Schools rather than extend them. I should lay great stress upon that; there are a great number of Schools scattered throughout the country, of all kinds and descriptions, which, with inspection and a little assistance, might be rendered efficient Schools.

' When you give an opinion as to the necessity of improving, rather than extending, existing Schools, you may not have gone into the detail of the want of efficient Schools in the towns of Lancashire?—No one can have a stronger impression than I have of the want of Schools; but I believe that the improvement of Schools leads to their extension.

' Do you not think that it would be very practicable, supposing by any mode a sufficient fund was provided, to do both; that is, to improve, and at the same time gradually to extend, Schools for the humbler classes?—I quite think so; but to begin by extending is, I think, to begin at the wrong end; the first step should rather be to improve, and give efficiency to those which at present exist.

' Do not you think that one necessary accompaniment of the Board to promote education would be some system of Inspectors, who should make returns to the Central Board of the degree of efficiency of the Schools, and the number attending, and who should make periodical visits to inquire and look into the state of the Schools?—I think it would be essential.'

of the efficiency of that relief. (Hear, hear.) Whenever a grant of public money was made, the public had a right to know that it had been properly applied; and he was satisfied that the public would be contented if they knew, that with the money which they had granted the secular instruction was properly applied to the people, leaving the religious instruction in the hands of the Church' (hear.) On these observations the Marquis of Lansdowne remarked, 'Would the Right Reverend Prelate forgive him for stating, that it had never entered into the mind of any member of the Committee of Privy Council to use the Inspectors as agents to interfere, either directly or indirectly, with the religious education given in the Schools? What the Inspectors ought to interfere in was the more mechanical arrangements and improvements in education—improvements which ought to be introduced into all Schools, as they did not bear on any question of religion, but on a question which was all but of equal importance—he meant the training up of the scholars in those habits of discipline, of industry, and of employment (hear, hear), which ought to form part of every plan of general education.' (Hear, hear.)

On the propriety of a system of Inspection, and on the limits to be assigned to it, one fruit of the recent discussions in Parliament seems to be a concurrence of opinion in the highest authorities, and in the representatives of the Government and the Church.

The whole discussion tends to prove the importance, not to say the necessity, of an inquiry into the state of Education in England and Wales. Our precise statistical information is limited to a few districts in which the spontaneous exertions of individuals have collected facts. The knowledge we have of the extent of destitution is general only, and therefore not satisfactory to minds accustomed to a careful induction. Such an inquiry will doubtless prove of eminent service by stimulating the spontaneous exertions of society for the extension of education, and by diffusing information to guide its newly awakened zeal.

We may hope, by such means, also to obtain a more intimate acquaintance with the opinions of all classes on this momentous subject; and that the wants and moral and social peculiarities of different districts may be examined, so that when the period arrives that a more comprehensive measure can be submitted to the Legislature, it may be welcomed by a greater concurrence of popular opinion.

CHAPTER IV.

EXAMINATION OF THE MINUTE OF THE COMMITTEE OF COUNCIL OF THE 11TH OF APRIL, RESPECTING THE ESTABLISHMENT OF A NORMAL SCHOOL, WHICH MINUTE IS NOW SUPERSEDED BY THAT OF THE 3RD OF JUNE.

THE most important part of the plan originally submitted by the Committee of Privy Council to Parliament, was, as we have said, abandoned in consequence of the difficulty encountered in attempting to reconcile a due regard to the legitimate claims of the Established Church with a respect for the rights of conscience. Though the establishment of a Normal School has been for the present postponed, it may be useful to show what were the views of the Committee of Privy Council respecting the principles on which such an establishment ought to be conducted, and on the details of its internal economy. The departments of religious and general instruction, and of moral and industrial training proposed in Lord John Russell's letter to the President of the Council were included as elements of the plan of this school. It will be most convenient to consider the arrangements for religious instruction last.

The Committee of Council appear from that Minute to have been impressed with the fact, that throughout the country the number of schools for the poorer classes is inadequate to the reception of those who need instruction, but that this defect, from its extent and notoriety, appears to withdraw attention in some degree, from the equally lamentable inefficiency of the teachers commonly employed in the primary schools, arising from their imperfect attainments, their ignorance of correct methods of instruction, and still more from their want of skill in training the habits and developing the characters of the children, so as to prepare them for the persevering discharge of their duties in life. In many cases, the profession of the educator has fallen into the hands of persons who are destitute of means, not merely from want of ability, but from defects of character, and who resort to this calling after they have been proved to be unfit for any other. The exertions of the Clergy and Ministers in the religious instruction of the population would be materially assisted if the instruction of the children of the poor were given in such a form as not merely to inform their minds on their duties to God and to man, but to influence their habits and feelings, so that a sense of the true source of all moral and social obligations, might be not merely instilled as a precept on the understanding, but be imbibed from every part of the daily routine in such a way as to influence the life. It is feared, that the teachers now employed, often content themselves with requiring that the approved formularies be committed to memory.

In order to abate these evils the Committee of Council intended to found a school in which candidates might acquire knowledge necessary to the exercise of their future profession, and be practised in the most approved methods, both of moral training and instruction.

By such means alone can the parochial village, and town schools, as well as the endowed and charity and private schools throughout the country be supplied with teachers duly impressed with the great responsibilities of their vocation—entering on the discharge of their functions, as on a mission of truth and civilisation—and furnished with such attainments, such skill in the practice of their art— with minds and habits so disciplined, as to fit them to become at once the guides and the companions, the instructors and the foster parents of the children whose temporal and eternal welfare is committed to their care.

Such a school necessarily included a Model School in which children might be taught and trained, and it appeared expedient that it should comprise children of all ages from three to fourteen, in sufficient numbers to form an Infant School, as well as schools for children above seven. A considerable portion of the children were to board and lodge in the establishment, in order that the means of moral training might be proportionately more complete, and opportunities afforded to the candidate teachers for acquiring a knowledge of the method of regulating the moral condition of such a household greater than any which could be obtained in a school attended solely or chiefly by day scholars.

The Model School, thus formed, would have afforded examples of approved methods of instruction in each stage of proficiency and in each department of knowledge. The earliest information of all improvements would have been obtained; they would have been systematically examined, and introduced when approved, in that form which might appear to render them most easily applicable to the wants of the country. Industrial and moral training were to be developed, so as constantly to give a practical tendency to the entire instruction of the school, supplying the future handicraftsman, or domestic servant, with the knowledge required in his station, and reducing precept to habit.

The Model and Normal School were to have been beneath the superintendence of a Rector, acting under the regulation of the Committee of Council. The selection of teachers, and of candidates for the office of teacher, would have been a subject of great difficulty and importance. Diligent inquiry, under direction of the Committee of the Privy Council, concerning their previous habits and associations, an examination of their attainments, evidence of gentleness of disposition, and a fondness for the duties of an educator, together with a sense of the secular and religious responsibility of the office, would have been essential preliminaries to the admission of a candidate teacher.

The internal organisation of the Model School indicates the method of instruction which was to have been adopted. The Committee of Council proposed to arrange the classes n separate rooms, or sections of the same apartment, divided by partitions, so as to enable the simultaneous method to be applied to forty or fifty children of similar proficiency. The Committee intended also to use the gallery, commonly employed only in the Infant School, as a means of giving lessons on objects of sense, or requiring illustrations from objects of sense, to the older children in larger bodies than when assembled in the classes for mere technical instruction. The gallery would also have been used at periods when the teacher desired to assemble the children for serious moral admonition. Such arrangements would have enabled each teacher not merely to convey his instructions with greater success, shut out from the noise and confusion incident to the assemblage of large numbers in the same room, but to have cultivated moral relations with his scholars, who would gradually have learned to regard him with affection as well as respect, resulting from the paternal character of the discipline. All the lessons in which it is important that the sympathies should be awakened, as well as the understanding, might be conveyed by the teacher in a more impressive manner in a separate apartment than in the large hall of a school filled with some hundreds of children. Without such arrangements, the design of the Committee of Council to interweave moral training with the whole tissue of instruction would not have been fulfilled; and the teachers must have been content with whatever success they could attain in the merely *intellectual* advancement of their pupils.

The simultaneous instruction which the Committee of Council apparently intended to combine with the monitorial or mutual instruction prevalent in this country, depends for its efficacy on the fact that, by the simultaneous method, the mind of the teacher may be more constantly in contact with that of every child under his care. The moral agencies employed are, under such a method, greatly superior to those in operation where the child receives instruction chiefly, if not wholly, from a boy but little older than himself.

The successful prosecution of the simultaneous method supposes that the teacher is accustomed to a careful analysis of the subjects of instruction to their simplest elements, and that he proceeds by a suggestive method from the previous limits of the child's knowledge, that is, from the most simple and rudimentary facts to those which are the result of combination. In this process each step is accompanied by a corresponding exercise of the child's mind, which finds a natural pleasure in pursuing a process of induction stimulating it to exertion. To learn is no longer a task, but a pleasure; the teacher successfully appeals to the sense of utility and the natural desire to know and combine, which are ordinarily discouraged by the difficulties attending an opposite method. The discipline of the school naturally acquires a milder character with willing pupils than with the sluggish or perverse; and the educator depends on his skill in rendering the pursuit of knowledge attractive, rather than on a resort to the inferior stimulus of rewards and punishments.

The Committee were of opinion that industrial instruction forms an important element of the routine of a Model School, probably not only because it practically inculcates the great lesson of industry, but also because it tends to give a special character to the matter of instruction in the school, keeping it in close relation with the condition of workmen and servants, and engrafting whatever is new on habits and pursuits which are necessary and permanent.

The candidate teachers were to reside in the Normal School in order that their habits and characters might be under the constant observation of the Rector and his assistant teachers.

The class-rooms were to be so constructed as to afford the candidate teachers an opportunity of attending the lessons without distracting the attention of the children or of the teacher.

Means were to be provided for the instruction of the candidate teachers in the theory of their art, and for furnishing them with whatever knowledge is requisite for success in it.

The superintendence of their studies and the general regulation of their conduct would have devolved on the Rector of the School. He would have given lectures on the method and matter of instruction, and the whole art of training children of the poor. Each course of study would have been conducted by him, as well as the reading and the exercise and examination of the candidate teachers. The order in which they were admitted to the practice of their art in the school, and at length entrusted with the conjoint management of the classes, together with their ultimate examination and certificate would have been chiefly regulated by him.

The candidate teachers were to conform to such regulations respecting the internal economy of the household, as might have been issued by the Rector with the approval of the Committee of Privy Council.

In the Model School it would have been desirable to have had accommodation for at least 450 children, who should lodge in the household, viz., 120 infants, 200 boys and girls receiving ordinary instruction, and 50 boys and 50 girls receiving special instruction, leaving 30 children absent from sickness or other causes. Such arrangements would have enabled the teachers to conduct the school with complete success on the best methods, and thus to afford to the candidate teachers the best opportunity of acquiring the art of teaching.

But in order to enable the teachers to realise the application of these methods under all the limitations and obstructions which must arise in a small village or town day-school, it was deemed desirable that a day school of 150 or 200 children, of all ages and both sexes, should form part of the establishment.

Here the candidate teacher would have learned the limitations which the organisation and method pursued in the larger school must undergo when the numbers are reduced, and when all ages are assembled in the same room: and would have become acquainted with the expedients to be adopted under varying circumstances; for example when the number was even still further reduced by the prevalence of sickness, by the inclemency of the weather, or by the caprice of parents. He would have been taught how to communicate with the parents respecting the conduct, health, and progress of their children—respecting the payment of the school fees, the management of the children at home, and their observance of their religious duties morning and evening, and on the Sunday. The industrial training of children in day schools also has some peculiarities, and their moral training is liable to interference from the parents and other external circumstances, over which the teacher has little control, and is certainly limited in its operation to the period spent in the school and exercise ground.

The progress of education would probably soon, under the influence of the Normal School, have multiplied the number of Rural Schools of Industry, so as to have enabled the candidate teachers to visit other Model Schools near the metropolis, where they might have completed their acquaintance with the modifications required by limitations and obstructions incidental to the different situations of the schools. The teachers having charge of schools in London and its vicinity might have been admitted to the Rector's lectures, and to certain of his classes.

Teachers having charge of schools, whether in the metropolis or elsewhere, might, during the holidays common to such establishments, have been permitted to attend the school.

Conferences of teachers trained in the Seminary would probably have occurred, under regulations issued by the Committee of Privy Council; at those conferences the Rector might have presided—the teachers might have given an account of their schools, of the difficulties which they had encountered and overcome, and especially of any improvement in apparatus or method, &c. of sufficient importance for consideration.

That the benefits derivable from such an Institution are almost incalculably great appears to be universally admitted. The want of teachers thus furnished with all the acquirements necessary for their honourable station —thus trained in correct methods of teaching—with habits of thought and demeanour so disciplined as to enable them to sustain a moral dignity while they mingle with the sports, sympathise with the feelings, yet elevate the thoughts of children—capable of making knowledge attractive by the simplicity and kindness with which it is imparted—imbued with a deep sense of their religious responsibilities, and hallowing all their moral instruction by a constant reference to the sanctions of religion —the want of such men is felt by every clergyman and gentleman who takes an interest in the condition of the labouring families on his estates, and by every member of the middle classes who recognises in the present condition of the poor proofs of the fatal void in our national institutions.

Deeply, therefore, do we regret the difficulty experienced in devising any method by which the religious instruction of children and teachers can be reconciled in such an establishment, with due regard to the rights of conscience.

The regulations contained in the Minute of the Committee of Council of the 11th of April 1839, now superseded, were—

'Religious instruction to be considered as general and special.

'Religion to be combined with the whole matter of instruction, and to regulate the entire system of discipline.

'Periods to be set apart for such peculiar doctrinal instruction as might be required for the religious training of the children.

'To appoint a chaplain to conduct the religious instruction of children whose parents or guardians belong to the Established Church.

'The parent or natural guardian of any other child to be permitted to secure the attendance of the licensed minister of his own persuasion, at the period appointed for special religious instruction, in order to give such instruction apart.

'To appoint a licensed minister to give such special religious instruction, wherever the number of children in attendance on the Model School belonging to any religious body dissenting from the Established Church, is such as to appear to this Committee to require such special provision.

'A portion of every day to be devoted to the reading of the Scriptures in the school, under the general direction of the Committee, and superintendence of the Rector. Roman Catholics, if their parents or guardians require it, to read their own version of the Scriptures, either at the time fixed for reading the Scriptures, or at the hours of special instruction.'

These regulations had reference to the religious instruction of the children in the Model School only, and it was not the intention of the Committee of Council to propose similar regulations for the adoption of any other School, much less was this School intended in this respect as a type of schools to be established in different parts of the country. On the contrary, the sum voted by the Committee of the House of Commons was to have been distributed to Schools in connection with the National and the British and Foreign School Societies, with certain exceptional cases only, admitted in consequence of the inapplicability of the rules of those societies in neighbourhoods where extreme ignorance and destitution appeared to demand the interference of Government for the civilisation of the people.

The Committee of Privy Council appear to have considered it unnecessary to descend into an explanation of all the more minute regulations by which the instruction of the children in the principles of the Christian religion was to have been guarded; but their views appear in all their leading features to be so strictly in accordance with those of that able and pious prelate, Daniel Wilson, the Bishop of Calcutta, as developed in regulations which he proposed to the Committee of the Martinière, that we feel bound to state the most material parts of those regulations.[1]

This institution owed its existence to the following extraordinary circumstances:—An English private soldier by great merit rose from the ranks in India, was promoted to the rank of Major-General, and amassed a great fortune. At his death he bequeathed his wealth for general education, without reference to the creed of those who partook of the benefits of the institution to be founded.

It was the wish of the Bishop of Calcutta to have founded this institution on the express doctrines and discipline of the Church of England only; but finding that the intentions of the founder were that the benefits of the institution should be extended to all persons, without distinction of creed, he proposed and strenuously advocated the plan described in the report, comprehending, as he says, ' all the great doctrines of redemption, as held by the *five main divisions of the Christian world—the English, the Scotch, the Roman Catholic, the Greek, and the Armenian churches—as our fundamental principles—leaving the minister of each church to supply instructions on the sacraments and matters of discipline to the children of their own communions respectively.*' The following are extracts from the Report, signed by the Committee, and adopted unanimously by the Board, and, we may add, republished by the Bishop in his own vindication.

---

[1] The statements of the Bishop of Calcutta, and of his Chaplain and others, made it subsequently apparent that the regulations of the Martinière were adopted as special and exceptional provisions to meet a peculiar case. J. P. K. S. 1862.

'*Report, &c. of the Committee appointed to frame a Plan, &c.*

'I. Your Committee submit, that in order to meet the first rule adopted by the Honourable Governors, the religious instruction of the children must be divided into two parts,—*the one general, the other particular:* the one embracing the fundamental truths of Christianity, as they are held in common by the five great existing divisions of Christendom enumerated in the rule; the other relating to discipline, church government, the sacraments, and other matters on which differences more or less important exist. Your Committee consider that the first part should be taught, daily and publicly, to all the children by the head master of the School; the second, privately, and on particular days, by the ministers and teachers whom the parents of the respective children may, with the approbation of the Governors, select.

'II. The following are the main truths held in common, on which the public religious instruction should, in your Committee's opinion, proceed.

1. The Being of God; his unity and perfections.
2. The Holy Scriptures of the Old and New Testament, a revelation inspired by the Holy Ghost.
3. The mystery of the adorable Trinity.
4. The Deity, Incarnation, Atonement, and Intercession of our Lord and Saviour Jesus Christ.
5. The fall and corruption of man; his accountableness and guilt.
6. Salvation through grace by the meritorious sacrifice and redemption of Christ.
7. The personality and Deity of the Holy Spirit, and his operations and grace in the sanctification of man.
8. The indispensable obligation of repentance towards God, faith in Christ, and continual prayer for the grace of the Holy Spirit.
9. The moral duties which every Christian is bound to perform towards God, his neighbour, and himself, as they

are summed up in the Ten Commandments, and enlarged upon in other parts of the Holy Scriptures; all based on the doctrines above specified, and enforced as their proper fruits.

'III. As to the first of these branches of the religious instruction — the public and general — the Committee recommend that it be chiefly drawn from the Holy Scriptures themselves; such simple instruction being given by the masters and mistresses in a catechetical form as may be adapted to the capacities of the children, on the points which fall within the limits of the public teaching; all matters which belong to the private, or which touch on controversy, being sedulously avoided.

'With respect to versions of the Scriptures, your Committee will offer their opinion under a subsequent rule.

'V. The second branch of the religious instruction — the private and particular — will require no regulations from your Committee; it will be merely supplementary; so that what is, in the judgment of the parents and guardians of the respective children, omitted, or insufficiently taught in public, may thus be supplied. In this private teaching the entire Catechisms of the different churches, and the versions of the Holy Scriptures approved by them, may of course be freely used.

'VII. We come next to the subject of family devotional exercises, and the public worship of Almighty God.

'The daily morning and evening family prayers, your Committee suggest, should be read by the Head Master from a Form of Prayer extracted from different liturgies, which we have prepared, and which accompanies these rules. On these occasions all the children of both sexes, and all the masters and mistresses, with all the Christian members of the household, should attend.

'The family devotions should not exceed ten or fifteen minutes altogether in length.

'The masters and mistresses are to allow also a few minutes to the children for private prayer, before they retire to bed at night and when they rise in the morning.

'On Sunday mornings, your Committee think all the children should be conducted to their respective churches and chapels for the worship of the Almighty, in the manner and after the rites approved by their parents.

'On Sunday evenings they recommend that the ordinary family devotions be read, with the addition of a suitable sermon, to be approved of by the governors.

'The same to be done also on Sunday mornings, when circumstances may prevent the children from going out; with the addition of a Litany extracted from one or more of the Liturgies of different churches.

'VIII. As it respects versions of the Holy Scriptures, your Committee are not aware that the Greek and Armenian churches have any English version of their own. The English and Scotch churches use the authorised English version. It remains only that the case of the church of Rome be considered, which has long possessed an English version of its own — that of Douay and Rheims; we recommend that, whenever the Roman Catholic children are required to have the Holy Scriptures in their hands, and to learn lessons, or receive direct religious instruction from them, this version be permitted to be employed; the copies being of course without notes or indexes which touch on controversy, and the master taking care to range the children in different classes, so that no confusion may arise by the variations in the readings.

'As this, however, could not be done in family prayer, where all the children of all classes and each sex, as well as the Christian household, are assembled together, we are of opinion that the portions of Holy Scripture, directed to be read as a part of the doctrines, should be taken from the authorised English version: the selection being, of course, subject to the provisions of the foregoing rules.

'Your Committee do not know that they need proceed more into detail. Much will and ought to be left to the head master, if he be a man of piety, talent, discretion, and temper. His suggestions, founded on experience, will be of the greatest value. Much will also depend on the number, description, age, and capacities of the children. But your Committee feel a great confidence that by this union of public and religious instruction, on the basis of the great doctrines of redemption held by the universal church, with the private inculcation of what regards church discipline, the sacraments, and other matters of controversy, *the practical blessings of a Christian education may be conveyed to the children, without indifference and latitudinarianism on the one hand, or a spirit of debate and proselytism on the other.*

'DANIEL CALCUTTA,
'ROBERT S. LEGER, V.A.,
'JAMES CHARLES.

'*August* 31, 1835.'

It is scarcely necessary to add, that this Report is not inserted in this place on the presumption that it anticipates in all its details the plan which the Committee of Council had prepared. On the contrary, we have already been publicly informed, that on no occasion did the Committee of Council intend that different versions of the Scriptures should be used *in the same apartment* in the Model School, but only in separate rooms. We need not more particularly allude to other details upon which the Committee of Council have expressed no opinion; but we have quoted these extracts from this Report of the Committee of the Martinière, to show that one of the ablest and most pious prelates that ever shed the lustre of a comprehensive and highly-cultivated mind and of eminent Christian virtues on society and the church, has lent the authority of his name to regulations conceived in the same spirit of Christian charity as that part of the Minute of the Committee of Council of the 11th of April by which the religious instruction of the children in the Model School was to be regulated. By such means the Bishop of Calcutta believes 'the practical blessings of a Christian education may be conveyed to the children without indifference and latitudinarianism on the one hand, or a spirit of debate and proselytism on the other.'

This Report may at least serve as a complete answer to the question which the Archbishop of Canterbury asked in the House of Lords, respecting 'the meaning of general instruction in Christianity.' We refer him to the Bishop of Calcutta's solution of that question.

Then as to the Minute, 'Religion to be combined with the whole matter of instruction, and to regulate the entire system of discipline,' the Archbishop said, 'he was at a loss how this was to be carried into effect.' The answer is contained in the Report signed by the Bishop of Calcutta.

On this question, the Bishop of London quoted the opinion of Professor Thiersch respecting the Seminary of Teachers at Kayerslautern. We solicit our readers' attention to the very passage which the Right Reverend Prelate read to the House of Lords. The Professor, on whom the Bishop passed so just an eulogium, respects the ennobling sentiments of Christian charity which induced the Government, in the circle of the Rhine, to establish a common seminary for teachers. 'In the Bavarian circle of the Rhine,' he says, 'there is but one seminary for teachers. This is too little, both for the number of pupils to be instructed and for the wants of different confessions. It was rightly observed to me at the Training Seminary of Neuwied, by its excellent director Braun, that an institution of this kind flourishes better the more nearly it approximates to a family circle; and as its object is not so much instruction as education, that about thirty-six is the largest number it should contain. Besides, many arguments recommend the division of the seminary according to confessions of faith. I know and respect the motives which dictated that, in the circle of the Rhine, both confessions (Protestant and Romanist) should be united in a single seminary, in the advantages of which even the future rabbis should be allowed to participate. But it is conceivable, and the experience of other countries shows that it is found, that when seminaries are divided, toleration may be secured both among teachers and communities; indeed, that this is more effectually attained, the more each confession is secured in its real wants. Among these wants it would seem that the education and instruction of the persons to whom elementary Schools are to be intrusted must be especially included; and since such an education cannot be conceived unless its basis is firmly laid in the knowledge of some Christian confession, therefore the division of seminaries according to modes of faith, as happens in Nassau, in Prussia, and perhaps one may say in every other country, is necessarily required.' Apparently adopting the erroneous opinion that the plan of religious instruction proposed for the Model School only was to be extended to other Schools, the Bishop also referred, in support of his argument, to the opinion of M. Guizot, when, as Minister of Public Instruction in France, he was intrusted with the execution of the Law of the 28th of June 1833. This opinion was extracted from a circular addressed to the French Préfets on the 24th of July 1833. The Bishop quoted only part of the paragraph of the circular relating to this question; we will give the whole, and we shall then request our readers' attention to the opinion of M. Cousin in his Report to the Chamber of Peers, as the head of the Commission charged with the examination of the ' Projet de Loi' on Primary Instruction in 1833. M. Guizot says, 'In those communes in which the inhabitants profess different forms of religion recognised by the State, Schools particularly attached to each of these religious denominations may be established with consent of the Municipal Council, and under my authorisation. It is, in general, desirable that children whose parents do not profess the same religious opinions, should early contract, by frequenting the same Schools, those habits of natural good-will and tolerance which will grow into sentiments of justice and union when they become fellow-citizens. It may, however, sometimes be necessary, even with a view to the public peace, that separate Schools should be opened in the same commune for each faith.' So far the Bishop, who omitted what follows, 'You will be careful to transmit to me before the 5th of September a Report of the deliberations of the Municipal Councils on this subject, with your suggestions. It will possibly happen that in some communes of mixed faith, the elections will have sent to the Municipal Council men only of one religious denomination, and the Councils thus formed might show themselves inclined to support only one School, notwithstanding local circumstances, such as old and deeply rooted dissensions, the importance of the population, or some other cause, might render the opening of a second School very desirable. I recommend you to examine with the greatest care the remonstrances which may be made against the designs of the Municipal Councils. You will communicate with them to ascertain their opinion — you will then send it to me with your own—and you will inform me what is the number of inhabitants belonging to each religious community, as well as all the facts necessary to illustrate the decision I shall have to form.

'Bear in mind, M. le Préfet, that the efficacy, as well as the liberty of religious education, and the security of families in this respect, are the principal considerations which ought to guide the administration in this matter.'

We find nothing here but a provision against the intolerance of a dominant sect, which might abuse the regulations of the Communal School, so as to make its religious instruction agree chiefly, if not solely, with its own views, and be a subject of vexation or suspicion to the other religious persuasion.

But we may learn from M. Cousin's Report to the Chamber of Peers in what spirit the Law of Primary Instruction in France was conceived. Concerning article 2, the Commission say they 'cannot but applaud the homage rendered to liberty of conscience, and to the sacred rights of parents, by the declaration, that the wishes of parents shall always be consulted and complied with in whatever concerns the participation of their children in religious instruction.'

Again—'The ninth article of the project of the Government attached at least one public elementary School to each commune; and it is evident that to compel a commune to have *one*, was not forbidding it to have *several*, if it could maintain them; and that in this case the children of the commune should be distributed in the best way possible. A vast number of urban communes have several Schools; and then, instead of dispersing through them all the children of different communions, it is the constant practice of the local authorities to collect the children of one communion in one School, whenever they are numerous enough to compose a whole School, and the local resources allow it. The Chamber of Deputies has deemed this practice sufficiently important to find a place in the law. This is a fresh homage to religious liberty, to which we subscribe; and we propose to adopt the amendment of the Chamber of Deputies, wording it as follows:—"In case local circumstances permit, the Minister of Public Instruction may, after hearing the Municipal Council, authorise, as Communal Schools, the Schools more peculiarly attached to any one of the modes of public worship recognised by the State."

'Thus, when there is but one School, all sects will frequent it, and will there receive a common instruction which, without injury to religious liberty (placed under the perpetual security of Article 2), will strengthen the ties which ought to unite all the children of the same country. Whenever there are several Schools in a commune, the several sects shall be divided; but these different Schools shall all be established on the same footing, and with the same title: they shall all enjoy the same dignity, and all the inhabitants of the commune shall contribute to their common support; as, in a higher sphere, all the citizens contribute to the general tax which goes to the maintenance of the different churches. This measure of perfect tolerance appears to us conformable to the true spirit of religion, favourable to the public peace, worthy of the intelligence of our age and of the munificence of a great nation.'

Now it cannot be too constantly borne in mind that the

regulations of the Committee of Privy Council respecting the religious instruction of children of different sects in one School, related only to the Model School, and that, as we have said before, the Committee (with rare exceptions admitted on the plea of urgent necessity only) intended to confine the application of the money voted by Parliament to the assistance of Schools connected with the National Society and the British and Foreign School Society. The Bishop of London's argument was therefore addressed against a plan which was not contained in the Minutes of the Committee of Privy Council, and to represent which, as within their contemplation, would be an unwarrantable assumption. But if the spirit of the French Law, to which the Right Reverend Prelate appealed, be in harmony with his Lordship's views, we shall rejoice to reckon so able an advocate among the champions of civil and religious liberty.

The inferences which Professor Pillans draws from the practice of the German states to which the Bishop of London referred, and from the circular addressed by M. Guizot to the Préfets of France, are exactly the opposite of those which the Bishop of London conceives himself entitled to make. As we have quoted the extracts alluded to by the Right Reverend Prelate, we place in contrast with his inferences those of the able Head-Master of the High School, and now Professor of Humanity in the University of Edinburgh.

'Are you aware what is the system in Germany in that respect (of religion)?—I should say the arrangements in Germany upon that subject are extremely liberal, and, with every anxiety for religious instruction, provide at the same time for the cases of different religions with the greatest attention, and with the most perfect impartiality.

'Do you not suppose that a sufficient religious education could be conveyed without the conveyance, at the same time, of any peculiar religious doctrine?—I am disposed to think so as regards children, both because I think that the doctrines of our religion, as far as they have a tendency to influence the habits and practice of the young, may be separated and kept distinct from the peculiar opinions of any one sect, and because such opinions embodied in any school-books, I should consider as nearly ineffectual for any purpose at all, turning, as they generally do, upon points which are altogether beyond the comprehension of the young mind; and therefore it is that I think it most of all desirable to have a system of religious instruction for Schools founded upon the Scriptures, but directed only to those parts of the sacred volume which have a moral tendency, and which are likely to influence the conduct, cherish the best affections, and regulate the behaviour of the young. I am fortified in that opinion by the example of the German States, where the School instruction is founded on this principle, as well as of France, where the law on that head is very nearly a transcript of the German.

'Has it ever suggested itself to you, in the matter of teaching religion, that teaching theology is one thing, and inculcating religious habits is another?—Yes, I think that is obvious, though certainly not sufficiently attended to in practice.

'In the creation of religious habits, do not all sorts of Christians agree, as far as you have had an opportunity of considering the subject of teaching?—I think so.

'Supposing that we wanted to teach theology to pupils, the teaching of theology would be like the teaching of any other science?—It certainly requires a matured understanding to deal with subjects so deep and difficult; nor can it be a very profitable employment for the mind of a child to be turned to points of doctrine upon which, from its very nature, it cannot be informed.

'So that, in fact, the business of a teacher of the people, considering the matter of national education, would be to form religious habits; and those might be formed in a national School which did not impose any dogmata upon the minds of the pupils?—I should say so certainly; at the same time I wish it to be understood, that by dogmata I mean the peculiar tenets of any particular sect: the leading and distinctive doctrines of Christianity ought not to be omitted. It is these only, I conceive, that are within the province of the schoolmaster, his vocation being more of a literary than of an ecclesiastical character.

'Assuming that there is a general coincidence in all Christian sects, those truths might be taught in a national School, without trenching upon any religious differences that might exist between them?—I think they might.

'And, therefore, if there were a spirit of forbearance among the Christian sects at this time existing in England, there would, in reality, be no objection on this score to the institution of a national education?—Not the least, I should think. There is in the present day, as far as I have observed, less of excitement and mutual hostility between the different sects in Germany and France than in England; and, accordingly, in the ministerial and official instructions sent out to the prefect of the circle or department, as well as to the teachers themselves, they are strongly enjoined to encourage mixed Schools, where the children may practically learn the principle of toleration and mutual forbearance; and where that cannot be done, the authorities are invited to take every means to provide such religious instruction apart as shall be thought necessary, or even to form separate Schools. The last, however, they consider as a resource not to be resorted to, unless all means of uniting the two persuasions shall be found unavailing.

'Do you not suppose that the teaching of various sects in one School, under that system of Catholic faith, if it may be so called, would very much tend to promote general kindliness amongst the whole population?—I think so desirable an object most likely to be attained by such a joint and mixed system. Judging both from reason and experience, I should say it is a result that could scarcely fail to take place.

'Do you not think a true Christian feeling would be created by such a system of National Education?—I do.

'Do you consider that, in any way, the interests of

religion would be injured by such a system? — On the contrary, it appears to me that the amount of religious feeling and true Christianity would be increased very considerably by such an arrangement, inasmuch as we are all taught to believe, and cannot help believing, who are familiar with the Scriptures and the New Testament, that brotherly love is the first of Christian virtues.'

The religious instruction of the candidate teachers in the Normal School was, by the regulations of the Committee of Privy Council, to be in strict conformity with the tolerant principles which have characterised our modern legislation.

The regulation contained in the Minute of the 11th of April was as follows:—'The religious instruction of all candidate teachers connected with the Established Church to be committed to the chaplain, and the special religious instruction to be committed (in any case in which a wish to that effect is expressed) to the licensed minister of the religious persuasion of the candidate teacher, who is to attend the School at stated periods, to assist and examine the candidate teachers in their reading on religious subjects, and to afford them spiritual advice.'

Let us inquire whether the Dissenters of England are entitled to so much respect in the regulations of a Normal School. We may ascertain their title to consideration by examining the degree in which they have spontaneously assumed the charge of the primary education of the people of this country. If we find them in charge of a considerable amount of the primary education at present provided for the people, those who will not listen to right may perhaps be inclined to bend to necessity; or those who refuse to admit the principle must contrive to dispose of the fact. And here, we again find ourselves greatly indebted to the labours of the London and Manchester Statistical Societies. In the towns of Manchester, Salford, Liverpool, Bury, York, and Birmingham, comprising an estimated population of 713,000 inhabitants, the following Table exhibits the number of children receiving instruction in the Sunday Schools of different religious classes, and also affords similar information respecting the three divisions of Westminster, comprising 215,000 inhabitants

	Manchester, Salford, Liverpool, Bury, York, and Birmingham.			Westminster in Three Divisions.		
	No. of Schools.	No. of Scholars on book.	Average attendance.	No. of Schools.	No. of Scholars on book.	Average attendance.
Church Establishment	96	27,151	21,772	14	2115	1517
Dissenters	171	49,675	39,412	26	4152	2794
Catholics	16	5686	4563	—	—	—
Unconnected with any Religious Body	1	150	65	—	—	—
Total	284	82,662	65,812	40	6267	4311

NOTE. In the case of Birmingham, the average attendance is not specified; it is therefore presumed to be the same as the number of scholars on books.

The number of Sunday Schools in these towns under the Church Establishment was 107; under Dissenters, 197; under Catholics, 16; unconnected with any religious body, 4. The average attendance of scholars at the Church Schools was 22,841; at those of Dissenters, 42,206; at Catholic Schools, 4563; and at Schools unconnected with any religious body, 513.

The Table referred to in the note contains these facts in detail for the five northern towns.[1]

The religious profession of the teachers of the various classes of day and evening Schools in Manchester, Salford, Liverpool, Bury, and York, and in Westminster, is shown in the summary (p. 273), proving to what extent Dissenters have charge of the common daily instruction of the children of the middle and lower classes in the great towns of this country.

In the above classes of Schools, out of 2159 teachers, 1185 were members of the Established Church; 170 were Catholics; and 730 Dissenters; while the religious profession of 74 teachers was not ascertained.

[1] See Appendix, Table No. IV.

Explanation of Measures of 1839

	NORTHERN TOWNS.					WESTMINSTER.				
	Number of Teachers.	Established Church.	Catholics.	Dissenters.	Not ascertained.	Number of Teachers.	Established Church.	Catholics.	Dissenters.	Not ascertained.
Dame Schools	606	285	62	240	19	130	97	—	29	4
Common boys' and girls' Schools	455	209	60	163	23	129	100	2	22	5
Superior boys' and girls' Schools	324	177	11	130	6	129	110	—	17	2
Infant Schools	30	18	1	11	—	17	12	—	5	—
Charity and Endowed Schools	119	74	8	34	3	55	36	2	14	3
Evening Schools	165	67	24	65	9	—	—	—	—	—
Total	1699	830	166	643	60	460	355	4	87	14

We are indebted to the Reports of the Commissioners of Inquiry into the Condition of the Hand-loom Weavers for the following statement of the condition of popular education in the city of Coventry, and the contiguous weaving districts of the ribbon manufacture, as collected by their secretary, Joseph Fletcher, Esq.

'From an accompanying Table[1] it will be seen,

'1st. That the population of the City and Weaving District of Coventry in 1831, was somewhat more than 55,000, and must now, therefore, reckoning on an increase of 15 per cent., which that of the previous period more than justifies, be no less than 63,000.

'2nd. That the number of healthy children, *from two to fourteen years of age*, which the modern prevalence of Dame and Infant Schools in our manufacturing districts marks as the limits of the School ages, is therefore about 15,000, or nearly one-fourth of the population; the proportion of those from 5 to 15 in the City and County of

---

[1] It has not been considered necessary to reprint this Table in the Appendix in confirmation of the late Mr. Fletcher's statement, which was not challenged at any time. J. P. K. S. 1862.

the City in 1821, being between one-fifth and one-fourth, according to the census.

'3rd. That besides the children of the richer classes at the City Free Grammar School, and about twenty-five private Schools, there are 9369 children receiving instruction of some kind, so that the total number of children receiving instruction will be about *two-thirds* of those from two to fourteen years of age, while the other *third*, are under no School discipline whatever, even on the Sabbath.

'4th. That of the total number receiving instruction, only 2957, or scarcely *one-third*, receive any whatever in *private* Schools, at the cost of their parents; and of this number, excepting the children who attend the very few pay Schools which give an instruction similar to that of the ordinary Lancasterian Schools, *nearly the whole* are in Dame Schools, or subscription nurseries of the most wretched description, in which little attempt at religious instruction is made (though sometimes the Catechisms of different creeds are found in the same Schools), and which are best described by their usual name of 'out-of-the-way Schools,' from the children being sent to them chiefly to be out of the way of their parents or of harm.

'5th. That 6412, or more than *two-thirds* of the children receiving any instruction, *receive only public instruction*, which is already, therefore, a permanent institution, though on the voluntary system.

'6th. That of this public instruction, nearly two-thirds is, at the present moment, *in the hands of Dissenters*, with some few *Roman Catholics*, under whose management 4123 of these children are receiving all the schooling which they obtain; leaving only 2289 under the management of the *Church*.

'7th. That of the children receiving public instruction, 4150, or nearly *two-thirds*, are under only *Sunday School* teaching, which is chiefly religious, and, as a means of secular instruction, almost beneath notice; and of the total number of children receiving *only* this Sunday schooling, 3415, or nearly *seven-eighths*, are in the Schools of Dissenters; the predominance being yet greater in the country districts than in the city.

'8th. That 1510 children, or nearly *one-fourth* of those receiving public instruction, attend *unendowed* Day Schools, of the character of National Schools generally, with some few Infant Schools, in which the number of children attending those under the management of Dissenters, is, in the city of Coventry, approaching *two to one* of those attending the Church Schools; while in the Rural Districts, the poverty and dispersion of the Dissenting population, leave the *daily* instruction almost wholly to the Church Schools; and the *total* of children receiving instruction in public Day Schools, supported by voluntary subscriptions in the city and rural parishes jointly, is therefore divided between the Church Schools and the Dissenting Schools, in nearly the reverse proportion that is observed in the city.

'9th. That the *whole* of the remaining 752 children receiving public daily instruction, are in Schools more or less well *endowed*, of a character in few instances superior to National Schools, and nearly all under the management of Churchmen; and it is by the addition of these alone that the Church acquires a decided preponderance of 846, even in regard to the number of *day* scholars, to meet the overwhelming balance of nearly 3000 in the exclusively Sunday teaching.

'11th. That secular instruction, at all worthy of the name, being attempted only in the public Day Schools, and the few common Day Schools of superior character, the proportion of children under instruction to the population is rather 1 in 20 than 1 in 6, as the mere enumeration of the scholars of every class would indicate,—an enumeration assuredly in excess, through the prevalent desire of teachers to represent their Schools in the best light.

'12th. That much has been done by these several classes of Schools towards redeeming the labouring population of this district from a state approaching to absolute barbarism, cannot be doubted; any more than that somewhat of this has been pursued in a spirit of rivalry, where much more might have been accomplished by united efforts.

'And 13th. That there is still a want of any sufficient influence by which the rising generation of this district can be preserved from pursuing the like courses, and abiding in the same rudeness and misery which has been the usual lot of their predecessors.

'JOSEPH FLETCHER.

'3 *Trafalgar Square, Westminster,*
  '*July* 1, 1839.'

In the purely rural districts the Dissenters are not numerous. The inhabitants of agricultural parishes consist for the most part of the proprietors, the clergy, the farmers, and the labourers. Dissent has spread chiefly among the middle classes; but exceedingly less among the farmers than the inhabitants of towns. The gentry and clergy have little encouragement or assistance from the farmers in the erection or improvement of Schools. The common argument employed by the farmer is, that he had little or no instruction himself, and that he does not see why his labourers' children should be as well instructed as his own. No general sympathy in the improvement of the education of agricultural labourers can be expected, until proprietary Schools for the children of farmers have been established; and we hope that every intelligent landowner, and especially our aristocracy, will recognise the importance of thus providing such an education for farmers' children as shall enable the next generation to keep exact accounts of the income and outlay of their farms—to comprehend the mechanical improvements recently introduced into husbandry— to read with profit the treatises in which agriculture is treated as a science — to understand as much of general science as may enable them with less empiricism, and therefore with a greater chance of success, to conduct their trials of manures and composts on their different soils, and to avoid a waste of capital on experiments in draining, irrigation, &c., which are now often conducted contrary to ascertained principles. A taste for reading itself would assist the diffusion of a knowledge of improvements in agriculture, and would thus increase the intelligence and enterprise of a class of men who contribute so largely to the national wealth.

The clergyman might then rejoice to find his exertions for the erection and support of Schools for the children of labourers in the agricultural districts more cordially and steadily seconded by the farmers than they now are. He would also be able to reclaim from misappropriation educational endowments, on which parochial authorities have for a long time laid their hands; and among the labourers themselves would arise a stronger sense of the value of education to their children. At the present we fear we have for the most part to record, respecting the rural districts, a melancholy void in the means of instruction for the poorer classes. The exceptions to this rule are attributable almost solely to the interference of the proprietors of the soil, or of the clergy, to whose exertions we must owe any further advance which can at present be made.

But in the towns the influence of the middle class is, from their numbers and intelligence, predominant; and, consequently, that of the Dissenters is great. No Government could long exist in this country which should either neglect the legal right which the Established Church has to expect the protection and support of the Executive Government, or which, on the other hand, should refuse to admit that a large body of Her Majesty's subjects who dissent from the Established Church have a legal right to an equal distribution of all the secular advantages derivable from a Government supported by the public funds.

But when to the rights recognised by the law the Dissenters have superadded the claim arising out of the exertions they have spontaneously made to provide for education in some of the most important districts of this country, we are at a loss to know, on what pretence they can be excluded from sharing the secular benefits of any provision for National Education furnished at the public cost, or how the Government could have been justified, either in formally excluding them from the privilege of educating their teachers in the Normal School, or (which is equivalent to that) in imposing such religious observances on those teachers, or so inadequately providing for their entire religious freedom, as practically to have occasioned their exclusion.

Nothing would tend so much to increase the political power of religious denominations not agreeing with the Established Church, as to attempt a partial or exclusive distribution of any new civil advantages, after admitting them to a theoretical equality of civil rights. We believe it to be impossible to place on the statute book any such law; but once there, the clamour raised would be so loud and fierce, that any Administration must quail before it, and if Parliament did not listen to the indignant remonstrances of the constituency, this would become the sole topic of electioneering agitation until the new enactment was repealed.

Conceiving the application of the public funds to the exclusive secular advantage of any class of religionists impossible, we are of opinion that two courses only were open to the Committee of Privy Council in proposing the plan of a Normal School—

1. To establish separate Normal Schools for different classes of religionists.
2. To establish a Normal School open to all.

One principle our laws require should be preserved inviolate under all circumstances, viz., that the Established Church should suffer no detriment, but should hold her position among the religious denominations of this country, as the Church, whose head is the Sovereign, and whose institutions are interwoven with those of the temporal power.

If, then, separate Normal Schools were established for different classes of religionists, let us examine in what way an impartial distribution of the secular advantages of such institutions could have been secured. A Normal School being established for the Church, would it be necessary to establish a separate Normal School for each one of the numerous sects, or do those sects admit of some classification into groups, for each of which a Normal School might be provided? Clearly the latter is the only practicable plan, and the British and Foreign School Society is founded on a principle which provides Schools for the children, and a certain amount of training for the teachers, of the Orthodox Congregational Dissenters and of the Society of Friends. The plan of separate Schools for each sect is thus impracticable, and that of a common School for the Orthodox Congregational Dissenters is in practical operation. We may infer, from these premises, that the necessity of distributing impartially the secular advantages of such institutions under the plan of separate Normal Schools for separate classes of religionists would have required at least the following schools:—1. A Normal School for the Church.—2. A Normal School for the Wesleyan Methodists.—3. A Normal School for the Orthodox Congregational Dissenters, and for the Society of Friends. —4. A Normal School for the Roman Catholics. And it would have been necessary to make provision for any other classes by admitting them to the secular benefits of one or other of the above Schools without imposing any religious observances.

We are content to state, without comment, the scheme which appears to us to afford the only ultimately practicable alternative to the plan proposed by the Government. We do not hesitate to say, the concern of the Committee of Council to preserve the interests of the Church, while they exercised the authority confided to them by the temporal Head of the Church for the promotion of National Education, so as to protect the rights of conscience, could alone have induced the Committee to prefer the plan which they announced in their Minute of the 11th of April.

We have sufficiently vindicated that plan from the

charge of a tendency to promote latitudinarianism by our previous remarks—we have now shown what is evidently the only practicable alternative to the adoption of that plan.

One feature of the recent debates is a source of no little regret to the friends of education. The fact of the want of means of instruction for the people was admitted; but little or nothing transpired indicating that the extent of the void was known.—Had the fearful breadth of this chasm in our National Institutions been perceived, we cannot believe that so much time would have been expended in exaggerating every difficulty obstructing the extension of education to the entire people, whether those difficulties be referable to the religious divisions which unhappily separate the middle classes into hostile camps, or whether they originated in the opposition of any of the existing voluntary associations for primary education. Assuredly the privileges of the Established Church, and also the rights of conscience, must be respected, and the religious education of the people is of paramount importance. Neither are we inclined to disparage the value of any of the existing voluntary associations; but it is of infinitely greater importance that the feuds of sects and the interests of bodies incompetent effectually to deal with this national question, should not rob the people of England of the heritage which the Government, after periods of ruinous deprivation, was about to restore to them. The grievance would not be greater if the administration of justice was impeded, or rendered partial, by any attempt to extend spiritual jurisdiction from the Ecclesiastical Courts to the Civil, or to renew the interdicts upon the enjoyment of the civil advantages of society in consequence of some slight to the representative of the Church, or some interference with his spiritual power. But if the whole of this kingdom were placed under an ecclesiastical interdict; if marriages could no longer be solemnised; if the dead were left unburied; and the Churches closed, terrible though the calamity would be, we find a parallel to it in that wide-spread and demoralising ignorance which paralyses all the healthful influences of society, if it does not convert its elements into engines of mutual destruction.

APPENDIX

TABLE No. I.

District.	Estimated population at period of inquiry.	Children from 3 to 13 estimated, without deducting any from number living between 5 and 15, according to population returns.	Number attending superior private schools, and belonging to middle and upper classes.	Number of children of working classes from 3 to 13, for whom education should be provided, one-third being deducted from the whole number between 3 and 13 for those privately educated, or employed, or sick, or preventing by casualties from attending school, and also deducting the number attending superior private schools.	Number of children of working classes attending endowed and charity schools, and schools attached to public institutions, and infant schools.	Number attending dame schools, and common day schools.	Number uneducated in week-day schools.	Very ill Educated.	Uneducated in day schools.	Total uneducated, and very ill educated.
Manchester	200,000	50,000	2934	30,400	4103	11,624	14,641			26,265
Salford	55,000	13,750	882	8285	1776	3357	3172			6509
Liverpool	230,000	57,500	4080	34,254	13,500	11,336	9418			20,754
Bury	20,000	5000	174	3160	652	1648	860			2508
York	28,000	7000	716	3951	1296	1294	731			2025
	533,000	133,250	8786	80,050	21,957	29,259	28,822			58,061
Ratio to children of in attendance on	working school	Ratio classes	to who	population ought to be	1 in 24 / 1 in 5⅔	.	.			1 to 9 / 5⅘ to
Westminster (in 3 divisions). St. Martin in Fields, St. Clement Danes, St. Mary-le-Strand, St. Paul's Covent Garden, The Savoy, St. John & St. Margaret, St. George, St. James, and St. Anne, Soho.	50,000 / 54,000 / 111,000	10,000 / 10,800 / 22,000	1017 / 690 / 2429	5650 / 6510 / 12,371	1861 / 2718 / 3382	1124 / 1675 / 1944	2665 / 2117 / 7045			3789 / 3792 / 8989
	215,000	43,000	4136	24,531	7961	4743	11,827			16,570

Ratio to population	1 in 27	1 to 13
Ratio to children of working classes who ought to be in attendance on school	1 in 3	2 to 3

See Reports as to average expence of education in Schools, London and Manchester Statistical Societies.

The table contains the following results for

	Manchester, Salford, Liverpool, Bury, York.	Westminster, 3 Divisions.
Estimated population at period of inquiry	533,000	215,000
Estimated number of children between 3 and 13	133,250	43,000
Number of children of working classes from 3 to 13, for whom education should be provided	80,050	24,531
Number of children of working classes who attend endowed and charity schools, and schools attached to public institutions and infant schools	21,957	7961
Number very ill educated in dame and commnon day schools	29,259	4743
Number uneducated in week day schools*	28,822	11,827

* Of these several receive some instruction (chiefly religious) in Sunday Schools. See Table No. IV.

A Summary of the proficiency of the Prisoners in Norwich Castle, in Reading, &c. at the time of their commitment, taken at different periods from 1826 to 1835.

		Could not read at all.	Merely knew the Alphabet.	Could read only so imperfectly as to be of no utility to them.	Could read in the Testament, but could not write.	Could both read and write.	Total of those who could read, and of those who could read and write.	Total uneducated.	TOTAL.
1826	Feb. 7	153	24	40	45	89	134	217	351
	Mar. 8	173	28	49	51	99	150	250	400
	June 6	223	32	60	56	129	185	315	500
	Oct. 24	264	40	68	68	160	228	372	600
	Dec. 27	311	43	85	81	180	261	439	700
1827	Mar. 15	350	52	105	91	202	293	507	800
	June 13	393	57	119	109	222	331	569	900
	Oct. 16	430	60	128	124	258	382	618	1000
1828	Feb. 5	475	66	141	137	281	418	682	1100
	April 28	515	67	153	153	312	465	735	1200
	Sept. 1	554	72	167	169	338	507	793	1300
	Nov. 29	604	77	177	181	361	542	858	1400
1829	Feb. 4	641	81	187	197	394	591	909	1500
	April 4	678	88	205	207	422	629	971	1600
	July 13	718	94	215	221	452	673	1027	1700
	Oct. 21	750	99	228	237	486	723	1077	1800
1830	Jan. 21	793	100	242	253	512	765	1105	1900
	Mar. 29	822	105	262	273	538	811	1189	2000
	July 28	848	109	286	291	566	857	1243	2100
	Nov. 15	875	111	306	310	598	908	1292	2200
	Dec. 24	916	117	324	320	623	943	1357	2300
1831	Feb. 10	955	120	339	339	647	986	1414	2400
	May 4	989	123	351	357	680	1037	1463	2500
	Sept. 3	1019	127	366	378	710	1088	1512	2600
	Dec. 7	1052	129	381	395	743	1138	1562	2700
1832	Jan. 31	1084	133	398	415	770	1185	1615	2800
	April 9	1113	140	417	433	797	1230	1670	2900
	June 25	1146	147	428	445	834	1279	1721	3000
	Oct. 15	1175	152	449	461	863	1324	1776	3100
1833	Jan. 5	1204	157	459	479	901	1380	1820	3200
	Mar. 19	1238	166	470	494	932	1426	1874	3300
	June 18	1268	173	483	511	965	1476	1924	3400
	Sept. 27	1296	177	493	533	1001	1534	1966	3500
	Nov. 28	1330	186	499	555	1030	1585	2015	3600
1834	Jan. 16	1364	194	508	577	1057	1634	2066	3700
	Mar. 22	1397	204	521	599	1079	1678	2122	3800
	June 24	1428	211	534	617	1110	1727	2173	3900
	Oct. 23	1463	219	540	635	1143	1778	2222	4000
1835	Feb. 10	1499	222	547	651	1181	1832	2268	4100
	April 7	1542	231	554	675	1198	1873	2327	4200
	July 16	1581	237	561	693	1228	1921	2379	4300
	Nov. 4	1611	249	571	715	1254	1969	2431	4400

N.B. All recommittals are omitted, and also those prisoners who may have been committed for too short a time to come under the Chaplain's regular and continued instruction.

Manchester Statistical Society, 1834, 5, 6, 7.

	Church Establishment			Wesleyan			Independent			Wesleyan Association			Baptist			Calvinistic Methodist.			Methodist New Connection.			Catholic.			Unitarian.			Primitive Methodist.			Bible Christian.			Welsh Independent.			Of other Sects.			Unconnected with any Religious Body.		
	No. of Schools	Total Scholars	Avg. Att.	No.	Total	Avg.	No.	Total	Avg.	No.	Total	Avg.	No.	Total	Avg.	No.	Total	Avg.	No.	Total	Avg.	No.	Total	Avg.	No.	Total	Avg.	No.	Total	Avg.	No.	Total	Avg.	No.	Total	Avg.	No.	Total	Avg.
Manchester	25	10,284	7954	18	9066	6558	14	1059	2864	...	...	...	5	1533	1035	...	...	...	5	1453	1115	9	3880	3136	1	283	182	2	401	320	2	401	315	3	779	500	5	1057	827	...	...	...
Salford	9	2741	1900	5	2630	1766	4	1487	1138	1	213	134	...	...	...	...	...	...	2	553	332	2	612	539	1	221	128	1	702	318	1	98	83	1	176	166	3	170	122	1	150	65
Liverpool	27	6318	4902	11	2371	1859	11	2361	1747	6	890	662	6	833	628	3	673	585	3	404	265	2	700	440	2	325	282	1	160	110	...	...	...	...	...	...	4	333	235	...	...	...
Bury	5	1535	1188	2	892	780	...	990	840	...	...	...	...	...	...	...	...	...	1	412	400	1	155	110	1	330	250	*	*	*	...	...	...	...	...	...	1	116	80	...	...	...
York	15	1708	1263	4	941	577	...	498	281	...	...	...	...	...	...	...	...	...	...	...	...	...	...	...	1	60	40	1	40	30	...	...	...	...	...	...	1	...	...	...	...	...
Total	81	22,586	17,207	40	15,900	11,540	27	1395	6870	7	1103	796	11	2366	1667	3	673	585	11	2822	2112	14	5348	4225	6	1219	882	6	1303	778	3	499	398	4	955	666	15	1676	1264	1	150	65

* Included with Wesleyans.

	Number of Schools.	Number of Scholars on Books.	Average Attendance.
Church Establishment	78	22,064	16,759
Dissenters	132	37,821	27,558
Catholics	14	5348	4225
Unconnected with any Religious Body	4	672	513
Total	228	65,905	49,055

Similar information respecting the City of Westminster, founded on Reports of the London Statistical Society, to that given in p. 285.

	Church Establishment.			Wesleyan.			Independent.			Presbyterian.			Baptist.			Lady Huntingdon's Connection.			Dissenter not defined.		
St. Martin's-in-the-Fields, St. Clement Danes, St. Mary-le-Strand, St. Paul's, Covent Garden, and the Savoy	5	683	370	...	...	...	2	422	393	1	80	80	...	...	...	1	370	250	...	...	...
St. John and St. Margaret	4	751	579	1	330	220	6	842	439	...	...	...	1	140	105	...	...	...	1	65	30
St. George, St. James, and St. Anne, Soho	5	681	568	2	196	115	8	1287	882	2	285	170	1	135	110	...	...	...	...	...	...
Total	2115	1517		3	526	335	16	2551	1714	3	365	250	2	275	215	1	370	250	1	65	30

	Number of Schools.	Number of Scholars on Books.	Average Attendance.
Church Establishment	14	2115	1517
Dissenters	26	4152	2794
Total	40	6267	4311

FIRST STEPS AS TO PUPIL TEACHERS

4. *First steps in Workhouses and Schools of Industry for pauper children, in the apprenticeship of Pupil Teachers. A few brief extracts from Reports* (1837 to 1840).

THE first step which my memory recalls in the employment of Pupil Teachers occurred in a Norfolk Workhouse, in the case of a boy who became a Pupil Teacher there, and entered a Training College, and after some years' education became the master of a school. Having succeeded the late Sir Edward Parry in the administration of the Poor Law Amendment Act in Norfolk, the organisation of the workhouse schools for pauper children occupied my attention. I procured teachers from Mr. Wood's Edinburgh Sessional School, and from Mr. David Stow's schools in Glasgow, now the Free Church Training College. An organising Master from Mr. Wood's school (Mr. Horne, afterwards a master in Battersea Training College), successively resided in several workhouses of the Eastern Counties for a month or two. He reconstructed the school in each workhouse. Wherever the schoolmaster was capable, he placed him—with improved knowledge of method, a better organised and disciplined school, new desks, books, and apparatus—in charge of the training of the children, in humble learning, religion, and industry. If quite incapable, the teacher was removed, and another appointed. In the Gressenhall Workhouse of the Mitford and Launditch Union, Mr. Horne found an intelligent, active schoolmaster, who entered eagerly into all our plans. The garden, the school, and the workshops, when once organised, flourished under his care. Some of his scholars caught his spirit. Among these was a lad named William Rush, who rapidly rose to the head of the little school. The master fell seriously ill; William Rush, unbidden, though a boy of only thirteen years of age, took charge of the scholars. The master of the Workhouse found the school in its usual order. The whole discipline and routine of the garden, workshop, and class instruction went on unbroken. The Guardians were summoned to witness the phenomenon. Their Chairman—my late lamented friend, Mr. Fredk. Walpole Keppel of Lexham—entered at once into the merits of the case, and authorised the boy to continue his work in the school. I visited the workhouse, and at my suggestion William Rush was thenceforth regarded as the apprenticed assistant of the schoolmaster, who soon recovered, but afterwards employed Rush as his Assistant Teacher. This incident afforded a valuable hint, of which I availed myself in organising other workhouse schools. Generally we sought out the most promising boys, with a view to retain their services for a series of years as Assistant Teachers. Rush was afterwards sent to Norwood, and thence removed to Battersea Training School.

On taking charge of the Metropolitan District, I was early impressed with a conviction of the necessity of organising the establishments in which the pauper children, sent to be reared in the country under 'Jonas Hanway's Act,' had been grouped together from the houses of the dames, or others to whom they had been originally confided. I found in Mr. Aubin, at Norwood, an intelligent, honest, and active contractor—ready to adopt all reasonable improvements. He was, with equal good sense and kindness of disposition, desirous to be faithful to his young charge. The Guardians of the City of London Union first adopted my suggestions for the reorganisation of Mr. Aubin's Children's Establishment at Norwood. Aided by a grant of £500 per annum, which Earl Russell—then Secretary of State for the Home

First Steps as to Pupil Teachers

Department—made, this pauper childrens' asylum became the Norwood District School of Industry. It has since been transferred to Hanwell, where, under the faithful superintendence of Mr. Edward Carleton Tufnell, it is now the Central London District School for Pauper Children.

In Mr. Aubin's School of Industry at Norwood, and afterwards at Limehouse, Edmonton, and elsewhere, the system of Pupil Teachers was rapidly introduced. They were not all apprenticed, but by the consent of their guardians all were to be retained in the School for a series of years. William Rush and others were sent up from rural workhouses at the expense of their patrons[1], in order that they might have the advantage of the systematic instruction and training then provided at Norwood, and conducted by masters much more skilful than any in charge of the rural workhouse Schools.

While the earliest of these arrangements were in successful operation, I visited Holland, and found that in many of their features these plans resembled those adopted in the Dutch Schools. This confirmed my conviction of their value, and I was careful to justify them[2] by a reference to the experience of Holland in the Report on the Training of Pauper Children, and on District Schools, written in 1838. Again in a Report on the Norwood School of Industry, dated 1st May, 1839, occur the following passages. (*Ibid*, pp. 106-7-8.)

' For each class monitors have been selected, who are chiefly employed in superintending the mechanical daily routine; that is, in assisting the teacher in assembling the class in order, in procuring and preserving silence and attention, in distributing the books, slates, pens, &c., in superintending lessons in which moral training forms no element, such as writing and ciphering. From these monitors have already been selected those most distin-

---

[1] William Rush at the expense of Mr. F. W. Keppel.
[2] Report to Secretary of State for Home Department from the Poor Law Commissioners on the Training of Pauper Children, p. 46.

guished by zeal, skill, attainments, and gentleness of disposition, who are to be apprenticed, and reared as teachers. The organisation of each class will not be complete until it has at least one monitor and a pupil teacher; and when the pupil teachers have acquired considerable skill, and the arrangements for the instruction of the monitors are complete, it is believed that 100 children may with such assistance be instructed by one master alternately, in two classes of 50, and in the gallery. Such an arrangement, however, supposes that one of these classes shall be employed in writing, ciphering, composition, or drawing, while the other is receiving instruction from the master in reading, geography, and other matters of general knowledge. The monitors and pupil teachers sleep in a room apart from the rest of the children; they have also recreation in a separate garden, and in the evening receive instruction in a room situated there, where they also read and prepare the lessons for their classes on the succeeding day.

'The pupil teachers are distinguished by a uniform dress, and wear upon their arms the number of the class to which they are at the time attached.

'Some children of schoolmasters, and some of the most intelligent boys in workhouse Schools, have been sent to Norwood either by private individuals or by Boards of Guardians; and have, in consequence of strong testimonials of character, attainments, and fondness for the duties of a teacher, been admitted into the class of pupil teachers. In such cases it is required that each child shall be furnished with the uniform of the pupil teachers at the expense of his patrons; and that 5s. per week shall be paid for his board and lodging; and it is now necessary to require that they shall be apprenticed for a term of five years, after a certain period of probation, so as to secure their being so reared as to enable them rightly to discharge the duties of a teacher.

'The indenture of apprenticeship stipulates that the moral conduct and character of the pupil shall continue to be such as to afford the superintendent teacher a confident expectation of his success. Each child will undergo a formal half-yearly examination, at each of which successive periods he will be required to prove his qualification to complete his apprenticeship by his attainments in the several branches of instruction and School discipline. The subjects of examination will be so graduated as to test his proficiency and talent, rising in each successive half-year towards the examination required from candidate teachers, after a certain residence in the School.

'Each class contains 50 children, and is furnished with at least one pupil teacher and a monitor. Two classes of 50 children each have, besides their pupil teachers and monitors, one teacher and one candidate teacher attached to them; the teacher instructs each class alternately, or both classes together in the gallery; the candidate teacher listens to the instruction given in the gallery; or, when he has attained sufficient proficiency, occasionally assists the teacher in giving these lessons. The candidate teacher also instructs one of the classes at the desks alternately with the teacher, so that they are both always receiving instruction either from the teacher or candidate teacher. Candidate teachers are not intrusted with the instruction of the children until they have been some time in the School; and they are then first attached to those classes which require the smallest amount of skill, and the most slender attainments, and afterwards to those where greater proficiency is requisite. The means for instructing the candidate teachers at Norwood will require to be enlarged and improved, as soon as it is apparent that the demand for teachers trained in this School renders such measures expedient.'

In a subsequent Report, dated December 1st, 1840[1], occurs the following passage:—

---

[1] See Poor Law Commissioners Report to Secretary of State for the Home Department, pp. 129, 130.

'Mr. Aubin has, under your directions, taken the first steps towards the apprenticeship of some of the best conducted and most advanced boys as pupil teachers. If he be enabled, by the Boards of Guardians, to carry into execution this plan of retaining by apprenticeship some of the most promising children in the School, rearing them in the constant practice of the duties of teachers, and preparing them, by separate instruction every evening, for that vocation, he will be enabled gradually to establish his School on the sure basis of the "*mixed method of instruction*"—the characteristics of which it has hitherto only partially and imperfectly attained.

'Mr. Aubin's first attention should therefore be steadily directed, *to rearing up* within the School a body of well-instructed pupil teachers to assist the teachers in the general duties of the School. This, however, he has hitherto failed to accomplish; but I trust that arrangements which have recently been made will insure the attainment of this advantage.

'The introduction of greater precision in the methods of instruction, and the assimilation of those methods to the most approved forms, will necessarily depend on the degree of skill which the pupil teachers attain, and on the amount of assistance which they are enabled to afford the teachers.

'All progress in the introduction of correct methods must necessarily be slow, and subject to frequent embarrassments under existing circumstances.'

These extracts may suffice to mark the gradual development of the Pupil-Teacher system. In the month of January, 1840, some of these Pupil Teachers were removed from Norwood to the Training School (since called College) at Battersea, where their further progress will be found to be described in the Report on that School.

TWO REPORTS

DESCRIBING

THE ORIGIN OF THE TRAINING COLLEGE AT BATTERSEA,—THE INTRODUCTION OF SOME OF THE PUPIL TEACHERS AS STUDENTS, — AND ITS ORGANISATION AND PROGRESS.

PREFACE.

The two following Reports on the Battersea Training School record the history of the joint enterprise in which my friend, Mr. Edward Carleton Tufnell, and I were engaged for some years, without, so far as I can call to mind, any material difference of views as to principles, or in the management of the School.

But I have no right to hold Mr. Tufnell responsible for the style or colouring of these two Reports. As I was resident in charge of the School, it was natural that these Reports should be drawn by me. With the exception of the translation of the tabular account of the courses of instruction given in the Swiss Normal Schools, Mr. Tufnell is not responsible for more than a general, though, I am sure, a cordial, approval.

FIRST REPORT ON THE TRAINING SCHOOL AT BATTERSEA

TO THE POOR LAW COMMISSIONERS.

January 1, 1841.

GENTLEMEN,

The efforts made by your Assistant Commissioners for the improvement of the training of pauper children in the rural and metropolitan districts, made apparent, at a very early period, the great difficulty of procuring the assistance of schoolmasters and schoolmistresses acquainted with the principles on which the education of this class of children ought to be conducted.

Very little inquiry confirmed what was previously suspected, that the number of English schoolmasters acquainted with the organisation and discipline of elementary schools, and skilful in the application of approved methods of instruction, is exceedingly small, and by no means on the increase. Successive applications were made to those sources from which teachers are usually obtained in England, but these applications were almost invariably unsuccessful, for a variety of reasons.

The teachers trained in the Model Schools of the metropolitan and other societies enter those schools with the expectation of taking charge of rural or town day schools. They are not instructed in the management of schools of industry. They are not trained in that regulation of the habits of children at meals, in their dormitories, and during hours of recreation, which is essential to the success of a school of industry for pauper children. Moreover, the period during which they receive instruction and are trained in the art of teaching in these Model Schools is unfortunately very short. Such Schools possess slender funds applicable to the maintenance of the candidate teachers. The candidates, therefore, are maintained by their own meagre resources or are dependent on their friends, in the hope of being able, at the expiration of a short period, to take charge of a School; or they are maintained by the patrons or committee of some School, the mastership of which they are to assume, and which is probably in course of erection. Their attendance on the Model School seldom exceeds six months, and often does not extend beyond three. But little reflection is necessary to prove, that in six months they cannot acquire all the knowledge which is desirable, either of the principles, the matter, or the art of elementary instruction.

These Model Schools will ere long be re-organised, with more abundant resources for the training of the candidate teachers, and doubtless the teachers then trained in them will go forth much better prepared for the discharge of their duties than at present.

The introduction of works of industry, however, forms no part of the plan of the improved arrangements hitherto announced, and they afford no means of preparing teachers to learn that system of moral management which is essential to the success of Schools for pauper children.

The training of pauper children in a workhouse or district School cannot be successful unless the teacher be moved by Christian charity to the work of rearing in religion and industry the outcast and orphan children of our rural and city population. The difficulty of redeeming by education the mischief wrought in generations of a vicious parentage can be estimated only by those who know how degenerate these children are.

The pauper children assembled at Norwood, from the garrets, cellars, and wretched rooms of alleys and courts, in the dense parts of London, are often sent thither in a low state of destitution, covered only with rags and vermin; often the victims of chronic disease; almost universally stunted in their growth; and sometimes emaciated with want. The low-browed and inexpressive physiognomy or malign aspect of the boys is a true index to the mental darkness, the stubborn tempers, the hopeless spirits, and the vicious habits, on which the master has to work. He needs no small support from Christian faith and charity for the successful prosecution of such a labour; and no quality can compensate for the want of that spirit of self-sacrifice and tender concern for the well-being of these children, without which their instruction would be anything but a labour of love. A baker or a shoemaker, or a shop apprentice, or commercial clerk, cannot be expected to be imbued with this spirit during a residence of six months in the neighbourhood of a Model School if he has not imbibed it previously at its source.

The men who undertake this work should not set about it in the spirit of hirelings, taking the speediest means to procure a maintenance with the least amount of trouble. A commercial country will always offer irresistible temptations to desert such a profession, to those to whom the annual stipend is the chief, if not sole, motive to exertion. The outcast must remain neglected, if there be no principle, which, even in the midst of a commercial people, will enable men to devote themselves to this vocation from higher motives than the mere love of money.

Experience of the motives by which the class of schoolmasters now plying their trade in this country are commonly actuated, is a graver source of want of confidence in their ability to engage in this labour than the absence of skill in their profession. A great number of them undertake these duties either because they are incapacitated by age or infirmity for any other, or because they have failed in all other attempts to procure a livelihood; or because, in the absence of well-qualified competitors, the least amount of exertion and talent enables the most indolent schoolmasters to present average claims on public confidence and support. Rare indeed are the examples in which skill and principle are combined in the agents employed in this most important sphere of national self-government. Other men will not enable you to restore the children of vagabonds and criminals to society, purged of the taint of their parents' vices, and prepared to perform their duties as useful citizens in a humble sphere.

The peculiarities of the character and condition of the pauper children demand the use of appropriate means for their improvement. The general principles on which the education of children of all classes should be conducted are doubtless fundamentally the same; but for each class specific modifications are requisite, not only in the methods but in the matter of instruction.

The discipline, management, and methods of instruction in elementary schools for the poor, differ widely from those which ought to characterise Schools for the middle or upper classes of society. The instruction of the blind, of the deaf and dumb, of criminals, of paupers, and of children in towns and in rural districts, renders necessary the use of a variety of distinct methods in order to attain the desired end.

The peculiarity of the pauper child's condition is, that his parents, either from misfortune, or indolence, or vice, have sunk into destitution. In many instances children descend from generations of paupers. They have been born in the worst purlieus of a great city, or in the most wretched hovels on the parish waste. They have suffered privation of every kind. Perhaps they have wandered about the country in beggary, or have been taught the arts of petty thieving in the towns. They have lived with brutal and cruel men and women, and have suffered from their caprice and mismanagment. They have seen much of vice and wretchedness, and have known neither comfort, kindness, nor virtue.

If they are sent very young to the workhouse, their entire training in religious knowledge, and in all the habits of life, devolves on the schoolmaster. If they come under his care at a later period, his task is difficult in proportion to the vicious propensities he has to encounter.

The children to whose improvement Pestalozzi devoted his life were of a similar class,— equally ignorant, and perhaps equally demoralised, in consequence of the internal discords attendant on the revolutionary wars, which at the period when his labours commenced had left Switzerland in ruin.

The class of children which De Fellenberg placed under the charge of Vehrli at Hofwyl were in like manner picked up on the roads of the canton— they were the outcasts of Berne.

These circumstances are among the motives which led us to a careful examination of the Schools of Industry and Normal Schools of the cantons of Switzerland. These schools are more or less under the influence of the lessons which Pestalozzi and De Fellenberg have taught that country. They differ in some important particulars from those which exist in England, and the experience of Switzerland in this peculiar department of elementary instruction appears pre-eminently worthy of attention.

Those Orphan and Normal Schools of Switzerland which have paid the deference due to the lessons of Pestalozzi and De Fellenberg, are remarkable for the gentleness and simplicity of the intercourse between the scholar and his master. The formation of character is always kept in mind as the great aim of education. The intelligence is enlightened, in order that it may inform the conscience, and that the conscience, looking forth through this intelligence, may behold a wider sphere of duty, and have at its command a greater capacity for action. The capacity for action is determined by the cultivation of habits appropriate to the duties of the station which the child must occupy.

Among the labouring class no habit is more essential to virtuous conduct than that of steady and persevering labour. Manual skill connects the intelligence with the brute force with which we are endued. The instruction in elementary Schools should be so conducted, as not only to assist the labourer in acquiring mechanical dexterity, but in bringing his intelligence to aid the labours of his hands, whether by a knowledge of the principles of form or numbers, or of the properties of natural objects, and the nature of the phenomena by which his labours are likely to be affected. In a commercial country it is pre-eminently important to give him such an acquaintance with geography as may stimulate enterprise at home, or may tend to swell the stream of colonisation which is daily extending the dominion of British commerce and civilisation. Labour, which brings the sweat upon the brows, requires relaxation, and the child should therefore learn to repose from toil among innocent enjoyments, and to avoid those vicious indulgences which waste the labourer's strength, rob his house of comfort, and must sooner or later be the source of sorrow. There is a dignity in the lot of man in every sphere, if it be not cast away. The honour and the joy of successful toil should fill the labourer's songs in his hour of repose. From religion man learns that all the artificial distinctions of society are as nothing before that God who searcheth the heart. Religion therefore raises the labourer to the highest dignity of human existence, the knowledge of the will and the enjoyment of the favour of God. Instructed by religion, the labourer knows how in daily toil he fulfils the duties and satisfies the moral and natural necessities of his existence, while the outward garb of mortality is gradually wearing off, and the spirit preparing for emancipation.

An education guided by the principles described in this brief sketch, appears to us appropriate to the preparation of the outcast and orphan children for the great work of a Christian's life.

After a trial of various expedients, to which allusion has been made in preceding Reports, it became apparent that the means of embracing within one comprehensive plan the training of the 50,000 pauper children now in the workhouses did not exist in this country; and the importance of not abandoning these children to the consequences of the misfortunes and vices of their parents grew in proportion to the difficulties with which the subject was encumbered.

That which seemed most important was the preparation of a class of teachers who would cheerfully devote themselves, and with anxious and tender solicitude, to rear these children, abandoned by all natural sympathies, as a wise and affectionate parent would prepare them for the duties of life.

To so grave a task as an attempt to devise the means of training these teachers, it was necessary to bring a patient and humble spirit, in order that the results of experience in this department might be examined, and that none that were useful might be hastily thrown aside. Our examination of the continental Schools was undertaken with this view. A visit was made to Holland at two successive periods, on the last of which we took one of Dr. Kay's most experienced schoolmasters with us, in order that he might improve himself by an examination of the methods of instruction in the Dutch Schools, all the most remarkable of which were minutely inspected. A visit has been paid to Prussia and Saxony, in which several of the chief Schools have been examined with a similar design. Two visits were paid to Paris, in which the Normal School at Versailles, the Maison Mère and the Noviciate of the Brothers of the Order of the Christian Doctrine, and a great number of the elementary Schools of Paris and the vicinity, were examined. The Normal School at Dijon was especially recommended to our attention by M. Cousin and M. Villemain, and we spent a day in that School. Our attention was directed with peculiar interest to the Schools of Switzerland, in the examination of which we spent several weeks uninterruptedly. During this period we daily inspected one or more Schools, and conversed with the authorities of the several cantons, with the directors of the Normal Schools, and with individuals distinguished by their knowledge of the science of elementary instruction. The occasional leave of absence from our home duties which you have kindly granted us in the last three years respectively was mainly solicited with the view, and devoted to the purpose, of examining the method of instruction adopted in the Schools for the poorer classes on the continent.

This Report is not intended to convey to you the results of our inquiries. It may suffice to describe the chief places visited, and the objects to which our attention was directed, in order that you may know the sources whence we have derived the information by which our subsequent labours have been guided. We entered Switzerland by the Jura, descending at Geneva, and, having obtained the sanction of the authorities, were accompanied by some members of the council in our visit to the Schools of the town and neighbourhood. Thence we proceeded to the Canton de Vaud, inspecting certain rural Schools, and the Schools of the towns on the borders of the lake on our way to Lausanne. Here we spent two days in company with M. Gauthey, the director of the Normal School of the canton, whose valuable Report has been translated by Sir John Boileau, our fellow-traveller in this part of our journey.

At Lausanne we attended the lectures, and examined the classes in the Normal School and the Town Schools, and enjoyed much useful and instructive conversation with M. Gauthey, who appeared eminently well qualified for his important labours.

At Fribourg we spent some time in the Convent of the Capuchin friars, where we found the venerable Père Girard officiating at a religious festival; but he belongs to the Dominican order. The Père Girard has a European reputation among those who have laboured to raise the elementary instruction of the poorer classes, consequent on his pious labours among the poor of Fribourg; and the success of his Schools appeared to us chiefly attributable, —first, to the skill and assiduity with which the monitors had been instructed in the evening by the father and his assistants, by which they had been raised to the level of the pupil teachers of Holland; and secondly, to the skilful manner in which Père Girard and his assistants had infused a moral lesson into every incident of the instruction, and had bent the whole force of their minds to the formation of the character of the children. It was, at the period of our visit, the intention of Père Girard to publish a series of works of elementary instruction at Paris, for which we have since waited in vain.

Near Berne we spent much time in conversation with M. De Fellenberg, at Hofwyl. We visited his great establishment for education there, as well as the Normal School at Munchen Buchsee, in which visit we were accompanied by M. De Fellenberg. What we learned from the conversation of this patriotic and high-minded man we cannot find space here to say. His words are better read in the establishments which he has founded, and which he superintends, and in the influence which his example and his precepts have had on the rest of Switzerland, and on other parts of Europe. The town Schools of Berne and other parts of the canton merited, and received, our attention.

At Lucerne we carefully examined the Normal and Orphan Schools. Thence we proceeded through Schweitz, with the intention of visiting the colony of the Linth, in Glarus, but failed, from the state of the mountain roads. Crossing the lake of Zurich at Rapperschwyl, we successively visited St. Gall and Appenzell, examining some of the most interesting Orphan Schools in the mountains, particularly one kept by a pupil of De Fellenberg at Teuffen, the Normal School at Gais (Kruisi, the director of which, is a pupil of Pestalozzi), and the Orphan School of M. Zeltveger at Appenzell.

Descending from the mountains, we crossed the lake to Constance, where we found Vehrli, who had many years conducted the poor school of De Fellenberg at Hofwyl, now in charge of the Normal School of the Canton of Thurgovia, in a large mansion once connected with the convent of Kruitzlingen. Here we spent two days in constant communication with Vehrli and his pupils, in the examination of his classes, and deriving from him much information respecting his labours. From Constance we travelled to Zurich, where we carefully examined the Normal and Model Schools, both at that time considerably shaken by the recent revolution.

At Lenzburg we had much useful conversation with the director of the Normal School of the Canton of Aargovia; thence we travelled to Basle, where we visited the orphan house of the town, and also that at Beuggen, as well as other Schools of repute.

We have ventured to give this sketch of our journey in Switzerland as some apology for the strength of the opinion we have formed on the necessity which exists for the establishment of a training School for the teachers of pauper children in this country. Our inquiries were not confined to this object; but both here, at Paris, in Holland, and in Germany, we bought every book which we thought might be useful in our future labours; and in every canton we were careful to collect all the laws relating to education, the regulations of the Normal and Elementary Schools, and the bye-laws by which these institutions were governed. An abstract of these laws would form a most useful contribution to the literature of this country, which is well prepared to regard with respect the institutions of the free Protestant states of Switzerland.

In the Orphan Schools which have emanated from Pestalozzi and De Fellenberg, we found the type which has assisted us in our subsequent labours. In walking with M. De Fellenberg through Hofwyl, we listened to the precepts which we think most applicable to the education of the pauper class. In the Normal School of the Canton of Thurgovia, and in the Orphan Schools of St. Gall and Appenzell, we found the development of those principles so far successful as to assure us of their practical utility.

The Normal School at Kruitzlingen is in the summer palace of the former abbot of the convent of that name, on the shore of the Lake of Constance, about one mile from the gate of the city. The pupils are sent thither, from the several communes of the canton, to be trained three years by Vehrli, before they take charge of the Communal Schools. Their expenses are borne in part by the commune, and partly by the council of the canton. We found 90 young men, apparantly from 18 to 24 or 26 years of age, in the School. Vehrli welcomed us with frankness and simplicity, which at once won our confidence. We joined him at his frugal meal. He pointed to the viands, which were coarse, and said, 'I am a peasant's son. I wish to be no other than I am, the teacher of the sons of the peasantry. You are welcome to my meal: it is coarse and homely, but it is offered cordially.'

We sat down with him. 'These potatoes,' he said, 'are our own. We won them from the earth, and therefore we need no dainties; for our appetite is gained by labour, and the fruit of our toil is always savoury.' This introduced the subject of industry. He told us all the pupils of the Normal School laboured daily some hours in a garden of several acres attached to the house, and that they performed all the domestic duty of the household. When we walked out with Vehrli, we found them in the garden digging, and carrying on other garden operations with great assiduity. Others were sawing wood into logs, and chopping it into billets in the court-yard. Some brought in sacks of potatoes on their back, or baskets of recently gathered vegetables. Others laboured in the domestic duties of the household.

After a while the bell rang, and immediately their out-door labours terminated, and they returned in an orderly manner, with all their implements, to the court-yard, where having deposited them, thrown off their frocks, and washed, they re-assembled in their respective class-rooms.

We soon followed them. Here we listened to lessons in mathematics, proving that they were well-grounded in the elementary parts of that science. We saw them drawing from models with considerable skill and precision, and heard them instructed in the laws of perspective.

We listened to a lecture on the code of the canton, and to instruction in the geography of Europe. We were informed that their instruction extended to the language of the canton, its construction and grammar, and especially to the history of Switzerland; arithmetic; mensuration; such a knowledge of natural philosophy and mechanics as might enable them to explain the chief phenomena of nature and the mechanical forces; some acquaintance with astronomy. They had continual lessons in pedagogy, or the theory of the art of teaching, which they practised in the neighbouring village school. We were assured that their instruction in the Holy Scriptures, and other religious knowledge, was a constant subject of solicitude.[1]

The following extract from Vehrli's address at the first examination of the pupils, in 1837, will best explain the spirit that governs the seminary, and the attention paid there to what we believe has been too often neglected in this country—the education of the heart and feelings, as distinct from the cultivation of the intellect. It may appear strange to English habits to assign so prominent a place in an educational institution to the following points; but the indication here given of the superior care bestowed in the formation of the character to what is given to the acquisition of knowledge, forms in our view the chief charm and merit in this and several other Swiss seminaries, and is what we have laboured to impress on the institution we have founded. To those who can enter into its spirit, the following extract will not appear tinctured with too sanguine views:—

'The course of life in this seminary is threefold :—
'1st.—Life in the home circle, or family life.
'2nd.—Life in the school-room.
'3rd.—Life beyond the walls in the cultivation of the soil.
'I place the family life first, for here the truest education is imparted; here the future teacher can best receive that cultivation of the character and feelings which will fit him to direct those, who are intrusted to his care, in the ways of piety and truth.
'A well-arranged family circle is the place where each member, by participating

---

[1] See Table of the course of instruction in Appendix.

in the other's joys and sorrows, pleasures and misfortunes, by teaching, advice, consolation, and example, is inspired with sentiments of single-mindedness, of charity, of mutual confidence, of noble thoughts, of high feelings, and of virtue.

'In such a circle can a true religious sense take the firmest and the deepest root. Here it is that the principles of Christian feeling can best be laid, where opportunity is continually given for the exercise of affection and charity, which are the first virtues that should distinguish a teacher's mind. Here it is that kindness and earnestness can most surely form the young members to be good and intelligent men, and that each is most willing to learn and receive an impress from his fellow. He who is brought up in such a circle, who thus recognises all his fellow-men as brothers, serves them with willingness whenever he can, treats all his race as one family, loves them, and God their Father above all, how richly does such a one scatter blessings around! What earnestness does he show in all his doings and conduct—what devotion especially does he display in the business of a teacher! How differently from him does that master enter and leave his school whose feelings are dead to a sense of piety, and whose heart never beats in unison with the joys of family life.

'Where is such a teacher as I have described most pleasantly occupied? In his school amongst his children, with them in the house of God, or in the family circle, and wherever he can be giving or receiving instruction. A great man has expressed, perhaps too strongly, "I never wish to see a teacher who cannot sing." With more reason I would maintain, that a teacher to whom a sense of the pleasures of a well-arranged family is wanting, and who fails to recognise in it a well-grounded religious influence, should never enter a school-room.'

As we returned from the garden with the pupils on the evening of the first day, we stood for a few minutes with Vehrli in the court-yard by the shore of the lake. The pupils had ascended into the class-rooms, and the evening being tranquil and warm, the windows were thrown up, and we shortly afterwards heard them sing in excellent harmony. As soon as this song had ceased, we sent a message to request another, with which we had become familiar in our visits to the Swiss schools; and thus, in succession, we called for song after song of Nageli, imagining that we were only directing them at their usual hour of instruction in vocal music. There was a great charm in this simple but excellent harmony. When we had listened nearly an hour, Vehrli invited us to ascend into the room where the pupils were assembled. We followed him, and on entering the apartment great was our surprise to discover the whole school, during the period we had listened, had been cheering with songs their evening employment of peeling potatoes, and cutting the stalks from the green vegetables and beans which they had gathered in the garden. As we stood there they renewed their choruses till prayers were announced. Supper had been previously taken. After prayers, Vehrli, walking about the apartment, conversed with them familiarly on the occurrences of the day, mingling with his conversation such friendly admonition as sprang from the incidents, and then, lifting his hands, he recommended them to the protection of heaven and dismissed them to rest.

We spent two days with great interest in this establishment. Vehrli had ever on his lips, 'We are peasants' sons; we would not be ignorant of our duties; but God forbid that knowledge should make us despise the simplicity of our lives. The earth is our mother, and we gather our food from her breast, but while we peasants labour for our daily food we may learn many lessons from our mother earth. There is no knowledge in books like an immediate converse with nature, and those that dig the soil have nearest communion with her. Believe me, or believe me not, this is the thought that can make a peasant's life sweet and his toil a luxury. I know it; for see, my hands are horny with toil. The lot of men is very equal, and wisdom consists in the discovery of the truth, that what is *without* is not the source of sorrow, but that which is within. A peasant may be happier than a prince if his conscience be pure before God, and he learn not only contentment, but joy in the life of labour, which is to prepare him for the life of heaven.'

This was the theme always on Vehrli's lips. Expressed with more or less perspicuity, his main thought seemed to be that poverty, rightly understood, was no misfortune. He regarded it as a sphere of human exertion and human trial, preparatory to the change of existence, but offering its own sources of enjoyment as abundantly as any other.

'We are all equal,' he said, 'before God; why should the son of a peasant envy a prince, or the lily an oak; are they not both God's creatures?'

We were greatly charmed in this school by the union of comparatively high intellectual attainments among the scholars with the utmost simplicity of life, and cheerfulness in the humblest menial labour. Their food was of the coarsest character, consisting chiefly of vegetables, soups, and very brown bread. They rose between four and five, took three meals in the day, the last about six, and retired to rest at nine. They seemed happy in their lot.

Some of the other Normal Schools of Switzerland are remarkable for the same simplicity in their domestic arrangements, though the students exceed in their intellectual attainments all notions prevalent in England of what should be taught in such schools. Thus in the Normal School of the canton of Berne the pupils worked in the fields during eight hours of the day, and spent the rest in intellectual labour. They were clad in the coarsest dresses of the peasantry, wore wooden shoes, and were without stockings. Their intellectual attainments, however, would have enabled them to put to shame the masters of most of our best elementary schools.

Such men, we felt assured, would go forth cheerfully to their humble village homes to spread the doctrine which Vehrli taught of peace and contentment in virtuous exertion; and men similarly trained appeared to us best fitted for the labour of reclaiming the pauper youth of England to the virtues, and restoring them to the happiness of her best instructed peasantry.

We therefore cherished the hope that on this plan a Normal School might be founded for the training of the teachers, to whom the schools for pauper children might be usefully committed. The period seemed to be unpropitious for any public proposals on this subject. We were anxious that a work of such importance should be undertaken by the authorities most competent to carry it into execution successfully, and we painfully felt how inadequate our own resources and experience were for the management of such an experiment; but after various inquiries, which were attended with few encouraging results, we thought that as a last resort we should not incur the charge of presumption, if, in private and unaided, we endeavoured to work out the first steps of the establishment of an institution for the training of teachers, which we hoped might afterwards be intrusted to abler hands. We determined therefore to devote a certain portion of our own means to this object, believing that when the scheme of the institution was sufficiently mature to enable us to speak of results rather than of anticipations, the well-being of 50,000 pauper children would plead its own cause with the government and the public, so as to secure the future prosperity of the establishment.

The task proposed was, to reconcile a simplicity of life not remote from the habits of the humbler classes, with such proficiency in intellectual attainments, such a knowledge of method, and such skill in the art of teaching, as would enable the pupils selected to become efficient masters of elementary schools. We hoped to inspire them with a large sympathy for their own class. To implant in their minds the thought that their chief honour would be to aid in rescuing that class from the misery of ignorance and its attendant vices. To wean them from the influence of that personal competition in a commercial society which leads to sordid aims. To place before them the unsatisfied want of the uneasy and distressed multitude, and to breathe into them the charity which seeks to heal its mental and moral diseases. We were led to select premises at Battersea chiefly on account of the very frank and cordial welcome with which the suggestion of our plans was received by the Hon. and Rev. Robert Eden, the vicar of Battersea. Mr. Eden offered the use of his village schools in aid of the training school, as the sphere in which the pupils might obtain a practical acquaintance with the art of instruction. He also undertook to superintend the training school in all that related to religion.

We, therefore, chose a spacious manor-house close to the Thames, surrounded by a garden of five acres. This house was altered and divided so as to afford a good separate residence to Dr. Kay[1], who undertook to superintend the progress of the establishment for a limited period, within which it was hoped that the principles on which the training school was to be conducted would be so far developed as to be in course of prosperous execution, and not likely to perish by being confided to other hands.

In the month of January, 1840, the class-rooms were fitted up with desks on the plan described in the Minutes of the Committee of Council, and we furnished the school-house. About the beginning of February some boys were removed from the School of Industry at Norwood, whose conduct had given us confidence in their characters, and who had made a certain proficiency in the elementary instruction of that school.

These boys were chiefly orphans, of little more than 13 years of age, intended to form a class of apprentices. These apprentices would be bound from the age of 14 to that of 21, to pursue, under the guidance and direction of the Poor Law Commission, the vocation of assistant teachers in elementary schools. For this purpose they were to receive at least three years' instruction in the training school, and to be employed as pupil teachers for two years at least in the Battersea village school during three hours of every day.

At the termination of this probationary period (if they were able satisfactorily to pass a certain examination), they were to receive a certificate, of which mention will be made hereafter, and to be employed as assistant teachers under the guidance of experienced and well-conducted masters, in some of the schools of industry for pauper children. They were at this period to be rewarded with a certain remuneration, increasing from year to year, and secured to them by the form of the indenture.

If they were unable to satisfy the examiners of their proficiency in every department of elementary instruction,

---

[1] For which he pays half the rent and taxes, in addition to his share of the expenses of the school.

and thus failed in obtaining their certificate, they would continue to receive instruction at Battersea until they had acquired the requisite accomplishments.

The number of pupil teachers of this class has been gradually increased, during the period which has since elapsed, to 24. But it seemed essential to the success of the school that the numbers should increase slowly. Its existence was disclosed only to the immediate circles of our acquaintance, by whom some boys were sent to the school, besides those whom we supported at our own expense. For the clothing, board and lodging, and education of each of these boys, who were confided to our care by certain of our friends, we consented to receive £20 per annum towards the general expenses of the schools. Pupil teachers have been placed in the establishment by the Bishop of Durham, the Earl of Chichester, Lady Noel Byron, Frederick Walpole Keppel, Esq., the Board of Guardians of the Kingston Union, R. W. Blencowe, Esq., and our colleagues, Edward Senior and Edward Twisleton, and H. W. Parker, Esqrs.

Besides the class of pupil teachers, we consented to receive young men, to remain at least one year in the establishment, either recommended by our personal friends, or to be trained for the schools of gentlemen with whom we were acquainted. These young men have generally been from 20 to 30 years of age. We have admitted some on the recommendation of Lady George Murray, Lady Noel Byron, the Earl of Radnor, the Rev. Mr. Hoskins, of Canterbury ; the Rev. Mr. Wilkinson, of Holbrook, in Suffolk ; Leonard Horner, Esq.

The course of instruction, and the nature of the discipline adopted for the training of these young men, will be described in detail. This class now amounts to 9, a number accumulated only by very gradual accessions, as we were by no means desirous to attract many students until our plans were more mature, and the instruments of our labour were tried and approved.

The subjects of instruction were divided, in the first

instance, into two departments, which will be described in this Report; and over each of these departments a tutor was placed. Mr. Horne arrived at the opening of the school, and Mr. Tate on the 22nd of March, 1840.

The domestic arrangements were conducted with great simplicity, because it was desirable that the pupils should be prepared for a life of self-denial. A sphere of great usefulness might require the labours of a man ready to live among the peasantry on their own level—to mingle with them in their habitations—to partake their frugal or even coarse meals—and to seem their equal only, though their instructor and guide. It was desirable, therefore, that the diet should be as frugal as was consistent with constant activity of mind, and some hours of steady and vigorous labour, and that it should not pamper the appetite by its quality or its variety.

A schoolmaster might settle in a situation in which a school-house only was provided. Prudence might dictate that he should not marry, and then his domestic comfort would depend on himself.

No servants, therefore, were provided, with the exception of a matron, who acted as cook. The whole household-work was committed to the charge of the boys and young men; and for this purpose the duties of each were appointed every fortnight, in order that they might be equally shared by all. The young men above 20 years of age did not aid in the scouring of the floors and stairs, nor clean the shoes, grates, and yards, nor assist in the serving and waiting at meals, the preparation of vegetables and other garden-stuff for the cook. But the making of beds and all other domestic duty was a common lot; and the young men acted as superintendents of the other work.

This was performed with cheerfulness, though it was some time before the requisite skill was attained; and perfect order and cleanliness have been found among the habits most difficult to secure. The pupils and students were carefully informed that these arrangements were intended to prepare them for the discharge of serious duties in a humble sphere, and to nerve their minds for the trials and vicissitudes of life.

The masters partook the same diet as the pupils, sitting in the centre of the room and assisting in the carving. They encouraged familiar conversation (avoiding the extremes of levity or seriousness) at the meals, but on equal terms with their scholars, with the exception only of the respect involuntarily paid them.

After a short time a cow was bought, and committed to the charge of one of the elder boys. Three pigs were afterwards added to the stock, then three goats, and subsequently, poultry, and a second cow. These animals were all fed and tended, and the cows were daily milked, by the pupil teachers. It seemed important that they should learn to tend animals with care and gentleness; that they should understand the habits and the mode of managing these particular animals, because the schoolmaster in a rural parish often has a common or forest-right of pasture for his cow, and a forest-run for his pig or goat, and might thus, with a little skill, be provided with the means of healthful occupation in his hours of leisure, and of providing for the comfort of his family.

Moreover, such employments were deemed important, as giving the pupils, by actual experience, some knowledge of a peasant's life, and therefore truer and closer sympathy with his lot. They would be able to render their teaching instructive, by adapting it to the actual condition and associations of those to whom it would be addressed. They would be in less danger of despising the labourer's daily toil in comparison with intellectual pursuits, and of being led by their own attainments to form a false estimate of their position in relation to the class to which they belonged, and which they were destined to instruct. The teacher of the peasant's child occupies, as it were, the father's place, in the performance of duties from which the father is separated by his daily toil, and unhappily, at present, by his want of knowledge and skill. But the schoolmaster ought to be prepared in thought and feeling to do the peasant-father's duty, by having sentiments in common with him, and among these an honest pride in the labour of his hands, in his strength, his manual skill, his robust health, and the manly vigour of his body and mind.

The garden, on the arrival of our pupil teachers, was a wilderness of rubbish, withered grass, and weeds. Our first attention was directed to labours which were to insure the health of the students and pupil teachers, to invigorate their bodies, and make them strong and cheerful men. This was a matter of no mean importance. Many of the young men came to the school altogether unfitted for any common bodily exertion. Some, either from previous habits of inactivity, or from having followed some closely sedentary employment, were exceedingly weak. Slight labour in the garden produced profuse perspiration and exhaustion, or muscular cramps, pains, and even inflammation of the muscles of the chest. In two or three instances, the first attempt to labour in the garden (though cautiously commenced) brought on some slight febrile action, which confined the sufferer to the house for a day or two. Exposure to the weather was at first attended with colds or slight rheumatic attacks. In short, the young men were nearly all unaccustomed to any invigorating bodily exercise, and their first attempts to work required a certain period of transition, in which some caution was requisite.

At first, four hours were devoted every day to labour in the garden. The whole school rose at half-past five. The household-work occupied the pupil teachers altogether, and the students partially, till a quarter to seven o'clock. At a quarter to seven, they marched into the garden, and worked till a quarter to eight, when they were summoned to prayers. They then marched to the tool-house, deposited their implements, washed, and assembled at prayers at eight o'clock. At half-past eight they breakfasted. From nine to twelve they were in school. They worked at the garden from twelve to one, when they dined. They resumed their labour in the garden at two, and returned to their classes at three, where they were engaged till five, when they worked another hour in the garden. At six they supped, and spent from seven to nine in their classes. At nine, evening prayers were read, and immediately afterwards they retired to rest. The subject of the routine of study and labour will be spoken of hereafter, and subsequent alterations described; and the periods of labour and study are here briefly related in reference only to the earliest period of our proceedings.

The garden, it has been said, was a wilderness of weeds. The first care of the masters was, that it should be regularly trenched over its whole surface; and as the loam was rich and deep, the weeds were buried under three feet of soil. This trenching required vigorous exertion, as the soil had not been disturbed to that depth for many years. The teachers laboured in the trenches, and we occasionally joined. The work, therefore, gradually restored order. As the weeds disappeared, the ground was sown with such garden seeds as would yield the most abundant and useful crop for the household consumption. Attention was this year confined to the most obvious necessities, because the state of the ground required so much labour, that little time could be bestowed in providing a variety of garden-stuff as a means of instructing the pupils in horticulture. The ground, it was expected, would be reclaimed before the ensuing spring; and at that period more comprehensive and systematic instruction in gardening was to commence.

During the past year, however, the garden has yielded almost all the vegetables and a very abundant supply of fruit for the use of the school. As the year advanced, the crops were gathered and followed by others, cabbages and turnips succeeding the potatoes and peas; and where a large crop of mangel-wurzel had been grown for the cows, a green crop was sown for their consumption in the spring. The disturbance of the soil to so great a depth appeared to have the most beneficial influence on the trees. They bent under a load of fruit, by which the boughs of some were broken ere we were aware, and other boughs had to be disencumbered and propped for their preservation.

In these labours the pupils and students rapidly gained strength. They almost all soon wore the hue of health. Their food was frugal, and they returned to it with appetites which were not easily satisfied. The most delicate soon lost all their ailments. One young man on his arrival was affected with a rheumatic inflammation of the joints, attended with signs of feebleness of constitution, which created some apprehension that this chronic inflammation would incapacitate him. Some perseverance enabled him to work in the garden, and the gymnastic exercises and drill, introduced at a later period, restored him to great muscular vigour. Another had been a tailor, and probably had seldom quitted his shop-board. His first attempts at labour in the garden occasioned inflammation of the muscles of the chest, and severe muscular pains all over the body, attended with much nervous agitation. These symptoms disappeared in about a week or ten days, after which he resumed his work in some light occupations, and by degrees became inured to the more severe, until, after some time, he was the most expert and vigorous athlete in the gymnastic exercises.

The gymnastic frame and the horizontal and parallel bars were not erected until the constitutional and muscular powers of the pupils and students had been invigorated by labour. After a few months' daily work in the garden, the drill was substituted for garden work during one hour daily. The marching exercise and extension movements were practised for several weeks; then the gymnastic apparatus was erected, and the drill and gymnastic exercises succeeded each other on alternate evenings. The knowledge of the marching exercise is very useful in enabling a teacher to secure precision and order in the movements of the classes or of his entire school, and to pay a due regard to the carriage of each child. A slouching gait is, at least, a sign of vulgarity, if it be not a proof of careless habits—of an inattention to the decencies and proprieties of life, which in other matters occasion discomfort in the labourer's household. Habits of cleanliness, punctuality, and promptitude, are not very compatible with indolence, nor with that careless lounging which frequently squanders not only the labourer's time, but his means, and leads his awkward steps to the village tavern. In giving the child an erect and manly gait, a firm and regular step, precision and rapidity in his movements, promptitude in obedience to commands, and particularly neatness in his apparel and person, we are insensibly laying the foundation of moral habits, most intimately connected with the personal comfort and the happiness of the future labourer's family. We are giving a practical moral lesson, perhaps more powerful than the precepts which are inculcated by words. Those who are accustomed to the management of large schools know of how much importance such lessons are to the establishment of that order and quiet which is the characteristic of the Dutch schools, and which is essential to great success in large schools. A notion is prevalent in some of our English schools that a considerable noise is unavoidable, and some teachers are understood to regard the noise as so favourable a sign of the activity of the school, as even to assert, that the greater the noise the greater the intellectual progress of the scholars. The intellectual activity of the best Dutch schools is quite as great as that of any school in this country, and their average merit is exceedingly greater than that of the town schools of England; but a visitor seldom finds in a school of 700 children more than twelve persons speaking in the room at the same time, and those twelve persons are each speaking in a natural tone, and are distinctly heard. Such results do not depend solely or chiefly on the discipline of the drill-master, but they arise, in fact, from that minute attention to all the details of school organisation which secures the greatest amount of attention from the pupil, with the least amount of disturbance to his fellows. In the result, however, attention to the *posture* and to the *movements* of the children is by no means an unimportant element.

The training of the pupil teachers and students in the marching exercises had not, therefore, reference solely to their own habits and health—to their own love of order, cleanliness, and propriety, but to the influence of the formation of such habits in them on their future scholars. Neither was it deemed an unimportant element of the discipline and organisation of schools to enable the master to detect at a glance the cause of any disorder in inconvenient postures and ill-timed and inappropriate motions, which it is a part of the duty of an experienced master to control *by a sign*.

The gymnastic exercises were intended, in like manner, to prepare the teachers to superintend the exercises and amusements of the school playground;—to instruct the children systematically in those graduated trials of strength, activity, and adroitness, by which the muscles are developed, and the frame is prepared for sustaining prolonged or sudden efforts. The playground of the school is so important a means of separating the children from the vicious companions and evil example of the street or lane, and of prolonging the moral influence of the master over the habits and thoughts of his scholars, that expedients which increase its attractions are important, and especially those which enable the master to mingle with his scholars usefully and cheerfully. The schools of the Canton de Vaud are generally furnished with the proper apparatus for this purpose, and we frequently observed it in France and Germany.

The pupil teachers and students soon acquired considerable skill in these exercises. Their practice was interrupted by the equinoctial rains, but resumed as soon as the frost brought with it more settled weather, and will be steadily pursued.

The physical training of our charge was not confined to these labours and exercises. Occasionally Dr. Kay accompanied them in long walking excursions into the country, in which they spent the whole day in visiting some distant school or remarkable building connected with historical associations, or some scene replete with other forms of instruction. In those excursions their habits of observation were cultivated, their attention was directed to what was most remarkable, and to such facts and objects as might have escaped observation from their comparative obscurity. Their strength was taxed by the length of the excursion, as far as was deemed prudent; and after their return home they were requested to write an account of what they had seen, in order to afford evidence of the nature of the impressions which the excursion had produced.

Such excursions usefully interrupted the ordinary routine of the school, and afforded a pleasing variety in the intercourse between ourselves and the teachers and pupils. They spurred the physical activity of the students, and taught them habits of endurance, as they seldom returned without being considerably fatigued.

Such excursions are common to the best Normal Schools of Switzerland. It is very evident to the educators of Switzerland that to neglect to take their pupils forth to read the great truths left on record on every side of them in the extraordinary features of that country, would betray an indifference to nature, and to its influence on the development of the human intelligence, proving that the educator had most limited views of his mission, and of the means by which its high purposes were to be accomplished.

The great natural records of Switzerland, and its historical recollections, abound with subjects for instructive commentary, of which the professors of the Normal Schools avail themselves in their autumnal excursions with their pupils. The natural features of the country; its drainage, soils, agriculture; the causes which have affected the settlement of its inhabitants and its institutions; the circumstances which have assisted in the formation of the national character, and have thus made the history of their country, are more clearly apprehended by lessons gathered in the presence of facts typical of other facts scattered over hill and valley. England is so rich in historical recollections, and in the monuments by which the former periods of her history are linked with the present time, that it would seem to be a not unimportant duty of the educator to avail himself of such facts as lie within the range of his observation, in order that the historical knowledge of his scholar may be associated with these records, marking the progress of civilisation in his native country. Few schools are placed beyond the reach of such means of instruction. Where they do not exist, the country must present some natural features worthy of being perused. These should not be neglected. In book-learning there is always a danger that the thing signified may not be discerned through the sign. The child may acquire words instead of thoughts. To have a clear and earnest conviction of the reality of the things signified, the object of the child's instruction should as frequently as possible be brought under its eye. Thus Pestalozzi was careful to devise lessons on objects in which, by actual contact with the sense, the children were led to discern qualities which they afterwards described in words. Such lessons have no meaning to persons who are satisfied with instruction by rote. But we contend that it is important to a right moral state of the intelligence that the child should have a clear perception and *vivid conviction* of every fact presented to its mind. We are of opinion that to extend the province of faith and implicit unreasoning obedience to those subjects which are the proper objects on which the perceptive faculties ought to be exercised, and on which the reason should be employed, is to undermine the basis of an unwavering faith in revelation, by provoking the rebellion of the human spirit against authority in matters in which reason is free.

To the young, the truth (bare before the sight, palpable to the touch, embodied in forms which the senses realise) has a charm which no mere words can convey, until they are recognised as the sign of the truth, which the mind comprehends. In all that relates to the external phenomena of the world, the best book is nature, with an intelligent interpreter. What concerns the social state of man may be best apprehended after lessons in the fields, the ruins, the mansions, and the streets within the range of the school. Lessons on the individual objects prepare the mind for generalizations, and for the exercise of faith in its proper province. Elementary schools, in which word-teaching only exists, do not produce earnest and truthful men. The practice, prevalent in certain parts of the Highlands and Wales, of teaching the children to read English books, though they understand nothing of the English language, is about as reasonable as the ordinary mode of teaching by rote, either matters which the children do not understand, or which they do not receive with a lively conviction of their truth. The master who neglects opportunities of satisfying the intelligence of his pupil on anything that can be made obvious to the sense, must be content to find that when his lessons rise to abstractions he will be gazed upon by vacant faces. The mind will refuse a lively confidence in general truths, when it has not been convinced of the existence of the particular facts from which they are derived. From a master, accustomed to regard himself as the interpreter of nature, as the engrafter of thoughts and not of words, and who is endeavouring to form the character of his pupils by inspiring them with an earnest love for truth, the pupils will gladly take much upon authority with a lively confidence. From the rote teacher they take nothing but words; he gains no confidence; it is difficult to love him, because it is not obvious what good he communicates; it is difficult to trust him, because he asks belief when he takes no pains to inspire conviction. What reverence can attach to a man teaching a

Highland child to read English words, which are unmeaning sounds to him?

The excursions of the directors of the Swiss Normal Schools also serve the purpose of breaking for a time an almost conventual seclusion, which forms a characteristic of establishments in which the education of the habits, as well as the instruction of the intelligence, is kept in view. These excursions in Switzerland extend to several days, and even longer in schools of the more wealthy classes. The pupils are thus thrown in contact with actual society; their resources are taxed by the incidents of each day; their moral qualities are somewhat tried, and they obtain a glimpse of the perspective of their future life. It is not only important in this way to know what the condition of society is before the pupil is required to enter it, but it is also necessary to keep constantly before his eye the end and aim of education—that it is a preparation for the duties of his future life, and to understand in what respect each department of his studies is adapted to prepare him for the actual performance of those duties. For each class of society there is an appropriate education. The Normal Schools of Switzerland are founded on this principle. None are admitted who are not devoted to the vocation of masters of elementary schools. The three or four years of their residence in the school are considered all too short for a complete preparation for these functions. The time therefore is consumed in appropriate studies, care being taken that these studies are so conducted as to discipline and develope the intelligence; to form habits of thought and action; and to inspire the pupil with principles on which he may repose in the discharge of his duties.

Among these studies and objects, the actual condition of the labouring class, its necessities, resources, and intelligence, form a most important element. The teachers go forth to observe for themselves; they come back to receive further instruction from their master. They are led to anticipate their own relations to the commune or parish in which their future school will be placed. They are prepared by instruction to fulfil certain of the communal duties which may usefully devolve upon them; such as registrar, precentor, or leader of the church choir, and clerk to the associations of the village. They receive familiar expositions of the law affecting the fulfilment of these duties.

The benefits derived from these arrangements are great; not only in furnishing these rural communes with men competent to the discharge of their duties, but the anticipations of future utility, and the conviction that their present studies enfold the germ of their future life, gives an interest to their pursuits, which it would be difficult to communicate, if the sense of their importance were more vague and indistinct.

To this end, in the excursions from Battersea we have been careful to enter the schools on our route, and lessons have been given on the duties attaching to the offices which may be properly discharged by a village schoolmaster in connexion with his duty of instructing the young.

This general sketch may suffice to give an idea of the external relations of the life of a student in the training school, with the important exception of that portion of his time devoted to the acquirement of a practical knowledge of the duties of a schoolmaster in the village school. This may be more conveniently considered in connexion with the intellectual pursuits of the school. We now proceed to regard the school as a *household*, and to give a brief sketch of its familiar relations.

The period which has elapsed since the school was assembled is much too brief to enable us fully to realise our conception of such a household among young persons, to the majority of whom the suitable example had perhaps never been presented.

The most obvious truth lay at the threshold: a family can only subsist harmoniously by mutual love, confidence, and respect. We did not seek to put the tutors into situations of inaccessible authority, but to place them in the parental seat, to receive the willing respect and obedience of their pupils, and to act as the elder brothers of the young men. The residence of one of us for a certain period, in near connexion with them, appeared necessary to give that tone to the familiar intercourse which would enable the tutors to conduct the instruction, and to maintain the discipline, so as to be at once the friends and guides of their charge.

It was desirable that the tutors should reside in the house. They rose at the same hours with the scholars (except when prevented by sickness), and superintended more or less the general routine. Since the numbers have become greater, and the duties more laborious, it has been found necessary that the superintendence of the periods of labour should be committed to each tutor alternately. They have set the example in working— frequently giving assistance in the severest labour, or that which was least attractive.

In the autumn, some extensive alterations of the premises were to a large extent effected by the assistance of the entire school. The tutors not only superintended but assisted in the work. Mr. Tate contributed his mechanical knowledge, and Mr. Horne assisted in the execution of the details. In the cheerful industry displayed on this and on other similar occasions, we have witnessed with satisfaction one of the best fruits of the discipline of the school. The conceit of the pedagogue is not likely to arise among either students or masters, who cheerfully handle the trowel, the saw, or carry mortar in a hod to the top of the building; such simplicity of life is not very consistent with that vanity which occasions insincerity. But freedom from this vice is essential to that harmonious interchange of kind offices and mutual respect which we were anxious to preserve.

The diet of the household is simple. The fruits and vegetables of the garden afford the chief variety without luxury. The teachers sit in the midst of their scholars. The familiar intercourse of the meals is intended to be a means of cultivating kindly affections, and of insuring that the example of the master shall insensibly form the habits of the scholar. Every day confirms the growing importance of these arrangements.

It has been an object of especial care that the morning and evening prayers should be conducted with solemnity. A hall has been prepared for this service, which is conducted at seven o'clock every morning in that place. A passage of Scripture having been read, a portion of a psalm is chanted, or they sing a hymn; and prayers follow, generally from the family selection prepared by the Bishop of London. The evening service is conducted in a similar manner. The solemnity of the music, which is performed in four parts, is an important means of rendering the family devotion impressive. We trust that the benefits derived from these services may not be transient, but that the masters reared in this school will remember the household devotions, and will maintain in their own dwellings and schools the family rite with equal care.

Quiet has been enjoined on the pupils in retiring to rest.

The Sunday has been partially occupied by its appropriate studies. The services of the church have been attended morning and evening; and, besides a certain period devoted to the study of the formularies, the evening has been spent in writing out from memory a copious abstract of one of the sermons. At eight o'clock these compositions have been read and commented upon in the presence of the whole school; and a most useful opportunity has been afforded for religious instruction, besides the daily instruction in the Bible. Mr. Eden has likewise attended the school on Friday, and examined the classes in their acquaintance with the Holy Scriptures and formularies of the Church. The religious department, generally, is under his superintendence.

The skill which they have acquired in singing has enabled Mr. Eden to create from the school a choir for the village church, increasing the solemnity of the services by the manner in which the sacred music is performed.

The household and external life of the school are so interwoven with the lessons, that it becomes necessary to consider some of their details together, before the intellectual instruction is separately treated.

The boys who were selected as apprentices were rather chosen on account of their characters than their acquirements, which were very meagre. The young men who have been admitted as students have frequently been found even worse prepared than the boys of thirteen years of age, chiefly brought from Norwood, though some of these young men have been in charge of village and workhouse schools. Their acquaintance even with rudimental knowledge would not bear the test of slight examination. With pupils and students alike, it was therefore found necessary to commence at an early stage of instruction, and to furnish them with the humblest elements of knowledge. The time which has elapsed since the school has opened ought therefore to be regarded as a preparatory period, similar to that which, in Germany, is spent from the time of leaving the primary school to sixteen, the period of entering the Normal School, in what is called a preparatory training school.

As such preparatory schools do not exist in this country, we had no alternative. We selected the boys of the most promising character, and determined to wade through the period of preparation, and ultimately to create a preparatory class in the school itself. Our design was to examine the pupils of this class at the end of the first year, and to grant to such of them as gave proof of a certain degree of proficiency a certificate as *Candidates* of the training school. At the end of the second year's course of instruction, it is intended that a second examination shall occur, in which proficients may obtain the certificate of *Scholar*; and at the close of the ordinary course in the third year, another examination is to be held, in which the certificate of *Master* will be conferred on those who have attained a certain rank intellectually, and who support their claims by a correct moral deportment.

The means of determining this proficiency will be described hereafter.

Training schools, developed on this design, would therefore consist of —

    1. Preparatory classes of Students and Pupils.
    2. A class of Candidates.
    3. A class of Scholars.

And some students, who had obtained the certificate of Master, might remain in the school in preparation for special duties as the Masters of important *district schools*, or as Tutors in other training schools. These students would constitute

    4. A class of Masters.

Hitherto the training school has not passed the preparatory stage. No certificate of candidateship has been granted; and the examination of the qualifications of the students and pupils, by which they can acquire this certificate, will not occur till the end of March, at which period a certain number will have resided a year in the establishment. Another examination may probably take place on the 30th of June, and other certificates of candidateship may then be distributed to those who came to the school between March and June of last year.

The routine of preparatory classes was at an early period arranged according to the annexed Table, which regulated the daily lessons of the school until the members of the first class were employed as pupil-teachers in assisting in the instruction of the village school.

DAILY ROUTINE.

Half-past 5	Rise, wash, dress, and make beds.
Quarter to 6	Household work, viz., scouring and sweeping floors, cleaning grates, shoes, knives, &c., pumping water and preparing vegetables.
Quarter to 7	March into garden and commence garden-work, feed pigs, poultry, and milk cows.
Quarter to 8	March from garden, deposit tools, and wash.
8	Reading of Scriptures and prayer. (In the spring half an hour was commonly occupied in a familiar exposition of the passage of Scripture read.)
After prayer	Superintendents present reports.
Half-past 8	Breakfast.

		MONDAY.	TUESDAY.	WEDNESDAY.	THURSDAY.	FRIDAY.	SATURDAY.
9 to half-past 9	Classes united.	Reading in the Bible and religious instruction. Old Testament history.	Reading in the Bible and religious instruction. The Gospels.	Reading in the Bible and religious instruction. The Acts of the Apostles.	Reading in the Bible and religious instruction. The Epistles.	Committing to memory texts of Scripture.	Committing to memory texts of Scripture, or examination on the Scriptural reading of the week.
Half-past 9 to half-past 10	First class.	Mechanics. Arithmetic. Mentalarithmetic.	Arithmetic. Mechanics. Etymology.	Mechanics. Arithmetic. Mental arithmetic.	Arithmetic. Mechanics. Etymology.	Mechanics. Arithmetic. Mental arithmetic.	Weekly examination.
Half-past 10 to 11	Second class.						Ditto.
	Second class.	Etymology.	Mental arithmetic.	Etymology.	Mental arithmetic.	Etymology.	
11 to 12	Classes united.	Geography.	Geography.	Music.	Geography.	Geography.	Music.

12 to 1	Garden work, feeding the animals, &c. March to the house at 1, wash, and prepare for dinner.
Quarter-past 1	Dinner.

The Training School at Battersea

DAILY ROUTINE—*continued*.

	MONDAY.	TUESDAY.	WEDNESDAY.	THURSDAY.	FRIDAY.	SATURDAY.
2 to 3 . . . Classes united.	Mechanical drawing.	Map drawing.	Mechanical drawing.	Common and isometrical perspective.	Map drawing.	Weekly examination.
3 to 4 . . . First class.	Algebra. Grammar.	Use of the globes.	Mensuration. Algebra.	Use of the globes.	Algebra. Grammar.	Ditto.
4 to 5 . . . First class.	Natural history of birds.	Grammar.	Object lesson.	Grammar.	.	Ditto.
Second class.	Ditto.	Committing to memory arithmetical tables and rules of grammar, or mechanical formulæ.	.	Committing to memory arithmetical tables and rules of grammar, or mechanical formulæ.	Committing to memory.	

5	March to garden-work, feed pigs, poultry, &c., and milk cows.
6	March from garden, wash, and prepare for supper.
Quarter-past 6.	Supper.
7	Drill and gymnastic exercises.
8	Copying music or notes on geography, or mechanical formulæ, in the upper class-room. During this period the History of England is read aloud. Another class practising singing in the lower class-room.
9	Reading of Scriptures and prayer.
20 minutes past 9.	Retire to rest.

SUNDAY.

After divine service one of the sermons of the day is written from memory. In the evening the compositions are read and commented upon, and the Catechism or some other portion of the formularies of the Church is repeated, with texts of Scripture illustrating it.
Some of the elder students teach in the village Sunday-school.

The weekly examination was conducted orally during the day, until Dr. Kay's engagements in town rendered it necessary that some other method of examination should be adopted. As soon, therefore, as the attainments of the students and pupils appeared to warrant the experiment, an hour was daily appropriated to examination by means of questions written on the board before the class, the replies to which were worked on paper, in silence, in the presence of one of the tutors. This hour is, on successive days of the week, appropriated to different subjects; viz., grammar, etymology, arithmetic, mensuration, algebra, mechanics, geography, and biblical knowledge. The examination papers are then carefully examined by the tutor to whose department they belong, in order that the value of the reply to each question may be determined in reference to mean numbers, 3, 4, 5, and 6. These mean numbers are used to express the comparative difficulty of every question, and the greatest merit of each reply is expressed by the numbers 6, 8, and 10 and 12 respectively, the lowest degree of merit being indicated by 1.

The sum of the numbers thus attached to each answer is entered in the examination-book opposite to the name of each pupil. These numbers are added up at the end of the week, and reduced to an average by dividing them by the number of days of examination which have occurred in the week. In a similar manner, at the end of the month, the sum of the weekly averages is, for the sake of convenience, reduced by dividing them by four; and a convenient number is thus obtained, expressing the intellectual progress of each boy. These numbers are not published in the school, but are reserved as an element by which we may be enabled to award the certificates of Candidate, Scholar, and Master.

The examination papers are in our possession after the close of each week, and we select certain of them for our special examination, in order that we may form an opinion of the intellectual progress of each pupil.

The examination for the quarterly certificates will

necessarily also include the inspection of the writing, drawings, abstracts, and compositions. Oral examination will be required to ascertain the degree of promptitude and ease in expression of each pupil. They will likewise be required to give demonstrations of problems in arithmetic, algebra, and mechanics, on the black-board, to describe the geography of a district in the form of a lecture, and to conduct a class before us, ere we award the certificates.

The examination of the pupils will gradually rise in importance, and the quarterly examinations will be marked by a progressive character, leading to the three chief examinations for the certificates of Candidate, Scholar, and Master, which will be distinguished from each other, both as respects the nature and number of the acquirements, and by the degree of proficiency required in some branches which will be common to the three periods of study.

In another department of registration we have thought it important to avoid certain errors of principle to which such registers appear to be liable. We have been anxious to have a record of some parts of moral conduct connected with habits formed in the school, but we have not attempted to register *moral merit*. Such registers are at best very difficult to keep. They occasion rivalry, and often hypocrisy. On this account we did not deem it advisable to require that they should be kept; but it was important that we should be informed of certain errors interfering with the formation of habits of punctuality, industry, cleanliness, order, and subordination; and registers were devised for noting deviations from propriety in these respects. First, a *time-book* is directed to be kept, in which the observance of the hour of rising, and of the successive periods marked in the routine of the school is noted, in order that any general cause of aberration may meet the eye at once. Secondly, one book is kept by the superintendents appointed from among the students to inspect the *household work above stairs*, another in relation to the *household work below stairs*, and a third by the tutor having charge of *out-door labour.* In these books the duties assigned to each pupil are entered opposite to his name. The superintendent, at the expiration of the period allotted to the work, marks in columns under each of the following heads, — Subordination, Industry, Cleanliness, Order,— the extent of deviation from propriety of conduct by numbers varying from 1 to 4.

The register of punctuality in classes is kept by writing opposite to each pupil's name the number of minutes which elapse after the proper period before he enters the class. The sum of the numbers recorded in these books denotes the extent of errors in habits and manners into which any of the pupils fall, and directs our attention to the fact. Such records would, in connexion with the results of the examinations, enable us to determine whether, in reference to each period, a certificate of *Candidate, Scholar,* or *Master,* of the *first, second,* or *third* degree, should be granted.

The reports of the superintendents are presented to Dr. Kay immediately after morning prayers. The record is read in the presence of the school, and any appeal against the entry heard. At this period the relation which the entire discipline holds to the future pursuits of the pupils is from time to time made familiar to them by simple expositions of the principles by which it is regulated.

The tendency towards any error in the general conduct is indicated by the registers, and is at this period, if necessary, made the subject of mild expostulation.

Such expostulations have been needed in relation to such *precision* in the orderly management of the detail of *work* and *household service* as can perhaps only be attained by greater experience than the pupils have yet enjoyed.

The superintendents are chosen from among those students who appear to possess the requisite qualifications. We thus have an unexceptionable means of distinguishing with offices of trust those in whom we can place most confidence, and of preparing them for the discharge of their future duties by accustoming them to a mild vigilance, to fidelity, impartiality, and firmness. On the other hand, the rest of the pupils learn subordination to those who, on account of these qualifications, exercise a limited degree of control over them, and are thus prepared to occupy subordinate positions if it be found necessary that they should be employed as assistants.

The special training of those who may hereafter take charge of district schools for pauper children has been fulfilled, by charging certain of the superintendents with other details of the domestic arrangements. For this purpose a Steward has been appointed among the young men, who has cut and weighed the provisions, and kept accounts resembling the 'Provision Consumption Account' of a workhouse. The dietary has been found to preserve the pupils and students in florid health, under the physical and mental activity in which they have lived.

The dietary is hung in the steward's room, and guides him in cutting the rations for each meal.

It does not indicate the amount of vegetables and fruit in pies which are consumed; and it ought to be remarked that the fruit pies and vegetables have formed a wholesome and considerable part of the food of the household, which has perhaps been enjoyed with the greater relish as it is the product of the labours in the garden.

The influenza of the spring has been the only sickness which has occurred in the house, excepting those ailments which some of the students brought with them, and which disappeared as soon as they were accustomed to the routine of labour and instruction. Instead of sickness, numerous signs of increased strength, activity, and vigour are observed, which confirm the views by which the diet and the alternations of employment and study have been regulated.

This is the *household life* of the school. In proceeding to speak of the intellectual training, we premise that this report affords little opportunity for an explanation of the principles which have determined and regulated the preparatory course of instruction, and that we do not intend to anticipate the course which will be pursued in the future periods of study for the certificates of *Scholar* and *Master*. The questions which beset every step of this path could only be properly discussed in a work on pedagogy, resembling the numerous German publications on this subject. Brief hints only of these principles can find a place in the remarks we have to offer on the preparatory course.

The students have been stimulated in their application by a constant sense of the practical utility of their intellectual labours. After morning prayers, they are from day to day reminded of the connexion between their present and future pursuits, and informed how every part of the discipline and study has a direct relation to the duties of a schoolmaster. The conviction thus created becomes a powerful incentive to exertion, which might be wanting if those studies were selected only because they were important as a discipline of the mind.

The sense of practical utility seems as important to the earnestness of the student as the lively conviction attending object teaching in the early and simplest form of elementary instruction. In the earliest steps an acquaintance with the real is necessary to lively conceptions of truth, and at a later period a sense of the value of knowledge resulting from *experience* inspires the strongest conviction of the dignity and importance of all truth, where its immediate practical utility is not obvious.

Far, therefore, from fearing that the sense of the practical utility of these studies will lead the students to measure the value of all truth by a low standard, their pursuits have been regulated by the conviction, that the most certain method of attaining a strong sense of the value of truths, not readily applicable to immediate use, is to ascertain by experience the importance of those which can be readily measured by the standard of practical utility. Thus we approach the conception of the momentum of a planet moving in its orbit, from ascertaining the momentum of bodies whose weight and velocity we can measure by the simplest observations. From the level of the experience of the practical utility of certain common truths, the mind gradually ascends to the more abstract, whose importance hence becomes more easily apparent, though their present application is not obvious, and in this way the thoughts most safely approach the most difficult abstractions.

In the humble pursuits of the preparatory course, a lively sense of the utility of their studies has likewise been maintained by the method of instruction adopted. Nothing has been taught *dogmatically*, but everything by the combination of the simplest elements: *i. e.*, the course which a discoverer must have trod has been followed, and the way in which truths have been ascertained pointed out by a synthetical demonstration of each successive step. The labour of the previous analysis of the subject is the duty of the teacher, and is thus removed from the child.

The preparatory course is especially important, because the pupil's instruction is conducted on the principles which will guide him in the management of his own school. Having ascertained what the pupil knows, the teacher endeavours to lead him by gentle and easy steps from the known to the unknown. The instruction, in the whole preparatory course, is chiefly oral, and is illustrated, as much as possible, by appeals to nature and by demonstrations. Books are not resorted to until the teacher is convinced that the mind of his pupil is in a state of healthful activity; that there has been awakened in him a lively interest in truth, and that he has become acquainted practically with the inductive method of acquiring knowledge. At this stage the rules, the principles of which have been orally communicated, and with whose application he is familiar, are committed to memory from books, to serve as a means of recalling more readily the knowledge and skill thus attained. This course is Pestalozzian, and, it will be perceived, is the reverse of the method usually followed, which consists in giving the pupil the rule first. Experience, however, has confirmed us in the superiority of the plan we have pursued. Sometimes a book, as for example a work on Physical Geography, is put into his hands, in order that it may be carefully read, and that the student may prepare himself to give before the class a verbal abstract of the chapter selected for this purpose, and to answer such questions as may be proposed to him, either by the tutor or by his fellows. During the preparatory course exercises of this kind have not been so numerous as they will be in the more advanced stages of instruction. Until habits of attention and steady application had been formed, it seemed undesirable to allow to the pupils hours for self-sustained study, or voluntary occupation. Constant superintendence is necessary to the formation of correct habits, in these and in all other respects, in the preparatory course. The entire day is therefore occupied with a succession of engagements in household work and out-door labour, devotional exercises, meals, and instruction. Recreation is sought in change of employment. These changes afford such pleasure, and the sense of utility and duty is so constantly maintained, that recreation in the ordinary sense is not needed. Leisure from such occupations is never sought excepting to write a letter to a friend, or occasionally to visit some near relative. The pupils all present an air of cheerfulness. They proceed from one lesson to another, and to their several occupations, with an elasticity of mind which affords the best proof that the mental and physical effects of the training are auspicious.

In the early steps towards the formation of correct habits, it is necessary that (until the power of self-guidance is obtained) the pupil should be constantly under the eye of a master, not disposed to exercise authority so much as to give assistance and advice. Before the habit of self-direction is formed, it is therefore pernicious to leave much time at the disposal of the pupil. Proper intellectual and moral aims must be inspired, and the pupil must attain a knowledge of the mode of employing his time with skill, usefully, and under the guidance of right motives, ere he can be properly left to the spontaneous suggestions of his own mind. Here, therefore, the moral and the intellectual training are in the closest harmony. The formation of correct habits, and the growth of right sentiments, ought to precede such confidence in the pupil's powers of self-direction as is implied in leaving him either much time unoccupied, or in which his labours are not under the immediate superintendence of his teacher.

In the preparatory course, therefore, the whole time is employed under superintendence, but towards the close of the course a gradual trial of the pupil's powers of self-guidance is commenced; first, by intrusting him with certain studies unassisted by the teacher. Those who zealously and successfully employ their time will, by degrees, be intrusted with a greater period for self-sustained intellectual or physical exertion. Further evidence of the existence of the proper qualities will lead to a more liberal confidence, until habits of application and the power of pursuing their studies successfully, and without assistance, are attained.

The subjects of the preparatory course were strictly rudimental. It will be found that the knowledge obtained in the elementary schools now in existence is a very meager preparation for the studies of a training school for teachers. Until the elementary schools are improved it will be found necessary to go to the very roots of all knowledge, and to re-arrange such knowledge as the pupils have attained, in harmony with the principles on which they must ultimately communicate it to others. Many of our pupils enter the school with the broadest provincial dialect, scarcely able to read with fluency and precision, much less with ease and expression. Some were ill-furnished with the commonest rules of arithmetic, and wrote clumsily and slowly.

z

They have been made acquainted with the *phonic* method of teaching to read practised in Germany. Their defects of pronunciation have been corrected to a large extent by the adoption of this method, and by means of deliberate and emphatic syllabic reading, in a well sustained and correct tone. The principles on which the *laut* or *phonic* method depends have been explained at considerable length as a part of the course of lessons on method which has been communicated to them, and they will commence the practice of this method in the village school as soon as the lesson-books now in course of printing are published.

We have deemed it of paramount importance that they should acquire a thorough knowledge of the elements and structure of the English language. The lessons in reading were in the first place made the means of leading them to an examination of the structure of sentences, and practical oral lessons were given on grammar and etymology according to the method pursued by Mr. Wood in the Edinburgh Sessional School. The results of these exercises were tested by the lessons of dictation and of composition which accompanied the early stages of this course, and by which a lively sense of the utility of a knowledge of grammatical construction and of the etymological relations of words was developed. As soon as this feeling was created, the oral instruction in grammar assumed a more positive form. The theory on which the rules were founded was explained, and the several laws when well understood were dictated in the least exceptionable formulæ, and were written out and committed to memory. In this way they proceeded through the whole of the theory and rules of grammar before they were intrusted with any book on the subject, lest they should depend for their knowledge on a mere effort of the memory to retain a formula not well understood.

At each stage of their advance, corresponding exercises were resorted to, in order to familiarise them with the application of the rules.

When they had in this way passed through the ordinary course of grammatical instruction, they were intrusted with books, to enable them to give the last degree of precision to their conceptions.

In etymology the lessons were in like manner practical and oral. They were first derived from the reading-lessons of the day, and applied to the exercises and examinations accompanying the course, and after a certain progress had been made, their further advance was insured by systematic lessons from books.

A course of reading in English literature, by which the taste may be refined by an acquaintance with the best models of style, and with those authors whose works have exercised the most beneficial influence on the mind of this nation, has necessarily been postponed to another part of the course. It, however, forms one of the most important elements in the conception of the objects to be attained in a training school, that the teacher should be inspired with a discriminating but earnest admiration for those gifts of great minds to English literature which are alike the property of the peasant and the peer; national treasures which are among the most legitimate sources of national feelings.

A thorough acquaintance with the English language can alone make the labouring class accessible to the best influence of English civilisation. Without this, lettered men will find it difficult, if not impossible, to teach the vulgar.

Those who have had close intercourse with the labouring classes well know with what difficulty they comprehend words not of a Saxon origin, and how frequently addresses to them are unintelligible from the continual use of terms of a Latin or Greek derivation; yet the daily language of the middle and upper classes abounds with such words; many of the formularies of our church are full of them, and hardly a sermon is preached which does not in every page contain numerous examples of their use. Phrases of this sort are so naturalised in the language of the educated classes, that entirely to omit them has the appearance of pedantry and baldness, and even disgusts persons of taste and refinement. Therefore, in addressing a mixed congregation, it seems impossible to avoid using them, and the only mode of meeting the inconvenience alluded to is to instruct the humbler classes in their meaning. The method we have adopted for this purpose has been copied from that first introduced in the Edinburgh Sessional Schools; every compound word is analysed, and the separate meaning of each member pointed out, so that, at present, there are few words in the English language which our pupils cannot thoroughly comprehend, and from their acquaintance with the common roots and principles of etymology, the new compound terms, which the demands of civilisation are daily introducing, are almost immediately understood by them. We believe that there are few acquirements more conducive to clearness of thought, or that can be more usefully introduced into common schools, than a thorough knowledge of the English language, and that the absence of it gives power to the illiterate teacher and demagogue, and deprives the lettered man of his just influence.

Similar remarks might be extended to style. It is equally obvious that the educated use sentences of a construction presenting difficulties to the vulgar which are frequently almost insurmountable. It is, therefore, not only necessary that the meaning of words should be taught on a logical system in our elementary schools, but that the children should be made familiar with extracts from our best authors on subjects suited to their capacity. It cannot be permitted to remain the opprobrium of this country that its greatest minds have bequeathed their thoughts to the nation in a style at once pure and simple, but still inaccessible to the intelligence of the great body of the people.

In *writing*, they were trained, as soon as the various books could be prepared, according to the method of Mülhauser, which was translated and placed in the hands of the teachers for that purpose.

It is unnecessary to describe, in this place, a method of which the details will soon be accessible in the manual now printing.

It may be sufficient here to remark that both these methods are eminently synthetical. They depend for their success on the delicacy of the analysis which they put into the hands of the teacher, and by which they enable him to present the simplest elements of knowledge first, and then to proceed in a regularly graduated series to those combinations which, if presented in the first instance, would occasion the pupil much difficulty and consequent discouragement.

In like manner, in *arithmetic* it has been deemed desirable to put them in possession of the pre-eminently synthetical method of Pestalozzi. As soon as the requisite tables and series of lessons, analysed to the simplest elements, could be procured, the principles on which complex numerical combinations rest were rendered familiar to them, by leading the pupils through the earlier course of Pestalozzi's lessons on numbers, from simple unity to compound fractional quantities; connecting with them the series of exercises in mental arithmetic which they are so well calculated to introduce and to illustrate. The use of such a method dispels the gloom which might attend the most expert use of the common rules of arithmetic, and which commonly afford the pupil little light to guide his steps off the beaten path illuminated by the rule.

The analysis in the lessons of Pestalozzi is so minute as to inspire all minds, who have attained a certain knowledge of number by other means, with a doubt whether time may not be lost by tracing all the minute steps of the analytical series over which his lessons pass. The opposite practice of dogmatic teaching is so ruinous, however, to the intellectual habits, and so imperfect a means of developing the intelligence, that it ought, we think, at all expense of time, to be avoided. With this conviction, the method of Pestalozzi has been diligently pursued.

Whilst these lessons have been in progress, the common rules of arithmetic have been examined by the light of this method. Their theory has been explained, and by constant practice the pupils have been led to acquire expertness in them, as well as to pursue the common principles on which they rest, and to ascertain the practical range within which each rule ought to be employed. The ordinary lessons on mental arithmetic have taken their place in the course of instruction separately from the peculiar rules which belong to Pestalozzi's series.

These lessons also prepared the pupils for proceeding at an early period in a similar manner with the elements of algebra, and with practical lessons in mensuration and land surveying.

These last subjects were considered of peculiar importance, as comprising one of the most useful industrial developments of a knowledge of the laws of number. Unless, in elementary schools, the instruction proceed beyond the knowledge of abstract rules, to their actual application to the practical necessities of life, the scholar will have little interest in his studies, because he will not perceive their importance, and, moreover, when he leaves the school, they will be of little use, because he has not learned to apply his knowledge to any purpose. On this account boys, who have been educated in common elementary schools, are frequently found, in a few years after they have left, to have forgotten the greater part even of the slender amount of knowledge they had acquired.

The use of arithmetic to the carpenter, the builder, the labourer, and artisan, ought to be developed by teaching mensuration and land surveying in elementary schools. If the scholars do not remain long enough to attain so high a range, the same principle should be applied to every step of their progress. The practical application of the simplest rules should be shown by familiar examples. As soon as the child can count, he should be made to count objects, such as money, the figures on the face of a clock, &c. When he can add, he should have before him shop-bills, accounts of the expenditure of earnings, accounts of wages. In every arithmetical rule similar useful exercises are a part of the art of a teacher, whose sincere desire is to fit his pupil for the application of his knowledge to the duties of life, the preparation for which should be always suggested to the pupil's mind as a powerful incentive to action. These future duties should be always placed in a cheering and hopeful point of view. The mere repetition of a table of numbers has less of education in it than a drill in the *balance-step.*

Practical instruction in the *book-keeping* necessary for the management of the household was for these reasons given to those who acted as stewards.; accounts were kept of the seeds, manure, and garden produce, &c., as preparatory to a course of book-keeping, which will follow.

The [1] recently rapid development of the industry and

[1] It is somewhat remarkable that since this paragraph was written I should have received a letter from one of the principal Directors of a Railway Company, in which he informs me that the frequent occurrence of accidents had induced the Directors of the railway to make a careful examination into their causes. The Directors rose from this inquiry convinced that these accidents were, to a large extent, attributable to the ignorance of the men whom they had been obliged to employ as engineers, for the want of better; and to the low habits of these men, who, though they do not subject themselves to dismissal by such a defiance of regulations as to be found '*drunk*,' are in the habit of stupifying themselves with dram-drinking! The Directors of the Company had determined, that the proper remedy for these evils was to provide amusement and instruction for their men at night, and application has since been made to Mr. Tate, the tutor in mechanics, &c., in the Training School, to afford his assistance in delivering lectures on mechanics to the engineers, stokers, and other servants of the Company. A large room has been provided for these purposes, and it is understood to be the intention of the Company to draw their servants to this room by such amusements as may be more attractive than the tavern—to excite their attention to subjects of instruction appropriate to their duties by a series of popular lectures—and then to open classes, where they may learn mechanics and such of the elements of natural science as may be useful to them in their calling.

As a part of the amusements, application was made by one of the Directors to Mr. Hullah to open a class like those of the artisans of Paris, and to instruct them in singing on the method of Wilhem.—J. P. K. S.

commerce of this country by machinery creates a want for well-instructed mechanics, which in the present state of education it will be difficult adequately to supply. The steam-engines which drain our coal-fields and mineral veins and beds, which whirl along every railroad, which toil on the surface of every river, and issue from every estuary, are committed to the charge of men of some practical skill, but of mean education. The mental resources of the classes who are practically intrusted with the guidance of this great development of national power should not be left uncultivated. This new force has grown rapidly, in consequence of the genius of the people, and the natural resources of this island, and in spite of their ignorance. But our supremacy at sea, and our manufacturing and commercial prosperity (inseparable elements) depend on the successful progress of those arts by which our present position has been attained.

On this account we have deemed inseparable from the education of a schoolmaster a knowledge of the *elements of mechanics* and of the laws of heat, sufficient to enable him to explain the structure of the various kinds of steam-engines in use in this country. This instruction has proved one of the chief features even of the preparatory course, as we feared that some of the young men might leave the establishment as soon as they had obtained the certificates of candidates, and we were unwilling that they should go forth without some knowledge at least of one of the chief elements of our national prosperity, or altogether without power to make the working man acquainted with the great agent, which has had more influence on the destiny of the working classes than any other single fact in our history, and which is probably destined to work still greater changes.

Knowledge and national prosperity are here in strict alliance. Not only do the arts of peace—the success of our trade—our power to compete with foreign rivals—our safety on our railways and in our steam-ships—depend on the spread of this knowledge, but the future defence of this country from foreign aggression can only result from our being superior to every nation in those arts. The schoolmaster is an agent despised at present, but whose importance for the attainment of this end will, by the results of a few years, be placed in bold relief before the public.

The tutor to whom the duty of communicating to the pupils a knowledge of the laws of motion, of the mechanical powers and contrivances, and of the laws of heat, was committed, was selected because he was a self-educated man, and was willing to avail himself of the more popular methods of demonstration, and to postpone the application of his valuable and extensive mathematical acquirements. By his assistance, the pupils and students have been led through a series of demonstrations of mechanical combinations, until they were prepared to consider the several parts of the steam-engine, first separately, and in their successive developments and applications, and they are at present acquainted with the more complex combinations in the steam-engines now in use, and with the principles involved in their construction and action.

In *geography* it has been deemed important that the tutors should proceed by a similar method. The lessons on land surveying have familiarised the pupils with the nature and uses of maps. As one development of the art of drawing, they have been practised in map-drawing. For this purpose, among other expedients, the walls of one class-room have been prepared with mastic, in order that bold projections of maps might be made on a great scale.

Physical geography has been deemed the true basis of all instruction in the geography of industry and commerce, which ought to form the chief subject of geographical instruction in elementary schools. The tutor has first endeavoured to convince the pupils that nothing which presents itself to the eye in a well-drawn map is to be regarded as accidental; the boldness of the promontories; the deep indenture of the bays; the general bearings of the coast; are all referable to natural laws. In these respects the eastern and western coasts of England are in striking contrast, in appearance, character, and in the circumstances which occasion their peculiarities. The physical geography of England commences with a description of the elevation of the mountain ranges, the different levels, and the drainage of the country. The course, rapidity, and volume of the rivers are referable to the elevation and extent of the country which they drain. From the climate, levels, and drainage, with little further matter, the agricultural tracts of the country may be indicated; and when the great coal-fields and the mineral veins and beds, the depth of the bays and rivers, are known, the distribution of the population is found to be in strict relation to certain natural laws. Even the ancient political divisions of the country are, on inspection, found to be in close dependence on its drainage. The counties are river basins, which were the first seats of tribes of population. If any new political distribution were to be made, it would necessarily, in like manner, be affected by some natural law, which it is equally interesting and useful to trace.

Geography taught in this way is a constant exercise to the reasoning powers. The pupil is led to trace the mutual dependence of facts, which, in ordinary instruction, are taught as the words of a vocabulary. Geography taught in the ordinary way is as reasonable an acquisition as the catalogue of a museum, which a student might be compelled to learn as a substitute for natural history. A catalogue of towns, rivers, bays, promontories, &c., is even less geography than the well-arranged catalogue of a museum is natural history, because the classification has a logical meaning in the latter case, which is absent in the former.

The intelligent tutor should feel himself bound to acquire sufficient knowledge to explain to his pupil the mutual dependence of the facts which the map presents to the eye. Thus it is easy to explain why certain tracts are rich pastures, why others are arable; to account for the climate, productions, industry, and commerce of such a county as Lancashire, and to read its history in the natural features of its hills, valleys, streams, coal-field, rivers, and western site. London, originally the outport to Europe, now the outport to the world, presents a great problem, equally instructing and useful to work, compared with which the facts of its being the capital of England, and situated on the Thames (ordinarily taught), are as the ciphers detached from a numerical power. Its tidal river carrying vessels into the heart of the land; its position in relation to the old Norman possessions of the conquerors of this country; its subsequent position between the commerce of Europe and the richest tracts of England; the facilities which it affords equally for commerce with the East and the West Indies; the resources it derives from the Northumberland and Durham coal-fields, without which its prosperity would suffer a grievous blow from the rivalry of other outports to which coal-beds are readily accessible: these, and a multitude of other considerations, too numerous to relate in this place, constitute that lesson in geography which the mention of London suggests. Its very place in the map is determined by natural laws of the most positive character, and capable of strict definition.

Every county in England and Scotland is treated inductively in this manner, and its productions, the distribution of its population, &c., are referred to the operation of the natural laws on which, in the beneficent providence of God towards our country, they are dependent.

In like manner, but in more general terms, the great streams of our commerce are described and accounted for. The colonies of England form the first step beyond this country, and beyond a general description of the world; and then follow those nations with which we have the most intimate commercial connexion.

This geography is examined in relation to the great commercial activity of England, and the influence of our industry on the Christian civilisation of the world.

In like manner, the great internal changes of the country

are accounted for. The spread of agriculture over previously barren tracts; the drainage of former marshes; the influence of the coal-fields in creating great vortices of trade, to which all the domestic manufactures are drawn; the laws affecting the importance of the respective outports, &c. &c.; are topics of important illustrations.

For the delivery of this course of instruction the present books and maps are found exceedingly defective. No good school-books on geography exist, and the maps at present in use are mere outlines, neglecting most of the great features of physical geography, which is the basis, first, of the geography of commerce and industry, and then (in a natural series) of that statistical and political geography which should form a prominent element of the instruction given in schools for the middle classes.

Maps are wanted, in which the elevation and drainage of the country should be faithfully delineated, giving the chief coal-fields and mineral veins and beds; containing the soundings of the coast and harbours, and the chief means of internal commercial communication, such as canals, railroads, &c. On this basis should be depicted in colour the great agricultural tracts, as distinguished by soils; and the seats of the chief manufactures. Along the coast the chief streams of commerce should be shown; the fisheries; and the comparative amount of tonnage entering every port. The use of a few symbols would convey much important information respecting our internal relations.

Geographies should be prepared adapted to the use of such maps both by the teacher and by his scholars.

If such maps and books had been in existence, the tutors of the Training School would have been spared much labour, and the progress of their pupils would have been both more rapid and more satisfactory.

As a department of geographical instruction, the elements of the use of the globes, in connection with nautical astronomy, has been cultivated with some diligence.

The further progress of the pupils in the geography of commerce and industry will be accelerated by the lectures which will now be delivered three days in the week by Mr. Hughes, one of the Professors of the College of Engineers, who has been appointed lecturer on this subject.

The outlines only of the history of England have been read, as preparatory to a course of instruction in English history, which is to form one of the studies of the second year. The history of England has been read in the evening as an exercise in the art of reading, and the examinations which have followed have been adapted only to secure general impressions as to the main facts of our history. In the second year's course it is hoped that this general knowledge will be found useful.

Skill in *drawing* was deemed essential to the success of a schoolmaster. Without this art he would be unable to avail himself of the important assistance of the black-board, on which his demonstrations of the objects of study ought to be delineated. His lessons on the most simple subjects would be wanting demonstrative power, and he would be incapable of proceeding with lessons in mechanics, without skill to delineate the machines of which his lessons treated.

The art of design has been little cultivated among the workmen of England. Whoever has been accustomed to see the plans of houses and farm buildings, or of public buildings of a humble character from the country, must know the extreme deficiency of our workmen in this application of the art of drawing, where it is closely connected with the comfort of domestic life, and is essential to the skilful performance of public works. The survey now in progress under the Tithe Commissioners affords abundant evidence of the want of skill in map-drawing among the rural surveyors.

The improvement of our machinery for agriculture and manufactures would be in no small degree facilitated, if

the art of drawing were a common acquirement among
our artisans. Invention is checked by the want of skill
in communicating the conception of the inventor, by drawings of all the details of his combination. In all those
manufactures of which taste is a principal element, our
neighbours, the French, are greatly our superiors, solely,
we believe, because the eyes and the hands of all classes
are practised from a very early age in the arts of design.
In the elementary schools of Paris, the proficiency of the
young pupils in drawing is very remarkable, and the evening schools are filled with young men and adults of mature
or even advanced age, engaged in the diligent cultivation
of this art. Last midsummer, in some of the evening
schools of the Brothers of the Christian Doctrine, classes
of workmen were questioned as to their employments.
One was an *ébéniste*, another a founder, another a clock-
maker, another a paper-hanger, another an upholsterer;
and each was asked his hours of labour, and his motives
for attendance. A single example may serve as a type.
A man without his coat, whose muscular arms were bared
by rolling his shirt-sleeves up to his shoulders, and who,
though well washed and clean, wore the marks of toil on
his white horny hands, was sitting with an admirable copy
in crayon of *La Donna della Segiola* before him, which
he had nearly completed. He was a man about 45 years
of age. He said he had risen at five, and had been at
work from six o'clock in the morning until seven o'clock
in the evening, with brief intervals for meals; and he had
entered the evening class at eight o'clock, to remain there
till ten. He had pleasure, he said, in drawing, and that
a knowledge of the art greatly improved his skill and
taste in masonry. He turned round with a good-humoured
smile, and added, he could live better on less wages than
an Englishman, because his drawing cost him less than
beer. Some thousand working men attend the adult
schools every evening in Paris, and the drawing classes
comprise great numbers whose skill would occasion much
astonishment in this country. The most difficult engravings

of the paintings of the Italian masters are copied in crayon with remarkable skill and accuracy. Complex and exquisitely minute architectural details, such, for example, as perspective views of the Duomo at Milan, or the cathedrals at Rouen or Cologne, are drawn in pen and ink, with singular fidelity. Some were drawing from plaster casts and other models. We found such adult schools in many of the chief towns of France. These schools are the sources of the taste and skill in the decorative arts, and in all manufactures of which taste is a prominent element, and which have made the designs for the calico printers, the silk and ribbon looms, the papers, &c. &c., of France, so superior in taste to those of this country, notwithstanding the superiority of our manufactories in mechanical combinations.

These considerations lead us to account drawing an important department of elementary education. The manufacturers of Lancashire are well aware how difficult it is, from the neglect of the arts of design among the labourers of this country, to procure any skilled draftsmen to design for the cotton or silk manufacturer. The elevation of the national taste in art can only be procured by the constant cultivation of the mind in relation to the beautiful in form and colour, by familiarising the eye with the best models, the works of great artists, and beautiful natural objects. Skill in drawing from nature results from a careful progress through a well-analysed series of models. The interests of commerce are so intimately connected with the results to be obtained by this branch of elementary education, that there is little chance that it will much longer suffer the grievous neglect which it has hitherto experienced.

The drawing classes at Battersea were first exercised in very simple models, formed of oblong pieces of wood, arranged in a great variety of forms by the master, according to a method observed in the Swiss and German schools. These were drawn in common and in isometrical perspective, the laws of perspective being at the same time carefully explained, and the rules applied in each case to the object which the pupil drew. A very little practice made us aware that a method comprising a more minute analysis of form was necessary to the greatest amount of success. Some inquiries which were pursued in Paris put us in possession of the method invented by M. Dupuis; and a series of his models were purchased and brought over at the close of the autumn, for the purpose of making a careful trial of this method. Considerable difficulty was experienced in procuring the services of an artist to superintend the instruction; but at length the application of this method has been commenced, and is in progress.

The experience of the French Inspectors of Schools (at an early period after the establishment of the system of inspection) convinced them that, to the perfection of *skill in drawing form*, the practice of drawing from models is necessary. The best copyists frequently, or rather generally, were found to fail in drawing even very simple natural objects on their first trials. In the drawing schools at Paris, in which the most elaborate engravings were admirably copied, an Inspector would discover that the pupils were unable to draw correctly the professor's desk and chair. It became, therefore, evident that the copy could not stand in the place of the natural object. Copying works of art might be essential to one department of skill and taste, but it by no means necessarily gave skill in drawing from nature.

M. Dupuis was an Inspector, and, observing this defect, he invented a series of models, ascending from a simple line of wire through various combinations to complex figures. These models are fixed in an instrument on the level of the eye, and may, by the movement of the instrument, be placed in a varying perspective. By this means the pupil may learn to draw the simplest objects, and proceed by gradual steps through a series of combinations of an almost insensibly increasing difficulty, until he can draw faithfully any object, however complex. The instrument which holds the object enables the teacher, by varying its position, to give at each lesson a series of demonstrations in perspective, applying the rules to objects of a gradually increasing complexity, until they are understood in their relations to the most difficult combinations. Thus practical skill and theoretical knowledge are in harmony in this instruction. The taste may afterwards be cultivated by drawing those works of art best adapted to create a just sense of the beautiful in form and colour.

That which a workman first requires is mechanical skill in the art of drawing. Nature itself offers many opportunities to cultivate the taste insensibly; and skill can be acquired only by careful and prolonged practice in the art of drawing from nature. In the more advanced parts of the course, we shall be able to satisfy ourselves as to the best mode of using the skill acquired for the formation of the taste.

In the Normal Schools at Versailles, one year's instruction had sufficed to give the pupils a wonderful facility and skill in drawing from models. Some complicated pneumatic apparatus, consisting of glass, mahogany, brass, and in difficult perspective, was drawn rapidly, and with great truth and skill. It is not, however, our intention to carry the instruction of our pupils in this art further than is necessary for the industrial instruction of their future scholars.

Some of the reasons inducing us to attach much importance to the cultivation of *vocal music* have already been briefly indicated. We regarded it as a powerful auxiliary in rendering the devotional services of the household, of the parish church, and of the village school solemn and impressive. Our experience satisfies us that we by no means over-estimated this advantage, though all the results are not yet obtained which, we trust, will flow from the right use of these means.

Nor were we indifferent to the cheerfulness diffused in schools by the singing of those melodies which are attractive to children, nor unconscious of the moral power which music has when linked with sentiments which it is the object of education to inspire. We regard school songs as an important means of diffusing a cheerful view of the duties of a labourer's life; of diffusing joy and honest pride over English industry. Therefore, to neglect so powerful a moral agent in elementary education as vocal music would appear to be unpardonable. We availed ourselves of some arrangements which were at this time in progress, under the superintendence of the Committee of Council, for the introduction of the method of M. Wilhem, which has been singularly successful in France. It affords us great satisfaction to say how much advantage the pupils of the Training School have derived from the instruction they have received, during the development of this method, from Mr. Hullah, the gentleman selected by the Committee of Council to adapt the method of Wilhem, under their superintendence, to the tastes and habits of the English people. Mr. Hullah has devoted himself with unceasing assiduity and great skill to this important public duty; and his pupils will always remember, with a pleasure without any alloy, the delightful lessons they have received from him.

The method of Wilhem is simply an application of the Pestalozzian method of ascending from the simple to the general through a clearly analysed series, in which every step of the progress is distinctly marked, and enables the pupil, without straining his faculties, to arrive at results which might otherwise have been difficult of attainment. Wilhem has not in any respect deviated from the well-ascertained results of experience, either in the theory of music or in the musical signs; but he has with great skill arranged all the early lessons, so as to smooth the path of the student to the desirable result of being able to read music with ease, and to sing with skill and expression even difficult music at sight. The progress of the pupils at Battersea has been very gratifying, and, even in the brief period which has elapsed since the opening of the school, they sing music at sight with considerable facility.

They have received, on the average, only two lessons weekly, each of an hour's duration, and until lately have not been permitted to practise in the intervals, lest they should contract bad habits before their sense of time and tune had been cultivated. Of late, they have been permitted to practise daily for one hour. Their progress has necessarily been less rapid than it would have been had the entire method been previously arranged, as it now is, in a complete and logical series, as the result of Mr. Hullah's valuable labour. Much time has necessarily been expended in copying music, which will be spared to those who follow, and who, after Easter, 1841, will possess the volume and singing tablets published by the Committee of Council on Education.

Those who desire further proof of the importance of the method of Wilhem should visit the Normal School at Versailles, various day schools at Paris, and especially the great assemblages of the Working Classes, which occur almost every evening in Paris, for the purpose of receiving instruction in vocal music. The most remarkable of these probably is at the Halle-aux-Draps, where from 300 to 500 artisans are almost every evening instructed, from eight to nine o'clock, in vocal music. M. Hubert, a pupil of Wilhem, conducts this great assembly, by the method of mutual instruction, with singular skill and precision. We know scarcely anything more impressive than the swell of these manly voices when they unite in chorus.

If the music of Handel and Haydn were better known by the professors of music at Paris, assuredly this would be the place in which to display its most remarkable effects. Even in the singing of Wilhem's solfeggios in harmony, or of the scale in harmony, such a volume of sound was poured forth, that the effects were very impressive.

A method which has succeeded in attracting thousands of artisans in Paris from low cabarets and miserable gambling-houses to the study of a science, and the practice of a captivating art, deserves the attention of the public.

Mr. Hullah, in adapting the method of Wilhem to English tastes and habits, has both simplified and refined it. He has, moreover, adapted to it a considerable number of old English melodies of great richness and character, which were fast passing into oblivion, and which may be restored to the place they once held in the affections of the people, being now allied with words expressive of the joys and hopes of a labourer's life, and of the true sources of its dignity and happiness.

We have assisted in the development of this method, being convinced that it may tend to elevate the character of our elementary schools, and that it may be of great use throughout the country in restoring many of our best old English melodies to their popularity, and in improving the character of our vocal music in village churches, through the medium of the parochial schoolmaster and his pupils.

The pupils and students of the Training School now conduct the vocal music in the Hon. and Rev. Robert Eden's church at Battersea, and, under Mr. Hullah's superintendence, they also manage the instruction of the village school in singing.

When the preparatory course was sufficiently advanced, a series of lectures on the construction and organisation of elementary schools, and on the theory and art of teaching, were commenced. They have resembled those given in the German and Swiss schools under the generic term Pædagogik.

They have treated of the general objects of education, and the means of attaining them. The peculiar aims of elementary education; the structure of school-houses in various parts of Europe; the internal arrangement of the desks, forms, and school apparatus, in reference to different methods of instruction; and the varieties of those methods observed in different countries. The theory of the discipline of schools. Its practice, describing in detail the different expedients resorted to in different countries for the purpose of procuring order, decorum, propriety of posture and manner, regularity and precision in movements, and in changes of classes and exercises, and especially the right means of securing the reverence and the love of the children. This last subject naturally connects the consideration of the mechanical and methodic expedients with that of the sources of the schoolmaster's zeal, activity, and influence, on which much has been said. To these subjects have succeeded lectures on the great leading distinctions in the methods of communicating knowledge. When the distinguishing principles had been described, the characteristic features of the several methods were examined *generally*, and certain peculiar applications of each were treated. The application of these methods to each individual branch of instruction was then commenced, and this part of the course has treated of various methods of teaching to read, especially giving a minute description of the *phonic* method. Of methods of teaching to write, giving a special account of the method of Mülhauser. On the application of writing in various methods of instruction. Of methods of teaching to draw, giving a detailed account of that of M. Dupuis. Of methods of teaching arithmetic, in which the method of Pestalozzi has been carefully explained, and other expedients examined. This brief sketch may indicate the character of the instruction up to the period of this Report. Our desire is to anticipate as little as possible, but, on the contrary, to relate only what *has been done.* We have therefore only to add, that the instruction in Pædagogik is in its preparatory stage, and that the course will be pursued, in relation both to the general theory and practice, and to the special application of the theory and practice to the development of the village school, and of the training school, through the whole period of instruction, as that part of the studies of the pupils by which the mutual relations of these studies are revealed, and their future application anticipated.

We regard these lectures, combined with the zealous labour of the Hon. and Rev. Robert Eden, as the chief means by which, aided by the tutors, such a tone of feeling can be maintained as shall prepare the teachers to enter upon their important duties, actuated by motives which will be the best means of insuring their perseverance, and promoting their success.

The Brothers of the Christian Doctrine, who devote their lives a cheerful sacrifice to the education of the poorer classes of France, can be understood best by those who have visited their Noviciate and schools at Paris. From such persons we expect acquiescence when we say, that their example of Christian zeal is worthy of the imitation of protestants. Three of the Brothers of this order are maintained for a sum which is barely the stipend of one teacher of a school of mutual instruction in Paris. Their schools are unquestionably the best at Paris. Their manners are simple, affectionate, and sincere. The children are singularly attached to them. How could it be otherwise, when they perceive that these good men have no other reward on earth for their manifold labours than that of an approving conscience?

The *régime* of the *Noviciate* is one of considerable austerity. They rise at four. They spend an hour in private devotion, which is followed by two hours of religious exercises in their chapel. They breakfast soon afterwards, and are in the day schools of Paris at nine. They dine about noon, and continue their attention to the schools till five. They sup at six, and then many of them are employed in evening schools for the adults from seven till nine, or from eight to ten, when, after prayers, they immediately retire to rest.

No one can enter the schools of the Brothers of the Christian Doctrine without feeling instinctively that he is witnessing a remarkable example of the development of Christian charity.

With such motives should the teachers of elementary schools, and especially those who are called to the arduous duties of training pauper children, go forth to their work. The path of the teacher is strewn with disappointments, if he commence with a mercenary spirit. It is full of encouragement, if he be inspired with the spirit of Christian charity. No skill can compensate adequately for the absence of a pervading religious influence on the character and conduct of the schoolmaster.

The discipline of the Training School has been gradually developed with this design; and, under the faithful and judicious guidance of Mr. Eden, we trust, in the course of time, it may obtain some measure of success.

It is in this spirit that we have been anxious that the young pupils and students should, under the superintendence of Mr. Eden, and the immediate tuition of the master of the village school, undertake their duties in that scene of labour and instruction.

It is not our intention to say much on the arrangements which have been adopted in the Village School, which has been connected with the Training School only a few weeks. The first class of the Training School has been divided into two sections, one of which supplies pupil teachers to the Village School in the morning, and the other in the afternoon, each continuing their studies in the Training School at the periods not thus occupied.

The village school will, under the superintendence of Mr. Eden, be gradually developed as a school on the *mixed method* of instruction; but we cannot hope that anything like the precision in method which characterises the continental schools should be attained in it, excepting after prolonged and unremitting attention to all the details of its discipline and management.

Such attention continued through the course of the three years' instruction necessary to the certificate of Master, will, we trust, furnish the village school with such a class of educators as may enable it to realise the chief features of those schools which are most worthy of imitation in the Protestant countries of Europe; but before the expiration of the three years' course, we cannot hope it will be able to accomplish this design. At present, all that we feel warranted to say is, that we are very sensible of the great difficulties which lie in the way of success, and that much humble and patient exertion will be required to surmount them. The able and zealous superintendence of Mr. Eden affords the village school a prospect of success which, under less vigilant and intelligent management, we should despair to attain.

We have secured for the village school the advantage of the services of Mr. M'Leod, recently the principal master of the School of Industry at Norwood. He is aware of the great difficulty of assilimating an elementary school in this country to some of those forms of excellence which we have afforded him an opportunity of examining in Holland. He is therefore prepared to endeavour, by gradual improvements, in the course of time, to render the elementary school a scene in which the pupils of the Training School may prepare themselves for the skilful performance of their future duties. The success of these efforts pre-supposes so much improvement in his assistant teachers and in the scholars, that we deem it prudent not to venture to anticipate results which it must be very difficult to attain.

The examination of the third quarter of the residence of several of our pupils is now just concluded.

The mode in which the daily examinations are conducted has already been described. During the depth of winter, when the out-door labour is necessarily suspended, the place which these examinations occupy in the daily routine may be ascertained by the inspection of the subjoined Tables, pp. 362—3.

At the quarterly examination the usual routine is suspended, and examination-papers are prepared by the tutors, containing a series of questions, passing over the chief features of the studies of the quarter in each class.

The students and pupils have no intimation of the questions which will be proposed; but, three hours being allotted to each examination-paper, the questions of a particular subject (as for example grammar) are distributed to each pupil in the assembled class. The pupils then attempt the solution of all the questions without the aid of books, and without assistance from the tutors, or from each other.

At the expiration of the three hours the replies to the questions are collected, and in the afternoon, a similar plan is pursued with some other subject, the examination-papers of which are distributed without any previous intimation of their nature.

DAILY ROUTINE.

Half-past 5	Rise, wash, dress, and make beds.
Quarter to 6	Household work, viz., scouring and sweeping floors, cleaning grates, shoes, knives, &c., pumping water and preparing vegetables, and milking cows.
Quarter to 7	Reading of Scriptures and prayers.
Quarter-past 7	Superintendents present reports.
Half-past 7	Lecture on the theory and art of teaching, and on school discipline.
Quarter-past 8	Breakfast.
Quarter to 9	The first division of the first class go to the village school.

	Monday.	Tuesday.	Wednesday.	Thursday.	Friday.	Saturday.
9 to 10	(Second division, first class. Second class.	E. P. on mensuration. Arithmetic.	E.P. on grammar and etymology. Algebra.	Examination Papers — E. P. on mechanics. Arithmetic.	E.P. on arithmetic Mensuration.	E.P. on geography and globes. Arithmetic.	E. P. on problems. Algebra.
10 to 11	(Second division, first class. Second class.	Drawing. Writing on Mülhauser's method.	Algebra or mensuration. Grammar.	Drawing. Writing on Mülhauser's method.	Algebra or mensuration. Grammar.	Drawing. Writing on Mülhauser's method.	Grammar. Grammar.
11 to 12	(Second division, first class. Second class.	Etymology.	Practising arithmetic on Pestalozzi's tables. Mental arithmetic.	Etymology.	Practising arithmetic on Pestalozzi's tables. Mental arithmetic.	Etymology.	Arithmetic. Mental arithmetic.

12 o'clock	The first division of the first class return from village school.
12 to 1	Garden-work, feed the animals, &c. At 1, march to the house and prepare for dinner.
,,	A class practising singing in the hall.
Quarter-past 1	Dinner.

DAILY ROUTINE—*continued*.

		MONDAY.	TUESDAY.	WEDNESDAY.	THURSDAY.	FRIDAY.	SATURDAY.
Quarter to 2 .		The second division of the first class go to the village school.					
2 to 3 . . .		First division first class. Drill and gymnastic exercises in fair weather; in rough weather a lesson on drawing.					
3 to 4 . . .		Second class. Drill and gymnastic exercises in fair weather; in rough weather, reading. First division, first class. Examination-papers.					
3 to quarter to 4 . .	Second class .	Writing on Müllhauser's method.	Use of the globes.	Writing on Müllhauser's method	Use of the globes	Writing on Müllhauser's method.	Use of the globes.
4 to quarter to 5 . .	First division, first class.	Writing on Müllhauser's method.	Practising arithmetic on Pestalozzi's method.	Writing on Müllhauser's method.	Practising arithmetic on Pestalozzi's method	Writing on Müllhauser's method.	Surveying.
Quarter to 4 to quarter to 5	Second class. Examination-papers.						
Quarter-past 4 to 6	The second division of the first class return from village school.						
Quarter to 5	Classes united. On Tuesday, Wednesday, and Friday, lectures upon the geography of commerce and industry. On Monday, and Thursday, writing out the notes of the lectures on geography, preceded by an examination of a quarter of an hour's duration.						
Quarter-past 6	Supper.						
7 to 8 . . .	Classes united. Mechanics, Monday, Tuesday, Wednesday, Thursday, and Friday.						
8 to 9 . . .	Classes united. Biblical reading; lesson on the manners and customs of the Jews, and on geography of Palestine, &c.						
9 o'clock . .	Prayer.						
20 min. past 9	Retire to rest.						

SUNDAY.

One of the sermons of the day is written from memory.
In the evening these compositions are read and commented upon.

In this way, in three or four days, all the subjects of instruction in the Training School are brought under minute examination.

As soon as the answers are collected, they are examined, and the relative merit of each reply is ascertained. A mean number having been attached to each question, the merit of the reply is expressed in numbers above or below this mean, and thus the whole results of the examination may be tabulated, and the intellectual progress of each pupil ascertained.

The following series of questions were issued at the examination of the third quarter, which expired at Christmas. We submit them to you, because we are desirous that you should form an accurate opinion of the results of the instruction in the Training School during the preparatory course. The questions faithfully represent the general course of the instruction on the subjects to which they relate, and they are level to the capacity and attainments of the pupils.

In order that this may be more clearly evident to you, we have appended to the series of questions Tables containing the name of each pupil, his age, and period of entrance into the Training School, at the head of the columns. On the left side of each Table a column contains the number of each question, and in the next column the mean number indicating the comparative difficulty of the question; then, under the name of each boy the merit of the answer of each pupil is given in successive columns, and in the same manner, the merit of the replies to each of the questions respectively is tabulated.

In order that you may possess a standard from which to determine the relative merit of the rest of the replies, we have likewise placed, in an Appendix, replies to the questions from most of the pupils, the comparative merit of which may be estimated by a reference to the numbers in the Tables.

The answers to the questions on religious instruction have not been deemed simply an intellectual exercise, and the results in this case have not been tabulated. They were framed by the Hon. and Rev. Robert Eden, who has superintended the religious instruction of the Training School with unwearied assiduity. We are enabled to furnish you with a note, expressive of Mr. Eden's opinion of the general progress of the pupils in religious knowledge, during the three quarters of the preparatory course which have now elapsed.

Before submitting the questions to you, we are anxious to avoid one source of misconception, to which the plan of the school might be liable in consequence of our reluctance to anticipate results, by describing the course we intend to pursue in the future parts of the course of instruction. The technical instruction in that knowledge which it will be the duty of the pupils to communicate in elementary schools, occupies a much greater portion of the time in the preparatory course than that which will be allotted to such studies in the two subsequent years.

Every month will now bring into greater prominence *instruction, theoretical and practical, in the art of teaching.* The outlines only of a future course of instruction in this most important element of the studies of a training school have been communicated. Some of the principles have been laid down; but the application of these principles to each subject of instruction, and the arrangement of the entire matter of technical knowledge, in accordance with the principles of elementary teaching, is a labour to which a large portion of the future time of the pupils must be devoted.

Those studies which will prepare them for the performance of collateral duties in the village or parish have not been commenced.

The instruction in the management of a garden; in pruning and grafting trees; in the relative qualities of soils, manures, and the rotation of garden crops, is to form a part of the course of instruction, after the certificate of candidate is obtained.

A course on the domestic economy of the poor will be

delivered in the same year, which will be followed by another on the means of preserving health, especially with regard to the employments, habits, and wants of the working classes. Some general lectures on the relations of labour and capital will close this course.

Those parts of the present course of technical instruction which will obtain the largest share of attention in the year in which the *candidates* are trained, will be the geography of commerce and industry; mensuration, land surveying, and mechanics; and the history of England, treated chiefly in connection with the progress of civilisation, and especially of industry and the arts.

The religious instruction will develope itself, under the guidance of Mr. Eden, in its relations to those subjects of history in which it is desirable that the pupils should receive impressions consistent with Christian charity and truth.

This brief indication of that which lies immediately before the pupils of the Training School will, we trust, remove any apprehension which might be entertained that the technical character of certain of their present studies will overlay a large portion of the future course.

The spontaneous preparation for instruction in the village school, and which will require considerable and well-directed application to miscellaneous reading, will in itself be an obstacle to the continuance of the present extent of technical instruction. This spontaneous preparation must embrace many subjects collateral to the instruction in the school, but which must be communicated in a popular manner in an elementary school, requiring a re-arrangement of knowledge previously acquired in a technical form.

The chief source of any confidence we have in the course we have pursued, is derived from the inquiries respecting the routine of instruction in Normal Schools in certain parts of the continent.

We have, for your information, placed in the Appendix to this Report several Tables of the routine of studies in some of the chief Normal Schools in different parts of

Europe. A comparison of these Tables with the general sketch of the plans of the Battersea Training School, with which we have furnished you, will enable you to perceive how far our personal inquiries have guided us in the regulation of the Training School, founded under your sanction.

We lay before you the questions of the third quarterly examination at Battersea, and the tabulated results of the replies. In the first of these Tables, viz., that on grammar and etymology, we have given the age and day of the month when each pupil entered the school in the year 1840. It has not been deemed necessary to reprint these Tables in this place.

. . . . .

The preceding notes contain a few examples of the manner in which the questions have been answered, one being selected for each question, which, in conjunction with the numerical statements contained in the Tables, may serve as a standard of comparison by which the merit of the rest of the replies may be ascertained. It is a source of pleasure to us that a Maltese, confided to our care by the Maltese Government, notwithstanding the obstacles created by the want of a perfect knowledge of the language, occupies such a position in this examination as to justify our confidence in his success as the Teacher of a Model School in Malta, which is his destination.

The questions and answers afford better evidence than anything which we can say of the intelligent and persevering attention which Mr. Tate and Mr. Horne have paid to their duties. They have earned the reward of the affection and respect of their pupils, and if our own tribute of esteem can add anything to the satisfaction derivable from that source it has been freely accorded.

We are somewhat apprehensive that these questions may lead to erroneous opinions of our views. We are fully aware that all such tests must give a very imperfect idea of the real condition of a school, and in fact, from being necessarily confined to intellectual displays, omit all reference to what we have always considered to be the most essential, as it is the most difficult, object of our endeavours,—the formation of moral and religious characters. The progress that may have been made towards this latter object is incapable, as in the former, of being shown by written questions. We can only then solicit credit for our intentions in repeating with all earnestness, that we hold the end of all these intellectual demonstrations to be infinitely subordinate to the cultivation of the heart and feelings. We have no wish to send forth simply clever teachers; we believe, on the contrary, that the vice of several of the German Normal Institutions, which we have examined, has been the too great attention paid to instruction as distinct from education. The Swiss schools appeared to us to be mostly free from this defect, and to them we have chiefly resorted as models for what we have done.

It may also be objected to these questions, that some of them refer to subjects different from or beyond what it may be desirable or possible to teach in many schools. We admit the correctness of this statement, but deny the inference that some may attempt to draw from it derogatory to the utility of such studies for the purpose we have in view. The schoolmaster whose knowledge is strictly confined to what he has to impart, will frequently be at a loss, in attempting to explain many points that occur in his lessons, and puzzled with questions from the more intelligent pupils, whose unsatisfied inquiries will quickly generate a disrespect for their instructor. It is impossible to know or to teach many of even the lowest branches of knowledge thoroughly without some acquaintance with the theories and higher generalizations on which those inferior departments depend. But on this point we would refer to a higher authority, M. Guizot, with whose opinion on this subject, as well as in the following description of what a teacher ought to be, we beg to add our unqualified concurrence:—" A good schoolmaster ought to be a man who knows much more than he is called upon to teach, that he may teach with intelligence and with taste; who is to live in a humble sphere, and yet to have a noble and elevated mind, that he may preserve that dignity of sentiment and of deportment, without which he will never obtain the respect and confidence of families; who possesses a rare mixture of gentleness and firmness; for, inferior though he be in station to many individuals in the parish, he ought to be the obsequious servant of none; a man not ignorant of his rights, but thinking much more of his duties; showing to all a good example, and serving to all as a counsellor; not given to change his condition, but satisfied with his situation, because it gives him the power of doing good; and who has made up his mind to live and to die in the service of primary instruction, which to him is the service of God and his fellow-creatures. To rear masters approaching to such a model is a difficult task; and yet we must succeed in it, or else we have done nothing for elementary instruction."

The questions for this quarterly examination have been chiefly selected by the tutors. We do not propose that this course shall be pursued in the questions employed in the examination for the certificate of *Candidate*, or *Scholar*, or *Master*. We are of opinion that such institutions as this Training School (the further management of which we hope to superintend in entire subordination to your wishes) should be placed under the inspection of that department of the executive Government which is charged with the promotion of elementary education. The humble effort which we have made to place in your hands the means of providing schoolmasters for the workhouses, and especially for the district schools for pauper children, has not, we trust, been conducted inconsistently with the public interest; but we are anxious to afford the public the fullest warrant for confidence in the future management of this school, and we know no way of accomplishing this object so fully as by soliciting the periodical examination of Her Majesty's Inspectors of Schools, which we trust the Committee of Council on Education will allow. In the *quarterly examinations* of the Training School we hope for the assistance of one of Her Majesty's Inspectors, and we trust that, upon application from you, the Committee of Council will consent to associate one or more of their Inspectors with one of your own body, in selecting the questions for the *annual examination*, by which the certificates will be awarded; in determining the merit of the several replies; and in selecting the individuals who may be entitled to certificates.

In order that the selection of questions may have the necessary relation to the studies of the year, we propose to furnish the *examiners* with the weekly and quarterly examination-papers of the school, from which papers they will readily ascertain the range of the acquirements of the pupils in the several classes; but it will be expedient that every question shall emanate only from the examiners at the annual examination for certificates.

We are desirous that some standard of attainment should be fixed for entrance upon the preparatory course, and we wish to refer the examination-papers (employed to ascertain the acquirements of the pupils on their entrance) to the approval of the Committee of Council on Education; and that the replies, being prepared by pupils under the eye of an Inspector, at the end of a short probationary period, should be approved by their Lordships before each pupil is finally entered for the preparatory course on the books of the school.

We trust that, in this way, security will be afforded that any funds which may be devoted to the maintenance of this Training School will not be applied in any way inconsistently with the interests of the public.

We regard these securities to be indispensable to the permanent prosperity of such institutions. By the examination of the pupils at their entrance, and the submission of the examination-papers (prepared in the presence of an Inspector at the end of a short probationary period), we intend to exclude favouritism in the selection of pupils, and the interference of partial interests in burdening the school with unqualified students.

By the continual inspection of the school by able, independent, and impartial men, we hope to secure the most useful stimulus to the exertions of the tutors and pupils; to provide against self-deception on their part as to the condition of the school; and, above all, to afford the public the only sufficient security against the impression derived from appearances skilfully dramatised to prevent the disclosure of defects.

We are especially anxious that the certificates should be awarded by persons not directly interested in the management of the school, in order that a conviction of impartiality may prevail among the scholars, that the certificates may have more than the ordinary value of such documents, and that the public may have only a legitimate, and in all respects a well-founded, confidence in the results of the training.

We should much rejoice if the results of these preparatory steps towards the foundation of a training school were deemed sufficiently auspicious to warrant the confidence of the Commission and of the Government, so far as to procure for the future expenses of the school assistance from the public funds. In that case we feel that the Government would be entitled to require that no tutor or professor should be appointed in the school without their approval; that their sanction should be necessary to the dismissal of any tutor or professor; and further that, on the Report of their Inspectors, they should be entitled to proceed to remove any tutor or professor from his office.

We are also of opinion that the Training School would not be entitled to support, in any considerable degree, from the public funds, unless the estimates for the school were annually submitted for the approval of the Committee of Council on Education, and the accounts annually audited by one of their Lordships' Inspectors.

The expenses of the Training School during the preparatory course have been cheerfully borne by ourselves, with the exception of those payments which have been made on behalf of individual pupils and students, and the entirely unsolicited aid of three or four of our personal friends. We have not presumed to think that we were warranted in expecting confidence in plans which had not hitherto been put forth in this country, until we could place before you at least a partial development of our views. We have, therefore, avoided soliciting assistance from any one, and, to all inquiries on this subject, we have deemed it proper to suggest, that the personal confidence of friends would not insure the permanent prosperity of a training school, which could only flourish by deserving and obtaining the confidence of the public. Such remarks have not prevented Mr. Samuel Jones Loyd and Mr. George Cornewall Lewis from urging us to permit them to contribute each £100 to the expenses of this year. We have accepted these offers. The Bishop of Durham has not been content with the usual payment for the pupil he has placed in the Training School, but his Lordship has requested us to accept a more liberal rate of remuneration. Mr. George Norman, of Bromley, has also sustained the charge of a pupil, whom, however, he has not selected. The Earl of Chichester added £10 to the sum paid with a boy whom he recommended.

The efficiency of the school during the course of instruction in the ensuing year can only be maintained by a considerable increase of expense. The number of the pupils and students will probably increase to sixty in the early part of the spring. The attention of the tutors will necessarily be so much occupied with the preparatory studies of those who then enter the school that an additional tutor will be indispensable. Certain of the courses of instruction of this year cannot be pursued without the assistance of professors who will attend from day to day. We have already secured the attendance of Mr. Hughes, who lectures on the geography of commerce and industry, and of an artist to assist in the instruction in drawing and perspective. We regret to say that Mr. Hullah's services have been given gratuitously, and with a zeal and disinterestedness which would, we fear, place it beyond our power adequately to express the value which we attach to his admirable lessons on vocal music. We have further incurred a part of the charge of the master of the village school. We propose to appoint a well-conducted, intelligent, and skilful gardener to superintend the instruction in horticulture, which will now receive increased attention. The charge for the rent may soon increase by our encountering the necessity of occupying the entire house, with the exception of two apartments, which we each intend to reserve in the establishment, where we may confer with the tutors. The further expenses of furniture required by the increase of the number of pupils and tutors, the additional books, apparatus, and certain contemplated alterations which it will be impossible to postpone beyond the spring, will raise the expenses of the ensuing year (after all the payments for individual scholars are deducted) to a balance of £2000 at least.

We are prepared to sustain this expense, if it be necessary that the Training School should be carried through another stage of its development before it deserves the public confidence. In fact we consider ourselves bound to do so should we obtain no assistance, as we have entered into engagements with the pupils, which we must fulfil at whatever cost to ourselves. Considerable inquiry and observation have impressed us with the views on which the Training School is founded, and we have been desirous to make a practical trial of the principles and expedients which the experience of the Protestant States of Europe has sanctioned by a concurrent testimony. It would be grateful to us to receive an early assurance of confidence in the plans and principles which we have, with as much unreserve as is consistent with the limits of this Report, freely set before you; but we have not entered on our present undertaking without expecting that a sacrifice would be required of us, before the work was in a condition to obtain that confidence which we trust will not be refused.

We also trust that the exposition of the principles by which we have been guided will not be misconceived, as evincing so unwarrantable a confidence in our opinions as to lead us to indulge in dogmatism. We conceive we may sincerely entertain them, and endeavour to promote their diffusion, without any undue confidence in our own judgment, or want of respect for the opinions of others.

You will naturally expect that this free disclosure of our views and proceedings in relation to the Training School should be terminated by an account of the expenses we have incurred to the termination of the year 1840. We think it right to lay the balance-sheet of the expenses and receipts of the school, without reserve, before you. We have been careful to take receipts for all the payments we have made, and as we regard ourselves as labouring at the foundations of a public institution, in which our experience may be of some value to others, we shall feel obliged if you will direct the accounts to be audited.

We have endeavoured, by a scrupulous economy in every department, to render the expenses of the school as low as is consistent with its efficiency, and we have accordingly foregone many convenient arrangements not absolutely required, but which it would have been desirable to make.

Some expenses might have been reduced, had not the demands of our public duties rendered it impossible to give constant superintendence to certain details.

JAMES PHILLIPS KAY and EDWARD CARLETON TUFFNELL in account with the Training School, Battersea.

Drs.	31st December, 1840.				Crs.		
	£	s.	d.		£	s.	d.
To Cash from G. W. Norman, Esq.	25	0	0	By furnishing and repairs	444	6	11½
„ Lord Chichester	10	0	0	Clothing	91	12	1
„ S. Jones Loyd, Esq.	100	0	0	Books, stationery, &c.	76	15	7½
„ G. C. Lewis, Esq.	100	0	0	House account, viz., provisions, wages, and petty cash account.	564	7	4
„ Landlord repairs	200	0	0				
„	50	0	0	House account, viz., servants' wages	17	1	1
„ Sundries sold	14	13	3	Garden account	34	4	0
„ Mr. Philbrick	14	0	0	Rent and taxes (deducting Dr. Kay's rent)	103	5	6
„ for Students and Pupils	271	14	2				
Amount owing for dito ditto	196	19	4	Alterations and repairs (deducting Dr. Kay's charge)	340	6	4
Balance	1283	11	10	Bad bank-note	5	0	0
				Salaries	154	9	2
				Mr. Senf	70	0	0
				Bills unpaid	343	19	8
				Salaries due	20	10	10
	2265	18	7		2265	18	7

The balance of expenses for which we find we have to provide on the 1st January, 1841, is £1283, which we have accordingly devoted to the establishment of this school. This sum arises to a large extent from the expenses incurred in furnishing, repairs, and alterations. The rest is attributable to salaries and the charge of clothing and maintaining the boys selected from the best schools for poor children, and educated at our expense.

The expenses of Dr. Kay's own private establishment are of course all borne by himself, and his arrangements are in all respects separate.

> We have the honour to be,
> Gentlemen,
> Your obedient servants,
> JAMES PHILLIPS KAY,
> EDWARD CARLETON TUFFNELL.

To the Poor Law Commissioners, Somerset House.

Course of Instruction pursued in the

		Religion and Morals.	German Language.	French Language.	Arithmetic.	Geometry.	History.
1st Class and 1st School-year.	1st Half-year.	Geography of Palestine, Jewish Archæology. History of the Christian Church.	Grammar, exercises in reading and recitations; composition.	Exercises in reading, and translation of easy pieces of French into German; introduction to the grammar and etymology.	Elementary rules of arithmetic; Vulgar and Decimal Fractions.	The doctrine of parallel lines, properties of triangles, similar triangles.	History from the beginning of the world to the subjection of Greece to the Romans.
	2nd Half-year.	Faith and morals, as founded on revelation.	Grammar, continuation of exercises in reading and recitations, composition of letters, and speeches.	Continuation of the above; beginning of the translation of German into French; grammar; vocabulary.	Proportion; mental arithmetic.	Measurement of triangles, and straight line figures, planimetry.	From the building of Rome to the Westphalian Peace.
2nd Class and 2nd School-year.	1st Half-year.	Lectures on the Bible, with questions.	Etymology and logical exercises, recitations, and composition.	Continued exercises of reading and translation into German; grammar; syntax; translation from German into French; speaking.	Continuation of exercises in the elementary rules.	Further exposition of the properties of triangles, and of straight line figures.	History of Switzerland from the beginning to the Westphalian Peace.
	2nd Half-year.	Lectures on the Bible, with practical illustrations, and references.	Repetitions of the more difficult parts of grammar; more extended compositions; laws of poetry.	Continuation of exercises in reading and translation; conclusion of syntax; recitations of easy pieces.	Continuation of exercises in Proportion; Simple Equations.	The circle: elements of stereometry; easy questions in practical geometry.	History of Switzerland as it bears on that of the rest of the world to the present period.
3rd Class and 3rd School-year.	1st Half-year.	Deeper and more abstruse points of doctrine, with Scriptural proofs and practical illustrations.	The more important peculiarities of the German language: verbal expositions of the written exercises.	Further expositions of grammar; more difficult translations from and into French and German respectively; composition.	More difficult applications of the preceding rules	Continuation of planimetry; plain and solid angles; projection of straight line figures; questions in the above subjects.	General history from 1389 to 1815.
	2nd Half-year.	Continuation of the above	View of German literature; poetical exercises.	Continuation of the above; short sketch of French literature.	Quadratic and Cubic Equations; Logarithms, Properties of Numbers; Progression	Polygonal figures; elements of trigonometry; practical geometry; projection of bodies with straight or curved surfaces; sections.	General history from 1815 to the present time.

The Training School at Battersea

Normal Seminary at Zurich, Switzerland.

Geography.	Natural History.	Physics.	Singing.	Art of Writing.	Drawing.	Art of Teaching.
Introductory explanations the ocean and continents, with their respective divisions.	General introduction to natural history, description of elementary bodies, general characteristics of minerals.	...	Elementary exercises of the voice; easy choral exercises.	Exercises in German and Roman character, in legal writing, and in black letter writing, music, and stenography.	Sketches from objects placed before the pupil, and from nature; special exercises in shading.	...
Special geography of Europe.	Unmetallic minerals, metals, mountains, introduction of botany.	...	Melody, religious hymns and choral singing.			...
The most important points of mathematical and physical geography.	Systems of botany, description of plants, special information on the plants known to the pupils.	The common phenomena arising from the various properties of differently constituted bodies.	Further exercises in Sol-Fa, also with words, exercises in solo singing and choral singing.			Introduction to psychology, methods of instruction.
Geography of Asia, Africa, America, and Australia.	Introduction to zoology; classification and descriptions introductory to the natural history of man.	Acoustics, optics, heat, magnetism, electricity.	Continuation of the above, special exposition of the art of teaching music.			Further exposition of methods of instruction, and of the cantonal laws and regulations relative to schools; practical teaching in the primary school.
More extended expositions of mathematical and physical geography.	Natural history of man; further expositions of the natural history of the lower animals.	Further exposition of the above subjects.	Continuation of the above.	...	...	Fundamental principles of the science of teaching.
Special geography of Asia, Africa, America, and Australia.	Introduction to geology; fossils.	Further exposition of the above subjects.	Continuation of the above.	...	...	Practical teaching in the secondary school.

COURSE of INSTRUCTION pursued at the Normal Seminary in the Canton of Thurgovia, Switzerland, under the superintendence of M. Vehrli, in the Summer half-year of 1839.

HOURS.	CLASS.	MONDAY.	TUESDAY.	WEDNESDAY.	THURSDAY.	FRIDAY.	SATURDAY.	SUNDAY.
5 to 7	First / Second	Out-door labour. Out-door labour.	Out-door labour. Out-door labour.	Art of teaching. Out-door labour.	Out-door labour. Art of teaching.	Out-door labour. Out-door labour.	Art of teaching. Out-door labour.	Attending divine service, sacred music, teaching, in Sunday-school.
7 to 8	.	Breakfast.	Breakfast.	Breakfast.	Breakfast.	Breakfast.	Breakfast.	
8 to 9	First / Second	Natural history. Profane history.	Biblical history. Biblical history.	Profane history. Management of land.	Natural history. Profane history.	Biblical history. Biblical history.	Profane history. Management of land.	
9 to 10	First / Second	Grammar. Geometry.	Grammar. Arithmetic.	Natural history. Grammar.	Grammar. Geometry.	Grammar. Arithmetic.	Natural history. Grammar.	
10 to 11	First / Second	Singing. Grammar.	Singing. Grammar.	Grammar. Geometry.	Singing. Grammar.	Singing. Grammar.	Grammar. Geometry.	
11 to 12	First / Second	Arithmetic. Natural history.	Geometry. Natural history.	Geometry. Art of teaching.	Arithmetic. Natural history.	Geometry. Natural history.	Arithmetic. Art of teaching.	
12 to 1½	.	Dinner and gymnastic exercises.	Dinner and gymnastic exercises.	Dinner and gymnastic exercises.	Dinner and gymnastic exercises.	Dinner and gymnastic exercises.	Dinner and gymnastic exercises.	
1½ to 3	First / Second	Singing. Writing.	Writing. Drawing.	Drawing. Violin.	Singing. Drawing.	Writing. Singing.	Drawing. .	
3 to 4	First / Second	Geography. Arithmetic.	Arithmetic. Geography.	Arithmetic. Natural history.	Geography. Arithmetic.	Arithmetic. Geography.	Writing. .	
4 to 5	First / Second	Geometry. Reading.	Reading. Geometry.	Repetitions. Arithmetic.	Geometry. Reading.	Reading. Geometry.	. .	
5 to 6	.	Supper.	Supper.	Supper.	Supper.	Supper.	Supper.	
6 to 9	.	Garden-work, house-work, conversation.	Garden-work, house-work, conversation.	Garden-work, house-work, conversation.	Garden-work, house-work, conversation.	Garden-work, house-work, conversation.	Garden-work, house-work, conversation.	

COURSE of INSTRUCTION pursued in the two Classes at the Normal Seminary, Carlsruhe, in the Summer half-year of 1839.

HOURS.	CLASSES.	MONDAY.	TUESDAY.	WEDNESDAY.	THURSDAY.	FRIDAY.	SATURDAY.
7 to 8	First	New Testament.	Old Testament.	Geometry.	New Testament.	Old Testament.	New Testament.
	Second	New Testament.	Old Testament.	Catechism.	New Testament.	Old Testament.	New Testament.
8 to 9	First	Singing.	Geography.	Organ.	Geography.	Singing.	Natural history.
	Second	Profane history.	Composition.	Singing.	Organ.	Geography.	Organ.
9 to 10	First	Organ.	Singing.	Singing.	Singing.	Arithmetic.	Composition.
	Second	Arithmetic.	Grammar.	Geography.	Singing.	Singing.	Organ.
10 to 11	First	Grammar.	Geometry.	Singing.	Grammar.	Singing.	Grammar.
	Second	Singing.	Organ.	Grammar.	Profane history.	Grammar.	Arithmetic.
11 to 12	First	Singing and organ	Natural Philosophy.	Natural history.	Organ.	Organ.	Natural history.
	Second	Natural history.	Agriculture.	Singing.	Natural history.	Natural philosophy.	Singing.
2 to 3	First	Writing.	Agriculture.	.	Writing.	Agriculture.	Organ.
	Second	Drawing.	Arithmetic.	.	Drawing.	Arithmetic.	Art of teaching deaf and dumb.
3 to 4	First	Drawing.	Geometry.	.	Drawing.	Geometry.	Composition.
	Second	Writing.	Historical composition.	.	Writing.	Composition.	.
4 to 5	First	Geometry.	Historical composition.	.	Organ.	Geometry.	Singing.
	Second	Organ.					Singing.
	First	Piano and organ.	Organ.	.	Piano and organ.	.	.
5 to 6	Second	.	Organ.	.	Piano and organ.	Organ.	.

COURSE OF INSTRUCTION in the Normal School of the Canton of Vaud, at Lausanne, during the Winter of 1838—1839.

HOURS.	MONDAY.	TUESDAY.	WEDNESDAY.	THURSDAY.	FRIDAY.	SATURDAY.
8	Prayer, reading, and religious instruction (all).	As on Monday.	Idem.	Idem.	Idem.	Idem.
9	The art of teaching II).	General history (all).	The art of teaching (all).	Use of globes, first and second classes.	Swiss history (all).	Instruction in law and in the duties of a citizen, 1, 2, 3. Theme, 1, 2. Arithmetic, 3.
10	Geometry, 1, 2. The means of improving the health and condition of the people.	Arithmetic, 1, 2. Theme, 3.	Theme, 1, 2. Arithmetic, 3.	Composition, 1, 2. Mental arithmetic, 3.	Arithmetic, 1. Theme, 3.	
11	Botany, 1, 2.	Writing, 1, 2, 3.	Chemistry, then Zoology, 1, 2, 3.	Chemistry, then Zoology, 1, 2, 3.	Writing, 1, 2, 3.	Chemistry, &c., 1, 2, 3.
1	.	.	.	.	Exercises on the physical sciences, 1, 2.	.
2	Grammar, 1, 2, 3.	Drawing, 1, 2; reading 3.	Grammar, 1, 2, 3.	Drawing, 3 ; mental arithmetic, 1, 2.	Geometry, 3. Composition, 1, 2.	Writing, 3. Geometry, 1, 2.
3	Gymnastics, 1, 2.	Drawing, 1, 2.	Gymnastics, 3. Book-keeping, 1. Reading, 1, 2.	Drawing, 3 ; reading, 1, 2. Reading, 3.	Pedagogical exercises in mathematics, 1, 2.	.
4	Geography, 3.	Geography, 1, 2.	Geometry, 3.	Geography, 1, 2.	Swiss geography, 1, 2, 3.	.
5	.	Geography, 3.	.	Singing, 1, 2.	.	.
7	.	Singing, 3.	Singing, 1, 2, 3.	.	Singing, 1, 2, 3.	.

N.B.—The figures denote the different classes. The figure 1 being attached to the most advanced class.

COURSE of INSTRUCTION in the Normal School of the Canton of Vaud, at Lausanne, in the Summer of 1838.

HOURS.	MONDAY.	TUESDAY.	WEDNESDAY.	THURSDAY.	FRIDAY.	SATURDAY.
5	. .	Book-keeping (teachers).* Writing (pupils).†	Geography (teachers).	Geography (teachers). Writing (pupils).	. .	On the method of writing (teachers).
6	Prayer, Reading, and religious instruction.	As on Monday.	As on Monday.	As on Monday.	As on Monday.	As on Monday.
7	Composition (older pupils). Arithmetic (younger pupils).	Arithmetic (teachers). A theme (pupils).	Composition (teachers). Geometry (pupils).	Arithmetic (teachers). A theme (pupils).	Composition (teachers). Geometry (pupils).	Arithmetic (teachers). Composition (young pupils).
8, 9	The Art of teaching (all).	Use of the globes (all).	Art of teaching (all).	Instruction in the law and duties of a citizen (all).	Art of teaching (all).	Instruction in the law and in the duties of a citizen (all).
10	Geography (teachers) Mental arithmetic (pupils).	Grammar (teachers). Geography (pupils).	Geometry (teachers). Grammar (pupils).	Reading, with analysis of the grammar, structure, and meaning (all).	Grammar (teachers). Geography (pupils).	Geometry (teachers). Grammar (pupils).
11	Natural history (all).	Physics (pupils).	Natural history (all).	Natural history (all).	Pedagogical exercises on the physical sciences (pupils).	Reading (teachers). Arithmetic (older pupils).
2	A theme (teachers).	Drawing (teachers). Composition (young pupils).	A theme (teachers).	Drawing (pupils).	. .	. .
3	Gymnastics (pupils).	Drawing (teachers). Composition (young pupils).	Geography of Switzerland (teachers).	Drawing (pupils).	Gymnastics (pupils).	. .
4	Reading (pupils).	Reading (all).	Singing (teachers). Arithmetic (pupils). Singing (pupils).	Reading (all).	Singing (teachers). Arithmetic (pupils). Singing (pupils).	Practical geometry (pupils).
5	Mental Arithmetic (teachers).	Singing (all).	Singing (pupils).	Singing (all).	Singing (pupils).	. .

* Teachers are masters of elementary schools in attendance on the Normal School.
† Pupils are young men who have not had charge of elementary schools, but who are preparing for the duties of schoolmasters.

Course of Instruction pursued in the two Classes at the Normal Seminary in Eisleben, Prussia, in the Summer half-year of 1839.

Hours.	Classes.	Monday.	Tuesday.	Wednesday.	Thursday.	Friday.	Saturday.
7 to 8	First	Religious instruction.	Religious instruction.	Art of teaching.	Religious instruction.	Religious instruction.	Religious instruction.
	Second	Religious instruction.	Profane history.	Logic.	Religious instruction.	Profane history.	Logic or sacred history.
8 to 9	First	Profane history.	Logic.	Geography.	Profane history.	Logic or Prussian history.	Geography.
	Second	Arithmetic.	Thorough bass and organ.	Geometry.	Grammar.	Arithmetic.	Geometry.
9 to 10	First.	Reading.	Organ.	Thorough bass.	Art of teaching.	Reading.	Arithmetic.
	Second.	Thorough bass and organ.	Religious instruction.	Drawing.	Writing.	Religious instruction.	Thorough bass and organ.
10 to 11	First	Arithmetic.	Grammar.	Violin.	Arithmetic. Thorough bass and organ.	Grammar.	Organ.
	Second	Grammar.	Singing.	Drawing.	Examination.	Singing.	Writing
1 to 2	First	Art of teaching.	Natural philosophy.		Natural philosophy.	Natural History.	
	Second	Natural philosophy.	Reading.			Reading.	
2 to 3	First	Geometry.	Drawing.		Geometry.	Writing.	
	Second	Composition.	Geography.		Composition.	Geography.	
3 to 4	First	Thorough bass	Drawing.		Violin.	Writing.	
	Second		Violin.			Violin.	
4 to 5	First	Organ.			Organ.		

Note.—Three hours of singing, and one hour of instruction in the art of teaching, are also weekly given at indeterminate times.

Course of Instruction pursued by the Two Classes at the Normal Seminary at Schluchtern, Hesse Cassel.

Hours.	Classes.	Monday.	Tuesday.	Wednesday.	Thursday.	Friday.	Saturday.
7 to 8	First	Attend model school. Catechism. Bible explanations.	Attend model school. Life of Christ. Catechism. Arithmetic.	Attend model school. Catechism. Art of questioning. Arithmetic.	Attend model school. Life of Christ. Catechism. Bible explanations.	Attend model school. Life of Christ. Catechism. Arithmetic.	Attend model school. Catechism. Art of questioning. Arithmetic.
	Second						
8 to 9	First						
	Second						
9 to 10	First	Attend model school, or practise organ. Composition. Natural philosophy.	Attend model school, or practise organ. Thorough bass. Arithmetic.	Attend model school, or practise organ. Geography. Catechetical exercises.	Attend model school, or practise organ. Composition. Natural philosophy. Grammar.	Attend model school, or practise organ. Singing. Composition.	Attend model school, or practise organ. Geography. Arithmetic.
	Second						
10 to 11	First	Reading. { Singing.	Grammar. Violin.	Geometry. { Thorough bass. Writing.	{ Singing.	Geometry. Violin.	Grammar. { Singing. Writing.
	Second						
11 to 12	First	Attend model school, or practise organ.	Attend model school, or practise organ.	Attend model school, or practise organ.	Attend model school, or practise organ.	Attend model school, or practise organ.	Attend model school, or practise organ.
	Second						
1 to 2	First	Piano. Botany.	Drawing. Art of teaching writing.	Botany. Attend model school.	Piano. Botany.	Drawing. Attend model school.	Botany. Geography.
	Second						
2 to 3	First	Piano. Reading and explanation of German classics.	Piano. German history.	Biblical history. Geography.	Piano. Reading and explanation of German classics.	Piano. German history.	Singing.
	Second						
3 to 4	First	Piano. Religious instruction.	Piano. Art of teaching.	Reading.	Piano. Religious instruction.	Piano. Art of teaching.	
	Second						
5 to 6	First	{ Open air exercise.	Open air exercise.	{ Botanical excursions.	Open air exercise.	Open air exercise.	Open air exercise.
6 to 7	Second						

Second Period

Course of Instruction pursued in the Two Classes at the Fletcher Normal Seminary in Dresden. The course is of four years' duration; fresh pupils being received and departing every two years. Those that come in the fifth half-year would be placed in the second class of the following scheme, and at the end of the eighth half-year in the first class. Those entering in the first half-year would be in the second class till the fifth half-year.

Subjects of Instruction.	1st Half-year.		2d Half-year.		3d Half-year.		4th Half-year.		5th Half-year.		6th Half-year.		7th Half-year.		8th Half-year.	
	1st class.	2d class.	1st class.	2d class.	1st class.	2d class.	1st class.	2d class.	1st class.	2d class.	1st class.	2d class.	1st class.	2d class.	1st class.	2d class.
1. Biblical Knowledge		4 h.		4 h.						4 h.		4 h.				
2. Biblical History		4 h.		2 h.						4 h.		2 h.				
3. Bible Explanation	2 h.		2 h.		2 h.	,2 h.	2 h.		2 h.		2 h.		2 h.	2 h.		2 h.
4. Catechism		...		...		4 h.		4 h.		...		...		4 h.		4 h.
					common to both.		common to both.						common to both.		common to both.	
5. Art of Questioning	2 h.	...	2 h.	...	2 h.	...	2 h.	2 h.	2 h.	...	2 h.	...	2 h.	...	2 h.	2 h.
6. Catechetical Exercises		2 h.		...		...				2 h.		...		...		
7. Exercises in Thinking						2 h.		2 h.						2 h.		2 h.
8. Psychology and Art of Teaching		...		...		common to both.		common to both.		...		...		common to both.		common to both.
9. School Discipline		...		...		...		2 h.		...		4 h.		...		2 h.
10. General History		...		...		...		...		...		common to both.		...		...
11. German and Saxon History		2 h.		4 h.		3 h.		1 h.		...		2 h.		3 h.		...
12. Latin				common to both.		1 h.		common to both.		...		1 h.		1 h.		1 h.
13. Composition	common to both.		common to both.		common to both.		common to both.		common to both.		common to both.		common to both.		common to both.	
14. Arithmetic		4 h.		4 h.		4 h.		3 h.		4 h.		4 h.		4 h.		3 h.
15. Geography		3 h.		3 h.		...		1 h.		3 h.		3 h.		...		...
16. Natural Philosophy	...		...		2 h.		common to both.		common to both.		common to both.		common to both.		common to both.	
17. Writing	1 h.	2 h.	1 h.	2 h.	1 h.	2 h.	1 h.	2 h.	1 h.	2 h.	1 h.	2 h.	1 h.	2 h.	1 h.	2 h.
18. Violin	2 h.	1 h.	2 h.	1 h.	2 h.	1 h.	2 h.	1 h.	2 h.	1 h.	2 h.	1 h.	2 h.	1 h.	2 h.	1 h.
19. Singing	2 h.	2 h.	2 h.	2 h.	2 h.	2 h.	2 h.	2 h.	2 h.	2 h.	2 h.	2 h.	2 h.	2 h.	2 h.	2 h.
20. History of the Church		...		common to both.		common to both.		common to both.		...		common to both.		common to both.		common to both.
21. Geom·try		...		2 h.		2 h.		2 h.		...		2 h.		2 h.		2 h.
22. Grammar	1 h.	2 h.	1 h.	2 h.	1 h.	3 h.	1 h.	3 h.	1 h.	2 h.	1 h.	2 h.	1 h.	3 h.	1 h.	3 h.
23. Reading		2 h.		1 h.		2 h.		2 h.		2 h.		1 h.		2 h.		2 h.
24. Natural History		...		...		...		...		...		2 h.		2 h.		1 h.
25. Drawing	2 h.	2 h.	2 h.	2 h.	2 h.	2 h.	2 h.	2 h.	2 h.	2 h.	2 h.	2 h.	2 h.	2 h.	2 h.	2 h.
26. Thorough Bass	2 h.	1 h.	2 h.	1 h.	2 h.	1 h.	2 h.	1 h.	2 h.	1 h.	2 h.	1 h.	2 h.	1 h.	2 h.	1 h.
27. Organ	2 h.	2 h.	2 h.	2 h.	2 h.	2 h.	2 h.	2 h.	2 h.	2 h.	2 h.	2 h.	2 h.	2 h.	2 h.	2 h.
28. Piano	1 h.	1 h.	1 h.	1 h.	1 h.	1 h.	1 h.	1 h.	1 h.	1 h.	1 h.	1 h.	1 h.	1 h.	1 h.	1 h.

Note.—h. stands for the hours devoted to each subject of instruction during the week.

COURSE of INSTRUCTION pursued in the Three Classes at the Normal Seminary, Esslingen, Wurtemburg, in the Summer half-year of 1839.

HOURS.	CLASS.	MONDAY.	TUESDAY.	WEDNESDAY.	THURSDAY.	FRIDAY.	SATURDAY.
6 to 7	First	Arithmetic.	Art of questioning.	Geometry.	Art of questioning.	Arithmetic.	Methods of instruction.
	Second		Arithmetic.				Arithmetic.
	Third	Methods of Instruction.	Religious instruction.	Religious instruction.	Religious instruction.	Religious instruction.	
8 to 9	First	Attend model school.	Attend model school.	Attend model school.	Attend model school.	Attend model school.	Attend model school.
	Second	Geography.	Natural history.	Profane history.	Natural history.	Geography.	Profane history.
	Third	Piano or arithmetic.	Piano or geometry.	Piano or arithmetic.	Piano or geometry.	Piano or arithmetic.	Piano or geometry.
9 to 10	First	Methods of instruction.	Grammar.	Composition.	Grammar.	Composition.	Grammar.
	Second		Religious instruction.	Religious instruction.	Religious instruction.	Religious instruction.	Geometry.
	Third	Geometry.	Grammar.	Composition.	Grammar.	Grammar.	Grammar.
10 to 11	First	Grammar.					Examinations.
	Second	Thorough bass.	Geography.	Thorough bass.	Composition.	Recitations.	Examinations.
	Third	Grammar.	Grammar.	Composition.	Grammar.	Grammar.	Examinations.
11 to 12	First	Singing.	Religious instruction.	Religious instruction.	Religious instruction.	Religious instruction.	Singing.
	Second	Singing.	Methods of instruction.			Methods of instruction.	Singing.
	Third	Geometry or violin.	Arithmetic or piano.	Geometry or piano.	Arithmetic or piano.	Geometry or piano.	Arithmetic or piano.
1 to 2	First	Organ.	Organ or methods of instruction.	Organ.	Organ.	Organ or composition.	Organ.
	Second	Drawing.	Writing.	Recitations.	Writing.	Drawing.	Drawing.
	Third		Drawing.				
2 to 3	First	Organ.	Organ.	Organ.	Methods of instruction.	Organ.	Organ.
	Second	Recitations.				Recitations.	Arithmetic.
	Third	Writing.		Writing.		Writing.	Recitations.
3 to 4	First	Drawing.	Writing.	Methods of instruction.	Drawing.	Writing.	Piano.
	Second	Piano.	Piano.	Piano.	Piano.	Piano.	
	Third						
4 to 5	First	Methods of instruction.	Natural philosophy.	Art of teaching deaf and dumb.	Natural history.	Natural philosophy.	Art of teaching deaf and dumb.
	Second	Piano.	Piano.	Piano.	Piano.	Piano.	Piano.
	Third	Singing.	Geography.	Profane history.	Geography.	Profane history.	Geography.
5 to 6	First	Method.	Profane history.	Singing.	Methods of instruction.	Profane history.	Singing.
	Second	Thorough bass.	Thorough bass.	Singing.	Thorough bass.	Thorough bass.	Singing.
	Third		Natural history.	Singing.		Natural history.	Singing.

* Further instruction in instrumental music is given in the evening.

PLAN of INSTRUCTION pursued in the Three Courses, at the Normal Seminary at Lucerne, Switzerland.

Hours.	Monday.		Tuesday.		Wednesday.		Thursday.		Friday.		Saturday.	
8 to 9, or ½ past 9.	1st course. Arithmetic.	2nd and 3rd course, Grammar and school discipline.	1st and 2nd course, Religious instruction.	3rd course. Writing.	1st course. Geometry.	2nd and 3rd course. Composition.	1st and 2nd course, Religious instruction.	3rd course. Writing.	Same as Monday.		1st and 2nd course, Religious instruction.	3rd course. Geometry.
9 or ½ past 9, to 10 or 11.	Grammar and school discipline.	Arithmetic.	Grammar.	Religious instruction.	Composition.	Geometry.	Writing.	Religious instruction.	·	·	Grammar.	Religious instruction.
10 to 11.	·	·	1st course. Geometry.	2nd and 3rd course. Composition.	·	·	1st course. Composition.	2nd and 3rd course. Arithmetic.	·	·	Arithmetic.	Statistics of Switzerland.
11 to 12	·	Singing.	Singing.	·	·	Singing.	Singing.	·	·	·	·	2nd and 3rd course. Singing.
1st course.	1st course.	2nd and 3rd course.	1st course.	2nd and 3rd course.	1st course.	2nd and 3rd course.	1st, 2nd, and 3rd course.		1st course.	2nd and 3rd course.	1st course.	2nd and 3rd course.
½ past 1 to 3.	Art of teaching.	Geometry.	History.	Arithmetic.	·	·	Drawing.		Art of teaching.	Arithmetic.	History.	Geometry.
3 to 4.	Arithmetic.	Natural philosophy or history.	Writing.	Natural philosophy.	·	·			Arithmetic.	School discipline.	Arithmetic.	Natural philosophy or history.
6 to 7.	Gymnastics.	Geography.	Geography.	Gymnastics.	·	Geography.	Geography.	Gymnastics.	Gymnastics.	Geography.	Geography.	Gymnastics.

SECOND REPORT

ON THE SCHOOLS FOR THE TRAINING OF PAROCHIAL SCHOOL-MASTERS AT BATTERSEA

———o·o·̣·ọ·̣·oo———

London, December 15, 1843.

My Lord,

The Committee of Council on Education voted £1000 on the 14th day of November, 1842, towards the expenses attending the establishment of the schools for the training of parochial schoolmasters at Battersea, and their Lordships have also, during the present year, granted £2200 to enable us to carry into execution the plan for enlarging and improving the premises which is appended to this Report, on condition that satisfactory arrangements should be made for the future support of the schools.

We therefore consider it our duty to submit to your Lordship a general account of our proceedings since the publication of our Report in January, 1841; and to relate what arrangements have been made for the future management and support of these schools.

In the course of the four years which have elapsed since these schools were founded, we have had considerable experience of the difficulties which oppose the success of such establishments: we have been led to modify one part of our original plan, and the perspective of the future progress of the institution displays features in some respects different from those which we contemplated, when we stood upon the threshold of our experiment.

To record the results of our experience, and to narrate the reasons which have suggested changes in our original design, appear to us duties which we owe to the promoters of education in this country. Our desire is, that our errors may become beacons to those who follow, and our success a light on their path. We also think it important that some of the peculiar difficulties to be overcome in the management of such schools should be described, in order that they may not be encountered unawares. These are the reasons which induce us to submit to your Lordship some account of the progress of the Battersea Training Schools.

Our first step, on founding the institution, was to remove from schools which had been under our immediate superintendence, in connection with the Poor Law Commission, some of the most promising pupils. We were not indifferent to the impression that, in selecting the destitute children of pauper parents as the subjects of a trial of the transforming influences of a religious training, our success would not fail to increase the confidence of the public in the ameliorative tendency of national education, on the manners, habits, and feelings of the most neglected classes; we hoped that a more active sympathy might be inspired for the 50,000 pauper children who await the legislative interference of Parliament for their efficient education in religion and industry. But our chief design was to ascertain whether, by training youths for a series of years in the strict regimen, the exact and comprehensive instruction, the industrious and self-denying habits, and the peculiar duties of a Normal School, we should not be able to procure more efficient instruments for the instruction of the children of the poor than by any other means.

We had frequently visited the schools of the Brothers of the Christian Doctrine in France, and had spent much time in the examination of their *Ecoles-mères*. Our attention was attracted to these schools by the gentle manners and simple habits which distinguished the Frères; by their sympathy for children, and the religious feeling which pervaded their elementary schools. Their schools are certainly deficient in some of the niceties of organisation and method; and there are subjects on which the instruction might be more complete and exact, but each master was, as it were, a parent to the children around him. The school resembled a harmonious family.

The self-denying industry of these pious men was remarkable. The habits of their order would be deemed severe in this country. In the Mother School (where they all reside), they rise at four. After private meditation, their public devotions in the chapel occupy the early hours of the morning. The domestic drudgery of the household succeeds. They breakfast at seven, and are in the schools of the great cities of France at nine. When the routine of daily school-keeping is at an end, after a short interval for refreshment and exercise, they open their evening schools, where hundreds of the adult population receive instruction, not merely in reading, writing, and the simplest elements of numbers, but in singing, drawing, geography; the mensuration of planes and solids; the history of France; and in religion. Their evening schools do not close till ten. The public expenditure on account of their services is one-third the usual remuneration of an elementary schoolmaster in France, and they devote their lives, constrained by the influence of a religious feeling, under a rule of celibacy, but without a vow, to the education of the poor.

The unquestionable self-denial of such a life, the attachment of the children, and of the adult pupils to their instructors, together with the constant sense of the all-subduing presence of Christian principle, rendered the means adopted by the Christian Brothers, for the training of their novices, a matter of much interest and inquiry.

The Mother School differs in most important respects from a Normal School, but the extent of this difference is not at first sight apparent, and is one of those results of our experience which we wish to submit to your Lordship.

The *Mother School* is an establishment comprising arrangements for the instruction and training of novices; for the residence of the Brothers, who are engaged in the active performance of the duties of their order, as masters of elementary day and evening schools; and it affords an asylum, into which they gradually retire from the fatigues and cares of their public labours, as age approaches, or infirmities accumulate, to spend the period of sickness or decrepitude in the tranquillity of the household provided for them, and amidst the consolations of their brethren. The Brothers constitute a family, performing every domestic service, ministering to the sick and infirm, and assembling for devotion daily in their chapel.

Their novices enter about the ages of 12 or 14. They at once assume the dress of the order, and enter upon the self-denying routine of the household. The first years of their noviciate are of course devoted to such elementary instruction as is necessary to prepare them for their future duties as teachers of the poor. Their habits are formed, not only in the course of this instruction, but by joining the religious exercises; performing the household duties; and enjoying the benefit of constant intercourse with the elder brethren of the Mother School, who are at once their instructors and friends. In this life of seclusion, the superior of the *Mother School* has opportunities of observing and ascertaining the minutest traits of character, which indicate their comparative qualifications for the future labours of the order; nor is this vigilance relaxed, but rather increased, when they first quit the private studies of the Mother School, to be gradually initiated in their public labours as instructors of the people.

Such of the novices as are found not to possess the requisite qualifications, especially as respects the moral constitution necessary for the duties of their order, are permitted to leave the Mother School to enter upon other pursuits. During the period of the noviciate, such instances are not rare, but we have reason to believe that they seldom occur after the Brother has acquired maturity.

As their education in the Mother School proceeds, the period devoted every day to their public labours in the elementary schools is enlarged; and they thus, under the eye of elder brethren, assisted by their example and precepts, gradually emerge from the privacy of their noviciate to their public duties.

In all this there is not much that differs from the life of a young pupil in a Normal School; but, at this point, the resemblance ceases, and a great divergence occurs.

The brother, whose noviciate is at an end, continues a member of the household of the *Mother School*. He has only advanced to a higher rank. He is surrounded by the same influences. The daily routine which formed his domestic and religious habits continues. His mind is fed, and his purposes are strengthened by the conversation and examples of his brethren, and his conduct is under the paternal eye of his superior. Under such circumstances, personal identity is almost absorbed in the corporate life by which he is surrounded. The strength of the order supports his weakness: the spirit of the order is the pervading principle of his life: he thinks, feels, and acts, by an unconscious inspiration from everything by which he is surrounded, in a calm atmosphere of devotion and religious labour. All is prescribed; and a pious submission, a humble faith, a patient zeal, and a self-denying activity are his highest duties.

Contrast his condition with that of a young man leaving a Normal School at the age of 18 or 19, after three or four years of comparative seclusion, under a regimen closely resembling that of the Mother School. At this age, it is necessary that he should be put in charge of an elementary school, in order that he may earn an independence.

The most favourable situation in which he can be placed, because remote from the grosser forms of temptation, and therefore least in contrast with his previous position, is the charge of a rural school. For the tranquil and eventless life of the master of a rural school, such a training is not an unfit preparation. His resources are not taxed by the necessity for inventing new means to meet the novel combinations which arise in a more active state of society. His energy is equal to the task of instructing the submissive and tractable, though often dull children of the peasantry; and the gentle manners and quiet demeanour, which are the uniform results of his previous education, are in harmony with the passionless life of the seclusion into which he is plunged. His knowledge and his skill in method are abundantly superior to the necessities of his position, and the unambitious sense of duty which he displays attracts the confidence and wins the regard of the clergyman of the parish and of his intelligent neighbours. For such a life, we have found even the young pupils whom we introduced into the training schools at their foundation well fitted, and we have preferred to settle them, as far as we could, on the estates of our personal friends, where we are assured they have succeeded. Those only who have entered the Normal School at adult age have been capable of successfully contending with the greater difficulties of town schools.

But we are also led by our experience to say, that such a noviciate does not prepare a youth of tender age to encounter the responsibilities of a large town or village school in a manufacturing or mining district. Such a position is in the most painful contrast with his previous training. He exchanges the comparative seclusion of his residence in the Normal School for the difficult position of a public instructor, on whom many jealous eyes are fixed. For the first time he is alone in his profession; unaided by the example of his masters; not stimulated by emulation with his fellows; removed from the vigilant eye of the Principal of the school; separated from the powerful influences of that corporate spirit, which impelled his previous career; yet placed amidst difficulties, perplexing even to the most mature experience, and required to tax his invention to meet new circumstances, before he has acquired confidence in the unsustained exercise of his recently developed powers. He has left the training school for the rude contact of a coarse, selfish, and immoral populace, whose gross appetites and manners render the narrow streets in his neighbourhood scenes of impurity. He is at once brought face to face with an ignorant and corrupt multitude, to whose children he is to prove a leader and guide.

His difficulties are formidable. His thoughts are fixed on the deformity of this monstrous condition of society. It is something to have this sense of the extremity of the evil, but in order to confront it, that sense should become the spur to persevering exertion. We have witnessed this failure, and we conceive that such difficulties can only be successfully encountered by masters of maturer age and experience.

The situation of the novice of a *Mother School*, founded in the centre of a great manufacturing city, is in direct contrast with that of the young student, exchanging his secluded training in a Normal School for the unaided charge of a great town school.

If such a Mother School were founded in the midst of one of our largest commercial towns, under the charge of a Principal of elevated character and acquirements; if he had assembled around him devoted and humble men, ready to spend their lives in reclaiming the surrounding population by the foundation and management of schools for the poor; and into this society a youth were introduced at a tender age, instructed, trained, and reared in the habits and duties of his profession; gradually brought into contact with the actual evil, to the healing of which his life was to be devoted; never abandoned to his own comparatively feeble resources, but always feeling himself the missionary of a body able to protect, ready to console, and willing to assist and instruct him;—in such a situation, his feebleness would be sustained by the strength of a corporation animated with the vitality of Christian principle.

We are far from recommending the establishment of such a school, to the success of which we think we perceive insurmountable obstacles in this country. The only form in which a similar machinery could exist in England is that of a Town Normal School, in which all the apprentices or pupil teachers of the several elementary schools might lodge, and where, under the superintendence of a Principal, their domestic and religious habits might be formed. The masters of the elementary schools might be associates of the Normal School, and conduct the instruction of the pupil teachers, in the evening or early in the morning, when free from the duties of their schools. The whole body of masters would thus form a society, with the Principal at their head, actively employed in the practical daily duties of managing and instructing schools, and also by their connection with the Town Normal School, keeping in view and contributing to promote the general interests of elementary education by rearing a body of assistant masters. If a good library were collected in this central institution, and lectures from time to time delivered on appropriate subjects to the whole body of masters and assistants, or, which would be better, if an upper school were founded, which might be attended by the masters and most advanced assistants, every improvement in method would thus be rapidly diffused through the elementary schools of towns.

The first steps towards the establishment of such an institution for schoolmasters may be taken by the masters of elementary schools unaided, if they are disposed to adopt the system pursued in Holland of rearing pupil-teachers as apprentices in all the town schools, and completing their course of instruction by one year's training in a Normal School.

In Holland, the elementary schoolmasters of every great town form a society, associated for their common benefit. Their schools are always large, varying in numbers from three to seven hundred or even a thousand children, who are often assembled in one room. Every master is aided by a certain number of assistants of different ages, and by pupil teachers.

The course through which a youth passes from a position of distinction, as one of the most successful scholars, to that of master of a school, is obvious. He is apprenticed as a pupil teacher (an assistant equivalent, in the first stage, to the most superior class of our monitors in England). As pupil teacher he assists in the instruction of the youngest classes during the day, witnessing and taking part in the general movements of the school, and in the maintenance of discipline and order. He resides with his own family in the city, and before he is admitted apprentice, care is taken to ascertain that he belongs to a well-conducted household, and that he will be reared by his parents in habits of religion and order. Every evening all the pupil teachers of the town are assembled to receive instruction. The society of teachers provides from its own body a succession of instructors, by one of whom, on each night of the week, the pupil teachers are taught some branch of elementary knowledge necessary to school-keeping. One of the most experienced masters of the town, likewise, gives them lectures on method, and on the art of organising and conducting a school.

The society of schoolmasters meets from time to time to receive from each of its members an account of the conduct, progress, and qualifications of each pupil teacher in the town, not only in the evening class, but in the school duties of the day.

On the reputation thus acquired and preserved, depends the progress of the pupil teacher in the art of school-keeping. As his experience becomes more mature, and his knowledge increases, he is intrusted with more important matters and higher classes in the school. He undergoes two successive examinations by the Government Inspector, being first admitted candidate and afterwards assistant master, and he is then at liberty to complete his course of training by entering the Normal School at *Haarlem*, from which he can obtain the highest certificates of fitness for the duties of his profession.

This appears to us a course of training peculiarly well-adapted to the formation of masters for the great schools of large towns, and likewise for supplying these great schools during the education of the pupil teacher, with the indispensable aid of a body of assistant masters, without which they must continue to be examples of an economy which can spare nothing adequate to the improvement of the people.

The formation of a body of pupil teachers in each great town, thus instructed by a society of schoolmasters, is an object worthy of encouragement from the Committee of Council, who might at least provide the fees and charges of apprenticeship, and grant exhibitions for the training of the most successful pupil teachers in a Normal School at the close of their apprenticeship, even if the Government were indisposed to encounter any of the annual charges incident to the plan.

Few words are requisite to render apparent the difference between the life of a pupil teacher so trained, and that of a young novice in a Normal School. The familiar life of the parental household, while it exercises a salutary influence on the habits and manners of the young candidate, is not remote from the great scene of exertion in which his future life is to be spent. He is unconsciously prepared by the daily occurrences in his father's family, and by his experience and instruction in the day and evening school, to form a just estimate of the circumstances by which he is surrounded. He is trained from day to day in the management of the artful and corrupt children even of the dregs of the city, and enabled to apply such means as the discipline and instruction of a common school afford, to the improvement of the moral and intellectual condition of the children of the common people. He becomes an agent of civilisation, fitted for a peculiar work by habit, and prepared to imbibe during the two or three years he may spend in a Normal School those higher maxims of conduct, that more exact knowledge, and those more perfect methods of which it is the proper source. From such a period of training, he returns to his native city, or is sent to some other town, strong in the confidence inspired by his prolonged experience of the peculiar duties he has to perform, either to take a high rank as an assistant master, or to undertake the responsibility of conducting a town school as its chief.

These are the views which have led us to conclude that the admission of *boys* into a Normal School, as distinguished from a *Mother School*, is not a fit preparation for the discharge of the duties of a schoolmaster in a large town.

We have gradually raised the age of admission from 14 to 16, and thence to 18 or 20 years, and we are now of opinion that few or none should be admitted into a Normal School under the latter age.

Besides the reasons already stated why youths under 18 should not be admitted into such a school, there are some arising out of the internal economy of a Normal School of sufficient importance to deserve enumeration.

If youths are admitted, none who have arrived at adult age should be permitted to enter. The youth necessarily enters for a course of training which extends over several years; the adult student commonly enters for two years. The attainments of all are meagre on their admission. In the course of a few years, therefore, the youngest pupils are necessarily at the head of the school in their attainments and skill, which is a source of great discouragement to an adult entering such an establishment, and a dangerous distinction to a youth whose acquirements have suddenly raised him intellectually above all in his sphere of life. The tendencies of such a great disparity in the acquirements appropriate to the two classes of age are obviously injurious. We have experienced the consequences of this disparity as a disturbing force in the Training Schools, and to counteract these tendencies has required a vigilance and provident care, which has increased our labours and anxieties. Few things have been more pleasing than the readiness with which some of the oldest students who have entered the schools have taken their seats in the humblest positions, and passed with patient perseverance through all the elementary drudgery, though boys have held the most prominent positions in the first class, and have occasionally become their instructors. On the other hand, to check the conceit too frequently engendered by a rapid progress, when attended with such contrasts, we have suggested to the masters, that the humble assiduity of the recently entered adult pupil ought to secure an expressive deference and attention.

The intellectual development of the young pupils is a source of care insignificant in comparison with that attending the *formation of their characters*, and this could be accomplished with greater ease and certainty if they were the sole objects of solicitude. But, as members of an establishment into which adults are admitted in an equality or inferiority of position, the discipline is complicated, and the sources of error are increased.

For these reasons we prefer to admit into a Normal School only students of adult age, reared by religious parents, and concerning whose characters and qualifications the most satisfactory testimonials can be procured. The inquiries preliminary to the admission of a student should in all cases, where it may be practicable, extend to his previous habits and occupations, to the character of the household in which he has resided, and the friendships he has formed. In all cases those young men are to be preferred whose previous pursuits warrant some confidence in their having a predilection for the duties of a teacher of the poor.

Our plans have therefore tended to the introduction of young men of 18 years of age and upwards for a training of two years which we are led to regard as the shortest period which it is desirable they should spend in such a school.

Our pupils who have settled in charge of rural schools have been encouraged by the correspondence which has been maintained with the majority of them. They have been supported by the sense, that as long as they persevered faithfully in their labours, they had friends ready to help in any casualty. This correspondence has maintained the influence of the Normal School, when the labours of the masters prevented their writing to their absent pupils. We have also promoted a familiar correspondence between the students who have left the school and those who remain; and between all who have settled in life, in order that they may have a feeling of community of interest, and maintain among themselves an *esprit de corps*, the offspring of the public opinion of the school.

The main object of a Normal School is the *formation of the character of the schoolmaster*. This was the primary idea which guided our earliest efforts in the establishment of the Battersea Schools on a basis different from that of any previous example in this country. We have submitted to your Lordship the reasons which have led us to modify one of the chief features of our plan, but our convictions adhere with undiminished force to the principle on which the schools were originally founded. They were intended to be an institution, in which every object was subservient to the *formation of the character of the schoolmaster*, as an intelligent Christian man entering on the instruction of the poor, with religious devotion to his work. If we propose to change the means, the end we have in view is the same. Compelled by the foregoing considerations to think the course of training we proposed for youths does not prepare them for the charge of large schools in manufacturing towns, we are anxious that the system pursued in Holland should be adopted, as a training preparatory to the examination of the pupil teachers previously to their admission into a Normal School. Finding that the patrons of students and the friends of the establishment are unable, for the most part, to support a longer training for young men than one year and a half, we are more anxious respecting the investigation of their previous characters and connections, and more fastidious as to their intellectual qualifications and acquirements.

When the Battersea Schools contain their complement

of 50 students, the entire charges of the institution have been on the average, about £55 for each pupil: £30 have recently been required from the patrons or friends of the pupils towards the expenses of their maintenance and education. The average annual charge on the founders of the schools, has therefore been £25 for each pupil, or about £1250 per annum, when the school has been full.

If the number of pupils were augmented, the staff of masters would require to be increased, and the average expense would be about £20 each for 70 pupils, or £1400 per annum. The plans for the enlargement and repair of the school-buildings towards which your Lordships have voted us a grant of £2200, would provide convenient accommodation for 70 pupils, and for the residence of a Principal, an officer whose superintendence of the future progress of the establishment has become indispensable.

When 70 pupils are in course of training in the schools for one year and a half, upwards of 50 would leave the establishment annually, at an expense of £30 for the training of each pupil; or if the insufficiency of the resources of the establishment, and of the pupils conspired for the present, with the urgency of the wants of the public, to defeat this plan, and to render one year's training the maximum course, 70 pupils would leave the establishment annually, at an average expense of £20 for each pupil, or £1400 per annum.

When circumstances thus combine to prevent the residence of the students in the training school for a longer period than a year and a half, the inquiries as to previous character cannot be conducted with too much care, and *the first month of training should under any circumstances be regarded as probationary.*

Under these arrangements also, the impression produced upon the characters of the students during their residence is of paramount importance.

They are commonly selected from a humble sphere. They are the sons of small tradesmen, of bailiffs, of servants, or of superior mechanics. Few have received any education, except that given in a common parochial school. They read and write very imperfectly; are unable to indite a letter correctly; and are seldom skilful, even in the first four rules of arithmetic. Their biblical knowledge is meagre and inaccurate, and all their conceptions, not less on religious than on other subjects, are vague and confused, even when they are not also very limited or erroneous. Their habits have seldom prepared them for the severely regular life of the Normal School, much less for the strenuous effort of attention and application required by the daily routine of instruction. Such concentration of the mind would soon derange the health, if the course of training did not provide moderate daily exercise in the garden, at proper intervals. The mental torpor, which at first is an obstacle to improvement, generally passes away in about three months, and from that period the student makes rapid progress in the studies of the school. The tables and examination papers appended to Mr. Allen's[1] Report show the state of the pupil's acquirements, and how his intellectual powers are strengthened, when his course of instruction is completed.

These attainments, humble though they be, might prove dangerous to the character of the student, if his intellectual development were the chief concern of the masters.

How easy it would be for him to form an overweening estimate of his knowledge and ability, must be apparent, when it is remembered that he will measure his learning by the standard of that possessed by his own friends and neighbours. He will find himself suddenly raised by a brief course of training to the position of a teacher and example. If his mind were not thoroughly penetrated by a religious principle, or if a presumptuous or mercenary tone had been given to his character, he might go forth to bring discredit upon education by exhibiting a precocious vanity, an insubordinate spirit, or a selfish ambition. He might become not the gentle and pious guide of the children of the poor, but a hireling into

---

[1] The present Archdeacon of Salop,—then H. M. Inspector.

whose mind had sunk the doubts of the sceptic; in whose heart was the worm of social discontent; and who had changed the docility of ignorance and dulness, for the restless impatience of a vulgar and conceited sciolist.

In the formation of the character of the schoolmaster, the discipline of the Training School should be so devised as to prepare him for the modest respectability of his lot. He is to be a Christian teacher, following him who said, " he that will be my disciple, let him take up his cross." Without the spirit of self-denial, he is nothing. His reward must be in his work. There should be great simplicity in the life of such a man.

Obscure and secluded schools need masters of a contented spirit, to whom the training of the children committed to their charge, has charms sufficient to concentrate their thoughts and exertions on the humble sphere in which they live, notwithstanding the privations of a life but little superior to the level of the surrounding peasantry. When the scene of the teacher's exertions is in a neighbourhood which brings him into association with the middle and upper classes of society, his emoluments will be greater, and he will be surrounded by temptations which, in the absence of a suitable preparation of mind, might rob him of that humility and gentleness, which are among the most necessary qualifications of the teacher of a common school.

In the Training School, habits should be formed consistent with the modesty of his future life. On this account we attach peculiar importance to the discipline which we have established at Battersea. Only one servant, besides a cook, has been kept for the domestic duties of the household. From the table contained in Mr. Allen's Report, you will perceive that the whole household work, with the exception of the scouring of the floors and cooking, is performed by the students, and they likewise not only milk and clean the cows, feed and tend the pigs, but have charge of the stores, wait upon each other, and cultivate the garden. We cannot too emphatically state our opinion that no portion of this work could be omitted, without a proportionate injury to that contentment of spirit, without which the character of the student is liable to be overgrown with the errors we have described. He has to be prepared for a humble and subordinate position, and though master of his school, to his scholars he is to be a parent, and to his superiors an intelligent servant and minister.

The garden work also serves other important ends. Some exercise and recreation from the scholastic labours are indispensable. Nevertheless, a large portion of the day cannot be devoted to it, and when three or four hours only can be spared, care should be taken that the whole of this time is occupied by moderate and healthful exertion in the open air. A period of recreation employed according to the discretion of the students would be liable to abuse. It might often be spent in listless sauntering, or in violent exertion. Or if a portion of the day were thus withdrawn from the observation of the masters of the school, it would prove a period in which associations might be formed among the students inconsistent with the discipline; and habits might spring up to counteract the influence of the instruction and admonition of the masters. In so brief a period of training, it is necessary that the entire conduct of the student should be guided by a superior mind.

Not only by the daily labour of the garden, are the health and morals of the school influenced, but habits are formed consistent with the student's future lot. It is well both for his own health, and for the comfort of his family, that the schoolmaster should know how to grow his garden stuff, and should be satisfied with innocent recreation near his home.

We have also adhered to the frugal diet which we at first selected for the school. Some little variety has been introduced, but we attach great importance to the students being accustomed to a diet so plain and economical, and to arrangements in their dormitories so simple and devoid of luxury, that in after life they will not in a humble school be visited with a sense of privation, when their scanty fare and mean furniture are compared with the more abundant food and comforts of the training school. We have therefore met every rising complaint respecting either the quantity or quality of the food, or the humble accommodation in the dormitories, with explanations of the importance of forming, in the school, habits of frugality, and of the paramount duty of nurturing a patient spirit, to meet the future privations of the life of a teacher of the poor. Though we have admitted some variety into the ingredients of the diet, we have not increased the quantity, or raised the quality, of the food of the school, or added one element even of additional comfort to their life.

Our experience also leads us to attach much importance to simplicity and propriety of dress. For the younger pupils we had, on this account, prepared a plain dark dress of rifle green, and a working dress of fustian cord. As respects the adults, we have felt the importance of checking the slightest tendency to peculiarity of dress, lest it should degenerate into foppery. We have endeavoured to impress on the students that the dress and the manners of a master of a School for the poor should be decorous, but that the prudence of his life should likewise find expression in their simplicity. There should be no habit nor external sign of self-indulgence or vanity.

On the other hand, the master is to be prepared for a life of laborious exertion. He must, therefore, form habits of early rising, and of activity and persevering industry. In the winter, before it is light, the household work must be finished, and the school-rooms prepared by the students for the duties of the day. One hour and a half is thus occupied. After this work is accomplished, one class must assemble winter and summer, at a quarter to seven o'clock, for instruction. The day is filled with the claims of duty requiring the constant exertion of mind and body, until at half-past nine the household retire to rest.

By this laborious and frugal life, economy of management is reconciled with the efficiency both of the moral and intellectual training of the School, and the master goes forth into the world humble, industrious, and instructed.

But into the student's character higher sentiments must enter, if we rightly conceive the mission of the master of a school for the poor. On the religious condition of the household, under the blessing of God, depends the cultivation of that religious feeling, without which the spirit of self-sacrifice cannot take its right place among the motives which ought to form the mainspring of a schoolmaster's activity.

There is a necessity for incessant vigilance in the management of a training school. The Principal should be *wise as a serpent*, while the gentleness of his discipline, and his affectionate solicitude for the well-being of his pupils, should encourage the most unreserved communications with him. Much of his leisure should be devoted to private interviews with the students, and employed in instilling into their minds high principles of action. A cold and repulsive air of authority may preserve the appearance of order, regularity, and submission in the household; but these will prove delusive signs if the Principal does not possess the respect and confidence, not to say the affections, of his charge. He should be most accessible, and unwearied in the patience with which he listens to confessions and inquiries. While it is felt to be impossible that he should enter into any compromise with evil, there should be no such severity in his tone of rebuke as to check that confidence which seeks guidance from a superior intelligence. As far as its relation to the Principal only is concerned, every fault should be restrained and corrected by a conviction of the pain and anxiety which it causes to an anxious friend, rather than by the fear of a too jealous authority. Thus conscience will gradually be roused by the example of a master, respected for his purity, and loved for his gentleness, and inferior sentiments will be replaced by motives derived from the highest source.

Where so much has to be learned, and where, among other studies, so much religious knowledge must be acquired, there is danger that religion should be regarded chiefly as a subject for the exercise of the intellect. A speculative religious knowledge, without those habits and feelings which are the growth of deeply-seated religious convictions, may be a dangerous acquisition to a teacher of the young. How important, therefore, is it, that the religious services of the household should become the means of cultivating a spirit of devotion, and that the religious instruction of the School should be so conducted as not merely to inform the memory, but to master the convictions and to interest the feelings. Religion is not merely to be taught in the School—it must be the element in which the students live.

This religious life is to be nurtured by the example, by the public instruction of the Principal, and by his private counsel and admonition; by the religious services of the household; by the personal intercourse of the students, and the habits of private meditation and devotion which they are led to form; by the public worship of the church, and by the acts of charity and self-denial which belong to their future calling.

How important is it that the Principal should embody such an example of purity and elevation of character, of gentleness of manners and of unwearied benevolence, as to increase the power of his teaching, by the respect and conviction which wait upon a consistent life. Into the religious services of the household, he should endeavour to inspire such a spirit of devotion as would spread itself through the familiar life, and hallow every season of retirement. The management of the village school affords opportunities for cultivating habits of kindness and patience. The students should be instructed in the organisation and conduct of Sunday schools; they should be trained in the preparation of the voluntary teachers by previous instruction; in the visitation of the absent children; in the management of the clothing and sick clubs and libraries attached to such schools. They should be accustomed to the performance of those parochial duties in which the schoolmaster may lighten the burthen of the clergyman. For this purpose they should learn to keep the accounts of the benefit club. They should instruct and manage the village choir, and should learn to play the organ.

While in attendance on the village school, it is peculiarly important that they should accompany the master in his visits to children detained at home by sickness, and should listen to the words of counsel and comfort which he may then administer; they should also attend him when his duty requires a visit to the parents of some refractory or indolent scholar, and should learn how to secure their aid in the correction of the faults of the child.

Before he leaves the Training School, the student should have formed a distinct conception, from precept and practice, how his example, his instruction, and his works of charity and religion, ought to promote the Christian civilisation of the community in which he labours.

Turn we again to the contrast of such a picture. Let us suppose a school in which this vigilance in the formation of character is deemed superfluous; or a Principal, the guileless simplicity of whose character is not strengthened by the wisdom of experience. A fair outward show of order and industry, and great intellectual development, may, in either case, be consistent, with the latent progress of a rank corruption of manners, mining all beneath. Unless the searching intelligence of the Principal is capable of discerning the dispositions of his charge, and anticipating their tendencies, he is unequal to the task of moulding the minds of his pupils, by the power of a loftier character and a superior will. In that case, or when the Principal deems such vigilance superfluous and is content with the intellectual labours of his office, leaving the little republic, of which he is the head, to form its own manners, and to create its own standard of principle and action, the catastrophe of a deep ulcerous corruption, is not likely to be long delayed.

In either case it is easy to trace the progress of degeneracy. A school, in which the formation of character is not the chief aim of the masters, must abandon that all-important end to the republic of scholars. When these are selected from the educated, and upper ranks of society, the school will derive its code of morals from that prevalent in such classes. When the pupils belong to a very humble class, their characters are liable, under such arrangements, to be compounded of the ignorance, coarseness, and vices of the lowest orders. One pupil, the victim of low vices, or of a vulgar coarseness of thought, escaping the eye of an unsuspicious Principal, or unsought for by the vigilance which is expended on the intellectual progress of the school, may corrupt the private intercourse of the students with low buffoonery, profligate jests, and sneers at the self-denying zeal of the humble student; may gradually lead astray one after another of the pupils to clandestine habits, if not to the secret practice of vice. Under such circumstances, the counsels of the Principal would gradually become subjects of ridicule. A conspiracy of direct insubordination would be formed. The influence of the Superior would barely maintain a fair external appearance of order and respect.

Every master issuing from such a school would become the active agent of a degeneracy of manners, by which the humbler ranks of society would be infected.

The formation of the character is, therefore, the chief aim of a Training School, and the Principal should be a man of Christian earnestness, of intelligence, of experience, of knowledge of the world, and of the humblest simplicity and purity of manners.

Next to the formation of the character of the pupil is, in our estimation, the general development of his intelligence. The extent of his attainments, though within a certain range a necessary object of his training, should be subordinate to that mental cultivation, which confers the powers of self-education, and gives the greatest strength to his reflective faculties. On this account, among others, we attach importance to the methods of imparting knowledge pursued in the Normal School. While we have ensured that the attainments of the students should be exact, by testing them with searching examinations, repeated at the close of every week, and reiterated lessons on all subjects in which any deficiency was discovered, nothing has been taught by rote. The memory has never been stored, without the exercise of the reason. Nothing has been learned which has not been understood. This very obvious course is too frequently lost sight of in the humbler branches of learning—principles being hidden in rules, defining only their most convenient application; or buried under a heap of facts, united by no intelligible link. To form the character, to develope the intelligence and to store the mind with the requisite knowledge, these were the objects of the Normal School.

In the Village School a new scene of labour developed itself, which has been in progress since the period of our last report, and has now nearly reached its term. If we attach pre-eminent importance to the formation of character as the object of the Normal School, a knowledge of the method of managing an elementary school, and of instructing a class in each branch of elementary knowledge, is the peculiar object of the Model School attached to any training institution. In its proper province as subordinate to the instruction and training in a Normal School, it is difficult to exaggerate the importance to a teacher, of a thorough familiarity with the theory and practice of organising and conducting common schools. Without this, the most judicious labour in the Normal School may, so far as the future usefulness of the student as a schoolmaster is concerned, be literally wasted. It is possible to conceive that the character may be formed on the purest model; that the intelligence may have been kept in healthful activity; and that the requisite general and technical instruction may have been acquired, yet without the aptitude to teach; without skill acquired from precept and example; without the habits matured in the discipline of schools; without the methods in which the art of teaching is reduced to technical rules, and the matter of instruction arranged in the most convenient form for elementary scholars, the previous labour wants the link which unites it to its peculiar task. On the other hand, to select from the common drudgery of a handicraft, or from the humble, if not mean pursuits of a petty trade, a young man barely (if indeed at all) instructed in the humblest elements of reading, writing, and arithmetic, and to conceive that a few months' attendance on a Model School can make him acquainted with the theory of its organisation, convert him into an adept in its methods, or even rivet upon his stubborn memory any significant part of the technical knowledge of which he has immediate need, is a mistake too shameful to be permitted to survive its universal failure.

When we speak of the necessity of a thorough acquaintance with methods of organising and teaching in common Schools, we mean to *exalt* the importance of previous training of the character, expansion of the intelligence and sufficient technical instruction. Without this previous preparation, the instruction in the Model School is empirical, and the luckless wight would have had greater success in his handicraft, than he can hope to enjoy in his school.

For these reasons, among others, the attention of the students has especially of late been directed to the theory of the organisation of Schools, and to the acquirement of the art of teaching. Whatever degree of success has attended the introduction of changes in the organisation and methods of instruction in the village school is greatly to be attributed to the zealous co-operation of the Honourable and Rev. Robert Eden, who opened his Schools to our pupils, and has personally superintended the progress of these improvements with persevering activity.

It would be difficult in the brief limits of this Report to give a satisfactory account of the objects sought to be accomplished in the *organisation* of the Battersea Village School. This would be a subject more fitly discussed in a work on Method. General indications would only serve to mislead.

The *method of conveying instruction* is peculiarly important in an Elementary School, because the scholars receive no learning and little judicious training at home, and are therefore dependent for their education on the very limited period of their attendance at school. On this account nothing superfluous should be taught, lest what is necessary be not attained. The want of a fit preparation of the mind of the scholar, and the brevity of his school life, are reasons for adopting the most certain and efficacious means of imparting knowledge, so that this short period may become as profitable as possible. The regularity of the child's attendance, the interest he takes in his learning, and his success, will be promoted by the adoption of means of instruction suited to the state of his faculties and the condition of society from which he is taken. If his progress be obstructed by the obscurity of his master's teaching, and by the absence of that tact which captivates the imagination of children and rouses the activity of their minds, the scholar will become dull, listless, and untoward; will neglect his learning and his school, and degenerate into an obstinate dunce. The easiest transition in acquirement is in the order of simplicity from the known to the unknown, and it is indispensable to skilful teaching that the matter of instruction should be arranged in a synthetic order, so that all the elements may have to each other the relation of a progressive series from the most simple to the most complex. This arrangement of the matter of instruction requires a previous analysis, which can only be successfully accomplished by the devotion of much time. Such methods are only gradually brought to perfection by experience. The elementary schoolmaster, however highly instructed, can seldom be expected to possess either the necessary leisure or the peculiar analytical talent; and unless this work of arrangement be accomplished for him, he cannot hope, by the technical instruction of the Normal School, to acquire sufficient skill to invent a method by arranging the matter of instruction.

In order, therefore, that he may teach nothing superfluous; that he may convey his instruction in the most skilful manner, and in the order of simplicity, it is necessary that he should become acquainted with a *method* of communicating each branch of knowledge.

This is the more important, because individual teaching is impossible in a common school. Every form of organisation, from the monitorial to the simultaneous, includes more or less of collective teaching. The characteristics of skilful collective teaching are the simplicity and precision with which the knowledge is communicated, and the logical arrangement of the matter of instruction. Diffuse, desultory, or unconnected lessons are a waste of time, they leave no permanent traces on the memory; they confuse the minds of children instead of instructing them and strengthening their faculties.

Certain moral consequences also flow from the adoption of skilful methods of teaching. The relations of regard and respect which ought to exist between the master and his scholars are liable to disturbance, when, from his imperfect skill, their progress in learning is slow, their minds remain inactive, and their exertions are languid and unsuccessful. A school in which the master is inapt, and the scholars are dull, too frequently becomes the scene of a harsher discipline. Inattention must be prevented—indolence quickened—impatience restrained—insubordination and truancy corrected; yet all these are early consequences of the want of skill in the master. To enforce attention and industry, and to secure obedience and decorum, the languid and the listless are too often subjected to the stimulus of coercion, when the chief requisite is method and tact. The master supplies his own deficiencies with the rod ; and what he cannot accomplish by skill, he endeavours to attain by the force of authority.

Such a result is not a proper subject of wonder, when the master has received no systematic instruction in method. To leave the student without the aid of *method*, is to subject him to the toil of analysis and invention, when he has neither the time nor the talent to analyse and invent.

Some progress has been made in the introduction of appropriate methods into the Village School at Battersea.

In the introduction of the *Phonic method of teaching to read*, less has been practically done than the length of time expended in the production of the Manual would appear to justify, if it had been possible to accomplish much before the Manual and apparatus were prepared. The first and second books of the Manual are now complete, being printed, with the tablets for elementary schools, in new type, by Mr. Parker. The other books are almost ready, and all will be published without delay. The complete introduction of the Phonic method into the Village School will therefore encounter no further obstacle. Meanwhile the school has been the scene of all the early trials of the method. Mr. Senf, to whom the analytical labour, and the task of arrangement, was confided, resided in the Normal School, and from time to time conducted a class experimentally in the Village School. The task has since been confided to Mr. Tomlinson, who has prepared the reading lessons for the tablets and the Manual ; and Mr. Macleod, the master of the Village School, has practically tested the labours of these gentlemen, by his own experience of the method in conducting classes in the Village School. Mr. Tomlinson has also had charge of classes in London, in order that the method might not be published before its adaptation to English schools was proved by adequate experience. The limits of these pages do not permit us to enter upon the principles on which this method is based. It is perhaps sufficient to say, that it has been, in various forms, almost universally adopted in elementary schools in Holland, Germany, and Prussia.

The method of teaching *writing* invented by *M. Mülhauser*, of Geneva, and adopted in the chief Normal Schools of France, was introduced by us into the Battersea Village School, and taught there by Mr. Macleod. He has since given lessons to classes of the metropolitan schoolmasters at the School of Method formerly assembling in Exeter Hall, and now in St. Martin's Lane; and this method is adopted in many schools in London. Most of the principal improvements in this method have, since the public instruction given by Mr. Macleod, been adopted by the inventor of another method, who attended Mr. Macleod's classes for his own instruction. His copy-books and black-boards have been modified by the introduction of the most characteristic features of the method of Mulhauser; and, as there was no desire on our part to create a monopoly of instruction, we rejoice that this gentleman has become the propagator of the chief elements of this method. Some difficulty is frequently experienced in procuring the Manual and copy-books of Mulhauser through the country booksellers. This obstacle to its diffusion will be removed. The method is so simple, that any country schoolmaster of common intelligence may learn it, without trouble, from the Manual; and the books are sold at so low a price, as to be within the means of all.

The method of teaching *arithmetic* introduced into the Village School is a modification of that of *Pestalozzi*. By this method the theory of numbers, and the art of mental calculation have been taught both to the students of the Normal School and the village scholars. All the masters acknowledge the assistance they have derived from it.

We had seen the method of Pestalozzi cultivated in various parts of Europe, under different modifications, and, on visiting the Kildare Place Schools in Dublin, a few years ago, we found one of the most successful examples of the cultivation of this method, conducted by Mr. Irvine, now head master of the Lower School at the Royal Hospital, Greenwich. We never observed in any school greater expertness in mental calculation, than in the Kildare Place

Schools, nor so universal an aptitude for numerical combinations.

The method had been introduced into the Kildare Place Schools by Mr. Singh, of Wicklow, who had visited Pestalozzi at Iverdun, made himself acquainted with the method, and published in Dublin a Manual of Exercises for the use of the schools in connection with the Kildare Place Society.

Mr. Irvine was subsequently appointed head-master of the Lower School at Greenwich by the Lords of the Admiralty; and, notwithstanding the interruption of imperfect health, and many obstacles, has succeeded in establishing this method in his class.

He had also conducted classes, consisting chiefly of masters of elementary schools in London, at the School of Method, and there succeeded in creating interest in this new study, and in imparting considerable skill. It is greatly to be regretted that these labours exhausted his strength, and seriously impaired his health.

Mr. Tate, the mathematical master of the Training School, undertook the introduction of this method into that school, aided by the Manual of Exercises published by Tims of Dublin for Mr. Singh. Shortly afterwards Mr. Macleod also introduced the method into the Village School. Some months' experience led Mr. Tate to perceive that the Manual of Exercises might be condensed, and might be so arranged as to have a more evident relation to the theory and practice of the commercial arithmetic commonly taught in schools. With this view he was intrusted with the preparation of a Manual, which, after a prolonged trial, both in the Normal and Village Schools, is now ready for publication.

As soon as the Manual is published the lessons in the School of Method will probably be resumed. The Manual will be published cheaply by Mr. Parker, by whom the Tables necessary for instruction on this method will also be sold, both printed on sheets and painted on black boards.

The *method of teaching drawing from models* invented by M. Dupuis was also practised in the Training School. The development given to this method is due to the zeal of Mr. Butler Williams as a public teacher, and to the skill with which he has prepared a manual of the method. Mr. Butler Williams commenced his labours as a public teacher of this mode of drawing in the Battersea Village School, where he soon acquired, by his own efforts and ingenuity, such skill in the illustration of the method as to enable him to conduct with success the classes for drawing from models, which were immediately opened by him in the School of Method, and attended by schoolmasters, superior mechanics, and artificers. The public exhibition of the drawings made by Mr. Butler Williams' classes has established the efficiency of this method of teaching the drawing of form. Since that period, the pupils who executed these drawings have assembled in St. Martin's Church, and in a series of lessons have produced views of the interior. The elementary classes in the School of Method are re-opened, and an upper school of drawing from models has been established in a convenient gallery in Maddox-street, where Mr. Williams is now pursuing, experimentally, Dupuis' application of the method to the drawing of the human figure. The power of drawing from natural objects acquired by the artificers and schoolmasters who have attended these classes, together with the increase of their skill in design, have attracted Mr. Butler Williams' pupils to his course, and have also occasioned the opening of private classes in the new gallery in Maddox-street. It is also arranged that this course shall be required as a preliminary to an entrance into the classes of the Government School of Design at Somerset House, and for this purpose several new classes will immediately be opened.

The preliminary measures for the introduction of the *method of teaching singing*, invented by M. Wilhem, are related in your Lordships' Minute on that subject; but the success which has attended the labours of Mr. Hullah remains to be told. The primary object of the inquiries which Mr. Hullah was directed to make in Paris was the experimental introduction of this method in the Training Schools at Battersea, and the consequent preparation of the Manual. Here Mr. Hullah carefully pursued his early trials of the method, adapted it to English use, and gave the first demonstrations of its efficiency. The illustrations of Mr. Hullah's early lectures were sung by the pupils of the Training School; and when the method had been thus tested by a prolonged trial, the Manual was published, and the classes of the School of Method were opened at Exeter Hall. These classes were conducted at great expense, owing to the heavy charge made by the directors of that building for the use of the rooms, and for several incidental sources of outlay; yet, during two years, they have been maintained by the payments of the pupils, without the aid of subscriptions, or any grant from the Government, though the expenditure of the first year exceeded £3000, and that of the second year amounted to £2000, notwithstanding that Mr. Hullah's services were gratuitous, and that he remunerated his assistants. During the first year, 2657 members were in attendance on these classes, and during the second year 2325, and Mr. Hullah now has 1200 members in his upper schools, besides those attending the elementary classes, although in every part of London both elementary classes and upper schools are conducted by his pupils and assistants. The method has likewise been introduced by Mr. Hullah into the public schools of Eton, Winchester, the Charter House, Merchant Tailors' School, and into the school attached to King's College, London. It is, likewise, taught in St. Mark's College, Chelsea, the Whiteland's Training School, and the Central Schools of the National Society, in the Training Schools of the British and Foreign School Society in the Borough-road, in the Home and Colonial Infant School Society's Model Schools, in the Chester Diocesan Training School, in the

Model and Normal Schools of the Irish Commissioners in Dublin, in the Norwood Schools, and those of the Royal Hospital, Greenwich, and in the majority of well-conducted elementary schools both in town and country. Mr. Hullah is now Professor of Vocal Music in King's College.

The Manual is published in various forms, and the number of each of these forms sold by Mr. Parker may give some idea of the extent to which the method is diffused. We have, therefore, appended in a note a statement of the number of copies sold [1] About 130,000 copies of the first part of the Manual, Exercises, Sheets,

[1] *Statement of the Sale of Copies of Hullah's Manuals for Singing, December 12.*

Hullah's Manual	. . .	Part 1.	31,200	
		Part 2.	25,800	
				57,000
Exercises	. . . . .	Book 1.	95,000	
		Book 2.	44,300	
		Book 3.	31,000	
				170,300
Large Sheets	. . . .	1 to 10	1738	
		11 — 20	1170	
		21 — 30	672	
		31 — 40	550	
		41 — 50	417	
		51 — 60	325	
		61 — 70	290	
		71 — 80	242	
		81 — 90	531	
		91 — 100	214	
			5849	
			10	
				58,490
Hullah's Vocal Grammar	. . . .			1150
Tablets for Monitorial Schools	. . . .			173

Statement of the Sale of Copies of Mr. Hullah's Part Music.

	Class A.	Class B.	Class C.
Score, No. 1	3030	2100	1025
,, 2	1450	1250	680
,, 3	1050	730	500
,, 4	850	90	*
,, 5	820	*	*
,, 6	740	*	*
,, 7	360	*	*
,, 8	170	*	*
	8470	4170	2205

Those numbers marked * not yet published.

Training of Parochial Schoolmasters at Battersea 419

and Tablets are in use. Estimating that 100 children are under instruction in every case in which the large sheets and tablets are in course of sale, and that only one person receives instruction from each copy of the Manual, Grammar, and Exercises in course of distribution, upwards of 300,000 persons are now receiving instruction in singing according to this method in England and Wales, without reckoning those who have entered upper schools, and are now using the Part Music and Psalter. Mr. Hullah's Part Music is printed for three classes of voices, each class being also printed both in score and for each separate voice, in order to provide appropriate music for the practice of the upper schools. In the course of a few months 47,765 copies of the separate numbers of this Part Music have been sold, and 16,305 copies of the first number of each part in score or for a separate voice.

Mr. Hullah's labours for the diffusion of popular instruction in music are, for the present, completed by the publication of a Psalter.

Those methods of teaching grammar and etymology to which the denomination of *intellectual methods* had been given by the late conductor of the Edinburgh Sessional School, Mr. Wood, have been satisfactorily established, both in the instruction of the Village School and that of the Normal School. In the Normal School the course of instruction in grammar is more extensive, and a grammar

Statement of the Sale of Mr. Hullah's Part Music—continued.

	Soprano.	Alto.	Tenor.	Bass.	Summary.		General Summary.	
No. 1	3800	1900	2200	2250	Soprano	11,450	Class A.—	
2	1980	1090	1330	1390	Alto .	5930	Score . .	8470
3	1550	775	1100	1150	Tenor .	7675	Separate Voices.	32,920
4	1200	625	830	870	Bass .	7865		
5	1130	560	780	830			Class B.	4170
6	1000	520	710	750		32,920	Class C.	2205
7	450	260	425	425				
8	340	200	300	200				47,765
	11,450	5930	7675	7865				

of more refined analysis is employed than in the Village School, it being obvious the master ought to have a deeper insight into the construction of his native language than he can hope to impart to the scholar of a common school. In both schools, however, the aim of Mr. Wood to give a logical arrangement to the matter of instruction in these subjects, is followed.

These several *Methods* have now been tested by experience on the most public theatre, and have become an important part of the instruction of masters of elementary schools. The Manuals in which they are embodied, render their acquisition comparatively easy even to those who do not enjoy the advantage of receiving lessons in the art of teaching by them from adepts. The School of Method will place within the reach of the schoolmasters of the metropolis the means of acquiring the requisite skill; and the body of schoolmasters, whom the Normal Schools will annually disseminate, will diffuse them through the country. Every school conducted with complete efficiency by a master trained in a Normal School, will become a model to neighbouring schools which have not enjoyed similar advantages. On this account alone it is important that no student from a Normal School should commence his labours in the country, until he has acquired a mastery of the methods of teaching these necessary elements.

The arrangements for conveying instruction in these methods, have recently acquired a more definite form in the Training Schools, since the completion of the Manuals has enabled us to confide to Mr. Macleod, the master of the Village School, the course of instruction in the Phonic Method of Teaching to Read, in Mülhauser's Method of Writing, in the Arithmetic of Pestalozzi, in the art of managing and instructing a class, and in the art of giving lessons to a group of classes in the gallery, as well as such outlines of the discipline and organisation of schools as his experience suggests. To Mr. Butler Williams would have been confided the instruction in the method of teach-

Training of Parochial Schoolmasters at Battersea 421

ing drawing from models, and to Mr. May is intrusted that of singing after the method of Wilhem. The Rev. John Hunter, who is acquainted with the *intellectual methods* of Mr. Wood, conveys his instruction in grammar and etymology on those methods, and likewise the Biblical instruction, which is his peculiar charge.

On the theory of the discipline and organization of elementary Schools no complete course has hitherto been attempted in the Training Schools. Sufficient leisure has not been found for the completion of a Manual on this subject.

In a course of instruction extending over a year and a half, a student ought to spend three hours daily, during six or eight months, in the practice of the art of teaching in the Village School. When the course of instruction is necessarily limited to one year, four months should be thus employed, and during the entire period of his training, instruction in method should form an element of the daily routine in the Normal School.

By such means alone can a rational conception of method be attained, and that skill in the art of conducting a School and instructing a class without which all the labours of the Normal School in imparting technical knowledge are wasted, because the student has no power of communicating it to others.

The Battersea Training Schools were founded in the hope that they would be employed to assist the executive Government in supplying masters to the Schools of industry for pauper children, to the prisons for juvenile offenders, to the Schools of Royal foundation for the army and navy, to the Schools of the dockyards and men-of-war, and to the colonies.

The constitution impressed upon them was conceived with this view. We intended that these Schools should be under the direction of the State and in harmony with the Church.

The religious teaching was confided to the Honourable

and Rev. Robert Eden, Vicar of the Parish, and the Rev. J. Hunter, by whom the instruction in the Holy Scriptures, and in the Liturgy and Catechism, was conducted, and the religious discipline was superintended. Our desire was that the religious instruction should be positive; that it should be occupied with the exposition of truth; and that it should be copious, comprehending the great standards of our faith, so as to prepare the masters trained in the School to become in truth Christian teachers with all the strength of conviction and feeling.

In the asylum of indigence, and in the service of the State the law knows no distinctions of religion. It provides alike for the necessities of all whose services it demands. Pauperism is succoured without an inquiry into creeds, and crime is scourged without distinction of opinions. The Masters of Schools for such asylums by law belong to the Church of England, but we conceived they might be faithful to that Church without being intolerant to those who separate from her communion. We desired to rear Christian teachers, not antagonists of supposed error, but men regarding the Church with reverence and affection, and all Christians as brethren. We hoped that without adopting any previous *limits* for secular instruction, or acknowledging any rule but that of efficiency in the methods and matter of learning, the Schools might enjoy the confidence of the heads of the Church.

With these relations to the Church, and to those who separate from her communion, we desired to place the institution under the guidance of the executive Government, in order that the great Schools under its immediate control might be supplied with masters from this source.

The late Government left on Record the following Minute (*see Appendix*), approving the constitution of the Schools, and recommending that a grant towards the expenses incurred by their founders should be included in the estimates of the year.

The Committee of Council, over which your Lordship has presided, voted £1,000 in 1842, towards the expenses attending the establishment of the Schools.

Training of Parochial Schoolmasters at Battersea

This year your Lordship is aware, that we renewed our application for aid in a letter contained in the note at the foot of this page.[1]

[1] My Lord,—

You communicated to me the decision of the Committee of Council, on my letter, applying for a grant towards the establishment and support of the Battersea Training and Village Schools, and expressed on behalf of their Lordships a desire that the permanent prosperity of these schools might be secured. Their Lordships were pleased to grant £2000, on condition that the trustees of the school procured a lease of the premises which they now occupy at Battersea, and that the Committee could be satisfied that the schools were likely to be maintained in a state of efficiency for a reasonable period.

I did not hesitate to express to your Lordship my determination to do every thing that lay in my power to carry the wishes of the Committee into execution. I lost no time in making inquiries as to the terms on which it would be prudent to take a lease of the premises, and I now submit the result of those inquiries.

The schools have been conducted with the most rigid economy, and we have, therefore, avoided expending money on the repairs of the premises. Consequently, a considerable outlay on repairs is now unavoidable. I apprehend that about £400 would be required to put the premises into tenantable repair.

We have hitherto, likewise, been content with imperfect arrangements. We use one of the class rooms as a dining-hall. We have no convenient washing-room; the communication between the different parts of the premises is circuitous; and the domestic offices are not separated from that part of the building in which the students reside.

The greatest defect is, that the students sleep in common dormitories, each room containing many beds, placed near each other. I stated in my previous letter, that the whole body of students will now be adults, and the course of training limited to one year. The common dormitories were first occupied when boys only were admitted into the establishment, and when the course of instruction extended to three years. Separate dormitories have become necessary since we have admitted only young men. We propose to convert a range of stabling attached to the premises into a series of small separate bed-rooms, and to add another story to this and an adjoining building.

A lease of the premises without these repairs and alterations would be very undesirable. We have submitted to great inconvenience as long as we regarded the schools as provisional; but the improvement of the premises is indispensable to their prolonged occupation.

I lay before your Lordship, therefore, plans of the alterations in the premises, which are indispensable if we take a lease. They have been designed, and will be executed, on the most economical scale of expenditure. Mr. Cubitt has surveyed the premises, and furnished me with an estimate of the cost of these improvements, amounting to £2000, without including some general repairs which may be estimated at £200.

We should be unwilling to remove the training school from Battersea; our associations with the vicar have been harmonious; the parochial school,

After renewed deliberation the Committee of Council resolved to grant £2200 towards the expense of enlarging and improving the School buildings, on condition that a

which serves as our model school, has attained a degree of excellence, which, if we removed from this parish, could not be reached without the labour of years. We should not willingly commit the practical injustice of having raised this parochial school to its present state of efficiency, and then abandoned it, to the great injury of the parish, nor lose the aid of a school of such merit for the illustration of method to our pupils.

Having obtained the estimate of the cost of the projected improvements, I laid the plans and estimate before the landlord. He agrees to grant us a lease for seven, fourteen, and twenty-one years, and to contribute £400 towards the outlay, leaving £1800 to be provided for by your Lordships' grant. The grant of the Committee of Council will thus be reduced to £200, or barely a reasonable allowance for unforeseen contingencies.

We should hold the premises at a moderate rent, and I should be disposed to take a lease for seven, fourteen, and twenty-one years, and with the aid of their Lordships' grant, to expend £2200 on the improvements proposed in the plan which accompanies this letter, and on other repairs, under the following arrangements :—

That the students entering the School consist of four classes.

1. Those who provide the whole cost of their maintenance and education themselves, or by their patrons. These students will be free to settle where they please at the close of their course of training.

2. Those who provide £30 towards the cost of their maintenance and education, and who sign an agreement to serve the Government for five years from the period when they pass the examination for the first year's certificate. The subsequent regulations A and B apply to this class.

3. Those who provide £30 towards the cost of their maintenance and education, and give security for the payment of £25 within one year of the period when they leave the institution. These students will be free to settle where they please.

4. The trustees will offer every quarter an exhibition of £25 to the best candidate for admission, who may be able to pass a preliminary examination in religious knowledge, English grammar, etymology, and composition; arithmetic, as far as decimals; algebra, as far as simple equations; and the geography of Palestine and England. The trials will be conducted by the masters by means of examination papers and oral questions. The successful candidates will be admitted to one year's training for £30, without any condition as to future service.

5. The trustees will offer an exhibition every quarter to the ten students whose year of training expires in that quarter, upon trials by examination papers, oral questioning, and public teaching in the village school. They will award this exhibition to that student, whose proficiency in his studies, skill in teaching, conduct in the institution, and general character, shall appear to the Directors and masters most fully to warrant confidence in his success as the master of an elementary School. This exhibition for students of the first class shall consist of £25.

Students of the second class who have agreed to serve the Government, may fulfil the agreement without repaying £25 from their salaries: and the lease of the premises were taken, and that satisfactory arrangements were made for the permanent support of the institution.

We had expended upwards of £5000 in the manage-

training School will then have no claim on the Government for any payment on behalf of such student.

Students of the third class will by this exhibition free their sureties from the repayment of £25.

Students of the fourth class will gain a second exhibition of £25, and will pay only £5 for one year's training.

A. That students who belong to the second class shall sign an agreement to serve the Government as schoolmasters for five years after they obtain their certificates.

1. In any establishment containing a School under the executive Government.
2. In any School connected with the army, navy, or dock-yards.
3. In any institution for the reformation of criminal youth.
4. Or for the training of pauper children.
5. In any model School, partly or wholly supported by aid from the Committee of Council.
6. Or as inspectors or masters of model Schools in the colonies.

With a proviso that they shall not be required to serve for less than £50 per annum, and also, that if the salary exceed £70 per annum, they shall repay to the Government by annual instalments, in two years, the premium advanced on their behalf. An account shall be kept in the training School of the repayment of these instalments on behalf of the Government.

B. For every student signing such an agreement, the Government shall pay £25 to the training School, upon the presentation of a certificate from the Inspector, that the student has been instructed and trained for one year, and has, after the usual periodical examinations, obtained a diploma, certifying his good conduct, industry, capacity, and skill, the subjects upon which he has been examined, and the degree of competency he has acquired in each, which diploma shall be signed by the Directors, the vicar of the parish, and by the chaplain and masters of the training and village Schools, and countersigned by Her Majesty's Inspector of Schools.

Under this arrangement the trustees will assume the pecuniary risks of maintaining the establishment, and whatever responsibility may be connected with its management.

In order to conduct the establishment efficiently, it will be necessary to raise £500 or £600 annually by subscriptions beyond the grants of the Committee of Council, or of the patrons of students, and the payments of the pupils themselves.

I have no doubt that contributions to this extent can be secured, and that the stimulus which will be given to the Schools, if the Committee approve this arrangement, will ensure their prosperity.

On the other hand, the adoption of this arrangement, or of some similar plan, appears the only alternative to the immediate dissolution of the Schools.

I have the honour to be,
Your Lordship's most obedient servant,
J. P. K. S.

ment of the Schools; of this £1000 had been received from the patrons and friends of pupils towards the expenses of their training, and £1500 had been contributed by our personal friends (*see Appendix*) with unsolicited confidence and generosity. Our own expenses amounted to £2500.

We felt that in future the Schools could not be conducted without the aid of a Principal, and that our expenses would therefore rise from £1200 to £1500 per annum. We were unable to pledge our personal resources to this extent, and we could not claim the grant of £2200 offered by the Committee of Council without providing for the permanent support of the establishment by arrangements satisfactory to their Lordships. We felt it necessary carefully to deliberate on the course we should pursue.

The Battersea Training Schools had been founded with two distinguishing objects:—

1. To give an example of Normal Education for Schoolmasters, comprising the formation of character, the development of the intelligence, appropriate technical instruction, and the acquisition of method and practical skill in conducting an Elementary School.

2. To illustrate the truth that, without violating the rights of conscience, masters trained in a spirit of Christian charity, and instructed in the discipline and doctrines of the Church, might be employed in the mixed schools necessarily connected with public establishments, and in which children of persons of all shades of religious opinion are assembled.

Our first impulse was to remember the generous and unsolicited contributions by which our funds had been replenished, and to turn to those friends who had offered us this voluntary evidence of their sympathy. A little reflection, and the advice of some experienced friends, convinced us that, however successful such an application might be, a subscription for the support of the Schools, in the present agitated state of the public mind, would probably raise a new subject of controversy.

The Training Schools had to a remarkable extent escaped the fierce denunciations with which the success of almost every other effort for the improvement of Elementary Education had been menaced from one or other of the great parties, and we had no desire to expose them to the violence of party feuds, unless it were clear that some signal advantage could thus be obtained for the progress of an efficient religious Education based on the recognition of civil rights. We had no assurance that such an achievement could be won, by the exertions of so fluctuating a body as the subcribers necessary for the support of a charitable institution.

We were unable to fulfil our original design of devoting this establishment to the supply of masters to Schools connected with the executive Government, and especially to the great Schools of Industry for Pauper Children now existing at Norwood, Manchester, Liverpool, Sheffield, and about to be erected elsewhere. We therefore turned to observe in what sphere existed the greatest need of a supply of skilful and religious men, ready to devote their lives to the great work of spreading a truly Christian civilization through the masses of the people. Our personal experience had made us early acquainted with the absence of a growth in the spiritual and intellectual life of the masses, corresponding with the vast material prosperity of the manufacturing districts.

We had witnessed the failure of efforts to found a scheme of combined Education on the emancipation of infants from the slavery into which the necessities and ignorance of their parents, and the intensity of commercial competition, had sold them.

To arrest the progress of degeneracy towards materialism and sensuality, appeared to us to be the task most worthy of citizens in a nation threatened by corruption from the consequences of ignorance and excessive labour among her lower orders.

It is impossible that the Legislature should, year after year, receive and publish such accounts of the condition of the people as are contained in the Reports of the Hand-loom Weavers' Commission, or of the Commission on the Employment of Women and Children, or that on the Dwellings of the Poor and on the Sanitary Condition of Large Towns, without resolving to confer on the poor some great reward of patience, by offering national security for their future welfare.

These considerations have a general relation, but the state of the manufacturing poor is that which awakens the greatest apprehension. The labour which they undergo is excessive, and they sacrifice their wives and infants to the claims of their poverty, and to the demands of the intense competition of trade. Almost every thing around them tends to materialise and inflame them.

They are assembled in masses—they are exposed to the physical evils arising from the neglect of sanitary precautions, and to the moral contamination of towns— they are accustomed to combine in trades unions and political associations—they are more accessible by agitators, and more readily excited by them.

The time for inquiry into their condition is past, the period for the interference of a sagacious national forethought is at hand. We therefore felt that the imminent risks attending this condition of the manufacturing poor established the largest claim on an institution founded to Educate Christian Teachers for the people.

We have explained the relations which the Training Schools had to the Established Church of this country, and the circumstances by which that condition was determined. When, therefore, we perceived the resources recently collected by the Church to promote the spread of Education in the manufacturing districts, we felt that to contribute towards rendering the Education there provided efficient and comprehensive, was an object strictly consistent with the first of the intentions for which the instruction was founded, and we felt that the force of circumstances had defeated the accomplishment of the second.

After some correspondence with the Bishop of London,

we therefore requested the Committee of Council[1] to permit us to transfer the grant made by their Lordships

Council Office, Whitehall, November 20, 1843.

[1] MY LORDS,—

The Lord President communicated to me the result of your deliberations at the last meeting of the Committee concerning the application for aid towards the establishment and support of the Battersea Training School.

I was very sensible of the confidence in the founders and managers of that institution implied by your Lordships' grant of £2200, towards the expenses attending the enlargement and repairs of the school buildings. The condition of your Lordships' grant, however, demanded some deliberation. You required that satisfactory arrangements should be made for the permanent establishment and support of the schools.

Such arrangements it appeared could not be satisfactory to your Lordships, if entered into with private individuals only, unless they were prepared to pledge their private fortunes for the fulfilment of the condition.

The alternative that suggested itself was, that the schools should cease to be under the control of private persons, and that their future management should be confided to some public body, which, from its position, numbers, and character, could, with a reasonable prospect of success, assume the responsibility attaching to the fulfilment of the condition of your Lordships' grant.

Upon mature reflection, and after consultation with some friends, we felt that the public body, to which alone the schools could be confided, should be prepared to conduct them on the principles of the tolerant Church of England, and to acquiesce in the existing arrangements for the internal discipline and instruction of the schools, and for the training of the pupils for their peculiar vocation. These were the principles and the methods to which your Lordships had previously extended the sign of your approbation by a grant of £1000, and which you were now prepared to distinguish by a further grant of £2200.

With this conviction, I entered into communication with the Archbishop of Canterbury and the Bishop of London, proposing to them to put the schools under the management of a Committee of the National Society, disposed to carry into execution the plans upon which the schools had been founded.

I found the Archbishop and the Bishop both cordially disposed to acquiesce in this proposal.

They have since communicated with the principal members of the Committee of the National Society, and found them equally ready to concur, and I am informed that a special meeting of the Society will be held this week to consider and determine the question.

I therefore communicate to your Lordships the steps which have been taken towards the fulfilment of the condition of your grant, viz. that satisfactory arrangements should be made for the permanent establishment and support of these schools, and I request your approval.

I have the honour to be,
My Lords,
Your most obedient servant,
J. P. K. S.

The Committee of Council on Education.

for the enlargement and improvement of the buildings, together with the entire establishment, to the National Society.

This arrangement has since been completed, with the concurrence of the Committee of Council and the National Society, and we have now withdrawn from the direction of the Schools.

  We have the honour to be,
    My Lords, your obedient Servants,
      J. P. Kay Shuttleworth.
      Edward Carleton Tuffnell.

APPENDIX

Minute of the Committee of Council on Education, dated June 23, 1841.

The Committee had under their consideration a letter from the Poor Law Commissioners, dated the 6th of May, describing the urgent necessity of providing well-trained schoolmasters for pauper schools, and the expediency of enabling them to avail themselves of a training school lately established at Battersea from private resources, under the sanction and with the assistance of the clergyman of that parish.

Lord Duncannon further reported to the Committee the extreme difficulty recently experienced by the Commissioners of Greenwich Hospital, notwithstanding repeated public advertisements, in procuring adequately prepared masters and assistant-masters for the schools connected with that establishment.

Their Lordships were, therefore of opinion, that in an estimate to be laid before Parliament, a sum should be included for the purpose of enabling the Committee to defray such part of the expenses of the school at Battersea as may appear to be a reasonable compensation for the benefits derived to the Poor Law Commissioners, or any public institutions connected with the State, in obtaining schoolmasters under their direction, or that of any other department of the executive.

The Donors to the Battersea Training Schools.

The Viscount Morpeth	£500
The Duke of Sutherland	200
The Marquis of Lansdowne	100
The Earl of Radnor	100
Samuel Jones Loyd, Esq.	100
George Cornewall Lewis, Esq.	100
Seymour Tremenheere, Esq.	100
Rev. Mr. Brown	100
Mrs. Fydel	100
George Norman, Esq.	50
Total	£1459

THIRD PERIOD

THE MINUTES OF 1846

EXTENDING THE ADMINISTRATION OF THE PARLIAMENTARY
GRANT FOR EDUCATION IN GREAT BRITAIN TO

PUPIL-TEACHERS AND QUEEN'S SCHOLARS

THE SUPPORT OF TRAINING COLLEGES

THE AUGMENTATION OF THE SALARIES OF TEACHERS

THEIR RETIRING PENSIONS FOR LONG AND EFFICIENT SERVICES

DAY SCHOOLS OF INDUSTRY

A NORMAL TRAINING SCHOOL FOR MASTERS OF WORKHOUSE AND
PRISON SCHOOLS

PREFACE

THE following explanation of the Minutes of 1846 was first published in 1847 by direction of the Committee of Council on Education in defence of those measures, under the title of '*The School, in its Relations to the State, the Church, and the Congregation.*' J. P. K. S., 1862.

CONTENTS

CHAPTER I.

Preliminaries to the establishment of the Committee of Council on Education

CHAPTER II.

The nature and objects of the inspection of Schools, and the mode of appointing Inspectors . . . .

CHAPTER III.

The Minutes of August and December, 1846, considered in relation to their influence on the Schoolmaster, the School, and the Poor . . . .

CHAPTER IV.

The Minutes of August and December, 1846, considered in their Religious and Political Aspect . . . .

CHAPTER V.

The outlay from public grants and and private contributions required by the Minutes of August and December, 1846 . . . .

APPENDIX A.

The Plan for encouraging and aiding voluntary exertions for the Promotion of Education in Great Britain, proposed by Lord John Russell's administration in 1847 :—
  Minutes of the Committee of Council on Education in August and December, 1846 . . . .
  Regulations respecting the Education of Pupil Teachers and Stipendiary Monitors . . . .
  Support of Normal Schools . . . .
  Grants in aid of Day-schools of Industry . . . . . .
  Normal Schools for Training Masters for Workhouse Schools and for Penal Schools . . . .
  Minute on the Administration of the Grants for the Salaries of Masters and Mistresses of Schools for Pauper Children . . . . .
  Supplementary Official Letters . . . .

APPENDIX B.

The Origin, Procedure, and Results of the Strike of the Operative Cotton Spinners of Preston, from October 1836, to February 1837 . . .

APPENDIX C.

Annual Cost of Establishments, &c., for the Repression of Crime . . .

EXPLANATION

OF THE

MINUTES OF 1846

CHAPTER I.

PRELIMINARIES TO THE ESTABLISHMENT OF THE COMMITTEE OF COUNCIL ON EDUCATION.

The education of the working classes had not been regarded as of national importance in England until this century. The early ecclesiastical system which encouraged the admission of poor students into the schools of the religious foundations, was partly intended to provide for those indigent scholars who with little culture exhibited signs of superior natural capacity: and partly to satisfy the wants of the Church, by filling the ranks of the inferior orders of her clergy, and throwing across the complex woof of her hierarchy the thread of an order of men raised by genius alone. The parochial endowments for education were founded on the model of the richer foundations. They were chiefly grammar-schools, often enriched with exhibitions or scholarships in some college of one of the Universities, and thus opening to youth of humble origin access to the seats of learning.

The reigns of Edward VI. and Elizabeth were distinguished by a great policy, intended to consolidate the Reformation by the diffusion of learning ; and schools founded in those reigns were rendered still more accessible to the common people. But even these schools partook of the character of the more ancient foundations. They were institutions by which the learning of the Universities might be diffused among the middle classes, and portals through which they might enter the colleges; a postern only was left open for the poor.

The Reformation, however, gave birth to the idea that there is a certain amount of learning indispensable even for a man who earns his bread by manual labour. The teaching of the Catechism in the vulgar tongue was enjoined, as a part of the services of the Church. The proficiency of the humblest scholars was a necessary preliminary to the solemn rite of confirmation.

On this religious basis, the instruction of the humblest classes was not entirely neglected, but public opinion was not favourable to any other form of instruction. Protestantism vindicated the interference of reason in religion, to discriminate, at least, the authority to which we ought to submit, and proclaimed the sufficiency and completeness of the canon of Holy Scripture. But the formularies containing the doctrine of the Church were chiefly taught to the poor. The doctrines thus implanted were regarded as germs which would probably grow to maturity, and the vitality of which would, at least, destroy the noxious weeds of heresy.

The conception of what was necessary for the religious education of the poor seldom rose above this level. The art of reading was little cultivated; that of writing was almost universally neglected. The duties of schoolmasters, as set forth in the 79th canon[1], were applicable to the

---

[1] All schoolmasters shall teach in English or Latin, as the children are able to bear, the larger or shorter Catechism heretofore by public authority set forth. And as often as any sermon shall be upon holy and festival days within the parish where they teach, they shall bring the scholars to the church where such sermons shall be made, and there see them quietly and soberly behave themselves; and shall examine them at times convenient, after their return, what they have borne away of such sermons. Upon other days, and at other times, they shall train them up with such sentences of Holy Scripture as shall be most expedient to induce them to all godliness;

grammar-schools of an intermediate period, and in these schools the scholars were chiefly the children of the tradesmen of the small towns and villages, but few of the poor resorted to them. Until the close of the last century, it was not practically deemed of the highest importance that the Holy Scriptures should be universally accesible to the poor. Much less was any strong conviction entertained that, to promote the vital efficacy of Christianity on the great mass of the nation, the cultivation of the intellect was desirable, at least so far as to enable the common people to read the Scriptures with understanding, and to listen to their spiritual teachers with profit. Catechetical instruction, conducted on such principles, operated rather to the exclusion of error than to the circulation of truth—the effects were negative rather than positive.

The natural energies of society had occasioned the practical development of imperfect means for the education of the poor during the progress of the eighteenth century; but the Reformation in England failed to give birth to any national system of instruction for all the humblest ranks of society. The school did not become, as in Scotland, an institution in every parish, provided at the expense of the proprietors, and supported partly by an assessment on the land, and partly by the contributions of the middle classes and of the poor. The precepts and doctrines of Christianity were communicated to the great mass of the common people by catechetical and oral instruction from the pulpit. The school was not regarded either as a parochial institution indispensable for the completion of the ecclesiastical organisation, as in Scotland, or as any part of the means which ought to be employed by religious congregations, among dissidents from the Church, to instruct the poor as an act of Christian charity and zeal. The Government had not con-

---

and they shall teach the grammar set forth by King Henry the Eighth, and continued in the times of King Edward the Sixth and Queen Elizabeth, of noble memory, and none other.—*Extract from Canon LXXIX.*

cluded that it was expedient rather to prevent the growth of crime by sound instruction, than to attempt to repress it by police, or to eradicate it by a system of penal banishment, or to crush it by the punishment of death. The anarchical tendencies of ignorance among the great mass of the commonalty were not regarded as an evil in the polity of the State to be met by the diffusion of knowledge, but rather as eruptions, forming inevitable phenomena of social history, to be restrained by the interference of an armed force. The theory of government adopted coercion and punishment among its most active agencies; but to the great mass of the labouring classes the State was content with affording (as one of the conditions of the tenure of property) that security for life, which the laws for the relief of the poor had provided in the reign of Elizabeth.

Even the endowed schools, which had been founded chiefly in the reigns of Edward VI. and Elizabeth, being subject to no efficient supervision, and having also very imperfect constitutions for their management, fell into disorder, and not unfrequently into disuse. Their revenues were to a large extent absorbed by other local objects, or wasted by neglect, or rendered useless by their inefficient application.

The catechetical instruction of children had been much neglected during the eighteenth century. It had fallen into almost complete desuetude in the churches. Towards the close of this century, however, the Church and the religious congregations of England took the first step towards a provision for the education of the poor by the creation of Sunday-schools. These important institutions were the spontaneous growth of the zeal of religious communities for the diffusion of Scriptural knowledge, and were the first advance towards the cardinal idea that the school is an inseparable element of the organisation of a Christian congregation. Founded on a conception which has such vast relations (though then imperfectly foreseen), and fostered by intense religious zeal, the

Sunday-school, especially in the north and west of England, and in the seats of manufactures and mining, has supplied a means for the religious instruction of the people, which may probably, by the good providence of God, have contributed to save this country from some great convulsion.

The influence of the Sunday-school on public order and social progress must be regarded from two points of view. These institutions are most numerous and successful in the great towns which have been created on the coal-fields of Great Britain since the invention of the steam-engine. In such towns the labouring poor are employed during 12 or 14 hours in the day, and the occupations of the middle class are during the week incessant. Until Sunday arrives there are few or no opportunities for intercourse between the more wealthy and the working classes. The fact, that on the Sunday many thousands of the middle class devote three hours of their rest from the business of life to the pious office of instructing the children of the humblest ranks, shows how powerfully the cohesive influence of Christian charity has been in operation, between those elements of society among which repulsive forces abound.

The indirect influence of the Sunday-school has therefore been most favourable to social harmony and public order. Its direct influence is not less important. A large portion of the population chiefly owe the power to read, and whatever acquaintance they have with the Holy Scriptures, their connection with a religious congregation, and the influence of a religious example, to this school. It has also laid the foundations of public education for the poor deeply in the religious organisation of the country. The type of this school has to a great extent predetermined the constitution of the daily school, and provided the fabric which, by a natural transition, may be employed in the establishment of an efficient system of elementary instruction, tending, in harmony with the Sunday-schools, to complete the work of Christian civilisation, which has been so auspiciously commenced.

The establishment of Sunday-schools prepared public opinion for more general efforts to form voluntary associations for the promotion of elementary education by means of day-schools.

As the modern day-schools for the poor were a natural consequence of the Sunday-schools, the objects of elementary instruction received at first little extension. No experience existed to determine in what way the highest aims of education might be most certainly attained. No sympathy was awakened in the public mind for any other result than the acquirement of the almost mechanical arts of reading, writing, and cyphering. It was difficult to procure funds for these purposes. A severe economy of their resources was therefore indispensable to the existence of the day-schools. Under these circumstances the monitorial system was suggested as a solution of the question, how limited means could be most effectually applied, to the accomplishment of objects equally limited in extent; and from the labours of Joseph Lancaster and Dr. Bell the two great societies for promoting Education in England arose.

The National Society has successfully embodied the spirit and applied the resources of the Church of England to the foundation and support of parochial schools, in which the doctrines of the Church, as taught in her Catechism, are inculcated. The British and Foreign School Society, founded on the principle of religious equality, was established with the intention of uniting all Protestant congregations on the basis of the authorised version of the Scriptures without note or comment, and to the exclusion of all catechetical instruction.

From the voluntary labours of these two great societies, elementary education received its chief, if not its sole impulse down to the year 1833.

Until this period the Government had not intervened even to foster the operations of these societies. It was, therefore, a just tribute to the benefits which the country had derived from their labours, that when Parliament, on the motion of Lord Althorp in 1833, devoted an annual grant of £20,000 to the promotion of education in Great Britain, this money was applied in the first instance through the intervention of these two societies, to aid their resources and the voluntary contributions of each locality, in the erection of schools. The distribution of this grant was confided to the Lords of the Treasury, who acted on the recommendations of these two societies, apportioning the money according to fixed regulations.

Hitherto the education of the poor had depended almost solely on voluntary contributions; for the ancient endowments for education being without superintendence, and under local management, which had become inefficient, were almost useless. The grants in aid of voluntary contributions were made on conditions, which afforded only the minimum of security for the application of the public funds. It was required that the school building should be held in trust for the education of the children of the poor by a valid deed, that the building accounts should be liable to audit, and that the trustees and managers should make such reports, from time to time, as might be called for by the Lords of the Treasury. The Government by these means promoted the extension of education by voluntary efforts, but took no effectual step towards its improvement. The principle of voluntary action was not interfered with, but encouraged, and the basis on which voluntary associations had been organised was adopted as the means of progress.

Even this limited interference of the Government awakened new ideas as to the objects and aims of popular education. It was more clearly perceived that the Nation as well as the Church or Congregation had a direct interest in the solution of this question. The first act of the Government was a sign of confidence in the two great societies organised on a religious basis. By this act, the Government declared that it accepted the antecedent history of elementary instruction, as determining that the constitution of its schools should have a religious foundation, in harmony with the institutions of the country. The two societies differed in one important feature. The National Society made no effort at comprehension; its schools were founded on the doctrine of the Church; their religious constitution was in conformity with its discipline, and their management was confided to the laity of the Church, who co-operated with the parochial clergyman. The British and Foreign School Society desired to comprehend in the support and management of its schools all, whether Churchmen or Dissenters, who could co-operate in communicating religious instruction from the authorised version of the Holy Scriptures without any sectarian interpretation.

When, therefore, the Government determined to promote the erection of schools connected with these two societies, it recognised on the one hand the principle of separate, and on the other that of combined education. These two principles had been adopted by voluntary association. It remained to be seen which would predominate, or whether one of them might be accepted, as the expression of the views of Dissenting Communions, in combination with such members of the Church of England as were favourable to combined education, and the other of the majority of the clergy and laity of the Church of England.

Few or no schools were established on a purely secular basis. The whole elementary education of England tended towards a religious organisation. Combined schools, even among congregations of the different orthodox sects, became a rare phenomenon, and the new schools, in union with the British and Foreign School Society, chiefly originated in the zeal of dissenting congregations, and had a continually closer connection with their internal discipline. The British and Foreign School Society deserved the confidence of those politicians and churchmen who determined to consent to no system of national education inconsistent with civil and religious liberty, and of those statesmen with whom the civil rights of the minority were sacred.

Between the years 1833 and 1839, the province of the Government in promoting the education of the people attracted continually more attention. The interference of Parliament had necessarily caused the sufficiency of the existing means of education for the accomplishment of national objects to be called into question, and public opinion decided through all its organs in favour both of the extension and improvement of those means. These were the preliminaries which led to the creation of the Committee of Council on Education in 1839.

The period had arrived when the creation of a department, specially charged with the superintendence of whatever means the Government might employ for the promotion of education, had become a matter of general expectation. In the letter by which Lord John Russell communicated to Lord Lansdowne Her Majesty's intention to create the Committee of Council on Education, the principles which were to regulate its administration, and the objects to which it was to be devoted, were declared in the following words:—

'Much may be effected by a temperate attention to the fair claims of the Established Church, and the religious freedom sanctioned by the law.'

' On this subject I need only say that it is Her Majesty's wish that the youth of this kingdom should be religiously brought up, and that the rights of conscience should be respected.'

' It is some consolation to Her Majesty to perceive that of late years the zeal for popular education has increased, that the Established Church has made great efforts to promote the building of schools, and that the National and British and Foreign School Societies have actively endeavoured to stimulate the liberality of the benevolent and enlightened friends of general education.'

'Still much remains to be done; and among the chief defects yet subsisting may be reckoned the insufficient number of qualified schoolmasters; the imperfect method of teaching which prevails in, perhaps, the greater number of the schools; the absence of any sufficient inspection of the schools, and examination of the nature of the instruction given; the want of a model school, which might serve for the example of those societies and committees which anxiously seek to improve their own methods of teaching; and, finally, the neglect of this great subject among the enactments of our voluminous legislation.'

By the annual Parliamentary Grant, the Government had from the year 1833 promoted the extension of elementary education, but beyond confiding the schools thus erected to the superintendence of the two societies, it had assumed no direct responsibility for their efficiency. Yet it was not enough that convenient schools should be erected; nor even that the hours of labour for children of a tender age should be subject to some restriction, so as to afford them time for education. The first step towards the improvement of elementary education, was obviously the establishment of a system of inspection, by which Parliament and the country might be informed of the actual condition of schools aided by public grants. The next step appeared to be the creation of a Normal and Model School for the training of masters, and the development of the best methods, as well as to afford an example both of the organisation, discipline, and course of instruction, which might with advantage be pursued in elementary schools.

The assumption of a direct responsibility for the condition of the schools for the poor necessarily subjected the acts of the Government to discussion. The questions to be decided were of great importance and of the most exciting interest. On the one hand were claims on the part of the Established Church that education should be regarded as an ecclesiastical function devolving, both by divine authority and by prescription, as settled in the ancient ecclesiastical law, on the clergy. The 77th canon had declared that 'no man shall teach either in public school or private house, but such as shall be allowed by the Bishop of the diocese, or Ordinary of the place, under his hand and seal, being found meet, as well for his learning and dexterity in teaching, as for sober and honest conversation, and for the right understanding of God's true religion; and also except he shall first subscribe to the first and third articles aforementioned, simply, and to the two first clauses of the second article.' The claims of the Church were however asserted less, as inconsistent with toleration, than with the authority assumed by the Government to promote education.

On the other hand, various classes of dissenters and politicians, regarded the Government as the legitimate arbiter of civil rights, and called for its interference to establish a system of instruction on the basis of religious equality. Among politicians were some who regarded the school as a purely civil institution, and who consequently desired that education should be under the sole charge of the Government, and should be confined to secular learning. Others distinguished between the secular and the religious instruction, and while they imposed upon the Government the support and regulation of a system of secular learning, charged the clergy and the ministers of different religious communions, with the instruction of the children of the poor in religion. The British and Foreign School Society adopted the Bible without peculiar interpretation as the basis of religious education, and attempted to unite the Church and the orthodox sects on this ground.

These proposals were all forms of combined education on the principle of religious equality. It was also possible to create combined schools on the plan of religious toleration, in which the secular advantages of the schools should be open to all, without any requirement inconsistent with the rights of conscience.

When the Government intervened to promote the improvement of education, great principles were therefore necessarily brought into conflict. Many claims were put forth. Some acknowledged, but indefinite rights had to be defined. The authority of the Government, while its powers were only generally asserted, and without distinct limitation, excited apprehension. It remained to be ascertained how far the claims of the Church could be satisfied consistently with civil rights, and with the authority and duty of the State to promote the temporal well-being of its subjects. The constitution of society, as settled by institutions which were the growth of centuries, and by laws securing civil and religious freedom, was obviously the mould in which any system of education must be cast, and yet not so as to accept transient phenomena, instead of permanent principles.

Though therefore the proposals of the Government could scarcely have been more moderate, the whole question of the authority of the State and of the Church, of civil rights and religious immunities, and of combined and separate education, necessarily became subjects of controversy.

The Government had proposed in the constitution of the Normal and Model School that the religious instruction should be regarded as *general* and *special*, and that the general religious instruction should be given to the scholars by the master of the school, the special being reserved for the clergy and ministers of different communions, who were to impart it at hours set apart for that purpose. Under the term general religious instruction was intended such teaching from the Holy Scriptures as is pursued in the schools of the British and Foreign School Societies. Under the term special was intended such religious instruction as is contained in the catechism and liturgy of the Church, and in the catechisms of the several Dissenting Communions. It was at once apprehended that this Normal and Model School would become the type of schools to be founded by the Government.

The Government had, however, no intention to bring into discussion the question of combined education, nor to alter the constitution in which elementary schools, aided by public grants, had hitherto been founded. They proposed to continue to make grants to schools in connection with the National and British and Foreign School Societies, but to introduce inspection as a condition of those grants, and to establish a Normal School as a means of training masters of greater skill and attainments, as well as to afford an example of the working of such institutions. Their object was to improve without altering the basis of popular education; when therefore they perceived that the proposed establishment of a Normal School was misunderstood, that project was withdrawn.

The Government persevered, notwithstanding great opposition, in maintaining the establishment of the Committee of Council on Education, and invested that body with the power to inspect and report on the condition of all schools aided by public grants.

In every instance in which the authority of the State to interfere for the education of the people has been questioned, the doubt has been suggested by some antagonist authority. The abstract objection to the interference of the Government has been prompted either by some real practical grievance, or by the desire of some dominant majority to refuse an equality of civil privileges to the minority, or by a combination of these two causes. The abstract justice of the exercise of this power by the State would never have been called in question, if it had not appeared to threaten some existing interest, or failed to acknowledge some manifest social right. In France, where the Government and the University have represented the ideas prevalent during the Imperial and Revolutionary eras, the Roman Catholic Church has claimed the freedom of education, and the Jesuits have been the most able and persevering expositors of that doctrine. In Belgium, the Protestant Government of Holland had established a system of combined education, on the basis of religious equality, for Protestant and Roman Catholic communions. The authority of Holland was naturally odious in Belgium; and some great legislative and administrative errors had been committed by the Government, both in the courts of law and in the schools, wounding national instincts and rights as represented in language and local customs. But the sense of these injuries was inflamed and rendered intolerable by the industry with which the Roman Catholic clergy availed themselves of every means to irritate the public mind against the combined system of education. The impolicy of the Government of the Netherlands in other particulars might have failed to produce the Revolution of 1830, if the clergy of the Roman Catholic faith had not determined to resist a system of education, however efficient, which reduced the majority to the same level of civil rights with the minority of the religious communions, and which, for this purpose, excluded from the combined schools instruction in the peculiar doctrines of the Roman Catholic faith, reserving them as the separate duties of the clergy. These were the circumstances which induced the Roman Catholic clergy to proclaim the doctrine of the *freedom of education* from all interference of the State.

The immediate secular consequences of the success of this outcry from the Roman Catholic clergy in Belgium, were most disastrous. Throughout Belgium the King of the Netherlands had established schools after the model of those in Holland, distinguished for their admirable organisation, and for the skill, care, and success with which the instruction of the scholars was conducted. From the revolution until a very recent period, elementary education in Belgium has been in ruin; presenting an ominous contrast between the results of the power of the State directed with skill to the establishment of an efficient system of instruction, and the impotence of that *freedom of education* which (evoked to satisfy the claims of religious zeal, and to aid a patriotic resistance to the errors of a foreign government) produced in the schools nothing but failure or confusion.

Explanation of the Minutes of 1846

These are the most remarkable instances in Europe, in which the *freedom of education* from all interference of Government has been asserted. In both cases the objection arose from an authority antagonist to the State; in both that authority was a dominant religious party, and the objection embodied a double protest. One part of this protest consisted in a desire to possess in the schools full opportunity to inculcate the entire doctrine of the Church; the other part of this protest consisted in a refusal to admit the civil power to the control of education, lest it should grant equal privileges to the minority. The first of these two objections is reconcilable with civil and religious liberty; the second is subversive of it.

It is the characteristic of such controversies that the interests of the common people are sacrificed to those of the middle classes: the well-being of the State is postponed to promote the triumph of a party.

The authority of Government, especially in a representative system, embodies the national will. There are certain objects too vast, or too complicated, or too important to be intrusted to voluntary associations; they need the assertion of the power, and the application of the resources of the majority. The means for national defence, for the preservation of public order, and the maintenance of the institutions sanctioned by the law; the security of persons and property obtained by the protection of the law and the agency of the police, are among these objects. In like manner the municipal power provides, on principles settled by the legislature, for the regulation of local government, for police and the administration of justice, for the lighting and drainage of our towns, for the supply of water, and for the progressive improvements by which local abuses and defects are removed. These are all objects obviously too vast and too complicated to be accomplished by purely voluntary association. Many of them operate almost solely by restraint or coercion, and some interfere constantly with the individual will—even with the rights of property—and subordinate them to the general advantage. Yet there are persons who sanction a large expenditure by the State for the preservation of public order by the maintenance of the military organisation of the country, for the prevention or detection of crime by the establishment of an almost universally diffused police force, and who regard with complacency the annual outlay on the machinery of criminal jurisprudence, and the secondary punishment of offences, yet who deny that the State, which they permit to interfere by penal and coercive arrangements, may apply its resources even to promote the success of voluntary efforts for the education of the people.

To a statesman the condition of the great mass of the people presents a question of the greatest importance and interest. For the security of the life of the humblest wayfarer, the ministers of Queen Elizabeth charged the whole property of the country with a tax for the relief of indigence, which now amounts to five millions per annum. The liberty of the poorest is secured by the same statutes, and defended by the same legal authority as that of the highest. Some signs are beginning to appear that the condition of the poor has attracted the attention of the legislature in the improvement of the discipline of our gaols; in the amelioration of the criminal code; in the mitigation of all punishments, and the limitation of the penalty of death to murder, and a few crimes akin to it; in the attention now paid by Government to the sanitary arrangements of our towns, which has prepared public opinion for the adoption of a legislative arrangement intended to remove pestilence from the habitations of the poor; to promote the cleanliness and comfort of their dwellings, and thus to improve the morality of their households.

These are among the signs that the condition of the common people in England has become, in the opinion of statesmen, one of the chief tests of the prosperity of the nation, and of the stability of public order. The enactments which have restricted the hours of labour of women, children, and young persons in public manufactories, are among the earliest provisions for a great moral reformation intended to reach the condition of the entire body of the working classes.

There are social disorders not attributable to defects in the physical condition of the people. The mobs of machine-breakers, which resisted every improvement in the inventions of our manufacturing industry, *ignorantly* attempted to destroy the chief sources of their own domestic well-being, and of the national prosperity. The Trades Unions, which have endeavoured to limit the number of workmen in the best-paid employments; to prescribe a minimum of wages; to impose a uniform standard of earnings for the young and old, the feeble and robust, the industrious and the negligent, and to withdraw the workmen from the control of their masters, have for long periods rendered the working classes, particularly in Ireland and in the mining districts, the victims of their ignorance. They have adhered to these projects through many years, at the expense of great privations, and of a sacrifice of personal liberty such as no despotic government has ever been able to enforce, and with a frequent disregard of justice and humanity. The consequences have been most disastrous. Capital has been driven from entire districts; the labouring population has been dispersed; and if such combinations could become dominant, they would certainly destroy the manufacturing prosperity of this country. These are examples of a class of evils which arise from ignorance. It is difficult, but perhaps possible, to repress such evils, by giving summary and almost despotic powers to the magistrates, and by increasing the numbers, vigilance, and preventive authority of the police. But such measures are opposed to the spirit of our constitution, and the legislature has wisely determined to rely rather on the growth of intelligence among the great body of the people, than on the coercive powers of the law, for the correction of these disorders.

On the other hand, much social evil has its origin in the low condition of the morals of a people who have not been reared under the influence of an efficient system of religious education. Vast expenses are incurred by the country for the relief of those forms of indigence which are attributable to these causes. The whole apparatus of criminal jurisprudence and of secondary punishments, including the outlay on the constabulary force, involves an expenditure of two millions per annum. The provisions for the preservation of public order and the suppression of popular tumults, are an expensive barrier against the eruptions of popular passion. It is obvious to statesmen that to neglect the condition of the people is to permit society to be corrupted by domestic immorality; to render social order and the growth of national wealth insecure, by the combinations maintained by the prejudices of popular ignorance; to entail on the State the support of unnecessary indigence and physical suffering; to endanger public liberty itself, by increasing the need of coercive and penal arrangements, and vastly to augment the charge by which persons and property can be secured against violence and fraud, and public order preserved against anarchy.

The relief of indigence is not confided solely to private charity; nor the sanitary improvement of our towns to benevolent associations; nor the defence of property and public order to voluntary combinations; can it then become any great statesman to abandon to voluntary charity alone, that improvement of the moral and intellectual condition of the people on which such vast consequences depend?

That it is a function of the legislature to improve domestic morality and household comfort by education is apparent, because on the State devolves the duty of suppressing crime by coercive means and penal enactments. If public order may be preserved by the concerted arrangements of a highly disciplined military organisation, why may not the statesman seek, in the improved intelligence of the people, safeguards, surer and more consistent with personal freedom? Those who would create an alarm at the expenditure required for an efficient system of education, keep out of sight how much the national industry has been obstructed by combinations resulting from ignorance; what has been the cost of military establishments for the protection of society in periods of turbulence — how many millions have been annually expended on those forms of indigence which result from immorality or listless improvidence—how many millions the police force, the machinery of criminal jurisprudence and of secondary punishments engulf—and what is the annual waste in improvident expenditure occasioned by the immoral excesses and crimes of an uneducated people. Those who pretend that public liberty is endangered by the rewards which Government desires to give efficient schoolmasters and their assistants (representing it as the invasion of an army of Government stipendiaries), appear to forget how many thousand troops of the line are employed to protect the institutions of the country—how many thousand police to watch their houses and protect their persons—how many gaolers, warders, and officers of the hulks have charge of the victims of popular ignorance and excess—how many ships are annually freighted with their frightful cargoes to the pandemonium of crime in Van Diemen's land—how many overseers have charge of the convict gangs—and how vast is the outlay which sustains the indigence of orphanage and bastardy, of improvident youth, sensual maturity, and premature age.

The statesman who endeavours to substitute instruction for coercion; to procure obedience to the law by intelligence rather than by fear; to employ a system of encouragement to virtuous exertion, instead of the dark code of penalties against crime; to use the public resources rather in building schools than barracks and convict ships; to replace the constable, the soldier, and the gaoler by the schoolmaster, cannot be justly suspected of any serious design against the liberties of his country, or charged with an improvident employment of the resources of the State.

When, therefore, *freedom of education* from the interference of the Government becomes the war-cry of any party, will it not be suspected that they seek the interest of a class rather than the welfare of the nation; that they prefer popular ignorance to party insignificance; the liberty to neglect the condition of the people, rather than the liberty of progressive civilisation?

CHAPTER II.

THE NATURE AND OBJECTS OF THE INSPECTION OF SCHOOLS, AND THE MODE OF APPOINTING INSPECTORS.

HAVING in the preceding chapter related the preliminary circumstances which led to the formation of the Committee of Council on Education, we now proceed to describe its constitution, and the mode of its operation. Beside the abstract objections to the interference of Government in education, with which it was probable that such a step would be assailed, the structure of the Committee itself was described as unconstitutional, its members as irresponsible, and its powers as arbitrary. These were, however, only exaggerated expressions of alarm at the interference of Government in a new sphere, excusable perhaps, considering the difficulty of defining at an early period the mode of its operation and the limits of its authority, as well as the great interests disturbed by its existence. The Committee on Education, it was justly pleaded, was founded on the constitutional precedent of the Board of Trade, which also originated in the Privy Council, and continues to be one of its Committees.

The Education Committee is composed solely of responsible Ministers of State, acting under their oaths of office, all of them in Parliament, and liable to be there questioned or even impeached for their acts as members of this Committee. Its proceedings also are under the check of publicity, for all its correspondence and minutes might, by a vote of either House, be required to be submitted to Parliament without reserve, if the Committee did not always anticipate such a motion, by laying every document of any importance on the tables of both Houses. Lastly, no powers whatever are confided to the Committee of Council, other than to superintend the application of any sums voted by Parliament for the promotion of education in Great Britain. The regulations by which the distribution of these grants are determined are laid before both Houses, before the grant is submitted to the consideration of the House of Commons. Experience of the operations of the Committee of Council was however required to allay the apprehensions arising from these misconceptions. The Minutes of the Committee of Council presented to Parliament in 1839–40 occasioned only one distinction of importance between the proceedings of the Committee of Council on Education and those of the Lords of the Treasury. By the third regulation it was declared that 'the right of inspection will be required by the Committee in all cases. Inspectors authorised by Her Majesty in Council will be appointed from time to time to visit schools to be henceforth aided by public money; the Inspectors will not interfere with the religious instruction, or discipline or management of the school, it being their object to collect facts and information, and to report the result of their inspection to the Committee of Council on Education.'

Prior to the publication of the instructions to the Inspectors of Schools, the nature of this inspection was the subject of much misconception and alarm. It was apprehended, that notwithstanding the restrictions contained in the regulation which made inspection a condition of their Lordships' grants, it would become a system of vexatious interference with the internal discipline and management of schools, and an instrument by which the voluntary charity of society would be restrained in its operations, and thus chilled and extinguished.

The instructions issued to the Inspectors of Schools were, however, framed in a spirit which opposed a mild but effectual rebuke to these anticipations.

'3. In superintending the application of the Parliamentary grant for public education in Great Britain, my Lords have in view the encouragement of local efforts for the improvement and extension of elementary education, whether made by voluntary associations or by private individuals. The employment of Inspectors is therefore intended to advance this object, by affording to the promoters of schools an opportunity of ascertaining, at the periodical visits of inspection, what improvements in the apparatus and internal arrangement of schools, in school management and discipline, and in the methods of teaching, have been sanctioned by the most extensive experience.

'4. The inspection of schools aided by public grants is, in this respect, a means of co-operation between the Government and the committees and superintendents of schools, by which information respecting all remarkable improvements may be diffused whenever it is sought; you will therefore be careful, at visits of inspection, to communicate with the [1] [parochial clergyman, or other minister of religion] connected with the school, and with the school committee, or in the absence of a school committee, with the chief promoters of the school, and will explain to them that one main object of your visit is to afford them your assistance in all efforts for improvement in which they may desire your aid; but that you are in no respect to interfere with the instruction, management, or discipline of the school, or to press upon them any suggestions which they may be disinclined to receive.

'5. A clear and comprehensive view of these main duties of your office is at all times important; but when a system of inspection of schools aided by public grants is for the first time brought into operation, it is of the utmost consequence you should bear in mind that this

---

[1] In relation to the elementary schools of Scotland, the following passage is added in lieu of the words within brackets:—[presbytery of the bounds or the minister of the parish, in regard to all schools which are placed by law, or by the condition of their endowments or constitution, under the superintendence of the Church of Scotland, and, as respects other schools, with the minister of religion.]

inspection is not intended as a means of exercising control, but of affording assistance; that it is not to be regarded as operating for the restraint of local efforts, but for their encouragement; and that its chief objects will not be attained without the co-operation of the school committees;—the Inspector having no power to interfere, and not being instructed to offer any advice or information excepting where it is invited.

'10. The Committee doubt not you are duly impressed with the weight of the responsibility resting upon you, and they repose full confidence in the judgment and discretion with which your duties will be performed.

'My Lords are persuaded that you will meet with much cordial co-operation in the prosecution of the important object involved in your appointment; and they are equally satisfied that your general bearing and conduct, and the careful avoidance of whatever could impair the just influence or authority of the promoters of schools, or of the teachers over their scholars, will conciliate the confidence and good-will of those with whom you will have to communicate; you will thus best fulfil the purposes of your appointment, and prove yourself a fit agent to assist in the execution of Her Majesty's desire, that the youth of this kingdom should be religiously brought up, and that the rights of conscience should be respected.[1]'

The publication of instructions framed in this spirit tended to remove misapprehension and to establish confidence, which within a short period was confirmed by the arrangements which the Committee of Council made with the Church of England, with the Church of Scotland, and with the British and Foreign School Society, as to proceedings to be taken on the appointment of the Inspectors of Schools.

These three classes of schools differed essentially in their constitution, and in the nature of their religious instruction. In the Church of England schools, the re-

[1] Minutes 1839–40, p. 22, and vol. i. 1844, p. 22.

ligious instruction was confided to the superintendence of the parochial clergyman, and was enjoined to be given from the catechism and liturgy of that church, as well as from the Holy Scriptures. In the schools of the British and Foreign School Society, instruction in religion was confined to the Holy Scriptures without any peculiar interpretation or catechetical teaching, and was directed by the school managers, who were chiefly laymen. In schools placed under the superintendence of the Church of Scotland, religion was taught under the inspection of the Kirk Session and Presbytery, as well from the catechism of the Assembly of Divines as from the canon of Scripture.

The Church of England and the Church of Scotland were desirous that the religious instruction in their schools should be open to the examination of the Inspector. On the contrary, the British and Foreign School Society was understood (*vide* Minutes, 1842-3, p. 525) to prefer that the terms of their Lordships' third regulation of the Minute of the 24th September, 1839, should be adhered to, viz., that 'the Inspector should not be authorised to examine into the religious instruction given in the schools.'

As these three classes of schools differed so widely both in their constitution, mode of management, and in the nature of their religious instruction, and as opposite opinions appeared to be entertained by the Church of England and the Church of Scotland on the one hand, and by the British and Foreign School Society on the other, as to the propriety of authorising the Inspector to examine the religious instruction given in the schools, it was, after much consideration, determined that three separate classes of Inspectors should be appointed: one for schools connected with the Church of England; another for schools connected with the Church of Scotland; and the third for schools connected with the British and Foreign School Society.

The Committee of Council were of opinion that unless each Inspector possessed the confidence of the religious communion with which the schools visited by him were connected, he could not usefully co-operate with the school-managers. Their Lordships finally determined that in proceeding to nominate Inspectors they would consult the Central Board, watching over the interests of any distinct class of schools, in order to avoid the appointment of any persons who, especially on religious grounds, did not enjoy its confidence. Moreover, circumstances led to the practical conclusion, that no Inspector should be employed in the visitation of other schools than those for the examination of which he was appointed, except on the direct and formal invitation of their managers. With respect to the appointment of Inspectors of schools connected with the Church of England, their Lordships submitted to Her Majesty a Minute dated 15th July, 1840, on which was founded an Order in Council dated 10th August, 1840 (*vide* Minutes, 1839-40, pp. ix. x.). By this Order in Council it is settled that before the Committee of Council proceed to recommend to Her Majesty any person for appointment, as an Inspector of Church of England schools, their Lordships will consult the Archbishops of Canterbury and York, each with regard to his own province, and that without their concurrence their Lordships will not recommend any person to Her Majesty for appointment. It was also determined that if either of the Archbishops should at any time, with regard to his own province, withdraw his concurrence in such appointment, the Committee of Council should advise Her Majesty to revoke the appointment of such Inspector.

As it was the desire of the Church of England, that the religious instruction in schools connected with that Church should be examined by the Inspectors appointed in conformity with this Order in Council, it was agreed that the following instructions, formed by the Archbishops, relating solely to the examination of the religious instruction in Church of England schools, should be added to the general instructions issued to Inspectors of this class of schools:—

'In the case of schools connected with the National Church, the Inspectors will inquire, with especial care, how far the doctrines and principles of the Church are instilled into the minds of the children. The Inspectors will ascertain whether church accommodation, of sufficient extent, and in a proper situation, is provided for them; whether their attendance is regular, and proper means taken to insure their suitable behaviour during the service; whether inquiry is made afterwards by their teachers how far they have profited by the public ordinances of religion which they have been attending. The Inspectors will report also upon the daily practice of the school with reference to Divine worship: whether the duties of the day are begun and ended with prayer and psalmody; whether daily instruction is given in the Bible; whether the Catechism and the Liturgy are explained with the terms most commonly in use throughout the authorised version of the Scriptures.

'They will inquire likewise whether the children are taught private prayers to repeat at home; and whether the teachers keep up any intercourse with the parents, so that the authority of the latter may be combined with that of the former in the moral training of the pupils. As an important part of moral discipline, the Inspectors will inform themselves as to the regularity of the children in attending school—in what way registered—and how enforced; as to manners and behaviour, whether orderly and decorous; as to obedience, whether prompt and cheerful, or reluctant, and limited to the time while they are under the master's eye; and as to rewards and punishments, on what principles administered, and with what results. The Inspectors will satisfy themselves whether the progress of the children in religious knowledge is in proportion to the time they have been at school; whether their attainments are showy or substantial; and whether their replies are made intelligently or mechanically and by rote. The Inspectors will be careful to estimate the advancement of the junior as well as of the senior class, and the progress in each class of the lower as well as of the higher pupils. And in every particular case the Inspector will draw up a Report, and transmit a duplicate of it through the Committee of Council on Education to the Archbishop of the Province.'—*Vide* Minutes, 1839–40, p. 32.

The Committee of Council had, several months previously to this arrangement with the heads of the Church of England, communicated to the Education Committee of the General Assembly of the Church of Scotland, their intention to act in concurrence with that body in proceeding to recommend to Her Majesty any person for appointment as an Inspector of schools which were by law or by the condition of their endowments or constitution, under the superintendence of the Church of Scotland.[1] At a

---

[1] 'The Committee of Council direct me to inform you, in reply to your inquiries, that the Inspectors of schools aided by public grants are appointed by Her Majesty in Council, on the recommendation of the Committee of Council on Education; and, in order to afford you the fullest information respecting the duties of the Inspectors, my Lords direct me to transmit the inclosed copy of instructions addressed to the Inspectors for England and Wales. Instructions framed on the same principles, but modified so as to render them applicable to any peculiar circumstances in Scotland, will be issued to the Inspectors for that country. With respect to such modifications, my Lords will be glad to receive any observations from the Committee of the General Assembly.

'In these documents you will perceive that the inspection of schools is intended to be a means of co-operation between the Government and the ministers, local committees and trustees of schools, for the improvement and extension of elementary education; and my Lords embrace the opportunity of expressing their intention to co-operate with the Church of Scotland for the attainment of these results, as regards the schools which are placed by law, or by the condition of their endowments or constitution, under the superintendence of the Church of Scotland.

'In further reply to your inquiry, my Lords direct me to assure you that, with respect to these schools, my Lords will at all times feel it their duty to communicate and co-operate with the Education Committee of the General Assembly, and will direct copies of their Inspectors' Reports to be transmitted to the Committee from time to time.

'My Lords conceive this co-operation may best be promoted by selecting for the inspection of such schools gentlemen who possess the confidence of the Church of Scotland, while their acquaintance with all the technical details of elementary instruction, and their zeal for the education of the poorer classes, will afford a guarantee that they are fit agents for promoting

Explanation of the Minutes of 1846

subsequent period the Committee of Council communicated to the Committee of the British and Foreign School Society the following Minute in relation to the same subject:—

'The Committee of Council on Education having had under their consideration the memorial presented from the Committee of the British and Foreign School Society, respecting the inspection of schools in connection with that Society, it was resolved:—

'That their Lordships will communicate the Reports which their Inspectors may make respecting schools in connection with the British and Foreign School Society to the Committee of that Society, for their information.

'That when Inspectors, on the invitation of the Local Committees and Managers of schools, make suggestions to them respecting the discipline and management of their schools, such suggestions shall be reported to their Lordships, who will communicate these suggestions (with the reports on the condition of the school) to the Committee of the British and Foreign School Society, and will request their co-operation in recommending to the approbation of the Local Committee such of the Inspector's suggestions as their Lordships may approve'—(*vide* letter dated February 8, 1841, pp. 411—415, Minutes 1842-3).

In another letter Lord Wharncliffe conveyed to the Committee of the British and Foreign School Society an assurance that in the appointment of Inspectors of British Schools, no person would be selected for that office who did not possess the confidence of that Society,

---

the improvement and extension of such elementary education as may secure the religious and moral improvement of the children of the poor.

'The Committee of Council consider that much advantage will arise from their Lordships having the opportunity of consulting the Education Committee of the General Assembly with respect to the selection of the Inspectors of such schools; before, therefore, a recommendation of any gentleman for this office is made to Her Majesty in Council, my Lords will communicate the name to the Committee of the General Assembly for their observations.' *Minutes*, 1839-40.

and in whose appointment its Committee did not concur (*vide* Minutes, 1842-3, p. 537).[1]

It was not practically found necessary to make any arrangement for the inspection of any other class of schools, until the disruption of the Church of Scotland occasioned the withdrawal of a great number of schoolmasters from the communion of that Church, the transference of many *adventure schools*, and schools under the management of trustees, to the superintendence of the Free Church, and the establishment of numerous new schools under that Church. Mr. Gibson, who had been their Lordships' Inspector in Scotland, having withdrawn from the Established Church, was retained as Inspector of Schools not connected with the Established Church, until to his great experience and ability were confided (under the direction of the Education Committee of the General Assembly of the Free Church) the organisation of the schools which that Church might hereafter determine to form.

The principles on which the inspection of schools was founded ceased to be a matter of controversy. The instructions of the Committee of Council to their Inspectors

---

[1] Wortley Hall, Sheffield, Nov. 30, 1843.

'MY DEAR SIR,

'Upon further consideration of what passed between Mr. Forster and you and myself, on Monday last, I think it desirable, that you should be able, at your meeting with your Committee, to state to them exactly what the course is which the Committee of Council propose to pursue with regard to the appointment of Inspectors of Schools connected with the British and Foreign School Society. I therefore, for this purpose, refer you to pages 19 and 20 of the volume of the Committee of Council's Reports for 1839-40, containing a letter from Mr. Gordon, Secretary to the Education Committee of the Church of Scotland, and the answer of the Committee of Council upon the subject of the appointment of Inspectors for the schools in connection with that Church. Those are the precise grounds upon which we are desirous of placing the appointment of Inspectors for your schools, and no Inspector for them will be appointed without the full concurrence of your Committee.

'I earnestly hope that that Committee will be convinced, by the proposal of the Committee of Council to adopt that course, of their anxious wish to do every thing they can, consistently with their duty, to satisfy the British and Foreign School Society upon this important subject.

I am, &c.,
(Signed) WHARNCLIFFE.

'*Henry Dunn, Esq.*'

Explanation of the Minutes of 1846

were carried into execution with the utmost fidelity. Inspection was welcomed by the trustees and managers of schools so far, that throughout entire districts, schools which had received no pecuniary aid from the Committee of Council, invited the visits of the Inspectors, in order that the managers might have the advantage of the counsels of the Inspectors, and the schools receive a new impulse from their examination.

Besides the three great classes of schools described as having entered into definite arrangements with the Committee of Council, with respect to the inspection of their schools, their Lordships' grants in aid of the erection of school-buildings, &c., were, by a Minute of the 3rd of December, 1839, rendered accessible to schools not connected with the Established Churches of England or Scotland, or with the British and Foreign School Society It has been the practice of the Committee of Council to make grants in Scotland to all classes of schools connected with the orthodox religious communions of that country, as well as to schools of a mixed religious constitution, not distinctly connected either with the Church of Scotland or with any particular religious body. But in England few grants have been sought for schools not connected either with the Church of England, or with the British and Foreign School Society. Their Lordships have not hitherto in England been urged to remove the requirement in their Minute of the 3rd of December, 1839, which states that 'if the said school be not in connection with either of those societies (the National, and British and Foreign), the Committee will not entertain the case, unless some special circumstances be exhibited to induce their Lordships to treat the case as special.'

Their Lordships would probably upon application remove this preliminary requirement, but the principles which the rest of this Minute embodies, continue to regulate the administration of their Lordships' grants. This Minute has not been succeeded by any other which either supersedes or modifies it in any particular; it may therefore be received in all respects as an authoritative expression of the principles by which the distribution of grants to any class of schools, not connected with the Church of England, or with the British and Foreign School Society, is now in England determined.

It is obviously of importance therefore that this Minute, and especially that the conditions with which it concludes, should be carefully perused.

Minute of the Committee of Council of Education. 3rd December, 1839.

Their Lordships deliberated on the 9th Regulation of the 24th September, viz.: 'In every application for aid to the erection of a school-house in England or Wales, it must be stated whether the school is in connection with the National Society, or the British and Foreign Society; and if the said school be not in connection with either of those societies, the Committee will not entertain the case, unless some special circumstances be exhibited to induce their Lordships to treat the case as special.'

Resolved—That if such special circumstances be stated as to induce the Committee to entertain the consideration of any such case, their Lordships will require to be informed—

1. What are the objections which the applicants make to connecting the intended school with the National Society or the British and Foreign School Society.

2. To whom the superintendence of religious instruction will be confided in their school, and whether such religious instruction will be obligatory on all the children in the school, or whether the parent or natural guardian of any child may withdraw it from such religious instruction, or from any portion of it, without thereby forfeiting the advantages of the general education in the school.

3. Whether the Bible or Testament will be required to be read daily in the school by the children, and whether any and what catechism will be taught, and whether, if

the parents or guardian of any child object to such catechetical instruction, it will be enforced or dispensed with.

4. Whether the children who attend the day-school are required to attend the sunday-school, for the purpose of religious instruction, or to attend for Divine worship at any particular church or chapel, or whether the place of Divine worship is left to the selection of their parents solely, without their incurring, by reason of such selection, any loss of the privileges of the school.

5. Whether the school is to be connected with the congregation of any religious denomination, either by the erection of the school-house within the boundary-wall of the site on which a place of Divine worship is built, or by reason of its being chiefly supported by subscriptions from the members of such congregation, or in consequence of any rule limiting admission to any one religious denomination.

6. If it is intended that the school shall be so established and supported, the Committee must be informed what is the district from which the children will assemble in the school; what is the population of the district, and what portion of that population belongs to the religious denomination of the congregation with which the school is connected.

Resolved—That on these facts in relation to each case being presented to the Committee, and their Lordships being satisfied that the regulations of the 24th of September will in all other respects be fulfilled, they will limit their aid to those cases in which proof is given of a great deficiency of education for the poorer classes in the district; of vigorous efforts having been made by the inhabitants to provide funds, and of the indispensable need of further assistance; and to those cases in which competent provision will be made for the instruction of the children in the school, the daily reading of a portion of the Scriptures forming part of such instruction.

The Committee will further give a preference to schools in which the religious instruction will be of the same character as that given in schools in connection with one or other of the above-named Societies; and to those in which the school committee or trustees, while they provide for the daily reading of the Scriptures in the school, do not enforce any rule by which the children will be compelled to learn a catechism, or attend a place of Divine worship, to which their parents, on religious grounds, object.

This Minute is of the greater importance since the publication of the Minutes of the Committee of Council in August and December, 1846, inasmuch as it defines the classes of schools in which pupil teachers and stipendiary monitors may be apprenticed, in which masters having certificates may receive augmentations of salary, and to which in short their Lordships will be disposed to extend all the other benefits now consequent on inspection. It is, however, probable that the Committee of Council will no longer require that in such cases 'special circumstances shall be exhibited to induce their Lordships to treat the case as special.'

CHAPTER III.

THE MINUTES OF AUGUST AND DECEMBER 1846, CONSIDERED IN RELATION TO THEIR INFLUENCE ON THE SCHOOLMASTER, THE SCHOOL, AND THE POOR.

By the events which have been thus described, it had been determined that the assistance of Government for the promotion of elementary education should be distributed in aid of voluntary exertions, chiefly in connection with the Church of England and the British and Foreign School Society; with the Church of Scotland, and with those religious communions which united in giving instruction in their schools from the Shorter Catechism of the Assembly of Divines. A new condition was annexed to these grants, viz., that the schools thus aided should be open to inspection by officers appointed by the Crown, but who were not to interfere with the discipline or management of the school, nor even to examine the religious instruction, unless invited by the managers, but only to report the results of their inspection for the information of Parliament and of the public. Two great principles were thus established—the right and duty of the legislature to promote the extension and improvement of elementary education, and the interest of Parliament and the public in the condition of every school aided by the Government. The nature of the inspection by which this publicity was obtained was carefully defined in the instructions issued to Her Majesty's Inspectors. In order to satisfy the wish of the Established Churches of England and of Scotland, inspection was extended to the religious instruction of schools connected with those Churches; and as soon as the propriety of this extension of the objects of inspection was admitted, the Committee of Council agreed to consult the Archbishops of the English Church, each with regard to his own province, and the Education Committee of the General Assembly of the Church of Scotland, as respected Presbyterian schools, before they should proceed to recommend any person for appointment as an Inspector of Schools connected with these Churches respectively. In like manner, their Lordships consented to communicate with the Committee of the British and Foreign School Society, and not to appoint an Inspector of British and Foreign Schools without their concurrence. The inspection of schools was thus extended beyond the objects originally contemplated by the Government, and was placed in harmony with the religious constitution of the several classes of schools.

These arrangements having been made, the application of the Parliamentary Grant to the extension of elementary education proceeded without further interruption. Little could be accomplished in the improvement of the condition of the schools visited, because the Inspectors had no administrative function, for the Parliamentary Grant was then inapplicable to the support of schools; but the publicity given by the Reports of the Inspectors to the condition of elementary education (even in those schools which being recently founded were supported by the most active zeal) tended to bring about a more general acknowledgment of the incompleteness of that instruction which had been dignified with the name of education. The proposal made by the Government, in 1839, to establish a Normal School, awakened public attention to the important influence which such institutions might exert on the character of schoolmasters, and on the standard of instruction throughout the country. Shortly afterwards, a Normal School originated in the exertions of private individuals. This was followed by the establishment of several others, under the auspices of the Church, in London and in other dioceses. The British and Foreign School Society likewise established a Normal School in the Borough Road;

and the Church of Scotland, at a later period, one in Edinburgh and another in Glasgow. Eight of these Normal institutions received liberal assistance from the Government for their establishment, who also contributed towards the annual expenses of four of them.

Every new step, however, disclosed the poverty of the resources of the existing system. During the feverish excitement of controversy it was possible, by great exertions, to procure considerable funds for the promotion of education; but with the termination of the conflict, the tendency to personal sacrifices was exhausted, and the original languor returned.

It may be important to trace the consequences of this poverty of resources on the condition of the elementary school, on that of the Normal School, and on the profession of the schoolmaster. These subjects are necessarily so connected, as not to be capable of a separate treatment. The Reports of the Inspectors of Schools disclosed that in a great number of instances, even the primary arrangements for enclosing the school site, providing proper offices, completing the drainage and ventilation of the building, furnishing it with proper means of warmth in winter, and with desks and benches for the scholars, were either executed in a meager and insufficient manner, or were, in some cases, entirely neglected. The schools were generally found ill supplied with the apparatus of instruction; often, the only class-book was the Bible or Testament, desecrated as a horn-book, because indispensable for religious instruction, and on account of the low price at which it is sold by religious associations. If there were any other books, they were often in tatters. Black boards, easels, maps, and other indispensable apparatus of skilful instruction, were seldom to be found, except in the best schools.

The Reports of the Inspectors disclosed a relation between the imperfection of the school and the condition of the schoolmaster of the most painful character. Few efficient elementary schools exist in England, though the number of school-houses has of late years greatly increased.

The most prominent of the causes to which these defects are attributable is the fact, that the master of an elementary school is commonly in a position which yields him neither honour nor emolument. He has, therefore, a scanty knowledge even of the humblest rudiments of learning, meager ideas of the duties of his office, and even less skill in their performance.

There is little or nothing in the profession of an elementary schoolmaster, in this country, to tempt a man having a respectable acquaintance with the elements of even humble learning to exchange the certainty of a respectable livelihood in a subordinate condition in trade or commerce, for the mean drudgery of instructing the rude children of the poor in an elementary school, as it is now conducted.

For what is the condition of the master of such a school? He has often an income very little greater than that of an agricultural labourer, and very rarely equal to that of a moderately skilful mechanic. Even this income is to a great degree contingent on the weekly pittances paid from the earnings of his poor neighbours, and liable to be reduced by bad harvests, want of employment, strikes, sickness among the children, or, worst of all, by the calamity of his own ill-health.

Of late years he may more frequently have a small cottage rent-free, but seldom a garden or fuel.

Some portion of his income may be derived from the voluntary subscriptions of the promoters of the school—a precarious source, liable to be dried up by the removal or death of patrons, and the fickleness of friends.

Amidst these uncertainties, with the increase of his family his struggles are greater. He tries to eke out his subsistence by keeping accounts, and writing letters for his neighbours. He strives to be elected parish clerk, or registrar, or clerk to some benefit club. These additions to his income, if he be successful, barely keep him out of debt, and in old age he has no prospect but hopeless indigence and dependence.

To intrust the education of the labouring classes of this country to men involved in such straits, is to condemn the poor to ignorance and its fatal train of evils. To build spacious and well-ventilated schools, without attempting to provide a position of honour and emolument for the masters, is to cheat the poor with a cruel illusion. Even the very small number of masters now well trained in Normal and Model Schools, will find no situation in which their emoluments and prospects will be equal to those which their new acquirements and skill might insure if they should desert the profession of an elementary schoolmaster. Whilst their condition remains without improvement, a religious motive alone can induce the young men, who are now trained in Normal Schools, to sacrifice all prospects of personal advancement for the self-denying and arduous duties of a teacher of the children of the poor. Unless, therefore, concurrently with the arrangements made for training masters of superior acquirements and skill, efforts be also made to provide them with situations of decent comfort, and the prospect of a suitable provision for sickness and old age, they will be driven by necessity, or attracted by superior advantages, to commercial pursuits.

It may be well that the poor should give proof of the value they attach to the education of their children, by making some sacrifice from their earnings to promote the comfort of the schoolmaster, and should thus preserve a consciousness of their right to choose the school in which their children are to be trained, and to exercise some vigilance over the conduct of their master; but the social condition of the poor must be greatly superior to what the most sanguine can expect it will become in the next half-century, before they can afford to provide an adequate subsistence for the schoolmaster; and their moral and intellectual state must be at least equally improved, before they are prepared by the value they attach to the education of their children, to make sacrifices adequate to the remuneration of the teacher.

From the contributions of the poor, therefore, little

more can be expected in aid of the master's income, and that increase, if procurable, must be derived both from a more lively appreciation of the benefits of education to a labouring man, and from an improvement in his own means of subsistence.

But if it were otherwise, it may be doubted whether it would be a wise policy to make the schoolmaster dependent on the parents of his scholars for his entire income, for this would be to subject him to the caprices of the least intelligent classes, who would also certainly be the most vigilant and rigorous superiors.

Moreover, a provident charity can, by means of the village school, most gracefully interfere to elevate the condition of the poor, without undermining their independence or teaching them habits of servility; it would not therefore be wise to deprive the rich of a means of expressing their sympathy with the condition of the poor by means of a charity, in which the virtue of self-denial is not obscured by the degradation of the recipient.

The contributions which are annually dependent on the will of the donor, likewise afford him a most effectual means of stimulating the exertions of the master, and thus place the school to a great degree under the influence of the superior classes of society.

On these grounds, while on the one hand it may be doubted whether it is expedient to supersede either the weekly payments of the parents of the scholars, or the contributions of the more wealthy classes, by any fixed sources of income; on the other it is evident, that to leave the master dependent on the poor, and on the fluctuating charity of the rich, is to subject him, in the great majority of cases, to poverty in his office and to indigence and dependence when deprived of it by sickness or old age.

A certain portion of the schoolmaster's income should be attached to his office independently of all local sources of fluctuation and change; he should enjoy his house rent-free, and if possible be provided with a garden and fuel.

If then an estimate be made of his salary, on a scale equal to the position he ought to hold in society, one-third of this income should be certain. The smallest sum which ought to be secured to the master, besides a comfortable dwelling, should be £15 or £20, as part of an income of £45 or £60 per annum, and the condition of the master cannot be deemed respectably provided for, unless an income of £30 per annum be secured to him, besides what may be derived from school-pence, and from the contributions of the wealthy, which ought at least to raise this income to £90 per annum.

While the condition of the master is one of such privation and uncertainty, he has by the existing system of school instruction been placed in a situation, the difficulties of which are insuperable, even by the highest talent and skill, much less by men struggling with penury, exhausted with care, often ill-instructed, and sometimes assuming the duties of a most responsible office, only because deemed incompetent to strive for a livelihood in the open field of competition. Men so circumstanced, have been placed, without other assistants than monitors, in charge of schools containing from 150 to 300 scholars and upwards. The monitors usually employed are under twelve years of age, some of them being as young as eight or nine, and they are in general very ignorant, rude, and unskilful. The system of monitorial instruction has practically failed in this country because of the early period at which children are required for manufacturing and agricultural labour. It has been generally abandoned on the Continent on account of its comparative imperfection under any circumstances, but it was probably never exhibited under greater disadvantages than in England.

The earliest efforts of recent promoters of the education of the labouring classes were made in towns. The schools of towns are commonly large—the children are sent to work at a very early age—the population is migratory, and the school attendance short, irregular, and uncertain. One master was placed over a school containing for the most part from 200 to 400 children, and he was not supplied with any assistance, excepting what he could derive from the scholars committed to his charge. His own efforts to create an instructed class, which might render him this service, were constantly thwarted by the migration of the parents, by the removal of the child to work, and the extreme difficulty of combining the instruction and training of the monitorial class with such an attention to the whole school as would preserve order and discipline, and secure so much progress in the several classes as to furnish a proper succession in the first class of ripe scholars from whom to select the monitors.

Under such difficulties few masters succeeded in this country in creating and maintaining efficient monitorial schools, but they have succeeded exactly in proportion as they were enabled by local circumstances to retain the monitors beyond the age of 13 at the school, or were permitted by the trustees to pay them a small weekly stipend for their services, if they also gave them the advantage of separate instruction.

If this be the condition of the master, and if this be the character of the only assistance afforded him in the discipline and instruction of his school, is it a legitimate subject of surprise, that a very large proportion of the children attending elementary schools in this country should not even acquire the art of reading accurately, much less with ease and expression, and that all the higher aims of education should appear, notwithstanding constant school extension, to be unattainable? Can we wonder that the working classes should attach no value to an education so meager and worthless, and consequently that the school attendance of their children should not exceed a year and a half on the average throughout entire districts? Is it surprising that juvenile delinquency should be on the increase?

There are other features connected with the condition of elementary schools which are equally to be deplored. Too commonly their prosperity depends on the exertions and sacrifices of some benevolent individual. In Church of England schools, the labour and burthen of their maintenance often depend on the parochial clergyman; in Dissenting Schools, on some layman, who exhausts his resources and his time on the task of constantly rebuilding what always threatens to become a ruin. Even this want of sympathy of the laity of the Church, and the congregations of Dissenters, in the prosperity of their schools, is probably, in the first instance, a consequence of that inefficiency, which their apathy tends to perpetuate. The school exists, but produces no fruit; no one perceives that it exercises a civilising influence; when visited it is a scene of noise and disorder. It is obvious to a toil-worn member of the middle class of this country, that he has neither leisure, nor superfluous energy, to undertake the task of introducing order into this Babel. It fails to interest his sympathies; consequently elementary schools are visited by their supporters chiefly on the annual field-day of a paraded exhibition, when the children are initiated in a public imposture, and the promoters of the school are the willing and conscious dupes of a pious fraud.

The influence which the inadequacy of voluntary contributions, for the support of a system of elementary education, exerts on the condition even of the most prosperous Normal Schools, is not less remarkable.

The Normal Schools are at present supported partly by funds contributed by the Central Societies and Diocesan Boards, and partly by the sums paid by the patrons or friends of students to procure their settlement in the profession of schoolmasters, by obtaining for them the benefit of training in a Normal School.

As the Central Society contributes for the most part only half the requisite funds, or even less, the selection of the candidates for admission is narrowed to the class who are able and willing to pay for the admission of their children and dependents, and to the individuals whom they may present as candidates.

Unfortunately the tendency is to select young men wanting those natural energies, physical or mental, requisite for success in an independent career in life, and to seek, by means of the Normal Schools, to introduce into the profession of schoolmaster young persons, not from any peculiar fitness for this vocation, but rather on account of the absence of qualifications for any other.

The Principals of Normal Schools therefore complain, not only of their want of preparation for the course of instruction given in the Training Schools, because the candidates have not been grounded in ordinary elementary knowledge, but of the absence of the proper physical, mental, and moral qualifications. It is reported that a great number of the candidates and students of the Normal Schools show signs of scrofula, and that generally their physical temperament is sluggish and inert. They have too often had no further instruction than what can be obtained in an elementary school of average character, during the usual period of attendance, till 13 years of age. They do not for the most part enter into the profession from inclination, and it is therefore proportionately difficult to give the right moral direction to their minds, and to kindle in them energies equal to the difficulties they must encounter.

Ill-adapted as this class of students is for success in the Normal School, and likely as they are to fail in the elementary school when their training is (with whatever care) completed, the number of candidates presented by patrons and friends, on the terms of payment required by the Normal Schools, is barely sufficient to keep these schools in activity. There is therefore no opportunity for selection; and unless other sources be developed, even this imperfect supply is precarious, and liable soon to fail.

On these grounds it is of the utmost importance to the future prosperity of the Normal Schools, that the elementary schools should be rendered the means of educating a class of candidates for admission, who in their earliest youth should have been selected on account of their proficiency and skill, and whose progress in the several grades of monitor, pupil teacher, and assistant teacher, should not only have been the object of systematic care and continual vigilance, but whose ultimate selection should be made by the Inspector on the ground of their superiority, as proved by the experience of years, in all the qualifications required for success in the vocation of a schoolmaster.

On the other hand, it is important to provide for the Normal Schools a means of support which shall guarantee their efficiency by ensuring the application of the money to the completion of the training of teachers, whose instruction, character, and skill, have been the objects of years of vigilance and care.

The Minutes of the Committee of Council on Education, in August and December 1846, were intended to provide remedies for the evils which have been described in this chapter. Their Lordships desired to render the profession of schoolmaster honourable, by raising its character, by giving it the public recognition of impartially awarded certificates or diplomas, and by securing to well-trained or otherwise efficient masters a position of comfort during the period of their arduous labours, and the means of retirement on a pension awarded by the Government. They were also anxious to lighten their ill-requited toil in the school, by providing them with the aid of assistant teachers trained and instructed under their own eye, and adequate in number to the efficient management of the school.

The arrangements for rearing a body of skilful and highly instructed masters are to commence in the school itself, by the selection of the most deserving and proficient of the scholars, who are to be apprenticed from the age of 13 to that of 18. By the regulations determining the character of this apprenticeship, the school is to be in a condition fitting it to become a sphere for the training of a candidate for the office of schoolmaster. A great stimulus is thus offered to the scholars to qualify themselves by good conduct and by their attainments, for appointment as pupil teachers; to the promoters of the school to render its condition complete as respects fittings, apparatus, and the supply of books; and to the schoolmaster, so to order the discipline and instruction of the school, as to raise it to the proper standard of efficiency. But no requirements are made, limiting the discretion of the trustees, in the selection or dismissal of the master or mistress, in the dismissal of any assistant or pupil teacher, or either as to the books and apparatus to be used, the system of organisation to be adopted, or the methods of instruction to be pursued.

In each year of the apprenticeship, the pupil teacher is to be examined by Her Majesty's Inspector in a course of instruction, the subjects of which are enumerated in the regulations. Great care is to be taken that he live in a household where he will be under the constant influence of a good example. His religious instruction is to be conducted by the master of the school. In Church of England schools, this religious instruction will for the most part be under the superintendence of the parochial clergyman, but whenever the managers of the school are disposed to permit the apprenticeship in a Church of England school of a scholar whose parents do not belong to the Church of England, their Lordships have no desire to fetter their discretion in that respect, and would acquiesce in any reasonable arrangements which might be made between the managers and the parents for the religious training of their children. Though their Lordships have not by any of their Minutes attempted to enforce, they are nevertheless desirous to promote by their sanction and encouragement, such arrangements in Church of England schools as may provide for the admission of the children of persons not members of the Church of England, without any requirements inconsistent with the rights of conscience.

In schools not connected with the Church of England, the Committee of Council, acting on the third regulation of the 24th September, 1839, and on the Minute specially communicated to the British and Foreign School Society as related in the last chapter, will not direct the Inspector of such schools to examine the religious instruction of the apprentice. They desire to enable the promoters of schools connected with dissenting congregations, to accept the advantages impartially offered by their Minutes, without entering into any compromise of the opinions they entertain as to religious endowments. On these grounds their Lordships declare that they will accept the certificate of the managers of such schools that they are satisfied with the state of the religious knowledge of the pupil teacher. The Committee of Council thus intend to avoid making any requirement as to the character of such religious teaching beyond that contained in their Minute of the 3rd of December, 1839 (quoted in the last chapter), which states that 'the daily reading of a portion of the Scriptures shall form part of the instruction' of the school; nor do their Lordships require attendance on any particular Sunday school, or on any particular place of public worship; but at the close of each year will be satisfied if the managers certify that the pupil teachers have been attentive to their religious duties.

The scholars selected for apprenticeship will for the most part belong to families supported by manual labour; there is thus open to the children of such families, a career which could otherwise be rarely commenced. The first steps of their entrance into the honourable profession of a schoolmaster will be attended with an alleviation of the burthens, often ill-sustained by their parents, of supporting a family by manual industry. The pupil teacher will receive directly from the Government a stipend increasing from £10 at the close of the first year to £20 at the close of the fifth year of his apprenticeship. In many cases it is probable that the good conduct of the apprentice will secure additional rewards from the managers of the school, such as a supply of text-books on the prescribed subjects of instruction, or an annual grant of clothes, or an addition to his stipend. At the close of the apprenticeship, every pupil teacher who has passed the annual examination will be entitled to a certificate, declaring that he has successfully completed his apprenticeship. This certificate, as a testimonial of character and of attainments, would be in itself an invaluable introduction to the confidence of a merchant, or of the member of a learned profession, if the apprentice should then determine not to pursue the vocation of a schoolmaster. But the Government have extended their provident care even further. Every pupil teacher provided with a certificate at the close of his apprenticeship, may become a candidate for one or two employments under the patronage of the Government. In each Inspector's district, an annual examination will be held, to which all apprentices who have obtained their certificates will be admitted, to compete for the distinction of an exhibition entitling them to be sent as Queen's scholars to a Normal School under their Lordships' inspection. Such pupil teachers as are successful in obtaining a Queen's Scholarship, will thus be enabled to complete their training as schoolmasters, by passing through the course of discipline and instruction provided in a Normal School. They will thus have an opportunity of increasing their knowledge, improving their acquaintance with the best methods of instruction, and of becoming more experienced in the organisation and discipline of schools. At the close of each year's instruction in the Normal School, the students will be examined by one or more of Her Majesty's Inspectors, and upon such examination, their Lordships will award a certificate denoting one of three degrees of merit. Every master who leaves the Normal School with a certificate of the first degree of merit will be entitled to a grant of £15 or £20 per annum. If he obtain a certificate of the second degree of merit, a grant of £20 or £25 per annum; and for a certificate of the third degree of merit a grant of £25 or £30 per annum, on condition that the trustees and managers of the school of which he may have charge provide him with a house rent-free, and with a further salary equal to twice the amount of the grant.

A poor man's child may thus, at the age of thirteen, not only cease to be a burthen to his father's family, but enter a profession at every step in which his mind will expand, and his intellect be stored, and, with the blessing of God, his moral and religious character developed. His success will be acknowledged by certificates from authority. Honorary distinctions connected with solid advantages will be open to him. He may attain a position the lowest rewards of which are, that he shall occupy a comfortable dwelling, rent-free, with a salary of £45 or £60 per annum; and which may, if he complete his course of training be raised to a minimum stipend of £90 per annum.

Instead of having before him a life of arduous, ill-requited, and necessarily unsuccessful toil, if he had otherwise entered the profession of a schoolmaster, he will, on his settlement as master of a school, be enabled to organise that school with apprenticed assistants conducted by himself through a prescribed course of instruction from the age of 13 to that of 18. Thus aided by apprentices selected on account of merit, whose education will be completed under the eye of a vigilant inspection, his school will reward him by becoming a scene of order, and his scholars by their cheerful obedience and success. It will be the duty of the master to instruct the apprentices daily during one hour and a half after the usual school time, and to teach them the management of a school. If the numbers under his charge amount to 150, he may have six apprentices, and he will then receive a further addition of £21 per annum to his salary as a remuneration for the time and care bestowed on the education of these apprentices. A school so conducted could not fail to attract the confidence of the neighbouring poor. They would soon discover the great practical advantages of its discipline in moulding the habits, increasing the knowledge, and developing the mental energies of their children. They would perceive that education was not an unreal abstraction, affording no practical advantage, but a powerful means of promoting success in life, and of securing the happiness of their children.

On the other hand, if, at the close of his apprenticeship, the pupil-teacher shall be unable at the public competition to procure a Queen's Scholarship, the Government have opened to the unsuccessful candidates appointments in departments of the public service, which have hitherto been the objects of purely political patronage. The parents of poor families in the neighbourhood of any school will have an obvious interest in its efficiency, as a means of procuring for their children admission into departments of the public service with double or treble the wages of a working man, and the prospect of further promotion.

The Committee of Council have also shown a just consideration for the interest of the masters who, not having received a regular training in a Normal School, have at present charge of elementary education. Notwithstanding the low standard of acquirements, and the want of skill generally prevalent among the existing race of schoolmasters, there are among them men whose natural energies have triumphed over the difficulties of a neglected and ill-paid profession, and who, by self-education and natural sagacity, have attained a just reputation. The Committee of Council, desirous to avoid a practical injustice to such masters, and to offer incentives to all other teachers who may now have charge of schools, to qualify themselves for certificates, have resolved to admit untrained masters to an examination for three classes of certificates, corresponding with those to be granted in Normal Schools. The augmentation of salary annexed to such certificates will therefore be accessible to all meritorious schoolmasters; and, as it will not be necessary that a man of good education should, in order to enjoy this advantage, pass through the course of instruction given in a Normal School, the profession will probably attract men of character and acquirements.

The honour and emoluments of any profession are obviously among the chief inducements to its adoption.

Explanation of the Minutes of 1846

For the first time in the career of schoolmasters, they may obtain from authority the certificate of a successfully completed apprenticeship—the rank of Queen's Scholar, and three diplomas, denoting three degrees of attainments and merit. Through the whole period of their education, the Government offers rewards to stimulate exertions, and at length assists to establish them in a condition of comfort and respectability. These are circumstances likely in themselves to induce masters of schools to remain in their profession, even if we can suppose them to be insensible to motives of a higher character. But it is impossible to secure any position against vicissitude, and especially to prevent a deserving man from being plunged into privation by disabling sickness or infirmity, or robbed by unavoidable calamity of a provision for old age, Their Lordships have, therefore, rendered superannuation pensions accessible to masters distinguished by long and efficient services (adopting, as a minimum period, fifteen years, seven of which must have been spent in a school subject to inspection), and who by age or by any disabling infirmity are compelled to retire. It cannot be doubted that such arrangements will raise this profession in public estimation, by increasing its efficiency and respectability.

The Normal School is the most important institution in a system of elementary education. It has been before shown how desirable it is that the Normal School should be fed with students from the *élite* of the scholars educated in elementary schools. It cannot be expected that members of the middle class of society will, to any great extent in this country, choose the vocation of teachers of the poor. The system which renders Normal Schools dependent on that ambiguous support, rather intended to befriend persons of feeble character or physically infirm, than to give the largest amount of efficiency to elementary instruction, must impair the results which might otherwise be attained. To make every elementary school a scene of exertion, from which the highest ranks of teachers may be entered by the humblest scholar, is to render the profession of schoolmasters popular among the poor, and to offer to their children the most powerful incentives to learning. Every boy of character and ability who is first among his fellows may select this career, and in the majority of cases will do so. In his whole course he will be in vigorous competition with the pupil teachers of other schools; and thus the Queen's Scholars, who, after a public trial, are selected for admission into the Normal Schools, will be naturally the most gifted, and by persevering application, the best instructed and most skilful youths, which the elementary schools of the country can rear. Instead, therefore, of the complaint which the Principals of Normal Schools now make, that the students entering them are deficient in physical and mental energy, and for the most part in knowledge even of the humblest rudiments of learning; the Queen's Scholars who are after public competition admitted, will have passed through an elementary course of instruction in religion, in English grammar and composition, in the history of their country, in arithmetic, algebra, mensuration, the rudiments of mechanics, in the art of land-surveying and levelling, in geography, and such elements of nautical astronomy as are comprised in the use of the globes. Their skill in conducting a class will have been developed by five years' experience as assistants in a common school. To these attainments will in many cases be added a knowledge of the theory and skill in the art of vocal music, and also, in some cases, of drawing from models, or linear drawing. The Normal Schools, therefore, will be fed with a class of students much superior to that which now enters them.

The expense of supporting a Normal School in efficiency is a burthen too heavy to be borne by purely voluntary contributions. The cost of the maintenance and education of each student is about £50 per annum; the annual expenditure on a Normal School, containing 100 students, must therefore be £5000. If the training of each student be continued for three years, little more than 30 schoolmasters will annually enter the profession from such a school, and when the number of schools which ought to exist in the country is compared with this annual supply, it is obvious that if Normal Schools are to be the chief sources from which the ranks of this profession are to be replenished, the outlay for the support of such a system is in itself greater than anything which has ever been contemplated by a scheme of purely charitable contribution. Their Lordships have, however, by the plan of apprenticeship, at the same time provided both for the increased efficiency of the elementary school, and for the completion of a considerable portion of the training of the candidate before he enters the Normal School; it is probable, therefore, that the period of instruction in Normal Schools may in the case of Queen's Scholars be reduced from three years to a shorter term. The remaining expenses are in part to be met by assistance afforded by the Government. Every Queen's Scholar will have an exhibition of £20 or £25, which sum will be applied towards the expenses attending his education during the first year in a Normal School. At the close of that year, if he be successful in obtaining a certificate, a second contribution of £20 will be made to the school, so that in the first year of the training of a Queen's Scholar, four-fifths of the expense may be borne by the Government. At the close of the second year £25 are to be paid, and at the close of the third year £30, if the student obtain a certificate of merit in each year. In the two latter years, therefore, the Government will defray one-half of the cost of his training. With such liberal arrrangements for their support, it is probable that the number of Normal Schools will rapidly increase. A wide scope is still left for charitable contributions towards the erection of the requisite buildings, two-thirds of which outlay must be derived from private subscriptions; and in the maintenance of the schools, one-third at least of the expense will devolve on private charity, even if the Queen's Scholars should form a considerable proportion of the students entering the schools. One-half the charge of educating candidates who are not Queen's Scholars, will obviously devolve on private benevolence.

The efficiency of elementary schools will doubtless establish the confidence of the poor in these institutions, and increase the period of school attendance for their children. Some time must however elapse, ere parents struggling with poverty will consent to forego even those small additions to the weekly income of their families, which are derived from the humble earnings of their children at a tender age. The difference of popular opinion in Scotland on the advantage of education for the child of a poor man, as compared with that sentiment in England, is a remarkable proof of the natural influence of a system of national education, in raising the estimate among the poor of the value of mental and moral endowments. In Scotland, especially among the rural population, every labourer is willing to undergo privations to provide that education for his children which he deems essential to their success in this life, and to their preparation for another state of existence. This opinion is grounded not more on a shrewd estimate of the causes which promote the advancement of their children, than of that deep religious instinct which characterises the Scotch as a nation. There is nothing in the opinion of the poor in England as to the value of education, at all comparable to the sagacious foresight and profound and pious feeling which prompt the Scotch parent to make sacrifices for this object. The Committee of Council have however been unwilling, in the absence of such sentiments, to resort to any compulsory arrangements to procure school attendance. Such expedients they have regarded as ill suited to the genius of this country; they have been desirous to vindicate the parental right to determine the nature and extent of the education to be given to the child, and to promote the growth of a livelier sense of the benefits of education by the increased efficiency of the schools, and also by arrangements intended to show the labouring man, that considerable knowledge and mental cultivation are compatible with the hardihood necessary to sustain the rudest forms of toil, and to meet the privations of a labourer's life. With this view their Lordships have been disposed to promote the establishment of Schools of Industry. In rural districts, field-gardens may be advantageously connected with the school. The master may superintend the instruction of the scholars during half the day in the culture of a garden, and may devote the rest of the time to the ordinary school instruction. If the school field-garden were divided into allotments, for which a rent was paid by the scholars, the cultivation of these garden plots would afford a larger addition to the income of the labourer's family, than the earnings of a child in the casual employments of farming labour.

In the denser parts of great cities, a large, and possibly an increasing number of children have no training in any handicraft, but seek a precarious livelihood by coster-mongering; by casual employment in errands; and in small services to persons whom they encounter in the streets. Such habits naturally tend to mendicancy, va-grancy, petty thefts, and the criminal career and vagabond life of a juvenile delinquent. Such children have often no home; the father is dead, or has absconded; the mother may be a prostitute, or may have married and deserted her offspring; or the child has fled from the drunken violence or loathsome selfishness of his parents. Many sleep under the open arches of the markets, or of the areas of the houses of ancient construction; in deserted buildings, out-houses, and cellars, and rise in the morning not knowing where or how to obtain a meal. Others are driven forth by their parents to beg or to steal, and not allowed to eat until they have brought home the produce of their knavery or cunning. Some live in the haunts of professed thieves, are trained in all the arts of pilfering, instructed how to elude the police, and to evade the law. They are reared to regard society as their enemy, and property as a monstrous institution on which they may justly prey. The majority of this class of children are practically heathens. They probably never heard the name of Christ. Christianity has done nothing for them.

The most obvious advantage to be offered to such children is the means of earning a livelihood by training them in some handicraft requiring skill. If every such child had the opportunity of entering a workshop in which he could acquire the art of a smith, or a carpenter, or a cooper, or other similar trade, and after some hours of application was provided with a coarse but wholesome meal, it is not to be doubted that many, attracted not less by the sympathy which such arrangements would prove to exist for their forlorn condition, than by the opportunity of escaping from the misery of a life of crime and privation, would become assiduous scholars in such schools of industry. If also an hour or two daily were set apart for instruction in the general outline of Christian faith and duty, and in the rudiments of humble learning, how many children might we not hope would be saved from ruin. To promote such arrangements, their Lordships have offered assistance towards the erection of the requisite buildings, towards the purchase of tools, and for the encouragement of the master workmen by granting gratuities for every boy who, in consequence of skill acquired in the workshop, shall have become a workman or assistant in any trade or craft whereby he is earning a livelihood.

The domestic arrangements of the poor are often extremely defective, from the want of a knowledge of the commonest arts and maxims of household economy. A girl who works in a factory or a mine, or who is employed from an early hour in the morning until the evening in field labour, has little or no opportunity to acquire the habits and skill of a housewife. Even the rudest traditions of domestic thrift are liable to be lost, when public employment interferes so much with the proper training of the labourer's daughter at home. Commerce offers a larger variety of productions for the sustenance of the common people of this country, than of any other; but they are unacquainted with the use of any articles of food besides those which are of home production, with the exception of tea, coffee, and sugar. From these defects, a considerable portion of the earnings of the labourer is unskilfully wasted, his home is deprived of comfort which he might otherwise enjoy, and discontent often drives him to dissipation.

To remedy these evils it has been proposed to make the school itself a means of instructing and training girls in the arts of domestic economy. It has been conceived, that a considerable portion of the oral lessons given in the girls' school, might be devoted to the subject of household management, and that if a wash-house and kitchen were connected with the school, they might, by proper arrangements, receive a practical training in cottage cookery, and in the care of the clothes of a labourer's family. For the encouragement of such plans their Lordships have proposed to grant assistance towards the erection of the requisite buildings, and gratuities to the mistress for success in the instruction of her scholars.

The social tendencies of the plans contemplated in the Minutes of the Committee of Council on Education for August and December, 1846, are, therefore, to raise the character and position of the schoolmaster; to provide for him a respectable competency; to make arrangements for rearing a race of more highly instructed masters by the establishment and support of a larger number of Normal Schools; to feed those Normal Schools with candidates having much higher attainments and greater skill and energy than those which have hitherto entered them; to render the school popular among the poor, as a means of introducing their children to more honourable and profitable employments, and by its increased efficiency to create in the minds of the working class a juster estimate of the value of education for their children. These combined influences will, it is hoped, raise considerably the standard of instruction among the humbler classes, and promote the growth of a truly Christian civilisation.

CHAPTER IV.

THE MINUTES OF AUGUST AND DECEMBER, 1846, CONSIDERED IN THEIR RELIGIOUS AND POLITICAL ASPECT.

HAVING thus sketched the social tendencies of the measures contemplated in the Minutes of the Committee of Council for August and December, 1846, we are naturally led to examine their religious and political aspect. For this purpose a slight retrospect of previous events may be useful, in attempting to illustrate the adaptation of these measures to the state of public opinion, and the condition of society in this country. For many years prior to the creation of the Committee of Council in 1839, a conviction of the necessity of the interference of the State, to promote the education of the people, had gathered strength both in political circles and among many classes of Dissenters. On the other hand, the Established Church still cherished the desire and expectation, that the ancient function of the Church, as defined in her ecclesiastical law, might be revived, and that the education at least of the common people might be confided to her hands. Among the younger and more earnest members of her communion, lay as well as clerical, extensive plans for this end were cherished. At that time, however, it may be doubted whether, except among the able men who had formed these large conceptions, the civil aspects of elementary education had been sufficiently regarded by churchmen. The school it is probable was, in the conception of the majority of the clergy and laity, simply a means of spreading Christian truth, and of establishing the discipline and ceremonial of the Church in the convictions and sympathies of the great mass of the population. It was scarcely believed that it could enter into the conceptions of statesmen to regard religion as a primary and indispensable element of education. They imagined that the statesmen of this country relied solely on the cultivation of the intellect, and on the spread of secular knowledge, for the growth of a higher morality, and for the promotion of the public order and well-being of society; and while they justly repudiated the gross and mischievous error, that a purely secular knowledge was capable of establishing society on an immutable basis of social order, or was even necessarily connected with a high condition of public morality, it is to be apprehended that they had fallen into the opposite fallacy, and were not convinced how important it was to raise the intellectual condition of the people for the purpose of promoting the growth of true religion. Yet this was surely a strange want of foresight in those who would avoid the extremes of fanaticism on either hand, viz., that of presumptuous ignorance, and that of abject superstition. While these suspicions of the tendencies of the interference of the Government were entertained by the great body of churchmen, they had not arrived at any distinct conception of the amount of secular instruction which it was desirable to communicate to the poor. A considerable portion of the clergy and laity of this country confidently held the conviction that the inevitable tendency of an elevated secular instruction was to unsettle the minds of the working classes—to unfit them for a life of manual labour—to render them discontented with their station, and if such instruction were general it was feared that it would prepare an universal insurrection of the poor against the rich. Such as did not hold these doctrines with distinctness, did not believe that the state of the labouring poor could be materially improved by education; and were of opinion that the best condition that could be expected was that of quiet homage, which, though characterised by no energies, and accompanied with few virtues beyond patience and submission, was yet consistent with their highest conceptions of the condition of a race, which appeared to exist only to labour and to die. The ideas which were formed of the influences that Christianity might have on the minds and hearts of such a population were necessarily low. It may be doubted whether the Saxon serf under the teaching of the early English Bishops had not a livelier interest in Christianity, and was not a devouter and more consistent member of his Church than the pauper of the southern counties of England. Accordingly at that time little was attempted in the parochial school except instruction in reading and in writing, and the repetition of the catechism. The school had little or no influence on the intelligence — on the habits or character of the population, and as a means of inculcating religious truths it utterly failed.

On the other hand, there was much in the opinions of a certain class of politicians to justify the suspicions with which the clergy and a large body of the laity regarded proposals for the interference of Government in the education of the people. Among such politicians it was a favourite doctrine to represent the certainty of the exact sciences, the harmony that prevailed as to the results of experimental philosophy, and to contrast these conditions of scientific investigation with the almost endless diversities of opinion on morals and religion. Some went so far as to assert that it was obvious that religion ought to be excluded altogether from the education of the young, and to be examined only by a mature and vigorous intellect. According to them, the proper occupation of a young mind was to examine and contemplate in the laws of the material world, the proofs of a first great Cause, and to trace by the evidence of nature, the majesty, power, justice and mercy of the Supreme Being. Yet they did not include even in this chain of investigation, the history of man, the operation of all external causes upon his mind, or the inward emotions and outward acts of that spirit, which surely must in a higher degree exhibit a natural revelation of that great first and benignant Cause. According to this class of reasoners, that knowledge could alone be deemed divine which was capable of a rational demonstration commanding universal assent, and all knowledge in which such assent had not been obtained, must in every case but one necessarily be human. Leave then, said they, the dogmas of churches and sects to be examined by an intellect matured in the study of an exact philosophy, and present, for the first time, the choice of a religion to those whom you have thus taught to discriminate between falsehood and truth.

There were others whose views were more superficial, who proposed the diffusion of useful knowledge, not simply because of its influence in dispelling the anarchical tendencies of popular ignorance, in expanding the intellect, and promoting the refinement of manners, but who appeared to rely upon it as a moral panacea by teaching men how prudent it was to be wise, how useful to be virtuous, how politic to be honest, and that the greatest happiness of the greatest number was a condition certain to be attained by proving the convenience of virtue and the suicidal tendencies of vice.

To another class equally sincere, but who consider education as appertaining alone to civil government, the establishment of schools on a simply secular basis appeared the only practicable solution of the difficulties with which this question was encumbered. Agreeing among themselves in the civilising tendencies of secular instruction, and having no hope of reconciling the differences of rival religious parties, they conceived that the only way of removing these obstacles was the establishment of a school of purely secular learning, it being provided that religious instruction should be conducted by the ministers of the different communions at periods set apart for that purpose. Such politicians did not appear to foresee that a religious country could not tolerate a body of schoolmasters without religion; that it would be impossible to avoid a provision for the religious education of schoolmasters in Normal Schools; that the selection of the master of each elementary school would form an interminable subject of discord; and that while they ineffectually attempted to evade these difficulties in the elementary schools, it was impossible they should elude them in the constitution of the Normal School. On very different grounds indeed was it that Doctor Hook, at a recent period, witnessing on every side of him the frightful evils of a want of education among the poor, despairing that the energies of the Church could be effectually exerted for the removal of these evils, and having no confidence in what is called the voluntary system, invoked with a cry of despair the interference of the Government to found a system of secular education, leaving only to religious communions the establishment and support of Normal Schools. When Dr. Hook proposed that instruction in the elementary school should be confined to secular knowledge, he provided at the same time that certificates should be presented of the attendance of the child on Sunday, and on two other days in the week, on a school of religion to be founded and supported by the religious communion to which the parents of the scholar belonged. This proposal originated in the conviction that the secular instruction communicated by masters religiously educated, would be pervaded by a religious spirit, and that such instruction so given would form a most useful preparation for the religious teaching which the child was to receive on Sunday and on two other days in the week. By such means it is obvious that Dr. Hook expected to triumph over the radical defects of the school of purely secular instruction, and felt confident that by concentrating the energies of the country on the establishment and support of combined schools, the spirit of Christianity would inevitably penetrate the whole instruction even of the secular school, while the secular learning energised the instruction given in the school of religion.

Some years previously to 1839, however, a preference had been given to the establishment of a purely secular school, on grounds essentially differing from those which influenced Dr. Hook. The class of politicians who espoused these views were active, vigorous, and intelligent, and they did not fail, in the absence of any efficient system of instruction in the country, to obtain a considerable though transient influence on public opinion. When therefore the prevalence of such opinions among a certain class of politicians occasioned alarm in the religious communions of Great Britain, they not unnaturally adopted the unjust suspicion that the interference of Government must, in the very nature of things, be exerted for a system of education from which religion must be excluded. Yet these opinions were never entertained by the leading statesmen of either of the two great parties in Parliament. Lord John Russell, in his letter to Lord Lansdowne in 1839, had declared that ' it is Her Majesty's wish that the youth of this kingdom should be *religiously* brought up, and that the rights of conscience should be respected.'

This continued to a great extent to be the condition of opinions and parties at the period when the Committee of Council was established in 1839. At that period, as we have said, a body of young and able men had arisen in the Church, who did not despair of elevating the system of secular instruction imparted in her schools, and of bringing about a total change in the opinions of a majority of the clergy and laity as to the mutual influences of secular and religious teaching, and the necessity of both for the developement of a truly Christian civilisation among the poor. At the same time a considerable body of Dissenters, having confidence in the vigour with which the liberal Government of that day had defended the great interests of civil and religious liberty, anxiously claimed the interference of Government for the establishment of an impartial system of national education. They proposed a Board of Education, and the establishment of a vigorous inspection of schools; they claimed the application of a larger portion of the public resources, and appeared to be content that the Church should receive a share of the Parliamentary grants in a proportion corresponding to her exertions, if the Dissenting Communions, through the medium of the British and Foreign School Society, might obtain an equal degree of encouragement.

It was under these circumstances that, as has been related in the first chapter, the Committee of Council on Education was created by an Order in Council. That Committee has since its establishment continued to distribute the Parliamentary grants for promoting education, without deviating in any degree from the principles then espoused by the Dissenting, and especially by the Congregational Communions, and which were declared in petitions presented to Parliament during the education controversy of 1839.

Such being the condition of opinions and parties, it will be less useful for us to trace the gradual growth of the Parliamentary Grant from £30,000 per annum to £100,000 in 1846, or to describe in detail what have been the subordinate objects to which the Committee of Council have directed their attention, than to examine what indications of the state of public opinion have transpired since 1839, which may be presumed to have formed grounds for the adoption of the recent Minutes of the Committee of Council, dated August and December 1846.

One of the earliest proposals of the Committee of Council was the establishment, in 1839, of Normal and Model Schools. We have already said that these Normal and Model Schools were proposed, for the purpose of improving the instruction and training of schoolmasters, in order to awaken public attention to the importance of such institutions, and to offer an example of their organisation, course of instruction, and management. The constitution of the Normal School was necessarily declared by the Government, but though no such intention had been entertained, this constitution was at once regarded by almost all religious parties, as a type of the constitution of schools which the Committee of Council intended to establish throughout the country. The Normal and Model Schools were to be institutions of combined education, upon a religious basis. It was declared that 'religion was to be combined with the whole matter of instruction, and to regulate the entire system of discipline.' That 'religious instruction was to be regarded as general and special. That periods were to be set apart for such peculiar doctrinal instruction as might be required for the religious training of the children. That the chaplain should conduct the religious instruction of children whose parents or guardians belonged to the Established Church. That the parent or guardian of any other child should be permitted to procure the attendance of the licensed minister of his own persuasion, at the period appointed for special religious instruction, in order to give such instruction apart. That a licensed minister should be appointed to give such special religious instruction, wherever the number of children in attendance on the Model School belonging to any body dissenting from the Established Church should be such as to appear to this Committee to require such special provision.' It was intended, as before stated, that the general religious instruction should resemble that given in British and Foreign Schools from the Holy Scriptures, without peculiar interpretation, and that such doctrinal instruction should be given only at times set apart. The constitution of the Normal and Model Schools was to be one of combined education on a basis of religious equality. As the various religious communions refused to accept any assurance from the Government, that the constitution of this school was not to be regarded as the type of a predetermined plan of national education, the reception of this proposal must be regarded as that which would have attended an attempt to establish a system of combined education on the basis of religious equality. Considered from this point of view the results were most instructive, as to the state of public opinion and the condition of parties in the country.

This supposed scheme of combined national education received such unqualified and persevering opposition on the part of the Ecclesiastical Establishments of England and Scotland, and of the Conference and congregations of the Wesleyan connection, that it was not only very soon withdrawn, even as a constitution for the Normal and Model Schools, but the proposal itself so far endangered the existence of the Committee of Council on Education, that the Parliamentary Grant of 1839 was, after prolonged discussion, only carried by a majority of two; and the House of Lords voted, by a majority of 111, an Address to the Queen, which a considerable number of peers and prelates carried to the foot of the throne, praying that Her Majesty would be 'graciously pleased to give directions that no steps should be taken with respect to the establishment or foundation of any plan for the general education of the people of this country, without giving to this House, as one branch of the legislature, an opportunity of fully considering a measure of such importance to the highest interests of the community.'

Again, in the year 1843, another proposal, which was received as an indication of an intention to establish a system of combined education, was made by Sir Robert Peel's Government, in the education clauses of the Bill to regulate the employment of children and young persons in factories, and for the better education of the children in factory districts. These clauses provided for the establishment and support of schools.

The constitution of the schools thus proposed to be created, may be described as one of combined education on the basis of religious toleration.

The opinion of the Church of England, and the Church of Scotland, and of the Conferences and congregations of Wesleyan dissenters, had been unequivocally declared to be hostile to a system of combined education on the basis of religious equality. It remained to be seen among what parties a system of combined education, based on the principle of toleration, would find favour, and by whom it would be rejected.

On the announcement of this measure it was received with a simple and calm acquiescence by the Established Church. But the British and Foreign School Society, the Sunday School Union, and the Congregational Dissenters united with the Conference and congregations of the Wesleyan connection, and the other associations of Methodists, in vehement and persevering resistance. It is unnecessary to examine the circumstances, which had been accessory to this almost universal opposition of Dissenters to a measure, which embodied, with respect to education, the existing state of the law of this country as to religion. It cannot be doubted, that the House of Commons sympathised less with this agitation, than with that which had occasioned the withdrawal of the plan for the establishment of a Normal and Model School in 1839.

The leaders of the opposition in Parliament regarded the extreme form which the objections assumed with regret, and though wishing to aid Dissenters in procuring every reasonable guarantee for civil and religious liberty, were anxious that decisive measures for the education of the people should not be postponed. If, therefore, there had been any hope, that even a considerable section of the opponents of the measure would have considered modifications for the protection of their interests, they would certainly have been listened to with the utmost attention by the Government, and would probably have been seconded by the co-operation of the opposition, not in factious resistance to the administration of Sir Robert Peel, but with an anxious desire to assist him, in disentangling the complexed skein of this difficult controversy. The Government, therefore, with a regret which it did not conceal, but with the dignity of a wise forbearance, did not use the power which it undoubtedly possessed to pass this measure into a law, in opposition to the almost universal protest of the religious communions of England and Wales dissenting from the Established Church. This, which was esteemed the second measure of combined education brought forward by the Government, was therefore withdrawn.

In 1843 Mr. Roebuck, during the discussions on the education clauses of the Factory Bill, moved 'that in no plan of education maintained and enforced by the State, should any attempt be made to inculcate peculiar religious opinions; because, as such an attempt would be considered a plan for maintaining and strengthening an undue superiority of one sect over all others, the animosities and strife already existing among different religious denominations would thereby unhappily be greatly increased, and the cordial co-operation of all sects and denominations, which is absolutely necessary to secure the success of any plan of public education, rendered impossible.' This motion Mr. Roebuck supported with his usual acuteness and vigour, but it was lost by a majority of 96, the Ayes being 60, and the Noes 156.

There were still politicians and men of justly acquired and extensive influence among the Dissenting communions, who conceived that a system of combined education, on a purely secular basis, would obtain a more favourable reception from the country. A Parliamentary Committee had sat, apparently with a view to investigate this subject. The Central Society of Education, though it did not avowedly embody any positive declaration of opinion, and comprised among its supporters many gentlemen who had never embraced such a doctrine, yet by the general tendency of its publications, had indirectly supported this view with great ability. Other motions had been made in the House of Commons, supported by speeches delivered by veteran political economists, in which the attention of the Government had been called to this mode of solving the difficulties of the question. Such advocacy had, however, produced little or no effect on the opinions of churchmen, or of the majority of the religious communions dissenting from the Church. The possibility of establishing a system of combined education on this basis, however, attracted great attention when Dr. Hook, in 1846, demanded on behalf of religion and morality, and also on behalf of the Church which he had served with zeal, that all should unite to make a sacrifice of interest and prejudice, in short of everything but principle, in order that the power of the Government might be successfully exerted for the instruction of the poor. Dr. Hook possessed, in a pre-eminent degree, the confidence of high churchmen. No one could suspect him of any unworthy concession of the claims of the Church or of religion. When, therefore, he earnestly proclaimed his desire to relinquish, on the part of the Church, any desire for predominance; when he sought to place the Church on the same level with the Dissenting communions with respect to the education of the poor, and to forego his own preference for a system of religious education, rather than leave the poor in ignorance; this plan of providing for education was introduced to the consideration of churchmen under the most favourable auspices. They placed confidence in the sincerity of his zeal, and if any advocacy short of a concurrence of opinion among distinguished prelates could have reconciled the Established Church of England to such a plan, the vigour and ability with which Dr. Hook espoused this cause must have had this effect. On the other hand, among Dissenters, a very able and distinguished minister, Dr. Vaughan, the President of the Independent College at Manchester, and the editor of the British Quarterly Review, threw the weight of his character and the influence of his powerful advocacy into the same scale. Some of the leading journals of liberal politics likewise assiduously promoted the success of this proposal. It was impossible not to regard with interest the effect which might be produced on public opinion by such a combination in favour of a system of combined education on a secular basis. This experiment it appeared would exhaust, by a final test, the question of combining in one system of education the different religious communions of England.

The result of this appeal to public opinion seemed to be unequivocal. A great number of pamphlets appeared from the clergy of the Established Church, others from laymen and ministers of Dissenting congregations, all uniting in a rejection of the plan, and the majority of them calling upon Government to continue the system of encouraging the extension and improvement of elementary education, by grants in aid of schools connected with the Church of England and the Church of Scotland, with the British and Foreign School Society, and with the congregations of Dissenting communions. Mr. Edward Baines, jun., of Leeds, occupying a position of great influence in the metropolis of Dissent, addressed to Lord John Russell twelve letters of the most earnest deprecation and warning; entered into a controversy with Dr. Vaughan, though belonging to the same religious persuasion; and endeavoured with much success to excite among the non-conformists of England, not only opposition to the plan of Dr. Hook, but also to the abstract principle of the right of the Government to promote the education of the people. The great majority of churchmen therefore appeared to regard the scheme of combined secular education, though emanating from Dr. Hook, with disfavour, and Mr. Baines was successful in exciting among Dissenters a general alarm lest Government should be induced, by any combination of circumstances, to adopt this plan.

The Government had however never wavered in its adherence to the principle adopted in 1839, that religion should be mixed with the entire matter of instruction in the school, and regulate the whole of its discipline; and though the proposal of Dr. Hook might be regarded, by sagacious politicians, as one of great interest in determining the drift of public opinion, it was, in political circles, regarded as impracticable.

It is now necessary to take a brief restrospect of the progress of opinion among various ranks of society, on the subject of elementary education, from 1839 to 1846. The first efforts to raise elementary schools above the common level of the monitorial system, were made one or two years prior to the establishment of the Committee of Council on Education, and continued wherever opportunity offered after that period. Among efforts of this kind may be enumerated the organisation of the School of Industry at Norwood; the improvement of a considerable number of Schools of Industry under the Poor Law Commission; the system of instruction exhibited in some parochial schools, such as that of Battersea; the reformation of the Upper and Lower Schools of the Royal Hospital at Greenwich; the foundation of the Battersea Training School, and subsequently of St. Mark's College, of the Chester Diocesan Training School, of schools for the training of Schoolmistresses at Whitelands, Salisbury, and Warrington; the extension of the means of instruction for teachers, and the prolongation of their period of training in the Normal Schools of the British and Foreign School Society in the Borough Road; the foundation of Normal Schools in the Dioceses of York and Ripon, and Durham, with the commencement of similar institutions on a smaller scale in other dioceses; the erection of buildings for Normal Schools connected with the Church of Scotland in Edinburgh and Glasgow, and of similar institutions for the Free Church in both those cities; the fact that a considerable number of trained schoolmasters had been introduced by the Education Committee of the Wesleyan Conference from Scotland, to take charge of the day schools established by their congregations; the origin of a Dissenting Training School for Mistresses at Rotherhithe, and the establishment of another for Welsh teachers at Brecon. All these circumstances were proofs that the necessity of improving the condition of elementary education had at length attracted a large share of public attention, and was likely to call forth considerable exertions. The condition of the vast majority of elementary schools continued to be much as we have described it in the third chapter, but a great change had occurred in public opinion. The education of the poor was no longer a subject of popular apprehension, as likely to lead to social disorder. The best condition of the working classes of this country was no longer considered to be one of unenterprising contentment, uninstructed reverence, and unrepining submission. Public opinion appeared gradually to prepare itself for the effort, great and difficult though it might be, to overcome the obstacles to the establishment of a system of national education, by which the labouring classes might be made the intelligent supporters of order, and might adopt a faith not without knowledge.

The difficulties opposing the accomplishment of this great object, appeared to be insurmountable by private benevolence. The Normal Schools which had been established were struggling with great pecuniary embarrassment. The parochial schools were indebted to a great extent to the sacrifices made from the incomes of clergymen of slender stipends, often of humble curates. They still continued to be very meagerly furnished with the apparatus of instruction, and the teachers were generally unskilful, ill paid, and overworked, having to supply by their own untrained abilities, all the defects of the monitorial system. In schools not connected with the Church of England, the embarrassments had sometimes become extreme. Several of these schools were burthened with debts incurred at the period of their erection, at the time of Joseph Lancaster's teaching. Some schools had been sold for the redemption of these burthens; others exhibited in their accounts a continually increasing deficit. In all school committees, whether of the Church or of Dissent, the necessity of resorting to continual efforts to sustain the income of the school by public meetings, examinations, sermons, bazaars, fancy fairs, personal canvassing for subscriptions, canvassing by letter, and similar expedients, were confessed to entail a scarcely tolerable burthen of humiliating exertion on the promoters of schools. What had been accomplished towards the improvement of elementary education was rare and isolated. The common phenomenon was its disheartening imperfection, if not its complete failure. The question therefore presented to the Government, under the circumstances which we have related, was—is this condition inevitable? Has the failure of every proposal for the establishment of a system of combined education precluded the interference of the Government? Is there no other way in which the national resources can be applied to rescue the people from ignorance and vice, and from consequent crime and disorder? Can no expedient be devised, by which the State may be enabled to substitute the reward and encouragement of virtuous actions for a system of coercion and punishment? Are the common people necessarily and permanently (in the complications of modern civilisation) excluded from the possession of knowledge, from the softening influences of art, and from the transforming power of a well-grounded faith?

Little reflection is necessary to show why a Statesman should prefer a system of combined education. A combined school is in itself not a mere external sign of harmony. Where it is possible, such an institution might tend to soften the prejudices which may be fostered, when the population is reared in separate schools, obviously liable to degenerate into hostile camps, in which the scholars may be trained for future conflicts. A combined school also concentrates on one institution the resources which must otherwise be divided among several; and as it tends to diminish the expense of an efficient system of education, renders its establishment more easy. The principle of local assessment for the support of the school, of boards of management representing the rate-payers, and elected according to our popular forms of municipal government, together with the subordinate apparatus of an audit of accounts by public officers, and the complete publicity which attends all our civic arrangements; the fact that such a system being established by statute, would be in itself a purely civil arrangement, are circumstances which have strongly recommended the adoption of a system of combined education to the legislature. The means by which the interests of the minority may be protected from the encroachments of a too powerful majority when intolerant, are also, in a combined system of education, more within the control of Parliament, than in a system of separate schools. But experience shows, that against such arrangements the religious sympathies of the country revolt. Every system of combined education which has been proposed, whether on a purely secular basis, or on that of toleration, or on that of religious equality, has been rejected promptly, if not indignantly, by the religious communions of England.

According to the conscientious convictions of the religious bodies of this country, the school is a part of the machinery of a Christian congregation. They are of opinion, that its management should be confided to certain of the most respectable communicants of the Church, or to the elders, deacons, or class leaders of the congregation. The office of school manager is so strongly regarded by them as partaking a religious character, that in the Church it has been doubted whether it was not a purely clerical function; and though a more mature consideration of the subject has convinced churchmen that school management is a Christian office, devolving on the laity, not simply of right but as one which they may not avoid, there is the utmost unwillingness both in the Church and among the congregations of Dissenters, to commit the management of schools to other than religiously-minded men, who may fitly represent the congregation to which the school is attached. From the conviction that education is primarily a religious institution, have arisen the objections to the interference of the State, even for the purpose of improving all its secular arrangements, and raising the standard of its purely literary instruction. The perseverance of successive Governments in the adoption of the principle, that religion is the foundation on which education must be built, has vindicated Statesmen from the suspicion to which we have previously alluded, that they valued education solely because of their confidence in the influence of purely secular learning. But though the Church of England and the Church of Scotland, the Free Church of that country, and the Wesleyan Dissenters have no abstract aversion to State endowment, there is on all hands an insuperable objection to subordinate religion to purely civil authority. On these grounds it is obvious, that arrangements which should leave the election of the committee of school managers to the rate-payers of each school district, would to the religious congregations be intolerable. Experience also shows that the instruction in religion, given in separate schools, is seldom of that dogmatic character which delights to bring into undue prominence the distinguishing doctrines. In fact, such instruction treats generally of the Christian faith as common to all orthodox communions. Among the poor such differences are not perceived, and though this must often, it is feared, be attributed to their ignorance and indifference, yet the truth also is, that the danger to be incurred from the zeal of proselytism, by a child of 13, is small. On the other hand, it may be doubted whether the separate class-rooms of a combined school would not encourage more dogmatic doctrinal teaching, by apparently making it the duty of the religious instructor to dwell on those distinctions, which are the motives and apologies for religious divisions. It may further be apprehended, that the common basis of religious instruction in a combined school would prove a constant source of jealousy and suspicion, and thus disturb the management with continual bickerings, and array against each other, in the constituency of the school district, hostile parties for a perpetual religious feud.

Under these circumstances, the Government have apparently deliberated, whether it is desirable (for a problematical benefit, only to be obtained by a total change in the feelings of the religious congregations of this country) to persevere in efforts to establish a combined system of education. The demand for an improvement in popular instruction is urgent, and Lord John Russell, immediately after accepting from the Queen her commands to form an administration, announced his intention to employ the power confided to him for this purpose. It was desirable to ascertain, whether a system could not be devised, capable of adapting itself to separate schools, so as to encourage voluntary contributions for their support, to stimulate the activity of their management, and to promote their efficiency, by rendering it one of the conditions on which aid should be awarded.

The Minutes of the Committee of Council for August and December, 1846, which have been explained in detail in the third chapter, as far as they affect the interests of the school, the schoolmaster, and the poor, appear to have been the subject of prolonged deliberation by the Government. It is now important to show how the interests of civil and religious liberty are affected by this measure.

Many of the Dissenting bodies had, prior to 1839, and in that year, declared that they concurred in the justice and expediency of distributing the aid of Parliament, in proportion to voluntary contributions. In support of this view, some remarkable petitions were presented to both Houses, from which we have selected examples printed in the Appendix.[1] It is difficult indeed to conceive how such a system can be reasonably resisted, except the principle be admitted that the State has no right to interfere in the education of the poor. For those who assert the sufficiency of the voluntary principle to provide both the religious institutions and the schools of the country,

---

[1] This Appendix is not reprinted in this volume.

and who therefore would render the diffusion of each creed, and the schools of each sect simply co-extensive with its ability to maintain them, cannot on the ground of inequality object to the impartial administration of the Parliamentary fund, in proportion to the comparative exertions of each school committee. With the abstract objection to the interference of the Government, we have dealt elsewhere.

It is perhaps pardonable here to recapitulate.

In order to remove the scruples which certain nonconformist bodies might entertain to the acceptance of aid—partaking in their conceptions of the nature of religious endowment—the Government, as we have described in the second chapter, have carefully provided that their Inspectors shall not examine the religious instruction in such schools, and have made all grants to Dissenters arising out of the recent Minutes, on requirements relating to literary instruction alone. The certificate of the managers of the school, that they are satisfied with the state of the religious knowledge, is accepted in the stead of any examination. While therefore the school will be under the direction of managers selected from the congregation, and its religious instruction will be ordered according to their unfettered discretion, they may obtain assistance towards the improvement of the literary instruction of the scholars, on condition only of giving proof of the efficiency of such secular instruction. The Committee of Council will accede to the desire of the managers of Church of England schools, that the children of Dissenters shall be admitted to the privileges contemplated in these Minutes, without being required to learn the Catechism or Liturgy of the Church, if their parents object. If it should be found, that in any parish a Church of England school alone exists, that this school is aided by the Government, and that there are communicants of dissenting congregations too poor to provide for the education of their children, and who cannot conscientiously permit them to attend a school in which instruction in the Catechism and Liturgy is required from all the scholars ; it would become their Lordships to inquire, whether the managers of the school feel themselves under the obligation of duty to enforce this condition. Such a result would be to be regretted, and it is believed would be rare; but if it existed, it would become the Government to deliberate in what way education could be provided for the children of religious parents, who conscientiously objected to permit their children to be taught the Catechism and Liturgy of the Church.

Every School Committee will continue to hold in its own hands the power of selecting and dismissing the master; of determining the organisation, discipline, course of instruction, and methods of teaching, to be adopted in the school; of selecting the books; dismissing the pupil teachers or stipendiary monitors; in fact, of regulating in all respects its affairs. In the selection of the Inspector who may visit the school, the Government will consult the Education Committee, or other central authority watching over the interests of the schools of each religious communion. The Inspector will act under instructions restraining him from all interference with the discipline and management of the school. He will have no authority to direct, and will not be permitted even to advise, unless invited to do so by the School Committee. With these precautions against the exactions of authority, he will not fail to be useful to all schools which he may visit, by skilfully placing under the light of a searching examination, conducted in the presence of the managers, the actual condition of the school. The results of his experience will be available for their instruction and guidance. If they desire the assistance of the Government to enable them to provide for the apprenticeship of pupil teachers, he will become the organ of an impartial communication with the Committee of Council. If the master desire to present himself for examination for the certificate necessary to an augmentation of his salary, the Inspector will inform him what are the studies to be pursued, and the standard of acquirements to be attained, in order to procure this benefit for himself and for the school. If the augmentation of salary be granted, it will be withdrawn in any year in which the managers refuse a certificate of their satisfaction in the conduct of the master and of his attention to his duties. For a similar cause the stipend of the pupil teacher will cease. Yet the master and his assistant are described, by the objectors to this measure, as subservient to the authority of the executive, to a degree menacing the liberties of the country. It is, on the contrary, difficult to conceive any system by which the sympathies of the religious congregations could be more carefully consulted—by which their discretion could be left more completely unfettered—or which could afford effectual assistance, on terms more conducive to the interests of civil and religious liberty.

Considerable effort has been made to produce an impression that the Established Church of England will chiefly derive advantage from the administration of the Parliamentary grant, according to the Minutes of August and December, 1846; yet in point of the extent of the requirements which are conditions of grants under those Minutes, the advantage is certainly on the side of schools not connected with the Established Church. In British and Dissenting schools the Inspector will not examine the religious instruction. If the managers certify that they are satisfied with the state of the religious knowledge of the pupil teachers, the Committee of Council will not require further proof of proficiency, or that any catechism shall be used, or any particular form of religious instruction adopted, beyond the daily reading of a portion of the Scriptures in the school. When the managers of British or Dissenting schools certify, that the apprentice has been attentive to his religious duties, no requirement is to be made as to his attendance on any particular place of Divine worship. It is obvious, therefore, that the conditions of grants to Dissenting schools are much less stringent than those imposed on schools connected with the Church of England.

It has also been represented, that, by these Minutes, the clergy of the Established Church will enjoy a large amount of patronage and influence. The fact that they are required to assist the Inspector in examining the religious knowledge of the pupil teachers in Church of England schools, and, at the close of every year, to certify that the apprentices have been attentive to their religious duties, has been represented as conferring on the clergy an inordinate power, and a patronage so extensive as to threaten religious liberty. But the parochial minister has no authority in Church of England schools, in this or any other particular, which is not confided to the managers in British or Dissenting schools. Whatever patronage or influence is to be enjoyed by the clergy in the one case, is conferred on the managers in the other. In the arrangement itself there is a perfect equality.

We have made these remarks, without questioning whether it is in any degree fair to represent this power to award certificates of the state of the religious knowledge of pupil teachers, and of their attention to their religious duties, as a means of dispensing patronage and exercising influence. Such a representation involves a charge of corruption against the parochial clergy, and not less by inference against the managers of British and Dissenting schools. The zeal of the clergy and managers of schools for the religious instruction of the children of their congregations, is, in the mind of a controversialist, a corrupt ingenuity in entangling souls in the meshes of a spiritual policy. Her Majesty's advisers have not doubted that the predominating feeling among the clergy, as well as among the managers of Dissenting schools, would be a simple desire that the scholars should become thoroughly grounded in the doctrines, precepts, and evidences of Christianity, and should derive from their acquaintance with the material world a confirmation of their faith, and weapons with which to repel infidelity; but it has not been conceived that the managers could resort to a perversion of the authority confided to them, simply to bribe poor children to be of their party, without being of their faith.

But if any disparity should arise in the opportunities for the exercise of the supposed degenerate authority, that could be attributed only to one of two causes,—either to the fact that the condition of society in England is such that, by voluntary association, the Church of England has both the means and the will to erect and support more schools than the Dissenting communions; or to the fact, that certain bodies of Dissenters might, on whatever ground, refuse to participate in the advantages offered to them by the Government. If this disparity arose from the state of society, and were attributable to the greater numbers, wealth, and zeal of members of the Established Church, that would not constitute a political injustice, for it would be strictly consistent with the equitable principle, of applying the assistance of Government in aid of voluntary exertions. It is difficult to conceive, how the advocates of the voluntary system could object, that the number and efficiency of schools for the poor in any religious communion should bear an exact relation to the voluntary contributions of their supporters, and should carry with them whatever legitimate influence such institutions can afford.

On the other hand, if such disparity should arise from the determination of Dissenters to reject the aid of the Government, this would obviously be a self-inflicted privation, by no means inherent in the measure. Such an objection has its parallel in the opinions of those who object to any increase of religious endowments, or rather to the principle of religious endowment from resources in any degree national. That a minority should suffer for conscience' sake the deprivation of its worldly substance, or place itself in a position of persevering protest against institutions sanctioned by experience and supported by the law, must probably be the inevitable result of that freedom of opinion and action, private and public, which is happily secured to individuals and associations by the English constitution. But deference to such a minority is a question of public convenience and practical statesmanship. Few are prepared to appropriate to purely secular uses the tithes and other endowments of the Established Church. In such a case as the present, the minority would simply deprive itself voluntarily of its share of the means destined by the State to augment the resources of private charity. It is obviously within the power of the minority to show its attachment to its own principles, by the increased personal sacrifices of its members to fill the void which its rejection has occasioned. But it is impossible to admit, as a sufficient objection to the adoption of any measure which does not violate the first principles of justice, and which the majority conceive tends to the general advantage, the fact that a protesting minority claim the highest sanctions for the scruples which induced them to undergo privation, or submit to the spoiling of their goods for conscience' sake.

We will not attempt to add any force to this argument, by calling in question the sincerity of the professions of religious scruples against the reception of aid from the Government for the objects contemplated in the Minutes of August and December, 1846. Little time, however, has elapsed since the petitions from Dissenting congregations and other Dissenting bodies, in favour of State interference, were presented to Parliament in 1839. The basis of the grants of the Committee of Council on Education has in no respect changed from that declared in the Minutes of the 3rd of June and the 3rd of December, 1839; the same Statesmen are in power; the principle of aiding voluntary exertions by grants of public money is still in force; the instructions to Inspectors of schools, and their mode of appointment, remain unchanged; the constitution of the Committee of Council is exactly the same as in 1839. No pretence of partiality has ever been set up against the administration of the public money by this Committee. The only change that has occurred is, that it is proposed to extend the assistance which has hitherto been given only towards the erection of school buildings, from that object, to grants under the Minutes of August and December, 1846, for the support and improvement of existing schools. In the interval, the Established Church has, by great exertions and large contributions, availed itself to a great extent of the assistance afforded from the public funds. From whatever cause, the Dissenters have applied for this assistance to a much smaller extent. If this disparity be, in any degree, attributable to the comparatively feebler resources of Dissenting congregations, there is one feature in the Minutes of August and December, 1846, which ought to convince Dissenters, that these measures were framed in that spirit of equity which, while it deals justice to all, and refuses to be partial to any, rejoices in a just opportunity to assist the weak. Thus, though the grants for the stipends of pupil teachers and stipendiary monitors, and for the gratuities and pensions to deserving masters, are to be given on condition that a certain standard of efficiency has been attained in the school, and that the master, by his acquirements and character, merits encouragement; and though they will not fail thus to stimulate voluntary exertion, yet grants for these purposes are not to be made on condition of an equivalent contribution. This form of assistance is therefore available in schools, which by the natural energy and zeal of their promoters have attained a certain standard of efficiency, though the School Committee may be unable to make further pecuniary sacrifices.

The most astonishing objection which has been made against the operation of the Minutes of August and December, 1846, is that which declares, that they must operate to discourage and paralyse voluntary exertion. We have just said, that in the operation of these Minutes, some other forms of exertion are called forth than mere pecuniary sacrifices. Let any person make inquiry in his own neighbourhood from the masters of the schools by which he is surrounded, how often those schools are entered by visitors; whether there is a School Committee; when and where it assembles; whether, if there be a School Committee, it ever examines the scholars, or how often annually; and whether the master receives any and what amount of voluntary assistance in the instruction of the day-school, or of the evening-school; or the mistress, in teaching the girls to knit or to sew. The lamentable fact is, that except at some public annual exhibition dignified by the name of an examination, few or none of the subscribers enter an elementary school, from the commencement to the close of the year; that the schoolmaster is often without any other assistance, encouragement, or advice, than that of the clergyman, or in other cases, of some single member of the Committee of Managers.

In the generous rivalry which ought to exist among the schools of different religious persuasions, it is therefore obvious, that voluntary exertions, more valuable even than voluntary contributions, may accomplish very much for the improvement of the schools, by assiduous visitation, sympathy, and actual aid to the master in his arduous labours. By such exertions the school may be raised to that condition of order and efficiency which is required for the apprenticeship in it of pupil teachers; the master, if deficient in attainments, might, by the direction and assistance given to his studies, be qualified to receive and educate apprentices. These are forms of true charity more precious than money, which the regulations for the apprenticeship of pupil teachers are likely to call forth; they are also means of promoting education, independently of the mere wealth of a religious communion, and which therefore place zeal and the spirit of self-sacrifice on a level with money.

The tendency of this, however, as well as of every other part of the Minutes, will doubtless be to call forth increased pecuniary contributions. As the power to obtain assistance under these Minutes will depend on the efficiency of the master and of his school, the managers will be willing, where they cannot otherwise compensate for such sacrifices, to increase their subscriptions in order to send their master to be trained, to improve the fittings and apparatus, and to increase the supply of books for the school. In other cases, to procure a master who has obtained a certificate, and to raise his salary to the amount required as a condition of the augmentation offered by the Government; to build a residence for the master; to supply the pupil teachers with text-books for their studies, with clothes, or with an allowance in aid of their stipends; to hire a field garden, to erect workshops, or school kitchens and wash-houses, and to supply the remaining means of supporting a School of Industry. The Minutes are obviously destined to give a great impulse to the erection of Normal Schools. The Committee of Council have already, in their Minute of the 16th January, 1844, indicated what establishment Normal Schools require; and by their grants to St. Mark's College, the Battersea Training Schools, the British and Foreign Normal School, the Training Schools of Chester, of York and Ripon, and of Durham, have shown what is the character of the establishments which they are disposed to recognise. Such Normal Schools cannot be erected without a large outlay, about one-third of which is contributed by the Government. We have already seen that under the Minutes of August and December, 1846, from one-third to one-half of the expense of their support would have to be borne by voluntary contributions. But there is no doubt that the number of Normal Schools would rapidly increase, and consequently that the funds derived from private benevolence for their establishment and support would be at an early period greatly augmented. It is not improbable that £40,000 will be collected for the erection of Normal Schools in the ensuing year. Such an amount of contribution involves, with the usual amount of aid from the Government, an outlay of £60,000, and a provision for the training of 400 masters, at an expense of £20,000 per annum, one-third or one-half of which must also be derived from private charity. The settlement of trained masters (who have procured certificates) in improved elementary schools throughout the country, will necessitate the erection of schoolmasters' houses, the improvement of the school apparatus, a better and more constant supply of books, a better and more certain salary for the master, and in some cases assistance to the pupil teachers. Where these objects cannot be compensated for by personal exertions, the improvements will necessarily occasion an increase of pecuniary contributions.

On these various grounds we conceive the recent Minutes of the Committee of Council on Education to be consistent with the interests of religion, with political justice, with civil and religious liberty, and with the improvement of education by increased voluntary exertions, and therefore to deserve the confidence of Parliament and the country.

CHAPTER V.

THE OUTLAY FROM PUBLIC GRANTS AND PRIVATE CONTRIBUTIONS REQUIRED BY THE MINUTES OF AUGUST AND DECEMBER, 1846.

THE opposition which has been raised against the Minutes of the Committee of Council on Education of August and December, 1846, has assumed two other remarkable positions—the first of these is, an attempt to produce satisfaction with the present condition and prospects of elementary education; and the second, to excite an alarm at the outlay which may be incurred by the establishment of a system of National Education. The assumption from the first of these two positions is, that if the present state and future prospects of elementary education are so satisfactory, there is no necessity whatever for the assistance of the Government, and therefore that the great drain on the resources of the country, contemplated under the second form of objection, is a wanton and mischievous outlay. The second objection would, in the eyes of the English people, be insignificant, if there were no force in the first. It is no part of the characteristics of the English nation to withhold whatever money is necessary for the accomplishment of great and worthy objects. It would therefore be a great miscalculation to suppose that they would turn aside, like a startled horse from a shadow, at the prospect even of a possible future outlay of a million and a half annually, to improve the moral, intellectual, and physical condition of the great mass of their fellow-citizens. It has been justly observed that a nation which has, in little more than one generation, contracted a debt of nearly a thousand millions in warfare—which spent twenty millions to atone for the guilt of slavery—which has lately, in the defence of its frontier, strewn a nearly equal sum, together with the bones of its citizens, over the passes of Cabul and the deserts of Scinde, is not likely, by the mere dread of expense, to cast aside so vast an object as the education of the people.

Moreover, an outlay for such a purpose has no analogy with the direful expenditure of war; or even with the continual drain for national defence; or with the waste of national wealth occasioned by social tumult, domestic immorality, and crime; or with the means of repression and punishment which Government is compelled to employ. All these forms of expenditure may be regarded as unproductive, except as far as some of them may be protective; yet the expenditure on these objects forms the chief drain on the national resources. The Appendix C contains a necessarily imperfect estimate of the outlay occasioned by crime. In the Appendix B is an account of the loss sustained by the operatives, masters, and shopkeepers of Preston, in a strike which lasted only three months. The workmen sustained a nett loss of £57,210, the masters of £45,000, the shopkeepers of £4986. The total loss to the town amounted in three months to £107,196. The waste and expense of popular ignorance and crime alone consume several millions per annum.

Mr. Baines, the most indefatigable and able of the opponents of the Minutes of the Committee of Council, has endeavoured to excite alarm against their adoption by giving the following estimate of the outlay which he conceives might, in the course of years, be incurred.

Annual Expenditure, supposed by Mr. Baines.

	£
1. Grants to Normal Schools, for 1000 male students admitted each year on the average, £22 10s. for each	22,500
Ditto for 500 female students, at 2-3rds the amount per head	7500
2. Grants in aid of the salaries of Schoolmasters, 15,000, at £20 each	300,000
3. Grants to Schoolmasters for training pupil teachers and stipendiary monitors, 30,000 pupil teachers, at £9 for 2	135,000
30,000 stipendiary monitors, at £4 for 2	60,000
4. Salaries of pupil teachers and stipendiary monitors—30,000 pupil teachers, at £15 each	450,000
30,000 stipendiary monitors, at £10 each	300,000

Explanation of the Minutes of 1846

5. Grants to students in Normal Schools—3000 male students, at £25 each	75,000
1500 female ditto, at £16 13s. 4d. each	25,000
6. Gratuities to Schoolmasters for skill in training pupil teachers and stipendiary monitors—suppose 1500 to receive yearly £5 each	7500
7. School Field Gardens — suppose 2000, aided by grants of £5 each, for rent, &c.	10,000
Purchase of tools first year—may average yearly	1000
Gratuities to masters for teaching agriculture, say £10 each	20,000
8. Workshops for Trades—suppose 1000, aided by grants of (say) £5 each, for rent, &c.	5000
Purchase of tools first year—may average yearly	2000
Gratuities to masters for teaching, at (say) £10 each	10,000
9. School Kitchens and Washhouses — suppose 2000, at £5 each, for rent, &c.	10,000
Outfit, may average yearly	2000
Gratuities to mistresses for teaching, at (say) £7 each	14,000
10. Superannuation Pensions to Schoolmasters — not to exceed 2-3rds of salary and emoluments—suppose 1500, at £50 each	75,000
11. Grants for Workhouse Schools, Schools of Industry, and Penal Schools — Parliamentary grant already made for salaries of schoolmasters	15,000
Annual charge of Normal Schools for ditto	3500
Other expenses (say)	15,000
12. Grants, as at present, for building school-houses, and also the building of workshops, kitchens, &c. (say)	100,000
13. Salaries and travelling expenses of Inspectors—suppose 75, at £700 each	52,500
14. Expenses of the head office in London, clerks, &c. (say)	25,000
Total expenditure	£1,742,500

It cannot have escaped Mr. Baines' penetration, that the period, within which such an outlay could be incurred, must be almost indefinitely postponed by the vast amount of contribution required from private sources, as a condition of the grants under many of the heads of his estimate. With a view to show how long a time must elapse before the sums required from private contributions could be collected, it may be useful to furnish a statement of the amount which must be raised by charity alone under each head of Mr. Baines' estimate.

The Cost of the erection of Normal and Model Schools for the training of 4500 male and female students (supposed in Mr. Baines' estimate) at £150 for each, of which one-third would be granted by Government (therefore 4500 × 100 =) £450,000

Of this but little has been accomplished hitherto.

We will not enter into any estimate of the number of masters' houses and school-rooms to be erected, though that would, in our opinion, require a vast outlay.

Annual Amount of Subscriptions, &c., required as a condition of the Public Grants, to meet the Annual Expenditure in Grants supposed in Mr. Baines' Estimate.

	£
1. If, according to Mr. Baines' estimate, 3000 male and 1500 female students were trained in Normal Schools, about one-third of this expense would be borne by private subscriptions (4500 × £50 annual expense ÷ 3) =	75,000
2. Twice the amount of '*Grants in aid of the salaries of Schoolmasters*, 1500, at £20 each, £300,000'	600,000
3. Expense of clothes and books for one-half the number of pupil teachers and stipendiary monitors, or 30,000, at £5 each	150,000
4. Additional stipends to one-fourth of the pupil teachers and stipendiary monitors, 15,000, at an average through the apprenticeship of £10 each	150,000
5. Annual expenditure in books, fuel, light, apparatus, and repairs in 15,000 schools, at £30 each	450,000
6. One-half the rent of school field gardens, 2000, at £5 each	10,000
Purchase of tools annually after first year, at £5 each	10,000
7. Workshops for trades, 1000, at £10 each for rent	10,000
Purchase of tools annually after first year, at £5 each	5000
8. School kitchens and washhouses, 2000, at £10 each for rent	20,000
Annual expenses, at £200 each	400,000
Total	£1,880,000

Before, therefore, the money estimated by Mr. Baines would ultimately be required from the public resources to carry into execution the Minutes of the Committee of Council, the annual amount raised by voluntary subscriptions, collections, and school-pence, must rise to the sum of £1,880,000, and, which is perhaps more difficult, the schools throughout the country must be made thoroughly efficient. The Chancellor of the Exchequer need therefore have no apprehensions of any suddenly large demand upon the national income for education. It is obvious, that even if we were to admit, that Mr. Baines has accurately anticipated the largest outlay which this measure could entail upon the country (and he is not likely to have erred by an under estimate), the growth of this charge must be slow, inasmuch as it must be attended at every step, though not in all its forms, by equivalent contributions from private charity.

That the very gradual increase of the grant has been contemplated by Government, is obvious, because the sum to be voted in Parliament this year is to undergo no increase.

But there is another very obvious inference from Mr. Baines' statistics, which affords the most convincing proof of the fallacy of his assumption, that the present condition and prospects of elementary education are satisfactory. At present, there are scarcely any apprenticed pupil teachers in England. The only assistants which schoolmasters now have are, with rare exceptions, unpaid monitors, from eight to thirteen years of age. When a provision from the national resources for 30,000 pupil teachers, and 30,000 stipendiary monitors, or one trained assistant for every 25 scholars, is introduced into the estimate, no one questions that it is necessary to make some such a provision, either from private charity or by means of public grants. On all hands, it is admitted that the monitorial system has failed, and that it is necessary to substitute the services of trained apprentices between the ages of thirteen and nineteen for those of monitors between the ages of eight and thirteen. If, therefore, the aid of the State be rejected, voluntary charity will have to provide the whole charge of this arrangement.

In like manner, few masters have charge of elementary schools who have passed through any education comparable to that proposed to be accomplished by five years of apprenticeship to a skilful master, followed by two or three years' training in a Normal School. If, therefore, the efficiency of the schoolmaster is to be increased in all the elementary schools of England, to the standard contemplated by the Government, some such system as that proposed by the Committee of Council must be adopted, and the charge of erecting and supporting Normal Schools, if not in part provided for by public grants, must be wholly met by private charity.

The same remarks apply to the expense to be incurred for making provision for a sufficient income to support a trained schoolmaster in respectability and comfort. If education is to be within the reach of every working man — if the schools are to be well furnished; provided with sufficient books and apparatus; taught by skilful masters, and well-trained assistants, though we may demur to Mr. Baines' estimate as exaggerated, yet the outlay must eventually be considerable. Mr. Baines' estimate of the amount required to carry into execution the Minutes of the Committee of Council on Education (£1,742,500), together with the sums necessary to fulfil the conditions of the grants included in that estimate (£1,880,000), amount to £3,622,500. The proportion to be raised by subscriptions and school-pence would, however, be two thirds. Is there much hope that, from voluntary contributions and school-pence, two thirds this sum could soon be raised, and every school be made as efficient as the Minutes require? If, for the sake of argument, we should assume that an efficient system of National Education could not be maintained without a large outlay, the operation of the Minutes of the Committee of Council on Education would very slowly bring upon the State that portion of this charge which would have to be sustained from the public resources. Every fresh increment of expense would have to be met with an equal amount derived from private charity. The funds at the disposal of Parliament would have to meet no burthen for which private benevolence did not first spontaneously supply its offering. Such a system is therefore under the double check of public opinion as expressed in voluntary charity, and of the national feeling as it may find expression in Parliament. No system could be devised more dependent on popular favour. Unless the whole administration of public education should as cordially enlist the sympathies of the public, as associations purely dependent on voluntary subscriptions do, the sources of local charity would dry up; the conditions of the public grants would fail to be fulfilled, and the whole fabric would crumble into ruin. On the other hand, if the system were found to be inconsistent with public rights, or to operate in any way so as to give umbrage to Parliament, it would be under the check of an annual vote. During all the earlier stages of its progress, much vigilance would naturally attend its operation, and it would in each year be subject to such alterations as Parliament might require. While in its infancy, and therefore in the feebleness of immaturity, it would have acquired no powers of resistance to salutary changes. The plan, if necessary, might be moulded according to the will of the Legislature; and it is obvious that the Government have been of opinion, that a measure strictly tentative and experimental in its character, afforded the fairest chances of solving, in the course of years, all the difficulties of this most complex question.

With respect, therefore, both to the nature and the extent of the annual outlay from the public resources required for the execution of these Minutes, the power of Parliament will be continually exercised. For this reason, the introduction of a plan for the improvement of the education of the poor, in the form of regulations affecting the appropriation of a sum of money annually voted by Parliament, affords a much larger amount of security that public opinion will be continually directed to the subject, and will have an opportunity to exercise a legitimate control, through the press and the representative system, than if a measure were submitted in the form of a Bill for a complete system of education, and having been carried through all its stages, were subject to repeal only by a similar process.

The growth of the outlay contemplated under these Minutes must therefore be slow, not only because the amount derived from private charity must undergo an equal increase, but likewise because it will be under the annual control of Parliament, and subject to all those hindrances which prevent the rapid growth of expense in any public department. If in the course of some years, it should be found that the public interest in the education of the working classes, and the estimate of its importance among the poor had increased so far that the sums derived from school-pence, and from private subscriptions, and the efficiency of the schools, occasioned a demand for a considerable increase of the Parliamentary grant, and if public opinion in Parliament had watched the growth of this system with approbation, it would be within the power of Parliament to pass a measure giving the sanction of law to a system which had passed through every step of trial, and had, with whatever modifications, been sanctioned by experience.

APPENDIX (A).

THE PLAN FOR ENCOURAGING AND AIDING VOLUNTARY EXERTIONS FOR THE PROMOTION OF EDUCATION IN GREAT BRITAIN, PROPOSED BY LORD JOHN RUSSELL'S ADMINISTRATION IN 1847.

MINUTES OF THE COMMITTEE OF COUNCIL ON EDUCATION IN AUGUST AND DECEMBER, 1846.

COUNCIL CHAMBER, WHITEHALL, August 25, 1846.
By the Right Honourable the Lords of the Committee of Council on Education.

GENERAL MINUTE.

THEIR Lordships had under their consideration the sufficiency of the present number of Inspectors of Schools for the duties they have to perform, and

Resolved—That it would be highly expedient that all the schools which are under the inspection of the Privy Council should be visited at least once in each year: that the existing number of Inspectors appears to be insufficient, as, notwithstanding their constant assiduity in the discharge of the duties intrusted to them, it is found impossible to make arrangements for the inspection of schools oftener than once in two years.

Their Lordships are, however, unwilling to make so considerable an addition at once to the number of Inspectors as would be necessary for an annual visit to each school, but will recommend the appointment of three new Inspectors this year, reserving for consideration hereafter any further appointments which may be required.

Their Lordships had further under their consideration the Report of the Inspectors of Schools, memorials from certain Boards of Education, and letters from the clergy and others, representing the very early age at which the children acting as assistants to schoolmasters are withdrawn from school to manual labour, and the advantages which would arise if such scholars as might be distinguished by proficiency and good conduct were apprenticed to skilful masters, to be instructed and trained, so as to be prepared to complete their education as schoolmasters in a Normal School.

Resolved—That the Lord President cause Regulations to be framed defining the qualifications of the schoolmaster; the condition of Instruction in the school;

and the local contributions to be required as conditions on which annual grants of money may be made towards the stipends of apprentices in elementary schools; and further, cause indentures of apprenticeship to be prepared, declaring the duties of the apprentice and the nature of the instruction he is to receive; the periods of examination by the Inspectors of Schools, and the circumstances under which the indenture may be dissolved, in order that stipends increasing in each year of the apprenticeship may be granted in aid of local contribution.

It was further Resolved—That as the masters having charge of the instruction and training of school apprentices will be selected for their character and skill; and as the education of the apprentices will increase the labour and responsibilities of such masters, it is expedient that the successful performance of these duties be rewarded by annual grants in aid of their stipends, according to the number of apprentices trained by each master.

It was further Resolved—That it is expedient to make provision in certain cases, by a retiring pension, for schoolmasters and mistresses who, after a certain length of service, may appear entitled to such provision.

That the Lord President cause Regulations to be framed respecting the grants of such retiring pensions.

That it is expedient for the further encouragement of deserving schoolmasters, that small gratuities be annually distributed, under the authority of the Lord President, to schoolmasters whose zeal and success in teaching may, on the Report of the Inspector, appear to entitle them to such encouragement; and that Regulations be framed with reference to the distribution of such gratuities.

COUNCIL CHAMBER, WHITEHALL, 21st December, 1846.

By the Right Honourable the Lords of the Committee of Council on Education.

REGULATIONS respecting the EDUCATION of PUPIL TEACHERS and STIPENDIARY MONITORS.

THE Lord President communicated to their Lordships the Regulations which he had caused to be framed to carry into execution the Minute of the Committee of Council on Education of the 25th day of August, 1846, respecting the Apprenticeship of Pupil Teachers.

General Preliminary Conditions.

Upon application being made to their Lordships from the trustees or managers of any school under inspection, requesting that one or more of the most proficient scholars be selected to be apprenticed to the master or mistress, the application will be referred to the Inspector, and will be entertained, if he report—

That the master or mistress of the school is competent to conduct the apprentice through the course of instruction to be required:

That the school is well furnished and well supplied with books and apparatus:

That it is divided into classes; and that the instruction is skilful, and is graduated according to the age of the children and the time they have been at school, so as to show that equal care has been bestowed on each class:

That the discipline is mild and firm, and conducive to good order:

That there is a fair prospect that the salary of the master and mistress, and the ordinary expenses of the school, will be provided for during the period of apprenticeship.

General Rule.— The qualifications to be required of candidates and of pupil teachers in each year of their apprenticeship will be regulated by the following rules, in which the minimum of proficiency to be attained is precisely defined, in order to prevent partiality ; but their Lordships reserve to themselves the power to reward superior merit, by shortening the term of the apprenticeship, or by awarding the higher stipends of the later years of the apprenticeship to pupil teachers whose attainments enable them to pass the examination of one of the later years at an earlier period.

Pupil Teachers— Qualifications of Candidates.

The following qualifications will be required from candidates for apprenticeship: — They must be at least thirteen years of age, and must not be subject to any bodily infirmity likely to impair their usefulness as pupil teachers.

In schools connected with the Church of England, the clergyman and managers, and, in other schools, the managers, must certify that the moral character of the candidates and of their families justify an expectation that the instruction and training of the school will be seconded by their own efforts and by the example of their parents. If this cannot be certified of the family, the apprentice will be required to board in some approved household.

Candidates will also be required —
1. To read with fluency, ease, and expression.
2. To write in a neat hand, with correct spelling and punctuation, a simple prose narrative slowly read to them.
3. To write from dictation sums in the first four rules of arithmetic, simple and compound ; to work them correctly, and to know the tables of weights and measures.
4. To point out the parts of speech in a simple sentence.
5. To have an elementary knowledge of geography.
6. *In schools connected with the Church of England* they will be required to repeat the Catechism, and to show that they understand its meaning, and are acquainted with the outline of Scripture history. The parochial clergyman will assist in this part of the examination.

In other schools the state of the religious knowledge will be certified by the managers.
7. To teach a junior class to the satisfaction of the Inspector.
8. Girls should also be able to sew neatly and to knit.

Qualifications of Pupil Teachers in each Year of their Apprenticeship.

At the end of the first year pupil teachers will be examined by the Inspector:—
1. In writing from memory the substance of a more difficult narrative.
2. In arithmetic, the rules of 'Practice' and 'Simple Proportion,'* and in the first rules* of mental arithmetic.
3. In grammar, in the construction of sentences, and in syntax.
4. In the geography of Great Britain and Palestine.
5. In the Holy Scriptures and in the Catechism, with illustrations by passages from Holy Writ, *in Church of England schools*, the parochial clergyman assisting in the examination.

The managers will, *in other schools*, certify in this and in the succeeding years of the apprenticeship, that they are satisfied with the state of the religious knowledge of the pupil teachers.
6. In their ability to give a class a reading lesson, and to examine it on the meaning of what has been read.
7. In the elements of vocal music, in this and in succeeding years, when taught from notes.

8. In their ability to drill* a class in marching and exercises; and to conduct it through the class movements required for preserving order.

9. Girls should also be able to instruct the younger scholars in sewing and knitting.

At the end of the second year, pupil teachers will be examined by the Inspector: —

1. In composition, by writing the *abstract of a lesson, or a school report.
2. In decimal arithmetic*, and the higher rules of mental arithmetic. Girls will not be required to proceed beyond the rule of 'Compound Proportion' in this year.
3. In syntax and etymology.*
4. In the geography of Great Britain, of Europe, the British Empire*, and Palestine.
5. In the Holy Scriptures, Liturgy, and Catechism *in Church of England schools*, more fully than in the preceding year, the parochial clergyman assisting in the examination.
6. In their ability to examine a class in reading, in the rudiments of grammar and arithmetic; and, during the examination, to keep the class attentive, in order and in activity, without undue noise.

At the end of the third year, pupil teachers will be examined by the Inspector:—

1. In the composition of the notes of a lesson on a subject selected by the Inspector.
2. In the elements of mechanics*, or in book-keeping.
3. In syntax, etymology, and prosody.*
4. In the geography of the four* quarters of the globe. Girls in the geography of the British Empire.
5. In the outlines of English History.
6. More fully in the Holy Scriptures, Liturgy, and Catechism, *in Church of England schools*, the parochial clergyman assisting in the examination.
7. In their skill in managing and examining the second class in grammar, geography, and mental arithmetic.
8. The girls should have acquired greater skill as teachers of sewing, knitting, &c.

At the end of the fourth year, pupil teachers will be examined by the Inspector: —

1. In the composition of an account of the organisation of the school, and of the methods of instruction used.
2. In the first steps in mensuration*, with practical illustrations; and in the elements of land surveying* and levelling.*
3. In syntax, etymology, and prosody.*
4. In the * geography of Great Britain as connected with the outlines of English history. Girls in the geography of the four quarters of the globe.
5. More fully in the Holy Scriptures, Liturgy, and Catechism, *in Church of England schools*, the parochial clergyman assisting in the examination.
6. In their skill in managing and examining the first class in grammar, geography, and mental arithmetic, and in giving * a lesson to two or three classes grouped together.

At the end of the fifth year, pupil teachers will be examined by the Inspector: —

1. In the composition of an essay on some subject connected with the art of teaching.
2. In the rudiments of algebra*, or the practice of land surveying* and levelling.*
3. In syntax, etymology, and prosody.
4. In the use* of the globes, or in the geography of the British Empire* and Europe*, as connected with the outlines of English history. In this year girls may be examined in the historical geography of Great Britain.

5. More completely in the Holy Scriptures, Liturgy, and Catechism, *in Church of England schools*, the parochial clergyman assisting in the examination.

6. In their ability to give a gallery lesson, and to conduct the instruction of the first class in any subject selected by the Inspector.

General Rules.—In the subjects marked with an asterisk girls need not be examined, but in every year they will be expected to show increased skill as sempstresses, and teachers of sewing, knitting, &c.

In the examinations, the Inspectors will, in each year, observe the degree of attention paid by the pupil teachers to a perfect articulation in reading, and to a right modulation of the voice in teaching a class. A knowledge of vocal music and of drawing (especially from models), though not absolutely required, because the means of teaching it may not exist in every school, will be much encouraged. Every pupil teacher will be required to be clean in person and dress.

The number of pupil teachers apprenticed in any school will not exceed one to every twenty-five scholars ordinarily attending.

Certificate.—Every pupil teacher who has passed all the foregoing examinations, and has presented the required testimonials in each year, will be entitled to a certificate declaring that he has successfully completed his apprenticeship.

Stipendiary Monitors.—The Inspectors may, for some time, find in the rural district schools, in which all the general conditions required for the apprenticeship of a pupil teacher may be satisfied, but the master or mistress of which may be unable to conduct an apprentice even through the foregoing course of instruction. Their Lordships being desirous so to adapt their regulations to the condition of such schools, as by their improvement to enable them hereafter to provide for the training of pupil teachers, are disposed, for a few years, to encourage the managers to retain their monitors, by small stipends, to the age of seventeen, without apprenticeship, but under a form of agreement with the parents, on condition that the master give each monitor *extra* daily instruction.

For such an arrangement all the *general rules and preliminary conditions* previously enumerated will be required, and the following qualifications for candidates for such stipends:—

Stipendiary Monitors—Qualifications of Candidates.

The candidates must be thirteen years of age, and they will be required —

1. To read with fluency.
2. To write a neat hand.
3. To write from dictation sums in the first four simple rules of arithmetic, and to work them correctly.
4. To point out the parts of speech in a simple sentence.
5. *In Church of England schools*, to repeat the Catechism, and show a knowledge of its meaning, the parochial clergyman assisting in the religious examination.

In other schools, the managers will certify that they are satisfied with the state of their religious knowledge.

6. Girls to sew neatly and to knit.

Qualifications of Stipendiary Monitors in each Year.

The stipendiary monitors will be examined at the end of each year of service and will be required —

At the end of the first year —

1. To read with fluency, ease, and expression.
2. To write in a neat hand, with correct spelling and punctuation, a simple prose narrative, slowly read to them.

3. To write from dictation sums in the first four compound rules of arithmetic, to work them correctly, and to know the tables of weights and measures.

4. To point out the parts of speech in a simple sentence, and to give the rules of its construction.

5. To have an elementary knowledge of geography.

6. *In Church of England schools*, to show a general acquaintance with the Scriptures; the parochial clergyman, in this and the succeeding years, assisting in the religious examination.

In other schools, the managers will certify, in this and succeeding years, that the religious knowledge of the stipendiary monitors is satisfactory to them.

7. In schools where vocal music is taught, he should have commenced instruction from notes, and should give proof of improvement in each succeeding year.

8. Girls to teach sewing and knitting in this and succeeding years.

At the end of the second year —

1. To write from memory, with correct spelling and punctuation, the substance of a simple prose narrative, read carefully to them two or three times.

2. In arithmetic, to write from dictation sums in 'Practice,' and to work them correctly.

3. In grammar, to parse more difficult sentences, and give the rules of their construction.

4. To know the geography of Great Britain and Palestine.

5. *In Church of England schools*, to give illustrations of the Catechism from the Bible, and to show a more complete acquaintance with the Scriptures.

6. To give a class reading lesson, and examine it on the meaning of what has been read.

7. Girls to be able to cut out clothes.

At the end of the third year —

1. To write from memory the substance of a longer and more difficult prose narrative, and to show greater skill in composition.

2. In arithmetic, to write from dictation sums in simple proportion and simple interest, and to work them correctly.

3. In grammar, to be able to parse sentences, with a thorough knowledge of the rules of syntax.

4. To know the geography of Great Britain, Europe, and Palestine, and that of the outlines of the four quarters of the globe.

5. *In Church of England schools*, to possess a more extensive knowledge of the Holy Scriptures, and of the Liturgy and Catechism.

6. To examine a class in the rudiments of grammar, geography, and arithmetic.

At the end of the fourth year —

1. To prepare the notes of an oral lesson on a subject selected by the Inspector.

2. To work correctly sums in decimal arithmetic, and to show an acquaintance with the simple rules of mental arithmetic.

3. In Grammar to be examined in etymology.

4. To know the geography of the four quarters of the world, and especially of the British Empire.

5. To have a general knowledge of the outlines of English history.

6. *In Church of England schools*, to show a more perfect knowledge of the Holy Scriptures, Catechism, and Liturgy.

7. To examine the first or second class in grammar, geography, and arithmetic, and to give it an oral lesson, keeping the class attentive in order, and in activity, without undue noise.

Certificates of Character and Conduct to be annually required from Pupil Teachers and Stipendiary Monitors.

At the close of each year pupil teachers or stipendiary monitors will be required to present certificates of good conduct from the managers of the school, and of punctuality, diligence, obedience, and attention to their duties from the master or mistress.

In *Church of England schools,* the parochial clergymen, and *in other schools,* the managers, will also certify that the pupil teachers or stipendiary monitors have been attentive to their religious duties.

Salaries of Pupil Teachers and Stipendiary Monitors.

If these certificates be presented, and if the Inspector certify, at the close of each year, that he is satisfied with the oral examination and the examination papers of the pupil teachers or stipendiary monitors, and if those papers be satisfactory to their Lordships, the following stipends will be paid, irrespectively of any sum that may be received from the school or from any other source:—

	For a Pupil Teacher.		For a Stipendiary Monitor.	
	£	s.	£	s.
At the end of the 1st Year	10	0	5	0
„ „ 2nd „	12	10	7	10
„ „ 3rd „	15	0	10	0
„ „ 4th „	17	10	12	10
„ „ 5th „	20	0	0	0

Remuneration and Duties of Schoolmasters and Mistresses.

At the close of each of these years, if the pupil teachers have received a certificate of good character and of satisfactory progress, the master or mistress by whom they have been instructed and trained shall be paid the sum of £5 for one, of £9 for two, of £12 for three pupil teachers, and £3 per annum more for every additional apprentice; and, on the like conditions, £2 10s. for one stipendiary monitor, £4 for two, £6 for three, and £1 10s. in addition in each year for every additional stipendiary monitor.

In addition to the foregoing subjects of instruction, if the pupil teachers be skilfully trained by the master in the culture of a garden, or in some mechanical arts suitable to a School of Industry, or the female pupil teachers be instructed by the mistress in cutting out clothes, and in cooking, baking, or washing, as well as in the more usual arts of sewing and knitting, and the Inspector certify that the pupil teachers are thereby in a satisfactory course of training for the management of a School of Industry, the master or mistress will receive an additional gratuity, proportioned to the degree of skill and care displayed.

In consideration of the foregoing gratuity, and of the assistance obtained from the pupil teachers and stipendiary monitors in the instruction and management of the school, the master will give them instruction in the prescribed subjects, during one hour and a half at least, during five days in the week, either before or after the usual hours of school-keeping.

The stipends will be liable to be withdrawn by their Lordships on the report of their Inspector, on proof, of the continued ill health of the pupil teachers or stipendiary monitors, or of misconduct, want of punctuality, diligence, or skill, or failure in their examination, or in default of the required certificates.

SUPPORT OF NORMAL SCHOOLS.

Education of Schoolmasters and Mistresses, and Grants in aid of their Salaries.

Exhibitions on behalf of successful Pupil Teachers to Normal Schools — Employment of certain of them in the Public Service. Grants in aid of Expenses of Normal Schools, and of the Salaries of Masters and Mistresses educated therein.

The Committee of Council on Education had under their consideration their Lordships' Minutes as to the apprenticeship of pupil teachers in elementary schools.

It appeared further expedient to their Lordships, that the Lord President should authorise one or more of Her Majesty's Inspectors, together with the Principal of a Normal School under inspection, to submit to his Lordship, from among the pupil teachers who had successfully terminated their apprenticeship, a certain number of those who, upon competition in a public examination, to be annually held by such Inspectors and Principal in each Inspector's district, might be found most proficient in their studies and skilful in the art of teaching, and concerning whose character and zeal for the office of teachers the Inspector of the district could give the most favourable report.

That the Committee of Council on Education, on comparison of the testimonials and examination papers of these apprentices, should award, for as many as they might think fit, an exhibition of £20 or £25 to one of the Normal Schools under the inspection of Her Majesty's Inspectors.

That the pupil teachers to whom such exhibitions should be awarded, should be thenceforth denominated 'Queen's Scholars.'

That the exhibition should be liable to be withdrawn if the Principal of the Training School should be dissatisfied with the conduct, attainments, or skill of the 'Queen's Scholar.'

Their Lordships were also of opinion, that it might be useful to offer further incentives to exertion and good conduct among the pupil teachers, by opening to such of them as might not display the highest qualifications for the office of schoolmaster, but whose conduct and attainments were satisfactory, an opportunity of obtaining employment in the public service, under such regulations as may be hereafter adopted.

Their Lordships hope that the grant of an exhibition of £20 or £25 to the most proficient pupil teachers, to enable them to enter a Normal School, may diminish the difficulty, experienced by the trustees and managers of such institutions, of maintaining them in efficiency. In order still further to reduce the burden of such establishments, their Lordships will award to every Normal School subject to inspection a grant for every student trained therein, concerning whose character and conduct the Principal shall give a favourable report, and concerning whose attainments, skill in teaching, and general aptitude for the vocation of a schoolmaster, it shall appear to the Lord President, at the close of each of three years of training from the report of one or more of Her Majesty's Inspectors, and from the examination papers, that a certain standard of merit has been attained. Such grants shall be £20 at the close of the first year, £25 at the close of the second, and £30 at the close of the third year's course of instruction. This standard of acquirement shall not be so ordered as to interfere with the studies pursued in any Normal School, but shall be adapted to those studies, so, however, as to apply impartially to all such Normal Schools an equal incentive to exertion, by requiring efficiency in a sufficient number of the studies pursued in them.

Their Lordships will further grant, in aid of the salary of every schoolmaster appointed to a school under their inspection, and who has had one year's training in a Normal School under their inspection, £15 or £20 per annum; and in aid of the salary of every such schoolmaster who has had two years of such training, £20 or £25 per annum ; and of every such schoolmaster who has had three years of such training, £25 or £30 per annum ; provided he has upon examination obtained the proper certificate of merit in each year, on the following conditions :—

1. That the trustees and managers of the school provide the master with a house rent-free, and a further salary, equal at least to twice the amount of this grant.

2. That the trustees and managers annually certify that his character, conduct, and attention to his duties are satisfactory.

3. That the Inspector report that his school is efficient in its organisation, discipline, and instruction.

On the same conditions their Lordships will grant, in aid of the salaries of schoolmistresses appointed to schools under their inspection, who obtain similar certificates in a Normal School, two-thirds of the sums to be awarded to schoolmasters for each year's certificate of merit.

Retiring Pensions to Schoolmasters and Mistresses for long and efficient Services.

That a retiring pension may be granted by the Committee of Council to any schoolmaster or schoolmistress who shall be rendered incapable by age or infirmity of continuing to teach a school efficiently.

Provided that no such pension shall be granted to any schoolmaster or schoolmistress who shall not have conducted a normal or elementary school for fifteen years, during seven at least of which such school shall have been under inspection.

That in all cases of application for pensions a report shall be required from the Inspector, and from the trustees and managers of the schools, as to the character and conduct of the applicants, and the manner in which the education of the pupils under their charge has been carried on.

The amount of the pension shall be determined according to such report, but shall in no case exceed two-thirds of the average amount of the salary and emoluments annually received by the applicant during the period that the school has been under inspection.

A Minute of the grant of every such pension, and of the grounds on which it has been awarded, shall be published in their Lordships' Minutes.

GRANTS in aid of DAY-SCHOOLS of INDUSTRY.

Their Lordships had under their consideration Reports published in their Minutes on Schools of Industry.

Resolved—That when the managers of schools apply for aid to enable them to hire a field-garden for the instruction of the scholars, or to erect workshops in which handicrafts may be taught, or to provide a school wash-house or kitchen for the instruction of girls in domestic economy, their Lordships will be disposed, on the following conditions, to grant assistance towards the promotion of these objects.

1. School-Field Gardens.

If their Lordships are satisfied with the position of the field in relation to the school;

With the rent;

With the regulations for the management of the garden;

And with the competency of the master to superintend the work and give the requisite instruction;—

Their Lordships will consider whether it may be expedient to make an annual grant, not exceeding one-half the rent, so long as the Inspector may report that the field is skilfully and industriously cultivated;

To make a grant towards the purchase of tools in the first year; and

To grant a gratuity to the master in each year in which the instruction in industry is successful.

2. *Workshops for Trades.*

In schools situated in the denser parts of great cities, and intended to attract from the streets vagrant youths who are there trained in criminal pursuits, or accustomed to begging and vagrancy, if their Lordships are satisfied—

With the site, plan, and specifications;

And with the regulations for the management of the workshops, especially as respects the character of the persons selected as master-workmen, the share the scholars have in the produce of their labour, and the disposal of their work,—

They will, in the case of each application, consider the propriety of making grants for the erection of workshops.

They will also be disposed to contribute towards the purchase of tools in the first year.

In cases in which it may be desirable, in the first instance, to avoid the outlay required for the erection of workshops, their Lordships will entertain applications for assistance towards the hiring of a suitable building on the foregoing conditions, so long as the Inspector shall report that the handicrafts are successfully taught therein.

They will also consider the propriety of granting a gratuity to the master for every boy who, in consequence of the skill acquired in the workshop, shall have become a workman or assistant in any trade or craft whereby he is earning a livelihood.

3. *School-Kitchens and Wash-houses.*

If their Lordships are satisfied—

With the site, plan, and specifications;

With the competency of the schoolmistress to give the requisite instruction;

And with the regulations for the management of the school of industry—

They will be disposed to make a grant towards the erection of these buildings.

They will also consider the propriety of granting a gratuity to the mistress, in every year in which the Inspectors may report that the girls are successfully instructed in domestic economy.

In all cases of application for grants to establish Schools of Industry, it will be required that the schools shall be subject to inspection, and that the general system of instruction shall be found to be in conformity with the Minutes by which the distribution of the Parliamentary Grant towards the erection of school buildings has hitherto been regulated.

NORMAL SCHOOLS for TRAINING MASTERS for WORKHOUSE SCHOOLS and for PENAL SCHOOLS.

THEIR Lordships had further under their consideration the measures required to carry into execution the suggestions of the Secretary of State for the Home Department, for the establishment of Normal and Model Schools for the training of masters of schools for pauper and for criminal children.

Resolved—That a building be erected for the Normal School, providing accommodation for a principal, vice-principal, two masters, and for 100 candidate teachers.

That it be referred to the Lord President and Secretary of State for the Home Department, to cause plans to be prepared for this purpose.

That, as two years must elapse before this building can be ready for occupation, premises be in the mean time procured, in which the Normal School may be temporarily conducted; and that these premises be situated, if possible, near some workhouse or other school, which may serve as a practising school during the interval.

That, in connection with the Normal School, a Model School of Industry be erected, for the pauper children of some of the London Unions, who may be received into this school, either on contract by a steward with the Unions, or by letting the building to a district of Unions for the reception of children, under the direction of a Board of Management, according to the provisions of the 7 & 8 Vict. c. 101.

That, in connection with this Normal School, but distinct and separate from the school for pauper children, a school be erected for criminal children, and that plans of buildings for the School of Industry for pauper children, for this separate Penal School, be prepared and submitted to the Secretary of State for the Home Department.

That it be referred to the Lord President and Secretary of State for the Home Department, to cause regulations to be prepared for the management of the Normal School, and of the Practising Schools as connected with it, as well as for the Pauper School of Industry and the Penal School.

That an area of at least 10 acres is desirable for the Normal School, 10 acres for the Pauper School, and 10 for the Penal School, in order that training in gardening, and the management of a cottage farm, may be successfully pursued.

That the following general estimate of outlay on the buildings, and of annual expenditure, be approved:

Buildings.

The buildings of the Normal School	£10,000
The buildings of the Pauper School	5000
The buildings of the Penal School	5000
Annual charge of Normal School	3500

That it be referred to the Lord President and Secretary of State for the Home Department to direct the selection of the buildings required for the temporary management of the Normal School, and to determine the number of officers which may be required during the gradual growth of the establishment.

That the qualifications of the candidates for the offices of teachers in these schools be subjected to a careful examination, under the direction of the Lord President; and that the several schools be, from time to time, inspected by Her Majesty's Inspectors, and a Report thereon submitted to the Committee of Council, and transmitted by their Lordships to the Secretary of State for the Home Department.

MINUTE on the ADMINISTRATION of the GRANTS for the SALARIES of MASTERS and MISTRESSES of SCHOOLS for PAUPER CHILDREN.

The Lord President brought under the consideration of their Lordships a letter received from the Secretary of State for the Home Department, dated 18th November, 1846, calling their attention to the fact, that £15,000 was granted in the late Session of Parliament, towards defraying the expense of salaries of masters and mistresses of pauper schools, and to the importance of rendering grants for this purpose in future years, conducive to the increased efficiency of such schools.

The Lord President also communicated to their Lordships a paper, prepared at the request of Sir George Grey, on the administration of these grants.

From these documents, it appeared that there were upwards of 700 Workhouse Schools, and that little progress had hitherto been made in the establishment of Schools of Industry for districts of Unions, owing to the limitation of the radius of such districts in the Act of Parliament authorising their creation, and also to the limitation of the expense for which the rate-payers under this Act might be rated towards the erection of the requisite buildings. Their Lordships were of opinion, that it was expedient to employ Inspectors for the examination of Workhouse Schools, in order that by their suggestions to the Guardians, and upon their reports, measures might be adopted in the administration of these grants to procure the improvement of these schools.

Resolved—That it is desirable to train the pauper children now in workhouses in habits of industry.

That with this view, and for the purpose of improving Workhouse Schools, four Inspectors be appointed, with authority to examine the condition of schools for the education of pauper children; and to ascertain the character and qualifications of the persons employed as schoolmasters and mistresses, in order that unfit and incompetent persons may no longer be employed in that capacity, and that measures may be taken for awarding salaries according to the qualifications of the masters or mistresses, and the extent of the duties they have to perform.

That instructions be prepared for the guidance of such Inspectors.

SUPPLEMENTARY OFFICIAL LETTERS.

Committee of Council on Education, Privy Council Office,
Downing-street, March 11, 1847.

SIR,

I HAD yesterday to acknowledge the receipt of your letter of the 8th instant, in which you inquired whether masters of elementary schools, who have not been trained in a Normal School under the Inspection of the Committee of Council, 'are admissible to the advantages offered by their Lordships' Minutes of August and December last, provided that, upon the report of Her Majesty's Inspectors of Schools, my Lords find such masters to be efficient and deserving.'

It was very satisfactory to me to have been then enabled to state, that all such masters may enjoy the gratuities offered in their Lordships' Minutes, for the training of pupil teachers and stipendiary monitors apprenticed under the regulations of their Lordships, as well as the gratuities offered for the successful management of Schools of Industry, and for general merit.

I informed you also, that my Lords, being desirous to offer the strongest inducements to schoolmasters and schoolmistresses to render long and efficient services to the public had opened the prospect of a retiring pension to this class of teachers, and that the sole point of distinction which, in their Lordships' recent Minutes, had been left between this class of teachers and those who may obtain certificates of merit by a course of training in a Normal School under their Lordships' inspection, was the augmentation of salary to which the latter class will become entitled when provided with a house rent-free, and with a salary equal to twice the amount of the stipend granted from the Parliamentary Fund.

I was able at once to assure you, that my Lords did not intend that any injustice should be done to teachers whose merits and attainments equal those of masters and mistresses regularly trained in a Normal School under inspection, and provided with the required certificates of merit; as well as to intimate that their Lordships had under their consideration the important question, whether teachers who had not obtained such certificates at the close of a course of training in a

Normal School under inspection, should be admitted to an examination for certificates of merit.

The attention of their Lordships had been directed to this subject by numerous letters received from the trustees and managers, and from the masters of schools. My Lords had also before them the resolution of a meeting in Leeds, of the friends of the measure recently adopted by Government for the promotion of public education.

That resolution declares, 'That, as the benefits of Government aid are proposed to be confined to those masters and mistresses who have been trained in Normal Schools already under inspection, this meeting would beg leave respectfully to suggest that these benefits might, for the present, be extended to teachers who have not had that advantage, and who shall be reported to be duly qualified by competent examination.'

These communications having been carefully considered, I have now the satisfaction to say, that I am authorised to inform you that the Committee of Council on Education will cause regulations to be framed, for the purpose of defining the conditions upon which masters or mistresses of schools under their Lordships' inspection, who have not passed through a course of training in a Normal School, may be admitted to an examination for three classes of certificates, to correspond with those which are to be granted in Normal Schools.

Masters and mistresses who have not received such training, but who may, upon this examination, obtain certificates, will thus enjoy the augmentation of salary proposed to be granted, according to their Lordships' Minutes of August and December last, to teachers who shall have procured certificates of merit.

I am, &c.,

J. P. KAY SHUTTLEWORTH.

Mr. E. Salter, 68 Park Street, Hulme, Manchester,
    Secretary to the British Schoolmasters' Association.

---

38 Gloucester Square, Hyde Park, March 12, 1847.

REVEREND SIR,

I READ in the 'Patriot' newspaper this evening a letter to which your name is attached, addressed on behalf of the Committee of Privileges to ministers of the Wesleyan association, requesting them 'to use their best efforts to get a petition from every congregation in their circuits,' in order to induce 'the House of Commons not to vote any further sum of money to be placed at the disposal of the Committee of Council on Education, and to entreat the House to petition the Queen to dissolve the Committee by whom this pernicious scheme' (the Minutes for August and December, 1846) 'has been recommended, and to declare that the interests of the nation will be best promoted by the non-interference of Government as to the education of the people.' A form of petition is appended to this letter, and intended to be sent to every congregation connected with your Association.

For this purpose the letter commences with the following representation:—
'Her Majesty's Ministers having recently brought before Parliament certain Minutes of the Committee of Privy Council on Education, proposing that provision should be made by Government for training, supporting, and pensioning schoolmasters and mistresses, and for creating and supporting a widely-extended system of education, by which it is intended that the instructors of masses of the rising generation should become Government stipendiaries and expectants of Government pensions, to obtain which purposes they will have to secure the approbation of an Inspector appointed by Government, but who must also be sanctioned by one of the archbishops, and who is to remain in office only so long as such sanction is continued.'

If such was your interpretation of the intentions of the Government, I cannot wonder that you should have used your utmost efforts, in conjunction with the Committee of Privileges, to arouse the congregations of the Wesleyan Association to defeat so gross an injustice. But if you have misunderstood, and unintentionally very gravely misrepresented the plan developed in the recent Minutes of the Committee of Council, observe the consequences.

Every superintendent minister, placing confidence in your Committee of Privileges — every local preacher acting in obedience to the suggestions of his superintendent — and every congregation which may rely on the representations of its minister, will receive from your letter the impression that no school connected with the Wesleyan Association can partake of the grants offered by the Committee of Council in their recent Minutes, unless this school be subject to the visits of an Inspector, appointed with the concurrence of one of the archbishops, and liable to be dismissed by the withdrawal of the archiepiscopal sanction. They will believe that no Wesleyan pupil teacher can be appointed — no master can receive a gratuity — no teacher can be pensioned — no apprentice can be elected to a Queen's scholarship — and no candidate in a Normal School connected with the Wesleyan Association, can obtain a certificate, and the consequent augmentation of salary, unless he be examined by an Inspector appointed with the concurrence of an archbishop, and for whose continuance in office his grace's sanction is requisite.

Such a conception of the intentions of the Committee of Council would justify the appeal of the Committee of Privileges to the congregations of the Wesleyan Association, and such a representation is likely to rouse the superintendent ministers, the local preachers, and their congregations, to the utmost activity, to petition the House of Commons to withhold the parliamentary grant for the promotion of so 'pernicious a scheme.'

Accordingly, as your letter suggests, that 'it is important that the petitions should be numerously signed,' it is probable that on the ensuing Sunday (March 14th), as your letter is dated March 4th, the form of petition appended to your letter will be signed by great numbers of persons belonging to the congregations and Sunday schools of the Wesleyan Association. All will feel that a plan of education which thus imposes the interference of an ecclesiastical authority, as a condition of grants from the Committee of Council to dissenting schools, is an intolerable injustice.

You will rejoice to learn, that the danger which you apprehend to be impending over the schools connected with the congregations of the Wesleyan Association is a *delusion*.

The Committee of Council never made any grant to a dissenting school on such a condition as you have supposed. They have never acquired, either as a consequence of their grants, or otherwise, power to authorise any Inspector, appointed with the concurrence of an archbishop, to enter any British or dissenting school. The Order in Council of the 10th of August, 1840, makes the approval of an archbishop an incident in the appointment of *Inspectors of Church of England schools alone*.

Six other Inspectors have been appointed, in whose nomination the Archbishop has in no respect intervened, and *three more of this class* are about to be appointed. Their lordships have agreed (*vide* Minutes 1842-3, p. 537) that they will not proceed to recommend any candidate to Her Majesty as an Inspector of schools connected with the British and Foreign School Society, until they have consulted the Committee of that Society, and found that the candidate has their approval. In like manner, their Lordships have agreed to consult the Education Committee of the General Assembly of the Church of Scotland as to the appointment of any Inspectors of schools, which are by law, or by their constitution, connected with that church (*vide* Minutes 1839-40, pp. 19 and 20).

The Committee of Council have been of opinion that, unless each Inspector possessed the confidence of the religious communion with which the schools visited by him were connected, he could not usefully co-operate with the school managers. Their Lordships have, therefore, in proceeding to nominate Inspectors, been ready to consult the Central Board, watching over the interests of any distinct class of schools, in order to avoid the appointment of any persons, who, especially on religious grounds, did not enjoy their confidence. No Inspector is employed in the visitation of other schools than those for the examination of which he is appointed, except on the direct and formal invitation of their managers, which rarely occurs.

Schools connected with the Wesleyan Association would not, therefore, ever be entered by a Church of England Inspector, or by any Inspector who did not enjoy the confidence of the Committee of Privileges. If the managers of such schools desired the aid of Government to enable them to apprentice pupil teachers — to procure for these assistants exhibitions to Normal Schools at the close of their apprenticeship, or an augmentation of the salaries of their masters — the principle on which Inspectors of schools are appointed would oppose no obstacle to their application for such aid, for no person would be so employed who did not enjoy the confidence of the Committee of Privileges.

The opposite conception is a delusion, which the proceedings of the Committee of Council, as recorded in their Minutes, from the year 1839 to this date, disprove. Those Minutes contain abundant proof that the Committee of Council have, with unwavering impartiality, endeavoured on all occasions to protect the interests of the minority from civil injustice, while they have paid due respect both to the rights of conscience, and to the religious institutions and convictions of all classes of Her Majesty's subjects.

I am, &c.,
J. P. KAY SHUTTLEWORTH.

The Rev. Robert Eckett, 6 Argyle Square.

APPENDIX (B).

THE ORIGIN, PROCEDURE, AND RESULTS OF THE STRIKE OF THE OPERATIVE COTTON SPINNERS OF PRESTON, FROM OCTOBER, 1836, TO FEBRUARY, 1837.

(*Working Man's Guide Book,* 1839–40.)

Preston has, from an early period, been a principal seat of the cotton manufacture. In October last, there were in Preston and its vicinity forty-two cotton mills, giving employment to 8500 hands, and requiring about 1200 horse-power to work them, consuming about one twenty-first part of the cotton spun in the United Kingdom :

	£
And having a capital invested in them in buildings, machinery, &c., of about	550,000
And a working capital employed of about	250,000
Making a Total of	£800,000

The number of operative spinners employed in these mills was 660, each spinner having under his care on an average about 600 spindles.

The year 1836 was remarkable for great activity in the cotton trade; the master-spinners were making considerable profits, or at least such was the general belief, and the operative spinners were persuaded, with some truth, that they were not sharing in the general prosperity in the same degree as others of the same class in the neighbouring towns. Their net earnings — that is, what remained to them after paying the wages of the children employed by them as piecers — varied from 20s. to 25s. a week, and might be averaged at 22s. 6d., which was less than what was paid for the same description of work at the same period in other towns in the cotton districts, and particularly at Bolton, where the wages had recently been advanced, and which, in the disputes which afterwards arose, was assumed as a standard by the operative spinners of Preston.

It must here be observed, however, that the Preston masters had long been in the habit of adopting an uniform rate of wages, varying but little with the fluctuations in the state of their trade, whereas, in other places, and especially in Bolton, it had been the custom for the masters to raise the wages of their workpeople in favourable states of trade, and to lower them at times of depression. Such a practice, operating in conjunction with the almost universal want of economy and forethought amongst the working class, is necessarily very detrimental to the real interests of the operatives, giving them at one time a strong temptation to intemperance and excess, and at another reducing them to a very painful state of want and privation. Thus, in times of prosperity, the Bolton operative spinner may be receiving higher money wages than the spinner of Preston, but part of this differ-

Origin and Results of 'Strike' in Preston in 1836-7

ence is more nominal than real; for, if we take into consideration the comparative cheapness of the several articles constituting the expenditure of the working man in the two towns, we shall find that the advantage is, in no small degree, in favour of Preston, so that the same money wages will go further in the latter than the former place. In Bolton, the operative pays less for his coals; in Preston he pays less for provisions and house rent, and it is found that he has greatly the advantage over the former.

In October, 1836, while the spinners of Preston were receiving in money wages 22s. 6d. a week, those of Bolton were receiving about 26s. 6d.

There existed in Preston, previously to this time, a Spinners' 'Trades' Union, consisting of from 250 to 300 members, or less than one-half of the number of spinners employed there; but, inasmuch as it was a rule in many of the mills to give employment to those only who were unconnected with such institutions, its acts had been chiefly confined to relieving its own sick members, or contributing to the wants of other societies.

In October, 1836, on the occasion of the Preston spinners sending a deputation to Bolton and other places, to inquire into the current rate of wages, the 'Union' first began to assume a formidable aspect — numerous delegates, commonly called 'agitators,' began to arrive at Preston from Bolton, and the other places visited. Meetings were held; the disadvantages under which the Preston spinners laboured, as compared with those of Bolton and other places, were spoken of in exaggerated terms; the masters were denounced as unfeeling and tyrannical, and the efficacy of combinations, as a means of giving to the work-people a proper control over the proceedings of their masters, was pointed out and enlarged upon with great enthusiasm.

It may be proper here to observe, that none of the Preston people were officers of the Union, the affairs of the 'Union' being conducted by the delegates from other towns. Great excitement was produced, and nearly the whole of the spinners, not previously members of the Union, were induced or coerced by threats and intimidating means, to join the Union, and under this semblance of strength they, on the 13th of October, appointed a council, which commenced sitting at a public-house in the town.

The first act of the council was to wait on one of the most extensive houses in the town, who were known to be very strict in requiring from their hands an engagement not to belong to any 'Trades' Union,' and demand an advance in the spinners' wages, to which request the house refused to accede. Immediately after this, six spinners in the employment of this house became insubordinate, and were discharged, the remaining spinners threatening thereupon to leave their work, unless the six men were restored to work. The house then ascertained from their hands that they were in reality seeking, by advice of the spinners' council, to obtain the Bolton list of prices for spinning, the like demands being made simultaneously by the spinners to all the other masters in the town. The masters showed no disposition to give way to these demands made on them, and the result was, that all the spinners throughout the town united in giving notice to their masters of their intention to quit their work.

The masters now held a meeting, at which it was determined to offer the spinners an advance of ten per cent. on their gross earnings, or about 3s. 4d. per week, on the condition that they would detach themselves from the Union. This offer was in many instances accepted by individual spinners, but the council of the Union assuming the right to return an answer in the name of the whole body, rejected the offer of the masters, and renewed their demand of the 'Bolton List of Prices,' unaccompanied by any condition relative to the Union.

To these terms the masters refused to accede, and on Monday morning, the 7th November, the spinners discontinued their attendance, and the factories were closed.

From the following statement it would appear that the offer of an advance of ten per cent. on the previously existing rate of wages, was, in fact, setting aside the question of the Union, a concession of all the pecuniary advance that was demanded:—

	s.	d.
The gross weekly wages of the Preston spinner was	33	6
From which, if we deduct for the amount of the wages paid by the spinner to his piecers	11	0
There would remain for the net wages of the spinner the weekly sum of	22	6
To which, if we add the proposed addition of ten per cent. on the gross sum 33s. 6d. or	3	4
The result will be	25	10

which, taking into consideration the pecuniary advantages of cheaper living of the Preston spinners as compared with those of Bolton, was fully equal to the 26s. 6d. earned by the latter. From this it would appear that the struggle, on the part of the operatives, was rather to establish a precedent of successful resistance to the master, than to obtain any real and tangible benefit, inasmuch as the demand for the 'Bolton List of Prices' insisted upon by the operatives, amounted to a difference in the mode of reckoning the amount of wages for the work performed, which at Preston is computed by the yard, and at Bolton by the pound.

The operatives of Preston ceased working, and at the time of the turn-out, the 5th of November, they amounted, as was stated, to 8500 persons.

Of these 660 were spinners.
„ 1320 were piecers, children employed by the spinners.
„ 6100 were card-room hands, reelers, and power-loom weavers.
„ 420 were overlookers, packers, engineers, &c.

Making 8500 persons.

Of this number, it may be said, that only 660 (that is the whole of the spinners) voluntarily left their work, the greater part of the remaining 7840 being thereby thrown out of employment.

During the first fortnight of the turn-out no change was apparent in the condition of the work-people; some meetings were held both by masters and men, but nothing resulted from them. At the commencement of the second fortnight complaints began to be heard from the card-room hands, and from the shopkeepers of the town.

Early in December, when the mills had been closed for a month, the streets began to be crowded with beggars. The offices of the overseer were besieged with applicants for relief, the inmates of the workhouse began to increase rapidly, and scenes of the greatest misery and wretchedness were of constant occurrence. At this period the spinners were receiving from the fund of the Union five shillings a week each, and the piecers, some two and others three shillings a week; the card-room hands and power-loom weavers were destitute of all means of support, receiving no assistance except such as the masters afforded them, which (except in the cases of eighteen or twenty individuals who had not joined the Union) extended only to one meal a day for each person.

In December £100 was granted by the corporation towards relieving the general distress, and a meeting was convened for the purpose of raising a further sum, and of considering the most effectual means of putting an end to the turn-out, but nothing resulted from it.

Towards the middle of December, when the turn-out had lasted six weeks, it was evident that the funds of the Union were nearly exhausted.

By the end of December the distress had become universal and intense, and the masters came to the resolution of opening their mills, in order to give those who wished for it an opportunity of resuming their work. In doing so they announced their determination to abide by their former offer of an increase of ten per cent. on the rate of wages; but to require from those who should enter the mills, a written declaration to the effect, that they would not, at any future time, whilst in their service, become members of any Union or combination of workmen.

Immediately on the re-opening of the mills, which took place on the 9th of January, all the card-room hands rushed anxiously to their work, but the continued absence of the spinners rendered it impossible to give them employment.

At the end of the first week after the mills had been opened, forty spinners were at work, of whom eighteen were those who, as before stated, had not joined the Union, and the remaining twenty-two had never before been regularly employed in that kind of work.

In the course of the second week the number had increased to 100, of whom some were entirely new to the work, and three were seceders from the Union; and at the end of the third week there were 140 spinners at work; some of the additional forty having been procured from neighbouring towns. Besides this, in two of the factories a few self-acting mules, or spinning machines, were substituted for common mules, thereby dispensing with the services of the spinners.

As the number of spinners increased, of course a corresponding increase took place in the number of persons employed in the other departments.

Towards the middle of the fourth week the supplies from the funds of the Union suddenly stopped, and those who had depended entirely on this resource, had no alternative left but to endeavour to obtain re-admission to the factories.

On the 5th February, exactly three months from the day on which the mills were first closed, work was resumed in all the mills to its usual extent, but about 200 of the spinners who had been most active in the turn-out were replaced by new hands, and have since either left the town, or remain there without employment.

No systematic acts of violence, or violation of the law, took place during the turn-out. Detachments of military were stationed in the town to preserve order, but their services were not required. Some inflammatory hand-bills appeared on the walls, but without creating much sensation.

While the turn-out lasted, the operatives generally wandered about the streets without any definite object: seventy-five persons were brought before the magistrates and convicted of drunkenness and disorderly conduct; twelve were imprisoned or held to bail for assaults and intimidation; about twenty young females became prostitutes, of whom more than one-half are still so, and of whom two have since been transported for theft: three persons are believed to have died of starvation, and not less than 5000 must have suffered long and severely from hunger and cold. In almost every family the greater part of the wearing apparel and household furniture was pawned.

In nine houses out of ten, considerable arrears of rent were due, and out of the sum of £1600 deposited in the savings' bank, by about sixty spinners or overlookers, £900 was withdrawn in the course of the three months; most of those who could obtain credit, got into debt with the shopkeepers. The trade of the town suffered severely; many of the small shopkeepers were nearly ruined, and a few completely so.

The following estimate may be made of the direct pecuniary loss to all classes of operatives, in consequence of the turn-out:—

	£	s.	d.
The wages of the 660 spinners for 13 weeks, at 22s. 6d.	9,652	10	0
1320 piecers for 13 weeks, at 5s. 6d.	4,719	0	0
6520 card-room hands, weavers, overlookers, engineers, &c., &c., for 13 weeks, averaging 9s.	38,142	0	0
——— 8500			
Estimated loss sustained by hand-loom weavers in consequence of the turn-out	9,500	0	0
Estimated loss sustained by clerks, waggoners, carters, mechanics, dressers, sizers, &c., in consequence of the turn-out	8,000	0	0
Total	£70,013	0	0

From which must be deducted—

	£	s.	d.
Estimated amount of wages earned during the partial resumption of work, between the 9th of January and the 5th of February	5,013	0	0
Estimated value of relief given by the masters	1,000	0	0
Other private charity and parish relief	2,500	0	0
Allowance to the spinners and piecers from the funds of the Union	4,290	0	0
	£12,803	0	0
Leaving a net pecuniary loss to the whole body of the Preston operatives of	£57,210	0	0

But to the town at large it may be said the loss was that of the whole sum of £70,013, as the amount of the deductions are mostly of a charitable nature.

	£	s.	d.
Add to the loss to the Preston operatives	£57,210	0	0
The loss to the masters being three months' interest of £800,000, some of which being sunk capital was not only unproductive, but was taking harm from being rendered useless, has been estimated at	45,000	0	0
And the loss sustained by the shopkeepers from loss of business, bad debts, &c., &c.	4,986	0	0
Making the total loss to the town and trade of Preston, in this unavailing struggle	£107,196	0	0

APPENDIX (C).

ANNUAL COST OF ESTABLISHMENTS, ETC., FOR THE REPRESSION OF CRIME.

	£	£
Rates paid by Counties in England and Wales:		
Constables' rate	17,970	
Rural police rate	132,068	
		150,038
Paid by Votes of Parliament:		
Cost of prosecutions defrayed by the Treasury	21,000	
" " formerly paid from County rate	239,000	
" " relating to coinage	10,600	
Expenses of prison at Pentonville	19,934	
" " at Milbank	34,083	
" " at Parkhurst	12,463	
Expenses of criminal lunatics at Bethlem	3,935	
Issued from Consolidated Fund, for payment of the police of the Metropolis, including both the Police Courts' establishment and the		
Metropolitan police force £ 122,179		
Defrayed by rate on different parishes 210,500		
	332,679	
City of London: — Cost of police force	41,351	
Cost of police, defrayed by Corporate Towns in England and Wales	186,120	
Expenses connected with convicts, at home, at Bermuda, and at Gibraltar	62,330	
Freight of Ships employed in carrying Exiles, Stores, Provisions, &c.	35,622	
Votes for Convict Establishments, New South Wales and Van Diemen's Land	250,000	
		1,249,117
Expenses of criminal prosecutions, Scotland	64,610	
" of Central Prison, at Perth	6,693	
" of Prison Board for Scotland	8,986	
		80,289
Expenses of criminal prosecutions, Ireland	66,209	
" of Convict Depôt, Dublin	3,971	
" of Criminal lunatics, ditto	6,000	
" of Dublin police	36,000	
An equal sum levied by rate on inhabitants	36,000	
Expenses of constabulary force, Ireland, viz.,—		
Contributed from Consolidated Fund 271,497		
Amount raised by rate on counties, &c. 180,080		
	451,577	
		599,757
		£2,079,201

The above sum does not include any part of the cost of the judicial establishments of the country, since it would be necessary to maintain those establishments for the purposes of civil justice. It must be evident, however, that a fewer number of judges and other officers would suffice for that branch than is necessary for dispensing justice in both branches.

FOURTH PERIOD

TWO LETTERS TO EARL GRANVILLE, K.G.

IN 1861

1. ON THE RECOMMENDATIONS OF THE COMMISSIONERS APPOINTED BY WARRANT UNDER THE QUEEN'S SIGN MANUAL ON THE 30TH JUNE, 1858, TO INQUIRE INTO THE PRESENT STATE OF POPULAR EDUCATION IN ENGLAND, AS CONTAINED IN THEIR REPORT DATED THE 18TH MARCH, 1861, PRESENTED TO BOTH HOUSES OF PARLIAMENT BY COMMAND OF HER MAJESTY.

2. ON THE MINUTE OF THE COMMITTEE OF COUNCIL ON EDUCATION, DATED 29TH JULY, 1861, ESTABLISHING A REVISED CODE OF REGULATIONS FOR THE DISTRIBUTION OF THE PARLIAMENTARY GRANT.

LETTER TO THE EARL GRANVILLE, K.G.,

PRESIDENT OF THE COUNCIL AND OF THE COMMITTEE OF COUNCIL ON EDUCATION, ETC. ETC., ON THE REPORT OF THE COMMISSIONERS APPOINTED TO INQUIRE INTO THE STATE OF POPULAR EDUCATION IN ENGLAND.

MY LORD,

The Commission which has reviewed the Minutes of the Committee of Council, and the administration of the Parliamentary Grant for Public Education in England were called to the discharge of that duty, chiefly in consequence of the questions raised by the increase of the charge on the public revenue.

But the whole system was submitted to their scrutiny. They have, by a large majority, decided against relying for the support of elementary schools on the voluntary aid of parents and promoters. They have unanimously approved of the management of training and primary schools by the religious bodies; of the denominational character of the inspection; of the training of the teacher by his five years' apprenticeship, and two years' education as a Queen's scholar in a Training College. They even require that the proportion of pupil teachers should be increased from the present ratio of one in fifty on the average attendance to that of one in thirty. They do not alter the grants to Training Colleges. To the extent of 7s. to 8s. 6d. per scholar on the average attendance they subsidise the certificated and pupil teachers, who, in the proportions required by them would, at the present rate of aid, require 13s. $5\frac{1}{2}d$. But they provide a subsidiary grant, which might raise the aid to a successful school even to 15s. per scholar, so as also to meet in some degree that obtained from book and capitation grants under the present system. The Commissioners confirm the half-time system as applied to the associated labour of children in factories and other works, and recommend its extension.

They also perceive the necessity of encouraging evening schools, and recommend that grants be made for their organisation. The urgency of this need will be made daily more apparent by experience and discussion. They confirm the recommendations of the Report on the Training of Pauper Children published in 1840, and urge that these children should be removed from the workhouses and brought up in district schools. They recommend a steady progress in the development of reformatory institutions for vagrant and criminal children, and offer useful suggestions as to the schools of the army, navy, dockyards, and military asylums. A very able part of this report confirms the efforts made by successive keepers of the Great Seal to invest the Privy Council with important administrative functions as to certain endowments for education and for the poor.

The general result of the Commissioners' judicial examination of the existing system is therefore to erect a buttress to sustain it—apparently firm—if it could be regarded separately, from some suggestions which are like a dry rot in the new timber.

The grant from the Consolidated Fund is assessed on an annual value of £550,000,000; but the growth of the miscellaneous estimates within a few years has made successive Chancellors of the Exchequer jealous of the increase of each item. Calculations had been hazarded as to the claims which the present mode of administering the education grant would create on this fund. One principal question, therefore, to which the Commissioners had to direct their attention was, whether the Consolidated Fund could be relieved of any part of this burthen.

They have decided that the growth of income from school fees and from voluntary subscriptions must be so gradual, that no immediate and remarkable change in their proportions to the amount of public aid can be expected. One of the results of improved and extended education will, however, obviously be to develope the income from both of these sources until, in a quarter of a century, considerable relief may be had to the charge on the national fund. At least half a million annually may, within that time, be added to the present income from school-pence alone.

In searching for means of immediate relief to the Parliamentary grant, the Commissioners have examined the question of local rating. They had been warned that this subject had undergone anxious and prolonged scrutiny. The question presented is simply this—How can any part of the burthen of public education be transferred from an area of assessment of £550,000,000, on which the Consolidated Fund is charged, to one of £86,000,000, from which the county and borough rates are collected, without such a change as shall transfer the controlling and managing power altogether or substantially from the religious communions and the Committee of Council on Education to the ratepayers.

This question was examined during many months in 1851-2 by a mixed committee, representing all the religious communions of Manchester. The result of their deliberations was that no authority could be confided to the corporation of that city, or to any education committee appointed by it, except the administration of a capitation grant, upon terms which conferred mainly a power of registration and the rare arbitration of certain questions of civil and religious freedom. The bill framed on this basis was laboriously examined by a Committee of the House of Commons during two successive sessions of Parliament. Moreover, Lord John Russell's Borough Education Bill of 1853 was founded on this basis. Both these measures failed to secure support, because they were constructed on the principle of shifting a burthen from a wide area of assessment to one of less than one-sixth the capacity, without conferring local powers to economise the charge, or any substantial authority over its application. The corporations would not accept this illusive shadow of local government, with a real increase of their rates — cast on them for the relief of property six times greater than that locally assessed.

I speak of this the more emphatically, because I was responsible for aiding in the careful analysis of this question, so that the result might be brought before Parliament, in both forms, for public discussion.

My own impression finally was, that the ratepayers would not accept a transference of the charge of public education, in whole or in part, from the assessment of £550,000,000 of annual value to the local assessment of £86,000,000, without so substantial a transference of authority in the management of the schools, as would be subversive of that of the religious communions. If, for the sake of argument, we were to conceive that the control now exercised by the Committee of Council on Education over the Training Colleges, the apprenticeship, and the inspection, were in the hands of the ratepayers, I apprehend that civil and religious liberty would be in more danger from the dominant majority than from a department of representative Government watched by the religious bodies, under the criticism of the press, and subject to Parliament. This fear the elaborate investigation of the Commissioners confirms, by a new exhaustive process. They have doubtless examined numerous plans. Their scrutiny has resulted in one which consists in charging the county rates with an immediate burthen of £428,000 per annum, with the prospect of a very early increase to half a million. But they have not been able to confer on the County Committee of Education any other administrative functions than the appointment of examiners, who are to be certificated schoolmasters of seven years' standing, and who are to examine and register how many children can read, write, and cypher, in each school. The county board would thus have no real authority over the amount of the rates, except by appointing stingy examiners, and not the slightest influence in the schools, except by thus stinting their income to save the rates.

The transfer is itself a contradiction to Sir Robert Peel's policy, which removed the stipends of the teachers of pauper children and other similar charges from the poor-rates to the Consolidated Fund. The local administrative power acquired is so utterly disproportionate to the taxation imposed, that it rather oppresses than supports the principle of local administration, by transferring a central charge without giving the county board such authority as the magistracy have over the police, the prisons, the asylums, the bridges, and other objects of county expenditure.

This is not, therefore, decentralisation of anything but taxation. It is a removal of a charge of half a million from an area of £550,000,000 to one of £86,000,000, without giving any such control over the institutions to which this money is to be paid as exists in every other case.

There are certain words in the report of the Commission which the religious bodies must interpret for themselves. Among 'the direct effects which' they 'anticipate from this recommendation,' they state that (p. 338) '*it will secure as much local management as is at present desirable.*' Whether the increase of local management, in the future, is to be obtained by transferring to the County Board the examination of any Training College within the county, or of the pupil teachers and Queen's scholars, or by placing in its hands the appointment and direction of the inspection, together with a corresponding transference of the charge from the Consolidated Fund to the county rates, is not defined. But it must mean some or all of these things, or, on the other hand, such an interference by the County Board with the management of the schools by the Committees now appointed under their school deeds, as should give either the magistrates or the delegates of the ratepayers power to appoint and dismiss the teachers and regulate the details of school management.

This County Board is, therefore, either the thin end of the wedge of a total change in administrative action, or its power is too insignificant to justify the doubling of the county rates.

The grant administered for elementary education now amounts to £723,115. The Commissioners are of opinion that it can be restrained within the limits of £1,200,000, and will not increase to that amount for several years. The transfer of £500,000 from the Consolidated Fund to the county rates would secure no economy, and if unaccompanied with adequate local authority over education would be an unjustifiable expedient.

If, therefore, this charge cannot be justified as an economy of public funds, on what other grounds can it be defended?

The education department has for many years been in the condition of a juvenile hero outgrowing the suit of armour in which it was at first encased. Its helmet, greaves, and gauntlets have become instruments of torture. In other words, the building is too small — departments have swarmed out of it into neighbouring streets — its staff is too slender — and the provisional character of its arrangements has been injuriously prolonged. In their despair, the secretaries, worn out with the worry of an insufficient organisation, appeal to the Commission for relief.

The relief which the Commission offers is described as simplification. This consists in transacting the business of payment in forty county treasurers' offices and all the county banks, besides the education department, instead of as at present in the Council Office and the Post Offices only.

The cost of the present plan consists in the salaries of a few registering clerks in London, and in one-quarter per cent., paid from the education grant into the revenues of the Post Office. The payments are made by Post Office orders drawn in favour of each recipient of the grant, and sent to the correspondent of the school for distribution. The risks of confusion and misappropriation are thus minimised.

The plan proposed is, that the whole sum of grants due to a county should be paid in one sum periodically (it is not said whether monthly, quarterly, or annually), to the account of the county treasurer, accompanied by a statement of its appropriation to each school.

The correspondent of each school is to claim what is due to it from the county treasurer, who is to transfer the money to the local bank appointed by the correspondent. The cheques on this local bank are to be drawn in favour of each person who has acquired a claim to aid under the Minutes: the voucher of each payment is to be sent by the local bank to the county treasurer, who is to tabulate them for publication.

The complication consists in the employment of four agencies, besides the school managers, instead of two. The increase of expense would arise from the much larger number of clerks required to transact this business in each county treasurer's office than in one central department, and the employment of many unconnected banks in each county instead of the Post Offices, organised into one system strictly regulated by a central inspection and control, and which really make a profit out of the transaction. The risks of loss from error, confusion, and fraud, are obviously greatly increased by this complication. The clerk's work in the county treasurer's office, and the county banker's charge, would be a burthen on the county. The local bank could not afford to make minute payments and conduct the correspondence for less than one quarter per cent. of deduction from the grants to each school. All this involves an increase of complication, risk, and expense. The Commissioners do not announce any plan, but they leave an alarming suspicion that (as they expect such a simplification) this end will be sought under this scheme, by holding the examination of pupil teachers half-yearly in certain places, and sending their papers to a London office, where they are to be examined, and the apprentice passed or rejected without appeal. Yet the inspectors are to visit each elementary school as heretofore — they are to satisfy themselves as to the character and conduct of the apprentice — they are to hear him read, and observe his teaching and management of a class. Their report on the skill, character, and conduct of the pupil teachers, must be made either conjointly with that on the merely scholastic examination of the apprentices on paper, or separately. If conjointly, then both of these matters should come under the same eye for the primary report; otherwise there would be complication. If separately, then there must be delay, confusion, and conflict of authority. There would be no important change if the Inspectors are to conduct the collective examination of the apprentices on paper, or supposing they deputed the merely formal superintendence of this examination, then if the examination papers of the pupil teachers whose schools they have visited were to be brought under their review and reported on by them conjointly with their report on their character, conduct, and skill.

The Inspectors of late have availed themselves of every opportunity afforded by facilities of conveyance to assemble the pupil teachers of schools within a radius of four, six, or eight miles, for their scholastic examination; but they have thus brought together those pupil teachers whose schools they had visited or were about to visit. This has saved trouble to the Inspectors by the use of the same exercises for apprentices in the same year, and it has enabled the pupil teachers to work their papers with less interruption than is often possible on the day of the Inspector's parochial visit. But there are limits of convenience, as to distance and means of conveyance, in this which cannot be overstepped without mischief. Few managers of schools would like their pupil teachers to go more than ten miles from home. A journey of twenty miles (ten each way) in a farmer's open spring-cart, on a cold, wet day — a luncheon on cold bread and meat — and five hours' head work on examination papers — would endanger the health of many apprentices and their teachers accompanying them.

A distance of five or six miles should be the limit.

The system of apprenticeship has succeeded so as to secure the approbation of the managers of schools, of the Principals of Training Colleges, of the Inspectors, and of this Commission. But it has succeeded mainly because of the way in which the hourly influence of the teacher, and the authority of the clergy and the managers, have been in harmony with the final report of the Inspector, to whose judgment and experience all are inclined to defer, because he acts from personal communication with all concerned, and not as a mere scholastic calculating machine, but as a moral arbitrator. If there be any material change in this plan, I should expect the system of apprenticeship to give continually less and less satisfaction, and ultimately to fail.

But the proposals of the Commission, for the consolidation of the annual grants into three capitation grants, are also liable to serious objections.

The grants proposed to be paid from the Consolidated Fund, are—

First. A grant of 5*s.* 6*d.* to 6*s.* in schools containing less than sixty children, and from 4*s.* 6*d.* to 5*s.* in schools containing more than sixty children, to be paid per head, on the average number of children attending the school, where a certificated teacher is employed.

Secondly. A like capitation grant of 2*s.* 6*d.* where one duly qualified pupil teacher is employed for every thirty children in average attendance.

Thirdly. A payment of 20*s.* on the average attendance of children under seven in infant schools, without examition or condition.

In page 586, the Commissioners report that the present payments from the Parliamentary grant, for certificated teachers, amount to 3*s.* 5$\frac{1}{2}$*d.* per head on the average attendance of scholars in Church of England inspected schools, to 3*s.* 3*d.* per head in British inspected schools, and 4*s.* 4*d.* per head in denominational schools; and for pupil teachers (who are now employed in the proportion of one to every fifty scholars), the grant is at the rate of 6s. 2¾d. per head.

The grants to teachers and pupil teachers in Church of England inspected schools, amount together to 9s. 8½d. per scholar in attendance. But if one pupil teacher were now paid for by the Committee of Council for every thirty scholars in average attendance, the grant would be at the rate of 10s. per head for that alone.

A proposal, therefore, to raise the capitation grant, on account of the employment of certificated teachers, from 3s. 5½d. to 5s. 6d., and at the same time to depress the rate of grant for pupil teachers, from what would be 10s. under the present system to 2s. 6d., ought not to have proceeded from a Commission which approves the pupil teacher system so heartily, that it proposes to insist on an increase of more than one third of their relative numbers. The managers are called on to decide whether they will incur a charge of 10s. per scholar for a grant of 2s. 6d. per scholar. Throughout England and Wales, more than three-fifths of the children attend the same school less than two years, and more than two-fifths less than one year. If, therefore, it be replied that the managers might make up the difference by the fourth capitation grant proposed by the Commissioners for every child who may pass an examination in reading, writing, and arithmetic, the answer is, that there would obviously be more risk of failure than of success, since the migration of scholars is so frequent. The rate of capitation grant which the Commission propose to give on the average attendance, where certificated teachers and pupil teachers respectively are employed, is obviously an error which, in practice, would produce only confusion.

The capitation grant of 20s., on the average attendance of children in infant schools under seven, is to be given without any examination, or, so far as I can perceive, any other condition than the attendance of the child in a building of a certain size which can be reported to be not unhealthy.

This mode of administration would be novel, and, if expedient, might save all trouble but the keeping of registers. If the managers of infant schools are entitled to this confidence, good ground would have to be shown why it should not be extended to the managers of schools having children above seven years of age. If such a principle were adopted in practice, the whole machinery of Public Inspection, Apprenticeships, and Training Colleges would have to be disused or disconnected from the Education department, for it would have no administrative value whatever. All that would be needed for the administration of such an unconditional capitation grant would be a pay office and local audit clerks to examine registers of schools and certify claims founded on the attendance thus recorded. This cannot be the intention of the Commissioners, yet it is the necessary consequence of their proposal as it stands.

If even the infant schools to be thus aided were required to employ certificated teachers and pupil teachers in the present proportions, they would receive at least 20s. per scholar from this form of grant; whereas the Committee of Council obtain the same result for 9s. 8$\frac{1}{2}d$. per scholar on the average attendance.

The Commissioners might have continued the present system of aiding infant schools, if they had not obviously shrunk from the contradiction of paying for the machinery of education trained and acting under inspection in these schools, while they repudiate the sufficiency of that system in boys' and girls' schools.

Turning from the capitation grants proposed by the Commission to be paid from the Consolidated Fund to that which is proposed to be charged on the county rate, we encounter a new principle of administration as applied to elementary schools. The Commission desire to increase the proportionate number of scholars who are able to pass an examination in reading, writing, and arithmetic. For this purpose, they propose to make a capitation grant in a form which, in schools having only certificated teachers, might attain a maximum of from 9s. to 10s. 6d. per head on the average attendance; which in those that had also the required number of pupil teachers might reach 7s. per head; and in schools which had neither certificated teachers nor pupil teachers might reach any sum short of 22s. 6d. per head.

No condition is inserted in the scheme requiring subscriptions in any proportion to meet this fourth form of grant, for it is intended to encourage schools founded by independent or adventure teachers; nor is any stipulation even made as to school-pence. The limitation in these respects applies only to the amount of grants from three sources of capitation collectively.

This fourth form of grant will be found to operate, as far as it goes, as a premium on discarding certificated teachers and pupil teachers, and on limiting instruction to reading, writing, and arithmetic. It is proper to illustrate its tendencies by extreme cases.

We might suppose a man, broken down in character, without a certificate, and without the technical knowledge required to obtain one, though with skill enough to teach reading, writing, and arithmetic. He registers himself as a schoolmaster, takes a cottage with a deserted loom-shop, or garret, 20 feet by 24 feet, or 16 feet by 30 feet. In this he puts writing-desks, benches, and a grate or stove. At an outlay of a few pounds, and with the risk of five to seven pounds of annual rental he is a schoolmaster. He may be registered without examination (p. 96). He admits pupils solely with a view to claim the largest possible sum from the county rate. His scholars pay threepence or fourpence per week, conditionally that if regular in attendance for 150 days in the year, and if they pass their examination in reading, writing, and arithmetic, one half the school-pence is to be repaid to them. No scholars are admitted unless they can pass a certain preliminary examination. The children prepared by good infant schools are canvassed for and brought to this adventure school. He may even get the best scholars of the parochial or congregational school to attend for 140 days by some inducement to which the managers would not stoop, or which, in their case, would be subversive of discipline. The whole school-time is concentrated on the three subjects of instruction. Nothing else is taught. If forty scholars attend and pass out of sixty, probably £13 would be received from school-pence, even though half were returned or lost; and the master could also receive £44 from the Government. He would have a clear income of £50 per year.

If we were to suppose such a man to have a patron willing to back him, either from opposition to the clergyman, or to the dissenting minister, or to the squire, or to the managing committee, or as a means of easily providing for one having claims of relationship or otherwise, or out of a spurious charity for a broken-down man, this grant may thus be made an effectual local blister, with the certainty of keeping the instruction limited to its lowest elements, without any moral redeeming qualities, and without any religious instruction. The Commissioners recognise the great moral and social benefits flowing from the schools of the religious communions. If, for the sake of argument, we were to admit that the arts of reading, writing, and cyphering would be more effectually taught on their plan, what becomes of the religious and moral influences, and the social bond?

But in an ordinary parochial school, which depends, as is too frequently the case, on some one individual for a third part or half of its resources (even supposing that the certificated teacher were employed), this grant would obviously, on the part of the teacher, be a strong motive to limit the instruction more and more to the three elementary subjects, and to concentrate all his efforts on them, in order to secure the 9s. or 10s. 6d. per head which would still be attainable under the proposed scheme of grants. He would thus save his patron's purse, and establish claims on his gratitude. In other cases, a niggard patron, or committee, or managers starved in their resources, would eke out these funds by the most stringent limitation of the instruction to that which would pay. They would aim at securing the largest amount of grant for teaching these elements only.

This effort endangers not merely the religious instruction, the general information of the scholars, but even their understanding of what they read and their orthography. They are not required to write from dictation, nor to be examined in the meaning of what they read. The largest amount of this capitation grant can be obtained by sacrificing the moral and religious instruction, the intellectual training and general information, and restricting the instruction to a mechanical drill in the reading, writing, and arithmetic.

But any capitation grant, the distribution of which is determined by the results of instruction in schools, is liable to the fundamental objection that the average period of the attendance of the majority of scholars is so short, that, as far as that majority is concerned, few schools would be paid for the results of their own work. In the specimen districts, 42·3 per cent. of the scholars (p. 659) had been in the same public week-day school less than one year, and 22·7 per cent. had been one year, but less than two years. These proportions for England and Wales are 41·65 per cent. of the scholars who had attended the same school less than one year, and 22·58 who had been one year and less than two years. With such migratory scholars, it is impossible justly to pay for work done in schools on any plan constructed to embrace those three-fifths of the scholars who attend school less than two years. The remaining 35·77 per cent. who attend more than two years are alone subjects for an examination of the results secured by the work of any school. This, however, is not the proposal of the Commission. Their proposal is to pay a capitation grant on every scholar who has attended 140 days in the preceding year, and can read, write, and cypher. A scholar cannot learn to read, write, and cypher so as to pass a public examination in two years, much less in 140 days. Any examination of the majority of more than three-fifths who attend less than two years must therefore obviously fail to ascertain how far even these elements have been taught to that majority in any school. If the remaining two-fifths who have been in the school more than two years were separated from the other scholars, and examined apart, some approximate estimate might be thus made of the work done in the school. If any grant could be devised founded on the results of the school work, it must be proportionate only to the proficiency of this two-fifths of the scholars. But the working of any such grant was long ago examined, and rejected as full of difficulties which appeared insuperable.

I purposely confine my remarks to those practical recommendations of the Commissioners which affect the administration of the aid now distributed from the Parliamentary grant. In as far as the Report of the Commissioners approves of the present system, that sanction has its value, as the result of a careful critical analysis by a body of able men, selected because they had no previous connection with this administration, and for the most part, none with the controversies attending its establishment. Their Report, in the main agreeing with experience, points to a statesmanlike perseverance in those efforts hitherto made with so much success, by the Committee of Council, to develope in the existing system all its civil and secular elements, in harmony with the religious, and also with liberty of conscience. But, where their Report departs from that system, I have endeavoured to show how difficult it is to do anything inconsistent with that experience.

The force which will ultimately transform the whole

will be the result of education itself. When the people know that they have even more interest in the education of their children than their rulers have, they will more and more take charge of it. They now bear two-thirds of the burthen; but that third which they do not pay has given value to what before was of little worth, and has thus created a transient power destined to pass from the Government into the hands of those who will take the charge. The transference of administrative power to the local managers and the parents will attend the gradual assumption by them of the payment of the pupil teachers, and of the whole of the stipends of the certificated teachers, consequent on the effects of education on some generations of parents, and on the middle classes.

The Parliamentary grant has hitherto been so administered by the Committee of Council as to stimulate the investment of large sums in school buildings, by giving about one-third of their value. Between 1839 and 1860 grants amounting to £1,076,753 have caused an investment of subscriptions amounting to £2,360,226 in school buildings, or altogether of £3,436,226. The grant has also promoted the rapid growth of the annual income of schools, by subsidies at a similar rate of one-third the whole annual outlay, so that probably two millions annually are now expended in the support of schools. The public grant may in a few years increase, with corresponding results, to £1,000,000 or £1,200,000, making in its progress adequate provision for the education of youth from school age to manhood; but at that point, by well-devised antecedent expedients, its increase may not only be arrested, but this annual aid may be converted into an instrument, in the hands of skilful administrators, by which all the rest of the work may be done in the most apathetic as well as in the most earnest districts. That result attained, a new series of operations may commence, by which the charge of public education may be gradually transferred from the Consolidated Fund to the local sources of income, school-pence and subscriptions.

Both of these operations will be accelerated by giving to the Privy Council sufficient administrative authority over the charities applicable to the education of the poor.

The hopes of the voluntary educationists would thus, step by step, assume the form of probabilities, or realities, through means which they have regarded with unwarrantable distrust. For, from the first, this system was composed of two elements: one of which—viz. the resource of Christian benevolence and parental solicitude—was by the natural consequences of success rendered capable of indefinite extension; while the other—the aid granted by Parliament—was destined as it grew to awaken a jealousy and resistance, greater in a geometric ratio than its increase. It was therefore clear from the first that if a system of aid from local rates were not adopted, the grant from Parliament must have an early limit and must then be regarded as an instrument for the development of that other element in the system, which was capable of indefinite expansion. All proposals for deriving support for public education in England and Wales from the local rates have failed—from Lord Brougham's early Bill to Sir James Graham's Education Clauses in his Factories' Bill in 1842—the Manchester and Salford Education Bill—and those of Lord John Russell and Sir John Pakington. To these failures, this Commission has added a proposal which, if it were practicable, is liable to the most grave objections. The question of deriving support for public education from the local rates is therefore probably settled in the negative.

But if it were not, it would be proper to observe at greater length on the difference between the tendencies of such a system, as respects its influence on voluntary support from parents and subscribers, when compared with that of the Parliamentary grant wisely administered. The tendency of the local rating system would be, not to stimulate but to benumb voluntary exertion. A subscriber might properly say, since local rates are by law established, 'I see no reason why I should relieve the purses of absentee proprietors, or of niggardly residents, by my contribution.' A parent would say, ' If the schools are provided by law and paid for from the rates, for the education of all who are disposed to send their children there, it is unjust to ask from me a payment so disproportionate to my means as school-pence. I will pay the rate which is proportionate to my means, but not the school-pence, which are disproportionate. I claim the education for my child as a citizen.' Thus the sense of parental duty would be superseded by the policy of the State, which would wean the child from the parent. It is evident that neither subscriptions nor school-pence would long be paid under such a system. The whole of the £3,000,000 annually required to educate two millions of scholars, would soon come to be charged on the local rates.

The opposite result of a gradual transference of the burthen to the local resources—school-pence and subscriptions—might be attained by a wise administration of the Parliamentary grant, after it had attained the maximum which I have indicated.

In the impatience felt that all is not yet done, it is forgotten that seven years—from 1839, when the Committee of Council was founded—were chiefly expended in a succession of almost mortal conflicts, as to the principles on which the system of public education should be founded. The Minutes of 1846, and those of 1853, settled the course of administration, which, with modifications of detail, has since been pursued. Fifteen years are but a brief period for a great national change. All permanently beneficial improvements are the slow growth of secular development. Up to this time, the Minutes of Council have had a remarkable success, out-stepping the expectation of their authors, but rebuking hasty generalisation, which had conceived that a national system of education could be extemporised on paper, approved in Parliament, and, when made law, have a universal existence like a new post-office administration, or a new tax.

These views, which are the gradual result of observation of the working of the education scheme, I desire to submit through your Lordship to the consideration of the Committee of Council on Education.

> I have the honour to be, my Lord,
> Your obedient servant,
> JAMES P. KAY SHUTTLEWORTH.

38, Gloucester Square, Hyde Park, W.
April 24th, 1861.

LETTER TO EARL GRANVILLE, K.G.

ON THE REVISED CODE OF REGULATIONS CONTAINED IN THE MINUTE OF THE COMMITTEE OF COUNCIL ON EDUCATION DATED JULY 29TH, 1861.

38, Gloucester Square, Hyde Park,
November 4, 1861.

MY LORD,

I had the honour to address to you a letter soon after the appearance of the Report of the Royal Commission, on the 24th of April, 1861.

That letter was confined to those practical recommendations of the Commissioners which affected the administration of aid from 'the Parliamentary Grant.' The period when the annual grant would come under the consideration of Parliament was not remote, and the direct bearing of those recommendations on the financial arrangements to be then discussed appeared to justify immediate comment. I had no doubt whatever that in doing this, I was loyally aiding the Committee of Council in disposing of impracticable suggestions.

Other parts of that Report were left without comment. Almost all the Managers of Training Colleges and elementary schools, in common with the most experienced Principals and Teachers, regretted that they were compelled to differ from the Commissioners, both on questions of fact, and on principles so critical that on them hinged the plan which the Commissioners proposed.

The committees of the great Education societies of the religious communions had confidence that nothing would be done by the Committee of Council on Education materially to derange, much less to subvert, the system which they had been encouraged by the Government to build up. On the 11th of July the Vice-President confirmed this confidence ' on moving the Education Estimate,' when he said (p. 11)—' If we have spent £4,800,000 in educating the people, private liberality has spent double that sum. In fact, the opinion as to what system of education is to prevail, will be regulated by the opinion of those whose hands maintain it :' Also, when he prefaced his statement of ' the outline of the Minute' with the ' assurance that the Committee need not be afraid that we contemplate any *coup d'état.*' (p. 25.) And again, when he said—' We think it would be rash and imprudent to sweep away a machinery which has been constructed with great labour, care, and dexterity,—which, although it may be complicated and difficult to work, has answered many of the purposes for which it was designed, in order to substitute the new and untried plan of trusting merely to the results of examination.' (p. 27.)

Those who bore in mind the fierce conflicts which had defeated every attempt to found national education on any other basis, and had observed that the churches and congregations had been at length weaned from a jealousy of the interference of the State, rejoiced in the prospect of the maintenance of this harmony. Gradually the limits of the authority of the several boards of education, the managers of schools, the inspectors, the teachers, and the Committee of Council on Education had been defined.

The several Education societies contributed invaluable services, and two-thirds of the permanent outlay in founding schools, as well as of the annual expense of supporting them. The Committee of Council appeared to think that they had made a good bargain for the civil Government, in stimulating, by such an outlay, the production of so large an income and the good management of schools. The money paid by Parliament rose to £750,000, but represented an annual outlay of more than two millions of money, the rest of which was derived from private and local sources.

The 'Revised Code' has been so interpreted by the managers and teachers of schools as to produce a conviction that it would destroy the existing system. I think it right faithfully to record their impressions. They say that the Code at once abrogates the principles on which the Parliamentary grant has hitherto been administered; for it condemns the method of examining results in the education of the pupil teachers, Queen's Scholars, and students in Training Colleges, pursued in the present mode of the inspection of the teacher's work in their schools. It abolishes the plan of paying for the efficiency of the machinery in the schools, subject to satisfaction with the state of the instruction. It releases the teacher from all direct obligation to the State, and at the same time renders his income much more uncertain and insecure. It cuts off about two-fifths of the annual grants of elementary schools. The abruptness of this change shakes the confidence of the managers of 7500 inspected schools in the Committee of Council on Education, for it requires them in one year to raise £175,000, in addition to their present resources, or to cut down to the extent in which they fail to do this, the machinery of their schools.

Contrary to the recommendations of the Royal Commissioners, it lops off a large part of the income of the Training Colleges. Their Principals declare that it further discourages them by making it certain that they will be supplied by quite an inferior class of Queen's Scholars — for the Code, contrary to all experience as to their sufficiency, apparently reduces the average stipend[1] and the time for the instruction of pupil teachers one-third. It proposes to mix them with evening scholars — for the most part rough youths learning only the humblest elements, when the instruction of the pupil teachers would be rendered almost if not quite impracticable. It renders

---

[1] Revised Code, Clause 47 (b).

their prospects less encouraging, by throwing the teacher's support wholly on the managers at a time when one-third of the managers' school-income is made extremely uncertain, and on the average reduced two-fifths. It renders the literary certificate purely honorary, and thus removes the chief motive for remaining two years in the Training Colleges. Under these circumstances one-half the Training Colleges would be closed, though built with direct encouragement from the Government not exceeding one-third their cost, at a large expense to their founders.

The effect of these changes would, in the opinion of the official representatives ' of the National and Church of England Education Societies; the British and Foreign, and Home and Colonial School Societies; the Wesleyan Education Committee; and of the Principals of the Metropolitan Training Colleges, assembled on the 10th of October,' be, ' to introduce into elementary schools a lower class of teachers, and to degrade the instruction in the schools.'

I trust your Lordship will permit me to submit to the Committee of Council the reasons why the promoters of schools are of opinion that this Revised Code is impracticable, without pulverising the existing system and destroying the connection of the Government with elementary education.

The vindication of the Revised Code is based on the denial that the existing system secures adequate results. By implication it attributes this alleged failure to a misdirection of effort. The teachers are too highly instructed, —they are above their work,—their daily instruction as apprentices and their residence in college must be shortened,—their education must be lowered to the level of their work,—that level is the teaching of reading, writing, and arithmetic, to scholars early absorbed by labour in agriculture or manufactures. This work ought to be done before eleven. No working man's child need be paid for after that age. The teachers have been mischievously pampered and protected. 'Hitherto,' says the Vice-President, 'we have been living under a system of bounties and protection; now we prefer to have a little free trade.' (p. 31.) The teachers must, like corn and cotton, be subject to the law of supply and demand. They and the managers must make the best bargains they can. The school managers must be paid only for work done. It is quite easy to test the work their teachers do, by examining every scholar in those elements which alone are the care of the State. If a fair proportion of the scholars learn to read, write, and cypher before they are eleven years old, nothing else is wanted. But to accomplish this—whatever has been the age at which a child first entered school—whatever his home training, capacity, or the comparative regularity of his school attendance,— any school which takes charge of him must either do so without State aid, or must by some art lift him up to a fixed standard of attainment, to be required between the ages, respectively, of 3 and 7,—7 and 9,—9 and 11, and 11 upwards. If he know more and can do more than is required at his age by this standard, he must be examined among those who are less proficient than himself.

The remedy devised in the Code for the defects of the existing system may be thus defined:—

The most certain way in which to secure the only results which are the legitimate concern of the State in elementary schools, is to examine each scholar in reading, writing, and arithmetic, and pay the managers a certain sum per head for each school attendance of every scholar who can pass an examination in each of these three elements, according to a standard of attainment to be required at fixed periods of age, and other conditions set forth in the Code.

As respects the foregoing vindication of the Code, as far as it is grounded on the alleged inadequacy of the results obtained under the existing system, the promoters of education maintain that they have, under all the difficulties with which they have had to struggle, produced so large

Against the Revised Code of 1861-2

an amount of the only results which were attainable in the time during which they have been at work, that they base the vindication of the existing system on those results.

The Royal Commissioners, however, cast a shadow of doubt on the public satisfaction with the progress of elementary education, by giving great prominence in this respect to the alleged failure of a large part of the scholars to read, write, and cypher. Archdeacon Sinclair, the Treasurer of the National Society, replies that 'in respect to National Schools in particular, it appears from the Reports of the Queen's Inspectors for the year 1860-61, that of schools under certificated teachers, the per centage reported to have been instructed " excellently," " well," or " fairly," was, in reading, 86·2 ; in writing, 87·9 ; and in arithmetic, 80.' The British and Foreign, and Wesleyan Education Committee reply in like manner.

I throw into a note the results reported by the Inspectors of Schools, as recorded by the Committee of Council for 1860-61, and extracts from the Inspector's Reports, for which I am indebted to Mr. J. Langton.[1]

The Committees of the great Educational Societies would not, however, be content to leave the question on this issue. They would say —

1. That the obstacles to the production of the results contemplated in the Report of the Commissioners in teaching reading, writing, and cyphering well, to three-fifths of the scholars, have been hitherto insurmountable.

2. That satisfactory results have been obtained —

   (*a*) In building and founding schools.
   (*b*) In getting rid of brutish incapacity to learn, gross habits, heathenism, and barbarism in their scholars, notwithstanding frequent migration, extreme irregularity of attendance at school, and the rareness of auxiliary home training.

---

[1] This note contained extracts from the Reports of Her Majesty's Inspectors giving a favourable account of the results obtained. It is excluded because of want of space.

(c) In teaching the elements, and giving general intelligence.

(d) In training the existing machinery of 23,000 pupil teachers, assistant and certificated teachers.

(e) In accomplishing all these results, while they have satisfied the feeling and convictions of the Church and other religious communions.

(f) In the moral and religious influences exercised by the schools as one of the most powerful agencies of civilisation; the value of which receives a signal recognition from the Commissioners.

Now, on these results the Royal Commission has given a favourable Report, with the exception already stated.

The first of the two preceding pleas of the promoters of schools may be demonstrated upon the elements collected by the Royal Commission in support of their plan of making a considerable part of the annual grants to schools dependent on the number of scholars who could pass an examination in reading, writing, and cyphering.

The Commissioners state their own proposition (p. 174) in the following words :—' Even under the present condition of school age and attendance, it would be possible for at least three-fifths of the children on the books of the schools, the 63·7 per cent. who attend 100 days and upwards, to learn to read and write without conscious difficulty, and to perform such arithmetical operations as occur in the ordinary business of life. This knowledge they might receive while under the influence of wholesome moral and religious discipline, and they might add to it an acquaintance with the leading principles of religion, and the rules of conduct which flow from them.'

The hindrances under the heads of school age and attendance are erroneously estimated in this formula.

National education does not depend simply on the school-training of one generation. The first generation of children in school inherit some physical incapacity to learn. Their instruction is hindered by the late age at which they enter, the extreme irregularity with which they are sent to school, and the early age at which they are withdrawn. They have no help at home from semi-barbarous parents; but on the contrary, much hindrance from bad example, rude household management, capricious and often harsh treatment, and the incapacity of the parents to understand the value of school training. The influence of the school is not fully felt, even in the humblest technical acquirements of the children, until the parents have been themselves trained and instructed in day and evening schools, and civilised by other influences.

The Commissioners have overlooked the condition of the people immediately before the constitution of the Committee of Council on Education. In the pauperised counties they were in a state resembling helotry. The labourers were bound to their parish by a strict law of settlement. They were largely dependent on the poor-rate. There were few or no schools. The population was ignorant and demoralised; it had the craft of the pauper, or of the pensioner on parochial doles,—of the poacher and the squatter on the common, but not the manly bearing of the independent labourer. Wages varied from 7s., in Dorsetshire and some parts of Suffolk, to 10s. per week in other counties. The income of an agricultural labourer's family on the average was £26 to £30 per annum, including harvest work and the earnings of children.

The manufacturing and mining districts had been peopled in fifty years with a vast population gathered from these pauper counties,—from wolds, moors, fens, and from the wild, desolate hills and glens of the border and of Wales. The villages and even the towns were rude, irregular, to a great extent unsewered and unpaved,— without proper water supply or police. Entire districts were without church or school, and religious teaching was supplied by voluntary agencies, while education was given almost solely in scattered Sunday Schools.

The last twenty-five years has witnessed a great municipal and religious revolution;—the last fifteen years a still greater change in education. When schools were planted twenty years ago in towns, villages, and rural parishes, almost the only teachers were either untrained men, who from some defect of body or health had been driven from the rougher struggles of life or muscular toil, or were self-taught Sunday School teachers, trained for three or six months in some central Model School.

They had to struggle, aided only by monitors under thirteen years of age, with the untamed brutishness of the wild or pauperised immigrant population,—with the semi-barbarism of children from coarse sensual homes,—with the utter want of consciousness in the population that humble learning could do their children any good,—with the then extravagant and harsh claims of an unorganised system of manufacturing and mining labour,—with the absence of previous training in the home or infant school, —with the late age at which children with no school-habits, savage, ignorant, incapable, wayward, or wild, came under their care,—with irregularity of attendance, — short school attendance in each year, and brief school time altogether,—constant migration of families,—and overwhelming ill-paid duties.

To grapple with these evils, the Government resolved to create a new machinery of public education. This new trained machinery of apprenticed pupil teachers, assistant and certificated teachers, has come into existence chiefly since 1847. The number in each year since that date has been as follows (p. 638, vol. i. Report of Royal Commission):—

At the end of Year.	Number of Certificated Teachers.			Number of Assistant Teachers.			Number of Pupil Teachers.		
	Male.	Female.	Total.	Male.	Female.	Total.	Male.	Female.	Total.
1849	. .	. .	681	. .	. .	. .	2424	1156	3580
1850	. .	. .	980	. .	. .	. .	3070	1590	4660
1851	845	328	1173	. .	. .	. .	3657	1950	5607
1852	1158	513	1671	. .	. .	. .	4011	2169	6180
1853	1541	756	2297	67	28	95	4308	2604	6912
1854	1859	977	2836	139	33	172	4500	3096	7596
1855	2242	1190	3432	173	48	221	4910	3614	8524
1856	2726	1647	4373	181	44	225	5800	4445	10,245
1857	3206	1960	5166	198	46	244	6773	5449	12,222
1858	3568	2320	5888	184	59	243	7673	6351	14,024
1859	4137	2741	6878	214	81	295	8219	7005	15,224

This corps of teachers has been like the raw recruits of an army suddenly raised—brought into the field in successive battalions, on the verge of an immature manhood, and placed, as soon as drilled, in the front of difficulties and dangers. They have had to take up everywhere the work of the untrained masters. They have been the pioneers of civilisation. Fourteen years have barely elapsed since their first companies took up their position, and their ranks are still full of the last batches of raw recruits. The schools hitherto founded have met the wants of barely one-half of the population. Every year has been adding to the experience of the Inspectors of schools, and of managers and teachers. But schools are not universal, and are not yet thoroughly efficient.

The teachers have had to contend with all the obstacles which defeated their untrained predecessors. If some of these hindrances be examined in detail, it will become apparent that the proposition of the Commissioners, that it is reasonable, under all these circumstances, to expect that three-fifths of the scholars should now have the attainments required by them, is a fallacy, founded on a neglect of these considerations. I have thrown into a note[1] a

---

[1] The manufacturing districts of Lancashire and Yorkshire have been fed by a constant immigration from the wolds of North Yorkshire and the border, and from the moors of Cumberland, Westmoreland, Derbyshire, the Pennine Chain, and Wales. A family enters a manufacturing village; the children are at various school ages, from seven to eleven. They probably

more minute description of certain typical classes of uncivilised scholars whom the teachers have had to train.

All these classes of children tend, if the school contain any other more fortunate scholars, to drag down their

have never lived but in a hovel; have never been in the street of a village or town; are unacquainted with common usages of social life; perhaps, never saw a book; are bewildered by the rapid motion of crowds; confused in an assemblage of scholars. They have to be taught to stand upright,—to walk without a slouching gait,—to sit without crouching like a sheep dog. They have to learn some decency in their skin, hair, and dress. They are commonly either cowed and sullen, or wild, fierce, and obstinate. In the street they are often in a tumult of rude agitation. In the school they are probably classed with scholars some years younger than themselves. They have no habits of attention, and are distracted by the Babel of sounds about them. The effort of abstraction required to connect a sound with a letter is at first impossible to them. Their parents are almost equally brutish. They have lived solitary lives in some wild region, where the husband has been a shepherd, or hind, or quarryman, or miner, or turf cutter, or has won a precarious livelihood as a carrier, driver of loaded lime ponies, or poacher. The pressing wants of a growing family have induced them to accept the offer of some agent from a mill. From personal experience of many years, I know that such children as these form a large portion of the scholars which the schools of the cotton and woollen districts have to civilise and Christianise. A large part of that better work has often been accomplished, and the benumbed brain has been awakened from its torpidity, and fitted for the reception of knowledge which there has not been time to give. The half-time system in factories, and the rule that no child under eight shall be employed in them, have been in operation little more than twenty years. Before this time the factory children of settled families were as brutish as they still are in mining districts. The children employed in bleach and print works have had only a limited and almost worthless protection from too early and excessive labour.

A different kind of brutishness is shown by a large class of scholars in the most degraded parts of great cities. A London child, living in a street of brothels and thieves' dens, with parents leading abandoned lives, spends his day in the kennel among sharp-witted, restless little creatures like himself. He is his own master. His powers of observation are singularly acute; his powers of decision rapid; his will energetic. He is known as the 'Arab of the street.' He learns a great deal of evil. Perhaps, he is an accomplished thief or beggar, or picks up a precarious living by holding horses, sweeping a crossing, or costermongering. Such children have of late years been netted in shoals,—got into schools,—have been won, tamed, and, in some degree, taught. But is it not a mischievous fallacy to say that the work done is to be measured by the proficiency of such children in reading, writing, and arithmetic? All that has been done has been against wind and tide. At home—misery, drunkenness, sullen despair, or the irritability of a dissolute life, drive the child into the street. Bad example at home lends its corruption to the foulness of the street of stews, and hiding holes. Are twenty scattered weeks, even if repeated in three successive years, enough to get instruction. They introduce elements of disorder. They overtax the energies of the teachers in striving to lift them somewhat nearer to a level of intelligence and decency. I have had experience during nearly twenty years of large schools, through which, until lately, has floated a constant supply of an immigrant semi-savage population, bred on the moors of the Pennine Chain. While this immigration of an uncivilised transient population continued, and the teachers had also the additional burthen of the half-time factory system, a staff of most skilful trained teachers, working with exemplary industry, failed to produce any results in the schools which would bear the application of the Commissioners' test. Yet the cost of these schools, since 1844, has seldom been below 30s. per scholar. Of late years the surrounding population has become settled,

rid of the wild, untamed barbarism of such children, and to graft on this civilisation that amount of knowledge of reading, writing, and arithmetic which the Commissioners say is so easy?

What has to be done in the case of the children who have hitherto worked, without protection and without instruction, in mines? From eight years of age they have sat eight hours daily in the black darkness, with their feet in the mud or running water, and the dripping roof of the mine overhead—opening and shutting the ventilating doors—or as they grew older dragging the corves or waggons.

Take Mr. Norris's account of the life of a potter's child, up to the age of apprenticeship (p. 184, Commissioners' Report):—'At eighteen months or two years old he is sent to one of the dames who gain a livelihood by taking care of young children whose mothers are at the factory. There, from seven in the morning to eight or nine at night, he is stowed away in a small room, without exercise or change of air, predisposing the constitution to consumption, which is a common malady in the pottery towns. This continues, on an average, for four years. He is then, at five and a half or six years old, sent perhaps to the National School, where he stays one or two, or at most three years; but during the latter part of the time he is sure to be kept away very much, to act as an occasional substitute for some other boy who is at work. At eight or nine (earlier if his parents are drunken or improvident, often at six or seven) he begins to work regularly for a journeyman potter, turning his jigger (the potter's wheel, to which steam seems never to have been applied), and earning from 1s. to 2s. a week. In a year or two a quick boy will begin "handling" (making handles for cups, &c.) or "figuring," and earn from 2s. to 4s. But by this time a great change has come over him,—he has been kept at work twelve or thirteen hours each day, and so, even if disposed to continue his school studies, has little time to do so; consequently he now reads badly, and writes worse; and, in short, nearly all he acquired at school is forgotten.'

and consists of families selected from the immigrant mass for their better qualities. The schools have begun to triumph over these formidable difficulties; but for reasons (which will be explained at length hereafter) the scheme of the capitation grant contained in the Code would still be unjust, and would disorganise the machinery of these schools.

These are some of the facts overlooked by the Commissioners, which prove that it is not reasonable to expect that, under the present conditions of school age and attendance, it would be possible for at least three-fifths of the children on the books in these schools—the 63·7 per cent. who attend 100 days and upwards—to attain the standard contained in the formula previously quoted from their Report.

The promoters of schools say, in reply, that the merely technical and mechanical results follow a large part of the moral and religious training, and never precede them.

They have satisfied the Commissioners with the moral and religious training of their scholars. They have, as shown by the reports of the Inspectors already quoted, obtained already no little success in these technical elements. That is the first step towards complete success. They are certain that the present teachers and their pupil teachers would soon—out of the degree of civilisation which the schools have created—evolve better results in all the elements of a sound English education, than have been attained in those parts of Scotland which have had parochial schools and a settled population since the Reformation.

But the promoters of schools entertain a just apprehension that the necessities of many schools would compel the managers to refuse to admit children who presented themselves with a standard of acquirements so much below that required in the Code, as to give no hope that they could, however skilfully taught, pass the examination; to turn out dull scholars, sluggards, and truants, though the fault might be in the want of local civilisation and home training. School managers emphatically say that the Revised Code overlooks the value of all this indispensable preliminary moral and intellectual training. It treats it as no part of the work done. It discourages it because it cannot test it, and therefore excludes it from all aid. Moreover, the clergy and religious communions regard with alarm the scheme which bases the whole of the annual grants on a technical examination in the purely secular elements of knowledge, to the entire exclusion of all the results of moral and intellectual discipline, and religious training and instruction.

That part of the negative proposition on which the Revised Code is built, which implies a misdirection of effort, will be replied to in detail in other parts of this paper. It will be more convenient, in the first instance, to examine the scheme in the Revised Code by which it is presumed that the work done in elementary schools is tested, as respects the three lowest elements; and the whole annual grants are in future proposed to be transferred from their present basis to a capitation grant, determined by this new and untried test.

The Appendix[1] contains those clauses of the Revised Code which relate to the examination, by the results of which the amount of this capitation grant is to be awarded.

I propose, first, to examine the practicability of making the whole of the annual grants, or any large part of them, dependent on the conditions of this scheme.

In the letter which I addressed to your Lordship on the financial recommendations of the Royal Commission, I stated that the working of any such scheme was long ago examined and rejected, as full of difficulties which appeared insuperable. I did not intend to say that a scheme of examination in the three lowest elements could not be devised, on the results of which a certain limited portion of the grant might not be made dependent. I had, in fact, advised the adoption of such a scheme in the last paragraph of the Minute of 2nd of April, 1853. But

---

[1] I have also caused the alterations proposed February 13, 1862, and then presented to Parliament, to be printed in the margin. Nine thousand copies of this paper had, however, been sold before these changes were proposed.

such an arrangement cannot be extended beyond a certain limit, and even within that limit would be attended with partial injustice.

I will quote the passage from the letter which I addressed to your Lordship on the report of the Royal Commission:—'Any capitation grant, the distribution of which is determined by the results of instruction in schools, is liable to the fundamental objection that the average period of the attendance of the majority of scholars is so short, that, as far as that majority is concerned, few schools would be paid for the results of their own work. In the specimen districts 42·3 per cent. of the scholars (Commissioners' Report, p. 659) had been in the same public week-day school less than one year, and 22·7 per cent. had been one year, but less than two years. These proportions for England and Wales are 41·65 per cent. scholars who had attended the same school less than one year, and 22·58 who had been one year and less than two years. With such migratory scholars, it is impossible justly to pay for work done in schools on any plan constructed to embrace those three-fifths of the scholars who attend school less than two years. The remaining 35·77 per cent. who attend more than two years are alone subjects for an examination of the results secured by the work of any school. This, however, is not the proposal of the Commission. Their proposal is to pay a capitation grant on every scholar who has attended 140 days in the preceding year, and can read, write, and cypher. A scholar cannot learn to read, write, and cypher so as to pass a public examination in two years, much less in 140 days. Any examination of the majority of more than three-fifths who attend less than two years must therefore obviously fail to ascertain how far even these elements have been taught to that majority in any school. If the remaining two-fifths who have been in the school more than two years were separated from the other scholars, and examined apart, some approximate estimate might be thus made of the work done in the school.'

This was a brief statement of a fundamental difficulty grounded on the—

1. Migratory state of the population in Great Britain, and the indifference or caprice of parents, who have had only brief experience of good schools. That difficulty alone appeared so insuperable an obstacle that others were not set forth. Those other objections may now be examined in connection with the capitation grant scheme in the Code, or with any modifications of it affecting any large part of the annual grants.

2. Scholars enter the school who are in a state of brutish ignorance, unreclaimed barbarism and incapacity, requiring many months of skilful elementary training. Even if they enter young, they cannot fulfil the requirements of the Code. But it would be worse than useless to reduce the standard of acquirements in the Code towards this class of scholars, who enter at nine or even seven years of age without the knowledge of a letter.[1]

---

[1] Extract from Report of Royal Commission :—

'It must also be remembered that the children are frequently grossly ignorant when they first come to school, having been either at no infant school or at a mere dame's school. This is illustrated by the following Table[a] of the state of knowledge of 369 boys, admitted or re-admitted to St. George's School, Sheffield, from August 1854 to August 1855':—

[a] The following Table is drawn up from the Admission-book or Register, and shows the state of education, or rather the ignorance of the children admitted into the St. George's Boys' National School, between 1st August, 1854, and 1st August, 1855. 369 were admitted and re-admitted during the above period.

Number who had never been in an infants' school.	Who could read words of two or three syllables.	Who could read monosyllables by spelling them.	Who could only tell their letters.	Who could not tell their letters.	Who could write their names.	Who could not write their names or letters	Who had never learnt any Arithmetic.	Who could do simple addition.	Who could do simple subtraction.	Who could do simple multiplication.	Who could do simple division.	Who could do addition and subtraction.	Who could do addition, subtraction, and multiplication.	Who could do the whole of the first four simple rules.	Who could do compound addition.	Who could do compound subtraction.	Who could do compound multiplication.	Who could do compound division.	Who could do reduction.	Who could do rule of three.	Who could do practice, &c.
226	61*	99†	70‡	139	97	272	291	5	1	1	1	16	12	6	3	3	2	1	3	9§	0

* This includes 8 boys who had previously been in the school, but on leaving work were re-admitted.
† This includes 3 who were re-admitted.   ‡ This includes 3 who were re-admitted.
§ This includes 6 who were re-admitted.

Such a change would be to fix the standard on the capacities and knowledge of savages, and on a transient remediable state of the population. Yet the reclamation of these children from barbarism is a good, greater far than mere technical instruction in the three lowest elements. This reclamation is not to be tested by mere technical examination.

3. Besides the brutish immigrants, and the street-taught children of cities, the school has charge of very dull scholars. They are inept from scrofula; from mismanagement in childhood; from the dissolute habits of their parents, entailing on them forms of brain torpor or disease. When the teacher expends a larger amount of labour on them than on clever children, the school could receive no aid for them under the 'Revised Code.'

4. The children of dissolute, or rude parents, indifferent to their education, attend with strange irregularity. They are not simply among the two-fifths who do not attend twenty weeks, but their attendance is most capricious. When away from school, its influences are counteracted by the worst home example—and by that bad school, the street, with its republic of vagrant little ruffians. They return after each interval demoralised. That is an insuperable obstacle to early success in technical instruction.

The degree of success attending the struggle with all these formidable difficulties cannot be tested by any such examination as that set forth in the Code.

We must suppose a settled population, in which most of the children enter an infant school at three years of age, and spend 140 days, on the average, in a good school, with a fair amount of home training and example, before we can even approach to the hope expressed by the Royal Commissioners, that three-fifths of the scholars may receive the amount of instruction which they are so sanguine as to expect.

But even in this case it is easy to show how sudden

would be the reduction of the annual grants, by the operation of the Revised Code, on these inspected schools, without taking into account the losses contingent on the absence of children on the day of inspection, or during sixteen and a half school-times in the preceding month, or on account of errors of judgment on the part of the Inspector, and on the incalculable, because indefinite, reduction of the grant which the Inspector may recommend under Clause 47 of the Code.

The actual loss I shall show by returns obtained from schools; but without such returns it was easy to foresee what the extent of loss would be. Only 35·77 per cent. of the scholars attend the same school more than two years, and 22·58 per cent. only one year and less than two years. The improved machinery of schools has been only gradually introduced in the last fourteen years; it is still comparatively inexperienced, and has to meet the wants of children whose parents for the most part have either had no instruction or only that of the Sunday-school. Under such circumstances, a reduction of about two-fifths of the annual grants of elementary schools might have been anticipated; or of £175,340 in the first year of the operation of the Revised Code. That anticipation is supported by the returns obtained from schools.

Some of the details of the conditions in the Code, as to attendance, deserve only brief comment. Such are those of Clause 41 (*a*), that no grant will be made for any scholar who has not attended $16\frac{1}{2}$ school times in the 31 days preceding the day of inspection, and of course who is not present at the examination.

School managers naturally ask whether this is to apply to a school inspected during or soon after any harvest; or after any holiday week, such as a fair, wakes, rush-bearing week, Whitsuntide, or Christmas; or after the usual school holidays; or after a period of very bad weather, in a district of bad roads, with a scattered population; or after a general prevalence of influenza, or any of the contagious diseases of children. They inquire, too, whether their grant for any child is to be subject to the consequences of discontent in a master under notice of dismissal; or to possible hurry, impatience, carelessness, or error of judgment in an Inspector; or to the dread of the scholars of examination by a stranger; or to the caprice of any ignorant, negligent, or ill-tempered parent who may choose to keep one or more scholars at home on the day of examination; or to meet the common daily claims of the households of the poor on the services of their children for nursing, errands, and other duties.

Nothing has surprised the promoters of public education more than the regulation which practically discourages the extension of school attendance beyond eleven years of age, by refusing the grant to such scholars. A very small percentage of such children belong to any other class than that supported by manual labour.

There are no provisions in the Code to meet the circumstances of children working, according to the provisions of the law, in bleach or printworks, or in mines. The same examination is prescribed for girls as for boys, and for half-time scholars as for those attending full time. Children between three and seven years of age (Clauses 43, 44) are required to read a 'narrative in monosyllables;' to 'form, on a black board or slate, from dictation, letters, capital and small, manuscript;' and to 'form, on black board or slate, from dictation, figures up to 20; name at sight figures up to 20; add and subtract figures up to 10, orally, from examples on black board.' The opinion of practical educators on these requirements from infants has been unanimous, as to their impracticability and injurious tendency.

If the principle of making a large part of the grant dependent on attendance and on this examination were defensible, these details might be amended. But the objection to this mode of apportioning the grant could not be remedied by raising the scale of grant, as has been proposed.

Suppose the scale were raised so as to make the whole amount of the annual grants equal to the sum now distributed. That change would not get rid of the injustice and absurdity of the consequent inequality of the sums allotted to schools in districts widely differing in their power to fulfil the conditions. It would still bear no proportion whatever to the work done, or to the true wants of the schools. The objection is one of principle, which is not to be overcome by any change of detail or scale. A capitation grant, based upon an examination of individual children, does not pay for the work done in the school. It is impossible by examination, without arrangements too minute and expensive to be practicable, accurately to test individually the work done in the elementary schools of a great nation. To do this, the following arrangements are indispensable:—An impartial examiner, on the entrance of each child (or within a short time afterwards—a week for example) must record its state of cleanliness, aptitude for school discipline and instruction, capacity, and actual acquirements. Then the Inspector, having before him these facts, and the number of days which the scholar has attended in each month of the preceding year, might form an approximate opinion on the work done in the school. He would still be ignorant of the amount of hindrances in the home of the child, but he might accept irregularity of attendance as a scale with which to measure these. But it is obvious that any system so minute and delicate presents insuperable difficulties, from the cost of the machinery required to carry it into execution. If, therefore, the scale of capitation grant proposed in the Code were raised, a short analysis will show how that change would operate.

According to the note at page 8 of the Code, a school of 100 children, under the average conditions of attendance ascertained by the Commissioners, would earn £64. 3s. 4d. But this note says that 'fifteen shillings = 180 pence, may be earned, according to the proposed scale, by an attendance twice per diem of 140 days.' Double the scale, and suppose a school with a settled population in a wealthy town, well organised for regular attendance, by the visitors of a religious congregation sending the children early to school, and keeping them there five years during 150 days in the year. Then at least £140 of capitation grant might be earned.

Suppose a school in a rude village of East Lancashire, with a migrant population constantly floating through it from the moors of the forests of Bowland and Pendle and the Pennine Chain, with scholars brutish, ignorant, irregular in attendance, without home training, with nothing but coarse or evil example; no sooner disciplined than they are removed. The children would probably not attend 100 days on the average. If classed according to age, as proposed in the Revised Code, a large proportion of them would be unable to pass the examination in the three elements, at the standard of acquirement required, for want of previous training, consequent ignorance, and incapacity. As soon as they were partially reclaimed, they would often migrate. Such a school, needing aid much more than the former, would earn, perhaps, a fourth part of the double capitation grant. The one would have an extravagant grant; the other one quite insufficient for its wants.

A similar result would, probably, defeat the improvement of schools in the colliery and iron districts, in the Potteries, and in the worst parts of great cities. In the purely rural parishes of such counties as Dorsetshire, and other almost exclusively agricultural districts, the very early labour of the children on the farms, and the interference of successive harvest and seed-times, make school attendance so brief, and interrupt it by such long intervals, that the child's poor capacity for school work and learning are subject to constant drawbacks. Moreover, there is no help at home. His parents, though skilful in farm work, are unlettered, and in all other respects ignorant,—perhaps as superstitious as where the impostor Thom succeeded in deluding the peasantry in Kent a few years ago. The progress of the young scholar, thus hindered, is very slow, and the results are meager. But the teacher's work is not less real, and is more arduous than in schools more favourably placed for progress, though he may fail to pass many scholars through the examination in the Revised Code.

The best of these various classes of schools would earn at least three-fifths of the amount of the capitation grant (as estimated in the note at page 8 of the Code); the rest would get, some two-fifths, others one-fifth, and some might utterly fail.[1]

The doubling of the scale of the capitation grant in the Code would not get rid of these inequalities. One class of schools under that double scale would earn from £120 to £140, another from £80 to £120, while many would not get more than £50 or £40, or even £30, for every hundred children, if the scale were doubled.

To fix an arbitrary maximum beyond which no school could obtain any grant, would be simply to reduce the motives to exertion (presumed to be given by the Revised Code) in all schools in which this maximum was likely to be exceeded. That evil would be exaggerated by doubling the scale.

This argument might be pursued through every variety of change, with a similar demonstration of insuperable difficulties.

Though the objections in principle to basing a large part of the annual grants to schools on the results of an individual examination of the scholars in the first three elements are thus fundamental and insuperable, it was intended by the Minute of details contemplated in the last paragraph of the Minute of the 2nd of April, 1846, to provide, to the extent of that supplementary grant, (1) for an examination of the scholars in reading, writing, and arithmetic, and (2) for an apportionment of the grant according to the results reported, having due regard to

---

[1] See Appendix A.

age, previous training, school attendance, and acquirements.

The design was to encourage attention to these elements, and to test and reward success by an approximate estimate of the work done in the school. But it never was conceived that the work done would be tested by a classification of the scholars solely according to age, and an examination according to an arbitrary standard of acquirements in each group of age.

I will state the details of the plan, and then shew that, on this plan, it would be impossible to determine the distribution of a large part of the annual grants to schools in different districts, without leaving too large a discretion to Inspectors in considering circumstances necessary for the avoidance of very unequal results.

To describe the plan, may give it some appearance of complexity from which it would be free in practice.

The Minute of details would have comprised the following arrangements:—

A schedule would be sent to the teacher a week prior to the Inspector's visit, in which the teacher would enter the following particulars:—

The names of all the scholars, arranged in the classes in which the school is organised for daily instruction, but with each class subdivided into the following sections, viz.:—

Separate sections containing successively the names of the scholars in the class who had—

(*a*) Attended at least 120 days in each of the two preceding years.
(*b*) Attended at least 100 days in the preceding year only, or at least 80 days in each of the two preceding years.
(*c*) Scholars who had attended a shorter time than either of the two preceding classes.

The scholars in each section—(*a*), (*b*), (*c*)—would be entered in the order of seniority, the oldest first.

Then the following particulars would have been entered, in successive columns, with respect to each scholar:—His age; the time spent in any other inspected school in each of three or four years previous to his entrance; the number of days' schooling in each preceding quarter of the last year.

The schedule would then contain columns in which the Inspector would mark, by numbers or letters, his opinion of the results of the instruction of any scholar examined in reading, writing, and arithmetic; and a last column for his estimate of work done in all other subjects. He would not examine every child, but only so many as appeared to him necessary to test the state of the section of each class.

He would record his opinion at the foot of each class.

Then, as a summary of the whole, he could recommend one-third, two-thirds, or the whole capitation grant to be given to the school.

I place in an Appendix (B) the form of the schedule, to make this statement more clear. The regulations as to school attendance, in the Minute of April 2, 1853, would have to be modified, if this scheme were made universal.

If the capitation grant thus awarded were kept within moderate limits, and were accommodated, in the standard required, to the character of schools in different districts, according to their facilities for success, though it would still only imperfectly test the amount of the work done in each school, it would make a much closer approximation to justice than the plan proposed in the Revised Code.

By limiting the capitation grant dependent on these results to 4s. 6d. per scholar, the following serious difficulties would be avoided. It would not be necessary—

1. To interfere with the augmentation grants to teachers suddenly or extensively.

2. Changes in the sources of the stipends of the pupil teachers might be made, adapted to the growth of local resources, upon conditions which would not cause alarm, because they would operate gradually.

3. The arrangement of the scholars in their ordinary classes, divided into sections according to the length of their school attendance; and the admission of a record of the amount of previous instruction in an efficient school, would reduce the inequalities in the operation of a capitation grant in unsettled and uncivilised districts, and in those in which the attendance of children is much interrupted by labour, such as half-time in factories, work in mines, &c., and harvest and other work. The estimate of the school-work done would be founded on a consideration of all these elements. But it is clear that such discretion could not be allowed to operate if the capitation grant were large.

The Inspectors should also have instructions to take into account the degree of civilisation in the district, and the period during which the school has had the services of a certificated teacher and pupil teachers. Here, again, the fact that the grant forms only a small part of the annual grants, would facilitate the exercise of such discretion, which would be impossible with a large capitation grant.

This plan differs from that in the Code—

1. In the mode of classification of the scholars for examination. The classification is not primarily by age. First, the scholars are grouped in their usual classes. Then each class is divided into sections corresponding to their periods of attendance in the school, and in each section the children are arranged according to age. The Inspector ows how long the teacher has had them under his charge.

The schedule also informs him how long they have been in any other efficient school, in each of four preceding years.

He is not to examine every scholar, but so many in each section as to enable him to test the condition of that section. He will enter the results in the proper columns for every scholar so examined.

He will then enter his opinion of each class in the school.

Against the Revised Code of 1861-2

He will, finally, recommend one-third or one-half of the whole of the capitation grant of 4s. 6d to be awarded.

Such duties would not make it impossible for the Inspector to examine the religious and other instruction, as well as the three lowest elements, without devoting a very great increase of time to each school. It would, therefore, not be necessary to increase the number of Inspectors so much as the Vice-President states (p. 31) in his speech would have been 'unavoidable' under the Code.

The duties of the Inspector under the Revised Code would have been most harassing to himself, and would have occasioned an amount of irritation and controversy between school-managers and the Education Department which cannot have been foreseen.

The unavoidable reduction in very many schools would have amounted to half the annual grants, in some to much more, and the average deduction would have been two-fifths.

The Inspector would have been the ostensible instrument of this reduction. He has hitherto exercised greater influence on the improvement of the schools by his experience and conciliation of co-operative efforts, than by his power to recommend the withdrawal of the grants to the teachers and pupil teachers for neglect and consequent unsatisfactory results, either in organisation, instruction, or discipline. His time, under the Revised Code, would be consumed in a mechanical drudgery which would necessarily withdraw his attention from the religious and general instruction, and from the moral features of the school. The organisation of the school could not be inspected, for it would be necessarily broken up into groups of age for the purposes of the examination. Scholars with attainments above the Code standard would be degraded to their groups of age, to be placed along with untaught savages, dullards, sluggards, and truants, unable to reach the standard. The managers and teachers would watch anxiously the trial of each child, which was to determine whether twenty-five shillings or nothing was to be awarded to the school.

The scholars of elementary schools are often much disturbed during an inspection, because the examiner is a stranger. He speaks, perhaps, in the most encouraging way, but in a tone of voice, with words and a manner, to which they are not accustomed. The very refinement, gentleness, and scholastic accuracy of the Inspector often puts them out. I have seen scholars examined one day by the curate in some part of one of the Gospels, and reply successfully to questions uttered by one with whose person, manner, voice, words, and method they were quite familiar; and lamentably fail the next day, when questioned with perfect fairness by the Inspector, who was a stranger.

But all Inspectors are not perfect either in manner, utterance, choice of words for poor children, method of examining them; nor in the skill, kindness, and patience required to bring out the true state of the child's knowledge.

This applies forcibly to such elements as reading, writing, and arithmetic, even if the examination is restricted (as apparently intended in the Revised Code) to the most mechanical results, without any examination in the meaning or grammar of what is read, or in that 'logic of the poor'—arithmetic.

If an Inspector enter a school with an abrupt manner and a harsh voice,—if he roughly interfere with the organisation,—scold one or two scholars,—or be hurried, for lack of time or patience,—he will never discover what the children know or can do in their school-work. They will be bewildered. He will get few juniors to read without strange hesitation and mistakes. Few will write correctly 1,000,003 from dictation. Very few will write with their usual skill. A large portion will fail in arithmetical trials, which they would have passed with ease if the clergyman or the master had examined them. Thus the true state of the school is often not known to the Inspector. Experienced Inspectors make allowance for these hindrances in their estimate of the state of the schools under the present form of inspection. That would not, however, be possible if an Inspector had to deal with purely mechanical results, as in the examination in the Revised Code.

But when the results of the Inspector's examination differed widely from that made during the preceding week by the clergyman and teacher, his function would be regarded as the instrument for disallowing the just claims of schools. It would soon become the most unpopular and irksome function in Great Britain. The Privy Council Office would be worried with numerous and reiterated remonstrances.

The policy of investing the Inspectors with such extensive administrative policy is in absolute opposition to all the previous maxims and experience of the Department. The apportionment of the public grant has been reserved as the special function of the President and Vice-President, aided by their secretaries.

Even the Department itself has never exercised any authority so large as that with which it is now proposed to charge the Inspectors. By their direct instrumentality £175,000 would be, in the first year of the operation of the Code, withdrawn from the annual income of elementary schools. The acts of the Inspectors in this operation are not to be subject to the review of the Office, except only under clause 46, section (*e*), if the Inspector cancels the whole annual grant, 'when there appears to be any *primâ facie* objection of a gross kind,' or under the circumstances related in the note below.[1]

This delegation of administrative authority over a large part of the grant to the Inspectors would place them in a position challenging criticism, and so vexatious, from the great uncertainty of the resources of the managers of the schools under the Revised Code, as to provoke attacks

---

[1] The grant is to be withheld altogether, ' (*a*) if the school be not held in a building certified by the Inspector to be healthy, properly lighted, drained, and ventilated, supplied with offices, and containing in the principal schoolroom eighty cubical feet of internal space for each child in average attendance;' and for other reasons, giving less scope to the Inspector's discretion.

upon their conduct of the examination and the justice of their decisions. The results of the examination of the managers, minister, or teacher, would be sent up to Downing-street in contrast with that of the Inspector, and as a protest against it.

By limiting the direct operation of the Inspector's discretion to 4s. 6d. per scholar, this jealousy would scarcely exist. The work done in the school would be more truly tested by the plan which I have proposed. In harmony with the organisation of the school, a limited capitation grant might be safely confided to the discretion of the Inspector, to be distributed in the proportion of one-third, one-half, or two-thirds the grant for each scholar who had attended according to the conditions of a Minute prepared for that purpose.

The abruptness of the change in the annual grants may be estimated from the following returns, which have been furnished from 523 elementary schools, having on the average 66,375 scholars in attendance. These schools, last year, received £43,564 as grants. The capitation grant of the Revised Code would reduce this sum to £25,073, even without taking into account the reductions which are discretionary with the Inspectors, or cannot be foreseen under the 47th clause, or which result from clause 46. The estimated loss, nevertheless, amounts to £18,491 in one year's operation of the Code on 523 schools, or to a loss of more than two-fifths of the aid hitherto received. Probably the loss ascertained by more extensive data will not widely differ from this.

The abruptness of this change would tend to discourage, if not paralyse, the exertions of the promoters of schools, and especially of the clergy; for it would not be probable, if it were even possible, that, under all the varied circumstances of elementary schools, the two-fifths to be thus deducted in one year from the annual grants could be supplied from their local resources, and the one-fourth cut off from the income of Training Colleges could be raised by general subscriptions. (See Report of Royal Commission, pp. 144 and 145, vol. 1).

One object of the Revised Code, viz., that of economising the public grant by developing local resources, would thus be certainly defeated by the abruptness of the demand on private contributions, and the perplexing and impracticable character of the scheme and its untried conditions.

The Parliamentary grant was not simply an instrument for creating, by a suitable training during apprenticeship and in the Training College, the machinery of a system of education, and for the introduction of this machinery into elementary schools, on the conditions and by the aid of the annual grants; it was a powerful stimulant to private exertions and sacrifices. The £4,800,000 expended by the Government have called forth[1] double that sum. All the phenomena of activity in the founding and supporting of schools and Training Colleges owe two-thirds of their vitality to the Parliamentary grant of one-third, and would languish without it. To withdraw this grant abruptly, or any large portion of it, would produce a great shock. Many schools must perish if the annual grants hitherto given were suddenly exchanged for the capitation grant under the Revised Code.

The Royal Commission confirms the report of Her Majesty's Inspectors as to the extent of the sacrifices made by the clergy in rural districts for the support of parochial schools.[2] The note at the foot of this page shews the nature and extent of the strain on their private means. The reduction of two-fifths in the annual grants would often, if not in the great majority of cases, have to be made up by the parochial clergymen; or, if he were

[1] See speech of Right Hon. Robert Lowe, M.P.
[2] 'In the second place, the landowners do not contribute to the expenses of the schools so liberally as the wealthy classes in mining districts or large towns, so that the burden of supporting the schools falls principally on the parochial clergy, who are very ill able to support it. This is set in a strong light by a letter published in the Appendix to Mr. Fraser's Report, from which it results that £4518, contributed by voluntary subscription, was derived from the following sources:—

unable to make this further contribution, he would have to dismiss his pupil teachers,— if he did not also lose the services of his certificated teachers.[1] Or, as an alternative (adopted with a personal disappointment which none who have not the life-work of a parish in hand can under-

		£	£	s.	d.	
169 Clergymen contributed		1782, or	10	10	0	each.
399 Landowners	,,	2127, ,,	5	6	0	,,
217 Occupiers	,,	200, ,,	0	18	6	,,
102 Householders	,,	181, ,,	1	15	6	,,
141 other persons	,,	228.				

'The rental of the 399 landholders is estimated at £650,000 a year.'—(Commissioners' Report, vol. i., p. 77.)

'The heaviness of the burden borne by the clergy is imperfectly indicated by such figures as these. It frequently happens that the clergyman considers himself responsible for whatever is necessary to make the accounts of the school balance; and thus he places himself towards the school in the position of a banker who allows a customer habitually to overdraw his account. He is the man who most feels the mischief arising from want of education. Between him and the ignorant part of his adult parishioners there is a chasm. They will not come near him, and do not understand him if he forces himself upon them. He feels that the only means of improvement is the education of the young; and he knows that only a small part of the necessary expense can be extracted from the parents. He begs from his neighbours, he begs from the landowners. If he fails to persuade them to take their fair share of the burden, he begs from his friends, and even from strangers; and at last submits most meritoriously, and most generously, to bear, not only his own proportion of the expense, but also that which ought to be borne by others. It has been repeatedly noticed by the school Inspectors, and it is our duty to state, that, as a class, the landowners, especially those who are non-resident (though there are many honorable exceptions), do not do their duty in the support of popular education; and that they allow others, who are far less able to afford it, to bear the burden of their neglect.' —(Commissioners' Report, vol. i. p. 78.)

[1] A 'Poor Parson' writes to one of the journals to ask how he can meet this abrupt change. He has schools with two certificated teachers and four pupil teachers. He can see no means of increasing the resources of his school from subscriptions. His two teachers receive from the Government £35 as augmentation, and £9 each for teaching two apprentices. The average stipend of the four apprentices is £60. The 'Poor Parson's' own income is £70. He asks how he is to provide for the annual expenditure of the school, and to pay in weekly instalments £60 to the pupil teachers besides the quarterly instalments of the teachers' salaries, even if a certainty existed of his being repaid. But with the exceeding uncertainty of the capitation grant, he says that he must dismiss the pupil teachers, and make his school a private speculation, conducted by his teachers, with a guarantee limited to the amount of his subscriptions. This is an example of a very large number of schools.

stand), he would convert it into an 'Adventure School,' conducted either by his certificated teacher or some untrained master, in which he would retain some influence by providing books and fuel, keeping the school premises in repair, and allowing the teacher to use them free of rent and taxes. The blow to the rural clergy would come so swiftly and suddenly as to stun them. They would in many cases abandon their hopeless struggle, and close their schools. When they had adopted one of the foregoing alternatives, they would inquire at the Rural-decanal Chapters whether this measure of public economy arose out of a jealousy especially directed against their order. Was the Church, they would ask, absorbing a larger share of the Parliamentary grant by her zeal and wealth than was intended by the authors of the Minutes of 1846 and 1853? Was it deemed to be a sound piece of state policy to conciliate the 'voluntary' and the 'secular' parties? Was there in the Privy Council Office an impatience at the complication of the denominational system and its obstruction to civil liberty? Was it intended to pulverise the existing system by a crushing blow, so that when nothing was left as a memorial of it but its ruins, there might be built upon its dust and ashes a rate-supported secular system in conflict with the schools which the Church and the religious communions, faithful to their principles, would struggle to maintain?

Apart from the embarrassment or destruction of the rural schools, the abruptness of the change will everywhere discourage instead of stimulating exertion. When two-fifths of the annual grants are in one year removed, there will be no hope, in the majority of cases, of making up, in one year, the deficiency.

The questions presented to the managers of large poor town schools will rather be:—To what reduction of emoluments will the teachers submit? Will the certificated teachers accept their salaries without any, or with what, compensation for the augmentation and gratuities hitherto conditionally provided by the Government? Will the pupil teachers accept smaller stipends?[1] Or can the services of one or more be dispensed with in future?[2] The confusion and embarrassment caused by these inquiries, and the extreme uncertainty in the amount of the capitation grant under the Revised Code, will be very unfavourable to the increase of private subscriptions. School pence cannot be suddenly increased without a reduction of the school income.

One of two courses might be pursued in the restraint or reduction of the public grant. The first course is to declare that the children of parents supported by manual labour in Great Britain shall have a less costly education,—all classes of their teachers shall be trained at less expense, shall be worse paid, and be fewer in number than they now are,— instruction shall be chiefly technical and quite elementary.

The second course is so to order any reduction of the public charge as that it shall not derange the existing machinery, or give the poor a lower class of instruction than they now have, while it tends to throw the charge of maintaining a system which has the cordial approbation of the Church and other religious communions more and more, in successive years, on the resources of Christian benevolence, and on the growing sense of the value of education among the parents of the scholars.

The Revised Code appears to proceed on the presumption that the first course is the best. Its abruptness and its provisions tend, in the opinion of the representatives of the great education societies, 'to introduce into elementary schools a lower class of teachers, and to degrade the instruction in the schools.'

But one-third of the annual grants might be, in ten years, derived from local resources without strain, if one-

---

[1] This will certainly not be possible in the manufacturing and mining districts, nor in towns, without taking a lower class.

[2] This will be inevitable, with a consequent loss of efficiency and lowering of the level of instruction in the school.

thirtieth part were deducted in each successive year, in order that it might be supplied by subscriptions, or school pence, as a condition of the payment of the remainder. A more rapid rate of reduction would cause more or less embarrassment, and would be less certain to secure the earnest coöperation of the clergy and laity in evolving the local resources of schools.

To disgust and discourage the managers of schools, who raise more than £1,250,000 annually from local sources towards the support of a system of public education the cost of which amounts to two millions annually, would be an act of gross impolicy, unless the intention of the Government were to sweep away what exists in order to make room for something else.

The abruptness of the change in the position of the managers is not more sudden nor greater than in that of the teachers. The amount and conditions of their emoluments, and the sources whence they are derived—their relations to their pupil teachers as to authority, time and opportunity of instruction, and to the Inspector of schools —are all gravely changed.

They have regarded their apprenticeship and studies in the Training College—their literary position there, and the certificate awarded for that and for two years' good management of their schools—as parts of a system in in which the Government had used the Parliamentary grant as an instrument to create and sustain an improved machinery in schools, by calling forth local intelligence, exertions, and contributions. The cost of creating this machinery would be thrown away if it could not be sustained. It could be sustained only by stimulating managers of schools to give sufficient salaries, and encouraging the best scholars to become apprentices at low stipends, by the prospect of salaries rewarding seven years' ill-paid preparation [1]—by giving the teacher as much security in

---

[1] In the cotton district pupil teachers could, on the average, earn one-third more in factories.

his position as is consistent with his large dependence on local fluctuating voluntary resources. The whole machinery has been thus fostered. To have thus cherished its growth is now described as an error—as a system of 'bounties and protection.' But it is forgotten that this has been the history of all English and of all national education whatever. Edward the Sixth and Elizabeth thus founded the Endowed Schools. The education at Eton, Harrow, Rugby, Winchester, Birmingham, and in every other public school of celebrity for the middle and upper classes, is largely endowed. The colleges of Oxford and Cambridge are proprietors of estates with an aggregate annual value of probably half a million; and they further reward their most distinguished scholars and fellows by their patronage of large endowments ecclesiastical and scholastic—in livings and schools. No fallacy is more transparent or more monstrous than that which assumes that knowledge, or whatever training is got in schools, is a natural want, certain to assert itself like the want of food, or clothing, or shelter, and to create a demand. The fact is the very reverse of this assumption. Otherwise an ignorant man's appetite for knowledge, a savage man's desire for civilisation, a heathen's thirst for revealed truth, ought to be in proportion to their destitution; whereas mental, moral, and religious destitution have no appetite—they have no desire—they make no demand. All statesmen who have wished to civilise and instruct a nation, have had to create this appetite. The desire for knowledge has been implanted in the population by founding schools. The demand for instruction has been called forth by middle class schools—by endowments for masters—by foundations for poor scholars—by bursaries and exhibitions, enabling those who are successful to go to college; and in colleges by sizarships, scholarships, prizes, fellowships, honours, rewards of every description. These honours open a career in the scholastic, legal, and clerical professions. That has been the practice both of English statesmen and the English people before and since the Reformation. That practice is the type, and part of the justification, of the Education Grant and its administration hitherto.

The teachers settled in elementary schools, therefore, did not expect that the arbitrary and indefensible application of a doctrine of political economy respecting supply and demand, bounties and protection, to a sphere of action in which it has never had any place in English statesmanship—to a sphere of moral action in which it is totally inapplicable—would cause an abrupt and total change in every element of their position.

Similar errors in the application of doctrines of pure economy to questions in which moral elements greatly predominate have been committed before. Thus, because, at the time of the reformation of the relief of indigence, the children of independent labourers were either without schools, or in very bad schools, it was said that the pauper children in workhouses ought not to be well instructed, lest their better education should operate as an encouragement to pauperism. The fallacy here consisted not simply in a neglect of the consideration that education is the most efficient antidote to hereditary pauperism; but still more in a cynical and sceptical denial of all moral obligation on the part of the State to these children.

In like manner, the protection of women, and of children under 13, from excessive labour in manufactories and mines, has been resisted as a violation of the principles of free trade. Trade, it is said, should be free from all State regulation. If this were so, trade might exist in slaves—or workmen might be reduced to the condition of serfs or slaves—or the physical and moral condition of the people might be subject to any degree of degradation, while the interference of the Government for the interests of the commonwealth would be shut out by an inexorable abstract principle of political economy.

The fallacy in the application of the principles of free trade to the education of the people resembles these.

The Parliament and the Executive Government are the guardians of our mixed constitution,—they represent the nation,—but they are collectively a power created by the people for the promotion and conservation of national interests. This central power is embodied in the word State. The central authority has a greater interest, collectively, in the intelligence and virtue of the people than any fragment of the nation can have. On that intelligence and virtue depend respect for the law,—the right discharge of civil functions and political franchises,—the due subordination to authority,—the harmony of classes, —the development of the natural resources of the country and its power,—the increase of commerce, wealth, comfort, and national contentment,—the public spirit of citizens,—the valour of armies and navies,—and the national patriotism in sustaining the constitution alike against invasion and against internal corruption or revolution. But the education of the mass is not a want to be so felt, when ignorance and coarse habits prevail among them, as to create a supply by the act of the uneducated classes. Education infiltrates from the upper and governing classes to the lower. All civilisation is primarily the work of inventive genius. The lesson such minds have to teach is first imparted to the upper and governing classes. Its benefits descend from them to the lower. These uncivilised classes are trained by example and discipline; they are, as minors are, the care of the governing classes in some form,—they do not seek to be civilised and taught, as an original and irrepressible want, but they are sought by the missionary, by the teacher, by the agent of industrial progress, and they are rescued, not by their own act, but by that of the State and the upper classes, to whom their progress has become a social and political necessity. But the State—that is, the most able governing minds in the counsels of the sovereign power—is more likely to perceive this want of the commonwealth than even the middle classes; for the collective dangers from national ignorance and barbarism are greater, and the cost of national pauperism, crime, and disorder, are more apparent to the Government than they can be to individuals. Consequently, the education of the people has, throughout Europe, and in this country, originated in a great degree with the State. But if we were to suppose that education received no aid from the central authority, or the national resources from taxation, it would still be an error to speak of free trade in education. The several education societies certainly have a friendly rivalry in their efforts to found and support schools, and to attract children to them. The State in no way interferes with their freedom in doing this; but it is not trade. This work is not done for pecuniary profit; it is done under the influence of a sense of moral and religious obligation, and a conviction that the wealth and strength of States, and domestic peace and prosperity, depend on the moral and intellectual elevation of the people. There is the utmost amount of civil and religious liberty for such efforts; there is no lack of freedom in such work, which however is not trade. To pretend that it is trade—and on that pretence to invoke the application of an abstract principle to shut out the aid of the State—is by a fallacy to attempt to limit the power of the State to promote the intelligence and virtue of the people, in which it has a larger stake than any fragment of the people, even than the Church established by law.

It is impossible, then, to justify any part of the Revised Code by an appeal to the principles of free trade. The teachers of elementary schools have not, under the Minutes of 1846, been so much the subjects of 'protection and bounties' as the masters of the endowed schools of Edward the Sixth and Elizabeth, or the masters or presidents and fellows of colleges, and the professors of universities. The creation of an efficient machinery for elementary education, by the apprenticeship of pupil teachers and the two years' training of Queen's Scholars, and the security afforded to certificated teachers by a partial and conditional endowment of their schools, were in strict harmony with all English statesmanship since the Reformation.

Were it possible to conceive that those who thus appeal to the principles of free trade had narrowed their conceptions of national education from the interests of the people to those of the schoolmaster, then their formula as to bounties and protection, though inapplicable to national interests, would at least be intelligible. They would say —It is inexpedient to protect by endowment the schoolmaster who has been reared by the influence and aid of the State,—it is better that he should be wholly dependent on the managers of schools.

But, in the first place, this—under the Revised Code—is not an accurate statement of the fact. Though the master is to make his bargain with the managers, they are to be aided by the State to pay him. The change, therefore, does not consist in the withdrawal of endowments.

The annual grants are now made to the managers, though their apportionment is defined. The managers, under the Revised Code, are to have more discretion in this matter. The pretence of the absence of bounty and protection in the Code, therefore, arises from a confusion of ideas. The managers would receive a reduced bounty, and would still be thus protected, though in a less degree. There would, therefore, be no free trade in schools. Those which had certificated masters and pupil teachers would receive the bounty and protection of the capitation grant. The transference of protection would be at the expense of the certificated teacher. He would have to make the best bargain he could with managers at a time when one-third of their annual school income—viz., that received in annual grants—would be reduced to two-fifths. This is the free trade of the Revised Code.

But if to regard the principles of all promotion of elementary education as identical with those of freedom in trade be erroneous, have the certificated teachers acquired any legal or moral claim to the continuance of their conditional grants in aid of local resources?

The Royal Commission reports:—'It may be said that the State has excited expectations in the minds of the teachers by the system of augmentation grants, which give them a moral right to their continuance; but we do not think that this is really the case. The fact that the present system is supported by sums voted annually, and not by a permanent charge on the Consolidated Fund, shows that the State is not pledged to its permanence. Indeed, it is notorious that it has grown up by degrees, and that ever since its origin the propriety of replacing or altering it has been under discussion. The arrangement by which a certain portion of the grant is appropriated to the augmentation of the teacher's salary, is an arrangement between the State and the managers, not between the State and the teachers; and it is for the benefit of the school, not for the benefit of the teachers. At present the average emoluments of certificated masters of all classes and denominations are £97, which considerably exceeds the amount which can be said to be in any sense guaranteed to the holders of certificates; nor is there any reason to believe that the managers of schools, under the modified system, would desire to reduce the salaries of their teachers.'—(*Commissioners' Report*, vol. 1, p. 149.)

In order to ascertain whether the opinion thus given by the Commissioners is applicable to the position of the certificated teacher under the Revised Code, it is desirable first to define, as accurately as possible, what that position would be as contrasted with what it now is. The augmentation grants, and the gratuities for instructing pupil teachers, hitherto conditionally paid to certificated teachers by the Committee of Council on Education, are withdrawn. The total annual reduction of these direct payments to them would be £98,171 5s. for the augmentation grants, and about £62,000 for teaching 15,500 apprentices, calculated at £4 gratuity for each. The number of certificated teachers actually teaching is said to be 7711; therefore the grants withdrawn would amount to upwards of £20 each. The reduction of direct grants would, however, be more than this sum for masters, and less for mistresses. Thus masters might have their salaries from all sources reduced from the average of £94 to £65 or £70; mistresses, from £62 to £44; and infant mistresses, from £58 to £40.

The 'protection' thus afforded by the State being withdrawn, what are the chances that this reduction would be made up by the managers?

School managers have, in the first place, to provide for a loss to their schools of £175,000 in the annual grants. They have further to pay weekly in advance the stipends of 15,500 pupil teachers or (15,500 × £15) £232,500 annually, before they receive the capitation grant, which implies this reduction of £175,000 from the sum which they have hitherto received in annual grants. This double operation is to occur in one year. First, £232,500 are to be paid, in the hope of an uncertain return; and then, £175,000 of the annual grants are to be withheld.

In Appendix A it will be seen that this would affect schools in very different degrees. The positive ultimate reduction in schools in different districts would vary from nothing to one-fifth; one-third; two-fifths; one-half; three-fifths; or three-quarters of the grants hitherto annually received.

In some cases, especially where the clergy had hitherto made up the annual deficiency in the school income from scanty personal resources, the school would be closed;—or the teacher could receive nothing in lieu of his augmentation or gratuity. Often the aid of pupil teachers would be given up. Very generally, if not universally, their number would be diminished.

The embarrassments in the finances of schools could not, however, be measured by these two elements. If pupil teachers were not apprenticed to the teachers, they would be much less amenable to discipline. Their motives for a steady perseverance in their engagements would be incalculably reduced by the great uncertainty introduced into the position of the certificated teachers.

Bound only by an agreement with the managers, terminable on notice, they would soon become dissatisfied with stipends one-third below the market value of their labour in the manufacturing and mining districts. The caprice of youth would have its way. Not half of them —perhaps not above one-third—would persevere to the end of their five years' service. Consequently, as the Revised Code produced its inevitable results, the school would approach more and more to the condition of the monitorial schools superseded by the system of pupil teachers. At every step of this decline, the efficiency of the school, for all purposes, would be impaired. The energies of the teacher would be taxed in proportion as his assistants were inexperienced, ill-instructed, unskilful, insubordinate, and childish. Even the number of these stipendiary monitors would often be reduced for want of school-funds. At the time when his salary was both reduced and uncertain, his task would be made intolerable. With the worse condition of the school, both subscriptions and school-pence would fall off.

The position of the teacher, with respect to the managers, would become extremely irksome. The amount of the capitation grant, with his reduced and ill-paid staff of half-mutinous assistants, would be dependent mainly on his personal exertions. Whatever his conceptions as to the most powerful agencies to civilise and christianise his rude scholars, he would have to work like a horse in a gin-wheel, at the routine of teaching the elements, according to the mechanical standard of the Revised Code. Reading would be taught with mechanical fluency, even if the children (like many Welsh and some Caffre and Indian scholars) understood little or nothing of what they read. Writing would be learned according to the Code standard, though lessons in dictation and composition were disused. Such last-named lessons would fall out of the observation of the Inspector for want of time, while he examined the scholars' mechanical skill in forming letters. The religious instruction and the moral training of the scholars, which the Royal Commission declare to be so satisfactory, must yield to the paramount necessity of earning a larger capitation grant, by the success of the scholars in attaining the mechanical standard of the Revised Code.

These circumstances would altogether change the relations of the teacher with the managers. Every act of his school discipline and instruction might alter the annual result. Some managers would try to make the teacher's salary mainly dependent on this result; some would insist on his teaching an evening school—hitherto forbidden—in order to augment the grant. Then the five hours' instruction of the pupil-teachers would be a farce. The regulations which thus reduce the instruction of pupil-teachers from seven and a half hours weekly to five, and permit this to be given in the evening school, are utterly inconsistent with all the antecedent Minutes of the Committee of Council. They look like a sneer at the care with which the teacher's health was 'protected' from overwork, and at the solicitude with which the training and instruction of the apprentices were provided for by the Minutes which they repudiate and contradict.

The theory of schools under the administration of the Education Grant, hitherto, has been, that it was necessary to create a machinery of education capable of exerting considerable religious and moral influence in the civilisation of the people; that it was expedient to protect and encourage the teacher as the agent of this change,— to place him in close relations with the religious organisation of the country, and to uphold him in a position above that of a needy dependant;—that the staff of unpaid or ill-paid monitors, under thirteen years of age, previously employed, should be displaced, and in their room apprentices introduced, who should be most carefully trained. There is the authority of the Vice-President for saying that these pupil teachers have more than earned their stipends by their services in the schools, when they do not enter the Training Colleges. The teacher thus aided was not to be worn out prematurely by a coarse, ill-aided and ill-paid drudgery. That, however, would be his fate under the Revised Code.

It is in the contrast of these two positions that the breach of faith with the trained certificated masters consists, rather than in the exact technical form in which their engagements as pupil teachers and Queen's Scholars, or students, have been assumed. Undoubtedly, the Revised Code would reduce the teachers' salaries; would load them with ill-aided work; and worsen[1], in all respects, that position in which it has hitherto been the object of the Government to place them. A large part of this evil is the simple and direct consequence of the abruptness of the change. Thus defined, the effects of the Revised Code would amount to an unexampled breach of public faith with a most meritorious class.

That the arrangement as to stipend was made between the State and the managers[2], as pleaded by the Royal Commission, is unimportant if it was made on the condition and with perfect security that the money should be paid to the teacher. Then, also, it is for the 'benefit of the school;'[3] but that benefit is to be derived through the teacher, whose remuneration was thus protected,— not simply by the grants, but by all the conditions binding the managers. The last plea of the Commissioners, that the average actual salaries exceed those guaranteed as a condition of the augmentation grants, has no application whatever to an abrupt change which would shake the stability of all school arrangements, and probably reduce their salaries below that level; nor does it apply to a scheme which worsens[4] the condition of the teacher, not merely in income, but in the quality and number of his assistants; in the amount and value of his work; in his relations to the managers of schools; and, necessarily, in his social position: a scheme which converts him into an ill-paid and overworked drudge.

[1] and [4] authority — *Milton.*
[2] Report, vol. 1, p. 149.
[3] Ibid., p. 149.

'The fact that the present system is supported by sums voted annually, and not by a permanent charge on the Consolidated Fund,'[1] and that the arrangements have 'grown up by degrees,' and have been liable to changes moderate and harmonious in character, might be pleaded in favour of some change which would operate gradually, and thus give time for the development of those local resources which, if subjected to an abrupt and harsh blow, would rather dwindle under discouragement, or perish in panic.

The managers of schools, as the Royal Commissioners anticipate[2], have no desire to alter the social position, the duties, or the remuneration of the teachers of schools; and they will probably resist with a rare unanimity the disastrous revolution threatened by the Revised Code. But the same solicitude and zeal would exhibit themselves, in harmony with the Committee of Council on Education, if they were called upon to augment by moderate annual increments the local resources of schools, so as to maintain in their present position the whole staff of teachers and apprenticed pupil teachers, with a corresponding reduction of the amount of the annual grants.

I have already stated that one-thirtieth part of these annual grants to teachers and pupil teachers might be cut off every year, until in ten years one-third had been reduced. As each thirtieth part was reduced, the remainder would, on this plan, be granted, on condition that the fractions withdrawn should be furnished from local resources. All the conditions of these grants would remain otherwise unaltered. The stipends of all classes of teachers, and their relative positions to each other,—to the managers, the Inspector, and the Committee of Council on Education, would remain unchanged.

This was one of those restraints on the growth of the Education Grant referred to in the letter which I addressed to your Lordship on the 24th of April, 1861, when I anticipated that the 'increase' of 'the public grant' might,

[1] Report, vol. 1, p. 149.   [2] Ibid.

after providing for evening schools and for the apathetic districts, 'not only be arrested, but this annual aid might be converted into an instrument, in the hands of skilful administrators, by which all the rest of the work may be done in the most apathetic as well as in the most earnest districts.'

The development of the whole scheme of such arrangements would require separate treatment. I allude to them now only because the gradual change in the administration of the annual grants to schools is an illustration of the principle which such a scheme would embody.

The effect of the Revised Code on the position and training of pupil teachers having been incidentally referred to, a brief recapitulation only is necessary here.

1. The stipend of the pupil teachers is, as a direct consequence of clause 47 (*b*), to be reduced from an average of £15 to one of £10 per annum.[1] Pupil teachers could not be obtained on these terms in the manufacturing and mining districts. For example, a girl can earn 12*s*. per week in the cotton district when she can manage two power-looms; at sixteen or seventeen, by managing three looms she can often earn 16*s*.; at eighteen, she can gain 18*s*. with four looms, and, if working *barèges*, she can secure a guinea as weekly wages. Young men can of course earn as much. The reduction of the average stipend in such districts in itself amounts to the substitution of stipendiary monitors, on short engagements of one or two years, for pupil teachers, with an apprenticeship and training of five years. In rural districts and small agricultural towns and villages, the reduction of the stipend would at once preclude the realisation of the hope entertained, especially in the case of girls[2], that apprentices might be derived from well-ordered homes of the middle classes. This hope is legitimate if due care be taken to insist on every precaution to shut out those who

---

[1] Revised Code, clause 47 (*b*); also clause 80.
[2] See the Pamphlet of Miss Burdett Coutts.

have bodily defects, or are feeble in health or intellect. With a rigid examination of candidates, the realisation of this hope would be an unequivocal advantage.

2. The reduction of the time during which the certificated teacher is required to instruct his apprentices, from seven and a half hours to five, and the permission granted that this instruction may be conducted in an evening school, would lower the tone and amount of the pupil teacher's instruction, if the provision as to the evening school were practicable—which it is not.

3. The withdrawal of all pecuniary value from the certificate would prevent the apprenticeship of the most desirable candidates, and greatly discourage the application of pupil teachers to their preparatory studies. Such of them as gained Queen's Scholarships would rarely, if ever, remain more than one year in the Training College. Many would not go to the Training College at all, but would avail themselves of the opportunity afforded them by the Code[1] to take charge of rural schools, and to get a certificate at twenty-one years of age by examination.

Taking all these provisions in connection with the pecuniary embarrassments of the school managers, the Revised Code undermines the whole system of apprenticeship, if it does not, by the abruptness and harshness of the blow, at once destroy it.

The disallowance of the grants towards the salaries of lecturers in Training Colleges operates in the same direction. The Royal Commissioners '[2]do not recommend any reduction of aid at present given to the Colleges in various forms.' '[3]It may be asserted that, though the money is well spent, and though the relation between the Government and the Training Colleges is satisfactory, the assistance given discourages private liberality, and that the withdrawal of a part of it would be compensated by private subscriptions. We (the Commissioners say) do

---

[1] Clauses 118 and 119.
[2] Report of Royal Commission, vol. 1, p. 143; and again p. 148.
[3] Ibid., p. 144.

not agree in this opinion. It appears probable that considerable difficulty would be found in obtaining subscriptions enough for these institutions. Private benevolence usually operates rather to relieve the evils which directly excite sympathy and attract attention, than to prevent their occurrence by contributing to the removal of their remote causes.' '[1] Some conveniences are attached to the present state of things. No other institutions stand so much in need of a permanent income and of a considerable degree of Government supervision, which, of course, can only be had at the expense of Government grants. To ascertain and to regulate the principles on which teachers should be trained is a difficult process, and requires the light of long and varied experience. If every Training College was self-supporting, and was entirely regulated by its own subscribers or committee, they would vary far more than they do now, and would lose the great benefits which they at present derive from the common course of examination imposed upon the students by the syllabus, and from the experience which the Inspectors derive from their annual visits, and make public in their reports.'

The repeal of auxiliary grants by the Revised Code, limitations and diminutions in the supply of students directly[2] and indirectly, and the reduction of the period of training, all operate to cripple the resources of the Colleges. Therefore, if the grants to lecturers be withdrawn, the whole, or most of the lecturers will be removed. This result will be consistent only with a lower level of instruction. Such a result cannot have been foreseen without an intention to degrade the curriculum of study. The Queen's Scholars and students would thus not merely remain in college only half the time hitherto occupied with their training, but would be taught by a less numerous and an inferior, because worse paid staff,— the work would be reduced, and a lower range of attainment would be required. This

---

[1] Report, vol. 1, p. 145. [2] Revised Code, clause 97.

degradation of the level and diminution of the time of the instruction of the Queen's Scholars and students, is in harmony with the policy adopted towards the apprenticed pupil teacher. Together they must be accepted as signs of a deliberate intention to put the education of the poor, under the Revised Code, into the hands of teachers whose knowledge, experience, aptitude, and skill, are all of a much lower order than those of the present certificated teachers and their assistants.

Yet the Report of the Royal Commission supports the present scheme of rearing the apprentices in schools, and of training the Queen's Scholars in Colleges. It shows (p. 65) 'the great popularity of the certificated teachers, and especially of the certificated mistresses.' Uninspected schools are said to be not so liberally supported as the inspected schools (p. 64):—'To lower the standard of popular education throughout the country by discouraging the employment of trained teachers, would be fatal' (p. 155). 'The training given in the Colleges is on the whole sound, though there are several drawbacks to its value' (p. 138). 'On the whole, however, we have expressed a favourable opinion of the intellectual training of the students. The moral condition of the Colleges, especially of the female Colleges, appears to be satisfactory' (p. 168). 'In these opinions we were fortified by the evidence as to the moral and intellectual character of those who, having passed through the Training Colleges, were found by our witnesses in the actual charge of schools. We cited from that evidence abundant proof that the trained teachers not only are comparatively far superior to the untrained, but are in every respect but one positively good' (p. 168). That defect is the teaching of the three lowest elements, and the Commissioners attribute it 'not to want of power, but to want of motive.'

Concerning pupil teachers the Commissioners say:— 'Almost all the evidence goes to prove that the effect of the presence of pupil teachers upon the condition of the schools is very beneficial, especially when it is compared with the influence exercised over the schools by monitors' (p. 102). 'The evidence of the Assistant-Commissioners is unanimous as to the superiority of schools in which pupil teachers are employed' (p. 103). 'Of the whole number of pupil teachers, 87·32 per cent. successfully complete their apprenticeship; and 76·02 per cent. become candidates for Queen's Scholarships, which most of them obtain. The 11·3 per cent. who do not become candidates for Queen's Scholarships, include those who either adopt other pursuits or follow the callings of a schoolmaster without going through the course of instruction given in the Training Colleges' (p. 107). The Commissioners then show that this 11·3 per cent. have rendered, 'year by year, services for the salaries received,' and 'that this salary is presumably not excessive, inasmuch as they might earn more in other callings' (p. 107). The Commissioners in their recapitulation (section vi., art. 2) further say:—'We have shown that the pupil teachers' action on the scholars is eminently beneficial, but more on the higher and middle classes than on the lower' (pp. 166, 167). Yet the overthrow of the whole of this machinery is certain under the Revised Code. The financial embarrassments of school managers are interwoven with those of the teachers and pupil teachers in such a way as to operate with a most pernicious, if not fatal, effect on elementary schools. The lower social and moral condition of future Queen's Scholars—their inferior capacity and attainments—the cutting off of 10 per cent. in the number allowed to each College—the reduction of the duration of their training one-half—the repeal of auxiliary grants, and the limitations and diminutions of the supply of students, directly and indirectly—all form elements of a fatal disorder in the Training Colleges. A lower curriculum will be adapted to the inferior training of the Queen's Scholars. One-half the Colleges must be shut up, or a double supply of teachers poured upon the country, not half trained, yet to compete with the well-trained certificated teachers, by taking lower salaries, and so to aid that competition in driving them to better remunerated occupations.

These changes could not occur without the ruin of the present system of elementary education. They would cause it to be displaced by one closely resembling that which preceded it. What are the advantages which it is conceived would be purchased by this disastrous revolution?

It is said that the administration in the central office is so 'complicated and cumbersome' that the system threatens 'to break down at the centre.' If it were so, the Revised Code would only give it partial relief in one way—in the annual grant department—to bury it under an angry storm of controversial remonstrance against the Inspector's awards of the capitation grant. The relief which the Revised Code gave in the central office would be purchased, as the Vice-President says (p. 31), by an 'unavoidable' increase in the number of Assistant Inspectors. In other words, the clerks of the Education Department would be replaced by Inspectors whose emoluments and expenses would in each case be three or four times as great. The duties of the Inspectors would not be simplified; they would be degraded into a complicated and cumbersome daily drudgery, as wearisome as picking oakum. The system would then break down in its limbs. Scholars and gentlemen would scarcely spend their lives in examining nearly a million of poor children in their imperfect skill in what is purely mechanical in reading, writing, and arithmetic. But when it is asserted that the work of the office is too complicated and cumbersome, I reply—that one day's work in the General Post Office involves more complication, and is encumbered with more details, than one whole year's work in the Education Department. That which is most complained of—the payment of individual teachers and assistants by money-orders—is in fact mainly effected by the Post Office Money-order Department, and is an insignificant part of its enormous load of work; yet the

Chancellor of the Exchequer is now wisely attempting, at the expense of an immense increase of this complication, to convert the Money-order Department into a National Savings' Bank of shillings. In like manner, it might be shown that the complaint of complication and burthen of work will bear no comparison with the administration of the Admiralty, with a navy scattered over the whole world. The reserve, the coast guard, the dock yards, arsenals, hospitals, pensions, courts-martial, promotion, and the whole theory of naval construction in a state of transition—certainly cumber the Admiralty with a complicated burthen. Nor could the work be for one moment compared with that of the whole War department, directing the regiments of the line and militia; inspecting the new battalions of volunteers; with the ordnance; the citadels of Great Britain and the Mediterranean; with the forces scattered through the colonies; the examinations for commissions; the recruiting department; the depôts; hospitals; the pension list; normal and model schools, and barracks' schools; and the colleges of staff, engineer, and artillery officers.

An addition to the present buildings of the Education Department is needed, in order conveniently to concentrate the work under one roof: the Examiners' department may be simplified by being reduced to a system of checks; an Inspector-General is required to hold the inspection well in hand, while more discretion is given to experienced Inspectors; a permanent Vice-President is needed, to preserve intact the traditions of the office, and give unity of principle to all changes. The labour of making individual payments of money, which seems a great bugbear, may be minimised by transmitting the annual grant in one sum to the correspondent of each school, provided each recipient to whom its portions are allotted sign a receipt in the schedule of the annual grants awarded.

The complaint of complication and load of work is to be met by an enlargement of the building adapted to this national work; the concentration of the responsibility for the Inspector's work in an Inspector-General, might relieve the office of a mass of details; the money payments may be simplified; the Examiners' work greatly reduced. No doubt many other like changes might be made.

2. The expense of the present system, and its tendency to increase, might be pleaded in favour of a system of economy of the public grant. I have already shown that the reduction projected under the Revised Code is so ill contrived that it would simply disorganise and ruin the schools which now exist. But it is desirable to ascertain on what principle, and in what way, the growth of the Education Grant can be restrained so as to avert such disastrous results as the catastrophe prophesied by Dr. Temple. Of those who are alarmed at the tendency of the public grant to increase, the Royal Commission are the most moderate and reasonable representatives. They say:—'According to the most careful estimate we have been able to make, which is based upon a calculation of an increase in the number of pupil teachers and in the augmentation grant, the extension of the general system to the whole country would cost about £1,300,000, if the unassisted public schools alone were brought under it. If the scholars in private schools were added, the sum would amount to about £1,620,000. And supposing an increase in the number of scholars of 20 per cent., in consequence of an improvement in attendance, it would be increased to about £1,800,000 yearly. To this sum, if the present system were unaltered, would have to be added a capitation grant for 2,300,000 children; and at the present rate of attendance, which is an increasing one, at least 800,000 of these would earn 6s. a head. This would make the whole grant amount to nearly £2,100,000 a year.' (Commissioners' Report, p. 314.)

The Commissioners contrast this estimate with my own, that with a full provision for aid in the creation and support of evening schools, and in the spread of the whole system to the apathetic districts, the public grant for education might be kept within £1,000,000 per annum, or at the utmost, £1,200,000. I expressed this opinion in my letter to your Lordship of the 24th April, 1861, in the following words:—

'The force which will ultimately transform the whole will be the result of education itself. When the people know that they have even more interest in the education of their children than their rulers have, they will more and more take charge of it. They now bear two-thirds of the burthen; but that third which they do not pay has given value to what before was of little worth, and has thus created a transient power destined to pass from the Government into the hands of those who will take the charge. The transference of administrative power to the local managers and the parents will attend the gradual assumption by them of the payment of the pupil teachers, and of the whole of the stipends of the certificated teachers, consequent on the effects of education on some generations of parents, and on the middle classes.

'The Parliamentary grant has hitherto been so administered by the Committee of Council as to stimulate the investment of large sums in school buildings, by giving about one-third of their value. Between 1839 and 1860, grants amounting to £1,076,753 have caused an investment of subscriptions amounting to £2,360,226 in school buildings, or altogether of £3,436,226. The grant has also promoted the rapid growth of the annual income of schools, by subsidies at a similar rate of one-third the whole annual outlay, so that probably two millions annually are now expended in the support of schools. The public grant may in a few years increase with corresponding results to £1,000,000 or £1,200,000, making in its progress adequate provision for the education of youth from school-age to manhood; but at that point, by well-devised antecedent expedients, its increase may not only be arrested, but this annual aid may be converted into an instrument, in the hands of skilful administrators, by which all the rest of the work may be done in the most apathetic as well as in the most earnest districts. That result attained, a new series of operations may commence, by which the charge of public education may be gradually transferred from the Consolidated Fund to the local sources of income, school-pence, and subscriptions.'

Now, what are the alternatives to the adoption of such a system?

First, we have the scheme of the Revised Code. This may be briefly described as an attempt to reduce the cost of the education of the poor, by conducting it by a machinery—half trained and at less charge; to entrust it to a lower class of ill-paid teachers, and generally to young monitors as assistants; to neglect the force of a higher moral and religious agency in the civilisation of the people, and to define national education as a drill in mechanical skill in reading, writing, and arithmetic. The State would pay less, and be content with a worse article. The cheapness of the result would, however, be no measure of its value,—it would be almost worthless. There is too clear and faithful a sense of duty in the Church and religious communions to acquiesce in such a scheme. It comprises impracticable details. It is an abrupt revolutionary change from all the traditions of the Department, and is destined to fail.

Secondly, the notion of the practicability of a rate-supported system has been refuted by repeated careful investigation and experiment. Sir James Graham's Education clauses in the Factories' Regulation Act failed in consequence of the united opposition of non-conformists. These clauses were framed on the basis of toleration,—they gave as much authority to the Church as was consistent with complete civil and religious liberty within the school. Churchmen reluctantly assented to them, and they were almost universally rejected by dissidents from her communion. The subsequent Bills, for the partial support of education from the rates, were intended to operate in harmony with the Minutes and administration of the Committee of Council on Education. They failed from two causes: from the suspicion with which all the religious communions shrink from giving even the shadow of authority in schools to the representatives of the ratepayers; and secondly, from the indisposition of the Town Councils, and other representative bodies, to permit the total or partial transference of the burthen of public education—with only limited authority over its administration—from an assessment of 550 millions on which the Consolidated Fund is charged, to that of 86 millions, from which the local taxes are raised. The proposal of the Royal Commission, as to county rates, was also wrecked upon this rock.

Thirdly, there remains the expedient of devising measures for the restraint of the growth of the public grant without destroying the efficiency of the existing system; while due provision is made for the extension of the system, with necessary modifications of detail, to rural parishes with very limited population,—to districts apathetic on account of the non-residence of proprietors, and the humble intelligence and means of the tenantry,—and to the worst parts of great towns and cities.

I have already given a statement with respect to the mode of administering a limited capitation grant, so as to secure attention to the three lowest elements, and another as to the mode of reducing the annual grants to schools one-third, so as to cause a supply from local resources of the money thus withdrawn.

This reduction of the annual grants was proposed to be effected in equal annual instalments in ten years. In like manner the whole of the grants might be reduced gradually by equal annual diminution, on condition that the sums withdrawn should be supplied from local resources. Thus, in fifteen years, the proportions of the whole grant to the whole money raised locally might be changed, from the present ratio of one-third grant and two-thirds private funds, to the proportion of one-fourth of Parliamentary aid to three-fourths of voluntary contributions. Applying this ratio to the extension of education to the whole of England and Wales—the Commissioners say that, 'in round numbers, the annual grants in 1860 promoted the education of about 920,000 children, while they leave unaffected the education of 1,250,000 others of the same class.' Accepting this statement as the basis of calculation, let us suppose that in fifteen years the present system could be extended so as to include these 2,170,000 children. The annual cost of this education, at 28s. per scholar, would be £3,038,000 annually. The present Parliamentary grant of £750,000 would provide for the whole of this extension, if the proportions of all the grants were altered from one-third to one-fourth gradually, by equal annual reductions, which would proceed *pari passu* with the whole phenomena of extension. Two millions and a quarter would thus be raised locally, to meet three-quarters of a million of public grants. One great source of the increase of local funds would consist in a gradual growth of income from school-pence. This would arise both from somewhat larger weekly payments and more regular attendance. If the average attendance of each scholar became thirty-six weeks annually, an advance of one penny per week in the school-pence of two millions of scholars would produce £300,000. This result may be attained without doubt in fifteen years. Three-halfpence advance, weekly, would produce £450,000 annually.

The principle of the change by which the growth of the public grant might be restrained, is sufficiently indicated in these arrangements. There is but one alternative. Either the education of the poor must be worse, in proportion as it costs the State less; or the restraint on the growth of the public grant, and the reduction of its proportions to private contributions, must be so ordered that Christian benevolence and the sense of duty in parents may have time to step in, and gradually sustain, by increased subscriptions and school-pence, the efficiency of schools.

The Government is responsible for the present character of schools, in all their details. It invented the pupil-teacher apprenticeship, and the Training Colleges. It convinced the religious communions, by the earnest advocacy of its own authorised agents, that the education of the poor ought to be raised to its present standard. It has vigilantly superintended the execution of its Minutes by its own Inspectors. At any moment it might have required more drill in elementary subjects by schoolmasters. One circular letter would have ensured the closest attention to the subject. It even neglected to carry into execution the last clause of the Minute of the 2nd of April, 1853, devised for this express purpose, in schools which might obtain that capitation grant. The whole curriculum of study has been regulated by its examinations of the Training Colleges, of certificated teachers, and of pupil teachers. This curriculum might have been modified at any time. The Government is therefore identified with what exists. The present level of popular instruction has been the result of its administration. The work is confessedly incomplete, but for its condition in this stage of progress, the Committee of Council is primarily, in all respects, responsible. It has, however, contributed only one-third of the cost. The £4,800,000 expended by the Government, have been met by double that sum raised locally. The total outlay in building, enlarging, and improving 27 Training Colleges has been £334,981, of which £101,641 were derived from the Government, and £223,339 from other sources. Yet the State, as the contributor of only one-third, arrogates to itself the right to say that all that is done is wrong, though the Education Societies, the Diocesan and Archidiaconal Boards of Education, the committees and Principals of Training Colleges, cling to the principles of the existing system, and to the great majority of its details. Especially, when the State has thus invented and stimulated a system which has cost its promoters £9,600,000, by an outlay of one-half of that amount of public money, it has incurred obligations to those who have expended nearly ten millions, in the confidence that the Executive was not a mere abstraction, but a power capable of contracting moral obligations. The character of a system of public education thus created, ought not to be abruptly and harshly changed by the fiat of a Minister, without the consent of the great controlling bodies and communions who have expended twice as much as the State. Even were Parliament to make such a change, it would be a national dishonour. It would be an act of repudiation ever to be remembered with shame.

But not only would such an abrupt change be disgraceful, it would be short-sighted statesmanship; it would be a present saving, with the certainty of an ultimate disastrous loss. Otherwise, all those who have depended on the growth of Christian civilisation for the diminution of pauperism and crime have been dreamers. The protection of the public peace from tumult—of private property from depredation,—the detection, pursuit, trial, and punishment of crime,—cost the nation £9,000,000 annually, without taking into account the loss of wealth by robbers, incendiaries, and rioters. Pauperism, which is the hereditary consequence of generations of ignorance, superstition, and the slow and partial emancipation of the people from a previous state of serfdom, costs £6,000,000 annually. This relief of indigence is simply a measure of police. The life of the indigent is protected, as at the very foundation of laws for the protection of property and the public peace. The alternative would be a vast increase of vagabondage, crime, and tumult.

But this system of police for the restraint of crime and pauperism, has little or nothing in it that tends to cure those disorders. All curative agencies are of a totally different character. They are purely moral agencies. Their operation is gradual; it is felt only in a generation of men, or in successive generations. Such agencies appeal to the faith of great Statesmen, who are alone capable of guiding nations. A Statesman who foresees the necessity of providing for a great though remote danger, threatening the independence of his country, trains the population to arms; inspires them with a martial spirit; year by year strengthens citadels and erects batteries on the coasts; accumulates the munitions of war; and creates a great navy. The arsenals and dockyards, the citadels and forts, after years of preparation, contain a vast accumulation of the means of national defence. The nation, too, is armed, disciplined, and filled with a patriotic spirit. That conception of the necessity of thus meeting a great emergency is the result of the experience which history records. In like manner, a confidence in the efficacy of moral agencies in the dimunition of crime and pauperism, results from a careful study of the history of the emancipation of the humblest classes of any European nation from serfdom, helotry, and villenage. The primary agent in this has been Christianity, which has taught the moral equality of all men in the eye of God. This idea, notwithstanding inferiorities of race, renders the slavery of accountable human beings ultimately impossible in Christian nations. It is equally impossible that responsible moral agents should be allowed to be the victims of mere animal instinct, of ignorance, of the want of moral, religious, and mental culture, in any Christian people. Crime and pauperism are—in the degree in which they now exist—the heir-looms of the state of serfdom. They are the signs of the partial nature of the emancipation of the people from a brutish condition in which they were used like more intelligent beasts of burthen. But that Statesman who refuses to make an immediate outlay on the religious education of the people, in order to humanise their manners, correct their habits, increase their intelligence, and raise their moral condition, or prefers to cripple such an outlay for the sake of some immediate paltry economy, is not only shortsighted, but he must in his heart disbelieve the efficacy of moral and religious agencies as antidotes to pauperism and crime.

The force of the confidence in these agencies which exists in the nation, may be measured by the fact that the Education Grant is the only part of the fund derived from national taxation which, by its expenditure, now produces a voluntary contribution twice as great, and which by a gradual change, extending over fifteen years, may be made to produce from local sources, contributions thrice as large, as the public grant. Would a Chancellor of the Exchequer be farsighted who should put this result in peril,‘ if not render it impossible, by an abrupt and harsh change?

Recently proposals have been submitted to successive Parliaments for a reduction of the county franchise to a rating occupation of £10, and of the borough franchise to one of £6. Nothing tended to defeat these measures so much as the alarm excited in the middle classes by the proceedings of the Trades' Unions. These combinations often attempted to regulate labour so as to interfere with the freedom of workmen, and dictated to capital so as to usurp the authority necessary to successful enterprise. The domination of the Unions was generally without the violence and vindictiveness of former times. But it was arbitrary — was often directed to objects so mischievous or impracticable, as to inspire a deep-seated aversion to the extension of the franchise by the reduction of the property qualification. That proposal for including a larger number of the most intelligent and morally deserving portion of the working classes within the pale of the constitution is indefinitely postponed. But all parties agreed in the importance of devising the means of sifting out the best representatives of the classes supported by manual labour from the mass, and conferring the franchise on them. The effect of a steady perseverance in a system of national education, such as is at present in operation, would be to raise such men within the pale of the constitution. The 23,000 teachers and pupil teachers will certainly all possess the franchise. They are nearly all children of parents supported by manual labour, or of persons not possessing the franchise. Their elevation is a type of the true and certain influence of the same kind of training on the mass. The fifty-eight millions annually expended on beer, spirits, and tobacco will be reduced. The money thus saved will be devoted to the rent of more comfortable houses, to better household management, to the education of the children. A better-housed population will soon have many heads of families within the pale of the present franchise.

To give the people a worse education from motives of short-sighted economy, would be, in these respects, utterly inconsistent with all preceding national policy. The idea that an ignorant, brutish people is either more subordinate or more easily controlled than a people loyal by conviction and contented from experience and reason, is exploded. The notion that the mass of the people are the sources of national wealth merely as beasts of burthen — that the nation has no interest in their intelligence, inventive capacity, morality, and fitness for the duties of freemen and citizens,— is a doctrine which would find no advocates. No Chancellor of the Exchequer would dare to avow that their sensuality was a prolific source of revenue which he could not afford to check. Why, then, is education to be discouraged by regulations which cut off all aid to children under seven and after eleven years of age? Why are the annual grants to be reduced two-fifths at one blow? Why are the stipends, training, and qualifications of schoolmasters to be lowered? Why is instruction in the school to be mainly concentrated on the three lower elements? If these scholars are in preparation for Confirmation in the Church, why are the following instructions to Inspectors, of August, 1840, to be rendered practically nugatory by the individual examination of scholars in the lower elements imposed by the Revised Code, viz.—'That no plan of education ought to be encouraged in which intellectual instruction is not subordinate to the regulation of the thoughts and habits of the children by the doctrines and precepts of revealed religion?' Why is this formidable, if not insurmountable, impediment placed in the way of the order that 'in the case of schools connected with the national Church, the Inspectors will inquire with special care how far the doctrines and principles of the Church are instilled into the minds of the children?'

3. One of the pleas for the Revised Code is, that it was necessary to reduce the annual grants to inspected schools and Training Colleges, in order to provide for the establishment of evening schools, and for the extension of education in the apathetic districts.

But the plan proposed for both of these objects in the Revised Code is impracticable, or nugatory in some of its essential features.

For example, as to evening schools: the master could not teach in them without the ruin of his health and the neglect of his pupil teachers; for to mix them with these rude evening scholars, struggling with the lowest elements, is an utterly indefensible proposal. The proposed payments to the evening schools are not such as to be a motive for exertion to establish them. The Code therefore provides no available machinery for evening schools, and no motive for founding them.

As to the apathetic districts, there are only two provisions in the Code which seem to afford them any practical aid; they are—the creation of the fourth-class certificate, and the permission to pupil teachers who have successfully completed their apprenticeship, to serve as teachers in small rural schools until their twenty-fifth year.[1] But

---

[1] 118. Pupil teachers who fulfil the conditions of Article 84, may, upon special recommendation by the Inspector, and upon consideration of their last examination papers, be provisionally certified in the lower grade of the fourth division for immediate service in charge of small rural schools, but after the holder's 25th year of age (completed) such provisional certificates must have been exchanged for permanent certificates (Article 60), or are *ipso facto* cancelled.

119. Rural schools, in order to fall under Article 118, must not contain more than 1200 square feet of superficial area in the whole of the schoolrooms and class-rooms, or they must be certified as not needing nor likely to be attended by more than 100 scholars.

Pupil teachers who have successfully completed their Apprenticeship.

84. At the close of the apprenticeship pupil teachers are perfectly free in

these arrangements would be frustrated by the want of resources in such schools under the Revised Code. They are, as will be seen by a reference to Appendix B, exactly the schools in which the capitation grant of the Code would be often the least productive.

Much experience has been accumulated as to the organisation of evening schools, which is quite without influence on the regulations of the Code. The employment of raw apprentices — youths of only 19 — in sole charge of rural schools, is open to the gravest objections.

I shall not venture now to enter further on the plan of administration to be adopted on these two important questions, but I have no doubt whatever that an effectual impulse might be given to the general introduction of good evening schools, and that the present system might be extended into the smallest rural parishes, and the most apathetic districts, without any considerable temporary increase of the Parliamentary grant. I have already quoted the passage in which I deliberately stated my conviction that the public grant, under a wise and provident restraint, would at no time exceed £1,000,000 or £1,200,000, and that above two millions of scholars might, in fifteen years, be well taught and trained in inspected schools, under certificated teachers, at an expense to the State then reduced to £750,000 per annum.

Can Parliament refuse this outlay, when it would represent three millions of annual expenditure, of which two millions and a quarter would be derived from local voluntary resources, and at least £1,125,000 from the school pence paid by the parents of the scholars? I

---

the choice of employment. Any person properly interested in knowing the character of a pupil teacher may apply to the Committee of Council for a testimonial, declaring that the pupil teacher has successfully completed an apprenticeship; or the pupil teacher, if willing to continue in the work of education, may become an assistant in an elementary school (Article 85), or may become a Queen's scholar in a normal school (Articles 92–107), or may be provisionally certificated for immediate service in charge of small rural schools (Articles 118, 119).

should feel the utmost confidence that the co-operation of the Education Societies representing the Church and the religious communions, would be given to produce this result. Under a wise, faithful, and sympathising administration, strenuously striving with the Education Societies to attain it, there would be the utmost moral certainty of its accomplishment

It is impossible in this letter to submit to your Lordship observations on numerous matters of detail, which would only encumber and obscure the drift of the general observations which I have felt it my duty to lay before you. But I hope your Lordship will give me credit for not having overlooked them, though I have found it impossible even to allude to them in this argument.

   I have the honour to be,
    My Lord,
     Your obedient Servant,
      James P. Kay Shuttleworth.

The Earl Granville, K.G., *President of the Council and of the Committee of the Privy Council on Education.*

APPENDIX A.

Extract from Revised Code.

Annual grants conditional upon the number and proficiency of the scholars, the number and qualifications of the teachers, and the state of the schools.

38. Schools may meet three times daily: viz., in the morning, afternoon, and evening.

39. Schools which do not meet more than once daily cannot receive grants.

40. The managers of schools may claim per scholar 1*d.* for every attendance, after the first 100, at the morning or afternoon meetings, and after the first 12 at the evening meetings, of their school, within the year defined by Article 17.[1] Attendances under Half-time Acts may be multiplied by two to make up the preliminary number. One-third part of the sum thus claimable is forfeited if the scholar fails to satisfy the Inspector in reading, one-third if in writing, and one-third if in arithmetic respectively, according to Article 44.

'*Proposed Alterations*' as presented to both Houses of Parliament on Feb. 13, 1862.

---

[1] The Commissioners estimate the cost of education at 30*s.* per annum (p. 345), and recommend that the average grant obtainable should be about 10*s.* per child, never exceeding 15*s.* per child.

Fifteen shillings = 180 pence, may be earned, according to the proposed scale, by an attendance (twice per diem) of 140 days = the attendance proposed by the Commissioners as reasonable to aim at. (p. 330.)

According to the estimate of the Commissioners, the education of every 100 children = £150, and according to a rough application of the Table at p. 172 of their Report to the proposed scale, the grant obtainable for the *attendance* of 100 children would be £64 3*s.* 4*d.*, *before* the reductions consequent upon examination and inspection. The average, therefore, including evening scholars, would probably not exceed 10*s.* per head. The calculation is as follows:—

Amount of Grant for 100 *Children at* 1*d. per Attendance after the First* 100 *Attendances.*

Out of every 100 children, according to the average of England and Wales (Report, p. 172), taking round numbers, and counting 1 day = 2 attendances:—

			£	*s.*	*d.*
20 make less than 100 attendances . . . . =	0	0	0
20 „ between 100 and 200 = (upon an average) 150, of which 50 at 1*d.* = 20 × 4*s.* 2*d.*	4	3	4
20 „ between 200 and 300 = (upon an average) 250, of which 150 at 1*d.* = 20 × 12*s.* 6*d.*	12	10	0
20 „ between 300 and 400 = (upon an average) 350, of which 250 at 1*d.* = 20 × 20*s.* 10*d.*	20	16	8
20 „ between 400 and 440 = (upon an average) 420, of which 320 at 1*d.* = 20 × 26*s.* 8*d.*	26	13	4
	£64	3	4

41. No claim may be made on account of—
   (*a.*) Any scholar, except in Group IV., who has given less than sixteen morning or afternoon attendances, or eight evening attendances, within the thirty-one days preceding the date of the return;
   (*b.*) Evening attendances by scholars under thirteen years of age;
   (*c.*) A third attendance on the same day;
   (*d.*) Scholars once passed in Group IV.

42. The claim is to be made, and the examination recorded, in a schedule of the following form, or in such a modification of it as the Committee of Council shall from time to time prescibe.

Article 41. (*a.*) Cancel.

(*b.*) For 13 read 12.

Article 42. Heading of second column. Cancel all the words after ('*Article* 17').

No. of each Child.	Name of every Scholar who has attended more than 100 separate Meetings of the School in the Year ending ——— 186 (Article 17), of which attendances 16 or upwards were within 31 days of the last-mentioned date.	Aged.		Total number of Attendances at separate Meetings of the School in the Year as per Column 2.	Amount claimed per Child at the Rate of one Penny per Attendance after the first 100 Attendances.	Examined by Inspector, and passed in			Order of Committee of Council that the amount paid (omitting all fractions of 1d.) be
		Years.	Months.			Reading.	Writing.	Arithmetic.	
1	GROUP I. A.B. C.D.			£ s. d.	£ s. d				£ s. d.
2	&c.								
3	GROUP II. E.F.								
4	G.H. &c.								
5 &c.	GROUP III. J.K. L.M. &c.								
	GROUP IV. N.O. P.Q. &c.								

43. Group I. is confined to children between 3 and 7 years of age.
  „ II. between 7 and 9 years of age.
  „ III. „ 9 „ 11 „
  „ IV. „ 11 and upwards.

Article 43. *After* '11 *and upwards*' add '*Children under* 6 *years of age, in those schools in which the Inspector is able to report that special provision is made for the instruction of infants, are not required to be individually examined. But the grants of* 1*d. per attendance do not begin to be made for them until after the first* 200 *attendances.*'

Appendix A. 641

Those scholars who attend in the evenings only (Articles 40–1), must be distinguished from the rest in Group IV., and entered therein *after* the rest.

44	Group I.	Group II.	Group III.	Group IV.	
Reading.	Narrative in monosyllables.	A short paragraph from an elementary reading book used in the school.	A short paragraph from a more advanced reading book used in the school.	A short ordinary paragraph in a newspaper, or other modern narrative.	But scholars attending in the evening only may be presented for examination in any group at the discretion of the managers.
Writing.	Form on blackboard or slate, from dictation, letters, capital and small, manuscript.	A sentence from the same paragraph, slowly read once, and then dictated in single words.	A sentence slowly dictated once by a few words at a time, from the same book, but not from the paragraph read.	Another short ordinary paragraph in a newspaper, or other modern narrative, slowly dictated once by a few words at a time.	
Arithmetic.	Form on blackboard or slate, from dictation, figures up to 20 ; name at sight figures up to 20 ; add and subtract figures up to 10, orally, from examples on black-board.	A sum in any simple rule as far as short division (inclusive).	A sum in compound rules (money & common weights and measures).	A sum in practice or simple proportion.	

Article 44. Heading of second column. Add '*excluding children under six years of age.*'

45. The grant may either be withheld altogether or reduced.

46. The grant is withheld altogether,—

(*a*.) If the school be not held in a building certified by the Inspector to be healthy, properly lighted, drained, and ventilated, supplied with offices, and containing in the principal schoolroom at least 80 cubical feet of internal space for each child in average attendance.

(*b*.) If the principal teacher be not duly certificated (Article 61).

(*c*.) If the girls in the school be not taught plain needlework as part of the ordinary course of instruction.

(*d*.) If the registers be not kept with sufficient accuracy to warrant confidence in the returns.

(*e*.) If, on the Inspector's Report, there appears to be any *primâ facie* objection of a gross kind. A second inspection, wherein another Inspector or Inspectors takes part, is made in every such instance, and if the grant be finally withheld, a special minute is made and recorded of the case.

(*f*.) If three persons at least be not designated to sign the receipt for the grant on behalf of the school.

Article 45. Add '*for causes arising out of the state of the school.*'

Article 45*. The Inspector does not proceed to examine scholars in reading, writing, and arithmetic for the grant, until he has first ascertained that the state of the school does not require it to be withheld.

Article 46 (*b*.). For 'full stop' after '(Article 61)' read '*comma,*' and add '*and duly paid.* Teachers certificated before 31st March, 1864, and who have not otherwise agreed with their employers, are duly paid if they receive not less than three times the grant allowable upon their certificates in Article 64–5 *of the Code of* 1860, *and they have a first charge to the extent of this grant, being one-third of such due payment, upon the money received by the Managers, under Article 42 of the Revised Code.*'

---

* *This number is provisionally retained in order not to disturb the numbers in the remainder of the Code.*

T T

47. The grant is reduced,—
  (*a*.) By not less than one-tenth nor more than one-half in the whole, upon the Inspector's Report, for faults of instruction or discipline on the part of the teacher, or (after one year's notice) for failure on the part of the managers to remedy any such defect in the premises as seriously interferes with the efficiency of the school, or to provide proper furniture, books, maps, and other apparatus of elementary instruction.
  (*b*.) By the sum of £10 for every completed number of 30 scholars after the first 50 in average attendance who are without a teacher fulfilling the conditions of Articles 61, or 75-83, or 85-7.
  (*c*.) By its excess above
   1. The amount of school fees and subscriptions; or,
   2. The rate of 15*s*. per scholar in average attendance
  } in the year defined by Article 17.

48. If the excess of scholars over the ratio of 30 to every pupil teacher has arisen from increased attendance of children since the last settlement of the school staff (Articles 56, 57), the forfeiture prescribed by Article 47 (*b*.) does not accrue.

49. In every school receiving annual grants is to be kept, besides the ordinary registers of attendance,—
  (*a*.) A diary or log-book.
  (*b*.) A portfolio wherein may be laid all official letters, which should be numbered (1, 2, 3, &c.,) in the order of their receipt.

(*e*.) Add* after the '*objection*' referring to foot note.

Article 47 (*a*). Add* after the word '*instruction*' referring to foot note.

(*b*) Cancel, and instead read '*by the sum of £10, if after the first 50 scholars in average attendance there be not either one pupil teacher fulfilling the conditions of Articles 75-83 for every 40 scholars, or one certificated, or assistant teacher fulfilling the conditions of Articles 61 and 85-7, respectively, for every 80 scholars, in average attendance. The forfeiture is reduced from £10 to £5, if the failure to comply with these Articles be confined to the examination of a pupil teacher (Article 82); but this reduction is made only once for the same pupil teacher, and not in successive years for the same school.*'

---

* *In Church of England Schools the Order in Council of* 10*th August*, 1840, *and the instructions to Inspectors relative to examination in religion, which are founded upon it, are included under this paragraph.*

APPENDIX B.

The inequalities in the operation of the capitation grant scheme in the Revised Code exhibited in different districts.

Rev. John Menet, Chaplain of the Hockerill Training School, Bishop's Stortford, in a letter to the Guardian, dated October 21st, 1861, gives the following results of his inquiries :—

1. 'That infant schools could not in the great majority of cases be kept open.
2. 'That new schools and schools in shifting populations would suffer enormously.
3. 'That boys' schools in particular parts of towns would suffer the least, and that some might gain more than they receive now.
4. 'That the largest grants would be earned where they are least needed, and that therefore the assistance given would be in inverse proportion to the need.'

No.		Last annual grant under Old Code.	Estimated grant under New Code.
1.	Boys' school in very shifting London population	£133	£97
5.	Boys' school in a manufacturing town	96	48
11.	Boys' school in a shifting London population	132	76
7.	Boys' school long-established, and including farmers' and middle-class children	38	39
14.	Boys' school, with very close approximation to H.M.I. standard	28	11
17.	Girls' school (ditto as to standard)	58	22
20.	Girls' school in a large town (ditto as to standard)	134	38
5.	Mixed under a mistress, scattered country population	30	13
2.	Infant school, very successful (average attendance, 150)	80	21
9.	Infant school, established a year, in a very low town population	61	8
8.	Infant school, London population	97	15

The returns which have been furnished to me by school managers, teachers, and others, give the following results :—

Rate of loss in annual grants under Revised Code.

Schools with semi-barbarous, migrant population in manufacturing districts—Villages . . . . . } From 2-5ths to 3-5ths.
        Towns . . . . From 2-5ths to 2-3rds.
Schools in dense and corrupt parts of old cities and large towns . . . . } From 2-5ths to 2-3rds.
Schools in pauperised rural districts, where the children are employed in numerous harvests, &c. . } From 2-5ths to 2-3rds.
Schools on wild moorland, with scattered population . From 2-5ths to 2-3rds.
Schools closely connected with a wealthy congregation in long settled and prosperous parts of a town . . } The whole previous grant would be obtained, or only one-fifth loss suffered.
Schools of a settled, well-employed rural population, in which the influence of the proprietors and tenantry are beneficially exercised . . . . . } One-fifth loss.
Schools in rural parishes, intermediate between those with wealthy and vigilant patrons, and schools in pauperised and apathetic districts . . . . } From 1-4th to 1-3rd loss.
Schools in rural parishes with bad roads—a scattered population—non-resident proprietors—tenantry indifferent—much harvest-work—and ill-endowed benefice for clergyman . . . . . . } Will either be closed or will become 'Adventure Schools.'

APPENDIX C.

Schedule of Scholars to be examined, with preliminary information.

Population of School district _____ School for Boys, Girls, or Infants. _____
Chief occupations of Parents _____
Number of years' service of any Certificated Teacher in School _____
Ditto ditto of Pupil Teachers _____ Number of Pupil Teachers in each of four preceding years _____
or Assistant Teachers in ditto _____

Names of Scholars arranged in their Classes in the following Sections, and in each Section in the order of seniority:— Class Section (1.) Those Scholars in the Class who have attended 120 days at least in each of two preceding years. (2.) 100 days at least in last year, or 80 days in each of last two years. (3.) Scholars who have attended a shorter time than preceding Sections.	Age at last Birthday.	No. of days' school attendance in each of two preceding years, or of last year.	No. of days' school attendance in each quarter of last year.				Approximate number of days spent in any other school having a certificated teacher in each of four preceding years.				Marks awarded to each scholar examined in highest merit, 40 merit, 20 competency.							Marks awarded to each scholar examined in other subjects.			Here the Inspector will record his opinion on the work done in each class. He will, on the summary of the whole work done, recommend one-third, two-thirds, or the whole capitation grant to be given.
			1st Quarter.	2nd Quarter.	3rd Quarter.	4th Quarter.	1861.	1860.	1859.	1858.	Reading.	Writing.	Cyphering.	Religious Instruction.	Dictation and Composition.	Grammar.	Geography.	English History.	
Class 1, Section I.																			
Class 1, Section II.																			
Class 1, Section III.																			

PRINTED BY SPOTTISWOODE AND CO., NEW-STREET SQUARE, LONDON.

These two Title-Pages are printed for the use of those who may be desirous to bind the volume published by SIR JAMES KAY SHUTTLEWORTH *in* 1853 *as the first of a Series of which the present volume is the Second.*

PUBLIC EDUCATION

AS AFFECTED BY

THE MINUTES OF THE COMMITTEE OF PRIVY COUNCIL

FROM

1846 TO 1852

WITH

SUGGESTIONS AS TO FUTURE POLICY,

BY

SIR JAMES KAY-SHUTTLEWORTH, BART.

VOL. I.

LONDON
LONGMAN, GREEN, LONGMAN, AND ROBERTS
1853

PUBLIC EDUCATION

AS REVIEWED IN

1832—1839—1846—1862

IN PAPERS BY

SIR JAMES KAY-SHUTTLEWORTH, BART.

VOL. II.

LONDON
LONGMAN, GREEN, LONGMAN, AND ROBERTS
1862